A COMMENTARY ON JEREMIAH

A Commentary on

JEREMIAH

EXILE *and* HOMECOMING

Walter Brueggemann

WILLIAM B. EERDMANS PUBLISHING COMPANY
GRAND RAPIDS, MICHIGAN / CAMBRIDGE, U.K.

© 1998 Wm. B. Eerdmans Publishing Co.
255 Jefferson Ave. S.E., Grand Rapids, Michigan 49503 /
P.O. Box 163, Cambridge CB3 9PU U.K.

Printed in the United States of America

03 02 01 00 99   7 6 5 4 3 2

Library of Congress Cataloging-in-Publication Data

Brueggemann, Walter.
A commentary on Jeremiah : exile and homecoming /
Walter Brueggemann.
p.   cm.
Includes bibliographical references.
ISBN 0-8028-0280-X (pbk. : alk. paper)
1. Bible. O.T. Jeremiah — Commentaries. I. Title.
BS1525.3.B75   1998
224'.207 — dc21   97-38350
CIP

Contents

Contents

vi

Abbreviations

ICC	*International Critical Commentary*
JSOT	*Journal for the Study of the Old Testament*
LXX	Septuagint
NRSV	New Revised Standard Version
RSV	Revised Standard Version
SBL	Society of Biblical Literature

Recent Jeremiah Study

These volumes on Jeremiah were written and published in the immediate wake of the turn of Jeremiah studies in 1986, with the publication in that year of the three formidable commentaries of William Holladay, Robert Carroll, and William McKane.[1] It was not yet possible at the time of my publication, however, to assess or appreciate fully how decisive these commentaries and the work around them were for the refocusing and redefining of Jeremiah studies.

Each of these three commentaries goes in its own distinctive direction, but the cumulative effect of the three is more important. In a magisterial effort, Holladay sought to push to its furthest reach the direct and concrete connection between text and specific historical location. Indeed, Holladay's work is important as a summary of the most notable gains of history-oriented study. And while scholarship since then has not followed him, his work is an important reference point in that regard.

1. William L. Holladay, *A Commentary on the Book of the Prophet Jeremiah Chapters 1–25* (Hermeneia; Philadelphia: Fortress Press, 1986), completed as *A Commentary on the Book of the Prophet Jeremiah Chapters 26–52* (Hermeneia; Minneapolis: Fortress Press, 1989); Robert P. Carroll, *Jeremiah: A Commentary* (Old Testament Library; Philadelphia: Westminster Press, 1986); William McKane, *A Critical and Exegetical Commentary on Jeremiah I, Introduction and Commentary on Jeremiah I–XXV* (ICC; Edinburgh: T. & T. Clark, 1986), completed as *A Critical and Exegetical Commentary on Jeremiah II, Commentary on Jeremiah XXVI–LII* (ICC; Edinburgh: T. & T. Clark, 1996).

Robert Carroll has contributed most decisively to the counterperspective that seeks to distance the text of Jeremiah from any recoverable historical connection. The alternative that Carroll has offered is that the book of Jeremiah is an "ideological" proposal that is an intentionally argued perspective that advocates a system of social values and interests, and that is undeterred by "historical facts." As will be clear, Carroll's new initiative has gained an important following in subsequent scholarship. In a closely argued, text-based analysis, McKane has paid particular attention to the dynamic development of the book of Jeremiah. He is especially to be thanked for his now justifiably famous phrase, "rolling corpus." The scroll of Jeremiah is an ongoing development over several generations, with many voices, interests, and advocacies contributing to its emerging shape.[2]

The cumulative effect of these studies is to loosen the grip of historical-critical methods on Jeremiah studies. Heretofore, as elsewhere in Old Testament studies, historical criticism was the single acceptable method of reading. Now it is clear, given current perspectives, that the book of Jeremiah is not a "record" of what happened, but rather a *constructive proposal of reality* that is powered by *passionate conviction* and that is voiced in cunning, albeit disjunctive *artistic form*. This means that the book of Jeremiah is a rich and open field for venturesome interpretation, none of which can claim to be "objective" and none of which is likely to dominate or defeat alternative perspectives. While the text of Jeremiah exhibits immense interpretive openness, in my judgment it is not endlessly indeterminate. It does indeed make its own convoluted advocacy, whether happily "canonical" or flagrantly "ideological."

In his recent assessment of new ventures in Old Testament theology, Leo Perdue has identified a broad range of ways in which theological interpretation of the Old Testament is now being done that are in general regarded as legitimate.[3] One of the virtues of his study is that for each model of Old Testament theology he mentions, he takes interpretation in Jeremiah as an exemplar of how the method and perspective work in relation to concrete texts. Readers new to the field can well make Perdue's

---

2. On this matter, see especially Christopher Seitz, *Theology in Conflict: Reactions to the Exile in the Book of Jeremiah* (Beihefte zur Zeitschrift für die alttestamentliche Wissenschaft 176; Berlin: W. de Gruyter, 1989).

3. Leo G. Perdue, *The Collapse of History: Reconstructing Old Testament Theology* (Overtures to Biblical Theology; Minneapolis: Fortress Press, 1994).

study a point of access. His focus on Jeremiah may suggest that the tradition of Jeremiah is (a) enormously supple for interpretive alternatives, and (b) is peculiarly generative and draws to itself imaginative interpretive energy. In many ways, new studies of the book of Jeremiah suggest that the book is a primal matrix in which both to face the immense problems of biblical faith and to appropriate the most elemental, demanding, and bracing dimensions of that faith for contemporary engagement.

I

I will briefly identify four thematics that are prominent in current study, each of which attests to venturesome interpretation that is no longer anchored in positivistic, historicist, objectivist claims. We may begin with the recognition that the tradition of Jeremiah is an *ideological offer* that seeks to authorize a particular authoritative version of reality. The development of scholarship in this direction is a reflection of our general intellectual situation, but it is the merit of Carroll to have made the point in influential ways. *Ideology* in Jeremiah studies, in broadest perspective, is an alternative to *historical* studies.

There is, however, an enduring problem connected with the term "ideology." Its dominant use is derived from Karl Marx, who employed the term to refer to distortions of reality, whereby vested interests deliberately skew and misrepresent reality. A less polemical use of the term is offered by Clifford Geertz, who takes "ideology" in a benign way to mean any public, sustained sense-making by a community. The problem with the term in Jeremiah studies is that our usage tends to vacillate between these two very different meanings.

On the one hand, it can be argued that the Deuteronomists shaped "the final form of the text" and so imposed their particular perception on the Jeremiah tradition. That Deuteronomic "ideology" is Torah-centered and so understands the exilic crisis of Israel that dominates the book of Jeremiah as a consequence of Torah-disregard. Such a reading is to use the term "ideology" in Geertz's way as a sense-making of lived data.

On the other hand, this use of the term easily shades over into a polemical Marxian usage that takes the Deuteronomic perspective as "distortion." I have the impression that this tendency revolves around two issues. First, the tone of the Deuteronomists is uncompromising and smacks of "authoritarian." Some uses of Marxian criticism regard any authoritarian statement (except one's own) as distortion, as though there is somewhere a more benign, innocent, less insistent offer of reality. Second and more to the point, interpreters who react against generic religious authoritarianism tend to treat any voicing of "God" in the text as "ideology," as though a "true presentation" of the exilic crisis can only be understood on a historical-human plane without reference to God. It will be clear, in my judgment, that the use of "ideology" in Jeremiah studies is not an innocent matter but itself serves ideological interests. One can notice, in any case, how far we have come from "history."

II

Proponents of "ideology" take a dim view of textual representations or interpretations that appeal to God, for "God" falls outside Enlightenment modernity and outside certain definitions of scholarship. I suggest that in contemporary study, as "ideology" functions as a "negative" tool for reading, so "canonical" is a "positive" theological effort, positive in that the God-claim of the text is taken seriously and affirmatively. Thus I suggest that "ideological" and "canonical" approaches are two sides of the same coin. Both are agreed that the text is no "objective presentation," but they are in deep disagreement over the assessment of any advocacy presentation of reality.

Canonical perspectives are offered especially by Brevard Childs and Ronald Clements, who insist that the book of Jeremiah, as we have it, is framed to make a large and serious theological affirmation.[4] Specifically the book of Jeremiah is arranged to speak, in sequence, about *the judgment of God* who in prophetic tradition brings Jerusalem to an end, and the *deliverance of God* who offers to the consequent exilic community an open historical possibility.

4. Brevard S. Childs, *Introduction to the Old Testament as Scripture* (Philadelphia: Fortress Press, 1979), 338-54; Ronald E. Clements, "Patterns in the Prophetic Canon," *Canon and Authority: Essays in Old Testament Religion and Theology,* ed. George W. Coats and Burke O. Long (Philadelphia: Fortress Press, 1977), 42-55; *Jeremiah* (Interpretation; Atlanta: John Knox Press, 1988), and "Jeremiah 1–25 and the Deuteronomistic History," *Old Testament Prophecy: From Oracles to Canon* (Louisville: Westminster/John Knox Press, 1996), 107-22.

I find it intriguing and ironic that, in substance, ideological and canonical interpretations are allied. Both agree about the theological intentionality of the text. All that is different is the elemental, personal response of the interpreter, which is, characteristically, more informed by personal religious history and passion than by any scholarly discernment. The two approaches together indicate that the tradition of Jeremiah is an open invitation for interpretive imagination that permits the passions, hurts, and hopes of interpreters to come to lively expression.

III

Both "ideological" and "canonical" approaches tend to view the tradition of Jeremiah "from the outside." Ideological interpretation that is resistant to God-claims of an authoritative kind measures the book by *Enlightenment norms* of autonomy. Canonical interpretation is largely a Christian enterprise that identifies in the book themes and accents congruent with a general theological consensus in *the Christian tradition*. It is, to some great extent, inevitable that we measure the book by prior interpretive commitments, either fideistic or skeptical. Such a reality cannot be completely avoided.

It is possible, however, to "go inside," to follow where the text itself seems to point, without premature judgments grounded in past interpretive commitments. Such "inside" work is never fully innocent, but it can be more-or-less so. I have reference to rhetorical studies that pay great attention to grammatical nuance, utilization of images and metaphors, and ironic hints that undermine every flat canonical or positivistic reading. This approach was especially championed by James Muilenburg, and has received great impetus from Phyllis Trible.[5] Such rhetorical analysis suggests that the text is endlessly subtle and, when we are attentive, resists every reading that gives closure.

In this context, attention should be paid to feminist readings that notice the powerful familial sexual imagery that at the same time seems to reflect and foster patriarchal assumptions and undermines and subverts

5. Most recently and most programmatically, see Phyllis Trible, *Rhetorical Criticism: Context, Method, and the Book of Jonah* (Guides to Biblical Scholarship; Minneapolis: Fortress Press, 1994).

the very assumptions it seems to endorse. This perspective is evident in the work of Kathleen O'Connor, Angela Bauer, Renita Weems, and Gale Yee.[6] Of course it cannot be argued that such a perspective is "innocent," so that we are able to see an interface or overlap between an insider's attentiveness and an outsider's "ideological" perspective.

The outcome of such a way of reading is to help us see that in the amazing artistry of the book, every reading, including those canonical and ideological and skeptical, is provisional. (It can be argued that the poetry is more open and the prose [Dtr] more prone to closure. In any case, the relation between prose and poetry is an endlessly vexed question.) But it is precisely those vexed questions that preclude any final reading, whether in the trust of canon or in the anger of ideology, or in the resistance of rational skepticism. The book becomes a place in which to remain and play and listen and notice. But every such notice may be a new one, because the God featured here will not be flattened or muted.

IV

In the end, the book of Jeremiah does not belong to the scholarly guild. It belongs more properly to the synagogue and the church, who have, all through the centuries, attended to its preservation and reading. This does not mean that the book of Jeremiah is reduced to conventional religious expectations. It does mean, however, that the book's proper climate is a community that expects to be addressed in dangerous and unsettling ways by the holiness that sounds here.

Because of its character and quality, however, the book cannot be held and contained even in such communities of faith. It is a public document. This means that beyond the preoccupations of scholars, and

6. Kathleen O'Connor, "Jeremiah," *The Women's Bible Commentary,* ed. Carol A. Newsome and Sharon H. Ringe (Louisville: Westminster/John Knox Press, 1992), 169-77, and "Broken Family Mended" (forthcoming); Angela Bauer, "Dressed to Be Killed: Jer. 4:29-31 as an Example for the Function of Female Imagery in Jeremiah" (forthcoming); Renita J. Weems, *Battered Love: Marriage, Sex, and Violence in the Hebrew Prophets* (Overtures to Biblical Theology; Minneapolis: Fortress Press, 1995); Gale A. Yee, *Poor Banished Children of Eve: The Symbolization of Women as Evil in Biblical and Related Texts* (New York: Continuum, forthcoming).

even beyond the containments of church and synagogue, this book purposes to address all who attend and listen. It speaks to and from and about deep public disruption. It dares to reflect on the ground of disruption, on the practice of survival in the midst of disruption, and on life possibilities beyond disruption.

It is a crisis-driven tradition. More than that, however, it claims and sounds the utterance of holiness in the midst of disruption, sounds about the Holy One, sounds from the Holy One that summon to honesty and to hope. It dares, in its artistically venturesome way, to ponder the odd connection between public disruption and durable, undomesticated holiness. No doubt questions of ideology, canon, and rhetoric are important. But they are penultimately important because the human questions are more urgent and more elemental than our scholarly categories.

The book of Jeremiah is of course context-specific. Except that readers over time have found a generativity and dynamic that regularly pushes beyond context to new contexts, both illuminating context and being freshly read by fresh context. It takes no great imagination to conclude that the present disruption of Western culture — heralded by the Jewish holocaust but ongoing in other circles of barbarism as well — is a fit place from which to engage the tradition of Jeremiah again. It is a daring notion that holiness is at work in our own barbaric setting, but no more daring than the parallel claim was in that ancient situation. It is odd that holiness set in disruption comes in literary, rhetorical artistry. That in any case is what we have here on our hands, to our endless benefit and our recurring dislocation. Our scholarly reading is never as mere scholars, but always as children of the disruption, left to wonder about the disruption as a venue for the Holy One.

Columbia Theological Seminary　　　　　　　WALTER BRUEGGEMANN
March 31, 1997

Introduction

Historical Context

The book of Jeremiah is reflective of and responsive to the historical crisis of the last days of Judah, culminating in the destruction of Jerusalem and the temple in 587 B.C.E. This crisis is the dominant and shaping event of the entire OT. The destruction evoked an extensive theological literature of which the book of Jeremiah is one major component.[1]

The last days of the 7th cent., the time of Jeremiah, witnessed the abrupt collapse of the Assyrian Empire and its prompt displacement by the Babylonians under the governance of Nebuchadnezzar. The Judean crisis must therefore be understood in the context of Babylonian imperial ambitions and expansionism. The power of Babylon to the north of Judah, however, was not the only foreign power with which Judah had to deal. Judah had to attend also to the Egyptians to the south, whose policy was to maintain Judah as a buffer against Babylonian pressure. Thus Judah was placed precisely and precariously between Babylon and Egypt. The Judahite kings in the years after Josiah (639-609) vacillated between Babylonian and Egyptian alliances. Finally Babylonian policy would no longer

---

1. See Peter R. Ackroyd, *Exile and Restoration,* Old Testament Library (Philadelphia: Westminster; London: SCM, 1968), and Ralph W. Klein, *Israel in Exile,* Overtures to Biblical Theology 6 (Philadelphia: Fortress, 1979).

tolerate such political double-mindedness and moved against Jerusalem to end its political independence.[2]

Jehoiakim (609-598), son of Josiah, played a daring game of "international roulette" between Egypt and Babylon, eventually evoking Babylon's first incursion into Jerusalem in 598. One outcome of the events of 598 was the exile of Jehoiakim's son Jehoiachin to Babylon, where he remained for many years as titular head of the dynasty. Many prominent citizens of Judah were deported with him. For the period of 598-587, yet another son of Josiah, Zedekiah, presided over the affairs of Jerusalem but in the end had no chance for independent action in the face of Babylon. During these years, there was an intense rivalry between the community in Jerusalem (over which Zedekiah presided), and the exilic community in Babylon (in which Jehoiachin was understood as the legitimate leader).

Babylon's final decisive blow against Judah came in 587. The Babylonian Empire terminated Judah's existence as an independent political entity. Jerusalem and its environs were made part of a governorship accountable to the empire. A second and even more extensive deportation of Jerusalem's citizens occurred, as part of a general strategy for consolidating the Babylonian Empire and maintaining power. This radical displacement raised in Judah and Jerusalem a range of critical questions, moral and religious as well as political.

It is therefore possible to understand and explain the events around 587 in terms of *Realpolitik*, that is, in terms of political tensions between states and the overriding military and imperial power of Babylon. The realities of the political, military, and historical process provide convincing proof of Judah's helplessness in the face of Babylonian power, a helplessness exacerbated by the unwise and weak leadership it received from its monarchy. The Jeremiah literature is familiar with the realities of imperial politics and is conversant with those modes of thinking. However, Jeremiah does not pursue a *Realpolitik* interpretation of Judah's crisis of termination and displacement, but offers a different, alternative reading of those events. As an alternative to a political analysis, the tradition of Jeremiah proceeds on the basis of a theological perspective.

2. For a general review of the period, see Bustenay Oded, "Judah and the Exile," in *Israelite and Judean History*, ed. John H. Hayes and J. Maxwell Miller, Old Testament Library (Philadelphia: Westminster; London: SCM, 1977), 435-488; and Miller and Hayes, *A History of Ancient Israel and Judah* (Philadelphia: Westminster; London: SCM, 1986), 381-429.

Theological Tradition

The literature of Jeremiah engages in anguished poetic reflection and didactic prose explanation about the cause of Israel's end and the destiny of those deported to Babylon. Jeremiah's reading is not shaped by power politics but by the categories of Israel's covenantal traditions of faith, which concern the holy purpose and power of Yahweh and the aches and hopes of the faithful community. As the categories of analysis and understanding shift from matters of international power to concerns of covenantal faithfulness, so also the modes of speech change. The odd result is that the great political event of 587 is discerned through passionate poetry and uncompromising theological analysis. Out of that poetry and analysis emerges a poetic anticipation of a new historical possibility for Judah — an anticipation that pushes powerfully beyond imperial permits and transcends the seeming prohibitions of the empire.

When the events of 587 are read from a theological perspective, Judah's destiny will be shaped finally not by power as the world judges power, but by the covenantal realities of Yahweh's sovereignty and power. We may identify three elements that are constitutive of this covenantal understanding of historical reality.

1. The governing paradigm for the tradition of Jeremiah is *Israel's covenant with Yahweh, rooted in the memories and mandates of the Sinai tradition.* That covenant taught that the sovereign God of Israel required obedience to covenant stipulations about social practice and power. Disobedience to those covenant stipulations would result in heavy sanctions (curses) that would be experienced as death or displacement.

When the events of 587 are read in the light of the claims of covenant, the Babylonian invasion and deportation are understood as the means of implementation of the harsh sanctions (covenant curses) already known and articulated in the Sinai tradition. The reality of Babylonian power is not denied, but is firmly subordinated to and incorporated into the intention of Yahweh. The book of Jeremiah thus mediates the reality of imperial politics through the theological claims of covenant.[3]

The mediation of political reality and covenantal faith is offered with

3. See John Bright, *Covenant and Promise* (Philadelphia: Westminster, 1976), 140-170.

amazing daring, in order to insist that there is a moral dimension to the termination and deportation. The destruction of Jerusalem wrought by Babylon is presented as a covenantal response of the God of Israel to Judah's refusal to adhere to covenantal requirements. Such a conclusion follows from the categories of Israel's faith, but to link the historical crisis to those categories is a bold interpretive act. Indeed, that Jeremiah's contemporaries could not discern the relation between imperial politics and covenantal theology is a central issue of the book.

This governing paradigm of covenant indicates that Jeremiah is in important ways related to and derived from the traditions of Deuteronomy.[4] This connection (generally affirmed in a scholarly consensus) is important because the book of Deuteronomy gives a clear and uncompromising presentation of the covenant relation in Israel's faith. Deuteronomy makes clear that Israel's life begins in Yahweh's act of mercy and fidelity, and that Israel's proper response is obedient listening. Moreover, Deuteronomy asserts that every dimension of Israel's common life is to be brought under the rubric of covenant obedience. Indeed, it articulates a strategy for making public life fully covenantal.[5] Finally, Deuteronomy most clearly presents the potential curses that will come upon Israel for disobedience. The convergence of Deuteronomy and Jeremiah is clear not only in terms of theological substance, but also in matters of style and forms of articulation. Jeremiah's proclamation and the entire book of Jeremiah operate on theological assumptions that are most clearly presented in Deuteronomy. The tradition of Jeremiah is not closed and reductionistic, but it is clear about the claims of covenant.

2. The book of Jeremiah, however, cannot be completely understood by simple reference to a notion of covenant violation and covenant curse,

4. For summary statements from the older criticism, see John Bright, "The Date of the Prose Sermons of Jeremiah," in *A Prophet to the Nations,* ed. Leo G. Perdue and Brian W. Kovacs (Winona Lake, Ind.: Eisenbrauns, 1984), 193-212; and J. Philip Hyatt, "The Deuteronomic Edition of Jeremiah," *ibid.,* 247-267. The Deuteronomic dimension of Jeremiah has been most programmatically argued by Robert P. Carroll, *From Chaos to Covenant* (New York: Crossroad; London: SCM, 1981).

5. Norbert Lohfink ("Distribution of the Functions of Power," *Great Themes from the Old Testament* [Edinburgh: T. & T. Clark, 1982], 55-75) has argued that in Deut. 16–18, one can discern a proposed "constitution" for organizing and authorizing a particular mode of public life.

the central assumptions of Deuteronomic theology.[6] Along with the paradigm of covenant, the book of Jeremiah affirms another theological claim, *the pathos of Yahweh*. In spite of Israel's obduracy and recalcitrance, Yahweh nonetheless wills a continuing relation with Israel. This will is rooted in nothing other than God's inexplicable yearning, which is articulated in Jeremiah as God's pathos, presented in turn through the pathos of the poet.[7]

Thus the severity of covenant sanctions and the power of God's yearning pathos are set in deep tension. This deep tension forms the central interest, theological significance, and literary power of the book of Jeremiah. This yearning pathos that is presented as God's fundamental inclination toward Judah is a departure from and critique of the primary inclination of Deuteronomic theology.[8]

The juxtaposition of covenant claim and pathos makes clear that God is, in the life of Judah, more complex, free, and less controllable than a simple scheme of retribution would suggest. It is this greater complexity in the character of God that the rich rhetoric of the book of Jeremiah seeks to articulate. The theological richness of Yahweh's character evokes and requires a subtle rhetoric that is full of ambiguity, passion, and incongruity. The book of Jeremiah is so powerful and compelling because it has a mode of expression appropriate to its astonishing subject.

The mediation of the claims of covenant through the surprising power of Yahweh's pathos permits the book of Jeremiah to move beyond

---

6. The simple structure of violation and curse is also central to the "prophetic lawsuit" of indictment and sentence; see Claus Westermann, *Basic Forms of Prophetic Speech* (Philadelphia: Westminster; London: Lutterworth, 1967). But the language of Jeremiah is closer to that of Deuteronomy (e.g., Deut. 28).

7. See Abraham J. Heschel, *The Prophets* (New York and London: Harper & Row, 1962), 103-139, 221-278.

8. It is worth noting that in Deut. 7:7, a classic text on the election, the verb *hashaq* is used: "The LORD set his love upon you." The RSV translation, "set his love on," is an anemic one. The verb suggests a passionate, craving physical grasping of another in powerful embrace. It is this dimension of passionate craving that is articulated in Jeremiah's vivid imagery, and that gives his poetry such power and poignancy. In this, the poetry of Jeremiah runs well beyond the restrained articulations of Deuteronomy. While the tradition of Jeremiah may be informed in this regard by Deuteronomy, the theme is much more fully utilized, so much more so that it amounts to an important departure from the tradition of Deuteronomy.

the crisis of exile and death in the 7th and 6th cents. to envision a newness that is wrought out of God's gracious resolve and powerful will. The move beyond covenantal sanction is unwarranted, but that move is possible because of God's magisterial freedom, through which God can and does act beyond warrants. Jeremiah's discernment and articulation of the free- dom and pathos of Yahweh enables the poet to break out of the tight categories of covenantal sanctions and move to an articulation of hope.

3. The third constituent element necessary to understand the theol- ogy of the book of Jeremiah is the *royal-temple ideology of Jerusalem.* This ideology articulated in the Jerusalem establishment, fostered by the king and articulated by temple priests, claimed that the God of Israel had made irrevocable promises to the temple and the monarchy, had taken up per- manent residence in Jersalem, and was for all time a patron and guarantor of the Jerusalem establishment. Jeremiah's work only makes sense as an antithetical response to that ideology.

The royal-temple ideology, embodied in temple liturgy and royal claims of legitimacy, asserted and imagined that it was an indispensable vehicle for God's way and blessing in the world. It was therefore assumed that the royal-temple apparatus was immune to covenant sanctions and to God's judgment. This ideology was the official religion of Jerusalem and no doubt was popularly embraced. The tradition of Jeremiah articu- lates a sustained challenge to the royal-temple ideology, insisting on the centrality of covenant commandment and dismissing the notion of im- munity from judgment. The counterclaim of the tradition of Jeremiah is rooted in the old radical theological tradition of Sinai and was, as events materialized, vindicated by the actual end of Jerusalem. History showed that, indeed, Jerusalem was not immune to judgment.

The painful experiences around 587 made clear the inadequacy of both the old covenant theology and the royal-temple theology. While the sympathies of the Jeremiah literature are clearly with the former, neither tradition had the resources to provide the way out of the despair of exile. The new circumstances around 587 required a new theological assertion.[9] In his rereading of the events around Jerusalem in his moment of procla- mation, Jeremiah therefore used various elements of already existing in- terpretation models. These models, however, are handled in ways that are

9. See Gerhard von Rad, *Old Testament Theology,* 2 (New York: Harper & Row; Edinburgh: Oliver & Boyd, 1965), 263-277.

freshly discerning and astonishingly imaginative. The outcome is that Jeremiah's rendering of Jerusalem's experience and destiny is a wholly new one that belongs peculiarly to this literature.

In arriving at this imaginative, subtle, and bold rereading, the book of Jeremiah:

(1) reinterprets the events of *Realpolitik* through the categories of covenantal obligation and covenantal sanctions,
(2) disrupts the claims of the covenantal (Deuteronomic) pattern of obligation and sanction by a disclosure of the pathos of God that will not be contained in the tradition of covenant, and
(3) utilizes the combination of covenantal motifs and divine pathos to critique and reject the claims of the royal-temple ideology.

By such creative transformation of the available traditions, Jeremiah asserts that the city will be dismantled by the will and power of Yahweh (and not by the decision of Babylon), and that a new community of covenantal possibility will emerge after the dismantling, as a free gift of Yahweh.

The Book

The book of Jeremiah is a complicated literary composition that has evoked much scholarly attention. During the last century, an approximate consensus has been reached among critical scholars that the book contains three layers of literature reflecting three layers of redactional activity: (1) the poetic utterances of the prophet Jer-emiah, (2) the narrative accounts of Baruch, and (3) the theological overlay of Deuteronomic theologians.[10] This consensus reflects a scholarly view that the literature has emerged through identifiable stages of editorial activity. There is not agreement, however, among scholars about the precise extent of each of these layers of literature, nor the process by which they came to be a part of the book.

That three-source critical consensus, however, is now open to serious doubts because scholars are no longer agreed that the character of the book can be understood according to such a mechanical literary process. The

10. For a review of scholarship, see Brevard S. Childs, *Introduction to the Old Testament as Scripture* (Philadelphia: Fortress; London: SCM, 1979), 342-344.

7

literary formation of the book is much more dynamic and processive than such a three-document proposal would allow. Moreover, the new stress on the canonical shape of the literature may diminish the pertinence of these older historical-critical questions. Nonetheless, the residue of the old scholarly consensus includes two important points to which scholars give general and broad assent.

First, there is a core of material that originated with the historical person of Jeremiah. Second, an extended process of editorial work has transformed and perhaps made beyond recovery the original work of the prophet. What we now have is a literature decisively shaped by a later traditioning process. Beyond the general conclusion that the book contains *material from Jeremiah* and *subsequent editorial activity*, there is no discernible agreement among scholars.

Attempts to refine or advance beyond the "three-source critical consensus" may be grouped in three scholarly positions.

1. The more conservative critical position, perhaps standing in closest continuity to the older critical scholarship, is represented by William L. Holladay[11] and by the well established commentary of John Bright.[12] This approach seeks to determine the date and exact historical setting of each textual unit. It asks specific historical questions of each passage. Moreover, this approach is inclined to maximize the role of the actual person Jeremiah by assigning as much material as possible to the prophet. The work of Holladay and Bright, therefore, is inclined to accept whenever possible the claim of the book of Jeremiah itself, that the materials do indeed stem from the work of the prophet.

2. In sharp contrast to this first approach is the dominant tendency of recent British scholarship, articulated especially by Robert P. Carroll,[13] but also by Peter R. Ackroyd[14] and Ernest W. Nicholson.[15] This scholarly

---

11. William L. Holladay, *Jeremiah: Spokesman Out of Time* (Philadelphia: United Church, 1974), and now *Jeremiah 1,* Hermeneia (Philadelphia: Fortress; London: SCM, 1986).

12. John Bright, *Jeremiah,* 2nd ed., Anchor Bible 21 (Garden City: Doubleday, 1978).

13. *From Chaos to Covenant.*

14. "The Book of Jeremiah — Some Recent Studies," *Journal for the Study of the Old Testament* 28 (1984): 47-59.

15. Ernest W. Nicholson, *Preaching to the Exiles* (Oxford: Blackwell, 1970).

position focuses on the Deuteronomic editing of the book of Jeremiah in the Exile, a generation or two after the person of Jeremiah. The canonical text of Jeremiah is understood to be the work of exilic editors and redactors who have recast and transformed the older material for the sake of the community in exile, under the influence of the tradition of Deuteronomy. This approach focuses on the constructive pastoral and theological intention of the community in exile that construed the tradition of Jeremiah in fresh directions in order to meet fresh religious needs. As a result of the exilic community's theological mediation of the Jeremiah tradition, we cannot recover with any certitude any of the actual words of Jeremiah. Indeed, we have no access to the person of Jeremiah or his words, except as mediated by the community, and to pose such an historical question is both futile and irrelevant. From this scholarly perspective, the book of Jeremiah is seen to have no interest in the person of Jeremiah, and thus neither should we. Pursuit of such historical questions about the person or the words of the prophet should be abandoned.

We are at an especially fortuitous time in Jeremiah studies, because in 1986, both Holladay and Carroll published commentaries that provide a sustained presentation of their quite contrasting arguments.[16] These two commentaries represent the major literary-critical developments in Jeremiah studies since the older three-source critical consensus. They are likely to determine the shape and parameters of scholarly conversation for a long time to come.

The two perspectives of Holladay and Carroll stand in sharp contrast to each other. Holladay is inclined to assign to the prophet Jeremiah as much as possible, whereas Carroll believes that the work of the original prophet is beyond identification or recovery, so weighty is the exilic recasting of the corpus. Despite the sharp contrasts of their literary assumptions, however, it is important to note that Holladay and Carroll proceed with quite parallel concerns. Both ask primarily historical questions, and

16. Holladay, *Jeremiah 1,* Hermeneia; Carroll, *Jeremiah,* Old Testament Library (Philadelphia: Westminster; London: SCM, 1986). Also published in this remarkable year in Jeremiah studies was William McKane, *Jeremiah,* 1, International Critical Commentary (Edinburgh: T. & T. Clark). The commentaries of Holladay and Carroll likely represent the extreme parameters of current discussion. McKane's is a close and technical study filling the long lamentable void in the ICC series. None of these commentaries was available in time for me to benefit in my work on chs. 1–25.

both are singularly concerned to identify the historical location of the text. Whereas Holladay is concerned in some way with "the quest for the historical Jeremiah," Carroll, so to speak, is engaged in a "quest for the Deuteronomic Jeremiah." Much is to be learned from both enterprises, but both leave matters of interpretation incomplete. There is a tendency to focus so much on questions of historicity and redaction that literary and theological questions of the text as it stands do not receive as much attention as might be desired.

3. A third perspective has been adumbrated by Brevard S. Childs, who proposes to subordinate historical questions to the canonical shape of the literature.[17] Childs recognizes and seeks to value both the "original Jeremiah" and the "Deuteronomic editor." He has taken the uncontested literary judgment that the "original Jeremiah" has been recast by Deuteronomists in exile and has shown how that editorial/canonical combination of "original" and "exilic" materials articulates the theological claim of God's judgment against recalcitrant Jerusalem and God's promissory act of newness.[18] The canonical shape of the book thus makes clear that God "watches over" the sovereign word of God, first to pluck up and tear down, then to plant and to build (Jer. 1:10; 31:27-30). The initial word of Jeremiah was a word of judgment, of plucking up and tearing down. A quite distinct second word of hope has been imposed upon the judgment of planting and building. The dual theme of judgment and promise is reflected in the editorial shaping of the canonical text.[19] The intent and effect of Childs's work is to free the double theological assertion and function of the text from its particular historical locus in the 7th and 6th centuries. Childs does not seek a Jeremiah dating with Holladay, nor an exilic placement with Carroll. He brackets out such historical questions for the sake of the text's twofold theological intention. A study of Childs' proposal shows the extent to which Holladay and Carroll, while drawing

17. *Old Testament as Scripture,* 345-354.

18. In a general way the "original work" of Jeremiah presents a statement of God's judgment and the "exilic material" articulates God's promissory work. Childs, however, is interested in the double theological intention, not in the historical placement of the various texts.

19. On the general structure of judgment and promise in the prophets, see Ronald E. Clements, "Patterns in the Prophetic Canon," in *Canon and Authority,* ed. George W. Coats and Burke O. Long (Philadelphia: Fortress, 1977), 42-55. The structure of the book of Jeremiah provides evidence for Clements's general notion.

opposite conclusions, are in fact addressing very similar questions, the very questions Childs critiques.

There is at present no scholarly consensus about these three quite different perspectives. It is not the interest of the present commentary to advance this critical conversation, nor to adjudicate between these several alternatives. It is perhaps enough to conclude that the theological tradition of the book of Jeremiah continues to be lively and energizing long after the end of the work of the prophet Jeremiah.

The Person of Jeremiah

In light of the preceding statement concerning the work of Holladay and Carroll, it is not surprising that the question of the "person of Jeremiah" is exceedingly difficult.[20] A more conservative view (Holladay and Bright) assumes that one can in some way reach close to the person of Jeremiah and reconstruct that historical person from the data. At the other extreme, Carroll concludes that the materials have been so completely reshaped that they provide no clues to the historical person and that there is no access. It may well be, however, that these alternatives put the question wrongly.

Every historical presentation of a personality is a mediation and a construction.[21] What we have of the person of Jeremiah in the book of Jeremiah is more like a "portrait" that reflects the taste and interest of the artist, rather than an objective report that is factually precise. At the same time, as Timothy Polk has argued, it can hardly be denied that in the midst of this complicated Jeremiah literature there is an anchoring reference to a powerful personality about which the editors had some knowl-

20. See David Jobling, "The Quest of the Historical Jeremiah: Hermeneutical Implications of Recent Literature," in *A Prophet to the Nations,* ed. Perdue and Kovacs, 285-297;and Timothy Polk, *The Prophetic Persona,* JSOT Supplement 32 (Sheffield: University of Sheffield Press, 1984).

21. Roy Shafer, *Language and Insight* (New Haven: Yale University Press, 1978), 8-18, argues that every personal presentation of a historical self is a "construction." He concludes that this is so even when a person presents himself or herself. That being so in our self-presentation, it is obviously so when any literary effort is made to "present" an historical person. Thus there can be little doubt that Jeremiah as given us in the book of Jeremiah is a "construction." See Walter Brueggemann, "The Book of Jeremiah: Portrait of the Prophet," *Interpretation,* 37 (1983): 130-145.

edge and some conviction.[22] That knowledge and conviction of the historical person, however, are given to us in ways that reflect the interests and faith of those who give us the data.

Thus I have no difficulty in speaking of the person of Jeremiah, while being aware that the only "person" of Jeremiah about which we can know anything is given us through an intentional construction. I have characteristically spoken in my exposition of "the poet," "the prophet," or "Jeremiah" as the agent behind and within the text. Such a reference is not naively historical. To speak of "Jeremiah" is to refer to the constructed *persona* of the prophet that is no doubt rooted in the actual reality, and that equally without doubt is mediated and constructed for us in a particular way. Such a reference is in part an expository convenience, for clearly there is an agent who is evoker and actor in the text. But such a reference to "Jeremiah" is also a recognition that there is a coherence in the text in some way reflective of and witness to concrete historical experience and faith. The determination whether such evidences point to a discernible historical figure or an imaginative literary construct is not required for this exposition, and finally adjudication of the matter is impossible. We know enough about tradition, context, and style to recognize "the voice" at work in the text, even if we name that voice with full recognition of the ambiguity, complexity, and uncertainty surrounding that portrayed person.[23]

An Interpretive Perspective

In my interpretation I have paid special attention to two emerging methods in Scripture study.

22. Polk has argued well the delicate interaction between the constructive tradition and the person of the prophet. Finally he comes down on the side of the "persona" as a purposed paradigm for the reading community: "In my opinion, it violates the integrity of the text, *qua* poetry, to replace the given literary context with the conjectured historical occasion of the writing process and so to construe the text as referring to authorial circumstances rather than to the subject as it is literarily defined" (*The Prophetic Persona*, 165).

23. Robert M. Polzin, *Moses and the Deuteronomist* (New York: Seabury, 1980), has utilized the notice of conflicting "voices" in the text to good advantage. His work is informed by the critical theory of V. N. Voloshinov.

1. *Sociological analysis* has recently become important in Scripture study.[24] In this method, one pays attention to the interests, ideologies, and constructions of reality that are operative in the formation and transmission of the text.[25] The biblical text is understood as neither neutral nor objective, but as located in, reflective of, and concerned for a particular social context that is determinative of its shape and focus. This approach is distinct from the older historical-critical approach because it does not seek specific historical placement but, rather, a placement within various social voices or dynamic forces. Interpretation requires attention both to the particular voice in the text and to the other voices in the situation with which this voice may be in dispute, tension, or agreement.

The use of sociological analysis in the reading of Jeremiah is complicated because the world of the text permits the sounding of many voices. We may surmise voices present in the situation of the text representing the old covenant tradition, the memory of hurt from Hosea, the legitimacy of the monarchy, the high temple theology of the priesthood, pro-Babylonian and pro-Egyptian political preferences, and the powerful families of nobility that are in tension with the royal family and may represent the old claims of rural elders. In reading Jeremiah one asks how these various voices interact with each other, which ones are allied against what other ones, and how they are variously presented as reflective of or resistant to the will of Yahweh. In a later generation of the Jeremiah tradition, we likely contend with pastoral voices among exiles, with the claims of the community that remained in Judah, and again with pro-Egyptian voices. It is not nearly so important to date passages as it is to attend to the interaction of these several forces that vied for influence and legitimacy.

The interaction of these different voices in Jeremiah tend to coalesce around one central issue. The text of Jeremiah articulates a dispute (re-

---

24. See Robert R. Wilson, *Sociological Approaches to the Old Testament,* Guides to Biblical Scholarship (Philadelphia: Fortress, 1984). While Wilson well articulates the method, a much more substantive and influential use of the method is by Norman K. Gottwald, *The Tribes of Yahweh* (Maryknoll, N.Y.: Orbis, 1979). Gottwald's sociological analysis has been instructive for me in understanding Jeremiah's radical critique of the urban establishment of Jerusalem.

25. On such social construction, see Peter L. Berger and Thomas Luckmann, *The Social Construction of Reality* (Garden City: Doubleday, 1966).

flective of a conversation in Jerusalem) about who rightly understands historical events and who rightly discerns the relation between faith, morality, and political power. The tradition of Jeremiah articulates a covenant-torah view of reality that stands in deep tension with the royal-priestly ideology of the Jerusalem establishment. The Jeremiah tradition insists that covenant fidelity is the clue to public well-being, and a violation of such fidelity will bring death to the community. The tradition of Jeremiah assumes and argues that the historical process in Judah is rightly perceived not by those in the temple establishment, but by the voice of covenant fidelity that is clearly marginal. The book of Jeremiah is nearly unambiguous in its conviction that the Jerusalem ideology is a mistaken, fraudulent notion of public life that can only lead to death. This central tension between perceptions of reality, reflective of a deep social conflict, is present in many — if not all — parts of the book of Jeremiah.

The use of sociological analysis enables the interpreter to place the dispute between covenantal and noncovenantal notions of life and community into the particular social life setting of the divided Jerusalem community. The articulation of the social forces at work in this dispute permits the ongoing power and pertinence of the Jeremiah tradition in subsequent generations and new social settings. The claims of the royal-priestly ideology repeatedly are embodied, generation after generation, in monopolistic centers of domination in every sphere of human life. These centers imagine they are immune from the risks and responsibilities of the historical process. Conversely, a passionate commitment to covenant stands in every generation and every circumstance as a critical alternative to such domination.

The text requires very little explicit "application" to see that centers of domination still lead to exile and death, and that covenantal alternatives, mediated by God's sovereign graciousness, continue to be a fragile offer of life. The text continues its authoritative claim in new situations because the same social realities recur, and because the same witness to the same sovereign God is pertinent in new situations.

2. *Literary analysis* (which does not refer to the old source analysis)

---

26. Among the better representatives of this approach in an expanding literature are the books of Robert Alter, *The Art of Biblical Narrative* (New York: Basic Books; London: Allen & Unwin, 1981), and *The Art of Biblical Poetry* (New York: Basic Books, 1985); Meir Sternberg, *The Poetics of Biblical Narrative* (Bloomington: Indiana

is equally important in present Scripture study.[26] In this method, one pays attention to the power of language to propose an imaginative world that is an alternative to the one that seems to be at hand — alternative to the one in which the reader or listener thinks herself or himself enmeshed. Literature then is not regarded as descriptive of what is, but as evocative and constructive of another life world.[27] In this method, one takes the "world" offered in the text as a possible alternative world without excessive reference to external historical factors and without excessive interest in questions of authorship. This approach permits literature to be enormously daring and bold, and often abrasive and subversive in the face of the presumed world of the listener. It places the listener in crisis, but also presents the listener with a new zone for fresh hope, changed conduct, and fresh historical possibility.

The conviction that literature is evocative and not merely descriptive has significance only as that conviction receives specific implementation. This requires a careful "close reading" of the text in which one pays attention to the use, repetition, and arrangement of words, shifts in voices, deliberate verbal strategies that cause breaks, surprises, contrasts, comparisons, ambiguities, and open-ended wonderment in the text. The interpreter focuses on the action and voice of the text itself and is not led away from the actual work of the text by any external reference or hypothesis.

This method of literary analysis is useful in the study of Jeremiah in three ways. First, one notices the powerful and provocative use of metaphor

---

University Press, 1985); Phyllis Trible, *God and the Rhetoric of Sexuality,* Overtures to Biblical Theology 2 (Philadelphia: Fortress, 1978), and *Texts of Terror,* Overtures to Biblical Theology 13 (Philadelphia: Fortress, 1984); and David M. Gunn, *The Story of King David,* JSOT Supplement 6 (1978), and *The Fate of King Saul,* JSOT Supplement 14 (1980). For the delicate relation between literary theory and literary method, see John Barton, *Reading the Old Testament* (Philadelphia: Westminster; London: Darton, Longman & Todd, 1984).

27. This perspective on biblical literature is especially derived from the work of Paul Ricoeur, *Essays on Biblical Interpretation* (Philadelphia: Fortress; London: SPCK, 1980). See the helpful introductory article by Lewis S. Mudge in that volume ("Paul Ricouer on Biblical Interpretation," 1-40). More directly, the work of Amos N. Wilder has best considered the cruciality of language for its evocative, imaginative power. See Wilder, "The Word as Address and the Word as Meaning," in *The New Hermeneutic,* ed. James M. Robinson and John B. Cobb, Jr. (New York and London: Harper & Row, 1964), 198-218.

and image. One must follow the daring use of the specific language of the text if one is to sense the intention of the text.[28] One becomes aware that the language is carefully and artistically crafted so that the text can never be summarized but only "followed" in its portrayal of a fresh reality that takes its life from the powerful, passionate speech of the concrete text.[29] It becomes clear then that *what is said* is congruous with and dependent upon *how it is said*.[30] Through its concrete language the text of Jeremiah can variously evoke a sense of creation that has massively regressed to chaos (4:23-26), an awareness of God's grief and sickness at Judah's obduracy (8:18–9:3), or the resumption of wedding parties in a land where all such social rejoicing had stopped (33:11; cf. 7:34; 16:9; 25:10). The boldness of the metaphors witnesses to and evokes radical endings and astonishing beginnings in the social process.

The concreteness and imaginative power of such speech invites a different discernment and experience of the world of Jerusalem and Babylon. In turn, it summons the listener to reject the ideological discernment of the world by the royal-temple establishment, which is shown to be false and which will only lead to death. The language of the text means to penetrate and expose the counterinterpretations of the "establishment" for what they are: misleading, misinformed notions that lead away from the power and possibilities of historical reality as an arena of God's rule and

28. James Muilenburg, "The Terminology of Adversity in Jeremiah," in *Translating & Understanding the Old Testament,* ed. Harry Thomas Frank and William L. Reed (New York: Abingdon, 1970), 42-63, has made an important beginning on these matters in the book of Jeremiah. Unfortunately, Muilenburg's acute and discerning analysis of the rhetoric of Jeremiah remains unpublished. For an appreciative assessment of his work that centered in Jeremiah, see Bernhard W. Anderson, "Introduction: The New Frontier of Rhetorical Criticism," in *Rhetorical Criticism: Essays in Honor of James Muilenburg,* ed. Jared J. Jackson and Martin Kessler, Pittsburgh Theological Monograph 1 (Pittsburgh: Pickwick, 1974), ix-xviii; repr. in *Hearing and Speaking the Word,* ed. Thomas F. Best (Chico, Calif.: Scholars Press, 1984), 14-23.

29. On the notion of "following" the text, see W. B. Gallie, "The Historical Understanding," in *History and Theory,* ed. George H. Nadel (1965; repr. Middletown, Conn.: Wesleyan University Press, 1977), 149-202. Gallie's treatment concerns narrative, but the same posture applies to all texts that have such passionate concrete historical intentionality.

30. On the profound connection between what is said and how it is said, see the careful analysis of Gail R. O'Day, *Revelation in the Fourth Gospel: Narrative Mode and Theological Claim* (Philadelphia: Fortress, 1986).

purpose. The "establishment" assumed a kind of political, moral, intellectual autonomy that the Jeremiah tradition critiques as false and deathly.

Second, it is crucial to our interpretation that Jeremiah's proposal of the world is indeed an imaginative construct, not a description of what is nor a prediction of what will be. Jeremiah is attentive to the data all around him, but the text itself is not intended as descriptive account, nor can it be assessed as such. It invites the listener to participate in the proposed world so that one can imagine a terminated royal world while that world still exists, and one can receive in imaginative prospect a new community of covenant faith where none has yet emerged. The text leads the listener out beyond presently discerned reality to new reality formed in the moment of speaking and hearing.[31]

Third, if the context of Jeremiah's work is the royal-priestly ideology of the Jerusalem establishment (as my sociological presentation above suggests), then the alternative imaginative portrayal of a covenant community is juxtaposed to that royal-priestly ideology. The text offers imaginative alternatives to established ideology in the conviction that God is at work to *create a new alternative community* ("to plant and to build"; 31:27-30). The freedom of liberated, faithful speech anticipates and evokes new public reality.

Thus the two methods of sociological and literary analysis, when utilized in Jeremiah, yield respectively a *critique of ideology* and a *practice of liberated imagination*. These two methods enable us to take a fresh look at critical theological issues in the Jeremiah tradition. A sociological analysis helps us see how the covenantal perspectives of the prophetic tradition stand over against royal ideology. A literary analysis helps us see how Judah is invited to act faithfully, even if that faithfulness is against the presumed interest and "truth" of the Jerusalem establishment.

When the text is read and heard as a critique of ideology and as a practice of alternative imagination, the text continues to have power and pertinence in many subsequent contexts, including our own.[32] Indeed, the

31. See for example Bernhard W. Anderson, " 'The Lord Has Created Something New': A Stylistic Study of Jer. 31:15-22," in *A Prophet to the Nations*, ed. Perdue and Kovacs, 367-380.

32. James A. Sanders ("Hermeneutics," in *The Interpreter's Dictionary of the Bible*, Supplement, ed. Keith R. Crim [Nashville: Abingdon, 1976], 406), has rightly suggested that "dynamic analogy" is a helpful way to interpret the text. He stresses

text has the powerful capacity to cause us to rediscern our own situation, to experience our situation in quite new ways, and to participate in our own historical situation with new liberty and fresh passion — liberty and passion that arise in and with faithfulness. Such a text, when read critically, characteristically assaults every "structure of domination" with its self-serving and misrepresenting propaganda, including our own military, technological, consumer-oriented establishment. Such a text, when read imaginatively, issues a forceful invitation to an alternative community of covenant, including a risky invitation in our own time to practices of justice, risks of compassion, and sufferings for peace.

This text does not require "interpretation" or "application" so that it can be brought near our experience and circumstance. Rather, the text is so powerful and compelling, so passionate and uncompromising in its anguish and hope, that it requires we submit our experience to it and thereby reenter our experience on new terms, namely the terms of the text. The text does not need to be *applied* to our situation. Rather, our situation needs to be *submitted* to the text for a fresh discernment. It is our situation, not the text, that requires a new interpretation. In every generation, this text subverts all our old readings of reality and forces us to a new, dangerous, obedient reading.[33] If such a subversive reading of reality appears to us unreal, too dangerous, and too costly, we must recognize that for most in the 7th and 6th cents. it was rejected for exactly the same reasons.

Indeed, everything depends on our reading and hearing this text. If we fail to hear this text, we may succumb to a fraudulent discernment of our situation. Like ancient Jerusalem, we shall imagine that the present is decided by the policies of the empire and not by the pathos of the holy, faithful God. Like ancient exiles, we may imagine that our situation is occupied only by despair and alienation, that God's arm is shortened and there is none to comfort. We shall miss the summons home, the faint beginnings of new laughter in Jerusalem, and shall still be submitting to

---

that the analogy must be "dynamic," that is, one that emerges out of one's own interpretation and experience. Thus I have not pressed analogies in my interpretation, but invite the reader to make those connections out of experience and interpretation.

33. David Tracy (*The Analogical Imagination* [New York: Crossroad; London: SCM, 1981], chs. 3 and 4), has shown how a "classic" must have continued, ongoing, and developing interpretation in order to be timely as well as timeless. Jeremiah is just such a tradition that is both timely and timeless, kept timely by repeated interpretation.

the empire when we could be on our way rejoicing. Everything depends on the text, for without this transformative, critical, liberating, subversive speech, we shall live in a speechless, textless world that is always misunderstood. Without the text we are at the mercy of powerful ideology, of misrepresenting propaganda, of anxieties that make us conformist, and despair that drives us to brutality. It is precisely the text in its odd offer of holiness and pathos, of rending and healing, that dismisses ideology, exposes propaganda, overrides anxiety, and offers forgiveness in the place of brutality.

A commentary as this one must focus on what the text of Jeremiah meant in its ancient speaking and hearing. But that ancient speaking and hearing keeps pushing into our present. What it "meant" has incredible power to "mean" now.[34] It meant then that Yahweh would work a powerful, savage, pathos-filled purpose with that people, and it still means that that purpose is at work among us. It meant that Yahweh could grieve a terrible ending, and it still means we face terrible endings over which Yahweh grieves. It meant that Yahweh had the resilient power to work a newness among the displaced, and it still means that Yahweh's resilient power is at work in such displacements. It meant and means that the prideful empire, the pitiful royal leadership, the self-serving religionists, the cynical forces in society, cannot have their way, for history with Yahweh is about another intention. To be sure, the meaning we receive from the text is nuanced very differently from its early "meant." Our meaning is transmitted through our Enlightenment modes of scientific and rational autonomy. We cannot so easily ascribe the shape of the historical process to a single agent. My comments intend not to be reductionist or blindly supernaturalist. We can only interpret in our own situation when we know the historical process admits of no easy interpretation. Nonetheless, this textual tradition in its anguish and in its buoyancy witnesses to an inescapable hovering of God that is oddly sovereign in ways that outdistance

34. The split of "what it meant" and "what it means" has been championed by Krister Stendahl ("Biblical Theology, Contemporary," in *The Interpreter's Dictionary of the Bible,* ed. George A. Buttrick [Nashville: Abingdon, 1962] 1:418-420), but in retrospect seems clearly to have been a misperception. See the criticism of Stendahl by James Barr, "Biblical Theology," in *IDB, Supplement,* 106. In this commentary it is assumed that what "meant" inescapably "means," and both the writer and the reader are engaged in that interpretive transaction.

our desperate modernity. Poetic anguish, lyrical expectation, metaphorical openness, and imaginative ambiguity are ways in which sovereign hurt and fidelity are mediated to us. This powerful mediating shocks our intellectual self-confidence and invites us to reengage life with courage, awe, and submissiveness. This commentary is about that other holy, passionate, powerful intention that plucks up and tears down, that plants and builds, that subverts and amazes.

The Word through Jeremiah

Jeremiah 1

Editor's Preface (1:1-3)

These verses are an editor's preface to the book of Jeremiah, with parallels in other prophetic books (Isa. 1:1; Hos. 1:1; Amos 1:1). The formula reminds us that the present book of Jeremiah is the result of a long, complicated editorial process. These verses appear simply to provide historical data about the setting of the book, but in fact this introduction addresses issues more serious than historical placement.[1]

The unit identifies Jeremiah in a double way, historically as rooted in the priestly traditions of Anathoth (likely derived from the conservative covenantal traditions of Abiathar; 1 Kgs. 2:26-27) and theologically as recipient of Yahweh's invasive sovereign word. These introductory sentences intend to identify and authorize Jeremiah as a vehicle for Yahweh's governing word spoken at a specific time and place.

1:2-3 These verses make clear, however, that the editor does not linger long over the person of Jeremiah. What is of interest is "the word of the LORD," mentioned twice. The word of the LORD is not identified with the words of Jeremiah, nor with the book of Jeremiah. There are here two

---

1. See Gene M. Tucker, "Prophetic Superscriptions and the Growth of a Canon," in *Canon and Authority,* ed. George W. Coats and Burke O. Long (Philadelphia: Fortress, 1977), 56-70.

levels of word, that of Yahweh and that of Jeremiah. This preface makes no judgment about their relation to each other. It is enough to recognize that the words of this book stand in some special connection to the word of Yahweh. The theological claim of these verses is that the life of Jeremiah and this text sound the sovereign voice of Yahweh.

The word of the LORD is not a romantic or floating spiritual notion. It can be precisely linked to a chronological process. The arena of Yahweh's governing word is lodged in the reigns of Josiah (626-609 B.C.E.), Jehoiakim (609-598), and Zedekiah (598-587). The word of Yahweh is borne by the prophet, but it impinges upon the royal reality. It intrudes into the neat chronology of the kings to give us early notice that another governance is here that will unsettle the neat, fixed chronology. The word opens royal reality to another governance.

The phrase "until the captivity of Jerusalem" provides the terminus toward which the book of Jeremiah moves. This is more than a chronological reference. It is an awesome and dreadful formula. It is a clue to the intent of Yahweh's word and a signal about the nature of the book of Jeremiah. No doubt the book contains passages after 587, and there are evidently elements of hope; but the canonical scheme announces that the end point of this prophetic tradition coincides with the end point of historical Judah and of viable Jerusalem. Nothing more, it is suggested in these verses, can be said or need be said after that terrible moment. The word is on the move toward exile. Nothing the kings can do will alter that massive bent to the historical process of God's people. The kings, alleged managers of the historical process, stand helpless and exposed in the face of that disposition of Yahweh. It is a theme we will encounter repeatedly.

As the book of Jeremiah now stands, these verses on exile *(golah)* have as their counterpart Jer. 52:27-34. These together form an envelope at beginning and end of the book, in order to assert that this entire literary tradition is preoccupied with exile, with its source in Yahweh and its embodiment in Israel, Yahweh's people. The working out of Yahweh's word as Jeremiah's word has as its purpose and intent the ending of Jerusalem, the dismantling of that royal world, the termination of the recital of kings in Jerusalem. It is as though in this terse preface we are given the entire plot to the book of Jeremiah. The whole book as it stands is a literary-theological disclosure of the unraveling of a royal world, of the disintegration of a stable universe of public order and public confidence. The man Jeremiah is thrust into the middle of that dismantling to bring the deathliness of Jerusalem to speech. It is as though the die is cast even before the person of the prophet appears. The kings are named who are the helpless, unwitting recipients of this terminating action. Most importantly, however, it is the speech of Yahweh that evokes the end. The known world is not ending in spite of Yahweh's governance, as though Yahweh were weak. Rather, it is ending precisely because of Yahweh's governance. What may appear to be weakness and failure on the part of Yahweh is in fact Yahweh's policy.

The book of Jeremiah is thus an unwelcome offer. If we enter, we are invited to accompany the painful, genuinely unthinkable process whereby the Holy City is denied its special character and is handed over, by the intent of Yahweh, to the ruthlessness of Babylon. Kings, of course, never believe history works that way. Kings imagine that royal decisions can shape public life. But this literary piece asserts otherwise. Because of Yahweh, the historical process is headed toward exile. That is where disobedient history finally leads. No escape is available. Here, such escape is not even hoped for, for that would be hope against the sovereign policy decision of Yahweh. There are chronological difficulties in this scheme, but those difficulties are modest compared to the overriding assertion that an ending is willed that is now brought to speech. And when it is spoken, the ending will not go away. We only wait and watch for the ending to materialize. The book of Jeremiah is a witness to that long torturous watch.

Jeremiah's Call (1:4-19)

The book of Jeremiah "redescribes" the historical process by which God's people *go into exile* and surprisingly, come *out of exile*. That redescription hinges on the powerful presence of Yahweh in the historical process through Yahweh's word that has its own free say, without reference to human strategies and calculations. The tradition of Jeremiah is a stunning reflection on the power of Yahweh's word to order historical events (on which see Isa. 14:24-27; 55:8-9). That decisive say of Yahweh, inscrutable as it is, is borne through the human agency of Jeremiah, whose spoken word turns out to be the governing word of Yahweh. This strange convergence of human agent and sovereign word is a fundamental assumption of the prophetic tradition, which is made without embarrassment. The text offers no explanation about how the prophetic word is a sovereign word of Yahweh. Human words turn out, often to our dismay, to be the governing word of Yahweh. The speech of Jeremiah is presented as decisive both for entry into exile and return from it.

1:4-10 These verses are commonly regarded as a "call narrative" of the prophet Jeremiah. The words reflect common stylized features of such a call.[2] Those standard and predictable features include:

- divine initiative (v. 5)
- human resistance (v. 6)
- rebuke and reassurance (vv. 7-8)
- physical act of commissioning (v. 9a) and
- substance of commission (vv. 9b-10).

Three understandings of the narrative are available to us.

1. The text reports the actual personal experience of Jeremiah. This has been the conventional interpretation, especially among those who are interested in the personality and "spiritual experience" of the prophet. On this reading, the text tells about how this known person received authority.

2. Because the sequence is so stylized, it is suggested that this is a liturgical report of something like an ordination service.[3] This interpretation lessens the personal intensity of the first view, but has the merit of lodging the authority of the prophet more decisively in the institutional life and social fabric of the community. The prophet does not receive authority as primitive "raw data," but authority is mediated through a community that acknowledges the authority claimed for the prophet. The authority of the prophet then is a much more public authorization and might illuminate why Jeremiah has as much access as he had to public officials. These verses suggest that in the liturgy he has been publicly recognized to have this special vocation.

3. It has also been suggested that the text reflects neither personal nor liturgic experience but is an editorial construction, according to literary

---

2. See Norman Habel, "The Form and Significance of the Call Narratives," *Zeitschrift für die alttestamentlichen Wissenschaft* 77 (1965): 297-323.

3. See Henning Graf Reventlow, *Liturgie und prophetisches Ich bei Jeremia* (Gütersloh: Gerd Mohn, 1963), 24-77.

convention, to give authorization to the text that follows this chapter.[4] While this may sound odd to us, such a judgment reflects the turn of contemporary scholarship away from the person of Jeremiah to the book of Jeremiah. From this perspective, the intent of this narrative is to affirm that the text which follows is not merely a human construction, but is in fact the purposeful governing assertion of Yahweh, who will have history move as Yahweh asserts it.

According to this canonical interpretation, the personal response of Jeremiah is rather incidental. There may be fear because Yahweh's word is a hard, dangerous word to speak. It is a sovereign word that changes the historical process, and finally that purpose can be resisted neither by the prophet nor by the king. If this third interpretation is a serious one (as I judge it to be), then the accent falls not on the personal struggle of the man, but on the substantive sovereign word of v. 10. At the most, the prophet is a bearer of this word that will decide the future of the city, the temple, the dynasty and, indeed, the nation. Interpretive interest is immediately shifted away from the person of the prophet toward the prophetic text. It is this shift away from the personal to the canonical that permits the speech of Jeremiah to have continuing interest and power for us.

The six verbs of v. 10 — "pluck up" and "break down," "destroy" and "overthrow," "build" and "plant" — are a pointed statement of God's way with the nations. The first four verbs are negative. They assert that no historical structure, political policy, or defense scheme can secure a community against Yahweh when that community is under the judgment of Yahweh. The last two positive verbs, "build" and "plant," assert in parallel fashion that God can work newness, create historical possibilities *ex nihilo,* precisely in situations that seem hopeless and closed. God works in freedom without respect either to the enduring structures so evident, or to the powerless despair when structures are gone. God alone has the capacity to bring endings and new beginnings in the historical process (cf. Deut. 32:39; Isa. 45:7; 113:7-9).

It may be suggested that this range of six verbs provides the essential

4. See Robert P. Carroll, *From Chaos to Covenant* (New York: Crossroad; London: SCM, 1981), 49-58. Carroll takes the call narrative as a literary device wrought by the Deuteronomic editors. Brevard S. Childs (*Introduction to the Old Testament as Scripture* [Philadelphia: Fortress; London: SCM, 1979], 348-350), relates the biographical material to the shaping of the canonical tradition.

25

shape of the book of Jeremiah in its present form (cf. Jer. 18:7-10; 24:6; 31:27-28; 42:10; 45:4).[5] The book of Jeremiah in its main thrust concerns *the ending of beloved Jerusalem,* an ending wrought by the purposes of Yahweh in the face of every kind of human resistance, and *the formation of a new beloved Jerusalem* wrought by the creative power of Yahweh against all the data and in the face of massive despair. Indeed, the coming and going of Jerusalem (and by inference any historical structure) is not according to its own capacity for life and survival, but only according to the sovereign inclination of Yahweh. The prophet (prophetic person, prophetic text) authorized to carry this word is derivative from and subordinated to the irresistible purposes of Yahweh. Thus the text makes a sweeping claim for God's free governance.

In the NT one can see how this same bold way of thinking is applied to the claims made for Jesus. In John 2:19 the verbs "destroy" and "raise up" appear. They are used with reference to the Jerusalem establishment, specifically the temple. But an important interpretive move is made so that the intent is to speak of the crucifixion and resurrection of Jesus. The value of observing this analogy is to see that, in those early claims for Jesus, the early Church derives its understanding of the historical process from prophetic faith, and perhaps precisely from Jeremiah. In both cases, Jeremiah and Jesus, the text invites one to reckon with the reality of discontinuity in the historical process out of which God can work a powerful newness, utterly inexplicable.

The conversations with and about the prophet in Jer. 1:5-9 are aimed toward God's magisterial governance expressed in v. 10. It is no wonder that the prophet resists, for who wants to bear such a burdensome and unwelcome word! But the word overrules its bearer. The message requires the messenger. What follows in the book of Jeremiah is a study of how this word of harsh endings and amazing beginnings has its way with specificity. We must not be unduly preoccupied with the person of the prophet who here is the way of God's specificity. In this unit the person of the prophet is not a subject but an object of God's overriding verbs. As the person of the prophet is subject to God's sovereign action, so also is

5. See the discerning analysis of Prescott H. Williams, Jr., "Living Toward the Acts of the Savior-Judge," *Austin Seminary Bulletin* 94 (1978): 130-139; and the canonical reflections of Ronald E. Clements, "Patterns in the Prophetic Canon," in Coats and Long, *Canon and Authority,* 42-55.

the history of Jerusalem, of Judah, and finally of Babylon. That sovereign action, to which v. 3 has already given notice, revolves around the inescapable reality of exile. Because there is this particular exile into which and out of which God's people must go and come, there must be this prophet to speak Judah into exile and out again.

1:11-16 In this passage are reports of two "visions" that support the claim of Yahweh in vv. 4-10. The first of these (vv. 11-12) concerns a play on words: *shaqed* ("almond") and *shoqed* ("watching"). We need not linger over the question of the phenomenon of vision.[6] The prophets obviously saw things others did not see and made connections that others missed. We do not have data about the experiential factors in such occurrences, and it is idle to speculate. In this text the point is not the almond tree, which must have been obvious to anyone who could look at bushes. The point is the *watching* that Yahweh does, and that was not so obvious to every observer. It is asserted that Yahweh's purpose (i.e., plucking up and tearing down, planting and building) has been unleashed in history. That purpose is a power at work in the midst of public life. While invisible, Yahweh attends to that resolve, guarantees it, and will see that it comes to fruition. The "watching" that Yahweh does is not unlike the patient, concentrated, intense watching in ambush of a leopard ready to spring (see 5:6 with the same word for "watch").

Elsewhere it is claimed that the watch of Yahweh has two stages (31:28), one negative and one positive. Both stages are guarded and vouchsafed by Yahweh until fruition. For the people of God this means it is ordained that there will be a painful ending and a stunning beginning. Such a way of thinking is alien to our positivistic modes which assume that all of history is made by human decision. That, of course, is what the kings in ancient Jerusalem thought as well. They took their own decisions too seriously. They imagined they were unfettered to do whatever they pleased as long as it worked. But this "watching" of Yahweh asserts that there is a shape, a flow, and an intentionality to history that cannot be nullified or evaded. That intentionality overrides all human posturing.

6. On the phenomenological issues, see C. Johannes Lindblom, *Prophecy in Ancient Israel* (Philadelphia: Muhlenberg; Oxford: Blackwell, 1962), esp. ch. 3; and the disciplined reflections of Susan Niditch, *The Symbolic Vision in Biblical Tradition* (Chico, Calif.: Scholars Press, 1983).

That certitude is the basis of human hope, and it is the basis of judgment against human pretension. Interpretation of the book of Jeremiah must at the outset face this odd view of the course of persons and nations.[7] Another governance is at work that finally must be honored and that will not be mocked. The prophet bears this awesome disclosure that makes all human governance provisional. For that reason, the disclosure is never welcome, for it jeopardizes the pretense of human management.

The second vision (1:13-16) becomes more concrete in implementing the mandate of v. 10. The word to be announced also becomes unambiguously negative. Verse 10 contains four negative and two positive verbs. For much of the text of Jeremiah, however, the two positives are kept in abeyance. The main claim of the text (and of the prophet) is the harsh ending now to come. In this vision the text becomes more specific about Yahweh's purpose against Judah. The occasion for the vision (which quickly becomes an oracle) is a stove that apparently faces south, suggesting a "hot threat" from the north. Again, it is not the vision but the construal of the vision that interests the text and us.

a. The vision concerns the coming of an unnamed, awesome, and dreaded nation that will invade from the north and occupy Judah and Jerusalem. The words are deliberately vague and imprecise. This is not political analysis, but poetic vision. The very vagueness makes it even more ominous, for there is no defense against such a hovering. What is undoubted is that Judah is thrust into the map of international reality. That entire map is governed and managed by Yahweh. Judah now must cope with the changing configurations of international power. It is beyond the interest of the text here that we speculate about the identity of the nations. Surely this is a veiled allusion to the massive expansion of the Babylonian Empire, which came out of nowhere in the lifetime of the prophet. Indeed, for the Jeremian analysis of world history, Babylon looms as the central fact, central save one other factor. That other factor is Yahweh's sovereignty. Nations rise and fall, come and go, according to Yahweh's magisterial purpose. These nations are "summoned" by Yahweh. They are, knowingly or not, simply agents of Yahweh's way among the nations. The great theological-political judgment of the book of Jeremiah is to see, assert,

7. Klaus Koch refers to this understanding of the historical process as "suprahistory" and "metahistory" (*The Prophets*, vol. 1: *The Assyrian Period* [Philadelphia: Fortress; London: SCM, 1982], 144-156).

and establish a congruity between the purposes of Yahweh and the reality of Babylon. Kings in Jerusalem noticed Babylon but missed Yahweh's sovereignty. In the end, they missed everything.

b. The trigger for the historical process of "plucking up and tearing down" is not political or economic. It is theological and moral. Judah has done evil (v. 16; RSV "wickedness"). It is important to render the word as "evil," because the "evil" of the nations (v. 14) is a response to the "evil" of Judah.[8] The decisive evil of Judah, which will lead to the end of all old arrangements of power and security, is the abandonment of Yahweh. Everything hangs on the First Commandment concerning exclusive loyalty to Yahweh (Exod. 20:3). The burning of incense and worshipping other gods is not a critique of "religious behavior." It is, rather, a critique of a fundamental shift in social practice and loyalty. Appeal to "other gods" is Jerusalem's attempt to secure its own existence by mobilizing divine power without submitting to Yahweh's sovereignty. Judah has preferred to trust in "the works of their own hands." In that way, Judah imagines it can have security while retaining control over its own destiny. The prophetic alternative insists that security only comes by submission, which entails yielding control.

The sin of Judah is an effort at theological, political, historical autonomy, the nullification of Yahweh's governance of public life. That problem of social autonomy is a contemporary issue, but it is not only a problem of modernity. It is a recurring temptation for every concentration of power to imagine itself self-sufficient and therefore free to order its life for its own purposes without the requirements of Yahweh (cf. Isa. 10:13-14; 47:8; Ezek. 28:2, 9; 29:3).[9] As we shall see, in Jeremiah it is the disregard and nullification of Yahweh's sovereign will (expressed in social practice, religious activity, and policy formation) that regularly evoke the dismantling to come.

1:17-19   The oracle that derives from the second vision (v. 13) continues, but we treat these verses distinctly because of the major rhetorical break

---

8. Patrick D. Miller, Jr., has shown how the prophetic notion of punishment corresponds with some precision to the affront (*Sin and Judgment in the Prophets*, SBL Monograph 27 [Chico, Calif.: Scholars Press, 1982]). In this case "evil" will be punished with "evil."

9. See Donald E. Gowan, *When Man Becomes God*, Pittsburgh Theological Monograph 6 (Pittsburgh: Pickwick, 1975).

that is evident. Verses 14-16 concern the public intention of Yahweh. Verses 17-19, by contrast, are concerned with the particular destiny of the person of Jeremiah, who must bear this unbearable word against an unresponsive people. The rhetorical shift is marked by "but you" (v. 17). The God of this oracle is not indiscriminate. This God does not flatten the judgment so that everyone is treated in the same way. An important distinction is made between the majority, who are unresponsive and so under threat, and this minority voice (Jeremiah), who holds faithfully to the purpose of Yahweh. In a quite practical way, there are hints of a notion of a faithful remnant.

In 45:5 the same rhetorical move is made with reference to faithful Baruch. In both cases, specific faithfulness is acknowledged against the main inclination of Israel. Indeed, these two "but you" speeches in 1:17-19 and 45:5 may at one time have formed an envelope for the entire text. These two promises may provide a clue to the editorial history of the book of Jeremiah. That editorial work was done by those who came after Jeremiah, who lived in the Exile, and who took the text seriously. These faithful people understood themselves to be recipients of the same "but you" assurances. These two "exceptions" to the general judgment against Jerusalem may open a way to hope in Israel. For hope of "planting and building" is carried in this situation only by the true faithful remnant who took seriously that Yahweh did watch over the historical process in the face of massive empires and in the face of massive hard-heartedness in Judah. (See the same minority of two who open the future in Num. 14:30.) The specific oracle to Jeremiah echoes the initial summons of Jer. 1:4-10.

a. The prophet is summoned to dress for combat. As he speaks the truth about Yahweh and Jerusalem, he inevitably collides with the dominant ideology of king and temple. This combat is reinforced by the "againstness" in which Jeremiah is set and that is rhetorically so heavy in these verses. He must be ready and so "girded" for his dangerous role.

b. The prophet is provided an assurance that consists only in Yahweh's promise of solidarity. Indeed, it is not even promised that Yahweh will do anything, only that Yahweh will be there. Thus, the unequal quarrel is established that juxtaposes God's sovereign word against the mistaken ideology of the Jerusalem establishment. Jeremiah and the prophehtic tradition of passion and poignancy carry that sovereign word; the mistaken ideology of the holy city has plenty of advocates and spokespersons. God promises to Jeremiah God's personal solidarity in the face of massive public resistance. The man Jeremiah, the book Jeremiah, the community gathered around this text, are located precisely in this unequal quarrel.

The issue turns on whether Yahweh really governs, because that governance is always slow, always invisible, always capable of other explanation. The question surfaces in the midst of the well-being of Jerusalem: will the city come to exile (cf. 1:3)? Or will it be safe, as the ideology claimed, because of reliance on old conventional promises? Will those traditional promises override the commission of "pluck up and tear down" as Hananiah urged (ch. 28)? The answer is not known in advance. The question is posed, and answered, at deep cost to Jeremiah, who must articulate the risky problem of Yahweh's governance. The promise of solidarity in the midst of such a quarrel strikes one as a weak resource. It struck Jeremiah so as well. But it is all that is ever offered Jeremiah, save capitulation to the ideology. And it is all that is offered to the community around the text. The assurances provided the "truth-speakers" against ideology are always thin and precarious, because the managers of the ideology seem to monopolize all the big, powerful promises. The unequal quarrel is underway in the text, hardly a fair fight.

We read the call narrative as a clue to the person of the prophet. But we read it also as a clue to the editing community that in subsequent time understood itself as heir to the harsh mandate and the thin promise. In some sense we dare to read it as a clue to the contemporary interpreting community that also struggles with the mandate and counts on the promise. Our exposition cannot easily sort out the distinctions of prophetic person, editing community, and interpreting community. They come together for us because at the outset we trust the canonical judgment of 1:1-3 in seeing the convergence between the specific words of Jeremiah and the overriding sovereign word of Yahweh. If we are to have either, we will have to submit ourselves to both the text and the governing word of Yahweh, which asserts exile, promises homecoming, and assures solidarity.

The Wild Vine

Jeremiah 2

This chapter contains some of the most poignant and richly imaged poetry of Jeremiah. It is marked by only two major speech formularies (vv. 1-2a, 4-5a), and the structure of the poetry is not easy to determine. Despite these stylistic difficulties, the intent of the poetry seems clear enough. The poetry is an assault on Judah's imagination, requiring Judah to see its actual situation differently, to understand the causes of that situation and its inevitable outcome. The dominant theme is evident and redundantly stated: Israel has been unfaithful to Yahweh and stands under harsh judgment. There will be a temptation in interpretation to summarize and reduce, and one must have the patience to stay with the poetic nuance and detail in order to hear fully the word given through the poem.

2:1-3a These verses are marked off as a separate poem by the rhetorical formulae, "The word of the LORD . . ." and "says the LORD." They function as a historical retrospect, providing a basis for what follows. These verses employ two distinct metaphors. First, Judah's relation with Yahweh is like a marriage. The honeymoon period in the wilderness is remembered and celebrated (cf. Deut. 8:2-4). This positive reading of the early covenantal period is in contrast to Ezekiel, who reads the entire history as one of estrangement. The language of the poet is covenantal: "devotion" *(hesed)*, "love" *(ahab)*, "following after" *(halak)*. In those days of manna, Israel was totally dependent on Yahweh and glad to be so. As we shall see, this metaphor of marriage is taken up in the subsequent poetry to make a

32

different point. One who has sworn such fidelity and loyalty is bound and belongs with and to the partner. One who has made such a bonding is not free to disregard or pervert it, which is what has happened in Judah.

This poetic reading of the relation of Yahweh and Judah is continued in Jer. 2:2b-3 with a very different metaphor, that of a harvest offering. The first produce of the season, the tenderest, is offered to Yahweh as acknowledgment that because the land is Yahweh's (cf. Lev. 25:23; Deut. 26:2-10) Yahweh is entitled to the early produce. Yahweh is entitled to Israel because Israel belongs to Yahweh. The governing word is "holy." Israel is completely devoted to Yahweh, existing for no other reason and available for no other use. This metaphor is congenial to the marriage imagery, where Judah is also totally devoted to Yahweh. That relation is also exclusive. Both Israel and Yahweh delight in it. As wife and as first-fruits, Israel belongs exclusively to Yahweh, and exists for no other purpose. This motif of belonging exclusively is central to the covenant between Yahweh and Israel (Exod. 19:6; Deut. 7:6).

The positive metaphors provide the context for the harsh and unexpected turn in Jer. 2:3b. Whoever eats this produce is guilty and receives evil. To eat (use) what belongs only to Yahweh is to pervert its proper use and distort this relationship. The interpretive link between vv. 2-3a and v. 3b is left unspoken. We are not told how the totally devoted bride/offering becomes a source of guilt. But clearly these two words, "guilt" (indictment) and "evil" (sentence), provide the structure for what is to follow.[1] The poet contrasts the present sorry situation of violation, fickleness, and brokenness with what was and what could be. The language is elusive as is so much of the poetry in Jeremiah. but its claim is not obscure. Not only is the honeymoon over — the whole relationship is deeply distorted. What had been a happy marriage and a joyous offering is now deeply perverted, seemingly beyond recall.

2:4-13   Scholars conventionally present this section as a clear example of a prophetic lawsuit[2] that expresses the disastrous incongruity between

---

1. On the lawsuit form, see Claus Westermann, *Basic Forms of Prophetic Speech* (Philadelphia: Westminster; London: Lutterworth, 1967).

2. See Herbert B. Huffmon, "The Covenant Lawsuit in the Prophets," *Journal of Biblical Literature* 78 (1959): 285-295; Prescott H. Williams, Jr., "The Fatal and Foolish Exchange: Living Water for 'Nothing,'" *Austin Seminary Bulletin* 81 (1965): 3-59.

faithful Yahweh and fickle Israel. The skeletal structure of these verses is therefore that of the lawsuit, but the meaning of these verses will be fully grasped only when one attends to the way in which poetic imagery and rhetorical delicacy give flesh and life to this skeleton. The lawsuit form ensures that this is not undisciplined, rambling poetry, while at the same time the poetry imbues the conventional form with new power. It is the way of the poem to require a fresh discernment of reality that calls Israel to accountability for its distorted relation with Yahweh. The text "spills a whole kaleidoscope of metaphorical false identities for Israel."[3]

2:4-8   Here is Jeremiah's classic indictment, asserting that Israel has forfeited its relationship with Yahweh. After the broad summons to indictment (v. 4), v. 5 functions as a general critique of Israel. The tone of the initial question is like the hurt of a wounded lover. The opening question, "What wrong did your fathers find?" is a legal defense of Yahweh in divorce proceedings. It asserts that there was nothing wrong with Yahweh. It follows, therefore, that the fault must lie with Israel. What was to be intimate has become distant. The dominant verb is "went after" *(halak).* In v. 2, the same verb ("follow") is used for fidelity. Now it suggests infidelity. The critique is that Israel went after other gods who are "nothing." And since one takes on the character of the god one follows, Israel predictably has become a "no thing" as well (cf. Hos. 9:10; Ps. 115:8). Loyalty one has toward any god is decisive for the shaping of human life. We become like the god we serve. Pursue a bubble and become a bubble.[4] The object of love determines the quality of love.

In Jer. 2:6, 8 we are told what Israel did wrong. "They did not say . . ." The recital of Yahweh's story was no longer on their lips. They disregarded their shaping memory. Where the story of Yahweh is forgotten, Israel disregards its peculiar covenantal way in the world, and soon loses its reason for being. Verses 6-7 recite the credo that they "did not say," that has been forgotten. That credo is dominated by the word "land": land of Egypt, land of deserts and pits, land of drought and darkness, land that

---

3. William L. Holladay, *The Architecture of Jeremiah 1–20* (Lewisburg, Pa.: Bucknell University Press, 1976), 45.

4. The Hebrew word *hebel* is the same as used in Ecclesiastes and there is regularly rendered "vanity." It bespeaks vapor or unreality, an appearance that has no real substance.

none passes through, plentiful land, defiled land, heritage. Israel's whole life is about land.[5] Yahweh's primal gift is land. Jeremiah is concerned with the sure-coming destruction, exile, and land loss. This passage suggests that where the story of the land is lost, the loss of the land itself will soon follow.

When the phrase "did not say" is repeated a second time (v. 8), we are given evidence of the result of such forgetting. Where there is such amnesia, one is not surprised that derivative requirements of humanness erode. Where the creed is distorted, public life becomes skewed. The entire leadership structure of the community is included in the indictment: priests, judges, rulers, prophets — civic and religious leadership. To "know Yahweh" (v. 8; cf. 22:16) is to practice justice. Where Yahweh is not known, justice is not embraced. The poet is not engaged in moralizing. Rather, he discerned the collapse of public institutions. Priests no longer provide serious leadership. Judges forget their central commitment to justice. Rulers forget that power is a trust from Yahweh. Prophets forget that God has summoned them. The indictment ends with a third "go after," so that 2:8 forms an inclusion with the same verb in v. 5. The community is unfaithful. It has lost its foundational point of reference.

2:9-13 From this massive critique follows the prophetic "therefore." The unavoidable outcome is that Yahweh will take Israel to court to establish Israel's fickleness. Israel went after other gods (vv. 5-8), instead of after Yahweh (v. 2). Yahweh does not want simply to terminate the relation, but is willing to struggle, perhaps to fix blame, perhaps also to recover the relationship. Either way, court adjudication becomes a crucial metaphor. Indeed, the whole of Israel's history is now read as a lawsuit. The events of exile and/or destruction so near at hand are the implementation of that judgment which God has already decreed.

In vv. 10-11 the situation is ludicrous. Israel has this utterly faithful

5. On the theme of land in Jeremiah, see Walter Brueggemann, "Israel's Sense of Place in Jeremiah," in *Rhetorical Criticism,* ed. Jared J. Jackson and Martin Kessler, Pittsburgh Theological Monograph 1 (Pittsburgh: Pickwick, 1974), 149-165; and, more recently, Walther Zimmerli, "The 'Land' in the Pre-exilic and Early Post-exilic Prophets," in *Understanding the Word,* ed. James T. Butler, Edgar W. Conrad, and Ben Ollenberger, JSOT Supplement 37 (1985), 252-255.

God for a partner, yet engages in "partner swapping." It is ludicrous because other people — Cyprus to the west, Kedar to the east — have lesser, unreliable gods and do not change. References to Cyprus and Kedar are inclusive: look everywhere from west to east! But Israel, in its recalcitrance, exchanges the only true God for the gods of Canaan, who cannot profit (v. 8). Israel has distorted things at the foundation, not being able to sort out what is real and unreal, what is true and false, what is life-giving and death dealing (Rom. 1:20-25). Adam C. Welch suggests that Israel trades gods because this one is too demanding.

> But the grace which gave much asked much; it demanded self-surrender. And without self surrender on the part of those who received it, grace became an empty word. No other nation changed its god, non-entity though that was. The reason for the constancy was that it all meant so little. There was no cause to forsake such gods, because it involved so little to follow them. Israel forsook Yahweh, because the relation to Him was full of ethical content. . . . Yahwism had this iron core in it. The iron core was that Israel could only have Yahweh on His own terms. . . . Yahwism was no colorless faith which was simply the expression of the people's pride in itself and its destiny. It laid a curb on men, it had a yoke and bonds. The bonds were those of love, but love's bonds are the most enduring and the most exacting.[6]

It is no wonder that the great cosmic powers, heaven and earth, observe this sorry situation and are stunned (Jer. 2:12). Heaven and earth in this poem (cf. Isa. 1:2) function as witnesses who guarantee oaths and who observe patterns of faithfulness and fickleness. Because heaven and earth know Yahweh to be the true God (cf. Ps. 96:11), Israel's shabby response to Yahweh is exposed for what it is. In this cosmic court there is no doubt about the guilty party.

Jeremiah 2:13 functions as a reprise that reiterates the main point. Israel has forsaken an initial commitment to Yahweh. The poem introduces the metaphor of living water and empty cisterns. Yahweh is the living water that originates as gift outside of Israel (cf. John 4:10). Israel need not generate its own water or conjure its own life. It is freely given by this gracious partner of a God who is owner and husband. But Israel has

6. Adam C. Welch, *Jeremiah, His Time and His Work* (1928; repr. Oxford: Blackwell, 1951), 183.

rejected such a free gift that embodies its very life, and wants to be its own source of life — which of course leads only to death. The metaphor is water, but behind it lies the metaphor of marriage. "Forsake" is better understood in terms of marriage. The wrong that brings judgment is to abandon a true and faithful lover for a life of fickleness. It is as destructive as it is stupid (contrast Isa. 54:6-8, when God is the one who abandons, but not to perpetuity).

The metaphor of broken marriage is intimate and domestic, but its importance is public and historical. Israel's life is a gift of this covenant partner. The metaphor of firstfruits concerns an initial uncompromising claim of Yahweh to use and enjoy. But that uncompromising claim has been compromised. Where the gift is rejected and the partner is abandoned, life cannot continue. The metaphors serve the programmatic statement of Jer. 1:10. There will surely be a plucking up and a tearing down of one so faithless, who in this poem is none other than Jerusalem.

2:14-37   This longer unit is not a poem with a clear literary structure. Rather, it weaves together a variety of themes and metaphors in subtle and intricate ways. Rhetorically it may function as Yahweh's court testimony against Israel, anticipated in v. 9. The effect of the poem is to show that Israel's attempt to live outside a relation with Yahweh and to find other life-support systems is sure to fail and end in exile. Here as much as anywhere in Jeremiah, we must let the poetry have its own say without holding too precisely or too closely to a sustained argument.

2:14-19   Verse 14 puts a rhetorical question that assumes the answer: no, Israel is not a slave or a servant. Israel has not become a prey to the nations because it was fated for that by a bad birth. Israel is, rather, a much-loved heir and did not need to have this happen. The destruction has not happened for reasons of destiny, but for reasons of Israel's choice (vv. 15-16). Israel (i.e., Jerusalem) finds itself at the mercy of ruthless foreigners. The double use of the verb "forsake" in vv. 17, 19 provides the reason (we have already seen the verb in v. 13). This trouble of a historical kind has happened because Israel has forsaken and abandoned Yahweh, has refused the marriage relation of v. 2, has refused the exclusive belonging of v. 3a, has refused to be the Israel God intended. Such a refusal may seem like freedom, but in fact it is death.

2:20-28 The foundational rejection of covenant with Yahweh is given in v. 20. Israel refused to be Yahweh's covenant partner, thinking autonomy was preferable. The poetry then presents a variety of perverted identities, with each one imagined to be proper and true. These verses attribute false assertions of identity to Judah:

- You said, "I will not serve" (v. 20).
- You say, "I am not defiled, I have not gone after the Baals" (v. 23).
- You said, "It is hopeless . . ." (v. 25).
- You say to a tree, "You are my father," and to a stone, "You gave me birth" (v. 27).
- They say, "Arise and save us" (v. 27).

Everything Judah says is false. Judah distorts reality and leads to destruction. Reality is the very opposite of what Judah says in these five assertions. Judah must accept its identity as Yahweh's covenant partner and vassal or die (v. 20). Judah is indeed defiled, a violation of the holiness of v. 3 (v. 23). Judah's relation with Yahweh is not hopeless but could be restored (v. 25). Judah trusts a tree and a stone, but they are neither Judah's future hope nor root progenitor (v. 27). Judah appeals to false gods, but they will not save (v. 27). The poetic strategy is to let Judah condemn itself out of its very own mouth.

Around these five false statements the poet has employed various images of distortion. In v. 21 the choice vine has become wild (cf. Isa. 5:1-7). In Jer. 2:23-24 Judah was to be a loyal partner but has become like a wild animal in heat, desperate to find any partner. In v. 26 Judah is like a thief who is exposed for mistaken action. By v. 28 Yahweh is prepared to leave Judah to its own hopeless resources.

2:29-37 As vv. 20-28 state the indictment, so vv. 29-37 now lead to the sentence. They begin in vv. 29-30a with Yahweh's self-vindication of innocence of wrongdoing. Yahweh has not betrayed Judah. No, it is the other way around. Judah has forgotten Yahweh (v. 32). The image of bridal ornaments serves to speak about something especially treasured and also to refer to the initial image of vv. 1-2. What is most treasured has been readily abandoned. By a distorted marriage relation, wickedness leads to judgment. The wickedness (v. 33) is infidelity that includes exploitation of the poor (v. 34). The result is that Egypt and Assyria will abuse Judah.

That, however, is not simply the working of international policies. It is rooted in Yahweh's final rejection of Israel as the covenant partner (v. 37).

Jeremiah dares to say that Yahweh's connection to Judah is not unconditional. There are limits beyond which this fidelity will not go, and Judah has now reached the limit. Yahweh is prepared to give Judah over to the consequences of its own choices. The outcome is the termination of the relation so celebrated in vv. 1-2. This relation with God is not a guaranteed state, but a relation that depends on responsiveness. When the relation is neglected and grows cold, Yahweh will terminate. What courage, what nerve it must have taken to recite such a poem which announces that Judah's status as Yahweh's partner is now over!

The convergence of religious fickleness, political whoredom, and covenantal disregard shows that the poet is engaged in an acute critical analysis. Yahweh is not a God who is slotted in religious categories, but Yahweh is always related to a social system of values, policies, and conduct. When Yahweh is rejected, covenantal values disintegrate and life becomes a frantic pursuit of self-securing. Judah is therefore on a course to death. That death may ostensibly come at the hands of the empire, but in fact it is Yahweh who will finally relinquish his precious partner. There are limits. Yahweh has tried and tried (v. 30), but now it is enough. The God of high hopes (v. 21) is now the God of pained disillusionment.

The poet struggles here, as frequently, with the incredible obtuseness of this people. Not only is there an abandonment of God, but covenantal sensitivities have so collapsed that Israel is unable to recognize the quality and shape of its actions. In the face of the data, so clear to the poet, Judah continues to maintain innocence (vv. 23, 35). It is as though Judah lives in a land of pretense in which its actions are not connected to anything, in which actions have no outcomes.

The rich play of metaphors of vine, camel, wild ass, thief, lover — all of this constitutes an invitation to Judah to see reality differently. The words press Judah's awareness in a variety of directions. The decisive metaphor is that of marriage and infidelity (thus the words, "forget, forsake, rebel, reject"), which ends in harlotry and harsh judgment. Yahweh speaks as a chagrined lover, a stern judge, a companion who wants to be on the way with Israel. But Israel is on *another way* (vv. 16-18), a way that can only lead to death. Life is given only in relationship with Yahweh, nowhere else. Nonetheless, Judah chooses another way.

Notice that the concern of the poem is properly theological — not moral, not political. The overriding issue is the refusal to have Yahweh as God. The consequences of Israel's great refusal are implemented in history. Israel is exposed to ruthless imperial powers. Jeremiah's discernment of the historical process never permits religious issues to be isolated from real public issues. Yahweh's governance appears in the dangerous realities of power politics. Jeremiah's theological discernment occurs in the midst of astonishing imperial politics. The rule of Yahweh, acted out among the emperors, brings death to a faithless partner.

Return to Me

Jeremiah 3:1–4:4

This remarkable poem resumes the metaphor of marriage introduced in ch. 2. The long section of 3:1–4:4 has a complex redactional history.[1] The basic intention of the unit is an indictment of Judah (Jerusalem) and a stern invitation to return to Yahweh. The poetic elements address this issue. The language of "house of Israel" (3:20) likely is a reference to the covenanted community and is politically undifferentiated. That is, it simply refers to the community of faith and could as well apply to Judah and Jerusalem as the northern community. It is also not impossible, however, that the poetry originally was addressed to the north, also called Israel, but then is reused with reference to the south. The poetry provides no direct clues with which to resolve this issue.

In the prose of vv. 6-11, however, the language is much more precise and differentiated. There Judah — the same Judah addressed in the poetry — is contrasted negatively with northern Israel. In the next prose section (vv. 15-18) a return of Judah to Jerusalem after exile is envisioned, as well as a gathering of northern Israel to Jerusalem. It is not necessary or possible to trace the details of redactional development. It is possible, however, to see in these three layers of the text a sequenced reflection on Judah and Jerusalem, first addressed as the community of faith; second, as a community more fickle than the north; and third, as the restored community.

---

1. See John Bright, *Jeremiah,* 2nd ed., Anchor Bible 21 (Garden City, N.Y.: Doubleday, 1978), 25-27.

Each element reflects a particular historical moment. They are joined together in 3:1–4:4 to provide a sustained reflection that encompasses the course of Judah's life with Yahweh, a life reflected upon throughout the tradition of Jeremiah.

We have seen the positive assertion of the marriage metaphor (2:1-2), and its negation in the triple use of the word "forsake." This poem seems to begin with an allusion to the torah teaching of Deut. 24:1-4.[2] In the torah text it is prohibited that a twice-married woman may return to the first husband when rejected by the second husband. For our purposes, the three important phrases in Deut. 24:4 are:

(1) "may not take her again,"
(2) "she has been defiled,"
(3) "bring guilt upon the land."

The first phrase prohibits the return to the first husband. The return is prohibited even if both parties want to reestablish the relationship. The second phrase asserts that the woman is "defiled" by the second husband, that is, rendered unacceptable to the first husband. The third phrase, in characteristic Deuteronomic fashion, links the defilement of the woman to the defilement of the land, so that both the woman and the land are contaminated.[3]

The torah teaching only provides the beginning point for the present poem. The poet exercises imagination and carries the metaphor in quite new and inventive directions. Yahweh is the first husband; "other lovers" (false gods, false alliances) are the second husband for whom Judah has forsaken Yahweh. Judah is the faithless wife of Yahweh. The designation of husband-wife established in the poem of Jer. 2 is assumed in the poem of chs. 3–4. Now the question in ch. 3 is: what can happen next? The

---

2. On the relation between Deut. 24:1-4 and Jer. 3:1, see Michael Fishbane, *Biblical Interpretation in Ancient Israel* (New York and Oxford: Oxford University Press, 1985), 307-312; Trevor R. Hobbs, "Jeremiah 3:1-5 and Deuteronomy 24:1-4," *Zeitschrift für die alttestamentliche Wissenschaft* 86 (1974): 23-29.

3. On the relation between treatment of land and treatment of women, see the discerning comments of Wendell Berry, *Recollected Essays 1965-1980* (San Francisco: North Point, 1981), 191, 215; and my expository comments on his thesis in "Land, Fertility, and Justice," in *Theology of the Land*, ed. Bernard F. Evans and Gregory D. Cusack (Collegeville, Minn.: Liturgical Press, 1987), 41-68.

crisis turns on the capacity of Yahweh, the first husband, to take back the wife, Judah, after defilement by a second relationship. Yahweh's capacity to take back is clearly precluded by the torah. Yahweh, in spite of the torah, nonetheless yearns for the return of Judah to the covenant. This yearning on the part of Yahweh violates the torah, yet Yahweh's great love for Israel is sufficient to risk God's own violation of the torah. The yearning also violates common sense and pride. No husband, so it may be assumed from social convention as well as the torah teaching, would be so vulnerable as to take back such a fickle wife.

Such violation of the torah, however, is the stunning point of the poem. Against all expectations which should lead to final rejection, Yahweh, the God of Israel, will risk humiliation and defilement.[4] Jeremiah here echoes the insight of Hosea on the vulnerable, risky love of Yahweh for Israel. God is unlike every human analogy (cf. Hos. 11:8-9: Yahweh is God, not "man"). John Calvin says it well: "But we have seen at the beginning of the chapter that there is a difference between God and husbands. As then God did not deal, as he might justly have done, with the Israelites, and did not execute a capital punishment, as he might rightly have done, and what was usually done."[5] The central point of Jer. 3:1–4:4 is that God is not like human analogies, but will take the fickle partner back. The remainder of this section is an invitation, a yearning, and an urging for "return."

3:1 Verse 1 takes up the torah teaching in three rhetorical questions. The answer to the first is clearly "no." No, Yahweh will not return to Judah. This "no" is supported by the second question, which asserts land pollution. The third question is in fact an indictment for adultery with "lovers." It implies that Israel cannot return to Yahweh. The action of

---

4. On the capacity of God to violate God's own torah, see W. Sibley Towner, *Daniel,* Interpretation (Atlanta: John Knox, 1984), 89, in his comment on Daniel 6:

> The corollary question is whether God is trapped by the immutability of his own law. One is sometimes stunned at the intensity with which the psalmist reminds God of his own commitments to crush the wicked and to slay the psalmist's own opponents. . . . We also have words to Israel that God is capable of transcending his own law. God's law is immutability, and yet God himself can suspend it if compassion so demands.

5. John Calvin, *Commentaries on the Book of the Prophet Jeremiah and the Lamentations,* vol. 1 (repr. Grand Rapids: Baker, 1979), 167.

Judah makes return impossible, both on grounds of torah restrictions as well as common sense. Such betrayal precludes reconciliation.

3:2-5 These verses extend the theme with a series of indictments and sentences. The savage indictment likens lustful Israel to an ambushing Arab. The irony is intense. One would expect a lone woman on the road to be ambushed. But, shamelessly, the woman assumes the role of ambusher, so desperate is she for any lover. Parallel to the torah provision, such an action pollutes the land, so that not only are the people of Judah unclean but the land is also unclean. (This theme is utilized by Ezekiel to assert that God cannot stay in such a polluted place [Ezek. 8:6].) Thus, the defilement of land anticipates not only the exile of Judah but also the departure of Yahweh, the decisive absence of God from Jerusalem. The concern of the poet is never only the two covenant partners, but also the land. It is betrayal and abuse of the land that requires exile from off the land.

The result of the pollution is conveyed through the "therefore" of Jer. 3:3: the pollution has caused drought (cf. Lev. 26:19 and, by contrast, Ezek. 34:26). Yet even in the face of such data, Israel is incredibly recalcitrant, refusing to blush (cf. Jer. 8:12). Judah is not only wayward, but ignorant. As a faithless wife she is so eroded in sensitivity that she is not even embarrassed over her action. Jer. 3:4 implies that Israel has attempted to restore relation with Yahweh by uttering an address of covenant loyalty, "father." The disjunctive "behold" of v. 5 tells Israel, however, that the evil actions override any verbal repentance. Israel's actions are so loud and decisive that verbal repentance is regarded as frivolous. Yahweh yearns for reconciliation, but it will be on Yahweh's terms — and that requires a real change, not merely a verbal gesture. So the waiting continues. The grieving husband waits with expectation, but not without requirement.

3:6-10 These verses pursue the same general theme, but are prose and are generally reckoned as a later addition. Judah is contrasted with Israel, the northern kingdom, and is found to be even worse (cf. Ezek. 23:4-11).[6] Judah

---

6. While this prose element may indeed be a later interpolation, the contrast between north and south is not unthinkable in the tradition of Jeremiah. Notice that in 7:12-15 a comparison is established. In that case the south is said to be like the north, not worse than the north as here.

is portrayed as even more calloused than Israel. The reference to Josiah may link this judgment to the failure of the Reform of 621 B.C.E. It is as though Yahweh believes that if the degradation to which Yahweh subjects Judah is deep enough, it will move Judah to change. But Judah is not moved and does not change. Instead the pathos of Yahweh is intensified, for Yahweh still expects a return. In such gestures as Jer. 3:4-5 Judah makes a move, but it is a false move *(sheqer).* This false move appears regularly in Jeremiah as a motif for dishonest covenant.[7] Even in its ostensible return, Judah continues to act out the very alienation that is at the root of the problem.

3:11-13   The poem resumes (after the contrasts made in vv. 6-10) with an intense urging to return to the relationship. Israel, the northern community, is invited back by Yahweh. This invitation likely reflects a Josianic appeal to the north. That is, the religious appeal is related to a political recovery of northern territory by Josiah. The appeal is the voice of an offended husband seeking his wife back, even against the torah, even in the face of humiliation. The ground for repentance is a threefold statement about Yahweh, for the basis of new possibility is only in Yahweh, not in Israel. Yahweh will not be angry (cf. Ps. 103:9). Yahweh is "merciful" (the term is again *hesed,* on which see Jer. 2:2). The third statement on Yahweh is an answer posed to the question in 3:5. Even this yearning husband does not envision return without condition. To come home the ex-wife must acknowledge her promiscuity (v. 13). The poet struggles to articulate the anguish of Yahweh, who on the one hand wants the relation and on the other hand will not relinquish his own self-regard. The tension so felt and spoken by the poet tears at the heart of God, who yearns, but who will not be mocked, trivialized, or used.

3:14-20   The poetic verses of this unit (vv. 14, 19-20) offer a second invitation to return. They affirm again that the covenant people have been fickle, but also that Yahweh will cause a homecoming. The emphasis in vv. 19-20, however, is not on the summons or the possible return but on the grief of Yahweh, who is variously an affronted parent or a betrayed husband. The poetry moves easily from one metaphor of familial relation-

7. See James Muilenburg, "The Terminology of Adversity in Jeremiah," in *Translating & Understanding the Old Testament,* ed. Harry Thomas Frank and William L. Reed (Nashville: Abingdon, 1970), 42-63.

ship to the other. Verse 19 is a reflective soliloquy on the high hopes God had for a relationship of trust and intimacy, how God had planned to give over to this beloved child the best of the land. But all those keen hopes have been destroyed by the fickleness of Israel, who preferred other lovers. Thus the basic form is a summons to return, but the substance pushes against the form to articulate the grief of God. According to the nuance of the rhetoric, the grief may not yet be completely hopeless about a restored future, but it is well on its way to hopelessness. The poet presents a profound conflict, in which the heart of God yearns in hope for Israel but also grieves over Israel's betrayal. In this moment the relationship could be resolved in either direction.

Verse 19 is among the most poignant in Jeremiah. The poet has taken the anguish of a parent as his medium (cf. Hos. 11:1-9). The poet portrays for us a parent who has labored and dreamed for the glorious day when the child will be old enough, responsible enough, and responsive enough to receive all that has been saved for the child from the beginning. The father wants to give the child this inheritance even more than the child wants to receive it. But the moment of gift never comes, because the child neither knows nor cares. The wounded father is left with the shambles of hard work and broken dreams and knows the bitter combination of deep hurt and heavy resentment.[8]

The intervening prose of Jer. 3:15-18 is thought by most scholars to be later, echoing motifs from Ezekiel. The promise of a new shepherd (v. 15) is closely linked to Ezek. 34. The transformation of Israel in Jerusalem sounds like the restoration of Jerusalem in later Ezekiel. The unity of Judah and Israel here articulated is either an echo or anticipation of Ezek. 37:15-23. These verses seem attached to Jer. 3:14 (which appears to be earlier poetry) concerning a return to Zion.

In their present location vv. 15-18 form an important counterpoint to the poetry of alienation. The poetry announces the fickleness of Judah and the pathos of God. The prose articulates God's resolve in spite of the fickleness. The dramatic contrast between fickleness and pathos is crucial for the canonical assertion of the text. The poem is clearly heavy with judgment, but the canonical form finally focuses on the restoration. The

---

8. On the pathos of this relationship, see James Muilenburg, "Father and Son," in *Hearing and Speaking the Word,* ed. Thomas F. Best (Chico, Calif.: Scholars Press, 1984), 283-293.

present shape of the text is arranged to hold in tension the motifs of Israel's fickleness and Yahweh's pathos. The prose indictment of Israel's fickleness is flat, direct, and unambiguous. But the countertheme of Yahweh's yearning pathos is a dramatic surprise. The fickleness of Israel should evoke Yahweh's anger, and indeed it does. But along with anger is Yahweh's relentless yearning for a restored relationship. Both prose and poetry are necessary to articulate this powerful surprise. The two inclinations are dramatically juxtaposed as poetry and prose, though we do not yet know which way the issue will be settled. In these verses filled with hope the completed tradition asserts that God's yearning for a relation is so powerful and so resilient that in the end there is a new relation wrought, not out of Judah's repentance, but out of Yahweh's resolve. But the restoration is only "in those days." The prose of hope does not cancel out the poetry of hurt, but it comes after and presumes the painful alienation. The juxtaposition is not unlike the poetic articulation of Isa. 54:7-8, in which both abandonment and restoration are governed by the same God.

We are now in a position to consider the canonical shape of this unit. Judah stands under indictment as a fickle wife (Jer. 3:2-5). Judah is more faithless than is Israel (vv. 6-10). Israel is also guilty, but less guilty and is invited to return (vv. 11-13). The first thirteen verses establish the failure of both north and south, Israel and Judah. But both communities are invited to return (in violation of the torah prohibition of Deut. 24:1-4). Israel is invited back (Jer. 3:12, 14), and Judah is assured return (vv. 14-15). Both Israel and Judah are restored to well-being and relationship (v. 18). The passage thus moves from utter faithlessness to astonishing restoration. The shift from faithlessness to restoration is accomplished because of Yahweh's resilient fidelity, fidelity in the face of fickleness, fidelity that is rooted in God's deep pathos (vv. 19-20). On the basis of *faithlessness* become *restoration* through *pathos,* a new possibility is envisioned for Israel and the nations (3:17; 4:2), grounded in "truth, in justice, and in uprightness." The marks of truth, justice, and uprightness now to be implemented are contrasted with the present condition of falseness, injustice, and perverseness. There is hope now grounded in God's passion, but it is hope that looks failure honestly in the face and moves beyond it.

3:21-25 A third element of the summons to return now follows after 12-14 and 19-20. The invitation is offered in v. 22, a summons plus an assurance that God will heal. It is not clear if this summons is to be taken at face value, or if this is a mocking at Israel's too-easy presumption upon Yahweh. In any case, vv. 21, 22b, 23 are an articulation of repentance, an acknowledgement of guilt, and a recognition that trust in other gods has been an exercise in futility. It is affirmed, ironically or not, that only Yahweh can be Israel's deliverer.

The concluding verses, vv. 24-25 (prose), are in the form of a confession of sin. The poetic verses initiated the repentance, but the confession here is much more serious. It contains a judgment on the history of Israel. Jeremiah 2:2 affirmed that there was a honeymoon period of fidelity, but here the infidelity is "from our youth" (cf. Gen. 8:21). That is, through the entire history of the covenant there never was a time of faithfulness. From the very beginning Israel has been seeking alternatives. The "shame" and "dishonor" of Jer. 3:25 continues the metaphor of the shamed woman, now twice rejected — first by Yahweh her husband and then by her subsequent lovers as well. She is therefore left scandalized and without a place of belonging. Her own actions have caused her to be utterly displaced, abandoned with none to welcome her to safety. Through her own stupid actions, Judah is rejected. Her life, apart from the intervention of Yahweh as her advocate, is in profound jeopardy.

4:1-4 It may surprise us that in the face of such a history of infidelity there is still a chance to return to Yahweh. That in itself is an astonishing possibility. In this concluding section God issues yet another invitation, but that invitation comes neither easily nor cheaply. Yahweh's invitation is demanding and rigorous as Yahweh now sets conditions for return. The conditions are introduced by "if" three times in the RSV (twice in Hebrew):

- if you return
- if you remove
- if you swear
- *then* . . . (only then . . .).

The conditions are that Judah must cast off all other loyalties and reclaim Yahweh as sovereign LORD. The last line of the condition recalls Judah to the great themes of covenantal faith: truth, justice, righteousness. The last pair of words ("justice" and "righteousness") is a classic prophetic formulation (cf. Amos 5:7, 24; 6:12; Isa. 5:7; 9:7; Jer. 22:3, 15). The price of return to Yahweh is to order human life according to covenantal norms.

The third element, "truth," reflects a peculiarly Jeremianic focus on the sense of falseness (cf. 9:3) that permeates the life of Judah.[9] Covenant with Yahweh requires the reconstruction of all of life with a new orientation. Yahweh yearns for a renewed relationship, but it is not a shapeless, desperate yearning. It is yearning for a relation in which Yahweh's sovereign will is taken seriously. Because Yahweh is finally sovereign, no other kind of relationship is thinkable or workable.

The "then" (consequence) of repentance and reorientation of life is the implementation of God's promise to Abraham (Gen. 12:3; 18:18;[10] 22:18; 26:4; 28:14). The restoration of covenant thus will benefit not only Judah but the other nations that derive new life from that covenant.[11]

Jeremiah 4:3-4 reiterates the requirements of return with three new imperatives. The two imperatives of v. 3 ("break up and sow") seem to draw upon Hos. 10:12, using images drawn from agricultural practices. The imperative "circumcise" seems to appeal to the imagery of Deuteronomy (Deut. 10:16; 30:6), which is the most demanding tradition of covenant. Indeed, this summons mobilizes the best memories of Israel to make an appeal to the contemporaries of the poet.

It is clear that this extended unit (Jer. 3:1–4:4) is a subtle and complex literary whole. In rough sketch, the movement of the poem is as follows.

(1) Appeal to the torah, only to move beyond the permit of torah (3:1a);
(2) Application of torah teaching in order to convict wayward Israel (vv. 1b-5);
(3) Contrast with Israel, showing Judah more unfaithful (vv. 6-10);
(4) First appeal for return (vv. 11-13);
(5) Second appeal for return (vv. 14-20);
(6) Third appeal for return (vv. 21-25);
(7) Fourth appeal for return (4:1-4).

9. See Thomas W. Overholt, *The Threat of Falsehood: A Study in the Theology of the Book of Jeremiah*, Studies in Biblical Theology, 2nd series 16 (London: SCM; Naperville: Allenson, 1970).

10. On the crucial theological placement of this text, see Jose P. Miranda, *Marx and the Bible* (Maryknoll, N.Y.: Orbis, 1974), 94-97.

11. On the continuing concern for justice and righteousness as it concerns a blessing to the nations (and not only to Israel), see Hans Walter Wolff, "The Kerygma of the Yahwist," in *The Vitality of Old Testament Traditions,* ed. Walter Brueggemann and Hans Walter Wolff (Atlanta: John Knox, 1975), 41-66.

This poem is a meditation on the theme of return. The torah of Deuteronomy explicitly states that the wife shall not return. The connections to Deut. 24:1-4 make clear that the dominant concern is neither spiritual repentance nor a moral reconstruction. It is about a relationship that has been violated beyond recall. Yahweh, the first husband, has been deeply affronted. Judah, the wayward wife, is now rejected, scandalized, and exposed. The second lover has clearly failed. According to torah, it is impossible to go back to Yahweh, the first lover. Yet this is a meditation precisely on the unheard-of possibility of such a return. The return is possible because both the need of Judah and the yearning of Yahweh fly in the face of the torah. The torah establishes that Judah has no right to return. The torah establishes that Yahweh has no obligation to take her back. The themes of guilt and betrayal are stated with overriding power and clarity.

None of that quite touches the central affirmation of the poem, however. The truth of the matter is that, after the requirements of torah are acknowledged, there is the unfinished business of the relationship that the torah cannot contain. That unfinished business is to see how, in what ways, under what circumstances, a reestablished first marriage is possible. It is clear from 3:1b-5 that Judah has no case to make for herself. This is reinforced by vv. 6-10, 24-25. Yet it is also clear in vv. 15-18 that Yahweh can do a new promissory act, even in the face of the torah. But neither of these touch the real issue. The real issue is that *Yahweh is hurt* and filled with humiliated indignation. Nonetheless, *Yahweh is open* to restoration. It is as though the poet cannot clearly come down on one side or the other, because the God known to the poet is in God's own heart unclear. The yearning and indignation are locked in deep tension. The repentance of 3:4 seems to signal the hoped-for intimacy of v. 19, but it is not serious repentance. The outcome of this poem is that repentance which restores relationship is demanding and costly, very likely more demanding and more costly that this partner can handle.

Notice how this poem stays at the level of relational imagery. There is no connection here to actual historical content. Nor is there any explicit ethical requirement made beyond the generalities of 4:1-4. This is indeed a poetic reflection that leaves everything open beyond the hurt, pathos, and yearning of the relationship. How the future of the relation is to be actualized is left open. The poem does not deal with political or ethical reality. It cuts underneath that to the wounded hope of God. What counts now is not fox-hole repentance in order to survive. What counts now is the reality of this husband, who with bitter yearning and affronted loyalty, still is open to a relation, even against the wisdom of the torah. If perchance the relation can be resumed, it will be outside the righteousness of the torah. It will be the odd righteousness of the first husband (Yahweh) who violates the torah for the sake of the relationship (cf. Ps. 143:1-2). Yahweh's powerful yearning risks defilement for the sake of covenant (cf. Luke 7:34-35)!

Terror on Every Side

Jeremiah 4:5–6:30

The preceding poetic unit has portrayed God for us as a wounded, betrayed lover and husband yearning for a return. Even at the end of the unit there is still the hope that Israel will "come home." The mood is starkly different as this next section begins. Now there is no such yearning. Now there is darkness and harshness. This is a very different voice of God, who has reached the limit of yearning and the far edge of compassion. John Calvin draws this conclusion: "God now shews that he was not, as it were, at liberty to forgive the people; 'Even if I would,' he says, 'I could not.' "[1] We see the other side of God's inclination, which is that, for all of God's considerable passion and compassion, God will not be mocked.

This long section includes some of the most poignant poetry of the prophet. It is largely lacking in explicit historical allusion. It offers an open-ended poetic reading of reality that could be heard in more than one historical context, which is what gives it such enduring power.[2] Most

---

1. *Commentaries on the Book of the Prophet Jeremiah and the Lamentations,* vol. 1 (repr. Grand Rapids: Baker, 1976), 252.

2. That the text is not so closely tied to historical placement enhances its enduring canonical power for the community. On the process of textualization and the resulting authority, see Werner H. Kelber, *The Oral and the Written Gospel* (Philadelphia: Fortress, 1983). While Kelber's work concerns the Gospels, the point is valid for the tradition of Jeremiah as well. This methodological awareness makes questions of historical reference less important.

scholars believe this poetry comes from the early period of Jeremiah's poetry, but that is not important for our purposes. It is a miscellaneous collection without a clear ordering or structure, but one may identify at least four recurring themes.

(1) Anticipations of an invading army dispatched by Yahweh;
(2) Prophetic ruminations on personal grief and judgment;
(3) Harsh visions of the end of the human, historical process;
(4) Statements of guilt and punishment, which follow standard prophetic motifs.

4:5-8 This is the first of the poems in which Jeremiah characterizes an invading threat sent by Yahweh from the north (cf. 1:13-15). There has been much scholarly speculation on the identity of this enemy.[3] Older scholarship identified it as the Scythians, based on enigmatic references in the ancient historian Herodotus. A judgment closer to the actual concern may suggest that it is the Babylonian armies who did indeed come against Jerusalem in 598 and 597 B.C.E. To try to specify an historical referent, however, is to miss the point. This is not an historically descriptive narrative. Rather, it is an act of poetic imagination that does not depend on historical referent. Its purpose is, rather, to evoke in the listening community an awareness and a sense that this religious, political enterprise (Jerusalem) which has seemed so secure is in fact under massive assault, and that any complacency or "ease in Zion" (cf. Amos 6:1) is misplaced and ill-informed. The poet does not want his listeners to make a political analysis, but to let the dangerous reality — that the world of Jerusalem is not what they thought it was — play upon their perception and imagination.

The erroneous perception of Jeremiah's audience has been deliberately misinformed by a royal-temple ideology that screened out covenantal

3. John Skinner, *Prophecy and Religion: Studies in the Life of Jeremiah* (1922; repr. Cambridge and New York: Cambridge University Press, 1955), 37-45, offers a review of the problem and the possibilities of historical identification of the "foe from the north." Concerning historical identification, he concludes: "The conclusion is very uncertain; but we shall lose nothing if we take the Scythian poems to be in the main imaginative anticipations of future calamities, always shooting ahead of the accomplished fact, but at the same time following more or less the development of a grave national crisis which was as real to the prophet's countrymen as it was to himself" (44).

reality and permitted self-deception.[4] The poetry seeks to penetrate that ideology with a harsh and eloquent dose of reality. Jeremiah 4:5-6 sounds the bugle of warning trumpeted by a sentry to the north. The enemy has been spotted. His listeners, however, do not hear any such warning, for they have been lulled into imagining there was no threat. The poet antic-ipates, long before the actual fact of invasion; but the poet shrewdly does not identify, for that would flatten the poetic invitation into a description without power. Were the enemy named, then a debate could ensue about how to meet the threat. But the poet wants no such debate. He only wants his listeners to notice.

In Jer. 4:7 the metaphor of a lion is used to characterize the invader, a metaphor used by Hosea (Hos. 5:14-15) for Yahweh. In our poem the lion is the enemy people, but in Jer. 4:8 this is linked to the irresistible anger of Yahweh. The poet does not urge any specific response beyond formal grieving. There is no suggestion that any repentance is possible or desirable. Now the die is cast. Mobilization has begun and will not be averted. Judah is at war. Jerusalem is under attack. The army may be Babylonian, but the real agent is Yahweh. That of course makes the danger massive, ominous, inescapable. Yahweh is now engaged in a dread military exercise against God's own beloved Jerusalem. The wounded warrior has become invading army. Judah is left only to grieve the death that is now sure. In the lyrical maneuver of this war poem the poet has deftly overwhelmed the Jerusalem estab-lishment and its claim to immunity from attack.

4. The "royal-temple ideology" is rooted in the Davidic oracle of 2 Sam. 7 and the temple dedication of Solomon in 1 Kgs. 8. In these two events of oracle and dedication, the family of David and the temple establishment were able to claim for themselves the patronage of and alliance with Yahweh as the God who had made an abiding commitment to that enterprise. While the establishment of temple and dynasty was a gift of God's graciousness, that gift became distorted so that the eternal purposes of God came to be identified with the policies and purposes of the urban establishment. This gave excessive legitimacy to the economic-political enterprise of the city and made its policies immune from criticism because of religious legitimacy. The outcome is the establishment of a self-serving, self-deceiving ideology that nullified every ethical demand and every historical ambiguity. Clearly the prophetic tradition in general and Jeremiah in particular stand in harsh criticism of this ideology. On the tension between the royal-temple ideology and a prophetic alternative, see Walter Brueggemann, "The Epistemological Crisis of Israel's Two Histories (Jer. 9:22-23)," in *Israelite Wisdom,* ed. John G. Gammie (Missoula, Mont.: Scholars Press, 1978), 85-105.

4:9-10   This small unit is a prophetic reflection on the preceding poem. It is as though Jeremiah articulates both sides of a conversation. First he announces the massive threat as a speaker for Yahweh (v. 9). Then he responds to the threat as though its weight only now sinks in (v. 10). Persistently the poet carries on a critique against the leadership that he regards as self-serving. In v. 9 he names them, king/princes/priests/prophets. All of them are inadequate for the real crisis that they did not believe would come. These lines either reiterate the chagrin of the leaders or mock their now-shaken self-confidence. When all forms of official leadership have failed, only Jeremiah remains to provide shape to public life. He now undertakes to do the one thing still pertinent. He prays. In v. 8 he had urged lament. Now in v. 10 he utters Judah's complaint for them. (The prayer is paralleled in Ezek. 11:13, where that prophet also grieves the end of the beloved people of God.)

The prayer of Jeremiah in Jer. 4:10 may contain some irony. There has been talk of well-being *(shalom)*, when the historical reality is destruction (sword). The official line was, "It can't happen here," but it can, because it is. There is a deep incongruity between what is recited as official cant and what is taking place. The possible irony is that Jeremiah blames Yahweh for the cover-up, as though Yahweh were the source of the self-deceiving ideology of the Jerusalem establishment. There has indeed been deception, but it cannot be blamed on Yahweh. Surely it is not Yahweh who said "Peace, peace" (cf. 6:14; 8:11). Rather, it was the royal leadership, precisely those named in 4:9. Thus these verses that are cast as lament are in fact an assault on the official royal ideology that has refused to face reality. The reality, according to this poet, is that Jerusalem is ending. The poet has discerned and articulated what the official leadership is unwilling and unable to see. The poetry has the effect of delegitimating the public leadership that has refused to face reality. Nothing remains to be done except to hold the funeral. Leadership that ultimately deceives will finally bring destruction.

4:11-18   After an introduction in vv. 11-12 that utilizes the images of wind and winnowing as metaphors for harsh judgment of the invading army, the poetry is resumed. The language in v. 13 is hyperbole, wanting to assert that this people (still unnamed) is massive, awesome, irresistible. This invader is so overwhelming that Judah is reduced to funeral songs, to sing of its own death. For one brief moment (v. 14) it is suggested that the washing of repentance might still permit rescue (cf. Isa. 1:16; Ps. 51:7). The poet clings to that thin possibility, but nothing comes of it. It is as though the hope for repentance is only an instant of wistfulness that the poet cannot in fact believe or entertain. There is a chance, but that slight chance is soon abandoned in the rush of the poetry. Jeremiah 4:15 returns to the dramatic characterization. The guards in the north, in Dan and in the tribe of Ephraim, send signals ahead. They warn Jerusalem by a series of communications that Jerusalem is next in line; nothing can slow down the terror and pace of this coming enemy. (On the role of the sentries in the north, see the contrasting function in Isa. 40:9-11; 52:7-10.) The juggernaut is under way and none can slow it.

In Jer. 4:17b-18 it is asserted that this invasion is not arbitrary, but is in fact the consequence of Israel's own disobedient life. We should not miss the massive and bold act of imagination that stands at the center of this poetic claim. The poet links the *internal failure* of social life in Judah and the *external threat* of Babylonian expansionism. They are linked as cause and effect, as sin and judgment. Judah has failed to trust Yahweh; *therefore* Babylon invades Judah. One could offer political and geopolitical explanations about the coming of the Babylonians, but the poet has no interest in such knowing analysis. It is the work of the poet to focus with single-minded passion on one aspect of reality to the disregard of all else. The poet here focuses on the failure and fickleness of Judah in response to the covenant expectation of Yahweh, who is variously father, husband, judge. Shameless and unlimited transgression finally will bring the downfall.

History is a process over which Yahweh is sovereign and through which that sovereignty is worked out. The rule of Yahweh is not done "supernaturally," but through historical agents — in this case, the coming of this unnamed but awesome army that will not be resisted. Surely this poem is not a scientific description of an actual army. It is a poetic invitation. It does not want to change political postures in Judah, for that is not the work of the poet, but to penetrate the religious indifference and covenantal recalcitrance from which policy comes. Thus the language is bold and daring, without responsibility for being factually precise. The prophet wants to bring the imagination of Judah into touch with the theological reality of judgment. The visible threat of the Babylonian army is only an occasion for speaking of covenantal realities. The real threat from the north (or from wherever) is in fact the inescapable and uncompromising rule of Yahweh.[5]

Disaster Follows Disaster (4:19-31)

This extended poetic unit shows the power of Jeremiah's prophetic poetry in an unmistakable way. In this unit five distinct metaphors are employed in rapid succession. There is a sharp discontinuity as the poem moves from one metaphor to the next, because no logical coherence is intended. The five metaphors are:

(1) Personal anguish and disruption because of an invading army (vv. 19-22);
(2) A scenario of the dismantling of all of creation (vv. 23-28);
(3) A scene of frantic escape (v. 29);
(4) The futility of a prostitute whose allure is empty and ineffective (v. 30);
(5) The death cry of a woman in labor, vulnerable to murderers (v. 31).

The extreme images all point to the stunning assertion that death is coming in Jerusalem soon. The metaphors are to be understood with powerful concreteness, yet they all point beyond themselves to this overriding fact of the historical crisis of Jerusalem.

4:19-22 As the text is now arranged, this portion of poetry (like vv. 9-10 after vv. 5-8) is a personal response to the public disclosure of vv. 11-18. No doubt Jeremiah constructed both pieces, the public warning and the personal response. Dramatically, the two poetic pieces are to engage each other, so that the rawness of the situation for both Judah and for the poet is clear. This piece (vv. 19-22) is presented not as public proclamation, but as a scenario of the prophet at home. But even there, apart from his public responsibility, he is intensely troubled. He is troubled so that his

5. On Yahweh's rule in history, see the comments of Klaus Koch, *The Prophets*, vol. 2: *The Babylonian and Persian Periods* (Philadelphia: Fortress; London: SCM, 1984), 25-32. Koch appeals to the metaphor of Jeremiah, "the way of Yahweh" as the form of Yahweh's governance.

stomach churns. His bowels twist in agitation, so deep is his alarm and his anxiety. He is anxious, unsettled, frightened, to the point of heart palpitations. The reason is the bugle, the approaching army, the enmity of Yahweh, the collapse of his world.

The poet has had a vision of a chain of disasters as the invading army moves toward the beloved city. Suddenly the threat is here, here in Jerusalem, here in his very bedroom. The poem is a fantasy of how close the coming destruction is, as close as his bedroom, as close as the innards of his body. He takes his listener inside his very own person as an attempt to pierce their numbed indifference. He dares to suggest that his wild anxiety is more real than their cynical self-confidence. The invasion dispatched by Yahweh is a real threat. The poet tries to enact the threat in the most intimate language he can express. He moves between the personal language about bodily sensations (v. 19) and the language of military plunder (v. 20). Then in v. 21 he speaks a lament. The poet sees the enemy flag. It is closer than he and his contemporaries ever thought it would be. He knows it bespeaks death for him, for the others, for the city. It is death as dramatic as a soldier pulling back the drapery of his bedroom (v. 20).

Then v. 22 breaks off the agitated portrayal of invasion as judgment. This verse, not integrally related to the preceding scene, is an impatient denunciation of his listeners. They are so casual, so indifferent, because they do not notice; they do not believe the poem. They cannot participate in its vivid images, because they do not think a destructive judgment can happen here. Their reaction is contrasted with the pathos of the poetry. As they are unmoved by the theological reality of Yahweh, as they are unmoved by the political realities all around them, so now they are unmoved by the poetry. The verse speaks of "my people." The first person pronoun is likely spoken by Yahweh. It is Yahweh who sees that the covenant partner is obtuse about everything that is important. The language is not unlike 8:7 and Isa. 1:3, both of which appeal to animals that are wiser than is Israel. The Israelites are not even termed guilty, simply stupid and foolish. They are so stupid that they do not notice the world of God's life-giving governance made available only by the poem.

This indictment of stupidity has a sadness to it. The poetry uses the word "know" twice, once with Yahweh as its object and once with doing good (that is, covenantal acts) as its object. Jeremiah 22:16 makes the same connection between knowing Yahweh and knowing to do good. Covenantal acknowledgement of Yahweh and covenantal obedience are intimately linked.[6] Israel knows about neither, and therefore Israel knows nothing about its own identity and proper role in history. Israel knows many things the world values — political cunning, military planning, theological propriety — but lacks the covenantal awareness that saves. Ignorance of covenant leads to invasion and destruction. The others may not yet know, but Jeremiah already has this knowledge tearing at his very person, even as it must tear at Yahweh.

4:23-28   In these verses the tone of the rhetoric escalates. Heretofore the poetry has focused on historical-political destructions. With these verses the picture becomes cosmic in scope. The fourfold "I looked" is a staggering study of creation run amok, creation reverted to chaos. The Creator waits for the world to become the world hoped for. Yahweh waits for Israel to become fully God's people. But each time the poet looks at the world, he sees more and more of creation being nullified, regressing to the murky condition of Gen. 1:2. Israel refused to embrace the ways of the Creator. Covenantal Israel held the staggering notion that human conduct matters for the well-being of creation (cf. Hos. 4:1-3). Working from that notion, the picture of this poem is grim. Since there has not been obedience, there will be no viable creation. Disobedience finally leads to chaos for the entire creation.

This poem is a step-by-step rhetorical dismantling of creation. Jeremiah 4:23 utilizes the words of Gen. 1:2, "formless and void," to express the resurgence of chaos and disorder that is experienced by the poet at every dimension of life.[7] Then in quick succession the poet char-

---

6. On knowing as covenantal obedience, see Herbert B. Huffmon, "The Treaty Background of Hebrew *Yāda'*," *Bulletin of the American Schools of Oriental Research* 181 (1966): 31-37; and Huffmon and Simon B. Parker, "A Further Note on the Treaty Background of Hebrew *Yāda'*," *Bulletin of the American Schools of Oriental Research* 184 (1966): 36-38. What is now clear in terms of ancient Near Eastern parallels had already been articulated by John Calvin, *Institutes of Christian Religion,* I, vi, 2 (Library of Christian Classics [Philadelphia: Westminster; London: SCM, 1960]), 72: "But not only faith, perfect and in every way complete, but all right knowledge of God is born of obedience."

7. The poets of the Exile are able to use the old traditions of chaos as a way of speaking about exile. The historical experience of exile is akin to the cosmic sense of disorder given in the old myths of chaos. See Isa. 45:18-19; 54:9-10; and Walter Brueggemann, "Weariness, Exile and Chaos (A Motif in Royal Theology)," *Catholic Biblical Quarterly* 34 (1972): 19-38.

acterizes the loss of "light" (sun, moon, stars), the failure of even mountains and hills to embody stability, the disappearance of humanity and the absence of birds, and finally the end of fertile land and functioning city. Wholesale dismantling follows massive disobedience. The power of chaos is so dominant, it is as though creation never happened. This sad turn of events is the result of Yahweh's action, for Yahweh's patience has finally been exhausted.

The form of Jer. 4:27-28 differs from the symmetry of vv. 23-26. In its main claims v. 27 seems to be a confirmation of the devastation that has just been pictured. The whole world comes unglued when Israel is disobedient long enough. The nullification is total, comprehensive, and without qualification (cf. 45:4). But the last clause, "yet I will not make a full end," comes as a surprise. The line seems to qualify and contradict what has preceded. Two scholarly explanations can be made. First, it has been held that the line is a late intrusion intended to soften the harshness.[8] Second, the negative "not a full end" can be textually amended to read, "I will make a full end of it."[9] However, such explanations seem contrived. A different reading is offered by John Calvin. Calvin interprets the line in terms of its harshness, "I have not made an end yet to the devastation," meaning God has yet more destruction to do.[10]

As an interpretive principle, we must seek to understand the text in its wholeness. This expression, "not a full end," is a serious counterpoint to its context, either for Jeremiah or for Yahweh. Thus we may best take it as an expression of uncertainty on Yahweh's part, wrought out of Yahweh's yearning not to destroy. Yahweh has been provoked to a harsh resolve from which Yahweh momentarily draws back. As we shall see elsewhere, it is this reluctance on Yahweh's part that becomes the ground for hope in the midst of exile, for the yearning on God's part persists, even in the face of the relentless devastation in this poetry. It is as though the very poetry of harshness moves God to new awareness of how precious

8. See George Adam Smith, *Jeremiah* (London: Hodder & Stoughton and New York: Harper, 1923), 116. Cf. Robert P. Carroll, *From Chaos to Covenant* (London: SCM; New York: Crossroad, 1981), 76-77, esp. n. 38.

9. See John Bright, *Jeremiah*, 2nd ed. Anchor Bible 21(Garden City, N.Y.: Doubleday, 1978), 33; and Wilhelm Rudolph, *Jeremia*, 3rd ed., Handbuch zum Alten Testamentum 12 (Tübingen: J. C. B. Mohr [Paul Siebeck], 1968), 32.

10. Calvin, *Commentaries*, 1:240-242.

Israel is in God's eyes, as though God cannot fully accept God's own poetic rendition of judgment.

Verse 28 returns to the devastation of vv. 23-27a. It characterizes both heaven and earth as engaged in deep mourning. Frequently the prophets use the metaphor of the earth mourning to refer to drought. The poem concludes with powerful resolve on Yahweh's part to persist until the old creation has been fully nullified. The life-giving functions of the earth will come to an end. The whole earth is now weak and diminished. Such a poem serves to delegitimate the regime, because it recalls that the only purpose and legitimation of the royal-temple apparatus is to ensure and implement the full effective function of creation. The grief (drought) bespeaks the ultimate failure of the regime to maintain the earth.

We may ask about the function of this dangerous poem. We must stress that it is a poem. It is not a blueprint for the future. It is not a prediction. It is not an act of theology that seeks to scare into repentance. It is, rather, a rhetorical attempt to engage this numbed, unaware community in an imaginative embrace of what is happening. The world is becoming unglued. The poet has the awesome burden of helping his people sense that their presumed world is in jeopardy, because God's holy patience is fully ended. When that patience is exhausted, creation is not permitted to continue its disobedient course. The verdict of initial creation was, "It is very good" (Gen. 1:31). Here the verdict is "It is very evil." Such evil finally must be answered for.

4:29-31　These verses continue the imagery of an invading army (cf. vv. 13-17), but with the poignant use of three additional metaphors, the last two of which are abrasive and quite unexpected. Verse 29 creates a scene in which the citizens of Jerusalem scramble for safety in the face of the invader. All poise and dignity are lost as they run for cover (cf. Isa. 2:10, 19, 21). Then in Jer. 4:30 the poem abruptly introduces the metaphor of a prostitute. The scene is ludicrous: the army comes, frightened people hide, but this desolate Jerusalem is so insensitive and brazen that she has not sense enough to hide. Rather, she dresses like any conventional street prostitute — red dress, gaudy jewelry, heavy makeup. Because Judah has been a harlot, the image of harlotry fittingly explicates the poetic indictment and does not surprise. This is Yahweh's partner, shamelessly acting out her fickle identity. What does surprise us, however, is that this unacceptable behavior continues in the face of the army. Any prudent prostitute would know that such troops are dangerous, not to be seduced but to be feared, because they work violence. Judah the whore continues to misunderstand her true situation of danger, continues to misjudge the real threat of invasion, confiscation, and seizure. Instead she stands idly in front of the mirror, preoccupied only with appearance, not with the reality of death on the move.

In v. 31 the metaphor is again dramatically shifted. Out of the resolve of Yahweh, the army still approaches, but now Judah is not an alluring prostitute. Now Jerusalem is cast in a new role as a helpless, exposed woman in labor. What catches the ear of the poet (and any who will hear) is the cry of pain. The cry sounds like a labor pain, only labor pains are to give birth, the work of newness. The poet listens more carefully. The cry of the city is in fact a cry for help, a death cry, for the invaders (sent by Yahweh) are about the predictable business of rape and murder. The metaphor belongs in the same trajectory with the image utilized in 2:2 as bride, in 3:1 as faithless wife, in 4:30 as prostitute. Jerusalem is a street woman who gives birth and is overwhelmed by the army in what should have been a moment of joy. The poet presses to find a metaphor raw enough to carry the truth. Jerusalem is under judgment, about to be done in. Jerusalem may not know it, but the city is as shameful as a prostitute, as helpless as a woman in labor, exposed and endangered now because the betrayed husband has had enough of fickleness and will tolerate no more. Death must come. No one stands with Jerusalem to grieve, or to rescue.

5:1-6 This part of the poem is structured in a standard way for a lawsuit speech. It consists in two indictments, first against the poor (vv. 2-4) and then against the powerful (v. 5), followed by a concluding sentence (v. 6). The prophet is called (much like Diogenes) to search for one responsible citizen of Jerusalem who will fulfill Yahweh's expectation for justice and fidelity. A close parallel may be in Gen. 18:22-32, where the search is to find enough righteous people so that the city may be saved. Yahweh's opening offer in our text is that one such citizen will permit the city to be saved and forgiven. Thus less is required in this poem than was required of Sodom. In Gen. 18 Abraham had to find ten such persons. Jerusalem is so degenerate that Yahweh will now settle for one. Only a hint of covenantal responsiveness will be sufficient for the rescue, but no hint of such responsiveness can be found.

No trace of obedience is found among the poor (Jer. 5:4). As a consequence, pardon is not possible. They are calloused and cynical, stubborn in their ways and will not turn (v. 3). What God seeks is reliability *(emunah),* but everything among the poor is mendacity *(sheqer).* The poor do not know the torah. It is no different among the powerful, however (v. 5). The poet expects them to do better because they are schooled in the torah. They have had a chance to learn the way of obedience and are therefore without excuse. Yet they, too, are engaged in self-assertion and self-sufficiency (cf. 2:20), and refuse to acknowledge or live according to the covenant that gives life. Forgiveness of Jerusalem is no more possible because of the great than because of the poor. Indeed, forgiveness is not possible because the necessary trace of obedience cannot be found.

The city has refused in all parts of the citizenry to accept its proper vocation as Yahweh's covenant partner destined for submission and obedience. The hoped-for obedience is not onerous, but it is nonetheless rejected. There is a fundamental misorientation in the life of the city. The poet works two themes. First, pardon is gracious, but it is not cheap. Forgiveness still requires coming to terms with Yahweh. Second, the pathology of the community is massive and pervasive. The community practices autonomy so much that Yahweh's proper summons to accountability is simply ignored.

After these indictments v. 6 is not unexpected, though its harshness is surprising. The "therefore" means judgment. The language of the judgment is in the metaphors of ferocious animals who will attack, rend, and tear: lion (cf. Hos. 5:14-15), wolf, and leopard. The metaphors may point to the devastation of an invading army. Or perhaps the images refer directly to the coming of Yahweh. Either way, juridical language has been transposed into the law of the jungle. Disobedient Jerusalem is at the mercy of beasts of viciousness (cf. Lev. 26:22). The most interesting of the three metaphors for animals is the third, the leopard. It is depicted as an animal crouching in wait, ready to spring on any who try to escape. Observe that the judgment, as conveyed through this metaphor, is not exile but death. The leopard is "watching," the same word used in Jer. 1:12. Yahweh is ready to spring from a crouch to complete the judgment that is due and imminent against Jerusalem.

5:7-13 This section of the poem continues the language of the lawsuit. It is largely an indictment characterizing the sin of Judah, but vv. 9 and 10 allude to judgment, which inevitably follows the sin just described.

The beginning point is a question, either whimsical or pained. It looks back to v. 1. Yahweh is desperately seeking a way of forgiveness. Yahweh is ready, willing, and yearning to forgive, but Yahweh will not engage in cheap grace. There must be a hint of a turn, a gesture of obedience. There is not a single sign of it to be found, which makes forgiveness impossible and nullifies Yahweh's positive intent. The governing word for the unit is *'azab* (v. 7), to "forsake" or "abandon," the same word we have seen in 2:13, 17, 19, with its primary allusion to marital fickleness as in 3:1. This metaphor continually reappears in the poetry, indicating the center of Jeremiah's interest.

The acting out of this abandonment is detailed in a variety of ways. It includes false worship (note the contrast with 5:2). The people swear by other than Yahweh, even in the face of Yahweh's blessing. The tradition knows that when Israel is satiated and full, it is vulnerable to temptations to displace Yahweh as partner (cf. Deut. 8:7-10, 11-17; 32:15-18). The spin-off and seemingly inevitable effect of such satiation is moral disorientation in human relations. The image of "lusty stallions" surely alludes to sexual infidelity and perversion, but it is also a metaphor for shameless self-assertion. Judah is too full of self. "Horses" in the OT are regularly found only among those who, like kings, assert their own power and seize initiative for their own lives.[11] This same fullness of self-sufficiency, which leads to moral disorientation, also leads to religious self-destruction through the mocking of God (Jer. 5:12-13). Yahweh is now trivialized so that Yahweh may be mocked (cf. Zeph. 1:12). Jerusalem imagines that it is immune from Yahweh's governance or threat. Indeed, Israel imagines that there finally is no accountability in the historical process because Yahweh is not an active agent. The prophets who are to bear witness to the initiative of Yahweh have neglected the message and so have forfeited their authority. Jerusalem has become a city without reference to God or to God's torah.

It is no wonder that God asks in indignation, "Shall I not punish?" (Jer. 5:9). This question is the other side of the question, "How can I pardon you?" (v. 7). God shall now punish. This God was disposed to forgiveness, but forgiveness in such a city would be a mockery. It would

11. On the sociological function of horses and a critique of their social function, see Walter Brueggemann, *Revelation and Violence: A Study in Contextualization* (Milwaukee: Marquette University Press, 1986).

64

make Yahweh appear to be a docile beggar and a helpless patron. Yahweh is neither a beggar nor a patron. This city has lost its chance for forgiveness and now stands under judgment. There is a harvest of judgment that must be worked (v. 10).

In v. 10 we have a qualifying remark (as in 4:27). This may be read as Yahweh's struggle to decide how to act toward Jerusalem. The data calls for destruction, yet for a moment in the poetry Yahweh resists the necessary conclusion. Yahweh's inclination toward forgiveness — even if it is for a remnant, even if the text is late — is powerful against the need for God's self-vindication. The dilemma is real for God.[12] It is real for Jerusalem. It is real in the situation. In that dilemma of Yahweh's struggle between vengeance and forgiveness hangs the destiny of Jerusalem. The poem resolutely makes the case for destruction, with no evidence presented on behalf of the city. The only impediment against such an act is found in Yahweh's inclination. The hope of saving rests only in Yahweh, not in Jerusalem. That salvation, against the overwhelming evidence, is a thin, scarcely articulated possibility. The community and its religious leaders have made light of Yahweh, have collapsed God's sovereignty, have reduced and trivialized God's majestic distance in an effort to eliminate judgment from the historical process. Such trivialization of God will not be effective, however. Almost as though in response to the mocking reductionism, the verdict is given in 5:13: Yahweh will do it!

5:14-17 This brief section resumes the theme of the invading army. It is futile for us to try to identify the specific army from the general description, because the language is not descriptive but imaginative characterization. Its purpose is not to communicate information but to create a sense in the listening community of what it is like to be on the receiving end of such an army. The poetic scenario invites Jerusalem to receive God's judgment ahead of the fact of military invasion.

This coming army is an old established power (v. 15). The coming army is ominous because its language is alien. Its coming is not a happening contained in Judah's categories of business as usual. It is a nation of giants whom Judah cannot resist (v. 16; cf. Num. 13:28, 33). It is not the identity

---

12. On the reality of the struggle for God, see J. Gerald Janzen, "Metaphor and Reality in Hosea 11," *Semeia* 24 (1982): 7-44. This one text from Hosea is characteristically true for the prophetic texts of God's pathos.

of the army but what it does that is important. The marauding action of the army is caught in the fourfold "eat" in Jer. 5:17. (The same verb is used in v. 14 to describe the fire that "devours.") The army will "consume/consume/consume/consume": harvest and food, sons and daughters, flocks and herds, vines and fig trees. The items listed here for confiscation by an occupying army are closely paralleled to those listed in 1 Sam. 8:11-17 concerning "the ways of a king." The occupying army may accomplish this seizure in a wild orgy of takeover, and the devouring will be barbaric. The parallel in 1 Sam. 8, which concerns the confiscating power of the governing agent, however, suggests another reading. The "devouring" could mean that the occupying nation will deny economic freedom and impose such a tariff that this feeble people will be taxed to death, like they would under the king in 1 Sam. 8. The threat may be of sustained occupation rather than a sudden invasion.

In whatever form the usurpation occurs, the central threat is the destruction of the fortified cities. The end of these cities means the end of organized life and the exposure of urban life to a variety of threats that the walls currently stave off. Urban life is under assault and is sure to end, bringing down with it all institutional and structural supports for public life. With the destruction of the walls, the coming of social chaos is not far behind. In Amos's oracles against the nations, the burning of the fortresses is targeted (Amos 1:7, 10, 12, 14; 2:2, 5). In the savage announcement of Hos. 2:9-13 there is an end to the public activities of an ordered community. Israel, like every community, has trusted in its social order, but that social order is now jeopardized as God unleashes judgment against the covenant-breaking community. The world as it is experienced in Jerusalem is under threat and sure to end, gobbled up ruthlessly by the greedy invader said to be an agent of Yahweh.

5:18-19 These verses provide slight but not reassuring relief from the poetry of devastation. In v. 18 the curious assurance that the destruction will not be total appears for the third time (cf. 4:27; 5:10). Yahweh's words here are curious precisely because the surrounding poetry sounds so final. Again the statement reflects indecision on Yahweh's part or, we may say, a debate in the community concerning continuity and discontinuity in the midst of devastation. No doubt some viewed this invasion as the real end. Others (e.g., Hananiah) regarded it as an interlude after which normalcy would be resumed.

But if Yahweh will not make a "full end," what then? Jeremiah 5:19 offers an answer. The single verse justifies Yahweh's judgment, and at the same time asserts that the sentence is not death but exile. First, we have again the word "abandon" *('azab)*. Israel's abandonment of Yahweh is the cause of the judgment and the justification for it. As a result of Israel's abandonment, Yahweh is within Yahweh's rights to terminate and destroy. But the remarkable word pattern in this verse concerns foreign gods and strangers in "a land not yours." Foreign *(nkr)* gods have been served. Life will be lived in a strange *(zar)* land. The use of the two words yields a pattern of disobedience/exile:

> serve *strange god — therefore live in strange land*
> serve *alien god — then live in alien land.*

The Exile is derived from and linked to the service of other gods. The presence of the word "abandon" helps to connect the whole image to the marriage metaphor. This attention to a "second lover" (cf. 3:1) leads to life in a "second land," which is a land without promise. History has a theological dimension because Yahweh's severe sovereignty finally will prevail. This history ends inevitably in exile.

5:20-31 The remainder of this chapter consists in a variety of poetic images that pursue the general prophetic motifs of judgment and sentence. What is of interest is the way in which these general themes receive particular poetic articulation.

The accusation against the house of Judah surfaces in the introductory summons of vv. 20-21. The governing word is "hear." The vocative addresses a people who are incapable of response, who are "without heart" (RSV "senseless"), who see not, who hear not (cf. Isa. 6:9-10). The envelope of Jer. 5:21 moves from *shema'* to *shema'*: "Hear . . . you who will not hear." Because "hear" is the foundational word for covenant responsiveness, this poem both summons to covenant accountability and acknowledges that it cannot happen (cf. Matt. 11:15).[13]

Jeremiah 5:22-24 combines a doxology about God's power and great-

---

13. On "listening" as decisive in the Deuteronomic tradition that informs Jeremiah, see S. Dean McBride, Jr., "The Yoke of the Kingdom," *Interpretation* 27 (1973): 273-306; and Patrick D. Miller, Jr., "The Most Important Word: The Yoke of the Kingdom," *Iliff Review* 41 (1984): 17-29.

ness with Israel's rejection of that great God. God's self-assertion in the doxology has motifs like those of 2 Isaiah (cf. Isa. 40:12-17; 44:21-28) and Job (5:8-15; 9:5-10), though the first person form used in Jeremiah is more forceful. The praise of Yahweh does not concern the history of Israel, but God's power in creation, the taming of chaos (Jer. 5:22), and the governance of the rain (v. 24). Yahweh is sovereign over all creation, but Israel will not acknowledge Yahweh's sovereignty even in its own life.

This countertheme of Israel's failure to acknowledge Yahweh is expressed in the question of v. 22. The question is a rhetorical one, however, because it implies the answer: Israel neither fears (cf. v. 24) nor trembles. In v. 24 Israel does not recite the credo of doxology (cf. 2:6-8). Where Israel does not say, think, or recite the sovereignty of God, Israel soon imagines it is autonomous, self-sufficient, and indeed, self-invented (cf. Deut. 8:17). The rhetoric of Jer. 5:22-24 focuses on the heart of Israel. The traditional call to Israel is to love and serve Yahweh with its whole heart, but here we meet the opposite.

- This is a people without heart (senseless) (v. 21).
- This people has a stubborn, rebellious heart (v. 23).
- They do not say in their heart (v. 24).

Israel's heart, the organ of covenant (cf. 4:4), has become alienated from Yahweh.

In 5:25-28 the poet traces what happens to a community with a disoriented heart.[14] The moral failure of Israel derives from its "practical atheism" (v. 21).[15] Israel is indicted for iniquity, sins (v. 25), wickedness (v. 26), treachery (v. 27). The result is that they are great/rich/fat/sleek, that is, satiated and self-sufficient (vv. 27-28). Israel exploits and abuses. The particularity of the offense is that they judge unjustly (cf. Deut. 16:18), they exploit orphans and fail to defend needy people (Jer. 5:28). The problem is systemic. The neglect is social. The outcome of Israel's infidelity is a society of rapacious exploitation, supported and legitimated by institutional structures. This poem points Israel back to the marginal

14. On the cruciality of the heart, see Martin Buber, *Right and Wrong* (London: SCM, 1952), 34-52, and his comments on Ps. 73.

15. On the notion of "practical atheism," see Gerhard von Rad, *Wisdom in Israel* (Nashville: Abingdon; London: SCM, 1972), 65 and *passim*.

ones for whom Yahweh has special regard. This affirmation about Yahweh is crucial and nonnegotiable for prophetic faith.

The structure of these verses conveys the close relation between the dysfunction of Israel's faith and the disorder in Israel's life:

- theological disorientation (vv. 22-24),
- general indictment (vv. 25-26),
- self-sufficient satiation as the outcome (vv. 27-28),
- abusive social practice (v. 28).

Where covenant with Yahweh is betrayed, covenant values in social relationships cannot be sustained. Interpretation of the poem must show the dialectical relation between the basic disorientation and its manifestation among "the least." Caring ethics without a core covenantal commitment is not possible.

Verse 29 asserts Yahweh's indignation and the necessity of judgment on Yahweh's part (cf. v. 9). God's yearning to forgive has turned to harshness. Verses 30-31 serve as a reprise to sound again the main theme of disobedience and judgment. The land has been defiled (cf. 2:7; 3:1-2). The leadership to whom the people turn is corrupt and self-serving (cf. Hos. 4:9). The last line of Jer. 5:31 contains an ominous question. It might be freely rendered, "What do you think will happen next?" No answer is given, but hints are everywhere in the poetry. The double use of *shema'* in v. 21 has suggested the two poles about which Israel must decide. The choice is stark without any ambiguity or maneuverability. One option is to listen, which might lead to a renewed people. The other option is to die. If the heart fails, as it has for Israel, the city will fail, too. The end is no longer negotiable.

6:1-8   This unit reiterates the warning of an invading army. The threat comes from the north as it characteristically does for Jeremiah, though of course it is again unnamed. The invitation to escape the coming devastation is perhaps premised on the traditional notion that some are given a permit and safe conduct to be exempted from the general destruction (e.g., Josh. 6:22-25).[16] Such a provision in the practice of war provides a basis

---

16. On the genre of the invitation to flee, see Robert Bach, *Die Aufforderungen zur Flucht und zum Kampf im alttestamentlichen Prophetenspruch,* Wissenschaftliche

for a remnant who may survive. The faithful are warned to escape. The poetic strategy is to indicate that most are unfaithful, most will not heed, most will not escape.

The poem mentions two results of this invasion. First, the urban elite is destroyed (Jer. 6:2). The prophets, who seem to harbor great resentment against the urban elite, delight in mocking and caricaturing the women who are the quintessence of such self-indulgent well-being (cf. Isa. 3:16-24; 47:1; Amos 4:1). Second, the city of Jerusalem will become so desolate that it will be a place for grazing, inhabited by shepherds who represent the lowest social class (Jer. 6:3; cf. Mic. 3:12, cited in Jer. 26:18). Thus, 6:2-3 provides a sharp contrast between well-bred urban women and low-grade shepherds. The one will be displaced by the other, as the city loses its role as a center of cultural refinement and economic monopoly. This is a concrete case in which first become last and last become first.

Verses 4-5 offer three quotes allegedly from the principals in the battle to come. The alleged statements are from the mouth of the invading army, designed to escalate and dramatize the sense of danger and threat. It is as though the poet takes us into the commander's tent to hear the specific strategy. The second of the three quotes shows the chagrin the successful army has at the setting of the sun, for it means the end of the battle for the day (v. 4b). The winners never want the darkness to come (cf. Josh. 10:12-13, on the extension of the day so that God's people may win). In Jer. 6:6 the commands are in the mouth of Yahweh, who, according to the poem, is the one who fights the battle against Jerusalem. It is Yahweh who directs the siege instruments. We are not told in vv. 4-5 who is speaking, but in v. 6 the speaker — and the leader of the battle — is identified. The army is not the real threat, but is only an agent of Yahweh, who is the real threat.

Verses 6b-7 contain the indictment that is the motivation for the invasion. Six terms are used: "oppression," "wickedness," "violence," "destruction," "sickness," "wounds." The term "wicked" is quite general, as is "destruction." The more specific terms "oppression" and "violence" are perhaps the most important.[17] Congruent with 5:27-28, these terms sug-

---

Monographien zum Alten und Neuen Testament 9 (Neukirchen-Vluyn: Neukirchener Verlag, 1962); and Patrick D. Miller, Jr., "The Divine Council and the Prophetic Call to War," *Vetus Testamentum* 18 (1968): 100-107.

17. On the semantic field of this vocabulary, see Thomas D. Hanks, *God So Loved the Third World* (Maryknoll, N.Y.: Orbis, 1983).

gest a social system in which the strong exploit the weak. The royal-temple system is under poetic assault because it sanctions systematic abuses that are practiced both by the king (cf. 22:13, 17; cf. Ps. 72) and in relation to the temple (Jer. 7:8-10). The last two terms, "sickness" and "wounds," state the consequences of exploitation: a society that does not function is immobilized and under judgment (cf. Isa. 1:5-6).

The concluding element of this unit (Jer. 6:8) is related to Yahweh's words of indecision and assurance, which we have noted elsewhere in the opening chapters of Jeremiah. A chance still remains, because Yahweh has not finally decided. The RSV rendering "be warned" is somewhat misleading. A more accurate translation would be "take correction" *(ysr)*. The imperative is not a warning or a threat, but articulates the hard discipline of serious nurture (cf. Deut. 8:5). The verb suggests that Israel may still be reshaped to avert judgment. It may not yet be too late, although the double "lest" of the verse indicates the real danger. The danger is that Yahweh may leave Jerusalem, and then the city would be utterly vulnerable. As a result the land becomes desolate. It is remarkable that, in the face of intense poetic rhetoric and imagery characterizing the scope of the invasion, an alternative to "the full end" still seems available. This uncertain yet possible alternative is reflective of Yahweh's anguish and pathos over the decision that cannot much longer be averted.

6:9-15 These verses reiterate the now familiar themes of judgment and sentence. Verse 9 begins the unit with a statement of gleaning, a figure that has come to stand for judgment.[18] The general indictment of v. 10 (cf. 5:21) is that Israel's ears are uncircumcised. Israel is not capable of paying attention. They mock and despise the word of Yahweh. They are unresponsive as covenant partners. This poetic unit, like others we have

---

18. The metaphor has become familiar to us in the crusading hymn of faith, "The Battle Hymn of the Republic," in the lines,

> Mine eyes have seen the glory of the coming of the LORD;
> He is tramping out the vintage where the grapes of wrath are stored;
> He has loosed the fateful lightening of his terrible swift sword;
> His truth is marching on.

John Steinbeck, in *The Grapes of Wrath* (New York: Viking; London: Heinemann, 1939), has used the same metaphor to characterize a very different social crisis.

considered, begins with a quite general theological point of disorientation and disobedience, and then proceeds to particulars.

The general sentence for this failure to hear is given in 6:11-12. The failure occasions the full, powerful release of Yahweh's wrath against every part of the city. This passage, unlike others that indict the leadership, includes all in the scope of disobedience — children, young men, husbands, wives, old folk (v. 11).

The judgment is that property will be reassigned, notably houses, fields, wives. The triad is the same as is stated in the commandment against coveting (Deut. 5:21). The reference to wrath in Jer. 6:11 is answered at the conclusion of this poetic unit (v. 12) with reference to the outstretched hand. The outstretched hand was positive intervention in the Exodus (cf. Deut. 26:8), but now it is negative intervention that brings destruction. The rhetoric of wrath is filled with passion and a lack of restraint. Language about the wrath of God is difficult for us to hear. We are wont to think that the love of God overrides such anger, but that surely is not the case in this portrayal of God. This powerful language has its theological rootage in the metaphor of a betrayed father and an abandoned husband. The wrath of God in Jeremiah is not that of an indifferent sovereign who crassly retaliates, but is that of one who is intimate in covenantal relation and therefore is wounded by infidelity and rejection. The yearning for return and restoration, which we have considered, feeds the hurt, which is then turned to anger. This poet does not flinch from the emergence of this enraged love, which will not be softened or compromised. The poet is willing to let God respond fully in God's hurt.[19] While such an outburst may not be congenial to popular theology, it is indeed congruent with the metaphor of hurt turned to vigorous rejection. The God whose outstretched arm saved now outstretches the same arm to terminate.

Jeremiah 6:13-15a makes the general indictment of v. 10 more specific. All persons, but especially the religious leaders, are indicted for their unprincipled economics. All — the least and the greatest — are greedy and deal falsely.[20] When one does not listen to the word of God the result is destructive social policy (v. 10). This community has lost every norm by which to evaluate and assess its rapacious and exploitative greed. That

19. On God's hurt, see Terence E. Fretheim, *The Suffering of God* (Philadelphia: Fortress, 1984).
20. The merism of v. 13 ("from the least to greatest") corresponds to the detailed listing of v. 11.

destructive social practice includes recitation of the royal-temple ideology which covers over the real issues and engages in massive denial and propaganda (v. 14).[21] The poet has already suggested the profound problems and unresolved issues facing this society. The regnant ideology, however, dares to speak of well-being *(shalom)* when the realities are otherwise. The official claims are plain lies, because social reality does not correspond to its ideology. The worst part of this ideological recitation (v. 14) is that the citizens of Jerusalem themselves believe it and are persuaded by it. They have lost their capacity for critical analysis and have a sense of shame about their own wrongdoing. It is precisely the royal ideology that precludes moral sensitivity and covenantal anguish over failure. It intends to keep critical questions muted, so that establishment policy may advance unchecked. This unit concludes in v. 15b (in correspondence to vv. 11-12) with an account of the destruction that is to be wrought by the hand of God.

6:16-21   The themes of critique and judgment in these verses do not come as a sustained argument, but as a rapid sequence of changing images. Verse 16 begins with a summons to return to the ancient ways.[22] This could mean a return to the torah (cf. v. 19) or traditional teaching, even sapiential instruction.[23] It is, in effect, inviting Jerusalem back to the old Yahwistic teaching that has not been contaminated by the operative royal ideology. There are older traditions — likely theological, certainly ethical — which will help Judah reorder its life. This return to ancient paths is not a nostalgic return to "old-time religion" or "the good old days," but a return to a more radical and dangerous memory that serves to end all present complacency and to subvert all present certitudes. The summons is rejected, however, in the very same verse: "we will not walk in it." To

21. On the power of propaganda to create official reality that denies human suffering and hope, see Jacques Ellul, *Propaganda: The Formation of Men's Attitudes* (New York: Knopf, 1965).

22. On the genre of recall to "ancient paths," see Norman C. Habel, "Appeal to Ancient Tradition as a Literary Form," *Zeitschrift für die alttestamentliche Wissenschaft* 88 (1976): 253-272.

23. On "the way" as a central metaphor for the substance of Israel's faith, see James Muilenburg, *The Way of Israel* (New York: Harper & Row, 1961; London: Routledge & Kegan Paul, 1962). On "the way" as a metaphor for the contemporary possibility of serious theology, see Paul M. Van Buren, *Discerning the Way* (New York: Seabury, 1980), 1-9 and *passim*.

walk on the ancient paths would mean to walk away from unbridled royal power, shamelessly exploitative temple postures, and economic practice that nourish the lives of the sleek and fat.[24] Israel rejects such a walk, because it clashes with the dominant values to which they are committed. This rejection is a rejection of Israel's primal identity.

In vv. 17-19 the speech revolves around the theme of "heed" *(q-sh-b):*

- give heed (v. 17),
- we will not give heed (v. 17),
- because they have not given heed (v. 19).

The first use is an invitation to obedience. The second is an indictment for disobedience. The third use is the ground for punishment. Israel does not listen because it imagines itself to be self-sufficient. The first "give heed" was to heed the warning of the trumpet of judgment. The third and most important is to heed "my words," "my torah." Israel has become a torah-less community, unfocused, disoriented (cf. 2 Sam. 12:9). The nations of the earth are called to witness against this torahless people bound for death. It is the torah that gives life (Ps. 19:7-9). When Israel gives up torah, it gives up Yahweh, which means giving up the chance for life.

In place of the torah, Israel has substituted cultic action (Jer. 6:20-21): frankincense, cane, sacrifices. Israel has devised a form of religion that reflects affluence, which can be safely administered, and which brackets out all questions of obedience. Jeremiah, along with the entire covenantal tradition, is clear that an obedient religion does not require or prefer cultic actions of self-serving (cf. Hos. 6:6; 1 Sam. 15:22-23; Amos 5:21-24; Matt. 9:13; 12:7). Right cult is always in the service of obedience to Yahweh. This unit concludes in Jer. 6:21 with a sentence introduced by the characteristic "therefore." The stumbling block to which the poet refers is not identified, but clearly is an impediment to life (cf. Hos. 4:5).

The passage is constructed around two pairs of motifs that are the inverse of one another. The first pair, ancient paths (Jer. 6:16) and true obedience (vv. 17-19), leads to life. The second pair, ritual activity (v. 20) and stumbling blocks (v. 21), leads to death. The juxtaposition of paths and stumbling blocks is telling. The first invites to an obedient walk. The latter

24. On the double use of the metaphor of way, in "going after" and "going from," see the use in 2:2 (positively) and 2:5 (negatively).

promises a danger when Israel decides to be on the way, whether in the ancient path or not. The internal juxtaposition contrasts torah words, which give life, and cultic actions, which are rejected as unacceptable. The poet skillfully contrasts the reliable elements of covenantal faith with the current practices that are self-indulgent. The prophetic critique asserts that Jerusalem religion has become a narcotic which precludes faithful criticism of destructive policy.

6:22-26   This is the final poetic treatment of the invading army.[25] Verses 22-23 describe the powerful coming of this unnamed threat authorized by God. The coming enemy is ruthless, shows no mercy, and is aimed precisely at Zion.

Verses 24-26 describe the reaction of frightened Jerusalem to the invading army. Israel hears the report of the coming army and is terrified and paralyzed by fear. It is not the action of the invading army, but simply reports of it that reduce Israel to trembling. Again the image of the pain of a woman in labor is used (cf. 4:31). The concluding line of 6:25, "terror on every side," is a special formula in the tradition of Jeremiah, and we shall comment on it later in more detail. It is sufficient here to note that the anticipated army puts Judah in profound jeopardy. The reaction of terror is appropriate. The terror felt by the city is articulated as grief (v. 26), an intense grief like the grief of the loss of an only begotten son. The grief is over the death of the whole people and the entire religious apparatus that legitimates the community. The ending of the city envisioned by this scenario is pathos-filled. "Terror on every side" refers to the enmity of God, behind and before, from which Judah has no route of escape.

6:27-30   This passage is a personal word to Jeremiah concerning his vocation.[26] The metaphor used identifies Jeremiah as the one who is authorized to separate precious metal from dross (cf. Isa. 1:22). Jeremiah

---

25. Other references to an invading army occur in subsequent texts. This poem, however, is the last in the group of poems commonly regarded as a distinct corpus, referred to by scholars as "the Scythian songs." We are not interested in the historical identity of the army characterized here, but in the sustained literary power of the reference.

26. These verses function, according to much scholarly opinion, as the conclusion to an extended rhetorical unit, perhaps beginning in 2:2-3 or more precisely in 4:5. See William L. Holladay, *The Architecture of Jeremiah 1–20* (Lewisburg, Pa.: Bucknell University Press, 1976), 57-97.

will separate out according to the uncompromising categories of covenant obedience and disobedience. The metaphor serves to articulate one more lawsuit speech. The indictment is in Jer. 6:28: stubbornness/rebellion/corruption. The sentence is in vv. 29-30, which threatens fire and ends with the verdict "reject" (cf. Hos. 4:6). Israel is all dross, so the smelter must retain none of it. There is here no allowance for remnant or for exile. The metaphor declares a decisive end. The smelter finds Jerusalem to be all dross, without value, and so it is to be discarded. The metaphor thus comprehends both the prophetic office of Jeremiah and the destiny of the city. One is as rigorous as the other is ominous.

The long poetic unit of Jer. 4:5–6:30 utilizes a rich variety of metaphors in a most imaginative fashion to present the persistent theme of judgment. The theme is articulated with these metaphors, each of which suggests another dimension to the reality of coming judgment:

(1) The announcement of an invading army as the judgment of Yahweh who will destroy (4:5-8, 11-18, 29-31; 5:14-17; 6:1-8, 22-26),
(2) Visions of the end (4:23-28; 5:6, 18-19) that show uncertainty about the finality of the end,
(3) Articulation of disobedience and punishment in lawsuit speeches (5:1-6, 7-13, 20-31; 6:9-15, 16-21),
(4) Personal protests and responses of the poet (4:9-10, 19-22; 6:27-30).

In various ways these poems announce that, because of covenantal failure, the trusted, legitimated Jerusalem establishment is about to end. In this section the prospect of repentance, of averting judgment, is sparse. In a very general way 3:1–4:4 and 4:5–6:30 function complementarily. The former is a grudging, pathos-filled summons to repent. The latter is largely a threat because the time for repentance is exhausted. Both themes are crucial for the prophet and for Israel. Clearly, it is the latter theme of judgment that finally matters in the tradition. Israel did not heed the summons of 3:1–4:4. The judgment of 4:5–6:30 comes to fruition. Through the move from 3:1–4:4 to 4:5–6:30, the poet articulates this covenantal God who moves back and forth between *pained hope,* like a grieving father, and *enraged judgment,* like an indignant sovereign. Yahweh can never be detached and indifferent. That the people of Jerusalem could be detached and indifferent indicates how little they sense either who Yahweh is or what is happening among them. The poetic scenario in this poetry is a bold act of "tearing down and plucking up."

Jeremiah's Temple Sermon

Jeremiah 7:1–8:3

This unit presents Jeremiah's so-called "temple sermon," perhaps the clearest and most formidable statement we have of the basic themes of the Jeremiah tradition. In its present form the words of the prophet are cast in prose that may suggest a Deuteronomic redaction. Scholars who tend to date materials around the person of the prophet date this sermon (on the basis of 26:1) to 609 B.C.E., early in the reign of Jehoiakim. Other scholars believe the text is heavily redacted and reflects theologians of the exilic period who want to justify the destruction of the temple. In either case, this text seems decisive for understanding the tradition of Jeremiah and for discerning the social context, tensions, and possibilities that belong to this theological tradition.

The temple sermon shows the prophet in profound conflict with the dominant temple ideology on which the state relied. The position taken here by the prophet could only be treated as treason by the state, because it destroyed the ideological underpinnings of the establishment (cf. 26:11). That dominant theology claimed that Jerusalem was inviolate because God had made unconditional promises. This royal tradition, albeit now distorted, is rooted in the temple and royal claims of David and Solomon. It was substantiated in the words of Isaiah a century earlier (Isa. 37:33-35),[1]

---

1. The critical matters related to the historicality of this text are very complicated. See Brevard S. Childs, *Isaiah and the Assyrian Crisis,* Studies in Biblical Theology, 2nd series 3 (Naperville: Allenson; London: SCM, 1967). Whatever precise conclusion is

and was regularly celebrated in the hymnic tradition of the Psalms (cf. e.g., Ps. 132:6-10). This ideology claimed that the unconditional promises carried by the temple establishment limited God's judgment in response to Israel's action. In such a view, obedience is not a crucial dimension of faith. In the text of ch. 7 Jeremiah frontally attacks such a claim as "organized hypocrisy,"[2] and insists that God's way with Jerusalem is fundamentally concerned for obedience.

7:1-15 This section presents the core of the proclamation credited to the prophet. Jeremiah is commanded to have his say in the temple, though we cannot determine if his action is *ad hoc* or a part of the program for a special festival. The main theme of the proclamation is articulated in vv. 3-4. Judah is confronted with only two options. Judah may "amend," which will allow it to stay in the land, or Judah will blindly trust the temple and its ideology. The key word in Jeremiah's proclamation is "false" *(sh-q-r)*. The prophet is not rejecting liturgy or temple claims in principle, but those formulations which are false, that is, incongruent with the torah and with the LORD of the covenant. The implicit counterpart, later made explicit, is that if Judah does not amend its ways, it will not be kept in the land but will be sent into exile. Land is not an unconditional gift, but is premised on torah obedience. Land cannot be held simply by reliance on the legitimating ideology of the regime, but requires a quite explicit obedience.

Verse 4 alludes to the words of the Jerusalem liturgy that were boldly, endlessly, and uncritically repeated. Jeremiah dismisses those words of the liturgy as banal and ineffective, and mocks the unthinking reliance on the status quo that they reflect and embody. The accent is on *trust:* do not trust in, do not count on, do not stake your life on. In one deft move, the prophet has exposed the dysfunctional character of the Jerusalem temple. The temple and its royal liturgy are exposed as tools of social control, which in a time of crisis will not keep their grand promises. The temple is shown to be not an embodiment of transcendence, but simply an arena for social manipulation. The poet delegitimates the temple claims of absoluteness.

---

reached concerning historicity, it is clear that that ideology which Jeremiah resists is in some way a legacy of the Isaiah tradition.

2. John Skinner, *Prophecy and Religion* (1922; repr. Cambridge and New York: Cambridge University Press, 1955), 175.

Verses 5-7 explicate the theme of v. 3 with an "if-then" argument indicating the conditionality of Judah's well-being. The introduction of an "if" of obedience aligns the text with the Mosaic tradition (cf. Exod. 19:5) and distances it from the unconditional promises claimed for David (2 Sam. 7:14-16). The first "if" in Jer. 7:5 is a repetition of the opening proclamation of v. 3. The second "if" makes torah obedience more explicit: "do justice, do not oppress sojourner, widow, orphan, do not shed innocent blood, do not go after other gods."[3] This is a summary of the main requirements of the torah. In v. 7 the "then" clause of consequence is a permit to stay in the land. These verses, then, explicate in detail the same perception of reality announced in v. 3. Retention of the land is not by inherent right, not by might, not by liturgy, but only by the practice of justice and obedience. The call to torah obedience is raised as a bold challenge to the claims of the state.

Verses 8-11 present the harsh realism of the prophetic alternative. In the preceding verses the speech of the prophet sounds as though "amending" is still possible. Now with the opening term "behold," however, the prophet announces a conclusion and a verdict that suggest the time for amending is past and the decision about land loss is already made. Thus, while vv. 1-7 seem to allow time for a change, vv. 8-11 seem to suggest that the time is past. The reality of exile hangs over the entire tradition of Jeremiah. That exile is presumed here is not unambiguously clear, but the rhetoric tilts in that direction.

These verses characterize two stages of Judah's disobedience. First, v. 9 is a catalog of Judah's massive disobedience of torah in the conduct of its public life. The catalog of disobedience is a direct reference to the Ten Commandments, one of two such catalogs found in the prophets (see the other in Hos. 4:2). Judah regularly violates the main claims of its covenant with Yahweh. Second, those who violate the torah then go into the temple to conduct liturgy as though they are obedient to the LORD of the liturgy. They have no sense of shame at the distance between their liturgy and their ethics. The piercing, biting question of Jer. 7:11 does not suggest that temple disobedience is the problem. Rather, the temple has become a place of refuge, hiding, and safety for those who violate torah through their life in the world. The torah violators attempt to hide in the sanctity of the ritual. The temple becomes a means of cover-up for the

---

3. Note that the word order is inverted in Hebrew for purposes of emphasis.

destructive way life is lived in the real world. This escapist use of liturgy is self-deceptive, for it will not protect Judah from the realities of the covenant. Since the text addresses the power establishment, it is fair to conclude that the crimes targeted are not simply individual acts of exploitation but are acts of the entire system, which proceeds at the high cost of human well-being.

In vv. 12-15 the argument reaches its stunning and devastating conclusion. The prophet draws a shocking parallel between Shiloh and Jerusalem. Everyone listening knew of Shiloh — that it was a northern shrine and that long ago it had vanished from history, destroyed because of disobedience. It was also a part of the rationale and self-understanding of the southern royal community that northern Shiloh and southern Jerusalem are precise opposites.[4] Whereas Shiloh is rejected by Yahweh and therefore destroyed, Jerusalem is chosen and valued by God, and therefore safe. The contrast between Shiloh and Jerusalem shows the power of self-serving, vested interest in shaping the truth claims of the royal ideology. The managers of the Jerusalem establishment could not believe Jerusalem might be treated by God as Shiloh was.

Jeremiah vigorously denies this self-serving, ideological contrast and argues that Jerusalem is just like Shiloh. It is just like Shiloh in that it must obey to survive. It is just like Shiloh in its profound disobedience. And therefore, it is just like Shiloh in that it must be destroyed. The Jerusalem establishment's main claims of legitimacy are harshly and summarily dismissed. One can hardly imagine a heavier, more sobering message. Jerusalem has no preferential option from God and must answer to the demands of the torah. In the face of Jerusalem's failure to meet these demands, the verdict can only be destruction and death. The Jerusalem temple is under death sentence, and a whole world of religious and political self-interest with it. Jerusalem enjoys no "safe-conduct" in the midst of its policies, faith, and decision-making.

The parallel drawn between Jerusalem and Shiloh invites our imag-

---

4. That self-serving Jerusalem ideology is precisely articulated in Ps. 78:56-72. See Anthony F. Campbell, "Psalm 78: A Contribution to the Theology of Tenth Century Israel," *Catholic Biblical Quarterly* 41 (1979): 51-79; and Richard J. Clifford, "In Zion and David a New Beginning: An Interpretation of Psalm 78," in *Traditions in Transformation,* ed. Baruch Halpern and Jon D. Levenson (Winona Lake, Ind.: Eisenbrauns, 1981), 121-141.

inative parallels. The people of Jerusalem could not imagine their own precious system to be in jeopardy like Shiloh. Nor can we imagine that our own system — industrial, military, economic, political — might be in the same jeopardy as Shiloh and Jerusalem. Drawing analogies in contemporary life is hazardous. But imaginative preaching invites us to dare such analogies as did Jeremiah. His analogy in his time was as risky as any we might propose.

Jerusalem will be an empty crater, just like Shiloh (cf. 51:34). The royal establishment of the Davidic dynasty has no special claim upon God. Everything depends on torah justice, which has been massively distorted and denied. Even Jerusalem must meet the same requirements as Shiloh. Yahweh will "cast out" even favored Jerusalem. Exile is coming. At least in these verses this prospect will not be averted. Practitioners of injustice will lose land and be displaced. It is a harsh, unqualified verdict.

We should note not only the radical character but also the discerning quality of this insight. Long before Karl Marx, the prophetic tradition has seen that religion may serve to legitimate the dominant class. Jeremiah is able to see and express quite clearly that such religion has an important positive social function. That positive social function, however, is subject to the critique of God's sovereign will. Thus religion that flies in the face of the character of God (who is allied with widows and orphans) cannot sustain a religious establishment.

7:16-20 Here we are given access to a private oracle received by Jeremiah concerning his vocation. The address "as for you" makes a distinction between the person of the prophet and the community under judgment, the same distinction we have found in 1:15-19.[5] The special instruction to Jeremiah, articulated with three negatives in 7:16, is that he is no longer to make intercession on behalf of Jerusalem, because Yahweh is past listening (cf. 15:1-3 for the same motif). God's patience is exhausted, and now there is no turning back. A lawsuit speech follows.

The indictment (7:18-19) characterizes the embrace of other gods, which is intolerable to Yahweh. The mocking description shows that

5. On the person of the prophet in relation to the community, see Timothy Polk, *The Prophetic Persona*, JSOT Supplement 32 (Sheffield: University of Sheffield Press, 1984).

worship of the "queen of heaven" has become a cottage industry that engages the entire domestic economy. The sentence (v. 20) is the release of the wrath of Yahweh, powerfully expressed with the fourfold "upon" (*'al*) (cf. 1:15-16). Judah's infidelity is so severe that Jeremiah's intercession must stop. The provocation is decisive. There is no religious act now available that could revoke this decision. Religion cannot override the cost of covenant nullification.[6]

7:21-28   These verses expand on the contrast already made in vv. 3-4 between covenantal obedience and manipulation in liturgy. The assault on the ideological claims and practices of the Jerusalem establishment is unqualified and relentless. On the one hand, it is asserted that the God of Israel has never been interested in sacrificial liturgy (vv. 21-22). Those practices are fundamentally alien to the character of the God of Moses. Such acts are not intrinsically wrong, but they are invariably allied with the dominant values of control and oppression. The practice of such sacrifice tends to serve and legitimate vested social interest, and thus takes aim against covenantal obedience.

On the other hand, what is commanded and required is listening (*shema'*, v. 23.) That is all. Verses 21-28 appear to be much influenced by the Deuteronomist, for whom listening is the primal act of covenantal responsiveness (cf. Deut. 6:4). Listening is readiness to be addressed and commanded, to have life ordered by Yahweh. Listening is to cede control rather than to retain control through religious manipulation and ritual acts.

In what follows, the verdict, "they did not listen," appears four times (Jer. 7:24, 26, 27, 28). The alternative to listening is autonomy (cf. 18:12). Israel organized its life for self-serving and self-sufficiency, thereby denying its character as a people bound in covenant with this One who is sovereign. According to the claims of this Deuteronomic tradition (which is to some extent a contrived scheme), there has been a steady, identifiable line of

6. The nullification of the promise of which Jeremiah speaks has its contemporary parallel in the notion that a nuclear holocaust would nullify all cultural continuities and all religious underpinnings for cultural continuity. See Robert J. Lifton, *The Broken Connection* (New York: Simon & Schuster, 1980). The intent of Jeremiah is to articulate a cultural break that in its emotive power is as strong as that articulated in quite different terms by Lifton.

prophets.[7] Judah has had sustained opportunities to become a community of obedient listening (2 Kgs. 17:13). The refusal to listen and respond has been massive and pervasive, however, and continues to the present moment. Thinking it could determine its own best interest, Judah refused to receive corrective discipline or nurture (cf. Jer. 6:8, where the same word "correction" [*musar*] is used).

7:29-34 The focus in this section is on Judah's evil and Yahweh's punishment. The language used to describe evil moves from the torah categories of vv. 5-7 into the more extreme language of defilement. It is argued that the whole land has been defiled (v. 30). God cannot govern and life is not possible in a land that is ritually unclean and unusable. Living in such a land may make people exiles even if they never leave the territory. The rhetoric about punishment also takes extreme form. It does not speak simply of destruction and exile, but offers imaginative scenes of massive, ungrieved death. In these verses language for both indictment and sentence is escalated, perhaps to establish more fully the guilt of Judah and the legitimacy of Yahweh's claim.

Verse 29 invites lament because Judah is rejected. The covenant is terminated, and Yahweh withdraws protective care from the city. Verses 30-31 characterize the pagan religious action of disobedience. Verses 32-34 describe the punishment that comes with such religious promiscuity. Verses 32-33 concern death, which is so massive and comprehensive that there are no adequate social forms to cope with the disarray. As a result, the dead go unhonored and unburied, and they are left exposed in the most ignoble manner, surely contributing to the pollution. Verse 34 describes the end of the conventional celebrations of life. Society draws so close to total death that any such celebration is impossible and unthinkable. Life becomes barbaric, and all structures of plausibility are discredited. The poet searches for the most extreme language to invite his listeners to embrace the chaos at hand.

8:1-3 This passage carries the image of judgment and death to one more extreme dimension. Not only will there be death, but even the dead who

7. On the Deuteronomic construct of prophetic continuity, see Robert R. Wilson, *Prophecy and Society in Ancient Israel* (Philadelphia: Fortress, 1980), 156-226. Jeremiah seems to be the principal example of the ways in which the Deuteronomic tradition has recast prophetic traditions.

previously have been honored and laid in their tombs will be dislodged. Not only will forms of civility in the present and future be dysfunctional, but past acts of civility will be nullified. Present wretchedness will nullify past decency. Nothing is sacred or honored or beyond the reach of the wrath of Yahweh now unleashed. The punishment here fits the sin: Judah has gone after the gods of the heavens; now the bones of the disobedient dead will be spread before those gods.[8] At the end, life is worse than death (v. 3).

The rhetoric of the text is not "realistic" in the sense that it describes what is known. Rather, it is an imaginative anticipation of what is as yet unknown and unexperienced, for which there is no precedent. But this future is boldly envisioned by the prophet. The judgment to come is so unprecedented that only such ominous images are adequate to communicate it. Biblical eschatology always pushes to the limits of our imagination. Poetic characterizations of God's new age of blessing and poetic scenarios of God's judgment are always extreme cases of imagination, in the NT as in the OT. Such extreme imaginations are to be taken seriously. But when the poetic mode of imagination is forgotten and such anticipations are treated as flat predictions or descriptions, they are sure to be misunderstood and distorted. In such a reductionism, poetic efforts are robbed of their imaginative power. Any language that is used must match the unprecedented character of the impending judgment. The language of 8:1-3 does that. Practically, it may have been sufficient to impress upon Judah the impending historical realities of exile and displacement, but the prophet is not engaged in practical reasoning. Jeremiah seeks to penetrate and break open the imagination of the self-satisfied community so that it will see that the present circumstance is so extraordinary in its departure from torah that there can be no business as usual, not for Judah and surely not for Yahweh. Business as usual is dysfunctional because the indignant power of God is mobilized against Judah, and that mobilization is irreversible. This text seeks language to match that awesome, devastating theological reality. The text offers a "limit expression" to match an anticipated "limit experience."[9]

---

8. On the "fit" between sin and punishment, see Patrick D. Miller, Jr., *Sin and Judgment in the Prophets*, SBL Monograph 27 (Chico, Calif.: Scholars Press, 1982).

9. On "limit expression" to match "limit experience," see Paul Ricoeur, "Biblical Hermeneutics," *Semeia* 4 (1975): 122-128.

The theologically abrasive nerve of this text confounds conventional notions of the Bible. Popular propensity is to stress the ultimate continuity of God's commitment to the religious community. When all else fails, God will still be faithful. But in this remarkable statement the text opts for a final discontinuity. We cannot of course claim that this notion is pervasive in the Bible. It is important to recognize, however, that the Bible dares this unthinkable notion, and that it was asserted to real men and women in real historical circumstances. The prospect of theological discontinuity is an important dimension of biblical faith. This text bears witness to one aspect of God's inscrutable way with God's people. This text asserts something about the human prospect that we would prefer be left unsaid.[10] The text of 7:1–8:3 ends without relief.

10. The contemporary analysis of Robert L. Heilbroner, *An Inquiry into the Human Prospect* (New York: Norton, 1974), dismal as it is, is in keeping with the Jeremian analysis of the human prospect seen through the prism of Jerusalem's future.

No Balm in Gilead

Jeremiah 8:4–10:25

This collection of poetic units (with a few prose elements) contains some of the most poignant imagery in Jeremiah. This material is commonly regarded as deriving from the earlier period of the prophet, largely from the prophet himself. Many of the same images and phrases reappear that are present in chs. 2–6. The main thrust of the poetry is to "redescribe" the people and the city as a community on its way to death because of its refusal to be faithful to Yahweh. The two formal elements of the lawsuit speech, indictment and sentence, are at the center of this poetry. That is, the poetry demonstrates that Judah, and not Yahweh, is guilty of abandoning covenant. As a result, judgment will come, either in the form of invasion, destruction and death, or exile.[1] What is most amazing in this section is the rich, imaginative variety with which the poetry can work and rework these few central themes. Engagement with the poetry requires not simply that we get "the main point," as that is relatively obvious. What matters is that we attend to the nuance of language and the suggestive, imaginative quality of the literature. A countertheme to the lawsuit of guilt and judgment is the expression of grief that is felt by the poet and, we dare believe, by Yahweh. Some of the most eloquent and pathos-filled poetry in 8:4–10:25 attends to this motif.

1. On the various ways in which the tradition of Jeremiah nuances the coming judgment, see the discussion of Christopher R. Seitz, "The Crisis of Interpretation over the Meaning and Purpose of the Exile," *Vetus Testamentum* 35 (1985): 78-97. This study is a part of his exhaustive dissertation from Yale.

Judah Turns from Yahweh (8:4-17)

This poetic segment consists in an extended characterization of the failure of Judah (vv. 4-13) and a statement of impending judgment (vv. 14-17).

8:4-7 In this passage the poem takes up the theme we have seen in chs. 3–4, the act of *turning away* and the prospect of *turning back*. It is taken for granted that Judah has turned away in disloyalty. That Judah refuses to turn back to a right relation is the astonishing thing that bewilders the poet. The primary poetic device is the word "turn" *(shub)*, which is used six times in vv. 4-6.

> If one *turns away,* does he not *return* . . .
> Why has this people *turned away*
> in perpetual *backsliding* . . .
> They refuse to *return* . . .
> Every one *turns* to his own course . . .

Judah's life consists in turning away from Yahweh, who is the only one who can give life. Jeremiah's analysis leads to a thin hope that Judah may turn back to life.

The summons of Yahweh, issued in pathos and in sternness, is that Judah should return to covenant loyalty. The inhabitants of Judah can only be genuine Israelites when they are turned to Yahweh. But Judah violated this identity received from Yahweh and has done so jealously. Turning away is not only disobedient, but unnatural, violating the true character of this people. The repeated use of *shub* is supported by the use of *niham,* "repent," in v. 6, which carries the same meaning. The main assertion of the poems of the early period of the Jeremiah tradition is that Judah is out of covenant relation and must intentionally return to the discipline of that relation.

The metaphor of fickleness as unnatural act is explored in vv. 6b-7 by comparison with other creatures of God (cf. Isa. 1:2-3). Every one of God's creatures has an ordered way to live. It is proper that a horse should boldly head into battle. It is proper that storks and other birds know when to migrate, when to come and go. They have an uncanny sense of knowing what behavior is proper, and when. The poet turns to creation imagery in order to comment on the right ordering of life.

This appeal to creation reveals that every creature is wiser than fickle Israel. Just as every creature knows how to live, Israel is to know Yahweh's justice, to know Yahweh's will and purpose for the proper ordering of communal life and the proper handling of public issues and neighbor relations. But unlike every other creature, Israel is stupid and does not undertake the behavior that properly belongs to its covenantal character. Israel's stupidity is supportive of the *shub* motif that identifies proper behavior as return to Yahweh and Yahweh's justice.[2] Israel violates its own character as Yahweh's covenant mate.

In these verses the poet juxtaposes covenant language (Jer. 8:4-6a) and creation language (vv. 6b-7). The former concerns fickleness and inability to return. The latter is about the violation of one's true character. The juxtaposition is a powerful one, because it asserts that Israel's true character as a creature consists in being faithfully obedient to Yahweh. In refusing this obedience, Israel violates covenant vows and violates God's created order as well. In this act of violation, Israel has ceased to be the creature God has intended.

The poem becomes more specific about Israel's violation in vv. 8-13. These verses are framed as two lawsuit speeches, each of which states an indictment and a sentence.

8:8-10 The first lawsuit (vv. 8-10) is mostly indictment, but vv. 9a and 10a are a sentence. The indictment is directed toward the leadership, which has misled the community by its own fickle practice. (On the indictment of leaders, see Ezek. 13.) The "wise," who are to handle the torah, and the scribes, who are to understand how life with God is ordered, are in fact false. They are the "experts," but they have reneged on their proper role. The falseness of Judah concerns a fundamental betrayal and distortion, indeed, a systemic distortion of what matters for Israel. Israel has "rejected" the purpose of Yahweh (Jer. 8:9a), which means they have acted autonomously. In v. 10b prophets and priests, along with scribes and lawyers, are condemned. The entire public leadership is guilty of acting only in self-interest. The covenantal foundations of communal life have been completely jettisoned by the entire leadership apparatus.

2. On the intent of the verb *shub*, see the thorough exploration of the theme in John M. Bracke, "*šûb šebût:* A Reappraisal," *Zeitschrift für die alttestamentliche Wissenschaft* 97 (1985): 233-244, and the literature he cites.

The result of such falseness is sure and unavoidable, because covenant violations lead to judgment. Since Israel's only ground of life is covenant, when that is ignored trouble is sure to come. Verse 9a is general and says that Jerusalem is "captured." Verse 10a is more explicit. It anticipates invading forces, an occupying army. What is to be lost are wives and fields, property and relation, the two objects that are not to be coveted (Exod. 20:17). In the prose of Jeremiah the threat of invasion is explicitly identified as Babylon. But the poet is not so specific, because his aim is theological and artistic, not descriptive. The poet asserts that when covenant violations eventuate in broken relations, anticovenant forces are unleashed that will undo all of life. What amazes one is the bold capacity of the poet to make connections between evident religious perversion and happenings in the historical process that are interpreted as punishment. Only such a poet with an odd view of reality would dare to assign such cause-effect relation to these seemingly unrelated events.

8:11-13   In these verses the motifs of the lawsuit are reiterated again. The indictment is in three elements. The first (v. 11) is quite familiar. The leadership has lied. They have deceived the people by announcing a situation of well-being that in fact denies reality. The official ideology of the royal-temple establishment made claims of "peace and prosperity" that failed to acknowledge the profound theological sickness that is destroying the community. The lie is probably not a deliberate falsehood. Rather, it is a deep distortion that is so skewed and blind that it denies and prevents seeing how things really are. This people is so stupid that it accepts the cover-up offered by the leadership. It cannot see the gap between the claims of the establishment and the reality of its life (cf. 4:22).[3]

The second indictment (8:12a) is a loss of shame. The inability to blush means that there is no outside reference point to whom one must answer and by whom one is measured. Faithful people blush in the presence of the faithful God because the contrast between Yahweh's hope and their conduct is so stark. When as here, however, the faithful God has been effectively banished, the fickleness is no longer recognized as embar-

3. The incapability of Israel to notice, to see, or to hear is most dramatically expressed in Isa. 6:9-13. See Gerhard von Rad, *Old Testament Theology,* 2 (New York: Harper & Row; Edinburgh: Oliver & Boyd, 1965), 151-155.

rassing.[4] Abraham J. Heschel has said that the "loss of embarrassment" is a decisive step toward loss of humanness.[5] Israel has taken that step through a presumption of autonomy, so that there is no one to whom to refer and therefore no norm that evokes blushing.

The third indictment is in v. 13. This judgment seems to have echoes of Isa. 5:1-7. Israel is characterized as a vineyard or a fig tree. Its task is to produce the fruits appropriate to its life and species, but there are no fruits, no produce. There is no ethical outcome of faith proper to Israel, no manifestations of covenant. There is a complete incongruity between the expectations of Yahweh and the failure of Israel, an incongruity so foundational as to require judgment and rejection.

On all three grounds, therefore, Israel is guilty of: (1) systemic denial of reality and pretense (Jer. 8:11); (2) loss of a reference for shame and therefore autonomy (v. 12a); and (3) failure to yield appropriate outcomes (v. 13). All three constitute failure to be genuinely Israel. The "therefore" of the sentence in v. 12b is inevitable: they shall fall and stumble. Notice how elusive the language is. It does not prescribe or predict. It is lacking in specifity and concrete reference. It is poetry, not policy. The poetry is uncompromising, however, in its conviction that nullification surely follows the refusal to be who one is intended by God to be. This community will be nullified if it rejects its vocation as God's people. Judah in its disobedience has passed the point of having alternative choices. That nullification is now lamentably, inexorably underway.

8:14-17 These verses, which seem like an interlude in the flow of poetry, are an imaginative presentation of the destruction that is already underway. Only in v. 14b is there another reference to guilt. Otherwise, this poetic element is a characterization of the judgment now set in motion against Judah. The dominant metaphor is military. In the face of the invading army (quite unspecified), Israel is summoned to retreat and prepare for

---

4. The absence of an effective norm is reflected in 2 Sam. 11:25, "Do not let this be evil in your eyes," which is contrasted with v. 27, "the thing was evil in the eyes of Yahweh" (author's translation). David is shameless because he fails to refer his conduct to the uncompromising righteousness of Yahweh. The shape and deliberate contrast between evil "in your eyes" and "in the eyes of Yahweh" is lost in most English translations.

5. Abraham J. Heschel, *Who Is Man?* (Stanford: Stanford University Press, 1965), 112-114.

siege. The enemy is from the north, as Dan (v. 16) is the northernmost territory. (On the ominous character of the north as a source of threat, see 1:13-14.) That invasion, before which Israel is helpless, is articulated in a variety of gripping metaphors. Israel will perish. Israel's water, its basic support, is poisoned (cf. 2:13). There is only terror. The invading army is coming on great, terrifying, imperial horses. The army that comes will follow a scorched earth policy, devouring everything along the way (cf. 5:17). In this moment of poetry the experience of the confusion, threat, and upheaval that comes with the invasion is made available to the listeners. It is not necessary to await the arrival of the army. The experience of dismay can begin now with the poem.

The metaphor changes in 8:17 to a snake. The shift from horse to snake is a stunning one, from the massive rush of power to slow, creeping terror. The figure is employed to communicate that the danger facing Israel is sure and unavoidable (cf. Amos 5:19). The community will be poisoned to death if it does not first die of fear — all because Israel has refused its proper role in history. The price of covenant nullification is nullification of Judah as a viable, historical community. The poet creates a scenario that shows the utter undoing of this historical entity that the royal-temple ideology promotes as perpetually guaranteed. History is governed by this betrayed lover, this disappointed creator who has been casually disregarded by Israel. The price of such disregard is massive and unavoidable.

Grief beyond Healing (8:18–9:3)

This poetic unit is one of the most powerful in the Jeremiah tradition. It is also one of the most pathos-filled. Its central images are sharply contrasted to the preceding ones in 8:4-17. Now it is not threat and terror, but dread, sickness, and sadness. The poet asserts that this people is "sick to death." The poetry also probably asserts Yahweh's "sickness to death" over the terminal illness of this beloved people. The formula, "says the LORD" in 9:3 is textually insecure.[6] The use of this formula, however, makes it likely that the pathos of God and of the poet here are indistin-

---

6. The phrase is lacking in the LXX. The change is not an incidental textual correction. It matters whose "voice" is sounded here, in terms of the weight and intent of the poetry.

guishable. With the formula attributing the poem to Yahweh, the pathos cannot belong only to Jeremiah. This is poetry that penetrates God's heart. That heart is marked by God's deep grief.[7] God's anger is audible here, but it is largely subordinated to the hurt God experiences in the unnecessary death of God's people. God would not have it so, but the waywardness of Israel has taken every alternative response away from Yahweh.

8:18-21 This section may best be understood as a dialogue between the liturgic *pretense* of Israel and the corresponding *pathos* of God over this people that understands nothing. It is structured so that the beginning and end speak the pathos. Within that envelope are two quotes from the liturgy, and at the center is God's dismissive question of indignation. Thus, the structure of this unit is:

    A   pathos (vv. 18-19a)
    B   question of the people concerning presence (v. 19b)
    C   God's question of indignation (v. 19c)
    B′   question of the people concerning timing (v. 20)
    A′   pathos (v. 21).

The pathos of God (or of the poet) in vv. 18-19a, 21 is a heartsickness of a betrayed lover or a yearning parent.[8] One sees the trouble of the lover or child, wants to head it off, but must stand helplessly while the disease

---

7. See Terence E. Fretheim, *The Suffering of God* (Philadelphia: Fortress, 1984), 135, 160-162.

8. On the helpless yearning and heartsickness of a parent over a child, see Frederick Buechner, *Now and Then* (San Francisco and London: Harper & Row, 1983), 54-55:

> To love another, as you love a child, is to become vulnerable in a whole new way. It is no longer only through what happens to yourself that the world can hurt you, but through what happens to the one you love also and greatly more hurting. When it comes to your own hurt, there are always things you can do. You can put up a brave front, for one, and behind that front, if you are lucky, if you persist, you can become a little brave inside yourself. You can become strong in the broken places, as Hemingway said. You can become philosophical, recognizing how much of your troubles you have brought down on your own head and resolving to do better by yourself in the future. . . . But when it comes to the hurt of a child you love, you are all but helpless. The child makes terrible

works to its dread conclusion of death. Yahweh (and the poet) could see it all coming long before the leadership in Jerusalem had an inkling, if indeed they ever suspected it. God's hurt (v. 21) is derivative from Israel's hurt. Unlike Judah, God recognizes and embraces Judah's hurt. God has no alternative. That is the kind of God Yahweh is. But the people, where the hurt has its locus, neither know nor care. Their ignorance and indifference make the pain much more intense.

The pathos of the poem is derivative from the cynical indifference of Israel that continues with business as usual in the face of sickness to death. In v. 19b the people are quoted as presuming and insisting that God must be present. After all, it is God's business to be present, and it is Zion's claim that God is present (cf. Exod. 17:7; Mic. 3:11). This people is so cynical as not to notice that the temple claims are dead and have failed (cf. Jer. 7). The temple is no longer God's habitat, and so the liturgy makes an empty promise and relies on a nullified claim. The fakery of such an appeal to the holy place of Zion as a place of God's presence is matched in 8:20 by an appeal to time. Now the quoted liturgy reminds God that the saving season is almost over. The community expects to be healed by a certain point on the calendar. God may be a bit behind schedule, so the community attempts to remind God about the proper order of events. But just as the promise of place is voided, so too the claim of time is irrelevant. God will not respond to any liturgic calendar or the state's "five year plan."

Both liturgic formulae of place and time assume that God will respond to the plans of the establishment. Those in Jerusalem who engage in acts of ideological self-deception imagine Yahweh to be only a patron and therefore available at particular times and places. Those conventions have been obliterated by the grief that makes all old practices null and void. Nothing will work now except radical repentance, but repentance is remote from Israel.

---

mistakes, and there is very little you can do to ease his pain, especially when you are so often a part of his pain, as the child is a part of yours. There is no way to make him strong with such strengths as you may have found through your own hurt, or wise enough through such wisdom, and even if there were, it would be the wrong way because it would be your way and not his. The child's pain becomes your pain, and as the innocent bystander, maybe it is even a worse pain for you, and in the long run even the bravest front is not much use.

At the center of this poem in v. 19c stands the reason for the rejection of old traditional claims. God's pathos is evoked by affront. God hurts because God is offended. The ground of the sickness to death is idolatry, the attempt to organize life around controllable objects rather than in reference to holy subject. The text moves from the center of v. 19c out toward both its beginning and its end. Yahweh is affronted by the idolatry. Israel is driven to fraudulent liturgical assertions, which reflect idolatrous miscalculation. Israel wishes for God's presence in place and on time, but in fact Israel is terminally ill because of idolatry and should entertain no wish. Wishful thinking is inadequate religion. Because Yahweh discerns the pathology as Israel does not, Yahweh is pressed to deep grief. The structure of the poem suggests that the reality of idolatry precludes healing and deliverance. Israel's close commitment to fake loyalties immobilizes the very power of God that would save.

8:22–9:3   In these verses, God, the power that now cannot (or refuses to) save, is driven from rage to painful wistfulness. Perhaps elsewhere (not in Jerusalem), perhaps in Gilead, outside the normal range of royal administration, there is a cure. Perhaps there, there will be a doctor who can make a difference (v. 22). But the yearning question of v. 22 remains unanswered. The reader (along with the poet and God) is required to deduce from the lack of answer that there is no help in Gilead either. Indeed, no healing is possible. The sickness is too deep. The idolatry is too pervasive. Judah refuses the medicine that is available.

The poet (and God) are pressed by this awareness to a new wave of grief. In 9:1-2 the poet utilizes the Psalmic tradition (Ps. 55:6-8), which is surely familiar to his listeners. The familiarity of this tradition does not lessen its poignancy, however. The poet wishes first that his head and eyes were more available for weeping (Jer. 9:1). The hurt in the face of Judah's death requires and evokes more grief, more crying, and more tears than his body is capable of transmitting.

God is inadequate for the grieving now to be done, for "my people" are very close to death. In a second figure (v. 2a) the yearning is not for more adequate tear ducts, but for an escape from this unbearable people. The decisive verb is "leave" *('azab),* a word we have seen in ch. 2 dealing with Israel's abandonment of God. Now it is God (or the poet) who yearns to leave, because the fickleness is beyond bearing. This is not a God who loves eternally. There is only so much this God will tolerate. Now it is time to depart because the affronts and betrayals have become a burden too great for God.

Jeremiah 9:2b-3 catalogues the ground of grief and the basis for God's abandonment. The scandal of Israel's violation of covenant is based in idolatry, a falsely-placed loyalty, and is embodied in adultery, unjust gain, slander, evil. The telling phrase is "falsehood *(sheqer)*, not truth *(emunah)* is mighty in the land" (author's translation). Every practice of fidelity — theological, moral, juridical, economic — has become a practice of fickleness and self-deception. This is rooted in the fact that "they do not know me," that is, they do not recognize Yahweh as covenant LORD. The pathos of the line, "they do not know me" echoes 8:7, 12. Judah has forgotten everything necessary to survival, forgotten commitments, forgotten shame, forgotten accountability, forgotten God. When that core commitment is disregarded, there are not enough arms, strategies, policies, prayers, or sacrifices to survive. The God "not known" is the one drawn to grief, because the end is sure. Yahweh now has no rescue mission that can be undertaken.

The poignancy of the poem is matched by an absence of specificity. The poetry is left open and inconclusive. It does not allude to particular acts or kings or invading armies. No doubt the poet and his listeners have something particular in mind. But what lets the poetry function in every generation as a powerful disclosure is the concreteness of the language that is porous enough to let it touch new historical specificities. The first articulation of the poem can always be freshly presented with new concreteness. Heard in a new situation, this poem will have its powerful say toward new concreteness, almost without interpretation. Each new rendering in new circumstance permits the poem to be God's grief-stricken word in a quite fresh way.

Neighbors Beware (9:4-11)

The historical existence of Judah is coming to an end. The specific mention of Jerusalem in v. 11 is the first concrete reference in this long poetic unit beginning in 8:4. But listeners who follow the poetry could not have missed the allusions all along the way. This historical institution Jerusalem is under final threat, because its relation with Yahweh has been monstrously violated. Contrary to the reading of reality promoted by the self-serving

95

establishment, city, temple, and throne all in fact depend on covenantal fidelity. This alternative reading insists that relational metaphors tell us more about historical consequences than the formal posturing of the people ostensibly in charge (cf. Mark 10:42-44). Prophetic poetry has more to tell us about Jerusalem's future than carefully-crafted government news releases, because the ones who authorize such releases seem to know so little about the realities.

9:4-6   These verses open with an indictment that focuses on social relations. Interestingly, the poet centers on the loss of honest speech between neighbors. The dominant modes of communication are now slander and deception. The poet believes that no public community can function properly unless communication is conducted in good faith. Such a poetic discernment may give us pause in our time when communication has largely become deft management of fraudulent symbols and images — in economic and religious life, in advertising and in public office. In v. 5 the decisive words (already seen in v. 3) are "no truth . . . only lies" (*emet* and *sheqer*). The poet observes that the fabric of human community has collapsed because neighbor no longer counts except as an object of exploitation. The outcome of such calculating speech, which uses people, is treachery. The alternative to all such destructive deception is to "know Yahweh," but that has been refused. The analysis offered by the poem is subtle. It recognizes that the rejection of covenantal, theological references and underpinnings invites the erosion of all viable human relations. The freedom of the true God keeps human interaction open and faithful. Where there is a loss or diminishment of that God, the loss of serious human exchange follows quickly and surely.

9:7-9   This passage, introduced by "therefore," is the predictable sentence following the indictment of vv. 4-6. God cannot and will not be indifferent to such a violation of everything hoped for. The first judgment is refinement and testing, a motif we have encountered in 6:27-30. We should not be misled by the metaphor, however. The metaphor of refining may suggest that God will find and save the good elements of society; but the poem in its passion asserts that there are no good ones. The metaphor of sifting is pressed to its extreme, to announce that all are tested. All are found wanting. None are exempt. (See parallel imagery in Amos 9:9-10.)

The sentence is interrupted in Jer. 9:8 with a return to the indictment that reiterates the theme of vv. 4-6. Verse 8 articulates an incongruity and contradiction between speech and intent, between public appearance and actual motivation. The language is powerful: a deadly arrow, an ambush. The neighbor is under assault in ways that make community impossible. The sentence in v. 9 is a "visit," a harsh coming of judgment in which God's very life must be avenged. God's honor is at issue, and finally God will not be mocked — even by God's precious covenant partner. The basis of threat from Yahweh is finally not moral, but theological. God is God and will manifest that Godness against this people who mock. No social establishment, not even this holy one in Jerusalem, can finally banish God's awesome self, God's own life. The manipulative posturing of Judah does not paralyze God, for God need not and will not be trapped in these manipulative postures.

9:10-11 Beyond the lawsuit speech (indictment in vv. 4-6, sentence in vv. 7-9), vv. 10-11 summon to lamentation (cf. Amos 5:16-17). Such a poetic move may reflect the poet's deep pathos and/or the historic sense that the end is now very close to fruition. The poetry concerns both historical realism and poetic discernment. Grief comes because creation is undone (cf. Hos. 4:3; Jer. 4:23-26). Because of social falseness, cattle, birds, beasts are gone. The ecosystem has collapsed. This is indeed "the day after" — the day after reckoning, after social disintegration, after fickleness, after death. The lamentation focuses on the beloved city. This is the return of urban creation to chaos, the end of the system, end of ideology, end of security, end of meaning.

This poetry is flung audaciously in the face of every self-deceiving ideological claim. The words of the poet work against every soothing patriotism, every self-confident creed, every ideological ploy. It is only a poem, but it is received as a truth-telling by the community around the prophet. The poet does not linger over the juridical elements. He is a pastor. His community can begin grieving because the die of historical dismantling has been cast. None in Jerusalem can avoid the loss by their policy or by their buoyancy. History under God's governance is not so easily or painlessly reduced.

The Land Laid Waste (9:12-16)

The prose of vv. 12-16 lacks the passion of the preceding unit and may reflect the more measured articulation of the Deuteronomist. The unit is in three parts. First is a question (v. 12) that reflects astonishment at the poetry. The announced judgment violates common sense. It simply does not seem plausible that the entire world will end. The announced judgment also violates the most cherished tenets of the royal-temple ideology. This verse, in a threefold question that may function as a rhetorical ploy, asks, how can anyone make sense of what is happening?

Second, the answer given in vv. 13-16 seems to say: it is not all that difficult, complicated, or obscure to understand. There are very good grounds for all of the destruction to come, and those grounds are derived from the old tradition. To understand this astonishing threat, one need only ponder the main claims of the covenant tradition that expose the false presuppositions of Jerusalem. But of course, Jerusalem is incapable of pondering the old tradition.

The reason for the indictment is given in three negatives and two positives. The negatives are: forsake torah (again, the verb *'azab*), not listen, not walk (v. 13). That is, this people has departed from the quite explicit demands of covenant. In Deut. 6:4 Israel's main summons is to listen. In Deut. 13:4 Israel is to "walk after . . . listen . . . cleave," which forms a nice contrast to our three verbs. The problem for our poet is that on all three counts, Israel is unresponsive.

The two positives (Jer. 9:14) assert that not listening leads on the one hand to autonomy (stubborn heart) and on the other hand to idolatry (serving Baals). The two are equated: self-reference and idolatry are two forms of an alternative to covenant with Yahweh, two forms of escaping obedience to the torah, two choices that cannot bring life.

The third element (vv. 15-16) is the judgment introduced by "therefore." The sentence is massive and unambiguous with a fivefold statement:

- I will feed,
- I will give drink,
- I will scatter,
- I will send,
- I will consume.

The sovereignty of God over the historical process extends even to Jerusalem. No ideology of throne or temple protects Judah from this relentless God. The sentence reflects an ambiguity about punishment that recurs in the tradition of Jeremiah. The threat is on the one hand by sword and on the other hand by exile (scattering), which permits a new possibility.[9] The tradition at different times says both. In this passage both possibilities are forceful enough to announce an end. The poet's intent is to offer rhetoric through which the scenario of termination is experienced as a real historical happening, even though much of the poetic rendition precedes reality. It is an act of rhetorical interpretation, but not for that reason any less serious. It is poetry that claims to disclose God's full intent, and the reason for it.

Zion in Mourning (9:17-22)

In these verses the invitation to public lamentation sounded in v. 10 is now treated more extensively. The poetry of grief means to enact in the imagination of Judah the end that royal ideology denies. Public grief is an art form that requires expertise, and this unit therefore summons the women who are specialists in grief. In v. 21 the coming of death is treated like an intruding agent in the night who sneaks in the window (like a thief; cf. 1 Thess. 5:2), enters the safest places — like showing up in the queen's bedroom in spite of all security measures — and works its will even among the young who are the sign of life. The image affirms that the coming of death cannot be fended off. It will penetrate behind every device of protection. In this city, on these streets, in these squares, the power of death is deliberate, sure, and irresistible.

In the end (v. 22) there will be a pile of corpses, perhaps from slaughter, perhaps from plague (cf. Jer. 7:32-33). The poet offers as many metaphors as he can to evoke the inescapable, dreaded reality. The final metaphor is the reaper who cuts down with none to gather back up (cf. Amos 2:13-14). The bodies shall be strewn in the land. The inhabitants of Jerusalem shall be scattered around the Fertile Crescent. The center has

9. On the juxtaposition of death and exile as a live theological issue in the interpretive community, see Christopher R. Seitz, "Theology in Conflict: Reactions to the Exile in the Book of Jeremiah" (Ph.D. dissertation, Yale University, 1986).

not held, and things do indeed fall apart for Judah.[10] The pretense of the city is now fully exposed. Death presides in this city that has so craved life but that has carelessly squandered its chance for life and now must relinquish it.

True Glory (9:23-26)

In this prose section two very different sayings are placed back to back. The first (vv. 23-24) is a magisterial epitome of the claims of Israel's covenantal and prophetic faith. It articulates a sharp contrast between two very different ways of life.[11] The two ways of life are articulated in contrasting triads. The first triad is the way of wisdom, might, and riches. These modes of self-sufficiency are condemned. This triad figured large in sapiential instruction and seems to be embodied in King Solomon (on which see Matt. 6:29). The wisdom teachers reflected on the gains of wealth and power (see especially Eccles. 1–2) and concluded that they did not bring ultimate well-being. The meaning of "wisdom" in this triad is more difficult, but in this context it apparently means "technique," the means to control the outcome of life through technical data.[12] As such, wisdom ranks with might and riches as being unable to bring well-being.

The contrasting triad of "steadfast love, justice, and righteousness" (v. 24) reflects a wholly different orientation, congruent with the character of God who delights in these qualities and insists upon them. Yahweh

10. The familiar lines of William B. Yeats, "The Second Coming," are peculiarly pertinent to Jeremiah.

Things fall apart: the center cannot hold;
Mere anarchy is loosed upon the world . . .
The best lack all connection, while the worst
Are full of passionate intensity.

11. See Walter Brueggemann, "The Epistemological Crisis of Israel's Two Histories (Jer. 9:22-23)," in *Israelite Wisdom,* ed. John G. Gammie (Missoula, Mont.: Scholars Press, 1978), 85-105.

12. On wisdom as a form of administrative power, see George E. Mendenhall, "The Shady Side of Wisdom: The Date and Purpose of Genesis 3," in *A Light Unto My Path,* ed. Howard N. Bream, Ralph D. Heim, and Carey A. Moore (Philadelphia: Temple University Press, 1974), 319-334.

champions and embodies fidelity, equity, and humanness in the community. Thus, Yahweh is contrasted with other gods who seek satiation (might, riches). If God is committed to covenantal life as marked by steadfast love, justice, and righteousness, it follows that the community is to be ordered differently in light of that which delights Yahweh. The saying posits a close cause-effect linkage between the delights of God and social policy in Israel that reflects covenant faith.

This rather simple statement of contrasts identifies the social values that lead to death and the social relations that lead to life. Clearly Jeremiah's contemporaries had made the wrong choice and had chosen death. In 1 Cor. 1:18-31 Paul takes up the language of Jeremiah. In critiquing the practice of the Corinthian church, Paul contrasts the wisdom and power of the world and the weakness and foolishness of the Cross. As with Jeremiah and Paul, the issues in our own time have not changed. The same demanding choice between human fidelity and equity on the one hand and the self-serving ways of worldly security on the other hand is present among us.

In the verses that follow (Jer. 9:25-26), a verdict is given on Israel's choices. Verses 23-24 presented the choices Israel was called to make. Verses 25-26 review the choice that was made and the destiny received. The opening formula of v. 25 looks to a future that may be distant, but nonetheless very certain. The sure destiny of harsh "visitation" is on both the circumcised and the uncircumcised. Indeed, those who ostensibly practice the form of circumcision are in fact the uncircumcised. (See a parallel use of the theme in Rom. 2:25-29.) This bold assertion argues that the ritual practice of circumcision is in fact a fraud that has no reality. The result is that the chosen people are as ritually unacceptable and disqualified as any other *goy*. It is not only a judgment on both Israel and the *goyim,* but an argument that there is no distinction. The people who presumed a favored position in fact have no distinguishing characteristics to which any attention is paid. Chosen status is harshly dismissed. Judgment is the same on all. This assertion of impartial judgment is the inversion of impartial grace, reflected in Deut. 10:17 and Acts 10:34-35.

The specific reference to the other nations (Jer. 9:26) seems to be quite incidental. The point of the list of nations is simply to assert that Judah stands among the uncircumcised, and so is on equal basis with the other nations. Attention is thus focused in v. 26 on Israel, "uncircumcised in heart." (On this formula, see Deut. 10:16; 30:6; Jer. 4:4.)[13] The heart is the organ of response and covenant-making. When the heart is uncircumcised, it lacks sensitivity and ability to function. When Israel's heart is not responsive to Yahweh (as it has not been in the experience of this poet), Israel can make no covenantal claim on Yahweh.

Unlike the other uses of the circumcision metaphor, this is not an imperative urging circumcision and, with circumcision, repentance. Instead the formula of circumcision is a final judgment given without any new chance being voiced. Yahweh's harsh visitation is coming. When it comes, this people is no more chosen than any other. Surface rituals will not save. All that would save is the covenant practice of steadfast love, justice, and righteousness. But according to Jeremiah, Israel rejected these practices long ago. The argument on circumcision here, though negatively stated, is an anticipation of Paul (Gal. 5:1-6), who sees that ritual cannot save. Only a reoriented heart can save, but that is now impossible for Judah.

None Like the Lord (10:1-16)

In Jeremiah's time as in our own, the critical faith issue is not atheism, but idolatry.[14] In Jeremiah's time the temptation was the attraction of the gods of Babylon. In our day the comparable temptation may be the gods of militarism, of nationalism, of naturalism, of consumerism, of technology. In both cases the temptation is to vest one's life hope in the things we ourselves generate, instead of receiving life as a gift from this One who stands beyond us and for us. Characteristically the Bible does not deny the existence of other gods. The Bible makes an assumption that the world is polytheistic. The other gods exist. They have seductive power, but what they lack is power for life. They cannot do anything, and in that decisive

13. It is worth noting that in Deut. 10:16-17 the command to circumcise the foreskin of the heart is followed immediately with the assertion that God is impartial and takes no bribe. That is, circumcision is a mark of covenant obedience, but it gives Israel no preferential status. The distortion of circumcision, as argued by Paul, arises when the command to obey is distorted to indicate a preferential status. That distortion is rejected by Jeremiah as by Paul.

14. On the centrality of idolatry rather than atheism in contemporary discussion, see Pablo Richard et al., *The Idols of Death and the God of Life* (Maryknoll, N.Y.: Orbis, 1983), 1 and *passim.*

test they are utterly unlike Yahweh, who has the power to give life and therefore also the power to judge life.

The text of Jer. 10:1-16 is organized as a litany of contrasts between the true God and false gods.[15] The false gods, and their foolish subjects who have manufactured them, are characterized in vv. 1-5, 8-9, 11, 14-15. These gods are characterized by a series of negatives:

- cannot move (v. 4),
- cannot speak,
- cannot walk,
- cannot do evil,
- cannot do good (v. 5),
- did not make (v. 11).

Three times they are described by the Hebrew word *hebel* (vv. 3, 8, 15; cf. 2:5), which means "vapor, nothingness, vanity." Jeremiah 10:14 says that these other gods have no spirit (i.e., no vitality) and are in fact "false." They cannot keep their promises. The contrast with Yahweh leads to the conclusion that they are unworthy of trust or loyalty, commitment or obedience.

We should not imagine that such would-be gods are merely religious projections. A critique of the idols must be more realistic and critical than that. First, the idols are linked to the way of the nations (v. 2) and the customs of the peoples (v. 3). They reflect the practices of noncovenanting peoples. Second, not only are the idols stupid and foolish (v. 8), but those who make and serve them are equally foolish. Third, the weight of the description falls on what the idols are made of — silver and gold, violet and purple. The false religion of the idols is therefore directly tied to the false economics around which Judah structures its life.[16] The idols are not only religious objects. They are commodities with economic value that lead to a false and destructive organization of community life. A misdirected religious loyalty is attached to a misorganized community life. Indeed, we may imagine that the poet wishes to comment on both at the same time, for religion and economics are intimately connected. The poet

15. See Jož e Krašovec, *Antithetic Structure in Biblical Hebrew Poetry, Supplements to Vetus Testamentum* 35 (1984): 76-85.

16. See Walter Brueggemann, "Old Testament Theology as a Particular Conversation: Adjudication of Israel's Socio-Theological Alternatives," *Theology Digest* 32 (1985): 303-325.

surely is not preoccupied simply with an abstract religious habit, but with the concrete practices that shape communal life.

Yahweh, the God of Israel, is contrasted to the idols in vv. 6-7, 10, 12-13, 16. There is none like Yahweh (vv. 6, 7, 16). Indeed, these verses demonstrate that there is no serious point of comparison. This one is a God with power to act. The wrath of Yahweh terrifies (v. 10). This God is to be feared (v. 7), as the other gods need not be feared. The decisive and powerful actions of Yahweh are seen in contrast to the other gods who do no actions. Unlike the idols, this God is capable of doing something that matters.

The verbs used to speak of Yahweh are indicative of the power of this God:

- He made,
- he established,
- he stretched out (v. 12),
- he utters,
- he sends up (makes rise),
- he makes,
- he brings out (v. 13),
- he formed (v. 16).

The language is of creation, which is done by Yahweh's powerful speech and by Yahweh's forming activity. The modes of creation of both Gen. 1 and Gen. 2 are captured in these verbs. In Gen. 1 God creates by powerful speech. In Gen. 2 Yahweh makes by acting, as a potter. Both modes are utilized in our text.

The appellations of Yahweh are stunning: "true God," "living God," "everlasting King," "portion of Jacob," "LORD of hosts." Yahweh is the true and reliable God (Jer. 10:10), contrasted with the idols of falseness (v. 14). This God does what has been promised and keeps commitments to the world God has made. This God is a living God.[17] This God has the power for life, the capacity to work a real newness, to cause life where there is only death and chaos. The everlasting King (v. 10) gives the assurance of keeping the world order against every threat of chaos. This king is able to constrain the

17. See Hans-Joachim Kraus, "The Living God: A Chapter of Biblical Theology," in *Theology of the Liberating Word,* ed. Frederick Herzog (Nashville: Abingdon, 1971), 76-107.

waters, to drive back the flood (v. 13). The name "portion of Jacob" links Yahweh to the election tradition of Israel in Genesis, and "LORD of hosts" is an old martial name celebrating power. The collage of terms and phrases credits this God with power both in creation and in history.[18]

This poem is content to state the contrast between Yahweh and the idols and is not compelled to draw any implications. The contrast is powerful enough. Israel has the option to be in relationship with and loyal to the God who can give new life. This God must be trusted and served and is never at the disposal of Israel. The alternative is to be allied with gods who have no power for life and cannot be trusted. The structure of the text requires a decision (cf. Matt. 6:24). It is a decision Israel does not want to make, and one that Israel characteristically makes wrongly. The total tradition of Jeremiah affirms that Judah is in the jeopardy which Jeremiah announces, precisely because it has abandoned Yahweh and embraced other gods who cannot give life.

The faith question raised by the sharp contrasts of Jer. 10:1-16 concerns the character of God and the nature of faith. False faith is linked to the idolatry of false gods and to the ideology of false imperial claims. Israel's source of life falls outside such practices. The text requires a choice, which is indeed life and death (Deut. 30:15-20). Those who practice idolatry are consigned to powerlessness. The alternative of the power of the real God is offered here, but Judah seems never to understand or embrace this singular life-giving alternative.

In some ways this text seems quite remote from us because we understand ourselves to be removed from the ancient temptation to idolatry and polytheism. We do not credit the presence of other gods in our religious conversations. If we do a careful analysis of the modern situation, however, important parallels emerge. That analysis may be aided by the thought of Karl Marx, who sees that idols are made out of the most precious commodities, silver and gold.[19] That is, we come to worship the

---

18. A similar cluster of terms and phrases occurs in like usage in John 1:19-51 concerning Jesus.

19. Marx has helped us see that it is not commodities in general that are the problem, but precious commodities — gold and silver — which are assigned transcendent value and so function as fetishes. On such fetishism in American consumerism, see John F. Kavanaugh, *Following Christ in a Consumer Society: The Spirituality of Cultural Resistance* (Maryknoll, N.Y.: Orbis, 1981).

things we have made, the creation and not the creator (Rom. 1:25). The analysis of Paul (and Marx) is paralleled by that of Sigmund Freud, who critiqued religion as an illusion that projected a yearning and social value on the things we have produced. Both Marx and Freud offer a critique of religion that is faithful to the tradition of Jeremiah. They assert that it is a lie when we try to derive the source of devotion, loyalty, and obedience from ourselves and the things we have made, whether that dimension of self is economic, political, psychological, or religious. The root of idolatry is to try to find ultimacy within the world of our own control and production.

The positive assertion of the text concerning Yahweh moves beyond the criticism of Marx and Freud to say what is true. With the positive assertions of the truth about Yahweh, biblical faith parts company with the critique of Marx and Freud, for it asserts that the holy, incomparable God of judgment and deliverance is not a projection out of our economics or philosophy.[20] This God — true and living — is a free agent who moves toward and against established reality according to his own irreducible purposes. It is this reality of genuine, holy freedom that is the ground of the prophetic judgment against Jerusalem, for God is not dependent on what is in the world. This same reality of genuine, holy freedom is also the ground of hope after judgment for Jerusalem, for God can do a newness not derived from what is old and now nullified.

The "smashing of idols" and the assertion of the true God are the proper work of prophetic poetry.[21] In our own time, we seem to be deeply — if not hopelessly — enmeshed in our self-created systems of security, well-being, and prosperity. But the enmeshment destroys us, for it talks us out of neighbor love, out of genuine freedom, and destines us to the anxiety of competence and finally to despair. That the source of life lies outside us and moves freely delivers us from being self-generated and

20. On a theological understanding of faith that is not simply projection, see Hans Küng, *Does God Exist?* (Garden City, N.Y.: Doubleday, 1980).

21. See Walter Brueggemann, " 'Vine and Fig Tree': A Case Study in Imagination and Criticism," *Catholic Biblical Quarterly* 43 (1981): 188-204. More programmatically, see Paul Ricoeur on demystification and assertion, respectively, in his two essays, "The Critique of Religion," in *The Philosophy of Paul Ricoeur*, ed. C. E. Reagen and David Stewart (Boston: Beacon, 1978), 213-222; and "The Language of Faith," *ibid.*, 223-238.

self-sufficient. The modern form of idolatry is finally autonomy, the sense that we live life on our own terms. But such autonomy is a lie. The truth concerns this other One. It was so for Jeremiah and his contemporaries. It is so now, for us.

Pack Your Bags (10:17-25)

This unit has the poet moving back and forth between public calamity and personal, grieved reflection. In vv. 17-18 the poetry concerns the public calamity of exile. The people are to be thrown off the land. For that reason, they are summoned in v. 17 to pack up and be ready to go. (The image of being packed for exile is echoed in Ezek. 12:1-16.) That same motif is resumed in Jer. 10:22. The "threat from the north," anticipated in 1:13-14, now draws close. This unnamed threat has the effect of reducing Judah to an uninhabited thicket. The dismantling of Judah is an historical loss of created order and a return to social chaos (cf. 4:22-26). The twin motifs of exile and devastation are thus sounded in these verses. Some will be carried away. Some will be killed. Both groups are under harsh judgment.

Such a scenario about which the poet is so sure drives him to personal, grieved reflection. Jeremiah 10:19-20 is a statement of the poet's anguish over the scenario of devastation that he envisions. The loss is an experience of death: death of home, death of children. The first person pronouns are numerous. These two verses may contain a word play on *hal* ("affliction") and *ohel* ("tent"). The posture of intense personal devastation may reflect the poet's actual condition, but it is also a rhetorical strategy. He wants the listening community to enter in prospect into the public disaster. He wants to lead the community into grief by an act of imagination that anticipates the actual event.

Only in v. 21 is any reason given for the coming of the announced devastation. The shepherds (i.e., the kings) have turned against the wisdom of obedience. Such failed leadership leads to a scattering, to exile. In Ezek. 34 a new shepherd is promised who will gather in homecoming, but here there is only scattering (see also Jer. 3:15). In a variety of images the poet articulates and grieves the scattering of Judah, the outcome of failed covenant.

Finally, vv. 23-25 are a reflective prayer that sounds much like the

107

prayers of complaint which come later in the book of Jeremiah. The premise of the prayer is stated in v. 23 in language that sounds sapiential (cf. Prov. 16:9–19:21). It is conceded that the human agent does not understand or decide. The inscrutable historical process is governed only by God, who need not justify or explain such action. The devastation to come upon Judah is inexplicable to Jeremiah, and the purpose of it is inscrutable.

The prayer of Jer. 10:24 is an act of repentance. In v. 25 the poet prays for God to act against the nations for their cruel treatment of God's people. It could be that the prayer of vv. 23-25a is only a personal one by the prophet, but its substance serves a public intent. Much later in the tradition (Jer. 25, 46–51) this very judgment against the nations is implemented, but not before Judah and Jerusalem are defeated. The reversal of the situation of Judah and the nations is sounded with the use of the verb "devour" in 30:16: "all who devour you shall be devoured." That is, this prayer of the poet is indeed answered, but not in time to avert the devastation. This prayer of 10:24-25 is offered against the devastation, but it is answered only after the fact. This grieving reflection leads to hope, but it is hope in a context of assault from God. In the immediacy of the situation, the wrath of Yahweh overrides a hope for deliverance.

The Covenant Broken

Jeremiah 11:1-17

This prose passage contains a formal, highly stylized statement of covenant theology. As a result, it is commonly regarded as Deuteronomic. Much critical attention has been given to the precise identification of the covenant that the unit proclaims, and there is much speculation about the historical process behind this text. Because the tradition of Jeremiah is profoundly linked to the book of Deuteronomy, many scholars hold that this text shows the inclination of the prophet in his early period to be a supporter and advocate of Josiah's covenantal reform (cf. 2 Kgs. 22–23).[1] However, such a view is tenuous and is excessively focused on historical issues. We may do better to follow the contours of the text itself without settling questions that lie outside the evidence of the text.

11:1-5   These verses are an initial summons to the prophet to articulate the covenant and its demands. There is no hint of what covenant, but the following verses make clear that it is the covenant of Sinai with its torah

---

1. On the possible relation of this text (and Jeremiah generally) to the reform of Deuteronomy, see the classic essays of H. H. Rowley, "The Prophet Jeremiah and the Book of Deuteronomy," *Studies in Old Testament Prophecy* (Edinburgh: Clark; New York: Scribner's, 1950), 157-174; and John Bright, "The Date of the Prose Sermons of Jeremiah," *Journal of Biblical Literature* 70 (1951): 15-35. Since these articles, the change in methods of interpretation has shifted the issue and made it much more complex and elusive.

demands. Here, as everywhere in the tradition of Jeremiah, the torah demands of the Sinai covenant are held in confrontational tension with the confident guarantees of the royal covenant so cherished by the power elite in Jerusalem. The seriousness of this Sinai covenant and its required obedience is evident in the negative of v. 3. The one who violates such covenant is "cursed." This is a radical either/or from which Judah cannot escape.

These verses present three overriding themes of the tradition. First, Judah and Jerusalem are required to listen (cf. Exod. 19:5-9; Deut. 6:4; 15:5). To "listen" means to be addressed, to know that life comes as a gift from another (cf. Jer. 7:21-28). This listening is not simply an auditory response, but requires obedient action. Second, the act of obedient listening permits the covenant formula of 11:4. This formula of mutuality and solidarity indicates that, through speaking and listening, through command and obedience, this God and this people now belong peculiarly to each other.[2] It is probable that the covenant formula as such is not much older than the book of Jeremiah (and perhaps the covenant of Deuteronomy).[3] But even if the formula is not ancient, it expresses a conviction that is foundational to Israel's faith. It is the mystery of Israel's life with Yahweh that Israel and Yahweh are on the way in history together and must take each other with ultimate seriousness.

The third theme of the tradition occurs in the stylized formula of v. 5. This Mosaic-Sinaitic claim is linked to the promise of land made to the ancestors in the book of Genesis. By the linkage of promise and

2. On the peculiar power of speech to bind in covenant, see Robert Alter, *The Art of Biblical Poetry* (New York: Basic Books, 1985), 212, who comments on "the quintessential biblical notion of the nexus of speech that binds man and God. . . . God speaks the world and man into being, and man answers by speaking songs unto the Lord."

3. Lothar Perlitt, *Bundestheologie im Alten Testament,* Wissenschaftliche Monographien zum Alten und Neuen Testament 36 (Neukirchen-Vluyn: Neukirchener, 1969), has most strongly argued that the notion of covenant originated in the circles of Deuteronomy (and Jeremiah) in the 7th century. However, such a judgment seems to be an overstatement and inherently implausible. Cf. the careful and judicious statement of Dennis J. McCarthy, *Treaty and Covenant,* rev. ed., Analecta Biblica 21A (Rome: Biblical Institute Press, 1978), 13-24 and *passim;* and most recently Ernest W. Nicholson, *God and His People* (Oxford and New York: Oxford University Press, 1986).

command, this text proclaims the covenantal condition of Judah keeping the land. That proclamation is set in the midst of an invading army and the immediate prospect of exile and land loss.

All three elements indicate that Jeremiah is here commissioned by Yahweh to express and summon Israel to the most demanding and elemental claims of covenant faith. The prophet is to insist that his contemporary community should shape its life according to the costly demands of solidarity with Yahweh.

11:6-8 These verses provide historical retrospect. Jeremiah is once again commissioned. His mandate is in the context of a historical memory. The old community was summoned to listen, but it did not. It had a very long history of not listening. Because the community did not listen, the covenant curses are implemented (cf. Deut. 28). Yahweh reminds Jeremiah that the old generation of Sinai and wilderness was judged for its disobedience (cf. Num. 14). The ancient memory of the Sinai covenant is structured as indictment ("did not listen") and sentence ("I brought covenant words on them"). The retrospect to Sinai serves to create a context for the immediacy of Jeremiah's present proclamation of broken covenant.

11:9-13 The historical retrospect on disobedient Israel is made contemporary in vv. 9-13. In v. 9 Yahweh speaks to Jeremiah for a third time. The charge that Yahweh brings against Judah is revolt, conspiracy (v. 9), a total rejection of Yahweh and of the covenant. The substance of the "revolt" against Yahweh is given in v. 10 in highly stereotyped language of the tradition. They refused to listen, they served other gods, they broke covenant. Notice the charge is completely lacking in temporal and circumstantial specificity. The sentence in v. 11 is equally lacking in concreteness. It is "evil" that matches the affront. Israel "did not listen." Now, as judgment, Yahweh "will not listen" (v. 11).[4] If Yahweh does not listen, this recalcitrant people will try alternative gods and sooner or later will discover that those other gods cannot save (cf. Deut. 32:38).

---

4. The match between Israel's failure to listen and Yahweh's decision not to listen is precise and intentional. On this type of correspondence, see Patrick D. Miller, Jr., *Sin and Judgment in the Prophets*, SBL Monograph (Chico, Calif.: Scholars Press, 1982).

11:14-17 In these verses the judgment on this disobedient people is stated in a peculiarly theological way. The prophet may not intercede. Yahweh will not listen. This rebellious people has forfeited its right to approach God, and no ritual activity will compensate. Access to the throne of life is now denied. The living tree of much fruit is now only a dead tree set for burning (cf. Matt. 3:10). The end must surely come.

The entire unit of Jer. 11:1-17 is a meditation on Deut. 6:4.[5] This people must listen. When Israel does not listen, it rejects the One who summons, it violates its identity, and it must be destroyed. The sequence of the chapter offers an outline of the old covenant formulary.[6] That sequence is now utilized to offer an entirely fresh reading of Israel's life with Yahweh:

(a) covenant foundation (Jer. 11:1-5),
(b) covenant violation (ancient) (vv. 6-8),
(c) covenant violation (contemporary) (vv. 9-13),
(d) harsh judgment, end of covenant relationship (vv. 14-17).

We may take this covenant preaching on its own terms, without settling all the critical questions of reference and editorial work. The text takes up the old conventional language of covenant and applies it to Jeremiah's contemporaries (and subsequent generations) without being exact about the connections. The religious assertion is that Israel has found other gods to serve. The religious foundation of life has collapsed, but the punishment is public and political. Covenant violation leads to historical destruction. For this community defined in covenantal ways, disobedience to covenant can only lead to death (cf. Deut. 30:15-20). The conclusion is so sure that prophetic intercession is precluded. The covenant relation is decisive both for Israel's life with God and for Israel's life among the nations. That decisive relation is now about to be nullified. When it goes, everything goes. Israel is bereft of its partner and so is dangerously exposed to the nations. Only the covenant relation guarantees Israel among the nations. Without it, Israel is in acute jeopardy.

5. On the cruciality of Deut. 6:4 for Israel's faith and especially for Jeremiah, see S. Dean McBride, Jr., "The Yoke of the Kingdom," *Interpretation* 27 (1973): 273-306.
6. See Klaus Baltzer, *The Covenant Formulary* (Philadelphia: Fortress, 1971).

A Hard Message to Stubborn Jerusalem

Jeremiah 11:18–20:18

These chapters of Jeremiah contain rich and diffuse materials. Beyond the identification of recurring themes and motifs, it is exceedingly difficult, if not impossible, to detect any sustained order or intentionality to the editorial process. One can detect here and there suggestions about the juxtaposition of certain elements, but that falls short of any general shaping of the materials. While there are some few elements of hope and an occasional didactic reflection, two central themes dominate this material. On the one hand, there is a steady insistence that Jerusalem will be destroyed, and the poet can find many ways in which to speak this word. On the other hand, interspersed with this theme is the countertheme of grief and anger on the part of the prophet for having to speak this hard message to a community that resists. Given that very general overview, it is necessary simply to take up the texts one at a time. As elsewhere in the book of Jeremiah, this material reflects both rich and imaginative poetry and disciplined prose assertion. There is a commonality in the general direction of all of the material.

A Lamb Led to Slaughter (11:18-23)

These verses comprise the first of a series of passages (11:18–12:6; 15:10-21; 17:14-18; 18:18-23; 20:7-18) called the Lamentations or Complaints

113

of Jeremiah.[1] They seem to be the most direct, candid, and intimate prayers that we know about in the OT. Thus it is suggested that Jeremiah, in addition to his bold words to Judah as a prophet, also carried on an intense and often stormy conversation with Yahweh. These passages are models for the depth of honesty that is appropriate in prayer. The hazard of such honest prayer, as we shall see, is that Yahweh can be equally honest and therefore abrasive in response to prayer.

Though the prayers are indeed direct, intense, intimate, and personal, it is clear that they follow a conventional form of prayer speech that is evident in the laments of the book of Psalms. This suggests that Jeremiah was so thoroughly saturated with the Psalter and its liturgic uses that he readily and naturally employed the speech conventions of this community. Or it may suggest, alternatively, that these prayers are an intentional imitation of such liturgic usage. My own judgment is that while the forms are important, they are used here in a way that evidences the power, courage, and imagination of an identifiable person.[2] Critical judgments that overlook the work of a creative personality in the poem fail, I suggest, to discern fully the offer of the poetry.

One may also ask whose "voice" is sounded here. Traditional interpretation holds that these are indeed the prayers of this one person, presumably Jeremiah. A recent suggestion holds that they are rather the speech of this person, Jeremiah, who acts as a mediator and who is in fact presenting the prayers of the community.[3] This notion, however, meets great obstacles because of the particular substance of the prayers, which concern personal pain, grief, and rage.[4]

1. On the complaints, see Gerhard von Rad, "The Confessions of Jeremiah," in *A Prophet to the Nations,* ed. Leo G. Perdue and Brian W. Kovacs (Winona Lake: Eisenbrauns, 1984), 269-284; and N. Ittmann, *Die Konfessionen Jeremias,* Wissenschaftliche Monographien zum Alten und Neuen Testament 54 (Neukirchen-Vluyn: Neukirchener, 1981). The latter recent work contains a complete bibliography.

2. On the power of the person of the prophet midst the conventionality of forms, see Timothy Polk, *The Prophetic Persona,* JSOT Supplement 32 (Sheffield: University of Sheffield, 1984).

3. Henning Graf Reventlow, *Liturgie und prophetisches Ich bei Jeremia* (Gütersloh: Gerd Mohn, 1963).

4. John Bright, "Jeremiah's Complaints: Liturgy, or Expressions of Personal Distress?" in *Proclamation; Presence,* ed. John I. Durham and J. Roy Porter (London: SCM; Richmond: John Knox, 1970), 189-214, has provided the most acute critique of Reventlow's hypothesis.

Rather than choosing between these opposing views, we may opt for a mediating position. These prayers were in the first instance the specific prayers of a person rooted in the language and faith of the Psalms. But as the prayers of Jeremiah were taken up as communal literature, they were seen to have a larger pertinence to the entire community. That is, they were not canonized and regarded as "Scripture" simply in order to preserve Jeremiah's personal prayers. Rather, they were taken up and valued because they were found to be a poignant vehicle for Israel's faith. The canonizing process generalizes these prayers and transforms personal prayer into an expression of community issues. The prayers turn out to have power and compelling authority beyond the intent of the original speaker, but not in a way that cancels out the terrible pain and faith that is evidenced in them.

This unit contains three elements that follow the coventional structure of the lament prayer: complaint (vv. 18-19), petition (v. 20), divine response (vv. 21-23).

11:18-19 *The complaint* serves to express the trouble the speaker is in, to describe it fully and intensely enough to evoke God's response.[5] The complaint is an accusation against an unidentified "they" (v. 19), who in v. 21 are identified as "the men of Anathoth," people from Jeremiah's home village (cf. 32:7, 9). Reminiscent of the language of the psalter (Ps. 44:11, 22), the complaint is of an innocent lamb about to be slaughtered. That language is given specificity in Jer. 11:19b by a quotation placed in the mouth of Jeremiah's adversaries. According to this alleged quotation, the prophet's adversaries are devising a scheme to eliminate him. The quotation includes a cluster of powerful words: "destroy, cut off, not remember." We have seen that the prophet opposed the royal-temple ideology in his repeated assertions that God had now determined the termination of Judah's life as organized around that ideology. We can imagine that Jeremiah had powerful enemies who wanted to silence such a treasonable voice.

11:20 *The petition* builds upon the complaint and makes a powerful request of God. Jeremiah did not deliver this unbearable message of judgment out of his own imagination (cf. 23:21-22). It is, rather, the

---

5. On this intentionality in biblical prayer, see Moshe Greenberg, *Biblical Prose Prayer* (Berkeley: University of California Press, 1983), esp. 11-14.

verdict of the One who sends him. This prayer thus reflects the assumption that Yahweh will protect the messenger who delivers the message of the LORD, unwelcome as it may be. The appeal is addressed to "Yahweh of hosts," and is therefore an appeal to God's regal power. In the opening of the petition Yahweh is reminded that he "judges righteously" (cf. Gen. 18:25), that is, that such a judge actively intervenes on behalf of the faithful to see that they are fairly treated. The petitioner clearly presents himself as the righteous one who is entitled to such positive intervention. Thus the petition is based on a fundamental conviction Israel has about God.

The actual petition is reduced to one phrase, "let me see thy vengeance." In Jer. 11:18 Jeremiah already "knew" of the trouble. Now he wants to "see" a fair resolution. Jeremiah is not in doubt as to where righteousness is located in this dispute. He is the righteous sufferer who is wronged by evil devices. The uneven and unresolved relation between the righteous ones and the wicked ones is presently all in favor of the wicked ones, who will prevail — unless Yahweh intervenes. When Yahweh intervenes, the balance will be shifted to the righteous one who is allied with Yahweh. The new possibilities depend completely on Yahweh's readiness to intervene.

The language of "evil/right" and the summons to Yahweh to "judge and test" is court language. The final noun of the petition, "cause," means a legal case. The petition addressed to Yahweh seeks positively for acquittal and negatively for a countersuit against the offender. When the juridical language is recognized, the plea for "vengeance" is not a request for blind capricious retaliation, but for the implementation of a just legal claim and the implementation of Yahweh's justice on which the speaker has every right to count.[6] This is the court petition of one unjustly treated, addressed to a reliable judge against the unjust perpetrators.

11:21-23 *The divine response* indicates that the court of Yahweh has heard and accepted the claim of the speaker as a righteous one. The response of Yahweh is a court verdict. The guilt of those who scheme against Jeremiah is established in v. 21. The men of Anathoth are guilty of trying to silence a prophet. That offense is scandalous in Israel, for

6. On vengeance as a legitimate concern in a legal frame of reference, see George E. Mendenhall, *The Tenth Generation* (Baltimore: Johns Hopkins University Press, 1973), 69-104.

prophets are constitutive of communal life (cf. Amos 2:12; 7:16; Jer. 26:18-19). The silencing of prophets diminishes the identity of Israel.

The sentence against the ones Jeremiah accuses comes in 11:22-23. It is introduced by a characteristic "therefore." Yahweh will visit upon the men of Anathoth with death by sword and famine until none are left. They had done "evil" (v. 18). Now they will receive evil. We have no evidence of the implementation of this decree, but its rhetorical effect is the vindication of Jeremiah. The decree shows that Jeremiah's word is indeed from Yahweh, and that the prophet enjoys the formal support of the One who sent him.

Beyond the vindication of the person of the prophet, this prayer and its answer present a philosophy of history characteristic of prophetic faith. The men of Anathoth rejected a view of the historical process that asserted the end of the known world of royal-temple power. The divine response verifies such an establishment-ending word, however. It asserts that this prophetic word is authentic and enjoys the authorization and protection of the righteous Judge. What is guarded and endorsed here is not simply the person of the prophet, but the prophetic word that is indeed attested as the very word of Yahweh.

The prayer and response thus are to be heard in two ways. First, in its initial articulation, it is vindication for the person and message of the prophet. Second, canonically the text moves beyond the person of the prophet to endorse a view of historical processes under God's troublesome governance. It bears witness to Yahweh's judgment and Yahweh's sovereignty, which will not be outflanked. That righteous will is not frustrated or averted by violent resistance. History has moral shape *(tsedaqah),* and those who mock that shape are subject to death.[7] The covenant curses of sword and famine follow where the overriding will of Yahweh is mocked. The "conspiracy of the Jerusalem establishment" (cf. v. 9) cannot withstand this sovereign intent articulated by the poet. The prophet as bearer of this sovereign intent may suffer, but in this poem the outcome of God's sovereign will is not coterminous with the fate of the prophet.

7. The power of *tsedaqah* as a force governing history has been well exposed by Klaus Koch, *The Prophets,* vol. 1: *The Assyrian Period* (Philadelphia: Fortress; London: SCM, 1983), 56-76.

Plight of the Righteous (12:1-6)

By common scholarly reckoning, this is the second "confession" of Jeremiah. It has important linkages to the first one in 11:18-23. The passage divides into two parts, complaint and answer.

12:1-4   *The complaint* raises the most fundamental question of faith, the reliability of Yahweh to stand by and look after faithful covenant partners.[8] Verse 1 states a premise: Yahweh is righteous. The whole Bible is based on that premise. It means that the God who makes promises will keep them and will intervene in powerful ways when the promise runs amok. The same premise is operative in 11:20 (cf. Ps. 73:1). Because this God gives trustworthy decisions, Yahweh is the one to whom the speaker (and all Israel) turns in times of vexation. On the basis of the bedrock assumption, the second part of Jer. 12:1 states the question of theodicy, which rings in the ears of Israel even to the present day: why do wicked people prosper? That wicked people do indeed prosper is beyond debate. The unspoken counterpart is: "righteous people like me do not prosper." The question is an immediate, intense, and personal one and cannot be distanced as a speculative issue. The question (sounded in parallel fashion in Job 21:7) makes clear that the prayer does not seek an explanation. This is not an occasion for a theological seminar. Rather, Jer. 12:2 makes clear that this is an accusation of God, which anticipates action. It is God who causes the unjust to prosper, and that is against our expectation of God, if indeed God presides over a morally coherent creation.

Verse 3 expresses the righteousness of the speaker, which corresponds to the righteousness of Yahweh in v. 1. This complaint is a serious suit filed by a righteous petitioner to a righteous judge. The two of them, so the poem claims, should agree about the accused wicked, who surely must be judged. Jeremiah knows he is under scrutiny from Yahweh (cf. 11:20), but he also knows confidently that he is innocent. On that basis he

---

8. This text poses the problem of theodicy more frontally than any other OT text. See the essays on the theme in *Theodicy in the Old Testament,* ed. James L. Crenshaw, Issues in Religion and Theology 4 (Philadelphia: Fortress; London: SPCK, 1983). On the social dimension of the problem, not sufficiently emphasized in the Crenshaw collection, see Walter Brueggemann, "Theodicy in a Social Dimension," *Journal for the Study of the Old Testament* 33 (1985): 3-25.

proposes a sentence against the wicked, which would be an important righting of a wrong. Echoing 11:19, the wicked should be set for slaughter. What his adversaries have proposed against him, he now wishes for them. Jeremiah 12:4 is in the form of a complaint, designed to support the charge of guilt already asserted. The argument is that there is a severe drought ("the land mourns"). The drought is caused by the wickedness of the wicked (Hos. 4:1-3), and that drought will undo creation.

The opponents of the prayer and the targets of the petition are not named. We may assume a carryover of the "men of Anathoth" from the preceding unit. Or more generally, it is those who resist the harsh prophetic poetry now being announced. In any case, we are dealing not with a theoretical matter but with an intense and urgent issue about a real conflict over social reality. We are not, moreover, dealing simply with private wounds. Rather, we are dealing with an urgent question about the moral shape of reality and whether the reading of reality offered by the prophet can be sustained. If it can be sustained, it will only be by Yahweh's attentiveness. This poem is admittedly about the person of the poet. But more than that, it is a matter of the power of truth in a society where falsehood prevails. The quotation with which v. 4 ends means that the legitimacy of the prophetic announcement is in jeopardy.

12:5-6 *The answer* is a surprise to Jeremiah and to us. One would have expected a supportive answer, as in 1:8 and 19. But not here. Here there is only a hard-nosed response which reprimands and warns that more severe demands are still to come. The present threat is modest compared to what will come, like the comparison of human footraces to horses, like the easy terrain to the demands of an uncharted jungle. The safe or domesticated land is contrasted with the Jordan valley, which was hot, well watered, and so inhabited by wild beasts. The awareness of this geography intensifies the power of the contrast. The danger to come for the prophet is like the danger of living in the threat of the ominous jungle of the Jordan. Worse is yet to come. The danger of prophetic truth will grow more severe as the judgment draws closer. The petitioner gets no assurance and no relief. If the petition reflects uncertainty about whether God is indeed righteous and reliable, the answer is that the speaker will have to live with that uncertainty. There will be no relief from the uncertainty. God's righteousness is not articulated here. The issue of God's reliable righteousness is held in abeyance. In the meantime, severe obedience is required.

119

Beyond the reprimand, the second element of the response is a warning (12:6). The voice of Yahweh here acknowledges that the conspiracy of resistance (11:9, 19) to the prophetic vision of reality is so pervasive that the poet should trust nobody. They are all untrustworthy. The warning is unequivocal: do not trust them. Perhaps the warning means that Jeremiah is cast as an isolated voice and must get used to his isolation. Or the warning may mean "trust me, Yahweh, and only me." Trust me instead of them. The isolation of the petitioner with this response is not unlike a citizen who learns of conspiracy in government but can find no place to report it, because everyone to whom report might be made is implicated in the conspiracy. Such a grasp of the realities of public life drives one into isolation and/or into life with God.

Notice, however, that the response of God in 12:5-6 completely evades the issue of v. 1 and the desperate petition. No response is made to the issue of theodicy. Yahweh's response is not unlike the whirlwind speech of Job 38–41, which simply overrides the theodic question. Those who raise this question are given no comfort. It is as though fidelity to Yahweh must be its own reward. The one who is faithful cannot expect that others will see and be changed. To serve such a God is not merely an act of dedicated loyalty and intentional decision-making. It is, rather, an inescapable destiny once one has grasped a certain reading of reality. The prophet is compelled to speak without any assured award.

The response only summons Jeremiah to more radical obedience. But the obedience itself is the only matter at issue. There is no hint that obedience leads to any benefit. Characteristically, Yahweh changes the subject and will not respond to the question of benefit. We are left with a God confessed to be righteous, who refuses to deal with the problem of wickedness. That is how the obedient regularly find the sovereign rule of God. The poet is left with his reading of reality, with a sense of incongruity, yet with a passion for a reading that awaits God's sanction.

The Pathos of God (12:7-13)

Now a very different voice speaks. It is the voice of Yahweh. Yahweh's voice in the preceding poem (12:5-6) was harsh and uncompromising. That same voice now announces the devastation of the land of Judah. The words are not, as we might expect, however, judgment or indignation. They are words of exhausted grief by this One who so treasures the land and now finds it so abused that it must be abandoned. The poem is enveloped by powerful words that tell the whole story of land and people. It begins in v. 7 with a triad, "I have forsaken . . . I have abandoned . . . I have given over." That thought ends in v. 8 with the broken, harsh verdict, "I hate her." The first verb, "forsake," has been often used in Jeremiah to remark on Judah's abandonment of Yahweh. Now it is Yahweh who abandons. Yahweh can stand the affront, the pain, and the grief no longer. The poem ends in v. 12 with the outcome: "no peace." Verse 13 explicates this outcome, but the dramatic climax is at v. 12. Yahweh has abandoned Judah. The result is absence of well-being. Everything depends on the embrace of Yahweh. When that fails, all else is failed. The poem permits Judah to reexperience that central failure which, prior to the poem, had not been noticed. Yahweh has withdrawn fidelity. When Yahweh withdraws, Judah is helpless and hopeless.

Verses 7-8 begin with a threefold use of "inheritance" *(nahalah)*. From the beginning Israel (land and people) had been Yahweh's special, intimate treasure (Deut. 32:9). The use of "inheritance" stakes out a claim. The land can be possessed by none other, for it belongs inalienably to Yahweh. Nor can the people imagine that the land is autonomous, for Yahweh has old and deep claims on this community. But all of that is over. Yahweh's beloved land is "handed over." Yahweh's intimate partner, beloved wife, precious son, is now written off. (The "handing over" is perhaps parallel to the surrender of Jesus to the authorities in Matt. 27:2; Mark 13:1, 10, 15.) The triple use of "inheritance" is reinforced in Jer. 12:10, with "my vineyard" (cf. Isa. 5:1-7) and the double use of "portion."

The metaphors in Jer. 12:8-9 suggest that this beloved people has been actively antagonistic to Yahweh. The images portray the strange wildness of a recalcitrant creation. The land is like a lion, hostile to Yahweh. The heritage is like a bird of prey, ready to spring and hunt and devour. The kings are destructive, ready to abuse. The images bespeak a situation of brokenness, antagonism, hostility, alienation in the land and the people. The poetry is wondrously abrasive in presenting the disjunction between the peaceably ordered kingdom of Yahweh's vineyard and inheritance, and this community now gone berserk in its destructive, rapacious way.

This contrasting play of images of beloved people/aborted community leads to the outcome in vv. 11-12. The language now is of terror, violence, destruction. Abuse of the land has turned heritage to desolation, precious portion to wilderness. Verses 10-11 have a fourfold use of "desolate." Israel's waywardness with the land has destroyed the life-giving potential of the land and the life-celebrating quality of the community. (This portrayal is reminiscent of 2:6-8, in which the good land is made desolate land.) The land has not been well treated. The people have not been well served. The result is that the land is unable to be the land Yahweh intended and hoped for. The community is unable to be the people Yahweh proposed.

It is no wonder that Yahweh grieves. Yahweh's pathos results from the fact that nobody notices and nobody cares. As a result of abuse by exploitive royal power, destroyers have come. They have not come because Yahweh is fickle or careless, but because Israel has distorted. And now comes the destroyer, the sword, and "no one lays it to heart" (v. 11). Verse 12b makes it clear that the invaders are not an accident nor are they unwelcome to Yahweh. The invaders are not an intrusion in God's rule, but in part an instrument of God's rule. Yahweh cries because the invaders are Yahweh's own instrument of anger and judgment. Yahweh has declared war on this beloved, recalcitrant inheritance. In v. 9 the poem summons wild beasts to "devour." Now in v. 12 it is Yahweh's sword that "devours."[9] Both uses of the verb presumably refer to an invading army, but the army is summoned by Yahweh, who is the One who wields the sword. The end result is that the land and the people are now utterly unproductive. The trade-off of thorns for wheat (v. 13) indicates that everything has come to a sorry, failed end. The language may refer back to the Creation narrative in which the land of blessing can only produce thorns (Gen. 3:18).[10]

The situation of the poem is concerned with (1) the indictment that the land has failed Yahweh (Jer. 12:8-11), (2) the judgment in the form of invasion, and (3) the outcome of nonproductivity. The initial statement of v. 7 produces the clue to all else. Yahweh's withdrawal causes fertility to end and exposes the land and the people to chaos. The last phrase of v. 13 is not unlike 4:26, which also speaks of the land reverting to chaos.

---

9. That Yahweh wields a "sword" is a notion very deep in the tradition of covenant. Already in Exod. 22:24 Yahweh wields a sword on behalf of the marginal. Now that same sword which guards Yahweh's purposes is turned against Yahweh's people and city.

10. An inversion back to a functioning, joyous creation, from thorns to cypress, from briars to myrtle, is envisioned in Isa. 55:12-13. That vision is still beyond the horizon of judgment in Jeremiah, however.

This poem is not descriptive. The poet's contemporaries could not yet see the failure of productivity. It is, rather, evocative and anticipatory. The poem seeks to look again at what is about to happen. It enacts a scenario for the land and the people that unimaginative observers would reject as remote from reality. They would have thought it remote because they were enveloped in an ideology that did not know that Yahweh could be driven to grief and finally to withdrawal. Thus the poem is a disclosure of the turmoil that goes on in the heart of God, which is then implemented in the life of Judah.[11] The poem enacts this strange future at two levels — theological imagination and political realism. The poem moves back and forth between them, even as the tradition wants the community to do. Theological imagination by itself seems lacking in specificity. But political realism by itself is inadequate for the pain that lies at the heart of the historical process. The failure of the community and the withdrawal of Yahweh come together. As 12:1 asserts Yahweh's righteousness, this unit defends God's action, which leaves Judah bereft. In this text the outcome is unambiguous, even though most in Jerusalem did not want to notice (cf. Lam. 1:12).

Judah's Neighbors Plucked Up (12:14-17)

This unusual prose oracle reflects a quite late situation in the tradition of Jeremiah. Apparently it is placed where it is because of the initial use of "heritage" *(nahalah),* thus linking this unit to the preceding passage, which begins in v. 7 with the same word and ends in v. 13 with the like-sounding word *nahal* ("weary"). This passage is a play on the word "pluck up" *(natash),* which has been identified as a governing word for the Jeremiah tradition in 1:10. In this passage the term is used in a variety of ways concerning both Judah and the nations.

The initial address (12:14) against evil "sojourners" (RSV "neighbors") refers to the other nations that have invaded and occupied Judah.

---

11. This turmoil in the heart of God is crucial to the entire poetic tradition of Jeremiah. What eventuates in public history is derived from God's pain. This motif has been dramatically articulated by Abraham J. Heschel, *The Prophets* (New York and London: Harper & Row, 1962), 108-130, 221-278; and Kazo Kitamori, *Theology of the Pain of God* (Richmond: John Knox; London: SCM, 1965).

The tone of the beginning is one of indignation, for the nations violated (smote) the heritage that had been designed only for chosen Israel. Yahweh is affronted at such a violation. The primary assertion of this oracle is the lead sentence of v. 14: "I will pluck up the nations from the land." With magisterial sweep, the prophet asserts Yahweh's sovereignty over the nations and announces that God will now displace the nations from the land of Israel. This odd assertion is consonant with the oracles against the nations articulated by various prophets.[12] For Jeremiah, God is in the business of plucking up, that is, displacing peoples who are disobedient. The Jeremiah tradition is mainly preoccupied with plucking up Judah, but here the shoe is on the other foot. No nation is named, but one thinks of Babylon in this context. Babylon has been Yahweh's agent in plucking up Judah and sending Judah into exile. But now the process is inverted and this nation is in turn to be plucked up and driven out. This inversion bespeaks the end of exilic occupation (cf. Jer. 50–51; Isa. 46–47). Such a verdict is best understood after the destruction of 587 B.C.E., after Babylon has done Yahweh's harsh work of destruction. If one links this statement to the historical facts, then this unit may allude to the conquest of Babylon by Cyrus and the Persians. The great theme is that finally all the states and empires must answer to the rule of Yahweh.

In Jer. 12:14c-15 the oracle moves away from its focus on the judgment of the other nations. It is as though the use of the verb "plucking up" draws the tradition back to Judah. In these verses, the verb is used to trace Yahweh's dealing with Judah:

(a) In v. 14c Judah will be plucked up from among the nations. Judah will be taken from exile where it has been placed by God and brought home. This is a surprising use of the verb, which is characteristically negative in the Jeremiah tradition. Here it is positive, implying rescue and homecoming (cf. Amos 4:11).

(b) In Jer. 12:15 the same verb is used in its more characteristically negative way concerning Judah. This statement alludes to the deportation and Judah's departure into exile.

(c) Then, in v. 15b, the positive plucking up of v. 14c is reasserted so that the final action of God toward the nations is compassion, home-

---

12. On these oracles, the most complete discussion in English is that of Norman K. Gottwald, *All the Kingdoms of the Earth* (New York and London: Harper & Row, 1964).

coming, and the end of exile for all nations. All of the nations are promised homecoming, each to its own land. This odd statement suggests that the action of a foreign nation in invading Judah, even if it is the will of Yahweh, is experienced by that nation as displacement. The outcome of the complex use of the metaphor "plucking up" is to announce that Yahweh will have compassion over the nations, even as over Judah.

Following this digression, vv. 16-17 continue the main theme of the oracle that began in v. 14a. These two verses take the characteristic language of Deuteronomic thought and apply it to the nations. The unit is presented as two symmetrical "if-then" statements, one positive and one negative. (For the same structure applied to Israel, see 1 Kgs. 9:4-7.) In this oracle the nations are treated exactly like Israel, subject to the same choices, possibilities, and threats.

The positive "if-then" statement of Jer. 12:16 asserts that the nations must learn the faithful ways of Israel, must submit to the torah, and learn to focus life upon Yahweh. If the nations do that, they will be established in the midst of Israel. The word "build" here is the counter word to "pluck up" in 1:10, so that a new season of well-being is promised to the nations. The negative counterpart of 12:17 is that if the nations do not listen *(shema')* and submit to the claims of the torah, they will be plucked up and destroyed. The nations will be nullified and eliminated from the historical process. The nations are treated as potential covenant partners for Yahweh and are offered the same terms of condition for covenant to which Israel is held accountable. Without compromising the demands of Yahweh, this is a remarkable articulation of a possible covenant beyond Judah's presumed special destiny.

Thus this prosaic oracle is a juxtaposition of two themes: (1) a provision of mercy for Judah, and (2) an extraordinary offer to the nations to be included in the scope of covenant well-being. The promises and threats made to the nations are the same as Israel has had since Sinai, which are classically expressed in Deuteronomy.

The historical placement of this text would seem to be late in the Exile. In substance (though not in style), the text offers hints that are not unlike the assertions of Second Isaiah, for there is talk of both homecoming for Judah and a displacement of nations, presumably Babylon. But what interests us is not the dating or location of the text. Rather, it is the remarkable theological claim of the text that is evoked by the word "pluck up" and its counterpart, "build." The exile and restoration of Judah are not unexpected. But the double "if-then" structure for the nations and the words "learn-obey" are remarkable. They suggest that the nations are invited in and judged by the standard covenantal norms. They are treated as is the chosen people Israel.[13]

The notion that the nations may be regarded along with Israel as peoples of Yahweh is a motif recurring in the Isaiah tradition. Isaiah 2:2-4 records a vision of the nations coming to Zion. But in that envisioned scenario, the preeminence of the Zion-David establishment is retained. Our passage has more in common with Isa. 19:23-25, which does not refer to either Zion or David. The Jeremiah oracle stands apart from Isa. 19:23-25, however, because it is explicitly torah-centered as Isa. 19:23-25 is not. The future of the nations is conditioned by the torah. The torah is made the explicit norm for the nations without reference to Israelite preeminence. The whole international process is envisioned as submission to Yahweh. The nations embrace the same obedience required of Israel and so are treasured by Yahweh. Otherwise, the nations, like disobedient Israel, will perish (Jer. 12:17).

Both an invitation to the nations to join the covenant and an offer of compassion to the nations are unexpected in the tradition of Jeremiah. This unexpected oracle, however, offers important theological resources in a social climate that is too prone to link God with country. Even in Israel, with its passion for election as chosen people, it is here affirmed that God may choose elsewhere outside Israel. Here it is asserted that every kingdom with a readiness for obedience has an opportunity for Yahweh's special compassion. No more than that is offered even to Israel and Judah in this tradition.

The Linen Waistcloth (13:1-11)

In as many different ways as possible, the tradition of Jeremiah asserts that Israel-Judah has violated its proper loyalty to Yahweh and so stands

---

13. See the comments of Wilhelm Rudolph, *Jeremia*, 3rd ed., Handbuch zum Alten Testament 12 (Tübingen: J. C. B. Mohr [Paul Siebeck], 1968), 83. Rudolph notes the parallel between "my house" in v. 7 and "my neighbors" in v. 14. Moreover, the criteria are reminiscent of Amos 1–2, in which Israel is judged by the same norms as the other nations.

under severe judgment. Here that recurring assertion is presented through the action of a symbolic gesture. The narrative action here, as is characteristic of the genre of symbolic act, has two parts — the action and its interpretation.

The action of vv. 1-7 has three commands by Yahweh to Jeremiah, each of which the prophet obeys. First, Jeremiah is commanded to buy the linen cloth and wear it (v. 1). He does so in obedience (v. 2). Second, Jeremiah is commanded to take the loincloth and hide it in the rocks by the Euphrates River (v. 4). (Because the Euphrates River is a very long distance from Jerusalem, it is not clear that this is the river that is intended. The Hebrew term might refer to a town in Benjamin, Jeremiah's own home region. Or perhaps the entire narrative is a fantasy journey. The identification of the site has no crucial bearing on interpretation.) Jeremiah obeys the command (v. 5). Third, Jeremiah is commanded after a time to recover the buried loincloth (v. 6). He does so in obedience (v. 7). Thus far the structure of the narrative is perfectly symmetrical. And thus far we are given no clue to the meaning of the action. There is an oddity even in this symmetrical structure, however. Why does Jeremiah wear the loin-cloth before it is hidden and recovered? What is the significance of this initial act of command and obedience? As we shall see, the first action does serve a quite intentional purpose. The concluding statement of v. 7, introduced by "behold," breaks the symmetry of command and obedience. This assertion in v. 7c is something of a verdict that prepares us for the interpretation. The recovered loincloth is ruined and good for nothing. This conclusion prepares us for the interpretive comments that now follow.

The interpretation of the action of vv. 1-7 in vv. 8-11 is more complex than might at first appear. The interpretation can, I believe, be read in reverse order from the three commands of vv. 1-7. The link between act and interpretation depends upon the parallel asserted between loincloth and Judah-Jerusalem. Thus the action is a parable about Judah and Jerusalem. What has happened to the loincloth is taken up as a commentary about the life of Judah and Jerusalem.

First, in vv. 8-9 it is asserted that Judah-Jerusalem, like the loincloth, is now seen to be ruined. This first interpretive insight thus correlates with the third command and act of vv. 6-7. Second, in v. 10, in the second interpretive comment, Judah is as far from Yahweh as the loincloth is from Jerusalem. Judah is removed from Yahweh by refusing to listen, by acting in stubborn autonomy, by going after other gods. The language of indictment is characteristic of Deuteronomy and corresponding parts of Jeremiah. Third, in v. 11, in the third interpretive comment, we have a correlation to the first command and act of vv. 1-2. There Jeremiah is to wear the loincloth, so that it should cling to his body. In parallel fashion, Judah is to cling, to cleave *(dabaq)* to Yahweh, to be as intimately linked to Yahweh as clothes to a man (on clothes and person; see Ps. 109:18-19, 29). The proper use of a loincloth is to be worn by a man. It is to be worn, not to be hidden and buried. Thus Israel's proper use is to cleave to Yahweh, not to be autonomous, stubborn, or committed to other gods. An improperly used loincloth becomes rotten and useless. An improperly postured Israel becomes rotten and worthless.

Thus, Jer. 13:1-11 forms a rough chiasmus.

1st command: buy and wear (vv. 1-2)	3rd interpretation: cling to Yahweh (v. 11).
2nd command: remove and hide (vv. 3-5)	2nd interpretation: Israel refuses Yahweh (v. 10).
3rd command: recover and find useless (vv. 6-7)	1st interpretation: Israel is worthless (v. 9).

The narrative of the symbolic act is climaxed in v. 7 with a verdict introduced by "behold." The interpretation is concluded in v. 11 with the verdict, "did not listen." An Israel that does not listen is as useless as a loincloth that does not cling to the man for whom it is purchased. The covenantal attentiveness of "hear" and "cling" is decisive for Israel's identity and value. When Israel hears and cleaves, Israel is a name, a praise, a glory — that is, designed to enhance Yahweh (v. 11). As the cloth makes a man, so this people is to enhance this God. But now Israel has no value to Yahweh, for Israel refuses the function and relationship to Yahweh for which it was "purchased" in the first place. (See the similar purchase metaphor in 1 Cor. 6:19b-20.)

The narrative is artfully constructed to make a shrewd identification of the proper historical function of Israel. The analogy of the loincloth is concerned with more than exile and rottenness. The first command and the third interpretive comment allude also to the proper use of the loincloth. It was taken for granted that the loincloth could be properly worn. That is its normal use. So also it was taken for granted that Israel could be properly oriented to Yahweh. That is Israel's normal purpose. But Israel refused and so is worthless. The parable is a comment on Israel's true identity and in fact replicates the entire history of Israel, both as intended for covenant and as having rejected covenant, and so being "good for nothing."

The Wine Jar (13:12-14)

This unit of judgment is an oracle, not a symbolic act, even though it appeals to a visible object: jars full of wine. The initial statement, which gives no clue to its meaning (v. 12), appears to be a proverbial saying or even a riddle. The saying, "Every wine jar will be full," seems designed to evoke an inquiry. Indeed, it is followed promptly by an inquiry (v. 12b). This in turn is followed by the explanatory oracle in vv. 13-14, which is a statement of judgment.

In the move from proverb (v. 12b) to statement of judgment (vv. 13-14), however, the language has shifted.[14] "Full with wine" has become "full with drunkenness." The latter term is a metaphor for destruction. The language suggests bitterness, lack of control, shame. While we speak of the "cup of blessing" in the eucharist, this is the cup of reeling and death (cf. Jer. 25:15-29; Mark 10:38-39; 14:36).

No indictment or ground for judgment is given. The resolve of God is firm and massive nonetheless. The harsh conclusion is addressed to all the principal people of Jerusalem (kings, priests, prophets). This unit sounds one more time the familiar theme: Jerusalem is under death sentence not from Babylon, but from Yahweh. God speaks a threefold negative against God's own exercise of compassion (Jer. 13:14). Israel's old habitual ruthlessness against Israel's enemies (Deut. 7:16; 13:8; 19:13, 21) is now utilized as ruthlessness against Jerusalem. The formula of ruthlessness articulates God's final resolve to destroy his own beloved city.

The first action of Yahweh is "I will fill" (Jer. 13:13). There will be ample wine to evoke drunkenness. But the intent of Yahweh's action is not clarified until v. 14: "I will dash." The figure of full wine jars is used to assert that all inhabitants of the community will be filled with drunkenness (v. 13). But the metaphor remains enigmatic, until it is recognized

14. See the interpretive comments of William McKane, "Jeremiah 13:12-14: A Problematic Proverb," in *Israelite Wisdom,* ed. John G. Gammie (Missoula, Mont.: Scholars Press, 1978), 107-120.

that drunkenness may be taken as a protoapocalyptic figure for instability and judgment (cf. 25:15-29). The notion of drunkenness here is not related to immorality, but to a loss of equilibrium, of being dizzy and un-balanced.[15] The image is of persons so unstable, as in a crazy drunk, that they will bump against and hurt each other. They will be helpless, unable to act differently or responsibly. They will be at the mercy of their condition, out of control. Indeed, the only one who could save them from this uncontrolled act of self-destruction is Yahweh, who made them drunk in the first place.

Yahweh, who instigated the condition of instability, will not in-tervene:

> I will not pity,
> I will not spare,
> I will not have compassion.

Self-induced destruction is permitted to work its own way without inter-vention from Yahweh. Israel's current drunkenness (instability resulting from lack of reference) will be permitted to run its full course. According to this metaphor, Yahweh does not actively intervene to destroy or punish. Yahweh only creates a condition of drunkenness, which leads to a hopeless conclusion. The last term, "I will not have compassion *from their destruction*" (author's translation), is heavy and decisive. It is the word we have seen as "spoil" in 13:7-9. The outcome is the same in the acted parable (vv. 1-11) and the oracular riddle (vv. 12-14). Worthless Israel is coming to a sorry end. The judgment and punishment come without any inter-vention by Yahweh. As a result, the deathliness of Jerusalem's own life will work to its destination of death. Their own drunken disorientation will be their destiny.

Last Chance to Repent (13:15-19)

This poem is another reflection of the ominous fate that the prophet anticipates for the Judean community. Verses 15 and 17 juxtapose two

---

15. McKane, *ibid.*, in parallel fashion shows that the subject of the unit moves from intoxication to "shattering."

uses of *shema'*, "listen/not listen." According to vv. 15-16 there is still time to listen. To listen would be to concede glory to Yahweh and, conversely, not to presume glory for one's own program and policy. The invitation of v. 16 (echoing Amos 5:18, 20) suggests that if Yahweh is honored, judgment and death will not come. But if Judah does not turn, then the judgment of darkness, stumbling, twilight, gloom, deep darkness is sure to come. The language is not precise, for the poet prefers to use impressionistic speech that is all the more dread-filled.

The alternative of "not listening" (Jer. 13:17; cf. 7:24-27) will lead to death. "Not to listen" asserts a statement of autonomy and a rejection of Yahweh, an act of self-serving pride and self-sufficiency. Such a choice on the part of Judah drives the poet to grief, for "not listening" leads to exile *(shebah)*. The linkage of *"not listen"* . . . *"exile"* is structurally the main claim of the prophetic lawsuit (cf. Amos 7:16-17; 6:4-7). The indictment is Israel's refusal to be addressed in covenant. The result is expulsion from the land. The reality of exile is rooted in violation of the torah, which Yahweh will not countenance.

Jeremiah 13:18-19 expounds the negative judgment of v. 17. The double use of *shema'* in vv. 15, 17 makes it seem as if Judah still faced a choice (cf. Deut. 30:15-20). But the exposition of Jer. 13:18-19 suggests that the positive alternative is long since forfeited. In v. 17 the decisive choice is already made in the negative. This twofold address contains a specific message and a more general one, both of which have a mood of grief. In v. 18 the grief is addressed to the king, presumably Jehoiachin, who is exiled into Babylon with his mother (cf. 2 Kgs. 24:12).[16] The verse is an announcement that the royal claim is now nullified. The crown is removed and the king and queen mother are treated like common exiles, or even slaves. The language of dethronement is parallel to that of Isa. 47:1-3, only there it is addressed to Babylon. In this disclosure of an ending, we have symbolization of the end of the entire reality of dynasty and temple, the forfeiture of the dynastic promise, all because of not listening.

16. Christopher R. Seitz, "Theology in Conflict: Reactions to the Exile in the Book of Jeremiah" (Ph.D. dissertation, Yale University, 1986), 164-171, has drawn a remarkable conclusion that the confused status of the monarchy in the period of Jeremiah was much influenced by the role of several competing "queen mothers." That is, which members of the royal family controlled power and lasted in power seems related to the various mothers of princes, who are identified in the text.

The specific address in Jer. 13:18 is matched in v. 19 with a more general comment about the whole territory of Judah. The language is vivid and decisive: "closed . . . none to open." Judah has become occupied land. Then the poet lets fall the decisive word "exile" *(golah)*. That reality is announced in v. 17, but now it is decisive. In v. 17 there had still been a wistful "if." That chance is now gone in v. 19.

Thus far in this chapter then we have three units — vv. 1-11, 12-14, and 15-19 — all of which make the same point, but in astonishingly different ways. All of them announce an ending. All of them credit Judah with conduct that has evoked this outcome. By inference, all of them exonerate Yahweh. The judgment is more than warranted.

The Shame of Jerusalem (13:20-27)

This is an exceedingly difficult text, one that most commentators prefer to treat very briefly. The main thrust is clear, but the specifics of the text are problematic. It is not clear who the various persona in the poem are. The oracle is addressed to Jerusalem (cf. v. 27; most commentators follow the LXX and insert "Jerusalem" as a vocative in v. 20).

The main theme follows the skeletal structure of the lawsuit speech. Jerusalem is again reminded of its enormous evil: iniquity (v. 22), the doing of evil (v. 23), lies (v. 25), abomination, and harlotry (v. 27). All of this will cause royal Judah to lose its way and end in humiliation. If this poem is a continuation of vv. 18-19, then it may be an oracle again addressed to the king, who is now, in the drama of the poem, deposed. The threat from the north in v. 20 (cf. 1:13-15, here likely Babylon) caused the king-shepherd to lose the flock over which he rules.[17] As the Babylonian invasion caused the sheep to be without a shepherd (cf. the deportation of the king), so it also caused the shepherd to be without sheep (cf. Isa. 53:6). The "beautiful flock" of Jer. 13:20 suggests the kingdom en-

---

17. The metaphor of shepherd-sheep to speak of king and kingdom is pervasive in the OT and is used in the Jeremiah tradition (cf. 23:1, 4; 25:34-36; 31:10). It lends itself nicely to the notion of exile, which is a scattering of the sheep. Clearly the shepherd has obligations to the sheep, on which see 23:1 and Ezek. 34. The general use of the metaphor connects the failure of the shepherd and the scattering of the sheep.

trusted to the crown. The same word, "beautiful," is used here for the flock as for the crown in v. 18. Both flock and crown are beautiful and prized. Now both are lost. Indeed, everything is lost.

A tone of grief is appropriate for the poet's scenario. Verse 21 is especially difficult. William L. Holladay proposes to read the first line, "when your lambs are missing," with an allusion to the parable of 2 Sam. 12.[18] But it is difficult to know (even with such an emendation) what that means in this context. The corrected reading seems to suggest that the king has lost what is most precious. That loss will cause pain and hurt like a woman in labor (Jer. 13:21b). The judgment to come "from the north" (v. 20) will, in any case, mean loss of what is precious. The loss will be wrenching. But, says the poet, the king and the people need not ask long what is the cause of the loss and exile. It is Israel's disobedience.

Verse 23 is a well known verse. Along with Ezekiel, Jeremiah takes the dimmest view of Israel's chance of obedience. Jeremiah's assessment of a possibility of change is specifically a comment on wayward Israel and not a more general comment on "human nature." The conclusion the poet reaches is that Israel is as sure to do evil as an Ethiopian has black skin or a leopard has spots. That is, evil has become so habitual for Israel as to be definitional. Israel no longer has any option or choice to exercise.

The result of this massive and irreversible disobedience is presented in three different metaphors. First, the disobedient people is blown like chaff (v. 24). The metaphor echoes Ps. 1:4 and refers to being "scattered." Thus the metaphor is yet another way to speak of exile. Second, the language of land apportionment is used (Jer. 13:25; cf. Mic. 2:1-5; Ps. 16:5-6). Here the language concerns assignment of a specific piece of territory to be held as personal property. The image is used ironically here, for the portion given is now exiled land, that is, land that is ritually unclean and religiously worthless (notice a positive use of the same matter in Jer. 32:1-15). Third, in 13:26 we have again the image of a humiliated slave in exile.

This elusive poem is clear in its main intent. Very simply, disregard of Yahweh leads to exile and the loss of all precious sources of well-being. But that very simple message is presented with a rich variety of suggestive images that run from a woman in labor (v. 21) to a humiliated slave girl

---

18. In a private communication. See also his commentary, *Jeremiah 1*, Hermeneia (Philadelphia: Fortress; London: SCM, 1986).

(v. 26). The abruptness of the figure of a woman being shamefully exposed is intended to shock by offering a scenario of the queen mother treated like a common prisoner of war (cf. Isa. 47:1-3a). The last lines of Jer. 13:27 are a dirge over dying Jerusalem. The city has become a corpse to be grieved. The corpse is ritually unclean, not a fit habitation for Israel, and certainly not a place suitable for Yahweh.[19] The poem is the passionate nullification of all royal claims, for royal history is relativized and negated by the overriding, nullifying claims of the covenant God who will not brook such defiant disregard.

The loss of royal splendor, the humiliation of proud Jerusalem, and the ensuing grief in the face of death are themes that appear in both vv. 15-19 and vv. 20-27. It may be that all of these verses (vv. 15-27) are one extended poem. I have treated them separately because v. 20 seems to make a new rhetorical beginning. The rhetoric of v. 20, however, may function only for dramatic effect inside a single poetic structure. In either case, the intent of the poetry is clear. The once proud royal establishment that focused on the queen mother is now destined for a deep humiliation and displacement. The first one is on the way to becoming last.

No Rain on the Land (14:1-22)

This chapter contains standard conventions of lamentation as they are known in the Psalms of Lament. The lament speeches in vv. 1-10 and 17-22 surround the prose section of vv. 11-16. That prose section presents a controversy between Jeremiah and alternative prophetic voices that are judged to be false. The connection between the grief of lamentation and the practice of false prophecy is one to ponder. Indeed, it is a false discernment of historical reality by the other prophetic voices that causes the grief and loss.

14:1-10 This unit is a lament poem with an answer in the form of a divine oracle. Verses 1-6 are the complaint that portrays the trouble. The situation characterized is a severe drought that causes the land to dry up

---

19. On ritual uncleanness, defilement, and divine absence, see Emanuel Feldman, *Biblical and Post-Biblical Defilement and Mourning: Law as Theology* (New York: KTAV, 1977).

and creation to wane. The crisis is most immediate for the farmers because
the animals depend on grass, which has dried up (cf. 1 Kgs. 18:5-6). The
severity of the drought is evidenced in that it now touches not only
marginal people but even the nobles, who always have the best water
supply. The devastation caused by the drought is sounded in a ringing
repetition: "no water" (Jer. 14:3), "no rain" (v. 4), "no grass" (v. 5), "no
herbage" (v. 6). The asses and jackals, the animals accustomed to forag-
ing, are in trouble. The drought causes the social processes of the community to come to a halt, because now nobles, farmers, cows, asses, and
jackals all have something in common. Life is under threat for all of
them.

   After the articulation of complaint, vv. 7-9 express Israel's characteristic petition.[20] In the liturgy imitated in these verses, Israel assumes
that the drought is caused by a failure in relation to Yahweh. For that
reason, the complaint begins with a confession of guilt (v. 7). According
to this prayer, Judah is willing to accept that drought comes from sin. The
appeal is therefore made not to Judah's merit, but to the sovereign way of
Yahweh. Yahweh is asked to act not because of Judah but for the sake of
God's own reputation ("name"; v. 7).[21] The prayer suggests that Israel now
waits on Yahweh and Yahweh therefore cannot let Israel down. Yahweh is
indeed the source of hope (cf. Lam. 3:21-24).

   The series of rhetorical questions in Jer. 14:8-9a are almost accusa-
tions, for they suggest that Yahweh has been a stranger, a sojourner, a
man confused, a helpless giant. Notice how the prayer, which opens in
an act of trust, is also an insinuation that Yahweh has not been fully
effective. While there is an admission of guilt, the focus is placed on
what is expected of Yahweh. The attempt to prod Yahweh by praise is
crowned in v. 9b with a majestic affirmation, "Thou, Yahweh, art in our
midst." In 8:19 a question had been posed about Yahweh's presence.
Some doubted Yahweh's presence and the evidence was unclear in that
text. But here there is no question of Yahweh's presence. Now that

   20. On complaint and petition, see the comments of Patrick D. Miller, Jr.,
Interpreting the Psalms (Philadelphia: Fortress, 1986), 48-63. His work is heavily
influenced by the seminal work of Claus Westermann.
   21. See the forceful use of this motif in Ezek. 36:22-32, and my interpretive
comments in *Hopeful Imagination: Prophetic Voices in Exile* (Philadelphia: Fortress,
1986), ch. 4.

presence is affirmed. The prayer is a statement of boldness that addresses a rather demanding expectation to Yahweh. Yahweh's proper role is to be present in saving ways. Yahweh's presence should be a guarantee of rain, or of whatever else it takes in order to have life. This kind of speech to God is a motivation in the lament form. Its function is to require of Yahweh what is expected of Yahweh.

Jeremiah 14:10 is a crushing response of Yahweh to the complaint. Structurally, Israel expects an answer from God to such a prayer. Characteristically, the answer is one of gracious attentiveness. The lament-answer form tends to be facile in conventional religion. As we have seen, however, Jeremiah is not shaped by conventional expectations. The poet departs from the predictable, benign response of the liturgy. An answer is given in v. 10, as the liturgy anticipates, but the prophetic answer is not the one normally expected (cf. Amos 5:18-20). The answer is an unwelcome one, reflecting God's abrasive freedom.[22]

The answer is a clearly structured lawsuit. The indictment in Jer. 14:10a is that Israel has departed from Yahweh. Such a waywardness is the opposite of faithfully "following after" in the way (cf. 2:2; 6:16). The sentence is that Yahweh does not accept Israel or its petition (cf. Isa. 1:15). Yahweh is not prepared to save Israel and instead remembers their disobedience. It is a harsh word, congruent with what we have found elsewhere. In the tradition of Jeremiah, there are limits beyond which Yahweh will not be pushed. Yahweh will not be presumed upon. Israel cannot endlessly violate Yahweh and then expect Yahweh's gracious attentiveness (cf. Jer. 7:8-10). The immediate issue of drought is superseded. Now the issue is survival. Yahweh is willing to let this people die, because they have turned away from the torah. Jeremiah must articulate this bold conclusion against the assumption of established royal religion that Yahweh would never reach such a verdict.

14:11-16 These verses interrupt the lament. The harsh prophetic word of v. 10 must have led to consternation in the community. The covenantal

22. James A. Wharton, "The Unanswerable Answer: An Interpretation of Job," in *Texts and Testaments,* ed. W. Eugene March (San Antonio: Trinity University Press, 1980), 37-70, has shown that even in the destabilizing answer to Job in Job 38–41 there is nonetheless an answer. The very reality of the answer is decisive for the faith of Israel.

situation is so deteriorated that serious conversation between Yahweh and Judah is not possible. Yahweh withdraws from the conversation, for there is nothing more to talk about. The prophet is forbidden by Yahweh to pray any more (v. 11; cf. 7:16; 15:1). Prophetic intercession keeps the conversation open, but now that avenue of conversation is decisively closed. Israel has reached the limit of Yahweh's patience and the edge of God's graciousness. Now there will be only covenant curse: sword, famine, pestilence (14:12). In these verses we are no longer dealing with drought, but with the entire catalogue of death curses. The curses stand in place of intercession and come only when the conversation is hopelessly terminated. There is here no qualification or mitigating factor, no chance that Yahweh will speak a different life-giving word. It is indeed the end. The end of the conversation means the end of Israel.

Jeremiah is plagued by the presence of other credible prophetic voices in the community who perceived reality very differently (vv. 13-16). (The best known is Hananiah in ch. 28.) This alternative opinion, rooted in royal-Zion theology, knew there was a judgment. This was never denied. The prospect of judgment was acknowledged even in the foundational royal text of 2 Sam. 7:14-16. According to this establishment view of the covenant, however, the judgment of Yahweh had limits. In due time, because of God's abiding love, the punishment will cease and God will value Israel. There are of course old assertions in the tradition to support this theology. Jeremiah, however, insists that Judah's relation to Yahweh has now vitiated those old assertions.

The issue is joined between the harsh, uncompromising character of torah religion and the buoyant assurances of royal-temple theology. Israel debated God's commitment to Jerusalem. Israel wondered if God's rejection of Jerusalem might go as far as total nullification. For the tradition of Jeremiah, there is no protective line drawn by graciousness against such rejection. There is no guarantee against nullification. This hard-nosed prophetic view is hardly admissable in the religion of anyone, least of all in a religion — like that of king and temple — rooted in the marvelous and unconditional promises of Yahweh.

The opponents of Jeremiah gave assurance of God's *shalom*. They directly contradicted the heavy conclusion of Jeremiah. But according to the Bible (which sides unambiguously with Jeremiah; cf. Jer. 23:9-22), those other reassuring voices are judged to be false and unauthorized. Those prophetic figures are themselves under heavy judgment for misrepresenting reality.[23] We are given no objective norm for weighing the merit of these two prophetic inclinations. The canon, however, votes clearly with the harsh line of Jeremiah and against a religion of easy assurances. The tradition of Jeremiah asserts God's freedom, even from God's partner. It is that very freedom that comes to expression in prophetic faith, in a "theology of the Cross," that is, in the most critical strands of Reformation faith.

When we ask how the canon made its decision for the harsher reading, we can suggest that since Jeremiah was vindicated by the events of 587 B.C.E., the judgment is made, in retrospect, on the basis of historical eventuality. But the biblical canon is shaped finally not by historical observation, but by theological judgment and conviction.[24] The canon-making community found in the words and tradition of Jeremiah something they sensed as true, rightly reflecting the character, will, and purpose of Yahweh. To judge Jeremiah to be true is a theological verdict which allows for something wild, dangerous, unfettered, and free in the character of Yahweh. We cannot accept this literature as canonical without allowing something of its verdict about the inclination of God. To assent, then, to the authority of Scripture is to accept this canonical verdict not only about literature, but also about the character of God. Such a paradigm leads us to think against false prophets who imagine that any particular historical arrangement is immune from God's judgment, or that any established mode of life claims God's unqualified support. None are immune from God's heavy expectations — not in ancient Jerusalem, not now among us.

14:17-22 This unit resumes the complaint of vv. 1-10, only now God does not answer. The opening formula of v. 17 is striking. It is as though

23. On the difficult question of "false prophets," see James L. Crenshaw, *Prophetic Conflict*, Beiheft zur Zeitschrift für die alttestamentliche Wissenschaft 124 (1971); and the old but still suggestive statement of Sheldon H. Blank, *"Of a Truth the Lord Hath Sent Me"* (Cincinnati: Hebrew Union College Press, 1955).

24. On the power and resilience of canon, see Frank Kermode, "The Arguments about Canons," in *The Bible and the Narrative Tradition*, ed. Frank McConnell (Oxford and New York: Oxford University Press, 1986), 78-96. In his *Forms of Attention* (Chicago: University of Chicago Press, 1985), Kermode has considered the power of canon in literature more generally, but the matter applies as well to Israel's normative literature.

the prophet is mandated by God to articulate the lament. The pathos of the poet, in this poetry, is presented as the pathos of God. This lament no longer concerns the drought. It speaks much more comprehensively of a more massive threat. It is tightly organized around three word pairs (v. 18), each of which expresses a totality. The threat is total: "sword and famine." It extends everywhere: "field and city." All leadership has failed: "prophet and priest." The whole community is in death. The cause is failed leadership, which means there is no knowledge of God, no capacity for covenant, no inclination for obedience, no attention to torah. Such a total failure can only lead to death. That death, brought on by failed covenant, is the basis for the grief of v. 17, a grief so deep that the tears are unending (cf. 9:1). The poet is moved by what he sees in his prophetic imagination that his contemporaries refuse to see. He grieves as one might grieve in anticipation of a nuclear war, though the leaders do not notice the danger. The poet sees invading armies and the devastation they inevitably bring. He sees a terrible wound for this people he loves. He sees the hurt as inevitable, but complacent Jerusalem does not believe it and does not notice.

The devastation is massive and pervasive. In the country the dead are strewn. In the cities corpses result from starvation. In the midst of all the death, the religious leadership continues business as usual. Jeremiah's poetry is not descriptive. It is evocative and anticipatory. The poet wants his community to look ahead and see where its actions and policies are leading. But official truth looks in another direction. It does not believe that present policy will lead to ruin and devastation. The poet goes on characterizing and articulating while the establishment goes on denying and not noticing. The poet is driven nearly to madness by this poignant vision that is refused and resisted. To the poet, the deathly future is obvious and unavoidable. But the powerful are too sure, too dulled. While the poet can envision a future not yet available, dark in its deathliness, the powerful in Jerusalem numbly assume it will always stay the way it is.

Finally, in 14:19a the complaint again addresses God. The poet wishes the other prophets in v. 13 were correct. But he knows better and does not believe them. On behalf of his desperate people, he addresses God. His address is part honest inquiry, part hope, part reprimand. The question is the same as in Lam. 5:22. The question expects that the answer is "Yes, I have utterly rejected," but it waits eagerly — and perhaps desperately — for a better answer. At last the poet can entertain the terrible possibility long enough to think the unthinkable. Yes, God might utterly reject Judah, might loathe Zion, David, temple.

The experiential evidence supports the theological conclusion of rejection. There is no healing, no *shalom,* no good — only terror (Jer. 14:19b). Israel characteristically expected well-being from God. That is what the Jerusalem religious establishment celebrated. But Jeremiah dared to draw a different conclusion. Jeremiah had to entertain the antithesis. He was able to imagine that God could and would finally reject. The power of the poet, however, is that he will not be satisfied with the answer that God has rejected Judah. The urgent, relentless petition continues. In v. 20, as in v. 7, there is an admission of guilt. In v. 21, as in v. 7, there is appeal to God's self-interest. The full force of the appeal now no longer rests on Judah's guilt or on Judah's merit, or even on God's commitment to Judah. The force of the appeal is the enhancement of Yahweh and Yahweh's throne. The poet urges Yahweh to act only to maintain Yahweh's reputation. Finally, hope against rejection depends on God's own character, because all covenantal grounds have been nullified.[25]

The prayer asks God to remember the covenant (v. 21; cf. Exod. 2:24). That is a dangerous prayer, because in Jer. 14:10 it has been asserted that God will remember. What in fact shall God remember? Shall Yahweh remember Israel's sin (as in v. 10) or God's own commitment (as in v. 21)? One memory leads to death. The other memory yields continued life and possibility. This poem gives no hint of which. Perhaps we wait until 31:34 to see what God will remember and what God will forget. In these laments, however, we do not yet know. The prayer for remembrance is unanswered, but no answer may be preferable to an answer like 14:10. Where there is no answer, there is still possibility as God broods over the options. The poet hopes that God will remember, but the poet does not dare prescribe the memory for God.

At last, in v. 22, there is a return to the theme of rain with which the poem began. It is conceded that only Yahweh can cause rain, and only Yahweh can give life. The sweeping assertion of v. 22 echoes v. 9b. It is an assertion to Yahweh of who Yahweh is, an urging that, in order to be the One in whom Israel hopes, Yahweh must give rain. It is doxology, but not disinterested doxology. Verse 22 is an act of praise that summons God

25. On hope when all appeals to covenant have failed, see Brueggemann, *Hopeful Imagination.*

to do what God characteristically and faithfully does.[26] The complaint has moved to doxology, but still God does not answer. We are not given God's response to either complaint or doxology. Indeed, in light of Israel's sin (vv. 7, 10, 20), the doxology has a hollow sound. Israel cannot endlessly disobey and expect all to be set right by an act of praise (see 7:10). The covenant is more serious than that.

This majestic chapter poses the question of the possible termination of Israel. It is clear that if Israel is terminated responsibility belongs to Israel, not to Yahweh. The literature, however, does not arrive at a conclusion about Israel's fate. It only probes and suggests. Indeed, it is in Israel's interest not to press for a conclusion. Better to leave the hoped-for alternative still available. The answer will come soon enough.

The Four Destroyers (15:1-4)

This is a highly stylized unit that announces the finality of judgment against Judah. All four verses pursue this general theme, but there are two quite distinct articulations of it. In vv. 1-2 there is a prohibition against intercession (v. 1) and a summary of traditional curses (v. 2). The prohibition precludes further intercession. It does so by naming Moses and Samuel, the great intercessors in Israel. Since their prayers are now rejected, clearly any lesser intercession is futile. The outcome of silenced intercession is the inevitability of curse. There is now nothing to deter or alter Yahweh's resolve. The fourfold summary of curse is much used in Jeremiah and Ezekiel, though the constituent elements vary. The assertion is that the entire arsenal of covenant curses is now to be executed; there is no hope. That same fourfold catalogue takes on a powerful function in apocalyptic literature as "the four horsemen" (cf. Rev. 6:1-8), though the elements are again slightly changed. The language is as harsh and weighty as the tradition of covenant permits.

In vv. 3-4 we have a related but quite distinct articulation of judgment. Again there are four destroyers, but now they are sword/dogs/birds/beasts. In contrast to v. 2, this set of four elements places most weight on the verbs:

---

26. On praise as a context for serious petition, see Karl Barth, *Church Dogmatics,* III/3 (Edinburgh: T. & T. Clark, 1960), 265-288. Barth asserts that praise is the beginning and end of prayer, but petition is "the factual order and essence of prayer" (267).

"slay, tear, devour, destroy." The verbs make this formulation more awesome and terrifying than the conventions of v. 2. In what must be Deuteronomic rhetoric, the ground of judgment is quite specific (v. 4). In 2 Kgs. 21; 23:26; 24:3 Manasseh is reckoned as the cause of destruction. In Jer. 15:4 the cause of destruction is also assigned to Manasseh, who stands as a paradigm for failed covenant. The beloved city stands under death sentence. Nothing, not even the prayers of this passionate poet, can operate against such a condition.

Yahweh Weary of Relenting (15:5-9)

These verses constitute a severe judgment on Jerusalem, which begins in the rhetoric of a lament. This is a statement placed in the mouth of God, who speaks in the first person. The rhetorical question of v. 5 is a lament. The expected answer to the question is that no one will pity, no one will bemoan, no one will turn aside. No one will care (cf. 30:14; Lam. 1:12). No one any longer cares about the *shalom* ("welfare") of Jerusalem. *Shalom* was the special gift of Yahweh, and now that Yahweh has ceased to care, no one else can be expected to do it. Kings may pretend *shalom* (Jer. 6:14; 8:11), but in fact no one cares, not even those responsible for caring.

One might expect that this passage portrays Yahweh as rejecting Jerusalem. But 15:6 asserts that Judah rejected first. Yahweh has rejected in response to Judah's terminating activity (see the play of mutual rejection of Israel and God in Hos. 4:6). The matter of who originally rejected is an important covenantal issue. The lament tradition of Israel (cf. Jer. 14:19) could imagine that Yahweh initiated the rejection, but Jeremiah is insistent. It is Israel, not Yahweh, who caused the collapse of covenant. The God who stretched out a powerful hand to save (Deut. 26:8) now extends that same hand to destroy (Jer. 15:6).[27] What began as Exodus is now terminated in an anti-Exodus gesture. The last detached line of v. 6 suggests that Yahweh's patience has come to an end. Yahweh had again and again "relented" (*naham;* cf. 18:8, 10; Amos 7:3, 6; Jon. 4:2) of a proposed punishment. Yahweh kept changing an announced, justified intention to destroy and making concessions to Judah. Every such change

27. On the "hand of Yahweh" as a means of rescue and wrath, see Patrick D. Miller, Jr., and J. J. M. Roberts, *The Hand of the Lord* (Baltimore: Johns Hopkins University Press, 1977).

costs God. Yahweh kept delaying the judgment, but now Yahweh is exhausted with such delays and will delay no longer (cf. Isa. 1:14; 43:24). The poem thus articulates not only the current mood of God, but reflects on the long history of frustration that has created this decision of God to reject. The poet builds the case that the rejection which ends in exile and destruction is because of Judah's exhausting conduct.

In Jer. 15:7-9 the series of judgments Yahweh now undertakes is reminiscent of the recital of Amos 4:6-11. In the recital of Amos, Yahweh implements curses in the hope that there would be a change on Judah's part. But the desperate hope of Amos is massively dissapointed: "yet, you did not return." The series in Jeremiah shows Yahweh's strenuous efforts to evoke repentance:

- I have winnowed.
- I have bereaved.
- I have destroyed.
- I have made widows.
- I have brought destruction.

These past acts are not presented as judgments, but as efforts to save. But God's harsh effort to save Israel did not catch on, "they did not turn" (Jer. 15:7). At the end of v. 9, after a series of verbs of completed action, the last verb looks ahead: "And the rest of them I will give to the sword before their enemies." After each harsh action there had always been a remnant. Now the remnant is also claimed for destruction, so that Jerusalem is fully nullified. Punishment as chastisement has now become punishment as termination. The God of Jerusalem is a God of enormous patience. But now that patience is spent. God is exhausted and will try no more. A people like Israel surely must die at the hand of a God like Yahweh. This God will be taken with singular seriousness. Israel will not practice such seriousness. An end must come.

Why Was I Born? (15:10-14)

This prose unit contains two distinct elements. Verses 10-12 seem to be a reflective lament by the prophet. He reflects that his life is overwhelmingly conflicted, that he is assaulted and maligned on every side. His cry of trouble/woe/misery is a complaint addressed even to his mother, as though he craves intimacy and solace. This bitter statement of self-regard is echoed in 20:14-18, which in turn is reflected in Job 3. The speaker finds himself in quarrels or in litigation on every front, nearly to despair.[28] Jeremiah 15:10b-11 declares that such trouble is indeed unwarranted. First, negatively, Jeremiah is innocent of any wrongdoing, and no valid charge can be brought against him. He has not engaged in the kinds of dealing that ought to evoke such hostility. He has not exploited, abused, or taken advantage of anyone (cf. a like statement of self-vindication in 1 Sam. 12:3-5 and, more generally, Job 31). Indeed, he has not practiced the social exploitation of which he accuses others. His words distinguish him from his contemporaries, who have violated covenant and now abuse him. Second, positively, he has done something good that matters. He has faithfully executed his ministry of intercession. He has been such an intense advocate of troubled Judah against Yahweh that Yahweh has had to tell him to desist. This statement of self-justification is an assertion that those who afflict him do not know what an advocate he has been. He is a faithful advocate but is treated as though he were an adversary.

The complaint of Jeremiah is a reflection of the costliness of such a ministry of candor and discernment.[29] Perhaps the community has preserved the statement of this text as it became aware that it is Jeremiah's threatening word of Yahweh that evokes the conflict. Jeremiah's many adversaries take issue precisely with his word of threat. The message is so hard that the messenger is at risk. When the message is so formidable, it is easier to focus on the messenger. Such risk is definitional for any who carry the word against established reality.

In Jer. 15:12, however, the speaker seems to recognize that even the effectiveness of his vocation as an intercessor with God is finished and must be given up. The die is cast. God has ordained the assault from the north. In 1:18-19 Jeremiah is made iron and bronze to withstand assault. Now, however, it is the invading army (presumably Babylon) that is the

---

28. The juridical cast of the argument is easily missed with the conventional rendering "strife." Hebrew *rib* might better be rendered as "litigation." Jeremiah is a man in formal dispute, a fact made evident both in the trial of ch. 26 and in the confrontation of ch. 36.

29. On candor as a mark of the ministry of Jeremiah, see Brueggemann, *Hopeful Imagination,* ch. 1.

real bronze and iron. Yahweh's purpose is so adamant that none can stop it, not even powerful intercession. No more than Hananiah can break the yoke of exile (28:2) can Jeremiah break Yahweh's relentless purpose. Judah is unable to see that the real danger is Yahweh's relentlessness, not Jeremiah's persistence. Even the prophetic insistence of Jeremiah, which itself is formidable enough, finally must submit to God's resolve. That resolve is more serious, more devastating, more sure than any word of Jeremiah.

One cannot be certain that 15:13-14 is a divine answer to this complaint, but it might be. This oracle is not an oracle of comfort for Jeremiah, who has complained of his trouble. Rather, it is yet another decree of judgment against Judah. All that Judah treasures (cf. 2 Kgs. 24:13-17; Isa. 39:5-7) is now given to Babylon by Yahweh, and no amount of prophetic intercession can stop it. The poet knows about the relentlessness of the historical process over which Yahweh presides. The subject changes from his personal vocation (Jer. 15:10-12) to the destiny of Israel. Finally what counts is not the prophet, but the sin of Judah and the response of Yahweh. The prophet is quite incidental to the real crisis now to be faced.

The juxtaposition of vv. 10-12 and vv. 13-14 may be evoked by the dual mention of land. In v. 10 the prophet is in conflict with "the whole land." In v. 13 there is spoil taken "throughout all your territory," and now in v. 14 there is exile to another land, one "which you do not know." The sequence thus is a move from the land of contention to the land of exile, in which contention is futile. The displacement is yet another way of seeing God's action against Judah, and seeing that Jeremiah's vocation is about this unthinkable displacement. The role of Jeremiah is lost in the overriding decision of Yahweh against Jerusalem, Judah, and the land. There is not a hint of vindication or comfort for the prophet. It is no wonder that the poet's cry of pain which is disregarded is now followed by another quite personal complaint addressed to God (vv. 15-21).[30]

---

30. The juxtaposition of personal pain and public destiny is delicate and complicated. One must not on the one hand excessively focus on the person of Jeremiah; but on the other hand, one must not ignore the lively presence of such a person in the text. Polk, *The Prophetic Persona,* has offered a carefully nuanced treatment of the problem.

Conditional Assurance (15:15-21)

This poetic unit continues the complaint-protest we have found in 11:18-23 and 12:1-6. As there, this poem reflects the shaping influence of the Psalms of Lament in the Psalter. It is likely that the lament form has been appropriated here to make a more personal and specific statement concerning Jeremiah's prophetic vocation as he is placed between the obduracy of Israel and the harsh sovereignty of Yahweh.

The initial words, "thou knowest," are abrupt. As the beginning of the poem, this is a remarkable way of relating to Yahweh. The opening words may be an act of trust and submission to the One from whom no secret can be hidden. But they may also be words of reproach to Yahweh, who knows and yet does nothing on behalf of the one who suffers innocently.

The lament contains three elements: the petition (v. 15b), a statement of innocence and fidelity as a motivation for God (vv. 15c-17), and a statement of complaint (v. 18). The petition consists in four imperative verbs: "remember," "visit," "take vengeance," "do not seize" (RSV "take away"). The imperatives suggest not only a statement of strong passion, but also an established relationship that permits bold and candid speech. The one who prays is in a position to make heavy demands on Yahweh, to insist that Yahweh remember and act. This petition is not the beginning of the relation. It rests on promises and previous interactions. The poet expects Yahweh to make good on those previous commitments. The four imperatives are curious because they ask God to be patient and not to "seize" the poet. This abrupt verb "seize" *(lqh)* is used in Amos to describe the prophetic call (Amos 7:15), and in Gen. 5:24 is used with reference to God's seizure of Enoch. Here the term refers to death. The petitioner therefore prays not to have his life terminated. He obviously knows his life to be in great jeopardy.

In Jer.15:15c-17 the poem gives motivations why God should heed the petition. The crisis in which the prophet finds himself is a result of his faith, his unswerving attachment to Yahweh: "for thy sake . . . I am called by thy name." The prophet has not resisted the prophetic mandate, but has delighted in the word entrusted to him by Yahweh. Verse 17 becomes even more specific. Because of his call, he is socially isolated and did not join in the usual social relationships. The statement of innocence is an assertion that the prophetic mandate has been the overriding reality of his life. He has not flinched from it or compromised in any way. Such a claim can rightly expect a positive response from Yahweh. The poet asks only for that to which he is entitled as a faithful partner and obedient servant.

The third element in the prayer (vv. 17c-18) is an accusation against Yahweh. The human sources of conflict (i.e., priests, kings, men of Anathoth) are not the cause of Jeremiah's situation. Yahweh is singled out as the cause of the trouble. The double use of "thou" in this unit places the poetic focus on Yahweh. The rhetoric of v. 18 introduces a new metaphor — sickness and incurable wound.[31] It is useless to speculate on the details of the illness. The sickness metaphor may be only a convention. The oddity for the poet is that sickness follows sin, but he has not sinned. He has in every regard been a faithful servant of Yahweh. For that reason, v. 18b contains an accusation that Yahweh is unreliable and does not honor pledges of solidarity and protection.[32] The imagery shifts from illness to a river or wadi. The image is of a wadi that dries up in times of drought, so that trees planted by it have no chance of life (against 17:8). Yahweh is marked by the indignant poet as an unreliable, untrustworthy stream that will not sustain life (contrast 2:13). The streams of living water have failed.

Jeremiah has been mandated with a burdensome word to his contemporaries. His word from Yahweh is harsh when contrasted with the claims of established religion or the word from other contemporary prophets. That he has evoked hostility is not surprising. What is surprising and disconcerting is that the One who sent him does not stand by him. The prophet turns out to be more faithful than the God who sent him.[33]

---

31. On the metaphor of "wound" in Jeremiah, see James Muilenburg, "The Terminology of Adversity in Jeremiah," in *Translating & Understanding the Old Testament*, ed. Harry Thomas Frank and William L. Reed (Nashville: Abingdon, 1970), 42-63.

32. This statement of the problem anticipates the poem of Job. In both Jeremiah and Job the problem of theodicy is raised because there is "punishment" for which there is no identifiable sin.

33. In this regard Jeremiah is like Moses, for in the exchanges of Exod. 32–33 it is clear that Moses will stand by Israel after Yahweh is prepared to abandon. William L. Holladay, "The Background of Jeremiah's Self-understanding: Moses, Samuel, and Psalm 22," *Journal of Biblical Literature 83* (1964): 153-164; and "Jeremiah and Moses: Further Observations," *Journal of Biblical Literature* 85 (1966): 17-27, has observed the commonality of the dramatic presentation of Moses and Jeremiah.

Jeremiah is utterly alone in the conflict over fated Jerusalem. The isolation from his human companions (15:17) could be overcome by communion with God, but his isolation extends beyond earth to heaven.[34] God does not stand by. God is not with him as was promised (1:8, 19).

On two counts we expect an answer from God. First, the lament form characteristically evokes an assuring answer from God.[35] Second, this poignant prayer, if it does not evoke an assurance, should at least provoke God enough to make a self-defense. The Job-like assault of 15:15-18 asks something from God that is congruent with God's promise.

In vv. 19-21 there is an answer from God, but hardly the one anticipated. The conventional answer of the lament form is an assurance of God's presence, power, and compassion. Here, however, the answer is not an assurance, but a condition. The first part of Yahweh's response (v. 19) is a play on the word "turn," which occurs four times:

> If you will *return,* I will *return* you . . .
> they will *turn* to you, but you shall not *turn* to them.
>
> (author's translation)

Jeremiah's interactions with Yahweh are not easy and reassuring. They are endlessly demanding so that even the form of "divine assurance" is utilized for the demand of Yahweh. What Jeremiah experiences of Yahweh is exactly how Judah must face Yahweh. The expected assurance for Judah is also rigorous demand.

This carefully constructed statement in v. 19 uses the verb *shub* four times, all of them calling for a reorientation in faithful covenant. The first two uses concern Jeremiah's relation to Yahweh. The turn of Jeremiah is the condition of Yahweh acting on his behalf as a faithful covenant LORD. No specifics are given, but the implication is that Jeremiah has not yet met Yahweh's rigorous expectation. Jeremiah must find ways to be yet more faithful. When Jeremiah does, Yahweh will act in new ways and sustain him. The second pair of uses of the same verb concerns Jeremiah

---

34. In Ps. 88:8, 18 God is directly responsible for the shunning.

35. Claus Westermann, *The Praise of God in the Psalms* (Richmond: John Knox, 1965), has shown this characteristic form. It is precisely the dramatic power of this characteristic that makes the harsh response of Yahweh to Jeremiah so shattering and noteworthy. This poetic exchange violates the form in which Israel had learned to trust.

and his human opponents. It is promised that when Jeremiah has turned in new fidelity to Yahweh, Jeremiah's opponents will then yield to him and not he to them. Jeremiah is required to be faithful. Everything depends on Jeremiah's new obedience. When he is faithful, his relation to God and to his fellows will change. God will return him, that is, restore him. His fellows will submit to him.

The continuation of God's promise in vv. 20-21 is more conventional, less demanding, and not stated conditionally. It echoes the initial promise of 1:17-19. God's solidarity with the prophet and readiness to rescue are precisely what is hoped for and not yet experienced. In 15:20-21 Yahweh speaks as the faithful God Israel has always trusted and found trustworthy. But even these assurances are finally governed by the "if" of v. 19. Everything depends on Jeremiah's reliance on and adherence to Yahweh. Everything depends on this for Jeremiah. Everything depends on the same reliance and adherence for Jerusalem. There are no alternatives.

This complaint-response poem can be read at two levels. On one level, it is the prayer of a faithful person in need of a faithful response from God. God does indeed attend to the faithful. Jeremiah's prayer operates on that claim and premise. To that extent, the prayer is simply another use of Israel's patterned speech of complaint, submission, and trust.

The tradition of Jeremiah, however, requires a second level of reading. The poet who protests and yearns is not simply a faithful person. He is a prophet with special words, peculiar mandates, and heavy risks. The issue, then, is not simply God's fidelity toward this one man, but the relation between the sender of a word and the carrier of that word. The word sent by Yahweh and carried by Jeremiah is that Jerusalem must die. It is a burdensome word, not to be spoken lightly. Jeremiah has the sense that he is "out there" alone, abandoned by the God whose word he speaks. The question of the prayer is, will God stand by the carrier of the message? Is the message important enough to God to sustain the messenger? If not, then the message is not to be taken seriously. The seriousness of the message is measured by the credibility of the sender.

Will the sender sustain the carrier of the message? The answer is given in the response of God. The basic assurance is "I am with you." The exposition of that premise is given in four powerful verbs: "save" *(yasha‘)*, "deliver" *(natsal)*, "deliver" *(natsal)*, and "redeem" *(padah)*. It is indeed a prayer answered. God is trustworthy and stands by the messenger. But the answer is conditional and given only after an enormous price has been assessed from the person of the prophet. That price is integral to the work of the prophet. Because the word is so scandalous, the carrier of the word is inevitably at risk.

A third dimension of reading is also possible. Erhard S. Gerstenberger has suggested that what was originally a personal prayer of the prophet has been processed so that now it becomes a word of assurance to the community after the destruction.[36] Specifically, vv. 19-21 (which parallel 4:1-2) is an assurance given to the community, looking to the repentance and restoration of the community. Thus the prayers of the prophet are taken up into the canonical memory of Israel because the isolation and alienation of the prophet bespeak the status of exilic Israel. The assurances of God are offered to the prophet as a pained person. But they are also offered to the community. The conversation Jeremiah has with Yahweh comes to be a conversation for the entire community. What Jeremiah knows in his prophetic vocation, Israel comes to know in its exile, where it also senses abandonment. As Jeremiah can address God abrasively, so can Israel in exile. As Jeremiah is pressed to more serious obedience by Yahweh, so is Israel in exile. As Jeremiah receives a promise of God's solidarity in trouble, so does Israel in exile. In exile, Israel found Jeremiah's prayer and experience of God to be paradigmatic for its own destiny with God as a people of troubled faith.

You Shall Not Marry (16:1-21)

This chapter consists in distinct elements that likely existed independently. They have, however, been brought together in a coherent statement of judgment (vv. 1-13) and hope (vv. 14-21).

16:1-13 The prose passage of vv. 1-9 announces no new themes, but it solemnly and harshly reiterates the unqualified judgment that is to come. In v. 2 the prophet is prohibited from having sons and daughters. The prohibition anticipates the mood of those who so fear nuclear holocaust in our time that they do not want to have any children who might be

36. Erhard S. Gerstenberger, "Jeremiah's Complaints: Observations on Jer 15:10-21," *Journal of Biblical Literature* 82 (1963): 393-408.

subjected to the terror. But characteristically, the text does not linger over the personal situation of Jeremiah. This is not simply a prohibition for the prophet, but it concerns all children born in Judah who are subject to the curses that will not be turned away (vv. 3-4). Notice that in these verses we have a triadic emphasis, "this place, this place, this land," in anticipation of judgment and exile. The land itself, along with the people, is under death sentence. The curses of v. 4 are a combination of those listed in 15:2 and 3. By focusing the curses on the children, the prophet attempts to articulate the most extreme case of judgment and pathos. It is an incredibly harsh announcement, reflecting the fact that Judah has come to the end of the road. The entire future is now under assault. In 29:6 the new beginning will concern sons and daughters. But not here. Here there is only an ending.

The second paragraph is structurally parallel to the first. In 16:5, as in v. 2, the prophet is given a personal prohibition which is then interpreted more generally in the verses that follow. In this second personal prohibition of v. 5, the prophet is precluded from acknowledging the death of the community or from participating in the grief. The grief of the end is massive; it is escalated even more by this prohibition against active expression of the grief.

The theological background for the prohibition is given in v. 5b. Yahweh has taken away his "peace" *(shalom)*, his "steadfast love" *(hesed)*, his "mercy" *(rahamim)*. The covenant relation now is over. This triad of words is among the most freighted in the covenantal speech of Israel. The first, *shalom,* may be peculiarly linked to the tradition of Jerusalem.[37] The other two are rooted in the old Mosaic-prophetic tradition reflective of God's deep commitment and powerful pathos.[38] The most fundamental commitments of Yahweh are now exhausted and terminated by recalcitrant Judah. The harshness of this announcement is surely a surprise in biblical faith and must have been a staggering surprise when first spoken. It has

37. See Norman W. Porteous, "Jerusalem-Zion: The Growth of a Symbol," in *Verbannung und Heimkehr,* ed. Arnulf Kuschke (Tübingen: J. C. B. Mohr [Paul Siebeck], 1961), 235-252.

38. On *hesed,* see Katherine Doob Sakenfeld, *The Meaning of Hesed in the Hebrew Bible,* Harvard Semitic Monograph 17 (Missoula, Mont.: Scholars Press, 1978); and *Faithfulness in Action* (Philadelphia: Fortress, 1985). On *raham,* see Phyllis Trible, *God and the Rhetoric of Sexuality,* Overtures to Biblical Theology 2 (Philadelphia: Fortress, 1978), ch. 2.

been a ready assumption (in ancient Jerusalem and among us) that God's covenant commitment is abiding. Indeed, in 2 Sam. 7:14-15 Yahweh has made an oath never to remove *hesed.* But Yahweh could not have foreseen the unthinkable situation of infidelity that caused all old promises to be under review. In the tradition of covenant, even Yahweh's gracious inclination depends finally on some appropriate response. Having waited so long for a response that never came, Yahweh finally retracts this initial, gracious commitment.

Where there is complete absence of fidelity on God's part, there is death. Israel cannot live apart from God's fidelity. No public grieving, no consolation, no rituals are permitted (vv. 6-7). No acts of consolation are permitted that might mitigate the starkness of the abrupt judgment. Yet not only acts of death are prohibited. The text takes an odd turn in v. 8. The subject of the text has been mourning (vv. 6-7). Now, as though to establish a rhetorical polarity, it is the house of feasting, of eating and drinking, that is prohibited. Verse 9 builds upon the changed future of v. 8. There is to be a cessation of all celebrative life, all new social beginnings. Taken together, "house of mourning" and "house of feasting" mean that all social interaction is now terminated. History stops. Community is over. There is no longer any public life permitted.

Clearly such a massive judgment is difficult for us to fathom theologically. In its first articulation, it is an attempt to say to the contemporaries of Jeremiah how drastic the situation is. God's sustaining presence is now forfeited and public life must experience and embody that forfeiture. As a text available for our subsequent use, this double prohibition is an invitation to ponder God's free sovereignty that will not be mocked or taken for granted. The other side of that sovereign reality is the recognition that all social, economic, and political systems are provisional and in jeopardy. Both social grief and public celebration are arrangements that endure only by God's gracious leave. If one reads from v. 5 directly to v. 9, one sees that celebrative social life depends on God's steadfast love and mercy. When those gifts of God are withdrawn, more than fellowship with God ends. Life with neighbor is also voided. Social possibilities become as "formless and void" as the darkness of primordial chaos (cf. 4:23-26). The poet moves back and forth between scenarios of cosmic chaos and social dysfunction as he strains for adequate words to express the ending now at hand.

Jeremiah 16:10-13 is a didactic reflection on the painful prohibitions of vv. 2 (3-4) and 5 (6-9). It is another opportunity to state the reasons for the judgment under which Jerusalem stands. Perhaps the threefold inquiry of v. 10 is ironic. The threefold "why, what, what" surely did not need an answer, because the reasons are obvious.[39] Jeremiah's contemporaries are so detached from the claims of Yahweh, however, that they are unable to recognize the realities that the prophet regards as perfectly obvious.

Verses 11-13 answer the inquiry of v. 10, articulating that which Israel should already know. The response is a clear lawsuit speech with indictment (vv. 11-12) and sentence (v. 13). The statement moves dramatically from "because" in v. 11 to "therefore" in v. 13. The reason for the judgment is stated in two stages. First, "your fathers" have forsaken (*'azab*) Yahweh (stated twice) and violated torah. Second, the present generation is worse. The present generation has not listened. The language of indictment is clearly an echo of Deuteronomic theology. The ultimate sins are autonomy and self-sufficiency, which are evidenced in not listening.

The sentence is exile, expulsion, banishment. The final fate is to trust in false gods who cannot save (cf. Deut. 32:37-38). The service of false gods is not only a sin chosen by Israel, but a fate decreed by Yahweh.[40] Judah is to be "out of this land." Yahweh's people are to be in another land, away from all life supports, even away from Yahweh.

The tradition of Jeremiah cannot consistently make up its mind if the sentence is finally death or exile.[41] They are dramatically the same, however, for such radical displacement is tantamount to death. The language of lawsuit is so familiar to us that we miss its bold intellectual claim about the historical process. It is urged that historical, public displacement is not to be understood according to sociopolitical necessities, but according to the sovereign requirements of Yahweh. "Not listening" leads to "hurling." Breaking covenant ends in exile. Judah has chosen for itself to receive "no favor" from Yahweh, who wants to give "favor." This last word of the paragraph falls heavily and decisively: "No graciousness."

39. The threefold interrogative is even more powerful in Hebrew, for all three interrogative pronouns are *meh,* thus "why, why, why?"

40. "False gods" as both sin and as punishment is a striking case of the correlation of sin and punishment, on which see Patrick D. Miller, Jr., *Sin and Judgment in the Prophets,* SBL Monograph 27 (Chico, Calif.: Scholars Press, 1982).

41. The tradition cannot decide which is the actual danger. Thus in v. 3 there is death in the land, but in v. 13 the danger is exile. Seitz, "Theology in Conflict," has suggested that this tension reflects not simply editorial activity, but a conflict in interpretation.

16:14-15   The decisive ending of v. 13 makes the abruptness of vv. 14-15 all the more stunning. These verses form a complete contrast to the preceding judgment, for they announce restoration of the people of Israel to "their own land." Critical opinion is unanimous that these verses are a late voice in the tradition. They reflect a later generation of exilic hope, for such hope was not available until after 587 B.C.E. These words may indeed reflect 2 Isaiah and the moment of homecoming evoked by that poetry.

That critical judgment seems secure. However, we should approach the text as it stands and not dissolve the deliberate juxtaposition of Jer. 16:10-13 and vv. 14-15. Both the statement of harsh judgment and of grand homecoming are a part of the canonical text. Both bear witness to God's resolve. Neither cancels the other. Yahweh has two actions to take toward his people (cf. 31:27-28). The first action of Yahweh is displacement. That is not lessened by 16:14-15. Amazingly, however, the second action of homecoming is not precluded by the first act of displacement. There is a homecoming, but dramatically as well as experientially, it does not nullify the pain, shame, and grief of exile that is burdensome and real.

The ground for this second move of Yahweh is found in the Exodus tradition. The generation of the Exodus was also a community of displaced slaves, hopelessly subservient to a ruthless empire that seemed ordained to perpetuity. The Exodus happened because of Yahweh's capacity to invert the historical process and create a new historical possibility that gives life to the marginal. Israel characteristically appeals to the Exodus memories in order to bear witness to the sovereign graciousness of Yahweh against all forms of imperial hopelessness and fatedness. Israel always returns to the Exodus for a "fix" on reality. Jeremiah 16:14-15 does more than return to the Exodus memory, however. This text of new historical possibility dares to say that the Exodus memory will now be superseded because Yahweh is about to outdo that miraculous act by an even greater miracle. This new act bursts out beyond Israel's best memory of liberation. This generation, right before our eyes, now becomes the participant in this new focus of all historical possibility.

The Exodus had been the point of reference from which Israel interpreted all its experiences. Now, in the present moment, there is a new decisive event to which all experience is to be referred. Every other experience is to be understood in terms of this remarkable action of God. Such a claim cannot be made without appeal to the tradition. But the appeal to tradition in these verses is made only to supersede that very tradition. The claim of the tradition is shattered by the new act (cf. 23:7-8; Isa. 43:18-19).[42] There is judgment and there is new possibility. There is exile and there is homecoming. There is death and there is resurrection. Both moves are characteristic of this God. Both moves are definitional for this faith, this people, this God. There is historical shattering, wrought because of infidelity. There is also historical creating in sovereign graciousness. Both belong in tension to Yahweh's character and are the central reality of Israel's life. These two verses do not nullify the "hurling out" of Jer. 16:13, but do assert that after the hurling comes the homecoming.

16:16-18   This unusual statement is difficult to interpret for two reasons. First, it is not clear who it is that is being hunted, fished, punished, and judged. The actual indictment of v. 18 could indeed apply to Judah, which is guilty of inequity, sin, pollution, and abomination. This unit is placed between vv. 14-15 and vv. 19-20. In that context the reference may be to the nations who are to be judged (cf. vv. 19-20), as the countertheme of Israel's rescue (vv. 14-15). But it is more plausible to conclude that these verses refer back to vv. 10-13 and refer to Judah. In that case, these verses assert the coming devastation of Judah from which none can escape.

Another difficult interpretive issue is that the figures of fisher and hunter are not clear. The terms "fishers" and "hunters" refer to agents who will seek out those who are to be judged. Those agents will be so efficient and thorough that none will escape. Such images appear to be metaphors that run toward apocalyptic perspectives. The judgment on the nations here is not unlike the protoapocalyptic images in 25:15-29. While the language is difficult and the references obscure, the verses clearly anticipate the judgment of Yahweh from which none is exempt.

The unit of vv. 16-18 falls into two parts. In vv. 16-17a Yahweh acts through these mysterious agents from whom no one can hide (cf. Amos 9:2-4; Ps. 139:7-12). The second part of the unit (Jer. 16:17b-18) contains more conventional language in which Yahweh acts directly in response to

---

42. A new interpretation of "old things" and "new things" in Isaiah is offered by Ronald E. Clements, "The Unity of the Book of Isaiah," *Interpretation* 36 (1982): 117-129; but I do not believe it touches this contrast in the text of Jeremiah between the salvific tradition and the new act of rescue that is anticipated.

"iniquity." "My inheritance" (i.e., Yahweh's land) is polluted by foreigners
— invading armies who bring their religious images and practices with
them, thereby making the land ritually unclean. The punishment is not
specified, but the penalty is "double," the same language used in Isa. 40:2
against Israel. Judah is to be judged massively by Yahweh for its idolatry
and abomination. The passage is elusive in its intent because the metaphors
are remarkably open and lacking in specificity. The comprehensiveness of
judgment, however, is abundantly clear.

16:19-21   This unit begins in a statement of trust. Such an initial statement of trust characteristically provides a basis for a prayer of complaint.
Only here the statement of trust is not followed by a complaint. It is,
rather, an anticipation of the time in the future when the nations will
submit to Yahweh. The poem thus expresses the anticipation that, in due
time, the nations will recognize and admit their failure and the inadequacy
of their gods. This will be expressed as a confession of sin on the part of
the nations, who will finally embrace Yahweh as the true God. The nations
will confess that their gods are "false" (*sheqer;* RSV "lies") and "worthless"
(hebel), that their gods are really "no gods." The affirmation that Yahweh
is "strength," "stronghold," and "refuge" contrasts with the failure of the
gods who are not reliable and cannot save. A covenantal prayer of trust is
used for a polemic against false religion. This is a stunning admission,
because it is tantamount to conceding the illegitimacy of the imperial
political enterprise as well. The inverse point is made in v. 21. As the idols
are seen to be false and worthless, so the true God, Yahweh, is now shown
to be powerful and mighty. The nations will concede Yahweh's power and
might as they become obedient to Yahweh's kingdom.

Chapter 16, as it now stands, seems to be composed of a variety of
fragments. As the chapter is now ordered, it is organized into two parts,
the two parts we expect in canonical shaping. Verses 1-13 are a statement
of judgment, in which God will remove all marks of covenant concern
(v. 5). Verses 14-21 consist in three quite distinct elements, but they form
a secondary unit of hope and new possibility. The three original units,
respectively, affirm that:

(1) Israel will come home (vv. 14-15),
(2) the nations will be judged (vv. 16-18),
(3) the nations will turn to Yahweh (vv. 19-21).

All three reflect a situation of "planting and building," which presumes the judgment has gone before and has been completed. The important affirmation is that Israel's history is now alive in a new way. That new life depends on the assertion of Yahweh's power and might, and the knowledge of Yahweh as the LORD of covenant (v. 21). Where God is known, history can begin again, even after massive judgment. These verses concern the new historical beginning made possible by Yahweh's sovereign resolve.

Judah's Sin Engraved (17:1-4)

This passage offers one more intense and solemn lawsuit speech against Judah. The indictment (vv. 1-3a) establishes the unbearable, undeniable guilt of Judah. The substance of the sin, expressed in quite stereotypical language, is worship of other gods — violation of the main claim of the torah. No details are given, for they are already known. Judah's idolatry has been adequately explicated elsewhere. The "bill of indictment" (i.e., the record of guilt) is permanently engraved so that it is irreversible, not to be changed, denied, or forgotten. It is written in the ultimate places of memory, on the heart and on the altar. This record on the heart is the very antithesis of the torah on the heart (31:33). Something will be written on the heart, either sin or torah. The mention of the altar in 17:1 may anticipate the more polemical mention of altar in v. 2, but here it is a public place of record.

The sentence of vv. 3b-4 consists of two elements. First, an unnamed enemy will seize the wealth and treasure of Judah (cf. 2 Kgs. 20:12-15). This was indeed accomplished by the Babylonians, who seized the temple and the related objects which constituted public wealth (cf. Jer. 52:17-23).[43] Second, the announcement is again made of loss of heritage and subservience in a foreign land (cf. 16:13). Violation of the torah (in this case, worship of other gods) results in historic displacement. The structure of prophetic thought (which Klaus Koch terms "metahistory")[44] refuses

---

43. See Peter R. Ackroyd, "The Temple Vessels — A Continuity Theme," *Supplements to Vetus Testamentum* 23 (1972): 166-181; and "An Interpretation of the Babylonian Exile: A Study of 2 Kings 20, Isaiah 38–39," *Scottish Journal of Theology* 27 (1974): 329-352.

44. Klaus Koch, *The Prophets*, vol. 1: *The Assyrian Period* (Philadelphia: Fortress; London: SCM, 1983), 70, 144-156.

to relinquish either theological claim or historical eventuality. Prophetic faith insists that the two are held together in Yahweh's sovereignty and at enormous cost to the people of Yahweh.

The separation of theological claim and historical eventuality is a perennial temptation and even a commonplace among us, with one or the other being prized to the neglect of the other. In this text the theological claim concerns *disobedience* of Yahweh. The historical eventuality concerns *destruction* by Babylon. The claim of Jeremiah is that the theological reality of *disobedience* and the historical actuality of *destruction* can only be understood together. Disobedience without an historical settlement is a misunderstanding of Yahweh's sovereignty. To explain destruction apart from disobedience is equally a wrong perception of Yahweh's rule. They belong together. To be sure, the prophetic, poetic tradition is aware that God's rule is not a mechanical management by fiat, nor a despotic absolutism. The prophets do not entertain such a naive supernaturalism. They know there is slippage, anguish, ambiguity, and human initiative. But the poetry is singleminded in witnessing to God's resilient presence in all such ambiguity. This insistence is not naive, simpleminded, or innocent, but it is indeed a relentless insistence. An untenable separation is made by "spiritualists" who choose theological claim over historical eventuality, or by "secularists" who choose historical eventuality and shrink from theological claim. Such a separation in either direction completely misunderstands the intent of biblical faith. Prophetic thought permits no such choices, no escape from the overriding tension of this linkage. *Disobedience ends in displacement.* A split between historical eventuality and theological claim may separate disobedience from displacement, but the prophets countenance no such illusion.

Like a Tree Planted by Water (17:5-13)

This is one of the more unusual sections of the tradition of Jeremiah. It contains four distinct elements. The first three appear to be sapiential sayings, while the fourth (vv. 12-13) is a doxology of judgment containing echoes of other Jeremiah texts. The unit no doubt has a complicated editorial history, but we have no access to that process.

17:5-8 These verses are a sapiential instruction which articulates "the two ways" of life and death. The language has close parallels to Ps. 1, but

158

the metaphors are more consistently developed and in tighter parallel here. Moreover, the invitation and threat in this context are drawn close to the crisis of Judah in Jeremiah's time. The form is conventional, with a single subject, "the man." The condemned man is the one who trusts in human power, whether military, economic, technological, or whatever (cf. Isa. 31:3). "Trust in man" may mean to trust human wisdom or human armaments, as the kings of Judah were wont to do. Both wisdom and armaments are ways in which a monarchy sustains itself apart from the requirements of covenant. The contrast to such might and power is found in Yahweh, who practices justice and authorizes covenantal relations (cf. Jer. 9:23-24; cf. 16:21). A person (or a community) who trusts falsely is surely headed toward death, expressed in the metaphor of a dried-up shrub. John Calvin suggests that this particular shrub is not simply dead but gives the "appearance of life," even though the root system is gone.[45] Calvin's interpretation suggests that while Jeremiah saw death, his contemporary situation still had "the appearance of life." It is the stark contrast between what is and what appears to be that evokes such pathos in the poet.

The poem contrasts such a person (or community) with one who trusts in Yahweh and who stays free of false reliance on either human power or human wisdom. The alternative choices offered in this metaphor are very much like the preaching of Isaiah, who appealed to kings to trust in Yahweh and not in foreign agents (Isa. 31:1-3; cf. 36:4-10, 13-20). The one who trusts only in Yahweh is destined for life, like a green tree with plenty of water. A destiny of either life or death is determined by the object of one's trust. False trust has important policy implications in Jeremiah's time, as in our own. This summons to singular faith is not a mere religious proposal, but requires policy decisions. The metaphor of withered shrub or watered tree is more intense and more compelling when it is remembered that the poem emerges in a culture that characteristically is desperate for water. The metaphor of water in such a context makes clear that trust is a life-and-death matter.[46] No tree or shrub can survive without water. There are no viable substitutes. Likewise, Judah will find no viable sub-

---

45. John Calvin, *Commentaries on the Book of the Prophet Jeremiah and the Lamentations,* vol. 1 (repr. Grand Rapids: Baker, 1979), 351-352.

46. See Amos 8:11-12 on the power of the metaphor. Critical judgment has often kept a separation between Jer. 2:13, for example, and this sapiential poem. Taken together, they articulate the conviction that Yahweh is the only source of life.

stitute for a genuine trust in Yahweh. Every alternative will lead to withering and death.

17:9-10　These verses are another wisdom saying, placed now as a commentary on vv. 5-8. The teaching contains two affirmations, which together assert an awful judgment. The first affirmation (v. 9) is that the human heart is fickle. The RSV rendering, "deceitful," recalls that this word (*'aqobh;* cf. Ps. 49:6; 2 Kgs. 10:19) is the term from which comes the name "Jacob," the one who "overreaches, deceives, exploits, takes advantage of." In Jer. 17:5 the heart is condemned for turning from Yahweh. This observation in v. 9 is not carefully formulated theology, but is a sapiential observation that human persons are characteristically untrustworthy and unfaithful. The statement about human character in v. 9 is matched by an affirmation concerning Yahweh in v. 10. Yahweh is the God from whom no secret can be hidden (cf. 16:17), who deals with human persons according to their just desserts. Human fickleness and divine accountability together lead to an inevitable judgment. The poem is not interested in theological speculation, but simply narrates what is evident in Jerusalem. The outcome of destruction is inevitable because the human heart will not change, and Yahweh will not cease to search the mind and heart to locate loyalty and fickleness. The juxtaposition of themes on human obduracy is paralleled in Gen. 3:1-8; 6:5. Here, as there, the overreaching human person seeks to hide and cannot. Yahweh outlasts every attempt at concealment.

17:11　This verse is an odd, isolated statement which, as is common in wisdom instruction, offers a lesson from an observed natural phenomenon. A partridge hen gathers little chicks that are not of her brood. That is, she collects what does not belong to her. One reading of this figure is that partridges are scavengers who take what is not theirs. Another is that the hen is so lustful that it will abandon any egg for the sake of a new venture. In her lust, the hen works against nature to create a false brood (cf. 8:7). In either case, the hen is cited to warn those who take what is not theirs (cf. 2 Sam. 12:1-4; Matt. 25:24). The poem does not pursue the metaphor very far, but turns it to the subject of riches gotten unjustly. In the end, unjust riches cannot be retained but will surely be lost. When wealth is gotten through injustice (cf. Jer. 22:3-14), it is no more proper than when a chick is seized by a scavenger hen.

Such wealth is improper, a violation of natural relations, and will surely be lost. The greedy rich are under judgment. Again, the teaching — as is typical of wisdom sayings — is detached from any context. In Jeremiah, however, the context in which that saying is heard is against the system of royal wealth. Such wealth will be lost and those who have it will be forsaken. It is as sure as a partridge not being able to keep what is not hers. The prophet skillfully takes up what must have been a conventional wisdom observation and transforms it into another harsh critique of an avaricious city.

17:12-13 These verses articulate a doxology of judgment. The brief poetic unit juxtaposes a hymn addressed to Yahweh and an indictment against those who do not embrace Yahweh. In v. 12 Yahweh is celebrated as enthroned. In v. 13 this exalted one is Israel's only hope. The remainder of v. 13 is built around the double use of "abandon" *('azab),* which now is linked to the use of the same verb in v. 11 concerning chicks who "leave" *('azab)* the hen. Yahweh is Israel's only hope. Israel in its stupidity has abandoned the only hope. As in 2:13, Israel has forsaken the only resource of life and so is destined to death by thirst and starvation. While 17:12-13 are originally unrelated to vv. 5-8, they are now brought together in the traditioning process. Taken together, they pursue the motif of water and life, of drought and death. In the marginal topography of Judah, where there is no water, all life will die (cf. Amos 4:7-8). The terrible incongruity is that Judah had a sure source of the water of life, and now has rejected it. The only outcome is death. This utilization of the theme of water and life illuminates the juxtaposition of Jer. 17:12-13 and 5-8. In both cases, water permits life (cf. John 4:10). In this prophetic rendering, "water" is taken to be covenant fidelity.

In sum, Jer. 17:5-13 contains an odd assortment of themes and rhetorical elements. John Bright suggests this section is "Jeremiah's 'miscellaneous file.' "[47] While the several elements are from different sources, they now form something of a unit, in which Yahweh's saving power (vv. 10, 12-13a) is contrasted with Israelite waywardness (vv. 9, 11, 13). Yahweh's sovereignty constitutes the offer of life. In these images, Yahweh does not intervene in judgment. Rather, life works its own destiny, and

47. John Bright, *Jeremiah,* 2nd ed., Anchor Bible 21 (Garden City, N.Y.: Doubleday, 1978), 119.

where there is no water (here, Yahweh) death is certain.[48] Yahweh's sovereignty and Israel's waywardness juxtaposed in this way present to Judah a limited range of possibilities.

The positive alternative is to turn to Yahweh in trust. Then Israel may live. The logic of the argument is the same as the "turn" summons of Amos: "Seek me and live" (Amos 5:4), or the Deuteronomic instruction to "choose life" (Deut. 30:19). The poetic rendering of Jeremiah, however, is much more subtle, requiring imaginative decisions more elemental than simple changes in behavior. The passage is bounded in Jer. 17:5 and 13, however, by the verb *sur* ("turn away from"), indicating that Judah has rejected the only way of life, and so comes death.[49] Israel must finally deal with Yahweh, the only source of Israel's future. Yahweh is the source of well-being (v. 8), the hope of Israel (v. 13a), the source of life (v. 13c). If Yahweh is rejected by the one who "trusts in man" (v. 5), like the deceitful heart (v. 9), like the greedy partridge (v. 11), like the ones who leave the living well (v. 13), death comes.

The context in which these wisdom sayings appear places them in the service of the harsh prophetic judgment over Jerusalem. The address of these sayings toward Jerusalem is not explicit, but clearly wisdom is now used to make the case that Jeremiah's Jerusalem has violated normal natural relations. Judah has as much chance of living as a shrub in the desert, a wanderer without water, a partridge taking a chick, a greedy one keeping wealth. The chance is nil, for "forsaking" leads to death. "Turning away" and "abandoning" are Israel's way of rejecting Yahweh and Yahweh's gift of life.

Be Not a Terror (17:14-18)

These verses resume the prayers of complaint and petition we have noted in chs. 11, 12, and 15. It is not clear why or in what way they are related to the immediate circumstance of ch. 17. Perhaps these verses provide a counterpart to the harsh lawsuit speech of 17:1-4, with the reflective

48. See Klaus Koch, "Is There a Doctrine of Retribution in the Old Testament?" in Crenshaw, *Theodicy in the Old Testament,* 57-87.

49. The double use of "turn aside" is reminiscent of 1 Sam. 12:20-21, a central text for the tradition of covenant which seems to lie behind the tradition of Jeremiah.

sapiential materials of vv. 5-13 leading to this passionate, needful prayer. The lawsuit announces a harsh future. Verses 5-13 suggest the common sense grounds (artistically wrought) about why this judgment is natural and inevitable. This rendering leads to the prayer, which may be both personal and public. The prayer then is a response of faithful, needful speech in the midst of a people that has not been faithful and does not know it is needful.

The brief prayer contains elements familiar in the Psalms of Lament:

(a) petition (v. 14a),
(b) motivation (vv. 14b-16),
(c) petition (v. 17a),
(d) motivation (v. 17b),
(e) petition (v. 18).

The initial petition is a personal one, asking for healing and deliverance. The poet throws himself utterly on Yahweh as the only source of healing. The poet's stance is therefore precisely opposite that of indicted Judah. The second petition (v. 17a) is the negative counterpart to the petition of v. 14a: "Be a healer . . . be not a terror." The poet has already known terror from God (cf. 20:10 on "terror on every side"). Now God is asked to change from terror to healing. The third petition, like the first, is also a personal one. It includes two personal requests: "Let me not be put to shame, . . . let me not be dismayed." These requests appeal to the standard assurances given in a salvation oracle (cf. 31:19; Isa. 54:4). The lament seeks to guide Yahweh into making such an assurance.

The main petitions in Jer. 17:18, however, are four requests for punishment of the poet's enemies: "put to shame . . . be dismayed . . . bring the day of evil . . . destroy . . ." This petition is the other side of the positive hope for self in vv. 14a and 17a. What the poet asks against his enemies is precisely what he himself wants to escape. It may surprise us that the prayer is so hostile. Such hostility bespeaks the courage and candor of prayer that is characteristic in Israel. Jeremiah prays against his adversaries knowing that God knows the heart and gives what is due (v. 10). The poet now asks that God give just due to the enemy, that is, punishment commensurate to the offense. The poet expects this of God and urges God to be faithful to those expectations.

The prayer offers several alternative motivations in an attempt to move God to act. First, in v. 14b the motivation is a statement of praise: "Thou art my praise." In v. 17b it is a statement of needful trust: "Thou art my refuge." The first seeks to enhance God. The second asserts Jeremiah's dependence and reliance on God. Both the praise and the plea seek to draw God into involvement with the situation of need, so that God should make Jeremiah's crisis God's own cause.[50]

Two other rhetorical features may be noticed. First, the prayer concerns the coming day of judgment. In v. 16 the poet asserts that in the past he has not wished such judgment on his enemies. He has not been preoccupied with retaliation. But in an abrupt change of mood, he does exactly wish for vengeance (v. 18). The poet believes that God's judgment is sure, he wants it soon, and he does not doubt who deserves judgment. The poet trusts in God's decisive sovereignty.[51] Second, three times in the poem a strong pronoun is used for God: "*thou* art my praise" (v. 14); "*thou* knowest" (v. 16); "*thou* art my refuge" (v. 17).[52] The threefold strong "thou" is matched by the threefold use of "*I*" (vv. 16, 18), also a strong pronoun.[53] Both pronouns are used for the sake of heavy emphasis.

The repeated use of such strong pronouns indicates that this relationship is one of intense communion. The relation in this moment of poetry is at a point of critical urgency. The one who prays is filled with hurt and rage, and entrusts vengeance to God. Such complaints are characteristically answered by an oracle of assurance.[54] In this poem, however there is no answer. The intensity of the moment and the dread of the situation break the conventional form. This faithful poet prays an unan-

---

50. Jeremiah prays out of the boldness characteristic of Israel's tradition since Moses. On the bold act of prayer that makes human need into an "interest" of God, see Greenberg, *Biblical Prose Prayer*, 10-18.

51. On vengeance as an act of sovereignty of a legitimate government, see Mendenhall, *The Tenth Generation*, 69-104.

52. The Hebrew verbal system has pronominal suffixes to indicate the subject of the verb. It also has a set of independent suffixes which may be used for additional emphasis. It is that "strong pronoun," "thou," which is used three times in this poem for special emphasis.

53. Parallel to the "thou" noted in the previous note, this unit also uses the strong pronoun "I" three times for emphasis. The juxtaposition of these two sets of pronouns is remarkable for the rhetoric of the unit.

54. On the oracle of assurance, see the recent study of Edgar W. Conrad, *Fear Not, Warrior*, Brown Judaic Studies 75 (Chico, Calif.: Scholars Press, 1985).

swered prayer. The hostility he faces from human agents is matched by the silence of God. No theological explanation is given for this silence on God's part. It is simply a reality in this anguished life of faith. God's silence to the poet corresponds to the absence of God announced to the whole people. God is no longer available, either to Israel or even to the poet. The poet experiences the very absence that is the destiny of Israel.[55]

Remember the Sabbath (17:19-27)

This prose passage is most unexpected in Jeremiah. The subject matter of sabbath is of course rooted in the old tradition of the Decalogue (cf. Exod. 20:8-11; Deut. 5:12-15).[56] The sabbath emerges as a matter of intense religious concern, especially after the Exile (cf. Isa. 56:4-5; Neh. 13:15-22).[57] For that reason, this prose unit is commonly regarded as later. We do know, however, that Jeremiah utilized the tradition of the Decalogue (cf. Jer. 7:9). Reference to the sabbath, therefore, is not necessarily alien to the tradition of Jeremiah and in itself is no reason to regard the passage as later.

The unit is divided into two parts, both concerning the sabbath. In 17:19-23 fidelity to sabbath is urged. Verses 21-22 urge obedience to the sabbath commandment with strong imperatives. Verse 23 follows as an indictment, indicating that Israel did not listen and did not obey, but violated the sabbath. This unit is dominated by the verb "hear" *(shema')*. In v. 20 there is a summons to listen, not unlike the classic Deuteronomic imperative of Deut. 6:4. In Jer. 17:23 the same verb is used twice to indict

---

55. On the dramatic power and significance of the absence and silence of God, see Andre Neher, *The Exile of the Word* (Philadelphia: Jewish Publication Society, 1980).

56. On the cruciality of the sabbath commandment for the Decalogue, see Patrick D. Miller, Jr., "The Human Sabbath: A Study in Deuteronomic Theology," *Princeton Seminary Bulletin* New Series 62 (1985): 81-97; and, more generally, Walter Harrelson, *The Ten Commandments and Human Rights* (Philadelphia: Fortress, 1980), 79-92.

57. The sabbath emerged as a crucial mark of Israel's distinctiveness in the exilic and postexilic periods, and had something of a polemical character to it. See Gerhard von Rad, *Old Testament Theology,* vol. 1 (New York: Harper & Row; Edinburgh: Oliver & Boyd, 1962), 79-84.

Israel. "Not listening" is the final disobedience. Life is not submitted to the will of Yahweh.

In the second half of the unit (vv. 24-27), the indictment of v. 23 strangely is ignored. In these later verses Judah is given a fresh chance. These verses are presented as a double "if . . . then" construct, in turn positive and negative. According to this text, Israel can decide afresh to keep covenant by way of keeping sabbath. The first "if . . . then" construct presents the positive option (vv. 24-26). If the community listens, it can be safe under a king and all Israel can be engaged in religious pilgrimage. The picture presented in these verses is of a great religious homecoming. The Jerusalem so much assaulted and critiqued by the covenant tradition is now the joyous goal of celebration. The negative option quickly follows in the second "if . . . then" construct (v. 27), however. If Israel violates sabbath and so breaks covenant, there will be massive destruction. Everything hangs on the sabbath, because the sabbath is the most dramatic sign that the will of God is honored and the life-giving power of God is trusted. To break sabbath means to violate God's will and to distrust God's gifts.

The pivotal role of the sabbath commandment in the future of this community may strike us as severe and peculiar. We must remember, however, that the sabbath becomes the identifying mark for the covenant community. Sabbath observance is understood as a deep rejection of imperial patterns of exploitation. It is the dramatic act whereby this people asserts to itself and announces to the watching world that this is Israel, a different people with a different way in the world, who will not behave according to the expectations of the imperial world. In the purview of covenant, the stability of political life (v. 25) and the effectiveness of worship (v. 26) depend on sabbath, an act that hands life back to God in trusting obedience.[58] If life is not handed over to God regularly, with discipline and intentionality, then the entire political-religious system will end in destruction.

This passage, like much else in Jeremiah, stakes everything on the centrality of God. It does so by distinctive appeal to the centrality of

58. See Matitiahu Tsevat, "The Basic Meaning of the Biblical Sabbath," in *The Meaning of the Book of Job and Other Biblical Studies* (New York: KTAV; Dallas: Institute of Jewish Studies, 1980), 39-52: "Every seventh day the Israelite renounces his autonomy and affirms God's dominion over him" (48).

sabbath. Sabbath-keeping is taken as a measure of obedience to Yahweh. While this focus on sabbath may link the passage to the concerns of the exilic or postexilic community,[59] the main claim is the same as the dominant tradition of Jeremiah. Obedience leads to life, though the specific form of obedience takes a different shape in each new generation and circumstance. In this case, sabbath asserts the cessation of destructive self-reliance, which is Judah's predominant temptation. We have seen that self-reliance is a central pathology of this people. Sabbath fidelity is one surrender of such self-reliance.

The Potter and the Clay (18:1-23)

This chapter contains diverse materials that must have had different contexts of origin, but in their present arrangement there is a discernable logic to the chapter. After the indictment (vv. 1-12) and the sentence (vv. 13-17), we have an expression of the opposition the poet had evoked (v. 18) and his prayer for help in the face of that opposition (vv. 19-23).

18:1-12 The narrative indictment of vv. 1-12 begins with a command to Jeremiah. He is instructed and he obeys. He goes as sent, and the result is a divine oracle. His observation in v. 4 prepares the way for the oracle that follows (vv. 6-12). Jeremiah observes that the potter completely controls the clay, can reshape it, and is not committed to any particular form for the clay (v. 4). The potter will completely reshape the clay until the potter has it the way he wants it.

The interpretation of this observation is rooted in the parallel drawn in v. 6. God can do to Israel whatever Yahweh chooses, just as the potter can the clay (cf. Isa. 45:9-11). Israel is not autonomous or independent, but is completely in the control of Yahweh. The oracle asserts Yahweh's complete sovereignty and Israel's complete subservience. That is the nature of the relationship, which finally cannot be avoided or denied.

The metaphor of potter and clay leads us to expect an unambiguous assertion of Yahweh's sovereignty. The argument that follows, however, is

59. See Robert P. Carroll, *From Chaos to Covenant* (London: SCM; New York: Crossroad, 1981), 215.

much more subtle. Jeremiah 18:7-10 are organized according to a double sequence of "if . . . if . . . then."[60]

A. 1. *If* . . . I declare . . . that I will pluck up . . . (v. 7),
    2. *if* that nation . . . turns from its evil (v. 8)
    3. *(then)* I will repent of the evil that I intended to do to it (v. 8).
B. 1. *If* . . . I declare . . . that I will build and plant it (v. 9),
    2. *if* it does evil in my sight . . . (v. 10),
    3. *then* I will repent of the good which I had intended to do to it (v. 10).

The first "if" (A.1, B.1) concerns God's decree. The second "if" (A.2, B.2) refers to a fresh decision on Israel's part. The "then" (A.3, B.3) expresses Yahweh's readiness to act in new ways in response to Israel's new behavior. In both sequences the first "if" is God's initial decision either to plant or to pluck up. The second "if" celebrates Israel's freedom. Israel is not fated but can act in new ways.

This mode of argument affirms, first, that God is free and can respond and, second, that Judah's obedience is of decisive importance. In light of both these affirmations, Judah is exhorted to choose carefully how it will act, for its future depends on its action. Yahweh's responsive sovereignty and Judah's determinative obedience are both constitutive of Judah's life.

In v. 11 an appeal is made that Israel should decide afresh. God has made a decree (the first "if," in v. 7), but that decree can be changed by Judah's action (the second "if," in v. 8). The argument asserts Yahweh's full sovereignty, consistent with the ability of the potter to control the clay. But the second theme, that Israel can take an initiative, violates the metaphor, for Israel has freedom that the clay does not have. The clay cannot challenge the potter, but Israel can act so that Yahweh will change. The narrative both uses the metaphor (to assert sovereignty) and violates the metaphor (to assert Judah's zone of freedom).

In v. 12, however, the prophet dismisses all of the freedom Israel

60. This sequencing is constructed from the rhetoric of the passage. The actual propositions do not all occur in the text, but this clearly represents the structure of the argument.

seemed to have in vv. 8-11. Now Israel's chance to change is nullified. The clay now can take no action free of the potter. There is no more time for turning. Judah has waited too long. Judah of course had had freedom of choice. But that freedom has now been forfeited through sustained resistance and stubbornness. The text is not interested in a theoretical question of free will. Rather, it addresses the pastoral reality that resistance to God practiced so long eventually nullifies the capacity to choose life. Israel's long-term resistance left it no longer able to choose life. Jerusalem's judgment is sealed because Judah has been too stubborn. Judah rejects God's plan which is for covenant obedience and chooses its own alternative plan that opts for autonomy and disobedience. Judah resolves to act autonomously, without reference to Yahweh.[61] Judah's plan is a plan of stubbornness which refuses the reality of God's sovereignty. Such a refusal ends in death. The narrative entertains a playful freedom out beyond the metaphor, but by v. 12 that freedom is ended and the potter completely controls the clay. Eventually the potter will quit on the clay because the clay will never turn out right. As the potter shapes clay (v. 4), so Yahweh shapes evil for Judah (v. 11).[62] The potter is not endlessly committed to working with this clay, if the clay is finally recalcitrant. The potter will finally quit, which means that the clay has no future.[63]

18:13-17   This poetic unit is nicely placed after the prose verdict of vv. 1-12. We have just been told that Israel will follow its own plan, against the plan of Yahweh, and that plan will lead to death. This poetic unit surely had no initial link to the preceding. Because of the editorial formula

61. As in other cases, the prophet places in the mouths of his opponents self-indicting words which are a polemical construction that would never have been uttered, but they are words reflecting actions and attitudes. We have seen a cluster of such alleged quotes in ch. 2.

62. Notice the reiteration of the word *yatsar* ("form") in vv. 4, 11.

63. The metaphor of potter-clay has an important and sustained use in the tradition, and Jeremiah's use should be understood in relation to other uses of the same metaphor. In 2 Cor. 4:7 the metaphor is used positively for a community of faith fully reliant upon and responsive to God. Between the deathly use of the metaphor by Jeremiah and the affirmative use by Paul stands the use of Isa. 45:9-10, which asserts that God's sovereignty over Israel (the potter over the clay) will cause Israel's rescue, even if the rescue takes a form that Israel would not prefer. All three uses stress God's sovereign power over the community of faith, whether in judgment or in mercy.

of judgment at the beginning of v. 13, however, this unit now functions to pronounce judgment after the harsh verdict of v. 12. The two units are connected by words which are rough homonyms. In v. 12 the RSV renders one term as "stubborn" *(sh-r-r)*; in v. 13 the RSV has "horrible thing" *(sh-'-r-r)*. Stubbornness and obstinate autonomy are Judah's "horrible thing." In this poem the "horrible thing" is done by the virgin, who should be completely devoted to her husband (cf. 2:2).

Jeremiah 18:13-14 appeals to natural phenomena to understand the grotesqueness of Judah. In v. 14 snow does not "leave" *('azab)* the mountains of Lebanon. It is always there. It belongs there. The crags of Sirion are the natural habitat for snow. Indeed, the snow of Lebanon cannot be snow anywhere else; it will disappear and cease to be snow if it is moved. The second metaphor of mountain stream reiterates the same claim. The metaphor affirms that as snow belongs in the mountains, Israel belongs with Yahweh, is always with Yahweh, cannot be Israel anywhere else. Yahweh is Israel's natural habitat, and to try to be Israel anywhere else will lead to disappearance. Elsewhere we have seen the verb *'azab* for Judah's leaving of Yahweh (2:13, 17, 19). Abandonment of Yahweh is the fundamental issue. Nobody ever heard of snow leaving the crags of Sirion. Nobody ever heard of Israel leaving Yahweh and still being Israel. Israel, like snow, will melt into oblivion if it leaves. When Israel leaves Yahweh, it ceases to be Israel.

The contrast to faithful, predictable snow which stays in its proper place is stated in 18:15-16, as the poem moves from nature to human behavior. Judah has forgotten Yahweh the way snow cannot forget the mountains. Verse 15 identifies the modes of forgetting as false worship, departure from tradition, and disobedience. The outcome of forgetting is that the land has become a ruin (v. 16). This outcome is inevitable. When the way of the LORD is abandoned, the land itself loses its life-giving capacity, because the capacity for life is in the gift of Yahweh, not in the character of the land itself. Baalism believed the land itself contained the gift of life. Israel's covenant faith knows that it is only Yahweh who causes the land to give life.

Forgetting Yahweh reduces the land to vulnerability and the people to deep humiliation. Verse 17 announces the specific form of judgment. It is like scattering before the wind — that is, exile. Israel will be blown away. Judah will be scattered the way the wind scatters chaff (cf. Ps. 1:4). Along with displacement, Judah will experience the absence of God (Jer.

18:17b). More precisely, Judah will experience God's "back" *('oreph)*, not God's face (cf. Ps. 13:1; 27:8-9). Where God's face is not seen, God's power is not available, and there is death. The removal of God's face likely asserts the nullification of the cultic apparatus in Jerusalem, which is designed to ensure God's presence.

This little poetic unit has a clear structure. It begins with a statement of judgment (Jer. 18:13). It then asks a rhetorical question which focuses on the fidelity of creation (v. 14). From the image of clinging snow and flowing streams, the poem moves from indictment to sentence, from "forgetting" (v. 15) to "scattering" (v. 17).

18:18   No doubt the harsh tenor of the prophetic message evoked hostility. Verse 18 suggests how pervasive and massive the opposition is. To "make a plot" ("devise a plan") suggests that the opposition to the prophet and his fearsome word is not simply an irrational, emotional response, but it is opposition that is formidable and intentional, that has developed a strategy for silencing this treasonable voice (cf. Mark 3:6). To "devise a plan" uses the same language as Jer. 18:12. As Judah is indicted for making its own recalcitrant plans (v. 12), so now we see those "plans" aimed both against Yahweh (v. 13) and against the prophet of Yahweh (v. 18). The plans of the opposition are an embodiment of the recalcitrant autonomy against which the prophet speaks.

Like the opponents of Jesus, the leadership "takes counsel." The triad mentioned (priest, wise, prophet) represents the power structure, the knowledge industry, and the religious authority of the establishment. That triad is matched by the three modes of authority that ordered the community: torah, counsel, word.[64] Jeremiah is perceived to be the enemy of all of these modes of authority. All of these established agents of public authority make common cause against this "voice of disorder." Those public leaders are adamant to maintain the status quo, immune to the notion that it is the very arrangement they defend which will result in exile and/or death. They perceive Jeremiah as a disruption, but they do not notice Yahweh, who sent Jeremiah as the unavoidable disrupter.

To "smite with the tongue" suggests public speech against the prophet. This is likely more than slander or gossip. Most probably, it means

---

64. On these modes of leadership and the corresponding modes of knowledge, see Walter Brueggemann, *The Creative Word* (Philadelphia: Fortress, 1982).

taking the prophet to court and filing public charges, with the hope of marking him as an enemy of the state (cf. 26:8-11). The word entrusted to the prophet has indeed made him a public enemy (cf. 38:4) and has isolated him from the main sources of public authority (cf. 15:17). As we shall see later, there were those who still supported him, perhaps at risk to themselves (cf. 36:19). It is worth noting that the support for the prophet comes not from the religious leaders but from civil authorities, perhaps those who themselves were increasingly alienated from the self-serving ideology of the royal-priestly apparatus.

18:19-23 The prayer of the prophet in these verses likely is an independent piece, but it has an appropriate place here in response to the conspiracy of v. 18. The prayer follows the general pattern of lament psalms and is dominated by petition. The verbs of petition articulate a series of requests:

- give heed, hearken (v. 19),
- deliver up,
- give over (v. 21),
- forgive not,
- nor blot out,
- deal (v. 23).

The petitions are reinforced by a series of jussives:

- let their wives become,
- may their men meet,
- may their youths be slain (v. 21),
- may a cry be heard (v. 22),
- let them be overthrown (v. 23).

The objects of this petition are not named, but the context suggests that they are the opposition identified in v. 18. Two things are clear in the petition. First, Jeremiah continues to trust in and look to Yahweh for well-being. His problematic situation drives him to more passionate faith and urgent prayer. Second, Jeremiah never doubts that he is entitled to good from Yahweh and is not embarrassed to seek good and insist upon it (v. 20). He prays as a righteous one who is entitled to God's intervention (cf. 12:1).[65] Jeremiah's petition is for God to implement covenant curses against his enemies, including the standard triad of famine, sword, and pestilence (18:21). The language of v. 22a moves beyond convention, however, and presents a visceral image of Yahweh's visitation. Jeremiah prays finally that justice should be done without forgiveness (v. 23).

Jeremiah provides two groundings for this petition. The prophet has done good even for his adversaries (v. 20). He has acted as intercessor (cf. 7:16; 15:1) and does not warrant their hostile response. His second ground of appeal is a theme recurrent in the prayers of lament: "Thou knowest" (18:23). This is an act of praise, but also a statement of profound trust. Jeremiah trusts the justice of God and is willing to entrust to God the response to his opponents. Jeremiah is completely confident that he will be vindicated and that his opponents will be found guilty.

The prayer begins with reference to "my plea" (v. 19). The language is juridical. It suggests that Jeremiah is in court, stands accused, and now turns to Yahweh for vindication. The ground of vindication is that he has faithfully spoken the word entrusted to him. He has acted faithfully as intercessor. He has practiced obedience, even if it was an unwelcome obedience. He asks no special mercy for himself and wants none shown to the others.[66] Already in 12:1-6 Jeremiah is troubled that God is not just. Here he pleads simply that God will be just and deal righteously with him because he is righteous, and deal appropriately with the wicked conspirators, who should be treated wickedly.

This chapter serves two different concerns. In vv. 1-17 the text concerns the obduracy of Judah and its coming exile and death. In vv. 18-23 we are concerned with the hostility evoked against the person of Jeremiah for speaking such a harsh word. The trouble experienced by Jeremiah and his harsh prayer (vv. 18-23) can only be understood in relation to the public issues of vv. 1-17. Finally, the issue is not the well-being of the prophet, but the validity of the judgment against Jerusalem. The evil "plans" made against Jeremiah (v. 18) match the evil

---

65. This prayer of vengeance which is rooted in and expresses confidence about one's own righteousness and the wickedness of one's opponents has a close parallel in Ps. 109:8-19. Again Jeremiah apparently utilizes a standard tradition of speech.

66. The juridical cast of the argument is much like that of Job, on which see Claus Westermann, *The Structure of the Book of Job* (Philadelphia: Fortress, 1981). Westermann shows the delicate interweaving of lament and lawsuit.

"plans" made in resistance to Yahweh (v. 12). When Yahweh's "plan" is rejected (v. 11), death will come. No amount of hostility against the messenger will modify the message. The clay finally will have to submit to the potter or be discarded. Jeremiah is clear that Judah has had options, and equally clear that Judah has chosen infidelity.

The Broken Flask (19:1-15)

We have considered the metaphor of potter and clay in 18:1-12. The same image is used again in 19:1-15 with much more sustained and devastating effect. Jerusalem will be nullified so that it "can never be mended" (v. 11).[67] The passage falls into two unequal parts. In vv. 1-13 we have a long summons from Yahweh to Jeremiah, instructing him in what he shall say and do. Then in vv. 14-15 we have a narrative of the prophet's actual actions. The long instruction to Jeremiah from Yahweh has as its counterpart a very terse narrative of compliance. The disproportion makes clear that the weight is borne not by anything Jeremiah says or does, but by the commanding word of Yahweh, which is the decisive element in this text. The speech of God dominates the text. Jeremiah's own words are only derivative from the words of God and bring those words of Yahweh to fruition.

19:1-13   The long speech of Yahweh here is organized around the two simple acts depicted in vv. 1-2 and v. 10. In vv. 1-2 the prophet is ordered to take an earthen flask and speak to the elders and senior priests. That is, he is to address the power structure. In v. 10 he is ordered to break the flask and speak again to the same representatives of the establishment. In both cases the earthen flask provides an occasion for an extended word of judgment. The initial act of vv. 1-2 leads to the long speech of vv. 3-9, and the act of v. 10 to the speech of vv. 11-13. The initial instruction assures that Jeremiah's effort is a quite public act, legitimated by the priests and elders who accompany him. The history-making word of Yahweh is not a secret matter; it happens in the midst of the public community.

---

67. The RSV has "mend," which renders the Hebrew *rapha,* most often translated as "heal." That Hebrew term reflects a correction of the text that is conventional and universally accepted.

The speech of vv. 3-9 is an extended lawsuit speech in three parts. The first brief element (v. 3) announces the main accent of the speech: Yahweh is now bringing evil upon Jerusalem, a judgment so severe that it will evoke a stunned, shocked response from all who hear of it.

The second element (vv. 4-5) is the indictment, which sounds themes we have frequently encountered and which echoes Deuteronomic phraseology. The dominant verbs are "abandon" and "profane." The first verb *('azab)* continues the dominant metaphor of marital infidelity, which we have seen frequently in the Jeremiah tradition. The second verb *(nakar)* means "to make alien or foreign." Jerusalem has been made alien. It is so abused that it has become an unwelcome, inhospitable place for Yahweh. The particulars referred to by these powerful verbs include wrong cultic practice ("burn incense") and wrong social practice ("innocent blood"). The reference to "burning sons" (v. 5) may be an allusion to Assyrian distortions,[68] but the phraseology is quite stylized and perhaps should not be taken too concretely. The general point is that all of life in Jerusalem is now ordered in ways that are alien to Yahweh.

The third extended element (vv. 6-9) has a "therefore" which corresponds to the "because" of v. 4. The lead sentence of the judgment asserts that coming events in the valley around Jerusalem will necessitate a new name for the valley. It will be called "the valley of Slaughter," for the killing done by Yahweh will be massive and unavoidable. This prediction of the fate of the city is made more specific in vv. 7-9, all of which culminates in the horrendous vision of v. 9. The rhetorical power of the verdict against the city is evident in the series of first person verbs in the mouth of Yahweh:

- I will make void
- I will cause to fall
- I will give (v. 7),
- I will make (v. 8),
- I will make (v. 9).

68. On the relation of this practice to Assyrian practices, see Morton Cogan, *Imperialism and Religion: Assyria, Judah and Israel in the Eighth and Seventh Centuries B.C.E.,* SBL Monograph 19 (Missoula, Mont.: Scholars Press, 1974). Cogan has persuasively argued that in this period Assyrian practices may have been attractive and seductive, but they were not systematically imposed. John W. McKay, *Religion in Judah under the Assyrians, 732-609 BC,* Studies in Biblical Theology, 2nd series 26 (Naperville, Ill.: Allenson; London: SCM, 1973), has argued in a fashion parallel to Cogan.

The action is sure, incontrovertible, and directly from the hand of Yahweh. There is here no mediating agent, such as the Babylonian army. The first person verbs make clear that it is Yahweh alone who takes these destructive actions.

The actual substance of the judgment appeals to the old covenant curse tradition. What now befalls Jerusalem are not novel acts, but the very threats which the torah tradition had long mediated.[69] There will be death by sword (presumably Babylon, but not specified). The simple announcement of death, however, is not rhetorically adequate. We are offered a picture of bodies piled up as food for birds (v. 7). The bodies will be uncared for, unprotected, and dishonored. The city, envisioned as a pile of ruins, will be a place of mocking (v. 8). The famine will be so great that people will desperately act as cannibals against neighbors and their own children (v. 9).

This judgment of God is no doubt stereotypical and hyperbolic. Its massive, relentless force is necessary to penetrate the complacent self-assurance of Judah that "it can't happen here." This prophetic speech makes the harsh claim: it can and it will. We are not sure what to make of this picture. It is a poetic scenario. The vision is one of rhetorical overkill in an attempt to suggest something comparable to the unthinkable death of a nuclear holocaust (cf. 8:1-3).[70] This picture is beyond historical realism, because the fate of Jerusalem falls outside such civil expectations. The rhetoric must match the passion of God, who has been provoked beyond any convention. The rhetoric runs beyond convention, because the social realities are beyond anything yet known in Jerusalem.[71]

After that intense scenario, the action of 19:10 is terse, and powerful because of its terseness. The verse is dominated by the stark word "break"

69. On prophetic use of the old covenant curses, see Delbert R. Hillers, *Treaty-Curses and the Old Testament Prophets,* Biblica et orientalia 16 (Rome: Pontifical Biblical Institute, 1964).

70. As Richard L. Rubenstein has argued ("Job and Auschwitz," *Union Seminary Quarterly Review* 25 [1969-1970]: 421-437), it cannot be claimed that the destruction of Jerusalem can be compared in scope, magnitude, or significance with the holocaust. I refer only to the rhetorical force with which the poet seeks to anticipate the judgment in the event. That rhetorical force is comparably present, even if the historical reality and significance is much less.

71. The extreme rhetoric utilized for this event suggests a case of using "limit language" to help Israel experience a "limit experience." See Paul Ricoeur, "Biblical Hermeneutics," *Semeia* 4 (1975): 107-128.

(shabar). The act evokes a second passionate comment (vv. 11-13). Verse 11 draws together the claims of this text in the most unambiguous way possible: like this earthen flask, so this city and this people will be broken. This narrative does not report sympathetic magic, as though the broken flask enacts the broken city.[72] "Sympathetic magic" is the notion that a dramatic act like the breaking of a pot may *cause* the destruction to which it alludes. While it is, in my judgment, too much to think the people in this text believed in such causation, there is no doubt that the dramatic act opened up a field of fertile imagination filled with dread and fresh discernment. The broken flask is a parabolic assault on imagination. The coming judgment is a firm resolve on the part of God. That resolve is all the more ominous because "it can never be mended" (v. 11). This is the point of no return. This destruction is not for chastening or for discipline. There is no invitation to repent. It is not intended to "teach a lesson." There is no escape clause. The judgment is final, massive, decisive, unarguable.

What an incredible word for this prophet of the covenant tradition! Jeremiah is utterly a child of the tradition of Moses. He takes to its conclusion what has been implicit all through the tradition. Since Exod. 19:5-6 the whole of Israel's life with Yahweh has been governed by this uncompromising "if." The whole enterprise is finished. There is in the purview of the prophet no hint of continuing care, no second thought on Yahweh's part, no yearning or wistfulness. This is the end of the tradition, the end of all things sacred.

Jeremiah is confronted by a royal establishment (and we may believe public opinion) that relied on the abiding continuity of God's covenant commitment. Against that, Jeremiah is a faithful interpreter of the Mosaic tradition. This outcome in destruction had been proposed from the beginning in this tradition of "if." Moreover, the prophet also offers a correct reading of historical events. Jerusalem is indeed destroyed! This really is an ending, whatever theological verdict one may render. Thus a *correct reading of public events* and a *faithful reading of the tradition* converge in this shocking and ominous text. The city now faces the very end that the covenant tradition had anticipated for the disobedient. God has not made an unconditional commitment to any historical construct — not even to Jerusalem. The tradition illuminates what is happening. The outcome of history vindicates the tradition.

72. Against John Bright, *Jeremiah,* 2nd ed., Anchor Bible 21 (Garden City, N.Y.: Doubleday, 1978).

Jeremiah is intensely immersed in both tradition and historical events. They come together in a stunning, almost unbearable verdict. Jeremiah 19:12-13 serves to expand the verdict of v. 11. The city has been rendered ritually unclean, a place where Yahweh cannot abide. As Yahweh finds the place uninhabitable, so the power for life departs. Where God's power for life is absent, death comes quickly.

19:14-15   Chapter 19 thus far is a decree from the mouth of Yahweh. Only now do we have narrated the speech of the prophet. It is striking that in this recounting of the prophet's response there is no mention of the earthen flask, no breaking of it, no travel with elders and priests. It is as though the prophet does not take the specifics of the command seriously. He simply stands in the temple and speaks. He goes to the heart of the city, the temple court, to speak his word. One may wonder about the reduction of all of Yahweh's words and command to act in vv. 1-13 to the simple statement of v. 15. Perhaps Jeremiah is not as enthusiastic about this heavy word as is Yahweh. Perhaps he does not want to engage in such rhetorical overkill. Perhaps he wants to soften the dramatic effect. Perhaps he believes the harsh judgment does not need to be voiced yet again with such eloquence.

For whatever reason, v. 15 gives only the essentials. The threat from Yahweh is an echo of v. 3: "I am bringing evil." Nothing is specified. Both the indictment and sentence of v. 15 lack specificity. The climactic indictment is "You did not listen." Everything depends on listening. Everyone suffers when there is no listening. Out of the tradition of Deuteronomy, not listening is the fundamental act of autonomy and bad faith. Not to listen is not to belong, not to concede sovereignty. Not listening is to claim one's own place and take one's own counsel (v. 7). It is to imagine one is free to order life as one wills, which leads to forsaking and making alien. Even Jerusalem in its splendor and dignity is not so free, so autonomous. Such a mistaken pretense leads only to death. That death is now at hand, says the poet.

Jeremiah in Stocks (20:1-6)

This passage appears to be a straightforward narrative report of an event in the life of the prophet. It offers a different form of rhetoric from the preceding chapter and perhaps is not originally related to it. However, the canonical juxtaposition of the two is not inappropriate. Jeremiah 19:1-15 is one of Jeremiah's most devastating speeches of judgment, leading to the conclusion "it can never be mended." Such a harsh word surely would evoke criticism and hostility from his hearers. We observe that criticism and hostility in 20:1-6, in which the administrative officer of the temple establishment treats Jeremiah to public abuse as an enemy of the establishment.

The leadership that is threatened by Jeremiah and that responds to him is embodied in Pashhur, who administers the temple. The confrontation of Jeremiah and Pashhur is not unlike that of Amos and Amaziah (Amos 7:10-17). Two views of reality clash and there can be no compromise. The action Pashhur takes on behalf of official truth is not a personal act of revenge, but is the public, "legitimate" procedure which deals swiftly and harshly with dissent. The temple complex claims to be the embodiment of God's presence and purpose, and therefore it cannot countenance the notion that Yahweh is against that very institution. Jeremiah is taken a political prisoner. The priest seeks to intimidate the prophet, hopefully to silence him.

Jeremiah is not intimidated or cowed. In response to this public punishment (Jer. 20:2), the prophet responds boldly and vigorously (vv. 3-6). Jeremiah's scathing response, rather than his punishment, is the point of the text. Jeremiah comes to see that the resistance he meets is not simply personal. The agents of the temple are enemies of God's word, and that word must therefore be uncompromising and unrelenting. (On the relation of personal opposition and opposition to the very purpose of God, see 1 Sam. 8:7.)

Jeremiah is not penitent or apologetic. He is immediately back on the attack against the baseless pretensions of the royal-temple establishment. His response is in three parts. First, he dramatically renames the temple administration (Jer. 20:3). A changed name witnesses to a changed reality. The temple was to bring *shalom,* but it brings *terror* (cf. 6:25). The administrative head of the temple is renamed "Terror on every side," or "Surrounded by trembling."[73] The temple (represented by Pashhur) and

---

73. On this phrase, see William L. Holladay, "The Covenant with the Patriarchs Overturned: Jeremiah's Intention in 'Terror on Every Side' (Jer. 20:1-6)," *Journal of Biblical Literature* 91 (1972): 305-320. Holladay sees the phrase as a subtle announcement of an inversion of all old covenant reliances.

the city are now marked by terror and not peace. The temple cannot keep its promises. The system is under judgment and has failed. It may mouth *shalom,* but it embodies terror. It is therefore subject to God's terror.

The prophet is not especially interested in Pashhur, however. Second, he is focused on the city and temple, enmeshed as they are in self-deception (20:4-5). The whole company of Pashhur — his associates, friends, accomplices — is under judgment. They are under a death sentence. Jeremiah appeals to the standard twofold form of judgment/sword and exile. (It is never clear when the invading armies will kill and when Israel will be deported. Rhetorically, the two futures of death and exile are treated as parallel.) The decisive statement in the mouth of Yahweh is, "I will give all Judah . . . I will give all the wealth . . . into the hand of their enemies." The word "all" is repeatedly used. The punishment is complete. There will be no escape. The Babylonian armies simply enact the decree of Yahweh. The priests are helpless against the resolve of God. The imperial seizure of temple treasury is narrated at the end of the book of Jeremiah (52:17-23). The critique of the temple apparatus serves to delegitimate the royal-temple ideology and its particular definition of the world.

Third, the oracle returns to Pashhur at its close (20:6). His personal destiny is exile, and finally death in exile. The judgment applies to the man, his family, and all his allies in the temple apparatus who have participated in the deception. (This destiny is not unlike that pronounced by Amos in Amos 7:17.) The final word of the verse is "false" *(sheqer).* The temple has not embodied the truth of God. The personal references to Pashhur (vv. 3, 6) form an envelope around the more public announcement (vv. 4-5). All three parts have the same aim, however. All of vv. 3-6, the personal and public words, announce the great historical reversal that is now decreed. Those at the center of the temple, the focus of well-being and security, are the very ones displaced and exposed to death. The very place that is to guarantee life has become the very seat of death. The symbolic world of Jerusalem is now effectively dismantled. The physical dismantling is still to be accomplished by Babylonian arms, but the dismantling is primarily accomplished by this prophetic word with its power to expose, indict, and displace.

I Have Become a Laughingstock (20:7-18)

This final, most pathos-filled complaint of Jeremiah now is placed to follow the prophet's extraordinary challenge to established religion (vv. 1-6). In 18:1–20:6 Jeremiah speaks a massive word of judgment. He does it boldly and unflinchingly, full of confidence, certain that he speaks the very truth God has entrusted to him. Such speech is costly, however, not only because of the external hostility and resistance that his word evoked (20:1-6), but because of the intense, personal toll of speaking against the very reality that must have been his own spiritual home. In announcing this harsh judgment of Yahweh, Jeremiah is not speaking only against the world of "the others" who are his adversaries, but against the very symbolic world he himself inhabits. The cost of such a harsh judgment is that the prophet predictably arrives at pathos, hurt, and despair.

The new rhetorical unit that begins in v. 7 stands in stark contrast to the preceding. Jeremiah is unflinching in his public speech (vv. 3-6). But after this defiant proclamation, we are permitted access to his conversation with Yahweh, which has a quite different tone. Now he joins issue with Yahweh over the cost of his public work. This poetic struggle with God is divided in two distinct parts — vv. 7-12 and vv. 14-18. Between them comes a curious doxological break in v. 13.

20:7-12 The prayer in these verses bears all the marks of a psalm of lament. While the poet uses that familiar genre, the personal poignancy of the poem corresponds to our general understanding of the pathos of Jeremiah. The poem opens with a powerful complaint against God (vv. 7-10). Although the lines complain about human hostility ("I have become a laughingstock"), the focus is on the ways of Yahweh, who seems not to be faithful and trustworthy. The complaint begins with an accusation that Yahweh has seduced him (v. 7). The verb rendered "deceived" could be rendered more strongly as "harassed," "taken advantage of," "abused," even "raped." Jeremiah finds himself helpless before Yahweh's power, which is overwhelming and irresistible, even if not trustworthy. Jeremiah admits the power of God, but concedes nothing else (cf. Job 9:19-27). The complaint only asserts Yahweh's raw, primitive power that overwhelms even the one who seeks to serve him. The words of the poem anticipate Job.

Yahweh's power is beyond challenge, and that places the prophet in an unbearable, "no-win" situation. On the one hand, Jeremiah is mandated

181

to speak against Jerusalem, but his speaking evokes deep hostility (Jer. 20:8). On the other hand, when he does not speak (in order to avoid the hostility) he is even more troubled, for the word of Yahweh is a burning compulsion to him (v. 9). The prophet has only two alternatives, and neither one works. When he speaks, Yahweh does not support him. When he is silent, Yahweh does not console him. He has this awesome burden from Yahweh, but without the accompanying power or presence of Yahweh. Yahweh has mandated him but has given him no visible support. The only way this awesome task could be endured is with Yahweh's reliable solidarity, and that is withheld.

Jeremiah's message has evoked a "whisper campaign" against him (v. 10). He is maligned by those who cannot bear his word and who want to dismiss him as an irresponsible dissident. In v. 3 Jeremiah had labeled his nemesis, Pashhur, as "Terror on every side" (i.e., he is a bundle of trouble and disturbance). But now the phrase is turned against Jeremiah himself. He is made the butt of attack and criticism. He now is the one who is accused as the bringer of trouble and terror. He is the object of harsh criticism and perhaps a conspiracy (cf. 18:18). In the face of his own fidelity and in the face of the weighty opposition he evoked, Jeremiah prays an urgent prayer. He asserts that he is in real danger (20:10), that he is in trouble because he has been faithful to Yahweh (v. 8). He insists that his danger is Yahweh's responsibility, that Yahweh must care and act. Jeremiah is without resource against his friends and associates who want to do him in (v. 10). He relies completely on Yahweh's advocacy.

A second characteristic element of the lament is the assertion of trust in Yahweh (v. 11). This statement of trust is almost contradictory to the complaint. Whereas Yahweh earlier had been accused of infidelity (v. 7), now Yahweh's powerful steadfastness is celebrated.

Jeremiah's assertion of confidence in Yahweh serves two functions. First, it is a statement of genuine trust. He has come to know that Yahweh's power is reliable and can be counted on. Second, it is a motivation addressed to Yahweh, reminding Yahweh of Yahweh's character and responsibility. Already in the call narrative of ch. 1, Yahweh had issued a "do not fear" to Jeremiah (1:8), much as a general might give to his troops. Yahweh promised to be with and for Jeremiah in the battle to come (1:17-19). Now Jeremiah, in his prayer, appeals to that metaphor to assert what Yahweh can do and to remind Yahweh of what must be done. Because Yahweh is such a warrior, Jeremiah is confident that the threats made against him will disappear, because they cannot stand against the mobilization of Yahweh.

The third element in this prayer (20:12) is a petition to Yahweh. The introductory lines echo 17:10. In that prayer it is affirmed that God tries the heart and gives people what they deserve. Here the prophet appeals to that same sure reality. Jeremiah does not ask for free grace, but only for an equitable settlement. He asks to be rewarded for his relentless obedience. The petition is lean and pointed: "let me see thy vengeance." He prays for the very vengeance for which the enemies ask (v. 10). Jeremiah does not take vengeance in his own hands. He only prays that Yahweh should enact the vengeance that is appropriate to Yahweh's own character.[74]

This prayer is an act of weakness and of power. Jeremiah is aware that he is weak and helpless. He cannot prevail, but he is confident that Yahweh can and will prevail. Michael Fishbane has seen how the word "prevail" dominates the poem.[75] The Hebrew word *yakal* occurs four times: "thou hast prevailed" (v. 7), "I cannot (prevail)" (v. 9), "we can overcome him" (v. 10), "they will not overcome me" (v. 11). Jeremiah prays about overcoming and being overcome. His only hope is that Yahweh will be his ally and not his enemy. When Jeremiah is alone, he is lost. He cannot withstand the enemy. But if Yahweh were to be his advocate, he is very sure of vindication, both because he is innocent and because Yahweh is powerful (2 Cor. 11:30; 12:9). Otherwise, he is hopelessly defeated by an alliance of Yahweh and his human adversaries. Either way it will be unequal. Without Yahweh, he is unequally weak; with Yahweh, he is unequally triumphant.[76] Everything depends on Yahweh. That is why the prayer is so urgent and passionate. Jeremiah must have Yahweh on his side. Only his prayer can summon and evoke Yahweh to stand with him.

---

74. See the discussion of vengeance in Mendenhall, *The Tenth Generation*, 69-104. This vengeance is not arbitrary and undisciplined, but is the embodiment of the rule of law. See Susan Jacobi, *Wild Justice* (New York and London: Harper & Row, 1983).

75. Michael Fishbane, *Text and Texture* (New York: Schocken, 1979), 91-102.

76. The attempt of Jeremiah to draw Yahweh into solidarity against a common enemy is illuminated by the analysis of "triangling" in family dynamics. See Murray Bowen, *Family Therapy in Clinical Practice* (New York: Aronson, 1978).

20:13   This verse is problematic and may not be a part of the original poem.[77] David J. A. Clines and David Gunn have shown, however, that the verse is the culmination of vv. 7-12, and is a fourth element of the lament psalm, resolution in praise.[78] Such a reading would suggest that the speaker is so confident of Yahweh's answer, of Yahweh's intervention, and of his own innocence that he anticipates a resolution as though it is already wrought. Thus the prayer moves dramatically, as Israel characteristically does in prayer, in four steps: complaint/trust as motivation/petition/praise.

Jeremiah cannot find satisfaction in the public arena, nor in social relations. He is finally driven to face the theological reality of his life and vocation. He is driven to God as his "only source of comfort and strength." In the face of God he is made aware of the deep, inescapable problematic of his life. Through its long history, Israel had found Yahweh to be sufficient solace in every threatening situation. In this verse Jeremiah turns to praise of God because he has found Yahweh to be adequate, reliable, present, decisive. Such a certitude was not anticipated by the poem, but Jeremiah is characteristically Israelite in arriving at this doxological conclusion. The God who was experienced as fickle at the beginning of the poem is forced by the prayer to become his powerful ally and advocate. Such a one as Jeremiah cannot hope for or expect more than that. But he can indeed expect and receive that much. The truth spoken even in the face of establishment hostility permits praise and solidarity with God. Jeremiah's lonely voice is a voice of truth. He finds himself allied with the God of all truth. Jeremiah does not find himself "prevailing" either with God or with his fellows, but the move from complaint to praise is itself a form of prevailing, finally the only form of prevailing that is available to Israel.[79]

77. Robert P. Carroll, *From Chaos to Covenant* (London: SCM; New York: Crossroad, 1981), 128, notes that v. 13 contains common hymnic elements. That in itself is not sufficient grounds for concluding it is an addition. It does in any case perform an odd function between vv. 7-12 and vv. 14-18.

78. David J. A. Clines and David M. Gunn, "Form, Occasion and Redaction in Jeremiah 20," *Zeitschrift für die alttestamentliche Wissenschaft* 88 (1976): 390-409; and " 'You Tried to Persuade Me' and 'Violence! Outrage!' in Jeremiah XX 7-8," *Vetus Testamentum* 28 (1978): 20-27.

79. That the petition should culminate in an act of trust (vv. 11-12) and in a hymn of praise (v. 13) is characteristic of Israel. Thus again Jeremiah follows the practice of Israel. On such statements of trust in times of distress, see Ps. 27:1; 73:25.

20:14-18 After the bold, confident conclusion expressed as praise in v. 13, we are shocked and taken aback by vv. 14-18. It is quickly clear that Jeremiah's complex and troubled life leaves more to be said even after triumphant praise. Verses 14-18 form a strange disjunction after the trust of vv. 11-12 and doxology of v. 13. It is as though the theological resolution and well-being expressed in vv. 11-13 cannot be sustained, because life is too raw. This does not make such trust and praise false, but they are not the whole truth. The full truth of Jeremiah includes a harsh counterpart. This bold and obedient prophet found himself in this moment of candid poetry alone, abandoned, hopeless, full of despair. Perhaps he is an unstable personality. No doubt his contemporaries found him so. The poem, however, gives us no warrant for a psychological analysis. We face a crisis of reality deeper than that. The measure of the crisis is that this cry, this curse, is not addressed to God or to anyone (vv. 14-15). The poet is bereft of anyone to whom address can be made, utterly alone with only shrillness against a hostile abyss.

The poetry moves abruptly from praise (v. 13) to the poison of assault upon everything that is near and dear. We are given no clue as to what might have evoked this poem of violent rejection and self-hatred. Perhaps this outpouring is triggered by the massive resistance Jeremiah encountered in his poetic vocation, or perhaps he is aware — in spite of the doxology — that God is not overly attentive. Or perhaps the poem is less focused and intentional than that. The curse speech may be an undifferentiated act of both deep exhaustion and a sense of futility about his vocation.

In any case, the verses are a cry from the depth (cf. Ps. 130:1). It is a cry so personal in character and so urgent that it lacks the focus of address. It is a wish hardly formed, not yet ready to be cast as a prayer. It is a yearning for "nonbeing," and in that regard is closely paralleled to the longer poem of Job 3. The poet wishes the day of his birth had never happened (Jer. 20:14). He knows of course that times of birth are awesome, specific, and irreversible (cf. 8:7), but he dares to imagine that his birth was not necessary and need not have been. The main assault in 20:15-17 is against the bearer of the news of his birth. He imagines the day of his birth. His father waited while the midwives worked. Then the news. Then rejoicing. But the waiting, the news, the rejoicing are all rejected. If only the news had not been brought. Jeremiah has made entry into this community only when the news of his birth is announced by the messenger. If the news had not been announced, he might have been unnoticed, unvalued, unassaulted, uncalled. The bearer of the message is rejected by Jeremiah because he did not need to bring the news. He could instead have suppressed the news and killed the baby. Perhaps there is subtle irony. As Jeremiah himself is rejected as a messenger, so Jeremiah would reject the messenger who caused him to be present and known in the world. Jeremiah knows all about messengers being rejected, and he wishes his birth message had never been delivered.

The poem ends with the great "why" question of human existence (v. 18); but it is not a general existential probe. The question is quite concrete. His urgent inquiry is more than simply the "why" of human existence. It is the "why" of being given a burden of "plucking up and tearing down," a message completely (and predictably) resisted. The issue is not existence, but vocation that shapes existence. Jeremiah's dread-filled question lingers unanswered, as we might expect. We do not know why, as Jeremiah does not know — because the ground and reason are hidden in the purposes of God.

Two facets of this poetic unit may be considered. First, how honest the Bible is! It does not deny or deceive about how costly the truth of God's word is. Such deep faith as Jeremiah's does not lead neatly to well-being, but to recurring crisis. The Bible knows about troubled, bitter faith that is left unresolved. Second, never does the poet finally curse God. While the poet seems to have gone berserk with curse, he also knows where the boundaries of faith are and how they must be honored. In a euphemism, Job's wife urges the cursing of God (Job 2:9), which Job will not do. Nor does Jeremiah. Nor does the poet curse his parents, who caused him to be. Indeed, there is no word uttered that would be a dishonoring of parents (cf. Deut. 5:16). In the bitterness and sense of abandonment that is experienced, that much of the relation still holds.

We must be aware of the odd (and, I judge, deliberate) juxtaposition of Jer. 20:7-13 and 14-18. These two poetic units are utterances of faith in tension. The second (vv. 14-18) does not cancel the first (vv. 7-13). One might imagine they should have come in reverse order, so that the doxology comes after the curse. But that is not how they are given. We do not know how to adjudicate between them. They are both given us as witnesses of this powerful, troubled faith. They both belong to this prophetic life of vitality and fidelity.[80] Such faith as Jeremiah's has seasons of trustful resolution and of bitter alienation. The two moods here in juxtaposition perhaps echo God's way with Jerusalem, which also knows about judgment and promise, about alienation and resolution. The alienation never quite reaches nullification.[81] The resolution seems never to be total. Both speeches of reassurance and of harsh protest are on the way. It is a troubled way, but it is the only way available to Israel.

There can be little doubt that this entire piece of poetry (vv. 7-18) partakes in *conventional forms* from the life of Israel, in turn lament and curse. There also can be little doubt that the poem reflects the *personal intensity and passion* of Jeremiah. The recognition of those two factors, however, still leaves us with the hard question of the public character of this poem. In what way or sense can the poem be the voice of public Israel? If the cry is only from the person of Jeremiah, then the poem has no larger or enduring interest. If, however, the poem is about the unwelcome, unbearable power of the Word, about the seductive way of God with the messenger, about the capacity to praise the God who sends the Word, about the despair evoked among those who embrace the Word, then the poem is a theological disclosure which concerns the whole community of the Word. In this way, I submit, the poetry of the person may be appropriated and appreciated by the canonical community which continues to reflect on the message to the community. In the long run the message is of more interest to Israel than is the personal anguish of the messenger. While they cannot be separated, it is only interest in the message that lets this poetry of the messenger be taken up into the awareness and memory of the community.

80. The antithesis of "vitality" and the "embrace of death" that Jeremiah approaches here is greatly illuminated by the subtle discussion of Robert J. Lifton, *The Broken Connection* (New York: Simon and Schuster, 1980), esp. chs. 12-15. Lifton (153-154) reviews a case study of a person who "swung between total submission and violent image-feelings." Jeremiah seems to swing precisely between "total submission" (vv. 11-13) and "violent image-feelings." Lifton observes that his subject experienced "the absence of an in-between capacity for anger and rage." I suggest that Jeremiah's poetic outbreak in vv. 14-18 is for him (and characteristically for Israel) the "in-between capacity for anger and rage" that limited the destructive force of images of violence.

81. On "nullification" and the capacity of God to work a newness in the "null-point," see Walther Zimmerli, *I Am Yahweh* (Atlanta: John Knox, 1982), 111-133, esp. 115, 133.

Judgment and Hope

Jeremiah 21:1–25:38

We group these several chapters together largely as a matter of convenience, because it is difficult to detect an intentional ordering. These chapters do cohere, however, around two themes: judgment and hope. The assertion of judgment is heavy, consistent, and non-negotiable. Beyond the judgment, these texts offer important hints of hope. Chapter 21 is a general statement of judgment; chs. 22:1–23:8 more specifically indict the kings, and 23:9-40 is a specific judgment against the prophets. The materials on kings and prophets are not in the first instant related to the general indictment of ch. 21, but the theme is common enough to make sense out of the placement of the materials. Chapter 24 issues a powerful, if surprising offer of promise, and ch. 25, in language that is extreme in the Jeremiah tradition, sounds both judgment and hope. These five chapters together assert that God is doing something radical concerning Judah and Jerusalem which is marked by an awesome and frightening discontinuity.

The Fire Next Time (21:1-14)

This passage, like much of the text, is set in the midst of the Babylonian threat. The first invasion by Babylon in 598 B.C.E. has left Jerusalem crippled and fearful, with the uncertain Zedekiah on the throne. The yet-to-come disaster of 587 is only vaguely anticipated, but not so vaguely as to avoid profound anxiety. The king is troubled. The chapter is arranged

188

as a question to which four answers are given. The first two answers, in vv. 3-7 and 8-10, are prose and are stylistically congenial to the question of vv. 1-2. The second two answers (vv. 11-12, 13-14) are poetic units that are intentionally placed here, though probably not originally articulated for this context.

21:1-2   The question posed to Jeremiah by the king and priest here is an urgent one asked in the face of a grave political threat. Judah knows that such political questions cannot be separated from the reality of God and God's purpose. The text intends high irony that the king and priest, leaders of the establishment which has resisted Jeremiah, are finally driven to the prophet as a last resort. Conventional forms of strategy and policy have failed. Finally the sovereign word of Yahweh must be taken into account (cf. ch. 37). Babylon is on the move. The king has no recourse except the prophet. The prophet has been perceived as an adversary of the throne, but now everything short of this adversary has failed. The imperative "inquire of the LORD" is not simply a directive to acquire factual data. The request includes a search for information, but it goes beyond information to urge a fresh commitment of loyalty to Yahweh (cf. Amos 5:4, 6; Isa. 55:6). The issue concerns a restored, trusting relation that goes beyond any new data. The question is to discern whether Yahweh is reliable and faithful in this crisis.

    Jeremiah 21:2 contains a marvelous rhetorical tension. The appeal is to "Yahweh's wonderful deeds," that is, the old memory of saving deeds that focuses on the Exodus. The inquiry is to find out if that economy of historical support is still operative. If the God who defeated Pharaoh is still available, then there is hope. That powerful appeal to the old saving traditions is undermined by "perhaps," however, which makes appeal to the tradition of mighty deeds tenuous at best. The question yearns and hopes that the prophet will give assurance that the old categories are still at work and that God will do one more "wonderful deed" to save, against rapacious imperial power from Babylon.

21:3-7   Jeremiah's answer, however, is not to the liking of the king, nor does it provide any ground for certitude. The first response is addressed directly to the king. It is dominated by a series of first person verbs: "I will turn back, I will bring together" (v. 4), "I will fight" (v. 5), "I will smite" (v. 6), "I will give (deliver)" (v. 7). The rhetorical pattern of this response is shaped by the old modes of faith. The same powerful verbs that have resounded in Israel's life are still operative. Yahweh still acts and still takes decisive initiative. Yahweh is still the subject of the great active verbs.

The astonishing surprise of the answer in vv. 3-7 is that the old rhetoric is now inverted, so that the great verbs of the tradition are now used precisely against Judah, and therefore in favor of Babylon. Jeremiah has reversed the credo tradition of Judah to use against Judah. It is Judah who will now be without weapons, utterly vulnerable, completely helpless (v. 4). The most telling inversion is in v. 5, which uses the particular language of the Exodus. The notion of "outstretched arm and strong hand" is an old formula (Deut. 26:8; Ps. 136:12), now used against Judah by Yahweh, who has become Judah's enemy.

Jeremiah 21:7 seems to be added in case the preceding is not quite clear. The initial invasion was to cause pestilence, sword, and famine, a conventional recital of curses. Verse 7 adds the proviso that if any do not succumb to these curses, they will nevertheless face the direct power of Babylon. This oracular statement envisions no escape. It is addressed to the royal dynasty and to the entire city. The climactic statement uses the old harsh formula originally enlisted to resist Canaanite ensnarement: "no pity, no sparing, no compassion." Zedekiah's inquiry is answered, and the answer is not ambiguous. As much as any text in the tradition of Jeremiah, this one announces the nullification of all of God's old commitments to this special arrangement. The pathos of the announcement is intensified because it is envisioned as a result of Yahweh's "wonderful deeds."

There is important and intentional irony in the juxtaposition of Zedekiah's request and the prophet's answer. Zedekiah had asked for assurance about Yahweh's "wonderful deeds" (v. 2). The prophet, especially in v. 5, answers in Exodus language, thus alluding to "wonderful deeds," only now inverting them so that they are deeds *against* Judah and not *for* Judah, as anticipated by the king.

21:8-10   The second answer is addressed to the people, not the king. While the first response drew on the tradition of the Exodus, the second answer draws on the tradition of the Deuteronomist. Interestingly, the judgment is not massive or ruthless. Yahweh offers an invitation parallel to Deut. 30:15-20. Whereas 21:3-7 announced only death, these verses allow a chance for life. The way of death is to stay in the city and resist

Babylon. To stay in the city means sword, famine, and pestilence (v. 9a). This part of the second response is parallel to vv. 3-7. The announcement is ideologically pure, offers no reservations, and is experientially probable. An occupied city is likely to foster famine and pestilence after the sword.

Verses 8-10, however, move beyond the vision of death with which vv. 3-7 end. These verses offer life, hope, an alternative possibility. To be sure, "this city" is under Yahweh's resolve for evil and cannot be saved (v. 10). Included in the reference to "this city" are the social ideology and policy of the throne and temple, and the power arrangements that sustain that ideology and policy. But individual persons need not go down with the city. The inhabitants of the city can escape. The judgment is against the arrogant temple and the self-serving monarchy. It is as though a distinction is made between "people" and "government," as we often do with reference to "the Russian people," or "the Cuban people." The oracle provides an out for the "people of Jerusalem." That is why vv. 8-10 are addressed to people, unlike vv. 3-7, which are addressed to the king. The alternative possibility is to "go out" to Babylon, to submit and find life.

It is worth noting that the verb "go out" (v. 9) is *yatsa,* the primary word for "exodus." Perhaps the usage is an accident, as it is a quite ordinary word. But in light of the explicit Exodus language (v. 5) and in light of the yearning for "wonderful deeds" (v. 2), it may be suggested that Judah's hope now is an exodus away from the "bondage" of Jerusalem to an odd "freedom" under Babylon. Perhaps this conclusion simply reflects the Deuteronomic bias in favor of Babylon. In any case, there was a lively, difficult, and urgent debate in Jerusalem about the possibilities still available. Some wanted to stay and fight. Others (including Jeremiah) saw surrender as a way of survival. While that must have been an ambiguous question for the contemporaries of Jeremiah, the book of Jeremiah insists upon a convergence between Babylonian policy and the will of Yahweh. Response to Yahweh now implies submission to Babylon. Because this convergence is now established in the canon, it cannot be explained simply on grounds of political calculation. The convergence is asserted on the basis of theological conviction. God wills submission as the door to a future community life.

21:11-12 The third answer is again addressed to the monarchy. It is probable that this is a free-standing prophetic oracle, with no particular reference to the question of vv. 1-2, nor to the immediate quandary of

Zedekiah. It is a conventional urging about the covenantal character of the dynasty and could have been uttered in many contexts. The address in v. 12 is formal and impersonal — "house of David." This word is addressed to any Judean king in any context. It is the voice of the old covenant urging a covenantal, obedient shaping of royal power and policy.

The structure of the passage is a double imperative: "execute justice," "deliver," followed by a "lest" of avoidable consequence (v. 12). The same structure of multiple imperatives followed by "lest" is found, for example, in Deut. 8:11-17 and Amos 5:6. The double imperative (Jer. 21:12a) articulates the insistence of the Mosaic, prophetic tradition that the purpose of the monarchy is to assure justice for the marginal, weak, and helpless. This insistence on the priority of social well-being is offered against the monarchy's temptation to self-seeking and self-serving. Only a commitment to justice will secure the monarchy.

The threat introduced by "lest" (v. 12b) is equally conventional. It introduces the standard threat of the royal apparatus being burned in judgment (cf. Amos 1-2). Its placement in this location may have been suggested by the reference to fire in Jer. 21:10. The tradition relentlessly asserts that concentrations of power (i.e., monarchies) that are inattentive to the weak will surely end in disaster. It is assumed by the poem that no strategy of state, no matter how wise or strong, can be a substitute for the simple connection of justice and well-being that is foundational to all social reality. Justice prevents destructive fire. Conversely, injustice brings destructive fire. No substitute for justice can preclude destruction, even though every established power imagines the linkage can be broken. There is a moral coherence to the political process, and that moral coherence is guaranteed by Yahweh, who finally cannot be ignored.

Verses 11-12 are lean and clear. They reiterate an old prophetic claim that the practice of justice is the source of well-being. Placed in this chapter, however, the two verses give a surprising answer to the question of vv. 1-2. In verses 11-12 there is still time and opportunity to avert the Babylonian fire. The chance for escape that is offered is drawn from the essential covenantal character of Israel. The possible escape from judgment in these verses does not come by submitting to Babylon, but by doing what is most characteristic for Israel, namely justice. Verses 1-2 asked for a "wonderful deed." There is need for a new wonderful deed, for the old wonderful deed of the Exodus has now been forfeited. There is still a chance for life, but the chance depends on justice from the royal establishment.

The first three answers to Zedekiah's inquiry of Yahweh are of very different kinds:

- vv. 3-8: inescapable destruction of the whole,
- vv. 9-10: a chance for escape by surrender and exile,
- vv. 11-12: a chance to save the whole by the practice of justice.

The three alternatives may represent different perceptions in response to different circumstances, but they also reflect different theological traditions. The first (vv. 3-8) asserts that Yahweh's only mighty deed will be to destroy. The second (vv. 9-10) believes that the mighty deed of saving will be mediated through the painful process of submission to Babylon and exile. The third (vv. 11-12) makes social justice a prerequisite for a saving deed, which is still an available option. This third is most powerfully rooted in the Mosaic tradition and least concerned to accommodate present circumstances.

21:13-14   The fourth answer is not in any direct way related to the preceding. It is a poetic fragment that lacks even the specificity of vv. 11-12. It apparently has no reference to either Zedekiah or Babylon. Its substance is most congruent with the first answer of vv. 3-7, though there is no specific link even to that statement.

The opening address to "inhabitant of the valley, rock of the plain" completely lacks a concrete reference. The oracle ostensibly is given against and in response to the question in v. 13b, "Who shall come down against us?" Perhaps the question is a request for information. More likely, it is a statement of defiance: that is, none would dare come against us; none would possibly succeed against us.

While the address of the oracle is unclear and the question is somewhat ambiguous, there is nothing unclear or ambiguous about Yahweh's answer (v. 14): "I will punish." Yahweh directly and personally will intervene in Judah's history. There is no mediating agent. Yahweh does not utilize Nebuchadnezzar. History is governed and judged by none other than Yahweh, who is able to intervene and can indeed enter any habitation. None are safe from Yahweh. The response of Yahweh contains elements of lawsuit. The sentence is fire; the indictment "the fruit of your doings." Judah's deeds evoke Yahweh's fire. The situation is not remote from that of vv. 11-12, but now Judah's circumstance is greatly deteriorated and therefore more hopeless.

It is difficult to know why vv. 13-14 are included here. The most likely reason is the mention of "fire," which coheres with vv. 10 and 12. Thus the latter three units all speak about a terrible destruction by fire. The notion that the city will burn reflects the deep antithesis of the prophetic tradition to urban monopolies of money, power, and religious pretense. God finds such self-serving concentrations of power deeply inimical to the covenant and to the possibility of humaneness. The image of fire evokes a harsh and total destruction.

If, as the text now stands, all four units are answer to the question of vv. 1-2, the king probably wishes he had not asked. The first answer (vv. 3-7) and fourth answer (vv. 13-14) offer no hope. The second answer (vv. 8-10) gives hope in exile, and the third answer (vv. 11-12) gives hope through radical social reorientation. None of these answers is bearable for the king and his company. The desperation of the situation had driven King Zedekiah to Jeremiah and to Yahweh. But no solace is given by the prophet. The question was asked with a hopeful "perhaps" (v. 2). At most, the response is a tenuous possibility, so tenuous that the king was unable to seize upon it. Zedekiah can only wait for "the fire next time."[1]

Oracles on the Kings (22:1–23:8)

The Jeremiah tradition is concerned with Jerusalem as a comprehensive social reality. But more particularly it is the king (and the dynasty) that embody the entire urban establishment. The conduct of the king is decisive for the weal or woe of the entire social system. The prophetic critique of kingship in this chapter has a double focus. On the one hand, as an embodiment of a self-serving ideology, the monarchy in principle is critiqued as disobedient and irresponsible. On the other hand, particular kings are handled in relation to specific items of conduct and policy. The tradition of Jeremiah takes a critical view both toward specific kings and toward the foundational claims of the institution of monarchy. Chapter 22 asserts that the trouble coming upon Jerusalem is trouble caused by the monarchy. While the entire chapter concerns the monarchy, a division may be usefully made between vv. 1-9 and vv. 10-30.

1. The phrase derives from the ominous formulation of it by James Baldwin, *The Fire Next Time* (New York: Dial, 1963).

The Royal House (22:1-9)

In vv. 1-9 we have a very general poetic unit concerning the Davidic house. This unit lacks contextual clues. Its pronouncement concerns the general attitude of prophets toward kings. The oracle is not dated, and the king is not named. It is a free-floating oracle which could have been used and placed in various contexts.

22:1-7 These verses consist of a quite stylized speech plus a poetic fragment. The address is formal, "King of Judah." Verse 3 lays down the main program of a covenantally-instituted monarchy. It begins with Israel's primary words addressing social responsibility, "justice and righteousness." These two words are found in the program of Ps. 72, in the royal corona-tion oracle of Isa. 9:7 (and its antithesis in Isa. 5:7), in the celebration of Solomon in 1 Kgs. 10:9, and in the sapiential rationale for kingship in Prov. 8:20. The two words taken together characterize social power and social practice in which there is strong support and care for the socially weak and marginal. (The critical statement of Ezek. 34:1-10 characterizes royal power that reneges on this central mandate.) The remainder of Jer. 22:3 gives details of what justice and righteousness entail, the language of which closely parallels the prophetic summons of 7:5-7. The entire pro-gram is care for the marginal and powerless. That is the business of kings.

Jeremiah 22:4-5 contains a quite symmetrical statement concerning the assured gains and losses related to the imperatives of v. 3. This unit is arranged in two parallel "if . . . then" structures, one positive and one negative. The positive promise of v. 4 indicates that if the monarch "listens," all dimensions of royal power, including horses and chariots, will be guaranteed. The negative counterpart in v. 5 is that if the king does not attend to justice and righteousness, the "house" (i.e., the temple and dynasty) will be leveled. The "if . . . then" structure of these verses is remarkable, for this rhetoric makes the monarchy explicitly conditional.

The question of conditionality is the subject of a very old dispute in Israel.[2] The Mosaic community knew the covenant was based on the

---

2. Jon D. Levenson, *Sinai and Zion* (Minneapolis: Winston, 1985), has in general resisted the bifurcation in the OT between conditional and unconditional aspects. However, I do not see how these tendencies when expressed concretely in the text can be harmonized.

fragile condition of obedience (cf. Exod. 19:5-6), but the royal ideology of Jerusalem regarded God's commitment as unconditional (2 Sam. 7:14-16; Ps. 89:24-37). Various articulations can be identified that fall between these two alternative interpretations.[3] The options in Jer. 22:4 and 5 may formally be symmetrical, suggesting that the monarchy still has a choice. But judgment for the monarchy is announced, because the monarchy has not and will not meet the requirements of justice and righteousness.[4] While this "if . . . then" argument may be a statement under the influence of the Deuteronomist, it is also consistent with the old Mosaic covenant tradition which we expect Jeremiah to articulate. The net effect of the "if . . . then" formula is to subordinate the monarchy to the torah, its requirements, and its sanctions.[5] This subordination deabsolutizes the monarchy and makes the king, like everyone else, subject to the demands of torah.

By themselves, vv. 4-5 suggest that Jerusalem still has a chance, if it will obey. The positive choice is still available. As the text stands, however, vv. 6-7 close off that option and announce judgment. Verses 6-7 are marked off rhetorically as an independent poetic piece. In their present context after vv. 4-5, however, they function to deny the possibility vv. 4-5 seemed to have offered. The time for a positive choice has passed. Judah and its kings are at a point of no return.

Verses 6-7 present a great reversal, in which the high one is brought low and there is no more chance for rectification.[6] The metaphor is that the dynasty is high, great, and majestic, like the fertile land of Gilead or

---

3. See Walter Brueggemann, *David's Truth in Israel's Imagination & Memory* (Philadelphia: Fortress, 1985), esp. ch. 4, for the continuing theological power of the David tradition. The split between conditional and unconditional is no doubt an ideal construct which permitted many different nuances in concrete expression.

4. This text is like 18:1-12, in that it announces a theoretical possibility of change but then the realistic conclusion is drawn that Judah is at the point of no return. The theoretical possibility is acknowledged, but is no longer available. On this strategy, see A. Vanlier Hunter, *Seek the Lord!* (Baltimore: St. Mary's Seminary & University, 1982).

5. The Deuteronomist also struggles with the relation of torah and king. The primary inclination of the Deuteronomist is to subordinate the king to the torah. See, e.g., Deut. 17:14-20; 1 Sam. 12:13-15, 25.

6. On the devastating reversal, see Isa. 2:9-22; 47:1-3, which is the antithesis of the positive reversal of 1 Sam. 2:6-8; Ps. 113:7-9; Luke 1:51-53. The Jeremiah tradition is fully informed by both modes of inversion.

the powerful cedars of Lebanon (cf. Isa. 2:12-17). Yet such height will not deter Yahweh. Yahweh will turn the fertile land into wilderness (Jer. 22:6b; cf. the contrast in Isa. 35:1-2). Agents of destruction will be dispatched by Yahweh (Jer. 22:7b). The best cedars will be cut and used only to fuel a fire of destruction. The poem moves at various levels of power. It moves in the direction of an apocalyptic conflagration. It also hints at the overthrow of a despised regime in which the oppressed sack and ravage all that remains when the power is gone. Faithful to the poetic and imaginative idiom, the destroyers are not named, but in the name of Yahweh they will commit massive destruction. The dynasty is under severe judgment, without invitation to repent. The live options given in vv. 4-5 are completely nullified. The monarchy has created for itself a situation of hopelessness.

22:8-9 These verses appear to be a prosaic clarification of what has preceded. In the poetry of vv. 6-7 no specific reason is given for the harsh judgment. These verses supply the reason with a simple "why . . . because" structure of question and answer. The answer is that they have forsaken "the covenant of the LORD their God." The punishment matches the affront. Israel "forsook" *('azab)* the covenant, and is now a forsaken people (cf. Isa. 54:6). Again the decisive term *'azab* is used, in parallel with worship of other gods. The harshness of judgment derives from the most fundamental violation of Yahweh's covenant. The contrast of this judgment with the condition of Jer. 22:3 is important. In v. 3 the conditions for continued covenant are ethical, without explicit theological reference. In v. 9 the reason for destruction is theological without ethical specificity. One may argue that the two different reasons reflect different theological traditions and different editorial layers. Or one may credit the tradition with understanding that the ethical conditions of v. 3 and the theological reason of v. 9 are in fact synonymous, a point made clear in vv. 15-16.

For all of vv. 1-9, the main point is that even such a powerful institution as the monarchy must meet elemental requirements of human compassion and responsibility in order to survive. The fulfillment of these requirements is glaringly absent in Jerusalem. The consequences are unavoidable and should not come as a surprise. Again, the text provides an unambiguous and remarkably disciplined conclusion. The text is an invitation for each new generation to reflect on the uncompromising condition Yahweh has set for historical well-being. The way of a people in history cannot, by any stratagem, circumvent the elemental requirements of humaneness. The historical process is finally and inescapably a moral process. The judgment of God is not "supernaturalist," but is worked out in the discerning dynamics of power transactions in social relations.

The Failure of Monarchy (22:10-30)

The remainder of the chapter now explicates these general statements through reference to specific kings. This section reads like a chronicle of kings during the years of Jeremiah and the last days of Judah.[7] A general review and critique of kings evidences the claim that kings are subject to assessment by the prophets, who represent the real governance of Yahweh. The prophets speak of Yahweh's rule which stands in tension with the rule of the Jerusalem regime (cf. Isa. 6:1). Such a prophetic review has the dramatic effect of destabilizing or delegitimizing absolute royal claims made by Davidic kings. The tradition of Jeremiah is preoccupied with the authority of the prophetic word as a decisive mode of God's governance, which inherently threatens the monarchy. That preoccupation in Jeremiah can be traced back to the call narrative of Jer. 1:4-10. Kings are assessed by their response to this strange governance of Yahweh.[8]

22:10-12 In these verses the first reference to a specific king includes a general poetic statement and a specific prose comment. The contrast in the poetry of v. 10 is between Josiah ("him who is dead") and Jehoahaz

7. See John Bright, *Jeremiah*, 2nd ed., Anchor Bible 21 (Garden City, N.Y.: Doubleday, 1978), 144-146. The important point is that the chronicle is subjected to a very particular criterion of assessment, namely justice and righteousness. For a critical historical assessment of these kings, without the particular theological norm of justice and righteousness, see J. Maxwell Miller and John H. Hayes, *A History of Ancient Israel and Judah* (Philadelphia: Westminster; London: SCM, 1986), 391-415.

8. As the Jeremiah tradition is now constructed, the word is addressed "to the nations and to the kingdoms" (1:10). Among these, clearly the first nation/kingdom addressed is Judah, i.e., the kings of this chapter. The claim of the tradition is that Yahweh's work of "plucking up and tearing down," of "planting and building" is the way in which Yahweh presides over the kings. Jeremiah is party to the notion that the monarchy, like the temple establishment, finally must answer to the God of the torah. Torah is a more elemental theological construct than is monarchy.

("him who goes away").[9] Josiah was an effective king who died in a military action and is much celebrated by the traditions of Jeremiah and the Deuteronomist (cf. 2 Kgs. 23:25). At his death, his son Jehoahaz was placed on the throne by a popular movement, but was immediately deposed by the Egyptians, who carried him into exile in Egypt (2 Kgs. 23:30-33). There he died (cf. 2 Kgs. 23:34). The poetic verse of our unit suggests that the real weeping in grief should not be for dead Josiah (Jer. 22:10). Josiah has escaped the trouble through his death and is now better off. It is his son in exile who faces the real problem and needs to be grieved, for exile is more cruel than an honorable death.

The refrain is constant in all three verses:

- never return (v. 10),
- never return (v. 11),
- never see the land (v. 12).

The unit asserts the dread and finality of exile. The king himself is of little interest to the tradition. He is, however, a sign of the failure and the judgment of the monarchy. The kings in Jerusalem, of which Jehoahaz (Shallum) is a sorry case in point, are unable to cope either with internal threat or with the resolve of God. Monarchy is no barrier against God's ultimate nullification of Jerusalem. Royal ideology and pretension are quickly dismissed. Grief for the king is in fact grief for Jerusalem, now under certain death sentence.

22:13-19   This unit has two parts. In the second part, Jehoiakim is named (v. 18) and vv. 18-19 are a funeral lament for him. The poetry is an anticipation of his death, in which he will be mocked, scorned, and dishonored. The poet skillfully discredits and dismisses the failed kingship of Jehoiakim by portraying a death in which there is no adequate funeral and no serious grief.

Verses 13-17 lack specificity, but the reference to a king and his father (v. 15) parallel the identity of father and son in v. 18. We may therefore understand this unit to be a contrast between the well-respected father, Josiah, and the contemptible Jehoiakim, who is the real subject of this

---

9. The king, Shallum, is mainly referred to elsewhere by his throne name, Jehoahaz. Cf. *A History of Ancient Israel and Judah*, 402.

unit. Josiah is simply a foil to this pitiful son Jehoiakim, who succeeded his brother Jehoahaz on the throne in 609 B.C.E. and lasted until 598. It is an irony of Judean history that Jehoiakim engaged in dangerous political exploitation and adventurism, evoking the wrath of Babylon, but died well and comfortably before the Babylonian Empire responded (2 Kgs. 24:5-7). The biblical tradition judges him to be contemptible. He brought upon his people costly trouble, which he himself did not experience.

The poetry of Jer. 22:13-17 has three elements. First, vv. 13-14 are a radical critique of the false use of power. The "woe formula" is an announcement that death will come. The formula anticipates a funeral for a governance whose death is already underway. This formula is not spoken in harshness, but in grief, concerning the inevitable outcome of long-term systemic irresponsibility on the part of the king. This critique is expressed in the verbs following the woe — "who builds," "who makes," "who says," "who cuts." All four verbs concern economic exploitation, rendering others subservient for the sake of self-aggrandizement. The key concern of the poem, stated at the outset, is injustice and unrighteousness (v. 13), precisely the antithesis of the imperative of v. 3. This king, apparently Jehoiakim, has violated the most elemental responsibility of covenantal kingship. He has violated what it means to be king in order to enhance his own prestige by his conspicuous consumption.

Second, vv. 15-16 are a stunning act of social criticism, the most poignant of its kind in the entire Bible. The poet raises the question of what constitutes legitimate social power. He asks with disdain if it is visible luxury that constitutes kingship. That rhetorical question is answered in vv. 15b-16 by comparison to Josiah, who "did justice and righteousness." Again the key terms, "justice and righteousness," occur, placed in contrast to the seductions of cedar and vermillion, marks of affluence. "Justice and righteousness" are a precise contrast to the base, self-serving values of Jehoiakim. As a result of his social policy of caring for the weak and needy, Josiah prospered and had secure rule. Josiah is characteristically regarded as the king who executed policies according to the covenantal requirements of the Deuteronomist. He is portrayed as the embodiment of the best of Moses' covenantal dream.

The final line of v. 16 is one of the most remarkable in Scripture. It equates "knowing God" with doing justice to the needy.[10] The equation

10. Jose Miranda, *Marx and the Bible* (Maryknoll, N.Y.: Orbis, 1974), 44-53, has most clearly grasped the radical subversiveness of this poetic unit.

needs to be seen in its full claim. It is not asserted that knowledge of God leads to justice, nor conversely is it claimed that social justice leads to knowledge of God. They are the same. One might, on the basis of this text, conclude that the practice of justice is the very reality of Yahweh. In this text we are very close to the contemporary conversation about *praxis* as the mode of faith. In the most radical terms, this poetry anticipates John Calvin's judgment that right knowledge of God comes through obedience.[11]

The third element in this section (v. 17) brings the two previous ones together. On the one hand, v. 17 reiterates the judgment of vv. 13-14. On the other hand, it continues the contrast of Jehoiakim with Josiah, for Josiah would never practice oppression and violence. Josiah had not succumbed to a self-serving royal ideology, but still understood that the king exists for the people. Jehoiakim is thus exposed as one who imagines he is autonomous and does not need torah. Such autonomy destroys its practitioner, and destroys society at the same time. Josiah is offered as a norm by which Jehoiakim is to be judged. No wonder the first word is "woe" (v. 13), as is the last word (v. 18; RSV "Ah!"). It is the only word the poet has for this king. Death is destined to come, and when death comes, the king not only dies but brings his city down with him.

Four possible statements of grief are suggested in v. 18, and all four are rejected: "ah . . . ah . . . ah . . . ah."[12] It is astonishing to have the death of the king envisioned, and then to have public grief precluded. The poet wants the utter shame and humiliation of this king to be clear. The poem is a dramatic act of delegitimation for a king who merits no honor.

11. John Calvin, *Institutes of the Christian Religion*, I, vi, 2 (Library of Christian Classics [Philadelphia: Westminster; London: SCM, 1960]). See also Charles M. Wood, "The Knowledge Born of Obedience," *Anglican Theological Review* 61 (1979): 331-340. Daniel W. Hardy and David F. Ford, *Praising and Knowing God* (Philadelphia: Westminster, 1985), argue and indicate by their title that knowledge of God comes through praise of God. Calvin, I think, would not disagree, for he would not make a deep distinction between praise and obedience, which are the two submissions through which God is known.

12. The term rendered in the RSV four times as "ah" is Hebrew *hoi*, which is a cry in prospect of or in the midst of death. The use of the term summons Judah to an imagined death scene and an appropriate response of grief. The point of the poem is that in a situation where grief is appropriate there will be no grief, because the king will not be lamented.

The dishonor is extended in v. 19. The king is to be treated in death as any other worthless animal carcass, simply disposed of in order not to disrupt the city. The scenario is a remarkably harsh one, appropriate for this most ignoble king. The ground of shame is named at the beginning of the unit in vv. 13-14 — injustice and unrighteousness.

That Jehoiakim apparently died a routine death with a routine royal burial (2 Kgs. 24:6) indicates that the poet's anticipation did not in fact occur. That does not detract, however, from the powerful assertion of this poem that kings as agents of injustice are sure to be dismissed as ignoble, irrelevant, and not grieved or remembered. In the world of royal ideology all kings are honored at death, no matter how bad they have been. But the poet constructs another world, a world of covenantal truth, in which the rule of kings is assessed differently. Through poetic imagination, faithful listeners are invited to break with the make-believe world fostered by royal interest and join the poet's world. The poem fights for the imagination of Israel, to wean Israel away from excessive fascination with the visible power in Jerusalem. The disgrace envisioned for Jehoiakim cuts through the facade of self-serving and self-righteous monarchy which flourished in self-deceiving Israel.

22:20-23   In this long poetic collection on kings the small unit of vv. 20-23 is an intrusion, but it is not inappropriate. Whereas the context asserts judgment on individual kings, these verses assert a harsh judgment on the whole community. We may observe four rhetorical factors that disclose the thrust of the poem. First, the poem begins and ends with "Lebanon" (vv. 20, 23). Lebanon as a geographical reality refers to a far boundary; as a metaphor it refers to pride and security. The poem addresses the community in its strength and prosperity (v. 21). The prophet identifies the crisis while Judah still thought there was no crisis. Second, there is a double "cry out" (v. 20), perhaps echoed in v. 23 with "groan." The cry is a desperate cry for help from someone who is vulnerable, weak, and abused. The juxtaposition of Lebanon and "cry" bespeaks an inversion. The strength of the establishment has been reduced to weakness, its competence to vulnerability and desperation (cf. Exod. 11:4-6). Third, in Jer. 22:21 there is a double use of *shema'*, "I will not listen . . . you have not listened." The decisive failure of Israel is that they did not heed Yahweh, from whom comes their life. Fourth, the verb and noun "shepherd" is *ra'ah/ro'eh*, which is matched by the word "wickedness" (*ra'*,

202

v. 22). These homonyms indicate the connection between the wickedness of not listening and the judgment of being cast to the wind, that is, blown away in exile. The poem ironically asserts that the wind that "scatters" will replace the shepherds that "gather." The once gathered community will be scattered in exile.

The poetic unit of vv. 20-23 begins and ends with reference to "Lebanon." However, this reference is in fact a reference to Israel. The metaphor "Lebanon" is applied to Israel because Israel under Jehoiakim has imitated Lebanon and now is trapped in the same destructive values as Lebanon.[13] Those values are symbolized by "cedar" (cf. vv. 14, 23). The community that relies on the commerce and affluence embodied in cedars is doomed for death as a community that denies covenant (cf. Isa. 2:6-8).

This poetic unit also announces the scattering of a community once powerful. The poetry means to lead reality, to construct for Israel a scenario of an exilic future, even while Judah imagined itself safe. While the subject is different from that of Jer. 22:18-19 and the judgment is much more massive, the primary announcement of exile and death is congruent with the preceding. A harsh, inescapable termination is coming, a hurt like birth pangs (v. 23), only now they are the pangs of death.

22:24-30 The last king mentioned in this unit is Coniah, better known as Jehoiachin (vv. 24-30). He is the son of Jehoiakim, grandson of Josiah. It is his destiny to ascend the throne in 598, just in time to reap the bitter benefits of his father's deathly policies. Within a year of his ascension he is deported to Babylon, where he endures a long captivity (cf. 52:31-34; 2 Kgs. 25:27-30). Jehoiachin receives two distinct treatments in biblical tradition. On the one hand, he bears the hopes of this people and keeps the thread of the royal promise alive; on the other, he is clearly helpless and historically impotent, as he has no chance to act on the hopes he embodies. In this passage Jehoiachin is not a figure of hope. He is only an object for deep pity.

13. For the capacity of Israel's poets to handle metaphors in powerful, subversive, and imaginative ways, see Carol A. Newsom, "A Maker of Metaphors — Ezekiel's Oracles Against Tyre," *Interpretation* 38 (1984): 151-164. See also Paul A. Porter, *Metaphors and Monsters: A Literary-Critical Study of Daniel 7 and 8*, Coniectanea Biblica, OT Series 20 (Lund: C. W. K. Gleerup, 1983; repr. Downsview, Ont.: Reproduction House, 1985).

This unit concerning the last king is divided into prose (Jer. 22:24-27) and poetic elements (vv. 28-30). In the prose of vv. 24-27 Jehoiachin is identified as Yahweh's "signet ring"; the embodiment and sign of dynastic hope, and one of the few assurances of any thinkable future (cf. Hag. 2:23; Zech. 3:8). Nonetheless, he is "torn off" (Jer. 22:24). God is portrayed as an indignant lover who removes a precious ring from his finger and throws it away, nullifying all the hopes and promises that the ring symbolized. The king is rejected. With him the royal line beginning with David is ended and the royal promise nullified. The king and his mother, the bearers of royal identity, are abandoned by God, given over to Babylon.[14] There they died a lonely, disgraced death (v. 26). What was asserted of Jehoiakim in vv. 18-19 is now enacted with his son. This boy-king will be thrown out of Jerusalem, even as the corpse of his father was envisioned as rejected. The royal history of temple and throne is now terminated, albeit only in an imaginative scenario. The historical reality of this poetic scenario became visible a few years later.

The poetic counterpart of vv. 28-30 is one of the most poignant and pathos-filled units in the Bible. The poet articulates the deep anguish of this humiliating rejection of the boy-king. The poet wants his listeners to focus on this boy on whom the whole Jerusalem establishment has staked its future. Now he is rejected, forgotten, disgraced. The metaphor is a broken pot not valued (v. 28; cf. 19:10-11). In the metaphor of potter and clay (already employed in 18:1-4), the potter could reshape and finally reject. Of course it is Israel and not the king who is the clay of Yahweh in chs. 18-19. Here the clay is handled with greater specificity. He is rejected as worthless. His rejection is echoed in Ps. 118:22. Jehoiachin is indeed a rejected stone.

The pathos, however, is not merely over the boy. Where the king is jeopardized, the whole land is vulnerable. The poet articulates a larger grief over the land, which now must die as well (Jer. 22:29). This dirge is lean and stark, and therefore powerful. The poet utters only three bold words: "land, land, land." The dirge is not even couched with the initial "O," which is added in the RSV. It is like the tears and sobs of one who can

14. The mention of the queen mother (v. 26) strikes us as odd. Christopher R. Seitz, "Theology in Conflict: Reactions to the Exile in the Book of Jeremiah" (Ph.D. dissertation, Yale University, 1986), 164-171, has persuasively suggested the cruciality of the queen mother for royal power, and derivatively why she should be expressly mentioned in this context. See also note 16 on p. 131 above.

only name the deceased's name over and over and over. It is important to note than in v. 29 this lean cry of grief belongs to Yahweh, who weeps over land and king. The death is so unbelievable. This good land (cf. 3:19) is now brought to death. Jeremiah 22:30 brings no relief from the death. Perhaps the pathos is not unlike that of a fourth-generation farmer in middle America who watched with choked tears while the bank foreclosed and auctioned the land for the mortgage. One can only say, "Land, land, land," when what has been home is now forfeited.

In Ps. 72 it is the justice of the king that brings prosperity in the land. Where there is no king the land cannot function. The dynastic promise rooted in 2 Sam. 7:13-16 is now terminated, albeit with grief and pathos. Not only is there no visible heir, but Yahweh has been pushed to a point of no return. There will be no heir. That great royal promise of 2 Sam 7:13-16 had appeared to be absolute and unconditional. It was in fact rigorously conditional (cf. Ps. 132:11-12). There would be an heir if the torah were obeyed. No obedience, no heir.

The "if" of Ps. 132:12 is consonant with the "if" of Jer. 22:4-5: the royal mandate is not unconditional. If one asks "why" about the fate of Jehoiachin in v. 28, or "why" more generally in v. 8, the answer is given in v. 9. The answer is the "because" of covenant violation. The invitation in v. 3 is premised on justice and righteousness. The indictment in v. 13 is precisely injustice and unrighteousness. Out of that wickedness of not listening (vv. 21-22), Jehoahaz (vv. 10-11) and Jehoiachin (vv. 24-30) are grieved; Jehoiakim is rejected (vv. 13-19); the city is dismissed (vv. 8-9), and the land is left wretched (v. 29). What could have been according to the promise of Yahweh now cannot be. The poet gives speech to the coming tears of Jerusalem. We dare think they are the tears of God (v. 29; cf. 9:1-2).

A Righteous Branch (23:1-8)

These verses bring to completion the general comment about kings. This unit continues the theme of ch. 22. It is organized around one very general indictment of monarchy and three quite unexpected promises.

23:1-2a The indictment in these verses is a general statement about kings ("shepherds"), parallel to the indictment of Ezek. 34. The "sheep" refer to Judah. There has been a scattering of the sheep (exile) because the shepherds have been inattentive to the sheep (cf. Mark 6:34). The shepherds have been remiss, because they have been preoccupied with themselves and their own well-being. The compelling metaphor of sheep and shepherd makes a powerful political statement. Mismanaged royal power is the single cause of exile. Neglected sheep will predictably be scattered.

The three promises of vv. 2b-4, 5-6, and 7-8 each begin with "behold." The placement of such promises in the Jeremiah tradition is unclear, especially when the promises are explicitly dynastic. The conventional judgment of scholarship has been that the hope passages are late and the dynastic promises are intrusive.[15] Whatever the historical and literary problems concerning these promises, the theological truth is that the tradition of Jeremiah asserts that the God who can nullify Judah can also work a new thing. Thus on theological grounds, these promise passages articulate Yahweh's resolve to work a newness in the face of historical realities and in spite of dynastic failure. The hope of God is not nullified because of Judah's failure. In the long run, and through anguish, God's hope overrides that historical, covenantal failure.

23:2b-4 The first promise asserts that God will act through no human agent, but will directly cause a homecoming. The verb "gather" is a precise resolution of "scatter" in vv. 1-2a, and stays with the metaphor of sheep. The gathering of sheep (as in John 10:1-18) refers specifically to the ending of exile. In our text, it is only after the gathering that new "shepherds" will be established, kings who will do what shepherds are supposed to do. The gathering from exile will be God's own action. Nonetheless there will be human shepherds who are the restored Davidic kings.

The double image of Yahweh as shepherd and of human shepherd reflects a tension (also seen in Ezek. 34:23-24) concerning the role of the Davidic dynasty in the Exile and beyond. There was surely dispute in exilic Judah about the cruciality of the Davidic house for the future. It is clear that the powerful claims for the Davidic house continued to be voiced in

---

15. The assignment of these promises to a later hand is characteristically not based on internal evidence, but on a more general theory of the prophetic literature. Cf. Robert P. Carroll, *From Chaos to Covenant* (London: SCM; New York: Crossroad, 1981), 147-48. A case is made by Bright and William L. Holladay for the assignment of these promises to Jeremiah in his later period. What is overlooked in both of these scholarly conclusions is the place of hope and promise in the tradition.

exile with a yearning for a restored kingdom. But there must also have been an alternative position among exiles which believed that no monarchy was needed when God reconstituted the community. With or without a human king, Judah's hope in exile concerns restoration of an ordered political life in which people are to be cared for, even as they have more recently been neglected. As with all these promises, this one holds together the power of God to create a newness and actual historical possibility. The new community which God gathers is regarded as a real historical possibility. The hope of Israel is concrete, this-worldly, and offered against the despair of present circumstances.

23:5-6 The second promise is the most explicitly Davidic promise in the tradition of Jeremiah (cf. also 33:14-16). The notion of a royal Branch is more appropriately expected in the tradition of Isaiah (cf. Isa. 11:1). The promise is so powerful and pervasive, however, that it also shows up in the tradition of Jeremiah. The usage asserts the conviction that God has not finally abandoned a commitment to the Davidic house. The Davidic possibility is envisioned as a king who will practice righteousness as was required in 22:3 and rejected in 22:13-14. In the days of this promised king (23:6) there will be a royal obedience which will make public life possible. One can see here exilic anticipations for the restoration of a valid public life, the very anticipations that the Christian community has found embodied in Jesus of Nazareth.[16] The new shepherd of the Davidic line is to implement a very old promise to "dwell securely" (v. 6; cf. Lev. 26:5; Ezek. 34:25).

This king will embody righteousness, to which his very name will attest. It is perhaps intentional and ironic that the "real king" anticipated is called "Yahweh is our righteousness" *(Yahweh tsidqenu)*, while the last king of the line up to 587 is Zedekiah ("Yahweh is righteous"). The coming king will be genuine "righteousness" *(tsedaqah)*, whereas the remembered King Zedekiah is not at all an embodiment of righteousness. That king bore the name; the coming king will embody the reality. The proposed name for the new king indicates a governance that brings well-being through justice.

16. It is worth noting that the promise articulated here is taken up in the "Common Lectionary C" in the use of Jer. 33:14-16 during Advent. Quite clearly, the Church has handled the text with reference to Jesus. Such a use requires an interpretive posture that recognizes that the text "does and does not" run toward Jesus.

23:7-8 The third promise asserts that the homecoming out of exile will be more dramatic than the initial Exodus. Liberation from Babylon will be so overwhelming that liberation from Pharaoh will be superseded and therefore not be remembered or spoken of. In 21:2 Zedekiah had asked about Yahweh's doing a new "wonderful deed." We have seen how ch. 21 employs exodus language negatively. In this promise the question of Zedekiah is answered. There will be a new wonderful deed which will displace the Exodus memory. Israel's hope outdistances even its powerful memory. The great gathering of liberated Judeans evidences that Yahweh is faithful and powerful. The land so grieved (22:29) now is a functioning homeland again.

We have seen that the old cannot be mended (19:11). Now God will work a newness (23:7-8). The newness is wrought precisely by God, and precisely in exile. There will be no newness by the operation of the old apparatus, and no newness prior to exile. Life will be lost — and then given again. This God presides over both loss and gift. Notice that the blessings announced are not guarantees of continuity. Rather, they bear witness to the deep discontinuity and imagine that God has power and will to assert the newness again, newness underived from what has gone before.

Oracles on the Prophets (23:9-40)

The traditioning process has brought together in this passage a number of originally independent materials which deal with the general theme of prophetic authority. We may divide the unit into three sections, though even these are likely formed from smaller literary fragments (9-22, 23-32, 33-40).

Jeremiah lived midst a variety of competing "truth claims," each of which purported to be a disclosure of Yahweh's will. In that dispute, there were no objective criteria by which to adjudicate the various claims. Jeremiah is one of the parties to that dispute. In these verses he makes his clearest argument for his version of reality, and makes it against the "truth versions" of others whom he dismisses as false.[17] While the vindication of

17. On conflict between prophetic voices, see James L. Crenshaw, *Prophetic Conflict*, Beiheft zur Zeitschrift für die alttestamentliche Wissenschaft 124 (1971); and Simon J. DeVries, *Prophet Against Prophet* (Grand Rapids: Eerdmans, 1978).

Jeremiah came through the anguish of the historical process, in the dispute itself it was not clear who was telling the truth and who had in fact discerned God's will and purpose. Jeremiah, against the other prophets, announced the end of Judah's "known world." The prophets who opposed him tried in various ways to soften the massive judgment he anticipated. Despite their protestations, that world did end as Jeremiah had announced. The tradition deduced from this outcome that Jeremiah had indeed stood in the council of the LORD. The canonical process that legitimated Jeremiah and excluded the other prophets with their rival message is a recognition of the truth of Jeremiah's perception.

23:9-12 Verses 9-22 are a general assault on prophetic voices that contradict Jeremiah.[18] Verses 9-12, however, are a more general indictment of religious leaders, both priests and prophets. The poet characterizes his deep consternation over the contrast between the words of Yahweh and the betrayals of that word. In vv. 10-11 he makes a connection between the wickedness of the leadership and what that wickedness does to the land. The tradition of Jeremiah is deeply concerned for the future of the land.[19] The land of Judah is so overburdened with evil that it cannot function. The linkage between bad leadership and the condition of the land is a powerful, imaginative assertion (cf. 22:28-30). Because of political abuse, the land is driven to grief and mourning, which take the form of drought. The land is reduced to deathliness because religious leadership is unprincipled and self-serving. Perverted religion produces public crisis. The conclusion of 23:12 is that religious leadership cannot hide in its sanctity, but will be punished.

23:13-15 These verses become more specific. Now the priests are not mentioned. The subject is the prophets, and by v. 15 it is specifically the "prophets of Jerusalem," whom we may take to be the hirelings of the royal-temple establishment. In 3:6-11 we have seen the comparison of

---

18. See Robert R. Wilson, *Prophecy and Society in Ancient Israel* (Philadelphia: Fortress, 1980), 249-251.

19. See Walter Brueggemann, "Israel's Sense of Place in Jeremiah," in *Rhetorical Criticism,* ed. Jared J. Jackson and Martin Kessler, Pittsburgh Theological Monograph 1 (Pittsburgh: Pickwick, 1974), 149-165; and Peter Diepold, *Israels Land,* Beiträge zur Wissenschaft vom Alten und Neuen Testament 95 (1972).

Israel and Judah at the expense of Judah. The same contrast is made here with the same result. The poet is not in fact interested in northern prophets. They are mentioned only as a foil to get at the southern prophets, whose disobedience is more profound than their northern counterparts. The Jerusalem prophets are morally unprincipled. They strengthen the hands of evildoers, that is, they support, endorse, and legitimate public policy that violates covenant (23:14). The verb "strengthen" is noteworthy, for it contrasts with the indictment against Jeremiah — that he "weakens" the hands of the leadership (38:4). The poet understands well the enormous power of religion to legitimate public policy. The religious leadership which opposes Jeremiah legitimates public policy uncritically, and in so doing it generates more wickedness. The outcome is that "all of them" (i.e., the entire population) are like Sodom and Gomorrah: worthy of destruction (cf. Gen. 19:1-29).

The indictment in Jer. 23:15 is not specific. The references to Sodom and Gomorrah and to adultery in v. 14 could suggest that the sins under indictment are sexual. These references do not stand alone, however. The adultery is paralleled by lies (v. 14), so that in all likelihood what is under indictment is a destructive, disobedient, noncovenantal way of ordering *every* aspect of community life. The poet understands that perverted sexuality goes along with a general distortion of public life that touches every phase of economic and political policy. In Ezek. 16:48-52 the metaphor of Sodom is used again with the contrast of Israel and Judah. There the sins of Sodom are "pride, surfeit of food, and prosperous ease," and lack of aid for the poor and needy. If that reference illuminates our poem, then the indictment is a general disregard of Yahweh's purpose of justice and righteousness. Jeremiah 23:15 summarizes the indictment and promises judgment on the distorting prophets.

23:16-17 These verses give more specificity to the conflict over the claims of the prophets. Jeremiah's opponents give assurance of *shalom* ("It shall be well with you"), and assert that no evil can come upon Jerusalem. These opponents are to be credited with some sophistication. They are surely not simply liars, or indifferent to moral matters. They may be quite conscientious, but are able to perceive reality only through the lens of Jerusalem ideology. Their commitment to divine sovereignty and moral sensitivity is filtered through a deep conviction about God's enduring commitment to king and temple. They trusted God's unconditional commitment to the Jerusalem enterprise. Jeremiah, however, dismissed their religious posturing as self-serving ideology which perverts reality and mocks God's truth. Jeremiah sees that Israel's faith is distorted to be a rationale for a particular political claim.

According to Jeremiah, the message of unconditional well-being *(shalom)* is false *(sheqer)*. The prophets' message of *shalom* misreads the historical situation and misrepresents the character of Yahweh, who is uncompromising about the concerns of justice and righteousness. As the message is false, so also the source of the message is false. Reliable prophetic announcement is given from God, but this message comes from the imagination of the prophets, not from God. That is, what claims to be truth is fantasy and wishful thinking. The "visions" of these prophets are not simply the result of personal idiosyncrasy, however. The minds and hearts of the other prophets are shaped by and in the service of the royal ideology. Their words are not private daydreaming, but systemically determined distortion.[20] Thus the contrast in v. 16 between "their own minds" and "the mouth of Yahweh" can be understood as a contrast between royal-temple ideology and the harshness of the covenant tradition. Those whom Jeremiah critiques offer only "vapor" for truth. Their "vain hopes" are not reliable and cannot be acted upon.

23:18-22 These verses reiterate the contention that the establishment prophets speak their own self-serving, uncritical message, unauthorized by Yahweh. These verses appeal to the "council of the gods," which meets to decide their will for the earth.[21] That council is presided over by Yahweh.

---

20. On systemic distortion, see Jürgen Habermas, *Legitimation Crisis* (Boston: Beacon, 1975). Habermas writes of the problems of modernity, but his analysis is helpful for our interpretive work, for Jeremiah was facing precisely the systemic distortion of reality done by the royal-temple enterprise.

21. Patrick D. Miller, Jr., *Genesis 1–11: Studies in Structure and Theme,* JSOT Supplement 8 (Sheffield: University of Sheffield Press, 1978), has explored the rootage of the "divine assembly" of the gods. In "The Sovereignty of God," in *The Hermeneutical Quest,* ed. Donald G. Miller, Princeton Theological Monograph 6 (Allison Park, Pa.: Pickwick, 1986), 130-31, 135-37, Patrick D. Miller, Jr., has explicated the theological significance of the divine assembly. It is noteworthy that he places the imagery of "divine council" under the rubric of Yahweh's sovereign authority. That is exactly what is at work in this text. See also E. Theodore Mullen, Jr., *The Assembly of the Gods,* Harvard Semitic Monograph 24 (Chico, Calif.: Scholars Press, 1980).

When a decision is reached, the council dispatches a messenger (sometimes a prophet) to announce the decision of the gods on earth (cf. 1 Kgs. 22:19-23; Isa. 6:6-8). The messenger who is dispatched has no freedom to give his own opinion, but can only give the verdict reached by the government in heaven.

Jeremiah claims to have stood in that council and been present when the decision about Jerusalem was made (Jer. 23:18). His message, authorized from heaven, is that Jerusalem will be destroyed (vv. 19-20). His claim of authority is expressed in the formula that is repeated throughout the tradition, "Thus says the LORD." That is, the message is from another source and it is not mine. The opponents of Jeremiah cannot legitimately say, "Thus says the LORD," because they have not been given a heavenly message, have not been present when the decree on Jerusalem was announced, have not been authorized or dispatched (v. 21). They have invented their own word and their own authority for the word (v. 22). Thus the dispute is not only about the substance of competing prophetic announcements, but also about the authority that lies behind and justifies those competing announcements. The contrast between Jeremiah and the other prophets can be traced back to the initial statement of Jeremiah's call. The words of 1:7 evoke the image of the messenger dispatched by the divine council:

> To all to whom I send you you shall go,
> and whatever I command you you shall speak. (1:7)

These claims about Jeremiah's vocation are precisely contrasted with the dismissal of his opponents:

> I did not send the prophets, yet they ran;
> I did not speak to them, yet they prophesied. (23:21)

Jeremiah is sent. They are not. Jeremiah is commanded. They are not.

Against this background of the divine council, the final adjudication among these various voices is made on the actual substance of the message. The verdict of the council is negative concerning Jerusalem, and any announcement to the contrary cannot have been generated in the divine council. It is a fantasy to announce well-being when the real verdict is judgment, wrath, and death. God decides God's own mind (in Hebrew, "heart"; v. 20), which is in contrast to the mind (heart) of the false prophets

(v. 16). God is not simply a human projection. The reality of God's heart and God's decision (v. 20) contrasts with the heart and fantasy of Jeremiah's opponents (v. 16).

Beyond the dismissal of the false messengers who do not tell the truth because they have had no access to the truth, this unit makes three additional assertions. First, the judgment against Jerusalem has now been mobilized and will not be deterred. It is sure to come (v. 20). Second, the talk of the earlier prophets had been a call to repentance. Genuine prophetic announcement should have wrought a change.[22] The poem presents a play on the theme of "turn." In v. 20 the anger of the LORD will not turn; in v. 22 people "would have turned." But now there will be no turning, either on the part of God or on the part of his people. Neither will turn. Third, in v. 20 the poet places a most ominous and dread-filled assurance at the center of this unity: "in the latter days." Presumably the latter days are after the destruction, perhaps in exile. Because the prophets have not had a true word, they have not turned Judah from evil. Because they have not turned Judah, God's judgment will not be averted. The awesome reality of God's sovereign rule will be evident as God's anger is implemented. The future of Judah, deathly as it is, is linked to the failure of prophecy.

23:23-32   The critique of false prophets continues in the prose of vv. 23-32. Verses 23-24 assert the sovereign freedom of God. God is not near and available (v. 23).[23] God is unavoidable (v. 24). That God should be "near" is a promise from the temple cult. The assertion that God is distant thus stands over against the temple ideology. God's distance enacts God's freedom, and if God is distant from the temple cult, God is also distant from these domesticated prophets. The claim about God in v. 24 also stands against the dominant ideology. Jeremiah resists the temptation to make God an uncritical patron of the establishment. False prophets always

---

22. Hunter, *Seek the Lord!*, has shown how the prophetic summons to repent is always a previous summons that is no longer possible. The previous summons is characteristically referred to in order to set a context for the present articulation of judgment.

23. See Werner E. Lemke, "The Near and the Distant God: A Study of Jer. 23:23-24 in its Biblical Theological Context," *Journal of Biblical Literature* 100 (1981): 541-555.

seek to draw God too near to favorite arrangements and so minimize God's sovereign freedom.

After this introduction which focuses attention on the character of God, the text turns again to the theme of false prophets. These verses do not state the content of the prophetic lies, though we may assume they are a continuation of v. 17. The text contrasts "lies" (vv. 26, 32) with truth (v. 28). The prophets opposing Jeremiah are false, but they could speak faithfulness. The substance of lies and falseness is that Yahweh's name is forgotten (v. 27), the word of Israel's God is distorted (v. 29), and God's name is taken in vain (v. 31). The effect of all such dreams, fantasies, and distortions is that Judah is led astray, away from God's will into a death-dealing disobedience (v. 32).[24]

We are not told what the specific point of acute conflict is. Verses 23-24 suggest, however, that in the name of the royal-temple apparatus the sovereignty of God has been reduced to uncritical patronage, and the mandate for justice and righteousness has been translated into security and order. God's word is like fire that burns and a hammer that smashes (v. 29). Every other prophetic word that is accommodating and anemic is recognized as an alien word and is not Yahweh's legitimate word. These other prophetic voices have become so perverted, so self-serving in their rejection of Yahweh's true character, that Israel's discernment of God is distorted. The judgment is upon the perverting prophets here, but the terrible end which eventuates will be upon the entire distorted community that can no longer discriminate between the truth of Yahweh's purpose and the falseness of futile attempts at control and self-securing (cf. Isa. 5:20; Ezek. 13:8-16).

Jeremiah 23:23-32 is indeed a dispute between rival prophetic voices which appeal to competing theological traditions. Behind the dispute concerning true and false prophets is a dispute about the character of God. The ideological prophets of the establishment celebrated and affirmed God's nearness and God's abiding commitment to and presence within the Jerusalem establishment. God had become a part of that social arrangement. In sharp contrast, Jeremiah bears witness to a God who is

---

24. This passage has important connections to Deut. 13:1-3, wherein it is asserted that prophets and dreamers will lead Israel away from Yahweh and into disobedience. In our text, Jeremiah locates this religious seduction with the prophets, on the one hand, and with the public political crisis of Jerusalem, on the other hand.

"afar off" — free, sovereign, and not a mere appendage to the established religion. The issue in the dispute is not about the content of a particular announcement, but about God and God's relation to Judah. Until Judah is clear about the character of Yahweh, it will never be clear about the discussion in the divine council, about whom the council may send to Judah, or what the message will be. Jeremiah is unambiguous about the message, because he knows clearly about Yahweh who will govern by his uncompromising will for justice and righteousness. The dispute begins and ostensibly concerns what the other prophets say and do. As the unit is completed, however, it becomes clear that the question of prophetic vocation is secondary to the foundational question of the reality and character of God. In this articulation of Yahweh's character, we are close to the central concern of the tradition of Jeremiah from which all else follows.

23:33-40   These verses are an appendix to the material concerning false prophets. The text appears to be a play on the word "burden" *(massa)*, the meaning of which is obscure. The term "burden" has a double meaning. It can mean an oracle that purports to be a disclosure from Yahweh (vv. 33, 35-36, 37-38). In this text the word also has a second meaning: a weight which Yahweh must carry and which leaves Yahweh exhausted (v. 33).[25]

The text is framed by vv. 33 and 39-40. In both the opening verse and the closing verses, the ones who speak "the burden" are threatened with exile. In v. 39 the threat of being "lifted up" *(nasa)* is linked to the "burden" *(massa)*. An additional wordplay is thus operative. The one who burdens *(massa)* will be lifted up *(nasa)*.

Within this frame, the text is highly problematic. Verses 34-38 seem to revolve around the relationship of the religious professionals to the word, the "burden," of God. There is a rhetorical pattern of alternation

25. Scholarship has not found a helpful explanation beyond the rather obvious point that the word is used in a double way as a homonym and that the power of the text depends on this double meaning. For critical attempts to establish linguistic grounds for the wordplay, see Henry S. Gehman, "The 'Burden' of the Prophets," *Jewish Quarterly Review* New Series 31 (1940/1941): 107-121; and William McKane, "משׂא in Jeremiah 23,33-40," in *Prophecy: Essays Presented to Georg Fohrer on His Sixty-Fifth Birthday,* ed. John A. Emerton, Beihefte zur Zeitschrift für die alttestamentliche Wissenschaft 150 (1980): 35-54.

between assertion and question. Thus in v. 34 the assertion of Yahweh's "burden" is prohibited, but in v. 35 the question about Yahweh's word is legitimated. Again in v. 36 the assertion of burden is prohibited, but in v. 37 the question is permitted. In v. 38 the assertion of the burden is again placed under judgment.

This rhetorical pattern suggests the following conclusion about the proper function of the religious leadership. The prophets and priests seem to presume that they can answer for God, and such presumption is summarily rejected in this text (vv. 34, 38). One can ask about Yahweh's burden, but one cannot presume to know it (vv. 35, 37). Presumptuous knowing, which closes one to true knowing (cf. vv. 23-24), results in being lifted up and cast out into exile. As elsewhere in the Jeremiah tradition, the religious leadership stands under indictment for attempting to curtail and control God's free and full sovereignty.

The Two Baskets of Figs (24:1-10)

This text is dated by the editors between the first deportation of 598 B.C.E. and the second, decisive deportation of 587 (v. 1). During that time, the exiled boy-king Jeconiah (Jehoiachin) was head of the exilic community in Babylon. After the people of Judah were exiled and away from their homeland, they came to be called "Jews." Thus we may refer to this exiled community as the "Jewish community." That reference, however, refers to the same covenanted community which concerns the whole of Scripture, the people of the covenant. It is only because of geographical displacement that the particular word "Jew" became useful and necessary. The community included prominent citizens and skilled artisans (v. 1; cf. 22:24-30). During the same period, the Jews who remained in Jerusalem were presided over by Zedekiah, uncle of Jehoiachin and the third son of Josiah. Zedekiah's status is unclear. Perhaps he is legitimately king (as in 2 Kgs. 24:18), or perhaps he is only regent for Jehoiachin. The uncertainty of his status is no doubt commensurate with the ambiguity and tension between the two communities.[26]

---

26. The dispute between the two communities is well documented and explored by Seitz, "Theology in Conflict." Seitz shows that the historical situation of the two communities evoked very different theological perceptions and conclusions.

The reality of two Jewish communities, one in exile and one in Jerusalem, is peculiarly important for this passage. There must have been rivalry and conflict between a community in exile and a community at home. On the face of it, one would imagine that the ones left behind (even if they are not the leading citizens) must have felt themselves fortunate for not having been deported. It must have been obvious to them that they were God's chosen — not only especially loved, but protected and entrusted with God's future. Given that self-understanding, it would be equally obvious to the ones in Judah that the Jews in exile were not in God's favor. Because they were the ones who suffered the punishment of exile, they must be rejected and judged by God.

This discernment of the historical process and the assignment of roles of favored and judged is the logical discernment. It must have been obvious to both communities, so obvious that it produced respectively a sense of arrogance in Judah and of dejection in exile. The Jerusalem community seemed to have ground for pride, even as the exilic community in Babylon had ground for despair.

The surprise of Jer. 24 is that it does not participate in that logical and obvious discernment. This text proposes a bold alternative interpretation of God's actions and the significance of these two Jewish communities.[27] This text is a polemic against what seems the obvious reading of God's intent in terms of affirmation and rejection. The text presents its alternative reading of historical reality through a vision, through which the prophet sees as others had not seen.

24:1-3 These verses report the vision of two baskets of figs.[28] The baskets of good figs and rotten figs suggest to the prophet communities of "good" and "evil." The oracle does not return to the figs, but instead moves away from the vision to the prophet's interpretation of what he has seen.

27. See Walter Brueggemann, "A Second Reading of Jeremiah After the Dismantling," *Ex Auditu* 1 (1985): 156-168; and David Noel Freedman, "The Biblical Idea of History," *Interpretation* 21 (1967): 32-49.

28. On the phenomenology of visions, see Susan Niditch, *The Symbolic Vision in Biblical Tradition*, Harvard Semitic Monograph 30 (Chico, Calif.: Scholars Press, 1983). The motif of a vision of figs is taken up in the OT elsewhere only in Jer. 29:17. Clearly the tradition is not interested in the phenomenology of vision.

24:4-7 These verses explicate "the good figs," who are the exiles in Babylon. The exiles are regarded as "good" by Yahweh. That is against the more conventional, obvious reading given by Jews in Judah that the exiles are objects of God's judgment. This oracle asserts instead that the exiles are the objects of Yahweh's special favor. Their goodness does not rest in themselves, but in sovereign assertions of Yahweh, who announces them to be good (cf. Deut. 9:6). The freedom of Yahweh in making such a dramatic assertion parallels that of Gen. 15:6, in which Yahweh "reckons" *(hashab)* Abraham to be righteous.[29] This is one of the most stunning theological claims in Jeremiah. The community in exile is the wave of God's future. Such a claim may indeed be self-serving propaganda, or it may simply be pastoral consolation for displaced people. It is nonetheless presented to us in the Bible as a theological verdict by this God who is now allied, by free choice, precisely with the community that the world thought had been rejected. It is indeed an act of free grace which creates a quite new historical possibility. The text thus bears witness to the conviction that this God can and will create a new community from among those rejected.

These exiles now are presented as the object and recipient of God's gracious intervention. God "set my eyes" upon them for good (v. 6). God resolves to return them from exile and to permit them to resume life in the land. In v. 6 the narrative utilizes the powerful verbs of 1:10. Now the positive verbs "plant" and "build" are operative. Indeed, "tearing down and plucking up" have already happened, and now God restores.

In 4:4 the poet had hoped for a change in Israel's heart. Now, however, the solution is more radical. Yahweh will give Israel a new heart (24:7). It is as though the narrative knows Israel can never change its inclination (cf. 13:23). The only chance of newness is due to God's radical and underived action. The gift of a new heart (see also 31:31; Ezek. 36:26) is done by God, because Israel cannot change its heart. Newness out of exile is wrought by God's powerful graciousness.

The purpose of the new heart for Israel is for the sake of a restored covenant with Yahweh: "They shall be my people and I will be their God" (Jer. 24:7). The covenant formula indicates that Israel's autonomy has now been happily displaced by an embrace of covenant. There is no hint that Israel

29. On the term in Gen. 15:6, see Gerhard von Rad, "Faith Reckoned as Righteousness," in *The Problem of the Hexateuch and Other Essays* (1966; repr. London: SCM; Philadelphia: Fortress, 1984), 125-130.

has changed. Rather, God has simply overridden former realities by his power to "regard" the situation afresh (v. 5). That sovereign "regard" makes covenant newly possible. Israel will now embrace its rightful character and live willingly in this relation with Yahweh: "They shall return to me" (v. 7). Israel is now to be who Israel finally must be, the people of Yahweh. God gives Israel "a heart to know" (v. 7a), and so Israel will return with "their whole heart" (v. 7b). Israel with a new heart can now live faithfully and joyously in covenant.

24:8-10 This last part of the speech looks at the other half of the Jewish community. The bad figs are those who were not in Babylonian subjugation but remained in Jerusalem. This is a radical, polemical reading of historical reality. Remaining in Jerusalem or fleeing to Egypt is now regarded as resistance to God's intent and therefore makes one subject to judgment (cf. 42:9-17). The practical effect of this judgment is to delegitimate the rule of Zedekiah. The ones in Jerusalem are not the real Israel of the future, and the one who governs there (Zedekiah) is not the real king of Yahweh's people. Here as elsewhere, the book of Jeremiah operates on the firm conviction that the history ruled by Yahweh has a decidedly Babylonian flavor to it. Those who do not submit to the Babylonian reality are in fact in rebellion against Yahweh's purpose.

The sentence pronounced against the Jewish communities in Jerusalem and in Egypt includes language out of the old curse tradition (cf. Deut. 28:37). Those who refuse Babylon shall be subject to keen ridicule and are to be abandoned and hopeless (Jer. 24:9). The sentence includes the standard threefold curse that is pervasive in the tradition of Jeremiah: "sword, famine and pestilence" (v. 10).

The vision and oracle of this chapter are of particular interest at two levels. First, one may observe how the *claims of a partisan community* come to be regarded as a *normative theological position*. There is no doubt that this text comes out of and reflects the community of Babylonian exiles.[30] The text is a partisan claim concerning who would exercise leadership among Jews and who would take initiative in the coming reconstruction of Judaism after the homecoming. That is, what is cast as religious reality is surely the mobilization of political opinion in a power struggle. While this partisan struggle may be the life setting for ch. 24, the Bible no longer

30. See Ernest W. Nicholson, *Preaching to the Exiles* (Oxford: Blackwell, 1970), 110-111.

presents this text as a self-serving claim. The rereading of history in ch. 24 is presented as a verdict rendered by God. The God of the Bible does indeed take sides in the midst of difficult historical conflicts. The passage may be very close to the cynical notion that winners write history, but we take the claim of this text as much more than that.

Second, we can see how drastic and astonishing are God's judgments in the historical process. The exiles devalued by the world are here identified as the bearer of God's future. This revaluation of the world's rejects is the surprise of the gospel, echoed in so many places. This revolution is evident in God's decision to choose "rabble" to form Israel (Exod. 12:38; Num. 11:4), in Jesus' decision to be friends with sinners (Luke 7:34), in the choice of the lowly, not the wise and the powerful (1 Cor. 1:26-27), in the choice of the stone that the builders rejected (Mark 12:10-11). This God seems indeed to *make* the future with those whom the world judges to be *without* a future.

The Cup of Wrath (25:1-38)

This is an odd and unexpected unit in the Jeremiah tradition. We have encountered nothing like it heretofore. It is a sustained and relentless announcement of God's judgment upon all the nations of the earth — even upon Babylon, who is regarded in most of the Jeremiah tradition to be God's agent. Now the one who has been God's agent stands under God's judgment. Judgment in Babylon, moreover, is inevitably news of rescue for Judah.

25:1-14 The first part of this peculiar chapter opens with familiar, conventional language. The passage is plodding prose, and surely is heavily influenced by the thought of the Deuteronomist. This chapter is rooted in the foundational assumptions of Israel's prophetic tradition, but moves beyond that tradition in articulating a very shrill philosophy of history. The first oracle is dated precisely to 605 B.C.E. (v. 1). That year was a pivotal time in the world of Jeremiah. In the geopolitics of the Near East that year, Babylon emerged as the victor in the battle of Carchemesh and the primal power of world politics.[31]

31. See a summary of the data by Miller and Hayes, *A History of Ancient Israel and Judah*, 403.

Verse 3 gives the date of 626 (thirteen years after 639). This date is reckoned by many scholars as the beginning of Jeremiah's ministry, though others take it to be the date of his birth.[32] Verses 3-7 present a view of the history of Judah from a prophetic-Deuteronomistic perspective (see also 2 Kgs. 17:7-18 and Zech. 1:2-6). This view asserts that (a) the prophets are sent by God, (b) the prophets called Judah to "turn," and (c) Judah refused in its stubbornness to turn. The entire history of Judah is presented as a long history of disobedience and resistance. Such a reading is extended and expanded in Ezek. 16, 20, and 23.[33]

This dismal verdict leads to the harsh sentence of Jer. 25:8-11, which is a summary of the anticipations that have been sounded in the tradition of Jeremiah. The dramatic rhetorical introduction of "Therefore . . . because . . . behold . . ." indicates that we are now at the battle line. The astonishing assertion which opens the argument is that the entire land will be given over into Babylonian control. We are now familiar with this Jeremianic judgment. What is new is that Nebuchadnezzar is explicitly referred to as "my servant" (v. 9).[34] Even alien rulers are utilized to work out Yahweh's purpose. Such a prophetic judgment is an act of theological courage and must have been galling to Judeans. A more palatable, positive counterpart is found in Isa. 45:1, which refers to Cyrus, king of Persia, as "my messiah." Even with such a positive prospect, however, Isa. 45:9-13 reports hostile resistance. If the positive notion that God uses Gentiles to save evokes hostility, we can only guess what was

32. On the chronology as it bears upon this date, see H. H. Rowley, "The Early Prophecies of Jeremiah in Their Setting," in *A Prophet to the Nations,* ed. Leo G. Perdue and Brian W. Kovacs (Winona Lake, Ind.: Eisenbrauns, 1984), 33-61; and William L. Holladay, "The Years of Jeremiah's Preaching," *Interpretation* 37 (1983): 146-159.

33. See Moshe Greenberg, *Ezekiel, 1–20,* Anchor Bible 22 (Garden City, N.Y.: Doubleday, 1983), 270-306, 360-388. Such negative recitals are an inversion of the old recital of God's mighty deeds of rescue. For a juxtaposition of the old recital and the inverted recital of disobedience, see Pss. 105–106.

34. On the theme of Nebuchadnezzar as the servant of Yahweh, see Thomas W. Overholt, "King Nebuchadnezzar in the Jeremiah Tradition," *Catholic Biblical Quarterly* 30 (1968): 39-48; and Werner E. Lemke, " 'Nebuchadnezzar, My Servant,' " *Catholic Biblical Quarterly* 28 (1966): 45-50. Overholt accepts the theological claims of the phrase, "Nebuchadnezzar, my servant," but Lemke has reservations on both critical and theological grounds.

evoked by the announcement that God uses Gentiles to judge. The implicit claim is that God governs gentile history as well as Israelite history (cf. Amos 9:7).

The dominant motif then is that God's sovereignty and governance is massive, irresistible, all encompassing. Yahweh's sovereignty is now turned against Judah. The concrete result is that the old curses will be implemented (Jer. 25:9; cf. Deut. 28:37; Jer. 24:9) and communal life will cease (25:10; cf. 7:34). It is noteworthy that in 25:9 the judgment is said to be "forever" *('olam)*. However, the word *'olam,* which we translate "forever" (RSV "everlasting"), does not mean an absolute, timeless future. Rather, it refers to all thinkable, foreseeable future. That future, however, is always left open for God's new and transformative action. God is not fated even by what is said to be "forever." The Bible asserts that in every circumstance God can work a newness which subverts and astonishes all that we regard as closed, settled, and absolute. At the end of the verdict (v. 11) the subservience to Babylon is for seventy years. The tension between "forever" and seventy years suggests redactional activity.[35] The first statement about "forever" is probably a prophetic verdict, unencumbered by historical specificity. It means "for all foreseeable future." The subsequent "correction" of seventy years may reflect the beginning of historical specificity. That is, either it intends to tone down the horror, or it means to keep the verdict in the realm of historical realism. It may also reflect the actual end of exile and the return of deportees to the homeland.[36]

The reference to seventy years begins to take the poison out of the

---

35. It is exceedingly difficult to know what is intended with "seventy years." It could be simply a traditional number which is appropriate for some matters, such as the duration of a destroyed city; it could be a reference to one generation span as a way of reckoning time, or it could be intended to refer to concrete dates. Cf. Avigdor Orr, "The Seventy Years of Babylon," *Vetus Testamentum* 6 (1956): 304-306, who argues that the apocalyptic tradition of "seventy years" began with a concrete chronological intention.

36. My propensity is to take the number as a limiting factor, but there is no doubt that the reference to "seventy" provides a source from which prophecy begins to move in apocalyptic directions. On that general problem see Michael A. Knibb, "Prophecy and the Emergence of the Jewish Apocalypses," in *Israel's Prophetic Tradition,* ed. Richard Coggins, Anthony Phillips, and Michael A. Knibb (Cambridge and New York: Cambridge University Press, 1982), 155-180.

"forever." It suggests that the harsh judgment is not final and is not to perpetuity. It begins to look beyond judgment to new God-given historical possibilities. Such a move does not lessen the harshness of the judgment. It is rather a disclosure of another dimension of this God who governs the historical process. This God does not "keep his anger forever" (cf. Ps. 103:9). This God chooses different possibilities and gives new gifts. On that basis, the figure of seventy years is a first whisper of hope in the midst of exile. This reference at the edge of Israel's thinking affirms that Israel is now facing Yahweh's second season, a season of new life.

In Jer. 25:12-14 we encounter a quite new move in the tradition. While the seventy years is not usually taken literally, the reference suggests that the hated Babylonian hegemony has its limits and its end point. The text moves on with a *waw* consecutive, rendered "then" (v. 12). God turns against Babylon. According to this philosophy of history, the very empire dispatched by God (v. 9) is now harshly judged by God. The judgment of God against the empire is because of the "iniquity" of Babylon (v. 12). Isaiah 47 provides a more detailed account of this same theological verdict. God did indeed authorize Babylon against Judah (Isa. 47:6). But Babylon, without mercy and with much brutality, overstepped its mandate and was too severe (Isa. 47:6). Babylon is caught in a "no-win" situation, for it is judged by criteria about which it knew nothing. Babylon did not know that Yahweh, even in judgment on Judah ("my people, my heritage") sets limits on what is to be done as punishment. The very agent of punishment is in turn now to be punished. This new posture against Babylon gives new possibilities for Judah's future.

God's work is not ended in the destruction of Jerusalem. God continues to be at work, supervising the nations. Therein lies hope for Israel in exile. The two-stage philosophy of history — Babylonian mandate, Babylonian punishment — indicates that history is finally still governed by Yahweh's compassionate attention to Judah. The same two-stage structure of mandate-punishment is implemented against Assyria (Isa. 10:5-19) and, in a less direct way, against Gog (Ezek. 38–39). The practical effect is that Judah judged now becomes Judah with fresh historical possibility.

The great Babylonian Empire, which seemed eternal and beyond assault, is now to be utterly reduced and finally nullified (Jer. 25:12).

Historical events implemented this verdict: in 537 Persia ended Babylonian imperialism. This text is not a historical comment, however. It is a theological assertion that no nation is finally autonomous and free of Yahweh's rule. Therein lies the source of Judah's judgment, and therein is the basis of Judah's hope. Yahweh rules.[37]

Verse 13 contains an interesting editorial note. In the very text of Jeremiah we find an explicit reference to "the book of Jeremiah." This phraseology makes clear that v. 13 is a late redactional layer of the book, for the writer of this text has already had in hand some version of the book of Jeremiah. Moreover, this later redactional activity seems to complete the book with a denunciation of Babylon (cf. chs. 50–51).

Jeremiah 25:13-14 asserts God's judgment against the empire. In the end, Yahweh's solidarity is indeed with Judah and against Babylon. This occurs, however, only at the end, after "seventy years," after the land had been destroyed. It is most important for Israel (and for us) that Yahweh is not immutable but reverses policy in light of God's own compassion.[38] Israel's hope is precisely in Yahweh's freedom to limit what was "eternal." This is the source of hope offered in our text. It is a sure hope, but it is given voice only in the "second reading" made by the tradition of Jeremiah in the midst of exile.

25:15-29 This section constitutes a startling passage in Jeremiah, expressed in an idiom we have met nowhere else in the tradition. The governing metaphor is "the cup of wrath" which is given by Yahweh and which all the nations are forced to drink. Its content is a sentence of wrath, destruction, and devastation from God's hand, delivered by the prophet and inescapable for the nations. The idiom ("cup of wrath") is apocalyptic (cf. Mark 10:38-39; Rev. 14:10). The metaphor expresses the rhetoric of

37. The general rubric for interpretation is Yahweh's sovereignty, a clue already presented in 1:10. For a critical analysis of such oracles, see Norman K. Gottwald, *All the Kingdoms of the Earth* (New York and London: Harper & Row, 1964).

38. On God's capacity for change through suffering, see Terence E. Fretheim, *The Suffering of God* (Philadelphia: Fortress, 1984); Jörg Jeremias, *Die Reue Gottes: Aspekte alttestamentlicher Gottesvorstellung,* Biblische Studien 65 (Neukirchen-Vluyn: Neukirchener Verlag, 1975); and Walter Brueggemann, "A Shape for Old Testament Theology, II: Embrace of Pain," *Catholic Biblical Quarterly* 47 (1985): 395-415. Jonah 4:1-2 is the clearest articulation of this reality. It is precisely Yahweh's fidelity that requires that God not be immutable.

prophetic judgment writ large.[39] It asserts that the whole world of international order is coming unglued, as God has purposed. Every nation will suffer. It is a vision of God's majestic and sovereign power, from which no nation, kingdom, or empire is immune.

The prophet receives instruction to carry the cup to the nations (Jer. 25:15-16). Already in 1:10 Jeremiah had been sent to the nations. The Jeremiah tradition understands clearly that Judah's destiny in the ancient Near East is connected to that of the other nations. (See this theme explicitly in 29:7.) If Yahweh seriously presides over Judah's future, then Yahweh must also govern the nations. The nations are not autonomous. They finally must answer to Yahweh. They must answer to Yahweh's good news for Judah, whom Yahweh loves.

The command of 25:15-16 is implemented in vv. 17-26. Jeremiah is obedient and delivers the cup. These verses constitute a roll call of the nations of the ancient Near East. All nations are under judgment.[40] Three items are of special interest in this inventory of nations. First, consistent with what we have seen of the Jeremiah tradition, the list begins with Judah and Jerusalem. Judgment begins in God's people (1 Pet. 4:17). Judgment does not stop with God's people, however. It moves out in every direction. Second, the first nation named after Judah is Egypt. The Jeremiah tradition is particularly hostile toward Egypt and regards it as a formidable foil to Yahweh's purpose.[41] Third, last in the list is Babylon (Jer. 25:26). It is almost as if the list deliberately holds off this name for dramatic effect. No nation is immune, not even mighty Babylon. For Jews in exile, the inclusion of Babylon in the list for judgment is decisive. This

---

39. See William McKane, "Poison, Trial by Ordeal and the Cup of Wrath," *Vetus Testamentum* 30 (1980): 474-492. McKane seeks to go behind the metaphor "cup" to find its concrete usage in trial, judgment, and punishment. See 16:7 for a parallel metaphor, "cup of consolation."

40. This large claim is already made for the Jeremiah tradition in 1:10. It is articulated in chs. 46–51, which in the Greek text (widely regarded as a preferred text) are placed in the midst of ch. 25. See J. Gerald Janzen, *Studies in the Text of Jeremiah.* Harvard Semitic Monograph 6 (Cambridge, Mass.: Harvard University Press, 1973), 115-116.

41. See Richard Elliott Friedman, "From Egypt to Egypt: Dtr[1] and Dtr[2]," in *Traditions in Transformation,* ed. Baruch Halpern and Jon D. Levenson (Winona Lake, Ind.: Eisenbrauns, 1981), 167-192. Friedman's analysis concerns the Deuteronomist, but his concluding comments note the related perspective of the Jeremiah tradition.

nation which seemed beyond all accountability is judged. In that judgment Judah has a basis for future and hope. There are no limits to Yahweh's mighty sovereignty and Yahweh's terrible wrath. The claims of vv. 12-14 are now given full expression in the apocalyptic specificity of vv. 15-26.

The prophet is instructed on what to do with "the cup." The first imperative in v. 15 is "take." The prophet is to "make drink." That imperative is repeated in the imperatives of v. 27: "drink," followed by the series "be drunk, vomit, fall." The nations will be undone by the "cup" from which they cannot avoid drinking. The view of the historical process expressed here presents a clear, coherent theory of punishment (vv. 28-29). Judgment begins with God's own people. That is not in doubt. But it moves from there beyond Judah.[42] That God judges Israel does not mean that God is indifferent to the other nations. All are accountable, and none escapes!

25:30-38 This section consists of a series of poetic fragments that have as a common theme the judgment of the nations. The first element (vv. 30-31) announces that God is about to work a judgment from his holy abode, which could be either Jerusalem or heaven (cf. 1 Kgs. 8:36, 39; Amos 1:2). No nation is mentioned as the object of judgment. This is poetry that, unlike the prose of Jer. 25:17-26, lacks specificity. The language is partly juridical. Yahweh has an indictment and will punish wicked nations. Individuals are not sorted out for particular attention as in 5:1-5, but nations are treated under single verdicts. The poem asserts that there are moral criteria to which whole nations must answer. In 25:32, an isolated fragment, the evil will reach everywhere, and in v. 33 the corpses will be too many to grieve. No specifics are given, but the picture is surely the result of invasion (sword), famine, or an epidemic (pestilence). God's judgment is mediated through such disasters. The picture proposed partakes both of realism and fantasy.

The last poetic unit (vv. 34-38) asserts judgment once more, this time addressed specifically to "shepherds" (rulers). The ones who seem safest are now the ones assaulted. Even the royal class has no protection.

42. The construction which moves from Judah to the nations contrasts with the pattern in Amos 1–2 which begins with the other nations and moves to Judah and finally to Israel. In both cases, the common theme of sovereignty and judgment is shown to pertain to both Israel-Judah and the nations.

It is usually the poor and marginal who cry in calamity, because they are more exposed to danger. Now, however, the cry comes from the center of society (cf. Exod. 11:6), because the judgment reaches into every protected place. No specific indictment is given beyond the reference to wickedness in Jer. 25:31. We surmise that the cause of judgment is that the nations do not practice the elemental requirements of justice, which apply in all regions of Yahweh's governance. The nations can never be strong enough or wise enough to avoid such a requirement.

The difficult and unusual text of ch. 25 suggests three conclusions.

(1) This text is not really a statement of punishment, but of Yahweh's sovereignty (cf. vv. 30-31). God has not abdicated God's governance. Finally, after a long, seeming indifference, God harshly calls all nations to accountability. All are found wanting and under heavy jeopardy.

(2) The countertheme to God's sovereignty is the denial of autonomy to the nation-states (v. 14). They seem to be autonomous and imagine themselves to be, but they are not. This is an exceedingly difficult theme in the face of modernity. The illusion of autonomy is powerful among us. Indeed, political powers in every time and place have imagined they were autonomous. The prophetic tradition relentlessly refutes such imagined autonomy.[43] The historical ordering of life among the nations has a moral coherence rooted in the reality of God's rule. God presides over the historical process and will not be mocked.

(3) There is no explicit hint of hope for Judah in ch. 25, except for the reference to a time limit (v. 11). Yahweh's sovereign rule over the nations has no instrumental purpose. It is not done for the sake of Judah. Nonetheless, insofar as the nations are called to accountability, and insofar as this includes Babylon, Yahweh's dreadful, inescapable sovereignty gives Judah its only possibility for the future. That Yahweh still rules the historical process and has not succumbed to Babylon or the gods of Babylon does indeed create a new chance for Judah. The Exile is not "forever" (v. 9). In the face of massive imperial power and cynical disregard of the moral dimension of human reality, God's sovereign rule is the only ground for historical possibility for God's people. Without the rule of Yahweh, Judah is at the disposal of the nations. Because of Yahweh's rule, however, Judah (and every vulnerable community) has a possibility in the historical

43. See Donald E. Gowan, *When Man Becomes God*, Pittsburgh Theological Monograph 6 (Pittsburgh: Pickwick, 1975).

process. This text asserts that the cynical, ruthless power of nations and empires is very real in the world, but such power is not the final reality. The final reality is in the One who "plucks up and tears down," who "plants and builds" (1:10). Yahweh is at work on both of these decisive, astonishing tasks which reshape life and evoke hope. There is a massive "cup of reeling," commensurate with massive human sin. The Jeremiah tradition shows God taking this sin with utmost seriousness. But there is, however, a second cup (Matt. 26:27; Mark 14:23) which is a cup of healing. It is then promised that the healing of God will overcome the reeling caused by God. In our text the second cup is held in abeyance. Here there is only reeling. God's people live in the midst of both cups. One is often bitter. The other is often held in abeyance. In the end the second cup is also "for all."

Truth Speaks to Power

Jeremiah 26:1–29:32

These four chapters can be grouped together, both for reasons of convenience and because of a common theme. The grouping is in part a matter of convenience, for it is clear that the four chapters do not form an obvious and natural literary corpus. They do, nonetheless, form an in-between group of chapters. On the one hand, ch. 30 begins a quite new grouping with its accent on promise and hope, and its poetic casting. On the other hand, ch. 25 stands by itself, so that most scholars understand it to be a climactic statement at the end of the first half of the book of Jeremiah. In any case, it is not likely that ch. 26 has any integral connection to ch. 25. Between chs. 25 and 30, then, are chs. 26–29, which may be grouped together by default.

More than that, however, can be said about this grouping. The four chapters do seem to make a sustained statement concerning a single theme. The text, completely expressed in prose, features a deep, partisan, ideological dispute concerning Judah's true situation vis-à-vis Yahweh, and therefore vis-à-vis Babylon. The "official view," voiced by the Jerusalem establishment and especially on the lips of Hananiah, is that (a) Jerusalem is safe and guaranteed by the promises of God, and (b) the Babylonian intrusion into Judean life is short term, after which there will be a prompt return to "normalcy." This official view, which counts heavily on establishment ideology, does not receive much direct expression in the text, but is the assumed and implied dominant view with which the prophet must struggle.

229

Against that self-serving view, Jeremiah (and the tradition of Jeremiah) voice a counterview of reality which functions to undermine and subvert the settled ideology of Jerusalem.[1] In this counterview, (a) Jerusalem is not guaranteed at all, but its existence and well-being are intensely conditioned by a resolve to keep torah, and (b) the Babylonian threat is a theological judgment on Jerusalem which is both long term and severe, and therefore not to be taken lightly. This counterview is variously articulated, but is rooted in the conditionality of torah, on which see 26:4-6.

In these chapters there is joined a crucial public issue concerning the political-theological assessment of Judah's actual place in the world. The person of Jeremiah is at the center of the dispute. The dispute does not, however, turn on his personal role, but on the theological-political realities of the situation.[2] There is, in ancient Judah, no unambiguous way to adjudicate this substantive dispute, no court of appeals which will give an objective verdict. The text as it stands is a testimony to Jeremiah's claim, and ultimately is his vindication. That is, in the end the text shows that Jeremiah is right in his assessment of the situation of Judah.

This unit begins in ch. 26 with the polemical proclamation of the prophet, a reiteration of ch. 7. This proclamation predictably evokes the hostility and resistance of the establishment, and Jeremiah is put on trial for his life (26:7-16). The intervention of powerful elders (vv. 17-19), among them Ahikam (v. 24), rescues Jeremiah. The following episode concerning the prophet Uriah indicates that, while Jeremiah may be personally rescued, the issue is not settled in his favor (vv. 20-23). That concluding episode in the chapter indicates that the dominant ideology has both the will and the capacity to silence a counterview and to crush its speakers.

As happens so often in Jeremiah, after the episode of ch. 26 set in the time of Jehoiakim (26:1), we are moved abruptly to another time, that

1. On the ideological dispute, see Henri Mottu, "Jeremiah vs. Hananiah: Ideology and Truth in Old Testament Prophecy," *The Bible and Liberation*, ed. by Norman K. Gottwald (Maryknoll, N.Y.: Orbis, 1983), 235-251.

2. For that reason, there is a problem with excessive stress on the historical person of the prophet. Larger policy issues are the main agenda of the text. The problem facing the Jerusalem establishment is not the critical voice of Jeremiah, but the conditional character of Jerusalem's well-being.

of Zedekiah in chs. 27–28. Clearly the tradition is not put together to make a chronological case.[3] Chapter 27 features a series of prophetic speeches in which the prophet asserts the reality of threat, and assaults the "good news" prophets who engage in massive denial. The same dispute which is generalized in ch. 27 is made direct, dramatic, and personal in the conflict with Hananiah in ch. 28. Finally, Jeremiah urges his contemporaries to prepare for the long haul of displacement (29:1-9) and again rejects false and easy assurances (29:15-32). The issue is clearly a major policy question in which this prophetic tradition asserts what the established ideology does not want voiced. The purpose of the book of Jeremiah is to present a counterview of reality, to say that which is most unwelcome to the ruling view of policy.

Only in 29:10-14 do we see a break in this theme of dispute, warning, and judgment. Here we can see the book of Jeremiah engaged once again in its two-stage notion of Yahweh's intention. After exile, there will be a homecoming. After "plucking up and tearing down," there will be "planting and building." But it will come only after.

Two matters surface in these chapters that relate to the larger themes of the book. First, the issue of true prophecy and false prophecy (ideology) is a recurring theme.[4] While the matter of what is true and what is false cannot be finally or objectively resolved, the book of Jeremiah as an enduring piece of literature clearly wants to insist on the truth of Jeremiah and his trajectory of interpretation.

Second, the unwelcome truth of Jeremiah concerns the reality of Babylon, a geopolitical reality taken as Yahweh's work in the world. Consistently in chs. 27–29 (with an initial warning in ch. 26), these chapters pivot on the Babylonian threat and the need to face it, a theme quite congruent with the Baruch narrative of chs. 36–45. The single exception to that emphasis in these four chapters is 29:10-14, in which the oracle

3. The same abrupt juxtaposition is evident in chs. 34–35. The former is in the days of Zedekiah and the latter in the time of Jehoiachim.

4. On the recent discussion of this dispute, see Thomas W. Overholt, *The Threat of Falsehood*. Studies in Biblical Theology, 2nd series 16 (London: SCM and Naperville: Allenson, 1970); James L. Crenshaw, *Prophetic Conflict*. Beihefte zur Zeitschrift für die alttestamentliche Wissenschaft 124 (Berlin: de Gruyter, 1971); and James A. Sanders, "Hermeneutics in True and False Prophecy," in *Canon and Authority*, ed. George W. Coats and Burke O. Long (Philadelphia: Fortress, 1977), 21-41 and the references to Quell and Buber.

envisions post-Babylonian reality (not unlike chs. 50–51). Thus, as in both the "Baruch narrative" and the "Oracles against the Nations," Jeremiah's theological argument in these chapters is saturated with Babylonian reality. The theme of Babylon is enmeshed in an argument about truth and falseness, so that the argument of the Jeremiah tradition is that the truth of Yahweh enunciated by the prophet concerns the cruciality of Babylon in any assessment of Judah's place in the world.

Thus the book of Jeremiah, exemplified in these four chapters, stays very close to political reality and urges Jerusalem to face that reality which it is prone to deny. That political reference is brought into close contact with Yahwism, so that Near Eastern geopolitics is understood theologically. According to this argument, Judah must at the same time reckon with the reality of Babylon, but also with Yahweh, who stands behind and sponsors Babylon and who then rejects Babylon for the sake of newness.

Thus the issue of truth and falsehood in theological discernment is not, in the book of Jeremiah, simply a matter of having right information or right discernment. It is, rather, an interpretive issue of recognizing that the transcendent will of Yahweh is completely coherent with socioeconomic, political processes.[5] It is in, with, and under Babylon that God is at work. The falseness of Jeremiah's opponents is not that they did not believe in and trust Yahweh, but that they tried to keep Yahweh apart from the world processes of their time. If trust of Yahweh is linked to geopolitics, as this tradition insists, then Jerusalem and Judah are much more at risk than the dominant ideology is wont to imagine. In the face of such a high risk, Judah is urged to face reality and to face "the truth" which comes packaged as torah repentance. This tradition will entertain no other sense of security, certainly no notion that Judah can count on unconditional promises from Yahweh. Judah is summoned by the prophet to live in a dangerous place, with no excessive assurances, but with only a summons to see in its immediate context the dangerous and decisive role of Yahweh. Interpretation of this tradition requires the continued adjudication of theological truth and falseness, an issue which brings theological claims very close indeed to socioeconomic realities. Without this latter reference, any attempt at theological truth will turn out to be false.

5. On the linkage of Yahweh and socioeconomic political processes, see especially Norman K. Gottwald, *The Tribes of Yahweh* (Maryknoll, N.Y.: Orbis, 1979), 608-621.

232

Jeremiah 26:1-24

Response to the Temple Sermon (26:1-24)

This narrative account of Jeremiah's public endangerment is presented as a comment upon his pivotal "temple sermon" in ch. 7. In the sermon of ch. 7, we were given no report on the response of his hearers. This text, conversely, treats the prophetic word itself only briefly (26:1-6) and deals at length with the response of the community. Thus chs. 7 and 26 relate as *proclamation* and *response.* The response puts the prophet in profound conflict with his community and its leaders and with its preferred theological conviction. This theme of conflict will be explored in greater detail in chs. 27–29. The conflict that arises from the dangerous decree of God places the messenger in jeopardy, because his construal of the city is a most unwelcome one. The conflict which dominates the text, however, is not a personal one. The overriding issue, and the overriding interest of the narrative, is not the person of Jeremiah. It is rather the sovereign purpose of Yahweh which will not be overcome, and cannot be silenced or dismissed.

26:1-6 These verses summarize the public proclamation of the prophet given in more detail in ch. 7. The words occur "in the beginning of the reign of Jehoiakim" (26:1). This king is the model of disobedience in the tradition of Jeremiah. From the outset of this reign, the word of Yahweh is an unwelcome word, systematically rejected and resisted by the government. We have no direct report of the prophet's actual speech. We have only notice of what Jeremiah is authorized by God to say. We assume he spoke exactly as he was instructed by God. The prophet is God's "device" or strategy for intruding into Judah's public process.

The decree of God places the future of the city precisely in the hands of those who are addressed. That is, the city is not fated by the will of God. The future all depends on what the people do. What they do will in turn determine what God does. The substance of the proclamation entrusted to Jeremiah is a sharp either/or. Either Jerusalem will turn and avoid God's evil, or it will not turn and receive God's evil. While policy questions may seem complicated, when construed by the prophet they are simple and abrupt. As in 18:7-8, the choice of obedience places in human hands the destiny of Jerusalem to be received from God. Judah has a chance (26:3). If, however, the chance is rejected, then Jerusalem stands under severe notice (vv. 4-6).

The "if-then" formula of vv. 4-6 places Jerusalem in a situation like that of the ancient shrine of Shiloh (cf. 7:12-15; Ps. 78:59-66). The choice is clear and exceedingly demanding. Judah must choose God's torah or be destroyed like Shiloh. The city must recenter its life around the purpose and will of Yahweh or cease to exist. The proclamation on the lips of the prophet asserts that the moral, covenantal factor is the key reality in the public process of Judah's life. In making this statement, the prophet contradicts the royal-temple ideology which imagined that the requirements of torah and the threats of the old covenant tradition were no longer operative for Judah. The prophet does not announce something new; rather, he announces something very old which had long since been dismissed as obsolete to the royal establishment. Insistence upon torah obedience relativizes the claims of authority held by human leadership. All present certitudes are thereby destabilized.

The response to his speech is quick and aggressive (Jer. 26:7-19). The prophet is brought to trial for his life. His threat to the city is judged by the religious leadership (priests and prophets) to be treasonable and worthy of death (vv. 7-9). His words are not for a moment considered by his hearers as a serious word from God, but only as an alternative political opinion which is immediately found unacceptable. The religious leadership has broad public support for finding him promptly guilty. The verdict, "You shall die," is a pre-trial opinion, perhaps a product of crowd psychology (cf. Matt. 27:22-23), or perhaps the filing of a formal charge. These accusers have already reached their verdict. It is the analogy to Shiloh that unnerves the religious leadership. The devotees of the city had imagined that Jerusalem had a privileged place with God and so was immune from the fate of Shiloh.

We are made privy to a courtroom scene in which the royal officers convene court "in the gate" (Jer. 26:10). The charges are lodged: he "prophesied against this city" (v. 11; cf. Amos 7:12-13).[6] This city is supposed to be immune to such criticism. Clearly the legitimacy of the city required keeping such a harsh critique unspoken.

---

6. It is worth noting that the charge made against Jeremiah distorts his actual words, much as the testimony of Amaziah distorted the words of Amos in Amos 7:10-17. Jeremiah did not simply prophesy against the city, but gave an invitation to repent. This invitation from the prophet has dropped out in the charge against him. His enemies mispresent him.

In response, Jeremiah testifies in his own defense (Jer. 26:12-15). He concedes that the charge is correct. He does not argue the point. His self-defense is twofold. First, the assault on the city which he has spoken is not his speech, but the word of God (v. 12). Second, this unwelcome word which is heard as threat is in fact an offer of rescue (v. 13). It proposes a way out of impending death, for it is not yet too late. It is indeed later in the reckoning of God than the leadership thinks. It is indeed very late, but not too late.

Jeremiah makes an important distinction between the words he must speak from God (vv. 12-13) and his own personal destiny (v. 14). The prophet speaks no word on his own behalf and is completely submissive to the authorities before whom he stands. His submissive gesture, however, is only a brief digression from his real issue, namely, the truth of Yahweh which he fears. In v. 15 the prophet returns to the main issue, the summons to torah as the only chance for life in Jerusalem. His opponents want to dispose of his message by a political-judicial maneuver. Such an urgent, ominous word, however, cannot be eliminated by disposing of the messenger. The message itself will have to be engaged, because it is from God.

The ultimate claim the prophet makes for his words is that God has spoken to him "in truth" *(emet)* (v. 15). Even his opponents do not claim that his word is false, only that it is prohibited. Thus the issue of genuine authority haunts the entire life and tradition of Jeremiah; the issue cannot be clearly disposed of, either by the tradition itself or by the opponents of the tradition. For that reason, the claim of the prophet is always fragile and sure to be challenged wherever it touches established ideology. In this chapter the opponents of the demanding word of God do not dispute the claim of authority. They do not seem to care if it is a word from God, for the defense of their way of life overrides any such theological question. They perceive, rightly, that the word of the prophet constitutes a significant threat to their ideological claims and therefore to their political power. Even if Jeremiah is authorized by God, his word is unwelcome. Thus the tradition poses a dramatic confrontation between the word of God and the false ideology by which the city lives. The opponents of the word imagine that if the word can be silenced, it will be nullified.

As long as the dispute is between Jeremiah and the religious leaders (priests and prophets), there can be no serious adjudication, because rival claims to authority end in a stalemate. Perhaps it is the religious leadership, the ones accustomed to giving legitimacy to societal claims, that have the greatest stake in the status quo. Alongside Jeremiah and his religious opponents, however, the narrative introduces a third voice, one that surprises us (vv. 16-19). It is the civic leadership, the princes, along with "all the people." Their intervention and verdict affirm the right of the prophet to speak. The princes do not assert that Jeremiah's word is true. They allow only that he has a right to speak and to be heard, because he speaks a word other than his own. Thus the princes resolve the dispute about authority by recognizing that a voice of prophecy must be taken with seriousness in the community.

The argument then takes an unexpected and decisive turn. In this controversy, certain "elders of the land," that is, those not a part of the urban establishment, cite a precedent in the tradition. The precedent that is cited is from Mic. 3:12, a prophet from a Judean village who a century earlier had spoken a harsh threat against the Jerusalem establishment. Moreover, it is asserted, King Hezekiah honored the prophetic word of Micah and did not execute the prophet as a traitor. On the basis of that remembered event, Jeremiah is acquitted. That is, a prophetic word spoken against the status quo of Jerusalem is not cause for execution of the speaker, but cause for repentance and a change in public policy.

Several things are of importance in this testimony. First, this is an example of "intertextuality," of the Bible itself quoting earlier texts from the Bible.[7] This prophetic tradition does not stand in a vacuum but relies on precedents. Second, the text quoted is from the prophet Micah, that is, a villager who looks askance at the claim of the urban center. Third, the ones who remember and testify are "elders." Hans Walter Wolff has suggested that it is the elders as village leaders who are rooted in old covenantal traditions and who maintain a vision of social reality and a historical perspective that was not preempted by royal definitions of reality.[8] Fourth, the Jeremiah tradition is shaped to assert that the city of

7. Michael Fishbane has made the most helpful and extended exploration of the practice of intertextuality. On this text, see his *Biblical Interpretation in Ancient Israel* (Oxford: Oxford University Press, 1985), 245-47, 458-460.

8. Hans Walter Wolff, "Micah the Moreshite — The Prophet and His Background," in *Israelite Wisdom*, ed. John G. Gammie (Missoula: Scholars Press, 1978), 77-84. On the social conflict of village and larger concentrations of power, see the broader argument by George E. Mendenhall, "The Palestinian Grass-roots Origins of New Testament Christology," in *Jesus in History and Myth*, ed. R. Joseph Hoffman and Gerald A. Larue (Buffalo, N.Y.: Prometheus, 1986), 79-86.

Jerusalem must, because of its very character, host prophetic voices which are critical of its own practice. It belongs to this community to receive prophetic voices, even when those voices are sharply critical of present social reality.

In one important regard, the offer of Jeremiah in this text is more generous than the text quoted from Micah. Micah offered no way out, but only announced a judgment. As this text casts the message of Jeremiah, there is an appeal for repentance, suggesting that it is not yet too late.

The tradition of Jeremiah has built this court trial into a focal drama. Through this confrontation, we are able to see that two perceptions of social reality are in deep and earnest conflict with each other. In short form, this is the old conflict between royal ambition and the memory of torah piety. The text suggests that Jeremiah is not an isolated figure, but he stands in a long tradition of covenantal memory and is the speaker for what must have been a live and insistent political opinion in Israel.[9] This tradition, voiced by the prophet and sanctioned by the elders, resisted the self-indulgent, cynical policies and practices of royal Jerusalem. They did not think that such easy "peace and prosperity" was a way to well-being, because the guarantees and requirements of the torah were being mocked and dismissed. Furthermore, where such requirements are mocked and dismissed, profound trouble is sure to come. Thus the theological verdict of the prophet and the socioeconomic, political interests of the village mentality converge against royal ideology. This exchange, then, is not only high prophetic drama, but can be understood in terms of sociological realism. A poet from the village of Moresheth in Gath (Micah) and a prophet from the village of Anathoth (Jeremiah) may share a critique of the capital establishment.

The implication of the precedent from Micah is that in the present, the power structure of Jerusalem should act as did Hezekiah a century earlier. Not only is Jeremiah acquitted, but the present king, presumably Jehoiakim, should replicate the "good king" Hezekiah. The latter is presented as a king who was not hopelessly enmeshed in Jerusalem ideology and who could respond to the claims and demands of the old tradition (cf. 2 Chr. 29-31). That is, the charge brought against Hezekiah and

9. On the social location of the prophet amid the social forces of his day, see Robert R. Wilson, *Prophecy and Society in Ancient Israel* (Philadelphia: Fortress, 1980), 245-49.

subsequently against Jehoiakim (cf. Jer. 22:18-19) is that Jerusalem's policy is unjust, and that injustice is an affront to the God of the Exodus. In terms of economic policy, that governmental perspective is a threat to the lesser landowners. The elders are asking the king to take those alternative traditions seriously, and not to be so singularly committed to the narrow economic interests of the Jerusalem operators.[10] The socioeconomic issues are not unlike those posed for Rehoboam (1 Kgs. 12:1-15), who like Jehoiakim was so committed to self-serving royal ideology that he would not heed the voice of the tradition. Such cynical obtuseness in each case can only jeopardize the throne and its security.[11]

Because the material concerning Jeremiah's dispute is then taken up in the later tradition of Jeremiah and reused in the exilic community, this dramatic exchange permits one other reading. Addressed to exiles, the text suggests that it is disregard of the torah tradition that has brought such trouble to the community. Therefore, in the Exile the reappropriation of the torah tradition is the only door of hope. Thus the prophetic voice seconded by the elders continues to insist, in each successive generation, that there is no alternative for this people except the embrace of torah, which entails systemic repentance.

The unrelated episode of Jer. 26:20-23 is an unexpected intrusion in the narrative. It concerns an otherwise unknown prophet, Uriah, who also reflects village life (Kiriath-jearim).[12] The case of Uriah is cited to make a contrast with Jeremiah in order to demonstrate the characteristically brutal policy of the crown, and to show that the danger to Jeremiah was real and serious. On this second occasion, the same king, Jehoiakim,

10. On Micah's concern for land policies and his critique of royal usurpation of land, see Albrecht Alt, "Micha 2,1-5 ΓΗΣ ΑΝΑΔΑΣΜΩΣ in Juda," *Kleine Schriften zur Geschichte des Volkes Israel* 3 (Munich: C. H. Beck, 1959): 373-381.

11. It is instructive that Barbara W. Tuchman, *The March of Folly: From Troy to Vietnam* (New York: Knopf, 1984), 8-11, cites King Rehoboam as a primary case of "the march of folly." The kings at the end of the dynasty in the time of Jeremiah only finish the destructive folly begun with Rehoboam. Tuchman concludes her comment, "The alternative course that Rehoboam might have taken, advised by the elders and so lightly rejected, exacted a long revenge that has left its mark for 2800 years" (11). Jeremiah is an interpreter of that "long revenge."

12. William L. Holladay, *Jeremiah 2*. Hermeneia (Minneapolis: Fortress, 1989), 109, suggests that both Micah and Uriah come from villages in the Shephelah, a linkage intended in the tradition.

was not deterred by the elders from his wrath against a prophet. Uriah had spoken words not unlike those of Jeremiah (v. 20). In this case, the prophet was extradited from Egypt and executed as an enemy of the state (v. 23). It is remarkable that the king was not content to have this unbearable voice of the torah simply leave the country in flight (as was the priest Amaziah in Amos 7:10-17, and as are many authoritarian governments in our own day). Rather, the king would settle for nothing short of Uriah's elimination. Thus the contrast is made deep and massive between the old critical covenantal tradition and the royal apparatus which unwittingly prepared for its own death by its crass and greedy policies. Judah is now so distorted in its perception of reality that the very voices of the covenant tradition which might save (i.e., the prophets) are regarded as a threat that must be silenced. The only voice which holds a promise of life is perceived as an unacceptable threat. The very torah which is the foundation for life in Judah is now intolerable.

We misunderstand if we imagine that the prophet is a lone religious authority standing against his community. Rather, he stands in the center of a deep public debate and dispute. Not only Jeremiah, but many elders could see plainly that the leadership of Jerusalem has abandoned the true identity of the community. Indeed, it is argued by the elders that such a prophetic voice which stands against current policy is constitutive for Judah. The prophet is as much an indispensable ingredient in the public life of Judah as are king and temple (cf. Deut. 18:9-22). When that voice of prophecy is silenced and that role nullified, Judah abandons its reason for being and its source of life.

The final verse of our text (Jer. 26:24), after the digression of vv. 20-23, concludes the narrative by reporting the outcome of the encounter. Unlike Uriah, Jeremiah is not executed. The source of rescue, however, was not the intervention or protection of Yahweh.[13] The narrative is much more realistic. It is not reported that the royal court was persuaded by the precedent of Micah. Rather, the rescue is reported in terms of political realism. Jeremiah had a powerful advocate in the family of Shaphan, no doubt representative of the influential families who were increasingly

---

13. In Jer. 36 the action of the princes in hiding Jeremiah and Baruch (v. 19) is said in v. 26 to be the action of Yahweh. Thus the human act and divine protection are equated. In our verse, no such linkage to God is suggested. The protection of Jeremiah here is human and political.

alarmed at the growth of royal power. Thus the prophetic word has its destiny resolved not only because of religious reality, but in the day-to-day realities of political influence and exercise. The rescue of the prophet is a quite human event. The word of God lives and works amid real historical realities. There the messenger is variously jeopardized and protected. It is there that the claims of torah must be decided upon. There is a coherence between the word of the prophet and the social yearning of part of the community, the part which understands the destructiveness of royal policy. This prophetic tradition knows that the true interest of the community is not contained in the narrow, self-serving, self-indulgent interests of the royal leadership. It insists that the true interests of the community lie elsewhere, rooted in the old tradition of torah.

The Yoke of Yahweh (27:1–28:17)

These two chapters belong together thematically, though they contain rather different materials. Chapter 27 is a fourfold decree from Yahweh that is formally all one speech. Chapter 28 is a narrative account of a face-to-face dispute evoked by the decree of ch. 27. The chapters have in common with ch. 26 the theme of the judgment of Jerusalem and the conflict between this torah-prophetic perception of Jerusalem and the dominant assumptions in the city. The substance of the judgment antic-ipated against the city, however, is quite different. In ch. 26 the judgment is the destruction of the city "like Shiloh" (v. 6); in chs. 27–28 the debate concerns not such final destruction, but how long the Exile will last. All of chs. 26–28 suggest an intense and ongoing debate about the future of the city and the nature and extent of its tribulation.[14]

Chapters 27–28 are removed chronologically from ch. 26.[15] They are set at the beginning of the reign of Zedekiah (27:1), that is, just after

---

14. Christopher R. Seitz, *Theology in Conflict: Reactions to the Exile in the Book of Jeremiah.* Beihefte zur Zeitschrift für die alttestamentliche Wissenschaft 176 (Berlin: de Gruyter, 1989), has explored the ways in which the book of Jeremiah is an exemplar and evidence of the interpretive disputes present in the community.

15. While the Hebrew text reiterates "Jehoiakim" as in ch. 26, there is a scholarly consensus, following an alternative textual tradition, that the name of the king in 27:1 should be Zedekiah.

the first incursion of Babylon into the city (598 B.C.E.). The first wave of Jewish exiles have been carried away (cf. 1:3; 52:28). By 598 it is established beyond dispute that the city of Jerusalem is not invincible. The deportation itself must have profoundly shattered the ideology within the city. Now the controversy concerns how long this displacement will last. The theological controversy concerns how long Yahweh will permit the Babylonian power to have its way against Jerusalem and its citizens. The question of *Realpolitik* concerns the durability and capacity of the empire. In the perceptual field of Jeremiah, the theological question of Yahweh's permission and the political question of imperial capacity and durability are the same question. Jeremiah insists that the *rule of Yahweh* and *Judah's response* to that rule are the only pertinent issues. That is, the prophet redefines the issue of politics. (It is of course true that his opponents also view international politics with reference to the character of Yahweh. Thus the difference is not in their political judgments, but in their discernments of God.)

27:1-22 This chapter begins with the dramatic action of Jeremiah in response to the command of Yahweh (27:2). Jeremiah publicly wears a yoke, which symbolizes Babylonian domination.[16] The yoke of Babylon is worn, however, not at the behest of Nebuchadnezzar, but at the command of Yahweh. It is Yahweh's yoke which Judah must now wear! The remainder of this chapter is a theological elucidation of that daring act.

27:3-7 This is a message ostensibly sent to the kings of the neighboring nations, all of whom were in the same subservient position to Babylon as was Judah. Perhaps the words suggest a conspiratorial meeting of subservient nations in Jerusalem to organize against Babylon, or perhaps the prophet simply appeals to the ambassadors regularly in residence in Jerusalem. Or perhaps the framing of the oracle to these nations is simply a device of the staging of the proclamation.[17] Either way, the speech reflects

---

16. S. Dean McBride, Jr., "The Yoke of the Kingdom," *Interpretation* 27 (1973): 273-306, has shown how the metaphor of "yoke" serves for submission both to political power and to the command of Yahweh.

17. Predictably Holladay relates the framing to an actual event, whereas Robert P. Carroll, *Jeremiah*. Old Testament Library (Philadelphia: Westminster and London: SCM, 1986), believes the framing to be only a literary strategy.

the global vision of prophetic faith. Moreover, it intentionally controverts all the usual assumptions of such international diplomacy, for it asserts that the real issue is Yahweh's will and not the apparent problem of Babylonian power. That is, in this oracle Yahweh preempts any claim of the empire.

The oracle addressed to the nations (vv. 5-7) is a freighted theological statement that has four elements:

(a) The foundational statement is in v. 5a: "It is I!" It is Yahweh and none other who is the creator of all that is, the earth, humankind, and the animals.[18] All are from Yahweh. All belong to Yahweh. All are accountable to Yahweh. The language of "great power" and "outstretched arm" is a reminder of Exodus language, bespeaking Yahweh's sovereign, unquestioned, incomparable power. The reminiscences of Exodus language are now in the service of a creation claim, befitting address to the nations who do not share Exodus faith but may acknowledge a creator God.

(b) From this large, uncompromising claim, it follows in v. 5b that Yahweh may dispose of any part of creation in any way that Yahweh chooses. Specifically Yahweh may assign power to anyone Yahweh chooses (cf. 50:44). These two elements together in 27:5 constitute one of the most remarkable statements of Yahweh's free sovereignty. Yahweh does not need to give explanation or justification, does not need to give account to the nations. The rhetorical intent of the announcement is to take the mind of Judah completely off Babylon. In such an assertion, the power and significance of Babylon are completely nullified. This claim for Yahweh assumes that in the beginning the nations were all parcelled out (cf. Deut. 32:8-9). They can, however, be redistributed at any time Yahweh wills, in any way. Yahweh does not need to respect old maps nor adhere to old power arrangements. The nations are put on notice about Yahweh's freedom.

(c) On the basis of the premise of Jer. 27:5, the specific decision of vv. 6-7a is one the nations will need to accept. "All these lands" (i.e., all the nations named in v. 3) are willed by Yahweh to be governed by

18. In a study of the Plague Cycle in the book of Exodus, Terence E. Fretheim, "The Plagues as Ecological Signs of Historical Disaster," *Journal of Biblical Literature* (forthcoming), has observed that the conflict between Pharaoh and Moses includes the devastation of the nonhuman world. In parallel fashion, it is noteworthy that the Jeremiah tradition refers to "the animals" when characterizing the way in which the creator God has turned creation over to the power of Babylon.

Nebuchadnezzar and the empire of Babylon. The empire is not an accident. It is Yahweh's intent, and therefore should not be challenged or resisted by the nations.

This is one of the most astonishing claims of the book of Jeremiah, pointing to one of the most pervasive assumptions of the Jeremiah tradition. Nebuchadnezzar is "my servant." The book of Jeremiah has a pronounced "pro-Babylonian cast." That is, the book envisions and entertains the convergence of the *will of God* and the *rise of the empire.* Prophetic faith does not live in a religious vacuum, but must take sides on the public issues of the day. This equation of Yahweh and the rise of Nebuchadnezzar may be political prudence, especially if this text is a late exilic text. It manages to turn submission to real, unavoidable power into a theological virtue. Or perhaps the prophet is simply a sympathizer whose political inclinations are pro-Babylonian and anti-Egyptian. Both factors of prudence and sympathy may indeed be operative. The canonizing process, however, claims more than prudence or bias. It claims that this affirmation of Babylon in light of Yahweh's will is a theological datum. The God of the Bible effectively tilts the international process. The literature dares to discern God's solidarity with a major world power. Accordingly, Yahweh's support of Babylon is to last three generations, that is, a long time past the present rulers (v. 7).

(d) In v. 7b, the announcement of the prophet takes a surprising turn. It is introduced by "until" (Heb. *'ad*). The promise of vv. 5-7 is not permanent. It has a time limit. The phrasing which follows indicates a quite complete and intentional philosophy of history. The text is not simply propaganda for the empire, but is a struggle concerning the tricky relation between the reality of God and *Realpolitik.* The text knows that the Babylonian Empire, even willed by Yahweh, is not absolute or permanent. In the eyes of Yahweh, the empire has a statute of limitation beyond which it cannot endure. In time, Babylon will in turn become subservient to others. Thus the same God who authorizes the empire anticipates its destabilization (eventually enacted in chs. 50–51).

We may propose practical explanations for such an "until." The simplest explanation is to say that this is a late exilic text, composed by those able to discern the erosion of Babylonian power.[19] Or one may say

---

19. This is the propensity of Carroll's commentary. In such a view, however, texts can only follow perceived reality and never be original. Such a procedure domes-

that the Bible writers are shrewd enough to know that every empire eventually exhausts itself in carelessness or overextension and comes to an end.[20] Such practical considerations are in principle not excluded from our interpretation. The canonical process, however, asserts more and other than this. The fall of Babylon will occur because Yahweh wills its ending as Yahweh has willed its rise. The particularities of 27:6-7 are not simply political prudence and "realism," but are theological affirmations that Yahweh does indeed govern the nations, sometimes to their advantage and sometimes to their destruction. We should not dismiss by reductionism the daring or the intense theological, intellectual work in such a claim. The prophet insists that the nations live in a world of moral accountability. This theory of the rise and fall of Babylon as willed by Yahweh is given more precise characterization in Isa. 47. There the rise of Babylon is because of Yahweh's anger with Israel (Isa. 47:6a). Conversely, the fall of Babylon is because it was excessively ruthless, that is, it showed no mercy (Isa. 47:6b).[21]

The claims of these two verses require a conviction that the human, historical enterprise is not meaningless or autonomous, but reflects an abiding governance beyond the will of either Babylon or Jerusalem. This abiding governance includes a great, expectant "until," at which time Jerusalem will be liberated. Thus this turn in the rhetoric of the sentence converts what has been a harsh judgment on Jerusalem into an act of hope.

---

ticates texts and tames them to "reality." Such a view does not allow for the authority or courage of the critical vision of the text. *Mutatis mutandis,* one may observe that one did not need to watch for the demise of the Soviet Empire to anticipate that it would surely come to an end, for such power cannot endlessly subjugate the human spirit. In like manner, one need not wait until after the fact to assert that the U.S. "colossus of the North" sooner or later will pay for and relinquish its grip on the peoples of Latin America.

20. Reference should be made here to the careful study of Paul M. Kennedy, *The Rise and Fall of the Great Powers: Economic Change and Military Conflict from 1500 to 2000* (New York: Random House, 1987). Kennedy of course does not include a theological factor in his analysis. The way he marshals his argument, however, makes clear that the rise and fall of the nations is not unrelated to the powerful, unavoidable operation of a moral dimension to public reality. While his analysis is not explicitly parallel to the prophetic tradition of the OT, the two are not without points of contact.

21. See Walter Brueggemann, "At the Mercy of Babylon: A Subversive Rereading of the Empire," *Journal of Biblical Literature* 110 (1991): 3-22.

The time of the turn is not specified, but the homecoming of Jews is as sure as the word itself. The very God who authorizes the deportation into exile is the very God who assures a return (cf. Isa. 54:7-8).[22]

27:8-11 These verses finally continue the decree to the nations from Jer. 27:3. While it is formally addressed to the nations, we may imagine that this is a rhetorical way of addressing Judah and more specifically King Zedekiah. In these verses, the pro-Babylonian claim of the prophet is made even more explicit. The unit consists of two unequal parts. In the first part, the listener is warned about what happens to nations who refuse the hegemony of Babylon which is willed by Yahweh (v. 8). Such nations are subject to the great plagues of sword, famine, and pestilence and will be destroyed.[23] These threats should not be understood "supernaturally." They are the predictable result of an occupying army. Thus the nation that does not submit to Babylon will be devastated by invasion and occupation. In the second part of this unit (v. 11), a nation that submits to Babylon will not be destroyed or exiled. That nation may be incorporated into the empire and its tax structure, but it will remain in its own place. It will not have the fabric of its own life disrupted. Thus the choices are devastating — death or submission. There is no third alternative. Submission permits continued life in the land.

Between the warning of devastation (v. 8) and the alternative assurance (v. 11), the text warns against false prophets (vv. 9-10). The language of the warning recalls the catalogue of Deut. 18:9-13. The substance of the warning, however, is simply that the false prophets are not pro-Babylonian; they seduce Judah into imagining a third alternative, namely, resistance to the empire. That is, such voices engage in religious fantasy not related to the power realities. There is actually no third alternative, and resistance will lead to death. Such a third alternative of resistance and independence is a false reading of social reality, as it is a false discernment of the will of Yahweh. Not to submit is to be crushed.

One should not draw easy parallels, but the situation is not unlike

---

22. See Walter Brueggemann, "A Shattered Transcendence? Exile and Restoration," in *Biblical Theology: Problems and Prospects*, ed. Steven Kraftchick et al. (forthcoming).

23. On such curses, see Delbert R. Hillers, *Treaty-Curses and the Old Testament Prophets*. Biblica et Orientalia 16 (Rome: Pontifical Biblical Institute, 1964).

the slogan "Better dead than Red" used so recently in the face of the perceived threat of the Soviet Union. "Dead" and "Red" were nicely said to be the options. The equivalent of "Red" is to be incorporated into the Babylonian Empire. The prophet urges "Red" rather than "dead." The prophet asserts that submission is now Judah's act of prudence, but it is also Judah's act of obedience to Yahweh. The alternative of resistance is a sure way to be "dead." The prophet makes a strong theological claim, but it is a theological claim that has important historical, political extrapolations. It is impossible, in the tradition of Jeremiah, to sort out what is political realism and what is theological discernment. The tradition refuses to have them separated. The convergence of the two constituted a devastating critique of the royal ideology of Jerusalem which imagined that the will of Yahweh was predictably on the side of Jerusalem safety. Such an ideology could hardly imagine that Yahweh's resolve could be aligned against Judah and not in its favor.

27:12-15   Here the same general message is asserted yet again, this time addressed specifically to King Zedekiah. It is likely that the announcement in Jer. 27:1-11, ostensibly addressed to the nations, is in fact addressed to the Jerusalem community in the years of Zedekiah. Now that address is made explicit. Once more the prophet voices a pro-Babylonian stance. We cannot here (as anywhere else in the tradition) determine to what extent this urging is prudence, bias, or an act of discerning faith. Perhaps it is all three, for discerning faith is not required to be imprudent or neutral. What resounds in these texts is the sure conviction that Yahweh governs the nations, both the great empire and the chosen community. No assertion of ideology, arms, or strategy can prevail against the will of Yahweh which is now being enacted. That irresistible will, as Jeremiah discerns it, is to submit to the yoke of Babylon, to yield to imperial policy. The specific command of v. 12 alludes back to the statement of v. 2, though the wording is somewhat different. The "yoke" of the empire is in this instant understood as the yoke of Yahweh. Subservience to Nebuchadnezzar is obedience to Yahweh. This inscrutable claim is not defended in the text, but it suggests a realism about faith. Submissiveness to political power may be (but is not always) an act of fidelity to the God who orders the affairs of the nations.

The alternative to submissiveness in this case is death, again by the great triad of covenant curses (v. 13). The lean political alternatives of vv.

12-13, either submission or death, are correlated to the religious question of true and false prophecy. More than anyone else in the OT, Jeremiah troubles over rival readings of historical realities, each of which claims to be faithful to Yahweh. The prophet clearly had powerful and articulate competitors and adversaries who urged either that Egypt was a better alternative than Babylon or that resistance was more faithful to Yahweh than was submissiveness.

Recommendation of resistance, claims this tradition, constitutes a "lie" *(sh-q-r)* (v. 14). Such a recommendation is an invitation to fantasy. Judah cannot resist Babylon, because God does not will such resistance. Such a fantasy will lead inevitably to disaster. Of course such a reading of reality cannot be made with objective certitude. Faithful discernment of God in the public process must always be done "in the middle of things," before the data are all in. That is what makes prophetic discernment so problematic and so urgent. Such a prophetic judgment requires the courage to declare without certitude. It is a religious judgment rendered with enormous political risk. But it is the only kind of religious judgment worth bothering with. The alternative is to remain silent and have faith dictated by events. Jeremiah dismisses a more "trusting" option not only as foolish, but as disobedient.

27:16-22   In this fourth section of the decree, the prophet addresses yet another constituency, the priests and the people. (We have already seen in ch. 26 that the priests are his primary adversary.) While the people are named here as an addressee, this word seems peculiarly addressed to the priests, for it concerns temple equipment. The substance of the first part of this section is by now familiar to us (27:16-17). Again the listener is warned against false prophets who were saying that the deportation of 598 would not last long. Only now it is not exiled people who would be returned, but it is the "temple vessels," all the gold and silver accoutrements which signify and enhance the worship of Yahweh.[24] Those temple vessels

---

24. Peter R. Ackroyd, "The Temple Vessels: A Continuity Theme," *Supplements to Vetus Testamentum* 23 (1972): 166-181 (repr. in *Studies in the Religious Tradition of the Old Testament* [London: SCM, 1987], 46-60), has demonstrated how the "temple vessels" function in the exilic literature as a sign and gesture of continuity in the disruption of exile. See his comments on our passage, *Studies in the Religious Tradition,* 54-56.

have now been profaned, mocked, and scandalized by removal, treated as so much indifferent hardware. The loss of such objects is passionately felt because it violates the highest symbolic, sacramental sensitivity of the adherents of the temple system. Again the conclusion is drawn: live by submission! Whoever says otherwise is engaged in a fantasy. Verses 16-17 simply reiterate the preceding announcement made to the nations (vv. 3-11) and to Zedekiah (vv. 12-15).

In v. 18, however, the argument advances in a new direction. Jeremiah throws down the gauntlet to the other prophets. If they want to speak about something important, if they want to make a difference, they should not fantasize about what is lost. They should rather devote their effort (through intercessory prayer) to making sure that Babylon does not come again to take what remained after 598. If they are able by their intercession to stop the empire from further usurpation, that will be an act of genuine authority, and all will know that these prophets are genuine. If Babylon is only the passing threat they imagine, they should be able to stop the flow of goods from the temple to the empire. That is, Jeremiah calls their bluff and requires that their easy word of assurance be put to hard test.

Immediately in vv. 19-22 the prophet refutes his own playful invitation to the adversaries. Even if the other prophets would accept the difficult task Jeremiah has given them, that task is futile. Thus by implication Jeremiah invites his false adversaries to a task they cannot possibly achieve, an impossible mission. From the perspective of Jeremiah and his tradition, not only will the first installment of temple equipment taken in 598 not be returned soon; but the remainder of temple vessels not taken at that time will be taken subsequently. There will not be a quick return (as the other prophets anticipate), but more harsh, intense treatment by the empire. Thus his opponents are doubly wrong.

In our handling of this text, it does not greatly matter if it is in fact dated after 587 when a second usurpation was enacted in Jerusalem. As it stands, the rhetoric of Jeremiah is anticipatory, asserting that God's sovereign will of "empire versus Jerusalem" will be brought to full, harsh fruition. Such a devastating eventuality is certain, even though many thought, hoped, and believed otherwise. The complete raiding of Jerusalem by the empire is as sure as God's rule is sure. Thus the prophet establishes dramatic and unbearable distance and tension between *the rule of God* and the *well-being of Jerusalem*. His opponents imagined that the rule of God and the well-being of Jerusalem were intimately allied. Events of the time supported the harder judgment of Jeremiah. Jerusalem has no "safe conduct" from its God.

Jeremiah's conviction about a second Babylonian seizure in Jerusalem is documented in the historical summary of 52:17-23. Indeed, that chapter is likely added to the literature from 2 Kgs. 25:8-20 as a vindication of Jeremiah's daring assertion in Jer. 27:16-22. Chapter 52 is a detailed summary of the Babylonian operation which includes the items mentioned in 27:19. Everything precious from the temple is placed under imperial control, thus scandalizing the faithful and placing in further jeopardy the ideology of Yahweh's commitment to Jerusalem.

This sequence of pro-Babylonian (i.e., pro-Yahwistic) announcments ends on a decisive and surprising note (vv. 22b). It is introduced by the word "until" *('ad),* echoing v. 7. This "until" asserts the prophetic expectation that Babylonian power is not absolute but provisional. The exile to Babylon is not for perpetuity, even though it is for a long time. The vessels of the temple will not forever be absent from Jerusalem, even though they will be absent for a long time.

This powerful "until" ultimately breaks the connection between *the destiny of Babylon* and *the will of Yahweh* which the prophet has so determinedly established. In the end, empire and Yahweh are not coterminous. As in v. 7, this "until" announces that the Babylonian Empire is an episode in God's history of sovereignty — an important episode, but only an episode, not to be taken with ultimate seriousness. What is ultimately serious is God's final resolve to restore Judah to its land. The restoration, however, does not negate the exile. This final note is not a capitulation to the voices of false hope earlier combatted by the prophet. This ultimate hope, judged by the canon to be genuine, is not a hope based on the collapse of the empire, but a hope rooted in God's positive and faithful regard for Judah, a regard which will outlast the Babylonian moment of domination. The long-term survival of the empire and its ultimate termination, in the reckoning of this tradition, both attest to the rule of Yahweh. The prophet is willing to discern the will of Yahweh in the midst of the empire, but not so that the two are equated. Jeremiah ends in agreement with his critics: there will be restoration. But it will not be soon or easy. In the end, Jeremiah's argument is of a quite different kind. He does the difficult work of affirming hope, but without grounding it in the ideology of the city.

28:1-17 This chapter includes a concrete and dramatic confrontation reflecting a continuing dispute about the programmatic decree announced in ch. 27. This narrative account is intentionally linked to the preceding chapter (28:1), but is made much more specific. The new voice in the dispute is Hananiah, a prophet who uses the same messenger formula as does Jeremiah to authenticate his speech: "Thus says the LORD" (v. 2). Like Jeremiah, he claims to be sent and authorized by Yahweh (cf. 23:21-22). His name is perhaps telling, for Hananiah means "Yahweh is gracious." His message is precisely that Yahweh is more immediately and powerfully gracious than Jeremiah can allow. Thus the dispute about the future of Jerusalem in the end is a dispute about the character and intention of God, for the life of Jerusalem flows from the life of God.

The first speech of Hananiah (28:2-4) directly challenges the preceding assertion of Jeremiah in 27:16-22. The Babylonian yoke of 27:12 is quickly a broken yoke at the hand of Hananiah (28:2). Babylonian domination will end, and with it, Judah's exile. The disaster of 598 will be undone, and of course, there is no prospect in the horizon of Hananiah for a later, second invasion and exile. Israel's life in all its parts will be resumed. Temple vessels will be restored (v. 3). The exiled king will be restored to power (v. 4). The positive and faithful inclination of Yahweh will result in full restoration and return to normalcy in Jerusalem.

Thus the issue is joined sharply and decisively. In a political dimension, there is a sharp disagreement about the future of the empire and how lasting Babylonian domination will be. Such political judgments, however, are rooted in competing convictions concerning the character of Yahweh and Yahweh's commitment to the Jerusalem establishment. It is not clear why Hananiah speaks this message and makes this judgment. The text does not probe his motivation or rootage at all. Perhaps he is a sheer opportunist who tells the king what the king most wants to hear. That possibility is a standard stereotype among us of a "false prophet." Likely matters are too serious and stakes are too high for such a surface assessment. Likely Hananiah had better and more serious reasons for his statement.

Two other explanations seem more cogent and more serious. On the one hand, Hananiah may be rooted in the royal theology of Israel, trusting in God's commitment to the temple and to the dynasty.[25] Thus the central

25. Carroll, 537, concludes: "So the prophets of v. 16 were right after all but were wrong about the timing!" The difference about the timing, however, is decisive.

issue is whether God would honor those longstanding commitments and much-celebrated promises to Zion. Hananiah's position then is not opportunistic, but is a reiteration of God's trustworthiness rooted in the normative theological tradition of Jerusalem. On the other hand and more specifically, Hananiah's message is congruent with the words of Isaiah a century earlier.[26] We know that Isaiah's words were vindicated in the astonishing deliverance of the city from the Assyrian threat in 701. There is no doubt that that miraculous rescue generated in Jerusalem supreme confidence that God is and would be the patron and guarantor of the holy city. Hananiah thus may be a disciple of the tradition of Isaiah and simply anticipates that God would again perform such an act of deliverance. Working from historical parallelism, the crisis of 598 did not seem so very different from the events of 701.

Whether Hananiah appeals primarily to the David-Zion traditions or to the memory of Isaiah, we may imagine that he spoke in good faith and believed he was articulating a serious form of bold and responsible faith. He is likely not a charlatan or a huckster. He is, nonetheless, judged by the canonical tradition to have been false in his faith. That falseness may be a judgment rooted in historical outcomes, for his anticipation was not in fact what happened. That is, the exile in Babylon was not short term, and the restoration was not quick, as he anticipated. Alternatively, Hananiah's falseness may be a theological judgment, for his word did not reckon with the stern, conditional quality of Yahweh's promise so championed by the tradition of Jeremiah. Either way, his hope rooted in an old, treasured memory, in this context, is an ideological distortion; it does not reflect what God is doing here and now. If the present-tense reality of God cannot be discerned, then any prophetic discernment is likely ideology. Thus yesterday's certitude has become today's distorting ideology.[27]

Jeremiah responds to the challenge of Hananiah (vv. 5-9). His re-

---

The other prophets want to collapse the two events of exile and return. The distance between the two, upon which this text insists, makes two experiences qualitatively and decisively different.

26. On the ideology of the temple and its delicate relation to the claims of the dynasty, see Ben C. Ollenburger, *Zion, the City of the Great King.* Journal for the Study of the Old Testament Supplement 41 (Sheffield: JSOT Press, 1987), 59-66 and *passim.*

27. On the ideological dimension of Hananiah in this narrative, see Mottu, "Jeremiah vs. Hananiah," 235-251.

sponse is in a quite public forum, for we are witnessing a crucial debate about policy (v. 5). The response of Jeremiah consists of three parts. First, he responds to Hananiah with the wish (perhaps ironic or even sarcastic) that Hananiah may be correct, that deliverance will be soon, and that exile will not be protracted (v. 6). The first word of the response is "Amen." If the word is sarcastic, it might be rendered, "Right!", dripping with mocking and disbelief. That hope for the quick rescue promised by Hananiah (perhaps voiced in disbelief) is quickly countered in vv. 7-8 with an adversative introduced by "yet" *(ak).* The tradition of Jeremiah is eager to place Jeremiah in a succession of prophets, so that he is not an isolated case. In this second part, the prophet appeals to "former prophets." The argument is that "real prophets" speak mainly of the covenant, of its requirements, and of its ominous sanctions for disobedience — war, famine, and pestilence. This argument does not in and of itself negate Hananiah, but it puts us on notice that Hananiah is against the mainstream of prophetic announcement. Thus the argument is that Hananiah is suspect because he does not say what prophets characteristically say. He is soft on the dangers of covenant disobedience.

In the third element of Jeremiah's response, Hananiah's word of "well-being" *(shalom)* can be tested (cf. 6:14; 8:11). It is not likely that Hananiah is correct, but the test is whether his word comes to fruition. Thus Jeremiah appeals to the test of prophets proposed in Deut. 18:22. For Jeremiah and the tradition of Jeremiah, a tradition so committed to and self-conscious of its memory, the burden of proof is on Hananiah, because he has taken a stand against the main strand of prophetic speech.

Hananiah's word can only be tested through the passage of time. It is as though Jeremiah anticipates Gamaliel, who counselled: "If this plan or this undertaking is of men, it will fail; but if it is of God, you will not be able to overthrow them. You might even be found opposing God!" (Acts 5:38-39). That, however, does not help much in the present, for decisions must be made and policies must be enacted. This criterion for assessing Hananiah seems almost for the sake of the canon. When the book of Jeremiah was ultimately framed, presumably in exile, enough time had passed to judge Hananiah and vindicate Jeremiah. "Peace" had not come as Hananiah had promised. God does not so promptly override God's own moral judgments. Whoever imagines that God will, is in fact false. Thus the text, even though set in a critical moment, has the long-term effect of establishing the authenticity of Jeremiah as the one who rightly discerned God's way with Judah. The "true prophet" must take into account the reality of God's free rule and the fact that even the well-being of Israel depends upon fidelity. There are no "quick fixes" for a people which distorts Yahweh's will. No ideology of continuity can deliver a quick rescue in the face of such fundamental distortion. While the dispute was urgent in the moment of Zedekiah, it is as though the canonical text is building a record of vindication for Jeremiah. The later community can remember and attest that there was in those difficult days one voice who spoke the truth. That one voice emerges canonically as an enduring witness and a recurring reminder.

Hananiah, however, is convinced, intransigent, and imaginative (Jer. 28:10-11). He is cast in the role of the antagonist necessary to the drama, but sure to be defeated. Jeremiah had worn yoke-bars as a sign of exile (27:2). Now the narrative returns to that initial notice. Hananiah dramatically breaks the symbolic yoke, thus articulating God's liberating action (28:10). Hananiah comments on his action by reiterating his judgment that in two years the Exile will end (cf. v. 3). His act is offered as a gesture of good news. The narrative leaves Hananiah's gesture unanswered and unrefuted. It is left lingering in the narrative, unresolved (v. 11).

Unfortunately, it is far easier to break a symbolic yoke than it is to override Yahweh's tough verdict or to break the reality of Babylonian power. Hananiah's symbolic act of breaking is a symbol without corresponding reality. Jeremiah, "after the breaking," makes one more response to Hananiah (vv. 12-16). The real yoke of exile is like iron, not like wood. It is unbreakable. It is unbreakable, not because it is hard metal, but because Yahweh's sovereign decree is for Babylonian domination. Jeremiah is unshakable in this discernment of reality. The God of this text is not an inevitable patron of state religion, but has enough distance and freedom from the royal apparatus to be for or against God's own people (cf. 23:23).

Jeremiah's response to the "breaking" is in two parts. First, he reasserts God's intention for public reality (28:14). God gives the world over to Nebuchadnezzar. Moreover, this authorized hegemony includes not only the human, political enterprise, but even the "beasts of the field." Thus Nebuchadnezzar has become God's "new adam" who will have his way in the world. The verdict could not be more sweeping. Second, after the assertion about public policy, Jeremiah addresses the person of Hananiah, the office of the prophet, and the matter of truth (vv. 15-16).

These verses constitute a lawsuit form aimed at Hananiah. The indictment is in v. 15. Hananiah has not been dispatched by Yahweh but is making up the good news on his own. The outcome is a "lie" *(sh-q-r)*.[28] Both the prophet and his word are a lie. In v. 6, Jeremiah had uttered the word "true" *(amen)*, perhaps in mocking or perhaps in hope. Now, however, that hope is dismissed. The verdict is "false" *(sh-q-r)*, not true *(amen)*. The sentence of the lawsuit is in v. 16: "Therefore, behold . . ." The sentence corresponds to the offense.[29] The offense was, "I did not send." The sentence is "I will send you." The RSV translation does not reflect the rhetorical correspondence. It renders, "I will remove," but the wording is, "I will send you now, for I did not send you to prophesy." That is, I will send you away from the earth, that is, to death. Hananiah had announced life for Judah, but his own destiny is certain death. Hananiah is a rebel against God and so must be dismissed. Jeremiah is impatient and heavy-handed with those who distort, mislead, soothe, and falsely reassure in Jerusalem.

The narrator adds tersely, "He died in the same year" (v. 17). Death was announced as a verdict in v. 16. In the same year the word comes to fulfillment. The report serves several purposes. It discredits Hananiah. It attests to the legitimacy of Jeremiah and his vocation. Moreover, it removes the hope of an immediate deliverance. As the messenger is eliminated, so the false message evaporates. It is worth noting that the terse conclusion makes no theological claim. It does not say that Yahweh destroyed Hananiah. Rather, it is a lean factual account. But of course, in this freighted, self-conscious narrative, such a factual report points beyond itself to the great theological issue of truth and falsehood. The issue of truth and falsehood is, however, not a theoretical issue. It concerns the will of Yahweh, the power of Babylon, and the future of Jerusalem.

The career of Hananiah in ch. 28 is only an episode which exercises no lasting impact upon the tradition of Israel. The distorting force of Hananiah passes quickly from the scene and the toughness of Jeremiah endures. By 28:17 we are made freshly aware that the prophetic announcement of ch. 27 is in effect. Yahweh is a hard sovereign. Jerusalem is under

---

28. On the role of the term *sh-q-r* in the tradition of Jeremiah and especially in chs. 27–28, see Overholt, *The Threat of Falsehood*.

29. On the characteristic correspondence of sin and judgment, see Patrick D. Miller, Jr., *Sin and Judgment in the Prophets*. SBL Monograph 27 (Chico: Scholars Press, 1982). So far as I can determine, Miller does not cite this particular case.

stern judgment. Jeremiah, the messenger of a hard sovereign, bears the message of stern judgment. No ideology or wishful religion can deny the intention of Yahweh in history as Jeremiah has voiced it. All the world can see is Babylonian imperialism. The community of this text, however, knows more. It knows that the real agent is not Nebuchadnezzar, visible as he is, but the God who "plucks up and tears down."

And we, long after Hananiah is gone, are left with this relentless text. We are left to ponder that, in a world of raw imperial power and in a world of well-wishing religious passion, there is this other claim made upon Jerusalem and every holy operation, upon Babylon and every concentration of world power. One cannot generalize from this specific case about power politics. The canonical shape of the story, however, keeps Jeremiah lingering as a witness into the very long future.

Correspondence with the Exiles (29:1-32)

This chapter has important connections to chs. 27–28. Those chapters asserted that the exile in Babylon after 598 would be extended over a long time. This chapter gives attention to those in exile since 598 who must find ways to live faithfully and hopefully in the midst of exile. In giving counsel to the exiles, this chapter implies a confirmation of Jeremiah's proclamation in chs. 27–28. The chapter has closest affinities with ch. 24, where the same exiles are addressed as the carriers of God's future.[30] On critical grounds, it is likely that the materials in chs. 24 and 29 reflect a later traditioning process in a subsequent generation of exiles. As the texts are now presented, both chs. 24 and 29 characterize Jeremiah as practicing pastoral care among the exiles. That pastoral care is expressed around two convictions: (a) there must be a realistic and intentional *embrace of the Exile* as a place where Jews must now be and where God has summoned them to obedience (29:5-7), and (b) there is *a long-term hope for return and restoration* that can be affirmed and accepted (vv. 10-14).

Both affirmations are important for the exiles and for the shape of the Jeremiah tradition. The first, which enacts "tearing down and plucking up," offers an alternative against romantic escapism and abdication. The

30. See Walter Brueggemann, "A Second Reading of Jeremiah after the Dismantling," *Ex Auditu* 1 (1985): 156-168.

second, which enacts "building and planting," speaks against ultimate despair. The two themes together correspond to the governing verbs of 1:10 and reflect the basic structure of the completed message of the Jeremiah tradition. While Jeremiah's word is characteristically one of judgment, it is striking that this voice of judgment brings with it a powerful voice of hope. The suffering of exile is for the OT the matrix in which the hope of God is most powerfully and characteristically at work.[31] The Exile is the place where God's faithful promises work a profound newness. Nowhere is this more passionately voiced than in the tradition of Jeremiah. Thus the completed tradition anticipates Paul: ". . . suffering produces endurance, and endurance produces character, and character produces hope, and hope does not disappoint us . . ." (Rom. 5:3-5).

29:1-3   These verses provide a frame for the pastoral letter of Jer. 29:4ff.[32] The letter is addressed to all those who were removed to Babylon in 598. There was important tension after 598 (and before 587) between those who had been deported and those who remained in the city of Jerusalem (cf. ch. 24). In his pro-Babylonian posture, Jeremiah concludes that the ones exiled are the bearers of Judah's hope for the future and the special object of God's attentive love and concern. This judgment about the exiles is congruent with the larger tendency of the Jeremiah tradition. It is to the latter that the letter is addressed, the ones who count for the future.

The letter is carried by royal messengers.[33] It is not known whether

31. See Walter Brueggemann, *Hopeful Imagination: Prophetic Voices in Exile* (Philadelphia: Fortress, 1986).

32. The form of the letter is perhaps to be taken seriously. It is not implausible that such a written communication could have been sent from Jerusalem to the exiles in Babylon. Cf. William L. Holladay, "God Writes a Rude Letter (Jeremiah 29:1-23)," *Biblical Archaeologist* 46 (1983): 145-46. Nonetheless, it is difficult to determine where the letter ends in this chapter. Perhaps it ends in v. 23, suggesting that the letter is a witness against the false teaching. In form, however, the letter is transmuted into a prophetic oracle. Except for the framing in vv. 1-3 (and the mention of other letters in vv. 25, 29-30), the chapter becomes a series of oracles which continue the debate and conflict of chs. 27–28.

33. It is important that one of the messengers is a son of Shaphan, suggesting a convergence of the fortunes of Jeremiah, the interests of the king, and the engagement of a powerful family that was pro-Babylonian in its politics (cf. 26:24, where another son of Shaphan protected Jeremiah).

they are dispatched for the purpose of carrying this letter or whether it is incidentally taken along with other business. Because the letter is such a public matter, and because Jeremiah had intense interactions with King Zedekiah, carrying such letters may have been routine business for any diplomatic courier. The verse following the substance of the letter was a quite public matter (29:29).

The letter purports to extend from v. 4 to v. 28. It is framed by the reiteration in v. 28 of the main admonition of v. 5; the accent is on the imperative verbs, "build, live, plant, and eat." This is the key pastoral advice of the message. Between these two framing verses (vv. 5, 28) is a series of prophetic oracles. The first is cast as a letter, but the later ones make little claim to the form of a letter and are simply oracles. The burden of the whole is that exile will be long and unavoidable, but not to perpetuity. Judah must accept exile as its proper place, and there must live its life and practice its faith.

29:5-7 Here is the most poignant statement of the long unit. In a series of imperatives, vv. 5-6 urge the development of sustained communal life in exile. Judah is to build and plant (cf. 1:10), to marry and to have their children marry. That is, Judah is to prepare for a long haul, because exile will extend beyond the present generation. Even in exile, Judah is to multiply just as the old enslaved community of Exod. 1 multiplied. Even in displacement, Judah continues to be the people over which God's promise for the future presides with power.

Then comes a stunning and remarkable turn in the letter (Jer. 29:7). This additional imperative reflects the Babylonian propensity of the Jeremiah tradition. It also reflects political realism, urging the exiles to accommodate their imperial overlord. "The city where I have sent you" is Babylon. Jews in exile are to work for the well-being *(shalom)* of the empire and its capital city. The well-being *(shalom)* of Judah is dependent upon and derivative from that of Babylon. This positive attention toward Babylon is very different from the deep resentment toward the imperial masters generally and Babylon particularly as expressed elsewhere (in the Jeremiah tradition, see chs. 50–51, and also Isa. 13-14, 47). Prophetic faith is powerfully realistic about the political situation of the Jews in exile. The Jews have no option to Babylon, which is God's chosen habitat for the exiles.

There is, however, more than realism in this assertion. The imperative bestows upon this vulnerable, small community a large missional responsibility. In this way, the community is invited into the larger public process of the empire. Such a horizon prevents the exilic community from withdrawing into its own safe, sectarian existence, and gives it work to do and responsibility for the larger community.

29:8-9   The text now returns to the recurring problem of false prophets, as already seen in chs. 23, 27–28. This particular warning reflects the concern of Deut. 13:1-5, which may identify the editorial hand at work in the completed text. The concern of the text is not a theoretical one about the nature of prophecy. The concern is a quite practical one, concerning the seduction of religious fantasy. The threat to the Jews is that they will be talked out of the reality of exile, invited to deny the real place where they must live their faith. Thus Jer. 29:5-7 affirms the real place of exile; the warning of vv. 8-9 is against an emotional, imaginative departure from that place, that is, engagement in an illusion. Prophetic faith is hard-nosed realism that is resistant to romantic, ideological escapism. No pretense based in religious fantasy can extricate God's people from their actual place in history. Those who permit religion to abrogate historical-political reality speak a lie.

29:10-14   While vv. 5-9 assert the reality of exile and the responsibility of being fully engaged with it, vv. 10-14 move the horizon of Judah beyond exile to assert the hope of return from exile. This is one of the most powerful, intense, and freighted announcements of return in all of Scripture. It is a rich inventory of Israel's primary formulas for hope of return. The reference to "seventy years" (25:11) is apparently a convention, perhaps not to be taken literally.

Moving beyond the actual circumstance of 29:5-9, the text makes a claim that is profoundly theological: Yahweh will keep the promise of homecoming (v. 10). That promise is rooted in God's long-term resolve for Judah. It had seemed through much of the Jeremiah tradition that God intended only evil for God's people. In the face of the *evil* of exile, however, the text asserts Yahweh's more fundamental interest in doing *good* for this people. This assertion does not nullify the long Jeremianic tradition of judgment. Rather, it moves through, past, and beyond judgment to assert Yahweh's final resolve. God has a long-term "plan" for Judah that is not defeated by particular historical circumstance. (On the "plan of Yahweh" for Judah, see Gen. 50:20; Deut. 4:29-31; Isa. 55:6-9.) Yahweh

258

exercises sovereignty even beyond the reality of Babylon. There is a future willed by God that refutes any despair which Judah has experienced. The juxtaposition of Jer. 29:5-9 and 10-14 explicates the deep judgment and the powerful purpose of Yahweh which are held together in tension, both in the heart of God and in the destiny of Israel.

Yahweh had seemed to the exiles to be hidden, absent, unavailable, and ineffective. In vv. 12-14a, however, God is now available (cf. Isa. 54:7-8). It is only required that Israel must "come, seek, and pray." That is, the exiles must engage in serious acts of piety and penance. More than that, Judah must reorient its life in exile. When Judah repents, Judah will find Yahweh to be faithful, available, ready and able to save. Precisely in a situation of hopelessness, Yahweh is announced to be the one who will overcome hopelessness and open a new possibility to Judah. Judah must only decide to seek its future exclusively from Yahweh. The exclusiveness is asserted in the characteristic language of Deuteronomy, "all your heart" (cf. Deut. 6:5; 13:3). Yahweh wills a people utterly devoted. And when there is such an utterly devoted people, life is made newly possible. This is an assertion of the gospel: God is available in the midst of despair and will override both the despair and the circumstances which generate it.

In the juxtaposition of Jer. 29:5-9 and vv. 10-14, we may observe a play on the word *shalom*. On the one hand, there is a contrast between the *shalom* which is a *task* for the exiles (v. 7) and a *gift* from God to the exiles (v. 11). On the other hand, the *shalom* of v. 7 is the welfare of the empire, whereas in v. 11 it is *shalom* for the community of exiles. Thus the two units together provide a subtle reflection on the subject of *shalom*, a subject which the exiles have on their mind even in their chaotic situation of displacement.[34] In the midst of the Exile, there is energy to meditate on and anticipate the possibility of *shalom* for Israel and for the world.

The God newly available in exile will act for the exiles (v. 14b). The conclusion of this oracle is dominated by first person verbs in the mouth of Yahweh: "I will restore, I will gather, I will bring you back." It is not denied that Yahweh has caused the Exile: "I have driven you; I sent you into exile."

34. In the exilic proclamation of 2 Isaiah, the subject of *shalom* is again articulated (cf. Isa. 52:7). Moreover, if *shalom* is the opposite of chaos (cf. Isa. 45:18-19), then *shalom* is understood as the opposite of exile. The promise of *shalom* and the task of *shalom* in our passage then are alternatives to the present disordered experience of exile.

Yahweh is not, however, fated to any decree of the past, nor is Judah in exile fated by Yahweh's old decree. God can do a new thing. This is a moment of a new decree from Yahweh which opens a new future from God for Judah. As *exile* is Israel's most devastating judgment, so *homecoming and restoration to the land* are Israel's deepest yearning and God's best gift. The God who has displaced Judah will now restore Judah. This is, in God's heart and in Judah's faith, a moment for radical newness, rooted only in God's good resolve.

The two units of vv. 5-9 and 10-14 express the core convictions of the Jeremiah tradition. They are hard-won affirmations. The counsel to settle in exile (vv. 5-9) is against the popular notion that the Exile is short and temporary. The counsel to look beyond exile (vv. 10-14) is against the temptation to despair. Both affirmations from the prophet are in fact counter to prevailing opinion. The capacity to entertain both of these affirmations is more than pragmatism, opportunism, and self-interest. Rather, it witnesses a robust dynamic in the textual tradition. It asserts that God has more than one thing to do with Judah, and Judah has more than one moment in its destiny. "True prophecy" is the capacity to say the right thing at the right time, a capacity not exercised by the prophets of optimism nor by the voices of despair. The canonical process is a conviction that Jeremiah rightly sounded both notes of faith at the right moment.

The remainder of this chapter shows the Jeremiah tradition in combat with alternative opinions. These verses reflect the deep tension in the Jewish community between 598 and 587, and no doubt in the same communities later on. Those who remained in Jerusalem after the deportation of 598 continued to believe they were favored by God and regarded themselves as the blessed carriers of Judaism. This was a natural, commonsense assessment. The tradition of Jeremiah, however, a tradition that voices a scandalous alternative, asserted that the ones in exile are favored by God and the ones in Jerusalem are to come under harsh judgment. Moreover, there were those among the Babylonian exiles who articulated the "Jerusalem line," to the chagrin and despair of the deported. In these verses Jeremiah counters that conventional Jerusalem view with his more difficult reading of historical reality. The claim of this tradition is that the ones apparently defeated through deportation are the community from which future Jerusalem will emerge.[35]

35. A Christian appropriation of this affirmation is evident in the christological claim that it is the rejected, scandalized One who is crucified, who is God's way to new life. See, e.g., 1 Cor. 1:18-25; Phil. 2:5-11.

29:15-19   The dispute over the truth of faith is treated in three distinct units. The first unit is framed in vv. 15-19 by two indictments (vv. 15, 19). Both indictments are critiques of the prophets who disagree with Jeremiah and who are regarded by the Jeremiah tradition as unprincipled ideologues and propagandists. The main indictment is that they did not "listen," for if they had heeded, they would not have disagreed with Jeremiah's proclamation. Between these two indictments is the sentence against the king (Zedekiah) and the community remaining in the city (vv. 16-18). The actual curse is conventional language in two formulas. First, the prophet names the three massive curses of sword, famine, and pestilence, which all arise with an occupying army (v. 17). Thus, in effect, the curse anticipates the second invasion of the imperial army. Second, in v. 18 that triad is repeated, but then the heavier threat is that the city will be "a curse, a terror, a hissing, and a reproach" (cf. Deut. 28:37). Using traditional language, the text anticipates the time when the city will be utterly destroyed and an embarrassment among the nations. The two formulas together in Jer. 29:17-18 anticipate (a) another occupation (sword, famine, pestilence) and (b) an ultimate devastation (curse, terror, hissing, reproach). These troubles will come because there has not been obedient torah-listening. Those clinging to the old uncritical hopes of the Jerusalem establishment, to the disregard of the torah, receive the heaviest indictment from the prophet.

29:20-23   In the second of these conflict narratives, the same charges as in vv. 8-9, 15, 19 are voiced, only this time with particular reference to two prophets. Presumably Ahab and Zedekiah were two prophetic adversaries, but we know nothing about them. Again the judgment is the same. They will be submitted to violent death at the hands of the Babylonians, because they pronounced a lie. That is, they did not comprehend and articulate who Yahweh really is and what Yahweh is doing. Their unreality about the historical prospects of Judah is rooted in their unreality about the demands of Yahweh. Their historical judgment is skewed because they did not treat torah religion seriously. They could not believe that God's demands are so serious that disregard would lead to trouble with the public process of history.

After the initial indictment and threat (v. 20), the text then reflects on how these two prophets will become a byword among the exiles (vv. 21-23). They will be a point of ridicule, but also a source of warning to others. The warning among the exiles is "Don't be like Ahab and Zedekiah." Since we know nothing about them, we cannot assess the charges made, except to note that the anticipated mocking of them departs considerably from the standard formulations we have had thus far concerning falseness. Thus the threat is worse than a conventional one. They are "roasted" by the king of Babylon (v. 22). Moreover, their affront is of a different kind: "They have committed folly in Israel [and] they have committed adultery with their neighbors' wives" (v. 23). It is difficult to know how to relate this quite personal charge to the more standard phrasing about false prophets. It may be that the true prophets had the wrong ideology but then attracted this more specific moral indictment. Or perhaps they were troublemakers in the community that had attached to them the more generalizing indictment about falsehood. Perhaps the charge of "adultery" is to be taken metaphorically in relation to falsehood. In any case, these prophets are treated as models of disobedience, used to warn against both moral corruption and theological distortion. The outcome of the oracle is to underscore the rule of Yahweh who will not be deterred from power, either by the empire or by distorting Jewish faith. Yahweh's governance is not altered or diminished by religious posturing or by political wishing. Those who resist the rule of Yahweh, both in its judgment and in its hope, will come to a sorry end.

29:24-32 Finally, one more opponent of Jeremiah is named. Presumably this adversary, Shemaiah, is also in Babylon. The letters he sends (vv. 25, 29) are intended in the present form of the text as a contrast and foil to the earlier letter of Jeremiah. The prophet among the exiles (Shemaiah) urges the priest in Jerusalem (Zephaniah) to exercise his priestly office by suppressing the prophets who are mad, that is, who contradict established opinion (v. 26; cf. Hos. 9:7). Specifically, Shemaiah urges Zephaniah to restrain Jeremiah, who has been speaking subversively. It is the same old issue one more time. The charge made against Jeremiah in Jer. 29:28 is a quote from the letter of vv. 4-5. Jeremiah, in his realism about the Exile, is ideologically unacceptable to this prophet. Thus the letter from Shemaiah is not only a counter to the letter of Jeremiah, but is in fact evoked by it and intends to refute it. The intent of Shemaiah is that the Jews should receive "better news," which means to deny their true situation in exile.

Zephaniah, the priest who is the target of Shemaiah's letter, shares the letter with Jeremiah but does not act on it (v. 29). Apparently he is allied with Jeremiah, or at least sympathetic to him. Predictably the consultation of v. 29 leads to yet another oracle from Jeremiah (vv. 30-32). This oracle deals only with Shemaiah, who is condemned as a liar (v. 31). He and his family are excluded from any future in Judah, because his teaching is an act of "rebellion" against God and God's intent for Judah. At the end of v. 32 this heavy oracle against a particular opponent takes a final positive turn. God will do *good* for God's people (v. 32). Thus we have a contrast between *good for Judah* and *evil for the deceiving prophet*. The *good* here echoes the *shalom* of vv. 11-14, which is homecoming. There will be a homecoming! It will, however, be in Yahweh's own time. It will not be soon or easy, but it is sure.

This is an exceedingly complex chapter, reflecting a deep divide and conflict in the Jewish community. It continues the dispute of chs. 27–28. Indeed, the issue with Ahab, Zedekiah, and Shemaiah is reminiscent of the issue with Hananiah. The canonical Jeremiah tradition accepted as *true* the pro-Babylonian stance of Jeremiah! On the one hand, this view resists the easy assurance that generates *false hope,* as in the case of Hananiah. This is the central issue in the conflict against Ahab, Zedekiah, and Shemaiah, who echo Hananiah. Against their optimism, Jeremiah urges realism. The hard claim of biblical faith characteristically resists easy, romantic renderings. On the other hand, as a subordinate counterpoint, Jeremiah affirms that there will be a homecoming in God's good time. This affirmation is against *weary resignation* which ends in despair, as though exile is a permanent fate.

Against both illusionary expectation and despairing resignation, Jeremiah speaks of God's powerful governance which both settles into exile and ends exile. Jeremiah seeks to extricate Yahweh's sovereign rule from every political compromise and qualification. It may, of course, be argued that Jeremiah's pro-Babylonian posture is itself a pragmatic compromise. Inside the claim of the text itself, however, this posture is affirmed as theologically correct, as congruent with God's own purpose. The purposes of God cannot be trimmed and fitted to any political resolution, either falsely assuring or misleadingly negating. God has God's own way, which is with utter freedom and, in the end, caring fidelity.

"The Book of Comfort"

Jeremiah 30:1–33:26

The primary work of the book of Jeremiah is to speak Israel into exile. While Jeremiah is given a twofold task in 1:10, "to pluck up and to tear down, to build and to plant," the negative theme is much more decisive for and prevalent in the book of Jeremiah. Indeed, the book of Jeremiah is framed in 1:1-3 and 52:12-30 to situate the literature toward and in exile. The primary burden of the literature is that Israel, Judah, and Jerusalem will be dismantled according to the intention of Yahweh.

The countertheme of "plant and build," however, is indeed present in the literature. It is that theme which governs chs. 30–33. The editorial process of the book of Jeremiah has grouped together in these chapters the primary materials voicing God's intention of newness and, derivatively, Israel's restoration after exile.[1]

We may identify three dimensions of the promissory materials which concern us. First, there are important historical considerations. In fact, the Exile was not the end of the Jewish community or of Jewishness. On the one hand, Jerusalem was not "emptied" by the Babylonians, but many Jews continued in the city. On the other hand, the Jewish community in Babylon developed an intentional and intense self-consciousness as a faith-

---

1. On the critical problems related to the promises in Jeremiah, see Siegfried Herrmann, *Die prophetischen Heilserwartungen im Alten Testament.* Beiträge zur Wissenschaft vom Alten und Neuen Testament 85 (Stuttgart: Kohlhammer, 1965), 159-241.

ful community in exile. This community understood and presented itself as a community in waiting, and preempted for itself the claim to be the "real Israel" which would shape post-587 B.C.E. Judaism.[2] Thus historical reality required that an honest portrayal of Israel with God should be amazed by and grateful for the survival and continuation of Jewishness. It turned out that "plucking up and tearing down" was not the last moment in Judaism. Something had to be said about that resilient historical reality.

Second, there is no doubt that the promissory passages function in a pastoral way to voice comfort, consolation, assurance, and hope for the exiles. It was not unreasonable that after 587 Jews in exile and in Jerusalem should have the sense that God had abandoned God's people, or at least was absent. The promissory oracles are in part evoked by such a sense of abandonment, intending to counter such a mood. In a very practical way, the promises serve to give Jews courage and energy to keep on keeping on.

Third, however, the historical and pastoral dimensions of these promises do not touch the reality of the Jeremiah text. Indeed, if there were no real substance to the promises of God, then they simply misread in terms of the historical facts, and they mislead in terms of pastoral crisis. In the end, the ground of hope and promise in Israel and in these texts is theological, that is, it is concerned with and for the character of God.[3]

2. The assertiveness and claim to preeminence of the Babylonian community of exiles is evidenced in the narrative reports of Ezra and Nehemiah as the initiators of what came to be Judaism. It is certain that this community in Babylon played a decisive role both in preserving the normative text for Judaism and in shaping the normative canon. While its claim to preeminence may be overstated, it is clear that the claim is rooted in actual reality.

3. A great deal of literature exists on the identity of the God of Israel as a God who makes and keeps promises. The primary and most influential in this regard is Albrecht Alt, "The God of the Fathers," *Essays on Old Testament History and Religion* (Garden City: Doubleday, 1969), 1-100. See also Gerhard von Rad, *Old Testament Theology* 1 (New York: Harper & Row and Edinburgh: Oliver & Boyd, 1962), 165-174; *Old Testament Theology* 2 (New York: Harper & Row and Edinburgh: Oliver & Boyd, 1965), 263-277; Claus Westermann, *The Promises to the Fathers* (Philadelphia: Fortress, 1980); and Walther Zimmerli, *Man and His Hope in the Old Testament.* Studies in Biblical Theology, 2nd series 20 (London: SCM and Naperville: Allenson, 1971). Note in the work of Zimmerli the important reference to Ernst Bloch. This strand of OT study was taken up in systematic theology in the decisive work of Jürgen Moltmann, *Theology of Hope* (New York: Harper & Row, 1967). The promissory element in Jeremiah is to be understood in the context of the more general promissory dimension of Israel's faith.

Historical criticism, in my judgment, has worked too hard at relating such promises to specific historical situations, seeking to explain the text in terms of context.[4] This sort of correlation tends to diminish the bold theological claim that the ground for assurance is not found in needy circumstance but in the character and resolve of God and in nothing other and in nothing less.

In the book of Jeremiah, the mandate "to build and to plant," that is, to restore, revive, and rehabilitate God's people and God's city, is presented as a resolve of God's own heart (cf. 29:11). The God of Israel (and of the book of Jeremiah) is in fact a self-starter whose speech grows out of a passion for a new beginning and whose speech guarantees newness, for what God says, God will do. The theological ground for the promissory claim depends on two factors. First, *God is faithful* to God's people and to God's promise (cf. 31:28). God does not quit or abandon or disregard. In these texts, particularly in 30:12-17 and 30:20, God's fidelity emerges with fresh power out of God's hurt and yearning for this people. Second, *God is powerful* and able, in spite of Israelite recalcitrance and in spite of imperial resistance, to work a newness in the real world of public power. *The faithfulness and the power of Yahweh* assure that in the depth of Israel's exile God will work a homecoming, in the face of Israel's death God will work new life. That is the substance and burden of these chapters.

In making such a theological affirmation that brusquely overrides historical circumstance, we are not yet at the wonder of these promissory texts. The wonder of these texts is that the resolve of God rooted in God's faithful and powerful character comes to expression in human speech, in poem and oracle and narrative. Thus God's resolve is voiced speech. It is the voiced speech heard in Israel that forms the text of chs. 30–33. This voiced speech is not to be understood as human description and observation of events as they unfold, as though the prophet is a historical commentator or chronicler. Nor is the voiced speech of promise simply human

---

4. Brevard S. Childs, *Introduction to the Old Testament as Scripture* (Philadelphia: Fortress and London: SCM, 1979), has paid primary attention to the canonical shape of the text. For Childs this means that the context of any passage of Scripture is not some historical situation, but the place where it is situated in the larger, completed text. Thus the promises of Jeremiah are to be understood, not in a sixth-century historical context, but as they are situated in chs. 30–33, between the disputes of chs. 26–29, and the Baruch document which follows in chs. 36–45.

hope or wishful thinking, the anticipation that somehow "things will get better." Rather, this speech on the lips of the prophet is God's self-announcement, God's self-resolve to which God's own self is committed in the face of resistant circumstance. That is, God has pledged to work a newness precisely where there is no evidence of such newness on the horizon.

As the promissory text embodies God's self-commitment, so the promissory text lingers in the exilic and postexilic community as an anchor for faith and hope in a context of fickleness and despair. That is, the text is not a prediction, but it is a promise to which Israel clings because of Israel's confidence in the promise-maker. The promissory text is not "used up" or exhausted in any fulfillment or partial fulfillment, but continues to stand, in situation after situation, in generation after generation, as a witness and testimony to what God intends that has not yet come to fruition.

The parlance of promise poses an intense theological problem for us in our interpretive modernity. Enlightenment epistemology is committed to a kind of technological positivism which believes that what is possible is contained in what is humanly available. Enlightenment epistemology programmatically excludes promise as a viable intellectual category, because promise rests upon and refers to power and resolve beyond human control. As a result, promises in the text have either been subjected to historical criticism to explain them (away) or have been generalized as to become innocuous or domesticated through trivialization. The outcome of all these strategies of criticism, generalization, and trivialization is that promise disappears as a category for faith in the midst of history.

An affirmation of promise as a mode for life and faith, however, persists in the text. It refuses to be banished from our horizon of reading and hearing. Moreover, it is striking and odd that while the notion of promise is enormously inconvenient in the midst of modernity, those who are marginalized by modernity — the poor, the oppressed, and the disadvantaged — find Israel's promissory speech to be credible speech. Those who find it unconvincing or inadequate to view the world through human control, or to see the world as finally meaningless, often do not find it irrational to trust another governance that enacts newness. It is the enactment of newness that is the subject of these chapters. To these chapters concerning promise (and others like them), the community of faith returns again and again, in a refusal to believe that present circumstance is the last word on human destiny. Newness is not only possible, but is promised. In the end, "building and planting" requires a wholly different perception of historical reality, a perception that regularly subverts and destabilizes all present-tense reality, for the sake of what God yet intends.

On the basis of 30:2, these chapters are referred to by scholars as "The Book of Comfort," presumably a collection or a scroll of promises through which God will work a new community and a new Jerusalem out of exile. This term for the collection applies most directly, according to common critical judgment, to chs. 30–31, and derivatively to ch. 33. Chapter 32 is of a different genre, a narrative rather than an oracle. Even in the narrative, however, the oracle of God in 32:15 (cf. also vv. 25, 37-41, 43-44) becomes the driving force of the narrative. The account of land purchase in ch. 32 keeps Jewish hope linked to the concreteness of historical reality. The newness this God will work out beyond the failure of Jerusalem and the domination of Babylon is never otherworldly or private, but always public, social, political, and economic. The form and substance of promissory oracles hold together the powerful resolve of Yahweh and the concrete possibilities of Jewishness revitalized. Others in addition to Jews (such as Christians) may use these texts, but in doing so, their future is always mediated to them through the peculiar discourse of Jewish promise.[5]

It is the power of this promissory tradition that is distinctive for Jewishness, and that authorizes and permits the strange, remarkable survival and witness of Jews. In his novel *The Thanatos Syndrome,* Walker Percy has a maladjusted priest conclude:

> The Jews as a word sign cannot be assimilated under a class, category, or theory. No subsuming Jews! Not even by the Romans. . . . This offends people, even the most talented people, people of the loftiest sentiments, the highest scientific achievements, and the purest humanitarian ideals.[6]

5. On the development, nuance, and history of promissory speech in the OT, see Claus Westermann, "The Way of the Promise through the Old Testament," in *The Old Testament and Christian Faith,* ed. Bernhard W. Anderson (New York: Harper & Row, 1963), 200-224.

6. Walker Percy, *The Thanatos Syndrome* (New York: Farrar, Straus & Giroux, 1987), 126. The same priest declares, "Since the Jews were the original chosen people of God, a tribe of people who are still here, they are a sign of God's presence which cannot be evacuated" (123).

These chapters of promise voice, in the sixth century and beyond, the relentlessness of Yahweh in the history of the Jews, relentlessness for newness which the world can neither evoke nor preclude. The promises require us to redefine the categories through which we sort out what is possible and what is not possible. In the end, nothing is impossible for this God (cf. 32:17, 27).[7] This God can indeed plant what has been plucked up and build what has been pulled down. The people who stay close to these promises are very odd people, who will never be "subsumed" either under the false promises of empires or under the large despairs of a failed city. After the failed city and the false promises of the empire, there persist these promises, the God who makes them, and the people to whom they are made. The promises, the God, and the people constitute an always new possibility in history, a possibility undaunted by the summarizing, subsuming categories of the empire. These chapters bear witness to that which the empire dismisses as impossible. The community of this text is insistently urged not to trust in what the world calls possible, for that way leads to despair, conformity, anxiety, and finally death. This community trusts instead in the impossibilities which exist first on God's lips.

Comfort for Israel and Judah (30:1–31:40)

The introduction to these two chapters is an instruction from God to Jeremiah: "Write in a book all the words that I have spoken to you. For behold, days are coming, says the LORD, when I will restore the fortunes of my people, Israel and Judah . . ." (30:2-3). These verses of instruction and authorization provide the clue to prevailing critical judgments about the chapters. These two chapters are called by scholars, "The Book of Comfort."[8] The phrase suggests two things. First, it is a book, a writing. Many scholars believe that these two chapters may have first existed as an

7. Cf. Walter Brueggemann, "'Impossibility' and Epistemology in the Faith Tradition of Abraham and Sarah (Gen 18₁₋₁₅)," *Zeitschrift für die alttestamentliche Wissenschaft* 94 (1982): 615-634.

8. William L. Holladay, *Jeremiah 2*, 148, provides a basic bibliography on these chapters. For a helpful summary statement in English, see Theodore M. Ludwig, "The Shape of Hope: Jeremiah's Book of Consolation," *Concordia Theological Monthly* 39 (1968): 526-541.

independent literary unit. In any case, there was some kind of editing process which has brought together in one place most of the promissory material of the book of Jeremiah. Second, the purpose of the book is to announce that "I will restore the fortunes of my people." That is, the subject of these chapters is God's good resolve for the future, which is homecoming for the exiles. Thus the chapters are a powerful statement of hope made to the exiles, announcing that the Exile will come to an end because God intends to bring the community back to its own land. We have seen that while 29:5-7 anticipates a long exile, 29:10-14 anticipates an end to exile and a homecoming.[9] Chapters 30–31 exposit in lyrical ways the foundational promises of 29:10-14. That is, God is still powerfully at work on behalf of Israel. The God who willed exile now wills homecoming. The God who plucks up and tears down is the very God who will now plant and build (cf. 1:10; 31:28). Exile is not a defeat or failure for God, but the arena out of which God works a glorious newness for God's beloved people and for God's treasured city.

These chapters enunciate a hope rooted in God's own resolve and fidelity, a hope addressed toward a people at the brink of despair, a hope issued in the face of and against the reality of the imperial prowess in Babylon and the utter failure of Judah. The text insists that the resolve of God is strong and active enough to create new possibility in the world, a possibility not generated by the Jerusalem establishment nor permitted by the Babylonian regime. The prospect of homecoming is the evangelical assertion that exile is not the last fate of God's people or of God's world: God's resolve overrides the deathly circumstance of the world, and authorizes and permits new life which did not seem possible in the season of displacement. The hope of this cluster of texts is rooted in nothing but God's intention, uttered against the recalcitrant circumstances of lived experience. The rhetoric of this little collection is complex, and the critical questions have yielded no consensus.[10]

9. The completed tradition of Jeremiah makes in turn two quite different theological emphases which are impossible to coalesce. On the one hand, the tradition of judgment works against complacency; on the other, the tradition of promise intends to counter despair.

10. On the critical questions, see the careful review by John Martin Bracke, "The Coherence and Theology of Jeremiah 30–31" (diss., Union Theological Seminary, Richmond, 1983); and *"šûb šᵉbût:* A Reappraisal," *Zeitschrift für die alttestamentliche Wissenschaft* 97 (1985): 233-244.

The main claim of the text is, however, not difficult or obscure. It is a stunning theological insistence that the historical process is subject to the powerful resolve of God to work a newness, to intrude into old power arrangements and firmly established patterns of reality, to rearrange, reshape, and make new. According to this assertion, any attempt to understand or assess or participate in the historical process without reckoning with this powerful resolve of God is sure to misconstrue and distort. The mode of the argument is mostly lyrical poetry. That lyrical poetry, however, should not be underestimated. It is the chosen mode of the tradition to voice what the closed discourse of power politics refuses and seeks to silence.[11] The oddness of this lyrical discourse in the ancient as in the contemporary world is that it moves in and through and beyond the very power arrangements which seek to silence it. And wherever it moves, it transforms and rehabilitates. This poetry is a means whereby the God of the Jeremiah tradition does indeed "plant and build" out of the very ruins of betrayed covenant.

30:1-3 These verses are a preamble to "the Book of Comfort." The prophet is authorized by Yahweh, the same Yahweh who destroyed Jerusalem, to record a new collection of words of Yahweh. In these verses there is joined together a statement about the mechanics of the origin of the literature and a high theological promise. The editors of the book of Jeremiah have a self-conscious interest in how *God's intention* becomes a *sacred scroll* (cf. 1:1-3; ch. 36).[12] This part of the text is established as the direct disclosure of God's new resolve.

The substance of the resolve concerns a new future for Israel and for Judah, certain but without a specified time: "Days are coming," the days when Yahweh's resolve will come to fruition. The new resolve of Yahweh is expressed in two notions, both introduced by first person verbs: "I will restore" *(shub)*, "I will bring back" *(shub)*. The first phrase is thematic for

11. On the power of such discourse to reopen the silence closed by censoring power, see Walter Brueggemann, *Finally Comes the Poet: Daring Speech for Proclamation* (Minneapolis: Fortress, 1989).

12. On redactional activity and the canonizing process, see Gene M. Tucker, "Prophetic Superscriptions and the Growth of a Canon," in *Canon and Authority*, ed. Coats and Long, 56-70; and the older discussion of Eduard Nielsen, *Oral Tradition: A Modern Problem in Old Testament Introduction*. Studies in Biblical Theology 11 (London: SCM and Chicago: Allenson, 1954).

hope in Jeremiah.[13] "Restore fortunes" means to give back to the covenant people the life, destiny, and well-being that belong to its identity as Yahweh's people. The phrase bespeaks rehabilitation of every aspect of life.

That phrase, however, lacks specificity. It is the second powerful phrase that makes concrete the programmatic theme of reversal. The second phrase concerns the end of exile and restoration to the land. Indeed, restoration to land is the central, quintessential hope of the Jeremiah tradition, and of much of the Bible. The land promise gives materiality to biblical faith; it concerns real life in this world. This tradition of hope knows that in the real world, no people or community will have dignity, security, respect, or well-being unless it has guaranteed land.[14] This is a conviction well understood by the contemporary state of Israel and by the Palestinians as well, by peasants in Latin America, and by Blacks in South Africa. The promise of God is to give that without which human life is endlessly precarious. The promise of Yahweh intends to overrule present land distributions, even those arrangements seemingly guaranteed by imperial decree. Indeed, the claim of the Jeremiah tradition (echoed by recent events in Eastern Europe) is that even imperial guarantees cannot resist the drive for secure land which is a dynamic of history over which Yahweh presides. God's envisioned future for this people concerns land redistribution on behalf of those who cannot secure land for themselves.

30:4-11 These verses include three distinct rhetorical units, which are grouped together in terms of their shared theme of God's rescue in the face of great odds. The poetic unit of 30:4-7 invites the listener into a situation of fear and unrest. The power of terror and dread is vivid perhaps as in the face of an invading army (cf., e.g., 4:13-22). Jeremiah 30:5a describes the external situation in general, and v. 6 portrays a response of enormous fear to the situation. The rhetorical strategy of v. 6 is to state a premise as a question: men do not experience the labor of childbirth? And yet "brave men" *(geber)* act like they are in labor. They hold their stomachs as in the enormous pain of childbirth. Of course their pain is not related

13. On the formula, see Bracke, "Coherence and Theology," 148-155.
14. Concerning the significance of land as the substance of God's promise, see W. D. Davies, *The Gospel and the Land* (Berkeley: University of California Press, 1974); and *The Territorial Dimension of Judaism* (Berkeley: University of California Press, 1982).

to childbirth. It is rather the pain of panic before the great day of turmoil caused by the power of God at work against God's people.

The ludicrous image of v. 6 may be turned in two directions. First, the metaphor of labor pains suggests the futility of this reaction to the danger. There are labor pains but no labor, birth pangs but no birth. Second, the military elite is mocked in what is a sexist image, soldiers acting like women in distress and fear (cf. 50:43; 51:30). The graphic portrayal of 30:5-7a leads us to be surprised by the dramatic conclusion of v. 7b: "Yet!" . . . Nevertheless . . . The powerful adversative preposition shows that the fidelity of God overrides the terror and panic. "He [presumably Judah, the frightened strong man] shall be rescued [presumably by Yahweh]" (NRSV). There is nothing in the scene of terror and panic which leads us to expect this reassuring conclusion. The outcome arises outside the scene of panic, wrought by the fidelity of Yahweh. With this abrupt preposition, a situation of grief and pain is turned to a situation of assurance. Thus the rhetoric itself voices the "turn" promised in v. 3. The terrified one is reassured.

Then follows a prose comment with a very different kind of affirmation (vv. 8-9). These verses give substance to the verb "rescued" *(y-sh-ʿ)* from v. 7. In that coming time, assured by God's fidelity, oppression will be overcome. Whereas vv. 5-7 stayed with the image of the frightened soldier acting like a pitiful woman, these verses step outside the image to the world of imperial oppression. Imperial oppression will be overcome (v. 8), and Israel will again have its own free government (v. 9). Yahweh is the subject of two strong, liberating verbs: "I will break, I will burst." Yahweh will overcome the subjugation caused by the Babylonian hegemony. The power of God is mobilized with reference to an actual concrete political reality, namely, the imperial "yoke."

Verse 9 reflects the conviction of some in exilic Judah that the Davidic dynasty will be reestablished. While this is not a primary expectation of the Jeremiah tradition, it is a live hope in the world of exilic Jeremiah (see 23:5-6; 33:14-16, 17, 22, 26; cf. Ezek. 34:23-24). These verses serve to introduce political specificity into Israel's hope, a political realism kept alive in the Christian tradition by seeing in the person of Jesus the power of God's promise to liberate from oppression (cf. Luke 4:18-19). The juxtaposition of Jer. 30:5-7 and vv. 8-9 is likely not happenstance. More likely, the daring poetry of vv. 5-7, which lacks political concreteness, generated and permitted the more realistic expectation of the prose verses. Thus if Yahweh is indeed to "rescue" these frightened strong men (vv. 6-7), there must be identifiable ways for such rescue. These verses suggest that the instrument of such rescue is the restored monarchy.

The quick rhetorical move from poetic imagery (vv. 5-7) to concrete political expectation (vv. 8-9) culminates in the poetic promise of vv. 10-11. These verses, centering in the magisterial "fear not," are an exile-ending announcement which has close affinities to the material of 2 Isaiah.[15] In this speech form, Yahweh asserts not only solidarity with Israel but a readiness to act on behalf of Israel in ways that will drastically transform Israel's exilic situation. In this form of speech, we are at the center of the notion that God's word of promise and presence does indeed impinge upon the historical process to save. The yoke of oppression is broken (v. 8), because Yahweh has announced an intention to intervene (vv. 10-11). The substance of the promise is that exiled Israel will come home and dwell in safety, the recipient of Yahweh's most powerful blessing (v. 10). The rhetoric marking the new life of the community is governed by Yahweh's strong verbs: "I will save" (*y-sh-'*), "I am with you to save" (*y-sh-'*). The double use of the verb *y-sh-'* echoes the promise of v. 7.

The remaining lines of v. 11 engage in two rhetorical moves which are interesting, but somewhat anticlimactic. First (v. 11b), there is a contrast between Israel and "the nations." The nations who oppress will be terminated,[16] whereas Judah will not be terminated. Thus the assurance of Yahweh goes against commonsense assessments of international politics in the sixth century. On the face of it, Babylon seemed guaranteed to perpetuity, and Judah seemed precarious. Seen in light of Yahweh's faithfulness, however, the situation of the powerful and the vulnerable is exactly inverted. The destinies of the oppressed and the oppressor are reversed.

Second, the last lines of v. 11 are an acknowledgement of reality which cannot be ignored, even in this lyrical promise. There really is exile. God really does punish God's own people. God does indeed take covenan-

---

15. On the text, see Edgar W. Conrad, *Fear Not Warrior: A Study of 'al tîrā' Pericopes in the Hebrew Scriptures.* Brown Judaic Studies 75 (Chico: Scholars Press, 1985), 108-115. On this formulation in a context of exile, see Walter Brueggemann, "Genesis 50,15-21: A Theological Exploration," *Supplements to Vetus Testamentum* 36 (1985): 46-53.

16. While "nations" is plural, in the context of the book of Jeremiah the reference is mostly likely to Babylon (cf. chs. 50–51).

tal disobedience seriously. Judah will be (and is) firmly punished. The conviction that the guilty must be punished is very old and central in the Mosaic memory that feeds the tradition of Jeremiah (cf. Exod. 34:7; Num. 14:18). Moreover, even the Davidic promise which gives large guarantees does not expect a future which is without moral payouts (cf. 2 Sam. 7:14).

Thus Jer. 30:11 contains several theological convictions which stand in some tension with each other. No doubt the ideas in tension — that Judah will not be ended, that Judah will be punished — reflect the ongoing conversation and dispute in exilic Judah about God's intended future for the community. There is punishment, but it is not ultimate. There is rescue, but it is not cheap. God is sovereign and will not be mocked; God is caring and not to be doubted. The ideas are not mutually exclusive, but they are not easily harmonized; it matters enormously in these several theological tensions where the accent is placed. The text leaves the matter of accent open, so that we are left to read and interpret with some freedom.

These three distinct units taken together — vv. 5-7, 8-9, 10-11 — articulate powerful faith, vivid rhetoric, and historical realism. In the end, it is asserted that God's sovereign purpose reshapes and reorders both Israel's despairing present and Israel's doubted but yearned-for future. In the process of adjudicating Israel's future, "the nations" are brought under the same sovereignty as that on which Judah must stake its life.

30:12-17 The theme of exile and return is here considered afresh through a different metaphor, that of sickness and healing. The most interesting fact about this poem is that it is bounded by two statements that blatantly contradict each other. The beginning point is a ruthless, candid diagnosis of diseased Israel (v. 12). God's people is terminally ill, beyond healing, sure to die. The end of the poem is a promise that God will indeed heal and restore (v. 17). Taken together, vv. 12 and 17 affirm that the one who is utterly beyond healing will be healed. The work of the poem (and our interpretation) is to trace the way in which Israel's faith and imagination move from the hopeless candor of v. 12 to the astonishing assurance of v. 17.[17]

Verses 12-15 revolve around the twin themes of guilt and illness. The sickness of Israel is beyond help. Israel, in its disease, is utterly

---

17. See Walter Brueggemann, "The 'Uncared for' Now Cared for (Jer 30:12-17): A Methodological Consideration," *Journal of Biblical Literature* 104 (1985): 419-428.

abandoned, disregarded by former allies ("lovers"). The figure suggests abandonment by fair-weather friends who will not stand by a loser, and who leave off friendship when sickness strikes. This people, in its theological pathology, stands alone in the international scene, helpless before the imperial threat that is authorized by Yahweh. There is for Israel no point in complaining about its deep jeopardy, for healing is not possible (v. 15). Moreover, the cause of the illness is no mystery. Sickness unto death is the outcome of sin, disobedience, and flagrant disregard of God. The diagnosis is unambiguous. Israel's desperate situation has a theological cause which produces a sociopolitical outcome. The nullification of Israel is willed by Yahweh. Clearly there can be no rescue from a sickness willed by Yahweh and warranted by disobedience. The poet daringly uses a medical metaphor to make a staggering affirmation about Judah. The politics of the Near East is read theologically! Judah is caught in a deep pathology of its own making, the pathology of infidelity and self-sufficiency.

The poem takes an abrupt turn in v. 16. We are not prepared for the "therefore" of that verse. In the prophets the term "therefore" characteristically introduces more judgment. More judgment, however, is not required or perhaps even possible after the pathos, harshness, and indignation of v. 15. What else could be said? We discover, however, that the "therefore" of v. 16 is a verbal trick. The term prepares us for one more message of judgment, but in fact the following lines offer exactly the opposite message — a word of God's powerful, healing intervention. The four word pairs of "devour-devour," "foe-captivity," "despoil-spoil," and "prey-prey" indicate a total, symmetrical inversion wrought by God's faithful power, an inversion whereby vulnerable, exposed Judah is protected, and all its powerful attackers are done in by the will of Yahweh.[18] Thus the poem witnesses to the inversion we have already seen in vv. 8-9, 11, whereby the strong are crushed and the weak one is guarded and guaranteed. This inversion again gives flesh to the promise of v. 3 concerning the restoration of Israel's fortunes. The one who has been a threat to Israel is now under severe threat from Yahweh. Yahweh is now actively at work on behalf of Israel's healing, and so deals decisively with the proximate curse of illness. It is odd that in vv. 12-15 it is Yahweh who

18. On the close correlation of sin and punishment, see Patrick D. Miller, Jr., *Sin and Judgment in the Prophets.* What is interesting here is that this prophetic mode of argument is now turned against the enemy of Judah.

causes Israel's terrible problem, but in v. 16 the nations are held accountable for the jeopardy of Judah. Yahweh was the enemy in vv. 12-15, but
has become Israel's friend and advocate in vv. 16-17. Yahweh has decisively
changed roles, which in turn decisively changes Israel's prospects for the
future. Thus in vv. 16-17 the poem changes tone and direction, reflective
of the change in Yahweh's disposition and the consequent change in Israel's
fortune.

Nothing has changed about the propensity of Israel. Israel is still
guilty, still sick, still under threat. Everything, however, has changed about
God. Between v. 15 and v. 16 there is a radical alteration in God's attitude,
perspective, and inclination. The indignant One has become the compassionate One.[19] God who would abandon Judah is now prepared to
intervene to save Judah. The poem traces in dramatic fashion, albeit with
elliptical articulation, the transformation of God from enemy to advocate.
Indeed, the changed fortune of Judah (v. 3) depends upon the changed
disposition of Yahweh. It is the changed disposition of Yahweh which
moves Israel's lot from exile to homecoming. The life of Israel depends in
both aspects (exile and homecoming) upon the inclination of Yahweh.

The crucial and most interesting point in the poem is the reason
given for God's decisive transformation. The final line of v. 17 seems to
give the reason for that change. In v. 14 God has asserted about the nations
that "they care nothing for you." God observes that the nations have
become indifferent. In v. 17, however, it is now the nations who mock
Israel in the same words, who say, "Zion, for whom no one cares." It is
powerful irony that God's own verdict in v. 14 is now on the lips of the
nations in v. 17. When that same verdict is sounded by the nations,
however, it evokes in Yahweh a response of caring solidarity. Yahweh had
been free to critique and condemn this people. However, when the nations
do the same as Yahweh had done, Yahweh is made freshly aware of deep
concern for Israel. In the mocking voiced by the nations, Yahweh is driven
to fresh saving action, becoming newly cognizant of a deep solidarity that
Judah's guilt and Yahweh's indignation have not mitigated. It is as though
in the depth of exile, in the bottom of Israel's terrible humiliation before

---

19. The same transformation of God is disclosed in Deut. 4. In Deut. 4:24
Yahweh is a jealous God but in v. 31 Yahweh has become a merciful God. In the
Flood narrative of Gen. 6–9, the same transformation of God occurs. See Walter
Brueggemann, *Genesis*. Interpretation (Atlanta: John Knox, 1982), 75-87.

the nations, Yahweh found depths of love for Israel about which Yahweh did not heretofore know. It is the situation of Israel's hurt which evokes in Yahweh fresh measures of love and resolve. Yahweh's transformed attitude and inclination dominate the poem and are good news for the exiles. There will be healing, because the diagnostician of vv. 12-15 has become the powerful healer in vv. 16-17. That healing wrought by a change in God bespeaks homecoming, restoration, and rehabilitation for this terminally ill people!

30:18-22   Given God's new resolve to heal Judah (vv. 16-17), the poetry now articulates a wondrous, sweeping scenario of the new historical possibility of restored Jerusalem. The poetry massively overrides any present inadequacy in the city, and focuses our attention on the newness decreed in an anticipatory vision. The poem begins with the "formula of rehabilitation" (cf. v. 3) which envisions an end of exile, an end that is rooted in Yahweh's "mother-love" ("compassion," *rhm*) directed toward the city which God loves (v. 18). There follows a picture of restored Jerusalem. The rebuilding, which is assured as God's own work and not a task urged on Judah, will mean the resumption of joyous liturgy, the glad sounds of birth and weddings (cf. 33:10-11), the return of ordered, prosperous life — all the antithesis of the shabby, poverty-ridden days just past. God will be at work to assure prosperity, prestige, dignity, and well-being (30:19). The promise is that "the good old days" (i.e., "as of old") can be experienced again.

Any who intrude or disrupt or "oppress" (presumably the nations) will have to deal with Yahweh, who is guarantor and protector of the revived city (v. 20b). Yahweh has changed roles; the destroyer has become the guarantor, and when Yahweh makes healing, restorative gestures toward the city, Israel's life is utterly transformed. Verse 21 suggests the reestablishment of the rule of law, though specifics are lacking.

In contrast to the present disorder, there will be an honorable leader with political authority, but also with liturgic legitimacy, for the term "draw near" implies access to cultic functions.[20] Perhaps this is an anticipation of the theocracy to come, when the leadership will be priestly (cf. 33:18,

---

20. The term rendered "prince" in the RSV *('dr)* may refer to any formidable leader. It does not necessarily or intentionally suggest a monarch, as the RSV rendering might imply.

21-22). Such specifics, however, are not at issue here. What is important is the restoration of legitimated order which will permit the community to function. These verses provide an impressionistic inventory of all that is required and promised for the resumption of a full communal life. The promise is capped in 30:22 with the formula of covenantal fidelity which redefines both parties.[21] Thus the tradition flings in the face of exilic disorder and despair the eloquence of God's new possibility. The poem intends to evoke and nurture a dangerous hope that becomes increasingly restless and ill at ease with the distortions, deprivations, and humiliations that presently go with occupation, defeat, and displacement. The poem summons and authorizes a community which believes promises and trusts the promise-maker to move beyond the present into a better world. Life begins again. That new beginning consists in real life in public categories, life guaranteed by the passion, care, and fidelity of Yahweh.

30:23-24 The preceding poetic units have voiced Yahweh's positive action toward Jerusalem. These two verses pause in the midst of that wondrous promise to articulate the dark, ominous side of Yahweh's saving action. Political reality dictates that Jerusalem cannot be restored until the occupying armies of Babylon are removed. Life cannot be normal again in Jerusalem until the imperial cause of the disruption is overcome. These verses are an assault on and warning against "the wicked" (plural). The language lacks specificity and might be variously assigned.[22]

In this context, however, the "wicked" must refer to the imperial power which oppresses (vv. 8, 11, 16, 20), and which precludes and prohibits restoration. The language must perforce be impressionistic, because the poet has no concrete strategy against Babylonian power. In its extremity, Israel does not engage in political analysis, but in sweeping, daring theological rhetoric. The real issue is not specific imperial policy,

21. On the formula, see Rudolf Smend, *Die Bundesformel.* Theologische Studien 68 (Zurich: EVS, 1963).

22. The same lines occur in 23:19-20. In that text the critique concerns the false prophets in Jerusalem. Here the lines appear to be aimed against "the nations." The reuse of the same lines suggests the supple way in which the tradition is open to varied use through fresh interpretation. On the general problem of "the wicked" as the enemy, see Steven J. L. Croft, *The Identity of the Individual in the Psalms.* Journal for the Study of the Old Testament Supplement 44 (Sheffield: JSOT Press, 1987), 15-48. It is clear that the terms have no stable referent, but are open to varied uses.

so the text urges, but imperial disobedience against Yahweh and imperial disorder against the people of Yahweh. The turn in power which will permit Judah to resume life is voiced in ominous, ill-defined threats of "wrath" and "tempest" which are vehicles for the anger which Yahweh has toward the wicked who violate God's people. In the end, there is a moral reckoning and even Babylon must answer to it. God is about to unleash a whirlwind of destruction against the oppressor, for the sake of beloved Jerusalem.[23]

This daring articulation of God's wrath which operates worldwide, however, is not capricious passion. The wrath is an action in the service of God's intention.[24] The vocabulary of judgment is escalated: "storm, wrath, whirling tempest, anger." The entire sequence drives toward the "until" *('ad)* in v. 24. It is the same "until" we have seen in 27:7, 22. The hard, demanding, uncompromising wrath of Yahweh is serious, but it is not ultimate. It has a purpose beyond itself. There is a turn in the rhetoric which marks a turn in God's disposition. The "until" opens vistas for Israel beyond the present situation. The wrath serves God's purpose, a purpose which exists in God's heart beyond the wrath. Thus the wrath against the marked oppressor is instrumental to God's larger intention (30:24a). The destruction that can topple even a great empire is identified by the poet as a strategy of God. The political process of intentionalism is understood in the enormous categories.

The poem ends with the enigmatic assertion of v. 24b: "In the latter days you will understand."[25] "The latter days" are whenever God's inten-

---

23. The unleashing of storm and whirling tempest is not to be understood as "supernaturalism." Rather, the terms bespeak a political revolution, the unleashing of a political, military assault which Babylon cannot withstand. This hint of threat becomes explicit in chs. 50–51, wherein it is Persian power which will be unleashed by God. The unleashing of such power against an established, seemingly impenetrable power is evident in recent time in the dismantling of the power of the Soviet Union.

24. On God's anger as an ordered act of sovereign policy, see George E. Mendenhall, *The Tenth Generation* (Baltimore: John Hopkins University Press, 1973), 69-104. In a little noticed article, G. Ernest Wright, "The Nations in Hebrew Prophecy," *Encounter* 26 (1965): 225-237, speaks of God's maintenance of God's "imperium." The same theme is voiced by Wright, *The Old Testament and Theology* (New York: Harper & Row, 1969), 121-150; and Patrick D. Miller, Jr., "The Sovereignty of God," in *The Hermeneutical Quest.* Festschrift James Luther Mays, ed. Donald G. Miller (Allison Park, Pa.: Pickwick, 1986), 129-144.

tion is implemented. Then God's largest intention will be clear, and this people which has understood so little will see and know. In the meantime, between now and "the latter days," the outcome of the historical process is hidden in God's heart, and Israel can only trust. The future is securely hidden in God's heart. Israel must walk by faith where it may not yet see. Israel may trust in the meantime that there is more in God's heart than wrath. This enigmatic conclusion asserts that the historical process, which on the face is destructive and chaotic, in fact is meaningful and structured in ways that only God can discern. The seeming chaos is a mode of God's majestic rule.

Chapter 30 is a statement of enormous complexity, utilizing a rich variety of literary forms. It moves in and out of the themes of God's anguish and fidelity, Israel's prospect for the future, God's resolve to save, God's readiness to rescue, and Israel's joy in the rebuilding. All of these themes serve the conviction that the future, characterized by Yahweh's covenantal fidelity, is firmly under the rule of God. On the one hand, Israel must not deny its bleak present. On the other hand, however, it must not take the present with ultimate seriousness. God's sure governance of the future stands as a powerful, palpable alternative to present despair. Even in this season of wrath, other days are coming, days of God's well-being and restoration. The poet provides a rich set of images as a bulwark against present-tense resignation. God's sovereignty precludes a deathly fate for Israel. Israel holds to powerful promises in order not to succumb to present despair.

31:1   This verse is a prose introduction for the nine promises that have been collected here. On the one hand, the assertion made by God is almost banal in its flatness. The covenant formula sounds so hackneyed. On the other hand, the statement can be understood as the most foundational promise God can make to exiles. It is the same covenant formula much used by Jeremiah and Ezekiel.[26] Most recurrent in exile when Israel felt abandoned, the formula intends to counter that sense of abandonment:

---

25. Cf. Jer. 31:26; Deut. 29:29. In key places the text acknowledges that there is something hidden about the very matters it seeks to disclose. That hiddenness recognizes not only that the future is not obvious, but that God's intention for the future lies well beyond human discernment.

26. Smend, 5-6, lists the several uses, especially as they pertain to the Exile.

"I shall be your God and you shall be my people." In exile, it is asserted that God will be present to and intervene for Israel precisely in its failure and humiliation. The process of God's loyalty is the process of tribes ("families," *mishpahot*) becoming one "people" *('am)*; thus the work of God is to gather and unify separated and scattered small social units of Israelites to form them into one viable community.[27] God in exile pledges to "form Israel" once again (cf. Exod. 19:6; 1 Pet. 2:9-10). Thus God will now do in exile what God did at the outset in Egypt, when God formed a new people out of disparate and hopeless social units.[28]

31:2-6 This promissory oracle affirms God's fidelity to Israel and, as a result, Israel's resumed life which is marked by joy and abundance. God is utterly faithful to Israel (Jer. 31:2-3). These two verses contain two of the most fundamental statements of God's fidelity to Israel: (1) "The people . . . found grace in the wilderness." This statement makes an allusion back to the wilderness sojourn in the ancient days of Moses, when God surprisingly gave sustenance in the wilderness (cf. Exod. 16:12;[29] Jer. 2:2). At the same time, however, "wilderness" is a reference to contemporary exile, so that the assertion not only remembers surprising graciousness in the past, but is a statement concerning God's powerful, gracious presence in Israel's contemporary circumstance of displacement. This is an example of how an old memory illuminates and redefines Israel's present circumstance. The formula asserts that the present reality of exile is not godless and not graceless.

(2) "I have loved you with an everlasting love." God asserts an abiding

27. Norman K. Gottwald, *The Tribes of Yahweh*, 237-340, has provided the most programmatic statement concerning the sociopolitical process of tribes becoming a unified people.

28. On the process of the formation of a new people, see the suggestive statement by Norman K. Gottwald, "Religious Conversion and the Societal Origins of Ancient Israel," in *Perspectives on the Hebrew Bible*. Festschrift Walter J. Harrelson, ed. James L. Crenshaw (Macon: Mercer University Press, 1988), 49-65. While Gottwald comments on the early period of Israel and not the exilic period, I cite the discussion because Gottwald shrewdly shows the interface between sociopolitical and theological aspects of conversion.

29. It is not unimportant that this narrative affirmation is lodged in the Priestly tradition, i.e., in an exilic text that shares the context and concerns of the "Book of Consolation."

fidelity to Israel. This statement is in considerable tension with much of the Jeremiah tradition, which suggests that God has terminated a relation with Israel. The tension cannot be resolved, because both statements of abandonment and fidelity are made, and both inclinations are present to Yahweh. This positive statement is characteristically made *after* the crisis of abandonment. Thus it is regularly in retrospect that such assurances of God's grace and presence are given, so that the statement does not in fact cancel or deny the recent, distressful past. Rather, the statement of grace and presence provides a basis on which to move beyond that terrible moment of distress into a new future, buoyed by God's reliable love. This statement does not abrogate older statements of discontinuity, but it now overrides them for the future.[30] Therefore God's freshly offered love *('hb)* issues in faithfulness *(hsd)* which gives impetus for the rehabilitation of Israel. Clearly the prophet is not a systematic theologian, but a poet who lives very close to the hurts and hopes of God's own heart. It is God's heart made visible here which gives Israel a new chance in the future.[31]

Israel will have all aspects of its life restored and revitalized (31:4-6). This poetic unit is dominated by the threefold "again" *('od)* which acknowledges that there has indeed been a decisive break in well-being. But that break will now be overcome. Thus "again" there will be building and restoration (v. 4a), as anticipated in the programmatic statement of 1:10. There will "again" be merriment, dance, celebration, and rejoicing, after all the party noise has ceased (31:4-6; cf. 7:34; 16:9; 25:10; 33:11). There will "again" be plenty and the earth will produce in abundance (31:5). "Plant," in the third element, is used as a term to balance "build" in the first element. The two terms together bespeak restoration of urban life and of agriculture, that is, all aspects of the community.

The restoration culminates in an invitation of pilgrimage to Zion (v. 6). That means the temple will be rebuilt and restored; to it will come worshippers from the north (Ephraim) in a reunited Israel. The love *('hb)* and faithfulness *(hsd)* of God (v. 3) issue in the revitalization of every aspect of Israel's daily and public life. The poem effectively holds together theological, socio-economic, and political dimensions of communal life; everything begins anew.

30. See Walter Brueggemann, "A Shattered Transcendence?"
31. See Walter Brueggemann, "A Shape for Old Testament Theology, II: Embrace of Pain," *Catholic Biblical Quarterly* 47 (1985): 395-415.

31:7-14 This promissory oracle in God's mouth asserts with exuberance the well-being, joy, and abundance that God will give to the restored, returned community. The oracle addresses the community itself (vv. 7-9) and the watching nations (vv. 10-12), followed by a summary statement of newness (vv. 13-14). The poem is a collage of Israel's best stock phrases for newness from God.

The community is summoned, invited, and urged to engage in praise (v. 7). Five imperatives are employed: "sing aloud, raise shouts, proclaim, give praise, say!" The substance of the proposed speech of Israel is either an imperative seeking God's rescue, or it is a declaration, celebrating it. Perhaps the verb intends to point in both directions, as imperative and as celebrative declaration. Either reading is powered by the decisive verb, *y-sh-'.* God announces what is to happen, introduced by "Behold, I" (v. 8). God is bringing and God is gathering. The term "gather" *(q-b-ts)* (vv. 8, 10) is a key word for the restoration of the exiles. Because of the destruction of Jerusalem, Jews have become fugitives, refugees, and displaced persons all over the known world. In these images God will bring them from all parts of the world, including the north (i.e., Babylon). Among those gathered will be the weak and the vulnerable, the blind, lame, and pregnant. They will be given power and legitimacy, which they themselves do not possess. The faithfulness of God makes possible a great homecoming procession of those valued by God whom the nations have devalued (cf. Isa. 35:3-6; 43:5-7). The homecoming throng will be deeply moved, overwhelmed with both memory and hope (Jer. 31:9a).

The language necessary to this overwhelming picture requires two metaphors. On the one hand, language of "lead," "brooks of water," and "straight path" evokes the picture of the good shepherd who seeks out the lost and brings them home (v. 9; cf. Isa. 40:11). On the other hand, the reference to the "first-born" suggests an Exodus motif (cf. Exod. 4:22), concerning the one especially valued and beloved, who receives God's special protection, care, and gifts. The shepherd who protects is the father who values. The metaphors are particularly telling because the community of the firstborn is constituted by the disabled. The two metaphors together bespeak a situation in which the last ones become the first ones; that is, the disabled ones become the firstborn. The "father" of the "first-born" takes those "orphaned" by the process of exile and makes them a home (cf. Hos. 14:3b).

284

The nations are addressed by God's firm resolve for homecoming for God's people (Jer. 31:10-12). The one who "scattered" now speaks (v. 10). It was none other than this God who caused exile; now the "scatterer" has moved to a new inclination and a new kind of activity. The One who scattered (i.e., caused exile) is the One who will now gather (i.e., bring home from exile). Again the shepherd image is invoked for the One who seeks and saves the lost ones. No single Jewish exile is lost from the wonder of a safe homecoming. The homecoming requires Israel's richest, most passionate vocabulary, to say fully what must be said about rescue. In v. 7 we have already had the verb "save" *(y-sh-ʿ),* and now in v. 11 we have "ransom" *(pdh)* and "redeem" *(g'l).* The latter phrase in v. 11 suggests that the hands of the oppressor were too strong for Israel to resist. The strong hand of Yahweh, however, is stronger than "hands too strong for him." The strong hand of Yahweh will prevail, and so Israel will be safe.[32]

Though the address to the nations continues in v. 12, that particular address seems almost forgotten. The poet simply describes the scene of the joyous return in power. Though many Jews in fact never left the homeland, and though Jews may have trickled back over a longer time, this is not the scene we are offered. The text of course is not descriptive reportage. This is rather a lyrical scenario, constructed for the most dramatic effect possible, in terms of the governing metaphor of exile and return. Israel's poetic tradition in exile imagines all the exiles coming home together in one great event, in a procession led by Yahweh.[33] In this verse the dominant image is of a well-watered land, which is a "good" from God, who knows where the good streams are. In that well-watered land (like a luxuriant garden), the best crops (grain, wine, oil) and the best animals (flocks and herds) will flourish, and there will be no more drought (languishing). Well-watered, productive land is one of Israel's ways of speaking about

32. Two clusters of uses evidence that "Yahweh's hand" concerns rescuing power. On the one hand, the notion occurs in the classic credo of Deut. 26:8 and similar uses. On the other hand, the motif is central to the "Ark narrative" of 1 Sam. 4–6, as Patrick D. Miller, Jr., and J. J. M. Roberts have shown in *The Hand of the Lord* (Baltimore: Johns Hopkins University Press, 1977).

33. Isaiah 40:10-11 offers one standard image of Yahweh at the head of a great, triumphant, celebrative procession coming home to Jerusalem. On the antecedents to this imagery for exiles, see Thomas W. Mann, *Divine Presence and Guidance in Israelite Traditions* (Baltimore: Johns Hopkins University Press, 1977).

God's rich blessing that makes abundant life possible (cf. Ezek. 34:25-31). Note well, the rhetoric moves beyond salvific language to creation, for the scope of the newness is utterly comprehensive. The poet strains to find language to match the envisioned newness.

The conclusion to this celebrative poem characterizes the new gifts of God given to the rescued (Jer. 31:13-14). This conclusion is introduced by "then" *(az)*. The "then" that is promised is sharply contrasted with the "now" which is still deathly and exilic. The key verb is "turn" *(hpk):* "I will turn" (v. 13), that is, God will invert and transform the total situation of Israel. The language here is closely related to and perhaps echoes the more intimate speech of Ps. 30:11:

> You have turned *(hpk)* my mourning into dancing;
> you have taken off my sackcloth
> and clothed me with joy. (NRSV)

This God has power to move against mourning and sorrow, the mood dictated by exile (cf. John 16:20). In their place God authorizes dancing, merriment, joy, comfort, and gladness. It will be "like priest, like people" (Jer. 31:14; cf. Hos. 4:9). The priests who receive a share of sacrifices will have more than enough; the people will be satiated with God's goodness ("bounty," *tob*). The structure of this section is a contrast of then and now; the poem celebrates both the coming "then" and the one who gives it. God has power to transform, and has promised to do so.

31:15-22 This poem reflects the tradition of Jeremiah at its most daring in the use of poetic metaphor, imagery, and strategy.[34] It begins by a careful listening at the very edge of Israel's horizon (Jer. 31:15). Jerusalem has listened too long to its own immediate crisis. Now it is invited in the poem to listen to a much older, much more pathos-filled voice. The sound comes out of the ancient past; Mother Rachel grieves over the generations, for all the lost children who are so vulnerable and so bru-

---

34. On this difficult unit, see Bernhard W. Anderson, " 'The Lord Has Created Something New': A Stylistic Study of Jer 31:15-22," *Catholic Biblical Quarterly* 40 (1978): 463-478 (repr. in *A Prophet to the Nations,* ed. Leo G. Perdue and Brian W. Kovacs [Winona Lake: Eisenbrauns, 1984], 367-380); and Phyllis Trible, *God and the Rhetoric of Sexuality.* Overtures to Biblical Theology (Philadelphia: Fortress, 1978), 40-50.

talized.[35] Mother Rachel is disconsolate for all the lost children of Israel, including the current generation of exiles. The weeping of the uncomforted mother easily traverses the generations, for all the lost ones are the same to this mother, regardless of their generation.[36]

God answers the disconsolate mother (vv. 16-17). The structure of vv. 15-17 is one of lament and response. The response in Israel is characteristically a response of presence, concern, intervention, and rescue. And so it is here. God's word to Mother Rachel is an invitation to wipe away the tears, to end the weeping (cf. Isa. 25:8; Rev. 7:17; 21:4). The children who "are not" will again "be," for they will come home. Thus the construct of lament-response is taken up to assert the resolution of homecoming for the grief of exile. The gift of hope overrides the despair of the lamenter.

After the mother grieves and God answers, the lost child speaks (Jer. 31:18-19). It is a speech of sorrow, regret, and repentance. It is an admission of resistance to the discipline of God. The speaker admits turning away, but now is ashamed at his own actions. God's response to the repentance of vv. 18-19 is one of pathos, comfort, and assurance (v. 20). As Mother Rachel has had unrequited pathos, so the God of Israel is moved by deep pathos. Indeed, God's response is not unlike that of Mother Rachel. There is, on God's part, an inclination to reject wayward Israel, and to be done with such painful, exhausting recalcitrance.

That inclination, however, is countered in the very heart of God. God's heart is profoundly torn. On the one hand, the cessation of speech which tries to blot out the painful name and deep memory of Israel will not ever finish with the son.[37] On the other hand, God's own memory of Israel is as compelling and powerful and palpable as the memory Rachel

---

35. On the reach of Rachel's grief across the generations, see Matt. 2:18. On that same voice in more contemporary accents, see Emil L. Fackenheim, "New Hearts and the Old Covenant: On Some Possibilities of a Fraternal Jewish-Christian Reading of the Jewish Bible Today," in *The Divine Helmsman*. Festschrift Lou H. Silberman, ed. James L. Crenshaw and Samuel Sandmel (New York: KTAV, 1980), 191-205; and Jonathan Kozol, *Rachel and Her Children: Homeless Families in America* (New York: Crown, 1988).

36. It is for that reason that Fackenheim and Kozol can claim that Rachel weeps even for twentieth-century children. All are equally treasured by this mother, who refuses to be comforted.

37. The verb for "remember," *zkr*, is expressed in the infinitive absolute, voicing the great force of the act of memory.

has of her children. God is reduced to trembling yearning, and finally finds that mercy wins over rejection.[38] The two infinitive absolutes of "remember" and "have mercy" indicate the power of God's positive resolve. The God who *utterly remembers* is the God who *utterly has mercy*. Thus v. 20 is a response to vv. 18-19, just as vv. 16-17 answer v. 15. In both vv. 16-17 and v. 20, God's response finally authorizes an utterly new beginning, putting behind (but not denying) all the grief of Rachel and all the waywardness of Israel.

God counsels a return along well-marked paths (the torah) (v. 21). The return is geographical (end of exile) and theological (end of resistance).[39] Astonishingly, Israel is addressed both as "virgin" (v. 21) and as "backsliding [RSV 'faithless'] daughter" (v. 22). Finally, the poem ends in an utter newness (v. 22). The virgin Israel (not the abandoned widow; cf. Isa. 54:4-8) is welcomed home. She is purged of her foolishness, is resolved to faithfulness, and is brought back to the land. The grieving Rachel is consoled; the wayward woman becomes the faithful woman now established in the land, prepared to have heirs and so to guarantee security. This rich and expensive range of metaphors (admittedly sexist in its manipulation of female roles) is used to render the awesome gift of homecoming, a new beginning both theological and geographical.[40] The use of these images suggests that the poet wants to voice not just a changed venue for Israel (homeland rather than exile), but also a genuine transformation that alters the very character of Israel and the modes of relationships in the community. Thus it is both a changed venue and a genuine transformation that matter for the ending of Israel's exile.[41]

31:23-26 This promissory oracle again anticipates resumed, renewed life in the land. This brief unit utilizes a number of interesting rhetorical

---

38. Again, the verb "have mercy" *(rhm)* is in the infinitive absolute.

39. On repentance and return as a primary theological motif in the Exile, see Hans Walter Wolff, "The Kerygma of the Deuteronomic Historical Work," in Walter Brueggemann and Wolff, *The Vitality of Old Testament Traditions* (Atlanta: John Knox Press, 1975), 83-100.

40. On the newness, see Anderson, " 'The Lord has Created Something New,' " 477-78.

41. The second dimension of a genuine and profound transformation is expressed variously as "a new heart" (cf. Ezek. 11:19; 18:31; 36:26), "new covenant" (Jer. 31:31), and "new name" (Isa. 62:2).

maneuvers. It reuses the thematic statement, "I will restore their destinies [RSV 'fortunes']." It promises that a celebrative song of Zion will again be sung in the land (Jer. 31:23). The "again" (RSV "once more") implies that there was a time when the song was not sung, that is, when the temple was discredited, God was absent, and the singing stopped. Now Israel will resume the old liturgical refrain which acknowledges that Zion is the place where God and God's people can meet. All around the temple and the city, life will resume in harmony and free from conflict (v. 24). This will include the towns and their inhabitants. It will equally include farmers and their flocks. Thus all aspects of the economy are named and included. They will all stand under the promise of God. God will minister to the weary and the faint, and will make them strong and vibrant. Again, the poem asserts God's resolve to invert completely every aspect of Judah's life.

Verse 26 is a most peculiar verse. Its rhetoric is apocalyptic, and it seems to allude to something like resurrection, with language of being asleep and being awakened. It is exceedingly difficult to know what is being talked about. Perhaps the verse suggests that this promise is a dream or a vision. Perhaps we should regard the scenario of vv. 23-25 as an act of imagination in which the speaker can envision reality beyond the present. We are told nothing about the present and its possibilities, but only about the future which is so unlike the present. This entire collection of promises, and indeed the hope of Israel in every exile, depends upon the capacity to imagine reality beyond present circumstances. Moreover, that act of imagination is not simply inventive fantasy,[42] but it is linked to the power and freedom of God as known in Israel's memory. Thus v. 26 indicates that this author fully understands what he is doing. He is voicing a dreamlike scenario of healing reality, not yet in hand, but already assured by the power of God. Hope is clearly understood as a dreamlike alternative imagination which accepts God's intent as more powerful than the present, seemingly intransigent circumstance.

31:27-30   This promissory oracle anticipates a new beginning for Israel and Judah, a new beginning after the old communities have been put to death. God asserts a powerful resolve to begin again, afresh, after a

---

42. On the crucial distinction between imagination and escapist fantasy, see the discerning statement of J. R. R. Tolkien, "Tree and Leaf," *The Tolkien Reader* (New York: Ballantine, 1966), 29-99.

complete failure. Verse 28 appeals to the six verbs which set the theme of the Jeremiah tradition in 1:10. The four negative verbs are intensified by the addition of a fifth one, "to bring evil." The most important matter in this verse is that the five negative verbs have all been fully enacted. There is no more threat in them. God has monitored ("watched," *sh-q-d*) the fulfillment of all the negatives and has kept track ("watched") until the promise of destruction has been fully actualized.

That review of the negatives, however, is only backdrop for the oracle. What counts now for the poem are the two positive verbs, "to plant and to build." The terms bespeak a full resumption of all of life. God is watching over these two verbs to bring them to fruition and to fulfillment. Thus the text uses all six verbs from 1:10. They are used here, however, in two distinct stages, so that the positive verbs come in sequence after the negatives. The poet proposes a two-stage philosophy of history which is crucial for the full acknowledgment of exile and the full practice of hope in the face of exile.[43] The negative has happened; the positive is only promised. The poem places us between the destruction already accomplished in 587 B.C.E. and the homecoming only promised but keenly anticipated. The oracle places us between a death already wrought and a resurrection only anticipated.[44] The text places the listener "in between" and promises that, in that in-between place, God is watching with powerful, intentional concern.

This assertion of God's watching echoes 1:10 (cf. *sh-q-d* in 1:11-12) and contrasts with 44:27 wherein God's watching is negative. It is easy in exile to conclude either that God is hostile to Israel or that events are completely out of control. This insistent text, however, refuses both the conclusion of God's hostility and the conclusion that matters are out of control. What is in fact happening, so the text asserts, is happening under the watchful superintending eye of God, who will not quit until all is accomplished. The God who watches over recalcitrant Jews in Egypt for

43. Childs, 345-354 and esp. 346, has shown how the literary history of the book of Jeremiah serves a two-stage theological statement.

44. Jacob Neusner, *Understanding Seeking Faith: Essays on the Case of Judaism*, vol. 1: *Debates on Methods, Reports of Results*. Brown Judaic Studies 116 (Atlanta: Scholars Press, 1986), 145, has shown how the language of death and resurrection pertains to the Jewish experience of exile and restoration. Indeed, the dominant Jewish paradigm Neusner presents operates in those categories.

evil (so 44:27) is the God who intends only good for the community that adheres to Jeremiah (so 24:6).

It is exceedingly difficult in our intellectual situation to believe in a larger purposefulness to public events, beyond our intention and discernment. That assertion of a larger purposefulness, however, is indispensable to fend off resignation and despair in situations of exile. God does indeed intend good (cf. 29:11).

That, however, leaves the question, is such goodness from God possible in a situation so burdened by the consequences of plucking up and tearing down? Will not the consequences be visited upon the children and the children's children (cf. Exod. 34:7)? In response to that question which must have been much alive among exiles, Jer. 31:29-30 is added to the promise of vv. 27-28. The two positive verbs, "plant and build," anticipate a newness from God. The proverb repeated in v. 29 apparently was popularly held and affirmed: children into the next generation are fated to the consequences of the deeds of their parents. In the context of exile, this proverb asserts that the generation of the Exile is fated to the consequences of choices made in Jerusalem prior to 587. The conclusion is that newness is impossible in the face of such a sure, heavy fate; the parents have already chosen the fate of the children and the children's children.

The text, however, finally refuses the proverb and declares it to be null and void. Each one (i.e., each new generation) can act out its own destiny and choose its own future with God. The refutation of the proverb, and therefore the dismissal of conventional wisdom, asserts that newness is possible for the generation of the Exile. God can indeed "plant and build" for and with and in that generation. Paul Joyce has shown that this statement is not an eruption of "individualism" in the community, as much interpretation has heretofore accepted, but simply is an assertion of newness possible for the new generation of exiles.[45] The newness to exiles made possible by the nullification of the proverb prepares the way for the promise of the next literary unit.

31:31-34   This oracle of promise is the best known and most relied upon of all of Jeremiah's promises. It has frequently been preempted by Christians in a supersessionist fashion, as though Jews belong to the old covenant

45. Paul Joyce, *Divine Initiative and Human Response in Ezekiel.* Journal for the Study of the Old Testament Supplement 51 (Sheffield: JSOT Press, 1988), 35-60.

now nullified and Christians are the sole heirs of the new covenant. Such a distorted reading of the text has been abetted by the rendering of old and new "covenant" as old and new *"testamentum,"* which was taken too easily and uncritically as the two "testaments" of Christian scripture. Thus the "new covenant" (i.e., new relation of God with God's people) became one of "two testaments," with the "New Testament" (and its community) being the "real" one.[46] Such a preemptive reading ignores the text itself. Moreover, such a rendering of the future could hardly be expected or cogent in the midst of these several promissory oracles which anticipate the reconstitution of the Israelite community.[47] Such a supersessionist reading in fact asserts the rejection rather than the reconstitution of Israel, a point not on the horizon of these oracles.[48]

It is clear, against such a Christian misreading, that the contrast of "old and new" concerns the Israelite community of covenant in both its parts. The "old" covenant belongs to that Israelite community which through its sustained disobedience forfeited covenant with God, even as it lost the city of Jerusalem. The "new" covenant now wrought by God also concerns the Israelite community. This is the community formed anew by God among exiles who are now transformed into a community of glad obedience. Thus we are right to posit a deep discontinuity between old and new, but that deep discontinuity is not between Jews and Christians, but between recalcitrant Jews prior to 587 and transformed Jews after 587 who embrace the covenant newly offered by God.[49]

---

46. See the discussion of Paul M. Van Buren, *A Christian Theology of the People Israel,* Part 2: *A Theology of the Jewish-Christian Reality* (San Francisco: Harper & Row, 1983), 28 and *passim.*

47. Van Buren, 255, comments on the text: "What was it that was to be new about it? Surely not a change of partners!"

48. This is a somewhat different reading from that of Van Buren. Van Buren suggests (155) not only that it is the same covenant, but that there is no room for discontinuity. I believe this view fails to appreciate the radicalness of the text, a radicalness that does not depend on Christian supersessionism.

49. Kornelis H. Miskotte, *When the Gods are Silent* (New York: Harper & Row, 1967), 409-415, offers a most helpful theological comment on the text. He observes: "The new covenant is new in that it finally becomes in simple truth a covenant. . . . So dreadful is the estrangement, so irreparable is the apostasy! Creating, establishing, disposing, God will have to call into being what is self-evident, so that Israel will finally be Israel in its own place, in time" (413).

This promise concerns a new covenant, a new relation, offered and given and established by God. It is given by God without reason or explanation, out of God's own resolve for the relation.[50] The second party who receives the new relation with God is the community of Israel and Judah (31:31). The contrast between old and new covenant is in its mode of reception. The old covenant from Sinai was resisted until it was broken and abrogated. The new covenant will not be resisted, because the torah — the same commandments as at Sinai — will be written on their hearts. That is, the commandments will not be an external rule which invites hostility, but now will be an embraced, internal identity-giving mark, so that obeying will be as normal and as readily accepted as breathing and eating. Israel will practice obedience because it belongs to Israel's character to live in this way. All inclination to resist, refuse, or disobey will have evaporated, because the members of the new community of covenant are transformed people who have rightly inclined hearts. There will be easy and ready community between God and reconstituted Israel.

From that basis, we are offered four derivative points about the coming covenant, all of which witness to the new communion wrought by God's powerful resolve:

(1) There will be genuine solidarity, expressed in the covenant formulary (v. 33).

(2) There will be full "knowledge of Yahweh." This theme is an important one for Hosea and for Jeremiah after him. On the one hand, as Hans Walter Wolff has urged, "knowledge of Yahweh" denotes a cognitive capacity to recite the saving tradition (2:6-8).[51] That is, such knowledge consists in knowing the identity-giving story. On the other hand, it is probable that "knowledge of Yahweh" means affirmation of Yahweh as sovereign LORD with readiness to obey the commands for justice that are the will of Yahweh. Thus when Jer. 22:15-17 speaks of "knowing Yahweh," it suggests obedience to God's commands for justice. It is not necessary

50. See Hans Walter Wolff, *Confrontations with Prophets* (Philadelphia: Fortress, 1983), 49-62.

51. See Miskotte, 412 and esp. n. 3, with references to Wolff and Zimmerli. See Herbert B. Huffmon, "The Treaty Background of Hebrew *Yāda'*," *Bulletin of the American Schools of Oriental Research* 181 (1966): 31-37; and Huffmon and Simon B. Parker, "A Further Note on the Treaty Background of Hebrew *Yāda'*," *Bulletin of the American Schools of Oriental Research* 184 (1966): 36-38.

(or even possible) to choose between these two meanings. Either or both
are possible for the newly constituted community of covenant. Thus
community both embraces a concrete memory and acknowledges a present
loyalty.

(3) There will be common, shared access to this knowledge which
evidences fundamental egalitarianism in the community. On the crucial
matter of connection to God, the least and the greatest stand on equal
footing. No one has superior, elitist access, and no one lacks what is
required. All share fully in the new relation. All know the story, all accept
the sovereignty, and all embrace the commands.

(4) The concluding statement may be the most crucial. The phrase
is introduced by *ki,* as though this line states the basis for all the foregoing.
All the newness is possible *because* Yahweh has forgiven. Indeed, beginning
again in and after exile depends upon Yahweh's willingness to break out
of a system of rewards and punishments, for the affront of Israel and Judah
could never be satisfied by punishment.[52] God has broken the vicious
cycle of sin and punishment; it is this broken cycle that permits Israel to
begin again at a different place with new possibility. This is an uncommon
statement, utterly Jewish, utterly grace-filled; upon it hangs the whole of
reconstituted Judaism out of exile. Jewish faith is deeply rooted in forgiveness.[53]

In this, of all Jeremiah texts, we must reflect on the Christian appropriation of the promise. The use of this text in Heb. 8:8-13; 9:15-22; and
10:16-17 provides a basis for a Christian preemption of the promise. This
preemption, however, misreads and misinterprets the text. Thus we arrive at
a profound tension between the OT text and the NT quotation, a tension

52. The exhaustion of punishment and the intrusion of forgiveness is expressed
in other language in Isa. 40:2. Miskotte comments: "And so it is that knowledge grows
out of forgiveness. And forgiveness remains the incredible miracle that wipes out time,
establishes time, and illuminates time" (414).

53. On the originary power of forgiveness, see Hannah Arendt, *The Human
Condition* (Chicago: University of Chicago Press, 1958), 236-243. Arendt (239, n. 76)
comments concerning Jesus: "It is his insistence on the 'power to forgive,' even more
than his performance of miracles, that shocks the people, so that 'they that sat at meat
with him began to say within themselves, Who is this that forgives sins also?' (Luke
7:49)." On the quite practical, public outcome of forgiveness, see Carter Heyward et
al., *Revolutionary Forgiveness: Feminist Reflections on Nicaragua* (Maryknoll, N.Y.:
Orbis, 1987).

reflective of a long history of Jewish-Christian competitive acrimony. The matter is not easily adjudicated, because the supersessionist case is given scriptural warrant in the book of Hebrews. My own inclination is to say that in our time and place the reading of Hebrews is a distorted reading, and we are back to the recognition of the Jewishness of the new covenant. At best, we may say that Christians come derivatively and belatedly to share the promised newness. This is not to deny Christian participation in the newness, but Christian participation is utterly grounded in Jewish categories and claims, and can have participation on no other terms. Moreover, this Jewish mediation of newness is left open as an act of profound grace to all who come under these commandments and allegiance to this God. It is of course possible to read this in terms of Jewish triumphalism, but such is not the intent of the text. Indeed, the text invites Jews (and belatedly Christians and others) to stand in grateful awe before the miracle of forgiveness, to receive it, and to take from it a new, regenerated life. Thus the promise occasions no arrogance or pride, but only genuine gratitude. The offer of newness is not narrowly construed, but it has at its core the commandments which God has given first of all to the Jews.[54]

31:35-37 Whereas Jer. 31:31-34 places its accent on discontinuity between old and new, the capacity of God to terminate and begin again, these two brief oracles place accent on continuity, on God's abiding and constant fidelity through historical disruptions. Whereas vv. 31-34 focus on Israel's recent experience of loss and displacement, these two brief oracles completely disregard historical specificity and focus on the abiding structures of creation.[55] The stress on continuity and creation embodies

54. The claim of the priority of Jews in the covenant is variously nuanced in the works I have cited by Van Buren, Miskotte, and Wolff. All of these scholars are agreed against any form of supersessionism. On the more general problem of supersessionism, see the discussion in *Hebrew Bible or Old Testament?* ed. Roger Brooks and John H. Collins (Notre Dame: University of Notre Dame Press, 1990), with special attention to the paper by Rolf Rendtorff.

55. The tension between 31:31-34 and 35-37 is reflective of the two strands of Israelite faith as articulated by Claus Westermann, "Creation and History in the Old Testament," in *The Gospel and Human Destiny,* ed. Vilmos Vajta (Minneapolis: Augsburg, 1971), 11-38; (with Friedemann W. Golka), *What Does the Old Testament Say About God?* (Atlanta: John Knox, 1979); and *Elements of Old Testament Theology* (Atlanta: John Knox, 1978), as respectively a theology of "deliverance" and a theology

the largest and most comprehensive ground for God's fidelity to Israel imaginable;[56] they do, however, cut against the grain of most of the Jeremiah tradition, for that tradition inclines to discontinuity rather than to continuity, to historical specificity rather than to creation. Thus in these two oracles, we are at the edge of the imaginative world of the Jeremiah tradition, in which the text strains to voice the most unshakable assurance it can muster. In both oracles, God's love for Israel is as sure and durable and credible as God's governance of the world itself.

The first oracle (vv. 35-36) consists in a doxology (v. 35) and an "if-then" statement of assurance (v. 36). The doxology seeks to establish the awesome power of the Speaker of the oracle, to indicate that this Speaker does indeed have the capacity to do what is promised. The doxology is governed by two participles, describing actions which God characteristically and continually does. First, "God gives": God gives the sun, the moon, and the stars their place and their ordering (cf. Ps. 136:7-9). Second, "God stirs up": God rules the sea and causes it to roar. Whereas the reference to sun, moon, and stars bespeaks order, the reference to the sea suggests disorder and surging chaos (cf. Jer. 5:22). God governs both order and chaos. Then, as in the doxologies of Amos, the story line of the doxology abruptly breaks off in awed exclamation.[57] Yahweh is Yahweh of the troops![58] Yahweh's awesome name matches and conveys Yahweh's awesome power to dispatch the creatures of heaven and earth.

---

of "blessing." The latter does not appear extensively in the tradition of Jeremiah. When we learn to look for that theology of blessing, however, we may find more of it than our conventional categories have permitted us to see.

56. James L. Crenshaw, "Introduction: The Shift from Theodicy to Anthropodicy"; and "The Problem of Theodicy in Sirach: On Human Bondage," in *Theodicy in the Old Testament*, ed. Crenshaw. Issues in Religion and Theology 4 (Philadelphia: Fortress and London: SPCK, 1983), 1-16, 119-140, has urged that when the historical categories of rescue became inadequate, Israel was driven to creation as a way of affirming sense in its experience. Such a development may suggest why 31:35-37 is included in the tradition of Jeremiah.

57. Concerning the doxologies of Amos, see James L. Crenshaw, *Hymnic Affirmation of Divine Justice*. SBL Dissertation 24 (Missoula: Scholars Press, 1975); and Werner Berg, *Die sogennannten Hymnenfragmente im Amosbuch*. Europäische Hochschulschriften 23/35 (Frankfurt: Lang, 1974).

58. When the "hosts" are understood as stars, then the accent on creation and the sovereign rule of God are more closely connected.

With such a doxological prefix, we are now prepared to take seriously the "if-then" formulation of 31:36. The "if" concerns the "fixed order" of sun, moon, and stars, the order just asserted in the doxology of v. 35. The point of the protasis is that this cosmic arrangement is utterly reliable. Thus the "if" is not a statement of conditionality (as it might appear to be), but in fact is a confident negation. It intends to assert that "never" will this fixed order cease. The cessation of sun, moon, and stars which God has authored is unthinkable and unimaginable. The "then" clause concerns Israel's status as the object of Yahweh's special love. The implied "never" of the protasis carries over into the apodosis: "never" will Israel cease.

This twofold implied "never" may be taken as an ontological assertion, thus giving Israel status not unlike sun and moon and stars as a fixture of creation. More likely this statement does not claim so much, but is a pastoral affirmation. Some must have taken the catastrophe of 587 as a sign of Israel's rejection by Yahweh (cf. 33:24).[59] Such a reading, this oracle asserts, is a terrible misreading, for even 587 cannot terminate the relation to which Yahweh is committed. This bold assertion, which is a very different assurance from that of 31:31-34, anticipates Rom. 8:38-39. Nothing, not even 587, can separate Israel from God's relentless love.

The second oracle is structured according to the same "if-then" pattern and makes the same affirmation (Jer. 31:37). Again, the "if-then" construct is not a statement of conditionality, but a twofold statement of "never." The heavens and the earth are never to be measured or explored;[60] Israel will never be rejected. The final line of the oracle is not indifferent to Israel's serious misdeeds, ". . . all that they have done." All that they have done is bad indeed, enough to evoke hostility and rejection; all of that evil, however, cannot undo God's powerful choosing. The connection between God and Israel cannot be abrogated from Israel's side; what God chooses, Israel cannot reject.[61] Israel is impotent to terminate the relation.

---

59. See the troubled, lingering, unanswered question of Lam. 5:20-22 and the liturgical verdict concerning the question in Isa. 49:14. The texts suggest that Israel's sense of abandonment was a powerful theological problem.

60. See the lyrical, doxological conclusions of Job 28, and the discussion of Gerhard von Rad, *Wisdom in Israel* (Nashville: Abingdon and London: SCM, 1972), 145-49.

61. This affirmation clearly runs counter to the statement of v. 32, that Israel "broke" *(prr)* the covenant. The two affirmations are there in the text, back-to-back.

Only Yahweh has made the relation, only Yahweh can nullify the relation, and Yahweh will not.

Two misreadings of this text are possible. On the one hand, it would be a mistake to consider this text as claiming ontological significance for the covenant structure, as if Israel is fixed in the cosmos like heaven and earth. The text does not claim this. On the other hand, in our modernity, it is not useful to consider that now the heavens can be measured and earth can be explored, thereby nullifying the promise made from an ancient view of the world. We must take the assertion on its own terms in its own context, as a pastoral, evangelical assertion of God's fidelity toward and solidarity with Israel, in and through the Exile. Israel's well-being rests with God's inclination; and God's inclination, as the sun, moon, stars, heavens, and earth attest, is relentlessly steadfast.[62] The episode of 587, harsh as it is, does not finally detract from the overriding reality of God's watchful, persistent fidelity.

31:38-40 This final promissory oracle in the chapter provides a surprising and remarkable climax to the series of promises in these two chapters. We have seen that 31:31-34 and 35-37 make very different points of emphasis, the former concerning discontinuity and historical specificity, and the latter concerning continuity and creation. Both of those promissory passages, however, are preoccupied with the relation between Yahweh and Israel. That is, the subject is intensely theological. This final promise (vv. 38-40) demonstrates the way in which Israel's faith in general, and the Jeremiah tradition in particular, are concerned with day-to-day concrete reality. This final promise does not attend to a more general God-Israel relation, but to the specific economic-political reconstruction of the city of Jerusalem. The oracle is filled with quite concrete geographical references to the city. The actual reference points are not known to us, but they are written or spoken by someone who is clearly familiar with the city. While it is most congenial to situate this oracle in the time of

---

Israel struggled with both statements. The interpreter is not free to opt for either one to the neglect of the other. The two affirmations provide the arena for Israel's ongoing theological work.

62. On the attestation of sun, moon, and stars in praise, see Terence E. Fretheim, "Creation's Praise of God in the Psalms," *Ex Auditu* 3 (1987): 16-30. See also von Rad, *Wisdom in Israel,* 144-176.

Nehemiah and that rebuilding of the city,[63] we must not disregard the enduring promissory character of the oracle. Thus the oracle is not simply reflective of a single rebuilding effort, but looms as a pervasive and enduring promise that marks the life and destiny of the city of Jerusalem in every time and circumstance. This oracle assures that Jerusalem in every time is a city under the powerful promise of God for rebuilding and for well-being.

The city of Jerusalem has indeed become a place of profanation (cf. 3:2; Ezek. 8–11). Now it is promised that this profaned city will be a place "sacred [RSV 'holy'] to Yahweh." The city which had become repellent to Yahweh, where Yahweh would no longer abide, now becomes an acceptable habitat where God will again dwell.[64] Thus the quite concrete geographical references are turned toward theological significance. The reconstituted city becomes once again the place where God will be present with healing, protective power.[65]

The acceptability of Jerusalem as a place of God's residence means that the whole bleak history of destructiveness (which has preoccupied the tradition of Jeremiah) will end. Thus in Jer. 31:40 it is asserted that the two negative verbs "uprooted" and "overthrown," which have been a leitmotif for Jeremiah since 1:10, are now eliminated from the vocabulary of Yahweh and from the life of Jerusalem. The long history of destructiveness evoked by Israel's disobedience has ended (cf. 31:27-28); now the counter-verbs from 1:10, "plant and build," can have full sway. It takes no great imagination, given the power of "plant and build" to overpower "uproot and overthrow," to see a new future for Israel, as stunning and profound as the ways in which resurrection nullifies and overrides crucifixion. Moreover, the final word about the silencing and annulment of these negative terms in the life of Jerusalem is "forever" *(l'olam)*, which the RSV renders "never again." That is, there will be no "plucking up" or

63. See Holladay, *Jeremiah 2*, 199-200.

64. The notion of the profane city being made holy to the LORD is parallel to the dramatic presentation of Ezek. 9–10, 43–44, in which the glory of God departs and returns to the city. See Ralph W. Klein, *Ezekiel: The Prophet and His Message* (Columbia: University of South Carolina Press, 1988), 172-79.

65. The lyrical anticipation of a "new Jerusalem" in Isa. 65:17-25; Rev. 21:2-4 thus is connected to a quite concrete passion for reconstruction of the ruins of Jerusalem. The metaphor must not be permitted to float off away from historical concreteness.

"overthrowing" ever again. One can see in the oracle an inchoate Zionism that will loom large in emerging Judaism. The city of Jerusalem now becomes the visible sign and evidence that God has turned the destiny of Israel decisively in a new direction of well-being. Where there has been uprooting and overthrowing, there will be building and rebuilding . . . forever!

Jeremiah Purchases Land (32:1-44)

This long prose passage seeks to find in God's resolve a way into the future for Israel, which has been seriously dislodged in the present. The chapter has its center in a quite specific, public, concrete, economic act (32:6-15). That specific act, which becomes the taproot of reflection in this chapter, generates an expansive and sweeping claim for the future (cf. esp. vv. 42-44).

32:1-5 The chapter begins in an odd way. The tradition of Jeremiah several times reiterates an encounter between the prophet and King Zedekiah (21:1-7; 37:3-7, 17-21; 38:14-28). This is yet one more report of such an encounter. The beginning point of the report is the delivery of another prophetic word (32:1). Two circumstances pertain: the city is under siege, and the prophet is under arrest (vv. 2-3a). The only speech in this unit is not "the word of the LORD," but the questioning speech of the king (vv. 3b-5). Thus v. 1 introduces a "word from the LORD," but what follows is a word from the king.

The king asks a question, but the substance of the question is a quote from the prophet, that is, a word uttered previously by the prophet. Thus "the prophetic word" is placed in the mouth of the king, who ostensibly had heard the message so often that he knew it by heart. The recurring message of the prophet that the king quotes is that the city will be taken and the king will be deported. While elsewhere the death of the king is anticipated, here what is promised is only an unequal, ominous meeting with the king of Babylon. The quote in the mouth of the king adds an ominous conclusion: "You shall not succeed" (v. 5). The staging of the entire speech of the king is "Why? (*maddua'*, v. 3b). Why does Jeremiah say this? Why does the prophet threaten the king? Why are the king and the city under assault?

Two observations are evoked by the question of the king. First, if the king had listened closely enough to quote the prophet as he does, the king might have listened closely enough to know the answer to his question. Second, though the king asks "why," this narrative in fact offers no answer. Thus vv. 1-5 present only a general background for the narrative to follow; the query of the king does not in fact relate in any specific way to what follows. All we know (yet again) is an inordinate threat to crown and to city. The king does not really ask for information, but makes a plea for rescue.

32:6-15 The core element in this chapter is the specific episode of land purchase here narrated. The word of Yahweh announced in v. 1 is now voiced in v. 6. The specific impetus for this public act is given in vv. 6-8. On the one hand, Jeremiah is forewarned (by the LORD) about his cousin's request (v. 7). On the other hand, the cousin makes the direct request as anticipated (v. 8). The convergence of Yahweh's forewarning and Hanamel's request authenticates that this act is indeed wrought by God. The actual imperative in v. 8 implicates Jeremiah in a land transaction at the moment when the land and its worth are jeopardized by a military occupation (vv. 1-5). Thus the "right of redemption" is an act to keep a family inheritance of land intact, just when circumstances made such an investment seemingly foolish. The family obligation (sanctioned by God) is taken seriously against all negative indicators from the sorry context. The obligation is to preserve and maintain the family inheritance of land.

Jeremiah acts to fulfill his cousin's imperative that is authorized by God (vv. 9-13). The narrative reports in a detailed way a carefully proper transaction in which appropriate public procedure is meticulously followed. There is a transfer of cash, the signing of titles and deeds, the verification of witnesses, and the public filing of copies of the transaction. Verse 12 suggests that there are ample witnesses, so that that can be no later question concerning the property or completeness and legality of the transaction. In this episode, we also have the first mention of Baruch, who is given a special position as the one who retains the deed of purchase (v. 12).

We may wonder why this episode receives such careful attention. Apparently the episode provides, in narrative form, clear title that this community facing deportation has an inalienable piece of land. That is, while the act contains one plot of land for one family, in the narrative presentation, that piece of land is paradigmatic of all the land which Israel held and now loses. Moreover, the public act (and its narrated report) put Jeremiah on public record as claiming that there is indeed "life after Babylon."[66] The prophet has put his money where his mouth is.

The narrative makes clear that while this is a carefully performed economic, legal act, it is not simply an economic or legal transaction. It is a land deal freighted with enormous theological significance. Baruch is commanded to deposit the deed where it is safe and where it will be an enduring witness into the long-term future. The act closely parallels and anticipates that of Seraiah the brother of Baruch in 51:59-64. Both acts that the brothers record and for which they make enduring deposits affirm the same reality of life after Babylon.[67] In terms of our reading the text, we may conclude that the safe place in which Baruch deposited the evidence, even after the "earthenware vessel" (32:14), is the biblical text itself. That is the only place in which the evidence of the land deal has remained. That evidence, however, is sufficient for Israel's long-term hope.

The entire transaction concerning the land comes into theological focus in v. 15. Now, in the mouth of God, we are given to discern the meaning of the economic, legal act. The triad of "houses, fields, vineyards" bespeaks the most common and characteristic elements of economic life. These items will "again be bought." The term "again" suggests a disruption and a cessation.[68] The invasion by the Babylonians will indeed cause the economy to come to a halt. A time will come when there will be no market for fields, houses, or vineyards, because people lack money or nerve. The invasion causes the economy to come to a standstill. But the land will be "born again." "Bought again" means that the economy will resume and regain its health. The community will begin to function again, and when the economy resumes Jeremiah will have staked out a crucial point of

---

66. See Peter Diepold, *Israels Land.* Beiträge zur Wissenschaft vom Alten und Neuen Testament 95 (Stuttgart: Kohlhammer, 1972): 129-131.

67. The references to Baruch (32:12; 36:4ff.) and his brother Seraiah (51:59-64) suggest that the family of Neriah (1) was skilled as a family of scribes and (2) belonged to the pro-Babylonian party in Jerusalem. On both counts, they were important to the developing tradition of Jeremiah.

68. The recurrence of the adverb "again" (*'od*) in exilic texts acknowledges both an honest recognition of discontinuity, and a deep conviction about rehabilitation after the discontinuity (cf., e.g., Isa. 54:9).

access for himself.[69] The entire process of vv. 6-15 holds together the theological reality of God's promise and the restoration of an economic infrastructure. This is a characteristic way in which the Bible holds together faith claims and the realities of public life. Unless both factors are present, the significance of this episode collapses. In the exercise of family economic responsibility, the prophet enacts the long-term fidelity of God as well. Jeremiah invests in God's promised future exactly when that future seems completely closed off.

32:16-25 The prayer of the prophet which follows the purchase of the land may have been placed here through an editorial process. It is, however, not inappropriate in its present place, for the conclusion to the prayer in v. 25 alludes directly to the climactic statement of v. 15.

After the transitional comment of v. 16, the prayer begins with a doxology (v. 17). God is named and then is identified as creator of all that is; the wonder of creation is sighted as evidence of God's power and freedom to do whatever God chooses. The way of creation is "by great power and by outstretched arm." This same sort of phrasing is more familiar to us in an Exodus recital, yet another area of God's power and freedom (cf. v. 21). Finally in the doxology, the prayer asserts that nothing is "impossible" for God. This extreme statement seems to allude back to Gen. 18, wherein what is not "impossible" for God is the birth of a child to an old, barren couple.[70] In the context of this chapter concerning exile, the doxology — which appeals to creation by implication to the Exodus, and to a birth to the barren — asserts that even the circumstance of exile cannot curb or limit or defeat God's great and powerful resolve, any more than chaos, bondage, or barrenness could thwart God's powerful intention.

After this thematic assertion, Jer. 32:18-23a provides a catalogue of the "impossibilities" God has wrought. The supporting evidence for praise to God is a highly stylized recital of Israel's canonical statement of God's gracious miracles. Yahweh is characterized by *hesed*, "steadfast love," which God has persistently "showed" to Israel. That statement of God's goodness, however, is balanced or even countered by the adversative statement that God

---

69. The act is at the same time a way of securing family property and of vindicating the faith voiced in the tradition of Jeremiah. That the land can later be reclaimed serves to announce that Jeremiah was right in his reading of history.

70. Walter Brueggemann, "'Impossibility' and Epistemology," 615-634.

repays *(sh-l-m)* guilt (v. 18). The two parts of v. 18 thus voice the fundamental tension in the character of Israel's God, a tension early articulated to Moses (Exod. 34:6-7), a tension evidenced in the wilderness tradition, especially Num. 14.[71] God is utterly faithful and exactingly severe.

Israel seems untroubled in its presentation of this tension in God, and is not obligated to find a way to resolve the tension. The doxological formulation of Jer. 32:18b-19a perhaps revels in the tension, and takes the very tension of God's faithfulness and judgment as the inescapable working of Yahweh's greatness and might. On the one hand, it is the God of such greatness and might who endlessly assesses the world, and who "rewards" all according to their just desserts. Thus the verbs "repay" *(sh-l-m,* v. 18; RSV "requite") and "reward" *(ntn,* v. 19) suggest a God of responsible retribution. On the other hand, v. 20 begins a recital of God's *hesed,* which is not at all guided by merit but by mercy.

The core memory of Israel completely disregards a retributive moral scheme and rejoices exuberantly in good gifts given by God which have not been warranted. This inventory of good gifts includes the signs and wonders of the Exodus and the gift of the land. These miracles, like the miracle of creation (v. 17), are accomplished by a strong and outstretched arm. The upshot of such generosity from God is a land of milk and honey. Thus in the recital, the prayer keeps the tension in God's inclination wondrously balanced, open, and unresolved.

After the recital of God's wonders, vv. 23b-24 speak out of a very different frame of reference, again returning to retributive sanctions. These verses are a programmatic lawsuit statement, offering a rationale for the Exile. The indictment of the lawsuit is that Israel did "not listen," did not "walk in the torah," did not "do." The sentence of the lawsuit, introduced by "therefore," refers to all these "evils" ("disasters"), specifically siege and its derivative visitations of sword, famine, and pestilence. These verses, like the events of 587 B.C.E., indicate that Yahweh in "repaying the guilty" has the last word. It is judgment against torah-breakers that finally prevails. This is indeed a primary claim of the book of Jeremiah, sustained by Israel's experience (587).

71. On this text and its bipolar theological function, see Katherine D. Sakenfeld, "The Problem of Divine Forgiveness in Numbers 14," *Catholic Biblical Quarterly* 37 (1975): 317-330; and Dennis T. Olson, *The Death of the Old and the Birth of the New.* Brown Judaic Studies 71 (Chico: Scholars Press, 1985), 129-152.

Except for v. 25! Indeed, the entire prayer beginning in v. 17 moves toward v. 25, surprising as it is after the reasoning of vv. 23b-24. For the most part, this prayer is focused on retribution. Except for the initial statement of "nothing is impossible" (v. 17) and the initial reference to "steadfast love" (*hesed*, v. 18), we expect nothing more beyond retribution. The move beyond a system of judgment begins with "Yet thou" *(we-attah)* (v. 25). Of course, finally Israel must reckon not with a system of sanctions but with the "Thou" who created the world, birthed the heir to the barren, and freed the slaves to become Israel.[72] This "Thou" is characteristically willing and able to move beyond prearranged payoffs and consequences to utterly new, inexplicable possibilities. This moment in exilic theology is such a moment when God moves beyond strategies and constraints of retribution. The land is invaded and occupied and has become worthless. The "Thou" of Yahweh, however, counters that outcome of worthlessness with a resolve and a promise: "Invest!" *(qnh)*. The promissory imperatives continue: Buy land and get witnesses, secure titles. Thus the verse names the matters Jeremiah performed in vv. 6-15. Do all these in faith, against the present data. The data is all Babylonian. God, however, speaks beyond Babylon to anticipate the liberation and revaluing of the land when it has been regarded as worthless.

This prayer is often dismissed as late, tendentious rhetoric. Such a verdict, however, misses the delicate, torturous, vibrant struggle of the text to find hope in exile. The voice of the text is honest and does not wish to evade or deny the awesome threat against Jerusalem which is the result of "not listening" (v. 23b) and which issues in terrible curses (v. 24). That moral severity is rooted in very old character traits of Yahweh (cf. v. 18; Exod. 34:7). That harsh element of Yahweh is readily acknowledged; it is not denied that Judah warrants every harsh action from Yahweh that it receives.

The prayer is not, however, a scolding. It is an act of amazement. It is mindful that Yahweh is not controlled or finally victimized by the reality

---

72. See the convergence of these several themes in Rom. 4:17. Hans Heinrich Schmid, "Rechtfertigung als Schopfungsgeschehen," in *Rechtfertigung*. Festschrift Ernst Kasemann, ed. Johannes Friedrich, Wolfgang Pöhlmann, and Peter Stuhlmacher (Göttingen: Vandenhoeck & Ruprecht, 1976), 402-414, has suggested that *creatio ex nihilo*, resurrection from the dead, and justification by grace are in fact parallel and synonymous claims. The same kind of identity of themes is present in this verse.

of disobedience and evil. This same God is marked by and free for *hesed*. The *hesed* seen in creation and Exodus now comes powerfully into play among the exiles. God intends a good life for this people after exile. Such a post-exilic destiny for Israel might seem to the exiles and to us utterly impossible. The possibility here announced is not first of all economic or political. It is rooted only in God's passionate freedom which issues in concrete newness. The world does not culminate on Babylonian terms, because God has post-Babylonian intentions for Judah.[73] Because of this "Thou," history for Judah and Jerusalem is open to outrageous newness wrought through the courage of the faithful. The act of faith commanded concerning the land is concrete and specific. It is because so much of faith rides on this act that the extreme care of Jer. 32:6-15 is taken. The move beyond exile to life in the land is the cause for doxology. Indeed, such a restoration of the land is a miracle on a par with creation. Life begins again, out of chaos!

32:26-41 The "prayer" of Jeremiah (vv. 16-25) evokes a response from Yahweh in the form of an oracle. Thus these two long prose sections are formally related as prayer (vv. 16-25) and as answer (vv. 26-41). In substance, however, they are two long theological reflections on the twin themes of judgment and hope, placed respectively in the mouth of the prophet and in the responding mouth of God.

Verse 27 is precisely symmetrical to v. 17 in all four of its parts:

	v. 17	v. 27
Initial ejaculation:	"Ah" *('hh)*	"Behold" *(hnh)*
Naming of God:	Lord Yahweh	Yahweh
Reference to creation as scope of sovereignty:	doxology	"all flesh"
Statement on impossibility:	conclusion	rhetorical question.

Thus v. 27 seems to echo and answer all the elements of v. 17 and prepare for the assertions that follow (vv. 28-41), even as v. 17 opens the

---

73. In the end, chs. 50–51 are canonically decisive. Most of the book of Jeremiah concerns the judgment of God wrought through Babylon. The defeat of Babylon in those concluding chapters creates space for the newness God will enact on behalf of this people.

way for the prayer of vv. 17-25. Verse 27 has Yahweh announce self as the cosmic sovereign. The question, "Is anything too hard for me?" echoes Gen. 18:14; it is a rhetorical question with an implied answer of "no." Thus the question corresponds to the assertion of Jer. 32:17. The oracle like the prayer concerns the God who acts beyond what Israel (or the world) thinks is possible.

The impossibility which God will work, according to both prayer and oracle, is twofold. First, God will work a massive judgment which is here expressed in a lawsuit form (vv. 18-36). It is not "impossible" for God to terminate Jerusalem. The more extended part of this divine asseveration is an indictment, detailing the wrongs of Judah (vv. 30-31a, 32-35). The affronts committed by "this city" against Yahweh are a quite generalized "evil" (vv. 30, 32); more specifically, the people of Israel and Judah "did not listen, they refused discipline" (v. 33, author's translation). That is, they regarded themselves as autonomous, outside the claims of the torah and beyond the obligations of covenant. Thus autonomy was the worship of other gods, which in fact are only projections of self-interest.

The sure outcome of such a rejection of Yahweh is that Yahweh will dispatch Babylon to destroy (vv. 28-29), so that the offending city is removed from Yahweh's field of vision (v. 31). The argument is a straightforward articulation of disobedience (vv. 30-31a, 32-35) and punishment (vv. 28-29, 31b). The disobedience is of the grossest kind, and therefore the punishment is most severe. If any in Jerusalem still believed the ideology that Jerusalem is inviolate, this oracle rejects such a view in the most unambiguous terms.[74]

In light of such an insistent statement, we are scarcely prepared for the second aspect of God's "impossibility" (vv. 36-41). The rhetoric marks a drastic turn in the oracle with "and now therefore" (v. 36). The "and now" *(we'attah)* characteristically marks a drastic break with a discussion of what is past, and makes an intense focus on the present which may stand in sharp tension with the past. The "therefore" is odd,[75] for it suggests that the facts of vv. 28-35 are the cause of v. 36. Nothing, of course, could be further from the intended shape of the argument. Verse 36 does not

74. For a positive presentation of the theological claims of the Zion establishment, see Ben C. Ollenburger, *Zion, The City of the Great King.*
75. Some versions of the text do not include the word.

follow in any way from the argument of vv. 28-35. Indeed, in v. 36 the text makes an enormous leap away from vv. 28-35 to God's second impossibility. Now the news is good. It has not been impossible to destroy the city. It also is not an impossibility, we are now told, that God will revive this city which is in ruins.

Verse 36 functions to tie the two impossibilities together, for v. 36 reiterates the judgment sounded against the city in vv. 28-29. Indeed, it is as though the text wants to establish continuity, so that we understand that the city now to be revived is in fact the city that has been destroyed. For the theological point being made, it is crucial that it is the same city. The issue of continuity in a crisis of deep discontinuity is not unlike the issue of the continuity of the crucified Jesus and the risen LORD, attested by Thomas's probing touch (John 20:24-28). As the resurrection of Jesus is the resurrection of the Crucified One, so the gathered city is the gathering of the city destroyed. That city is in the throes of heavy curses (Jer. 32:36). Those curses are, however, disrupted by the intrusive speech of God: "Behold!" (v. 37). The term matches the term in v. 27, thus creating a parallel in rhetoric as the two impossible acts of God are contrasted. This is followed by three powerful verbs through which Yahweh enacts a fresh and inexplicable intention: I will gather, I will return, I will settle. The verbs directly counter the negative "I drove them" (v. 37), so that the reverse of verbs serves God's intent to reverse exile. The rejected city is the place of God's great, impossible gathering.

These programmatic assertions are then followed by a series of theological statements reflective of Israel's best exilic faith, statements which find important parallels in exilic Isaiah and in Ezekiel (vv. 38-41). These statements include the following:

(1) The covenantal formula, "They shall be my people, and I will be their God" (v. 38).[76] This statement asserts utter solidarity between God and Israel, a solidarity sharply disrupted by the Exile, but now fully restored.

(2) A gift of a new heart, a new disposition toward Yahweh which permits full trust in God, which makes trustful obedience joyous (v. 39; cf. Ezek. 11:19-20; 36:26-27).[77]

---

76. See Smend.

77. On the "new heart," see Donald E. Gowan, *Eschatology in the Old Testament* (Philadelphia: Fortress, 1986), 69-83; and Joyce, 107-124.

(3) An assertion of an "everlasting covenant," one not to be disrupted or violated as exile disrupted and violated the old covenant.[78] Thus it is precisely the exilic situation of radical discontinuity that evokes and permits such a full statement of confidence and of continuity.

(4) The promise that God will act in complete fidelity *(emet)* to do good and to plant Israel in the land which had seemed forfeited (Jer. 32:41; cf. 1:10).

These four phrasings, characteristic of Israel in exile, give substance and depth and form to the large promise that God will "gather." This is what "gathering" means. Yahweh is resolved that Israel will now be fully blessed as God's people, so that none of the hurts or scars of the events around 587 and the Exile should remain. The word "faithfulness" *(emet)* suggests that Israel is now to benefit from God's powerful capacity to keep covenant.[79]

This double statement of prophetic prayer (vv. 17-25) and divine oracle (vv. 26-41) demonstrates how the tradition of Jeremiah understands and voices the problem of exile in relation to the fidelity of God.[80] The circumstance of Israel's experience in the time of the formation of this tradition required a two-stage statement of God's resolve. It would not do, on the one hand, only to state the destructive "impossibility," both because it was not by itself true and because it is not theologically adequate for the way of God's governance. On the other hand, it would not do to speak only of God's second possibility of restoration, for that would deny too much of the painful discontinuity and would in fact be a mode of "cheap grace." Both "impossibilities" are present in this oracular response of God. Both are essential, in sequence, to Israel's life with God. This twofold

---

78. The *berit 'olam* emerges as especially important in the Exile when the covenant of Moses seemed to have been abrogated. See Delbert R. Hillers, *Covenant: The History of a Biblical Idea* (Baltimore: John Hopkins University Press, 1969), 98-119.

79. On the delicate interplay of continuity and discontinuity in the covenant, see David Noel Freedman, "Divine Commitment and Human Obligation: The Covenant Theme," *Interpretation* 18 (1964): 419-431; and the fresh and vigorous argument of Jon D. Levenson, *Sinai and Zion: An Entry into the Jewish Bible* (Minneapolis: Winston, 1985), esp. 187-217.

80. Though the term is not often used for this text, the text in fact articulates a powerful proposal for a theodicy, holding together God's power and fidelity, and the experience of suffering in Judah.

structure of "impossibilities" is faithful both to Israel's experience and to the programmatic statement of 1:10. We may see in the two-stage presentation an anticipation of the Christian shaping of life in terms of death and resurrection.[81] While the casting of this twofold matter is of course in terms that are particularly Jewish (and only derivatively Christian), the twofold drama of grief and hope is in fact intrinsic to human experience, for those who have eyes to see. The commonality of this drama is well said by George Steiner.

> There is one particular day in Western history about which neither historical record nor myth nor Scripture make report. It is a Saturday. And it has become the longest of days. We know of that Good Friday which Christianity holds to have been that of the Cross. But the non-Christian, the atheist, knows of it as well. This is to say that he knows of the injustice, of the interminable suffering, of the waste, of the brute enigma of ending, which so largely make up not only the historical dimension of the human condition, but the everyday fabric of our personal lives. We know, ineluctably, of the pain, of the failure of love, of the solitude which are our history and private fate. We know also about Sunday. To the Christian, that day signifies an intimation, both assured and precarious, both evident and beyond comprehension, of resurrection, of a justice and a love that have conquered death. If we are non-Christians or non-believers, we know of that Sunday in precisely analogous terms. We conceive of it as the day of liberation from inhumanity and servitude. We look to resolutions, be they therapeutic or political, be they social or messianic. The lineaments of that Sunday carry the name of hope (there is no word less deconstructible).
>
> But ours is the long day's journey of the Saturday. Between suffering, aloneness, unutterable waste on the one hand and the dream of liberation, of rebirth on the other. In the face of the torture of a child, of the death of love which is Friday, even the greatest art and poetry are almost helpless. In the Utopia of the Sunday, the aesthetic will, presumably, no longer have logic or necessity. The apprehensions and figurations in the play of metaphysical imagining, in the poem and the music, which tell of pain and of hope, of the flesh which is said to taste of ash and of the spirit which is said to have the savour of fire, are always Sabbatarian.

81. See Neusner, 145 and *passim,* for those two stages in the decisive paradigm of Judaism.

They have risen out of an immensity of waiting which is that of man. Without them, how could we be patient?[82]

32:42-44   An additional oracle reiterates the same twofold drama of Israel's life with God. The rhetoric of 32:42 indicates the twofold character by "just as" *(ka-asherr)* and "so" *(ken)*. The one follows the other and is linked to it. In this brief oracle the destructive judgment of God is only alluded to in order to make the contrast between God's past deed of destruction and God's new action of restoration. The accent, however, falls completely on God's second act, that of restoration. The "good" (fortune) *(tob)* promised (cf. *tob* in vv. 40, 41) is restored, safe life in the land.[83] The substance of "good" is "fields shall be bought" (vv. 43, 44). That is, the promises of God are not theoretical or spiritual, but concern real life in a reordered, political-economic situation. Moreover, the revival of a full economy and an adequate property system touches all geographic regions of Judah's territory.[84] The whole land which is diminished shall now be utterly enhanced. The oracle anticipates a complete reversal of Israel's life into well-being.

The prayer (vv. 17-25) and the long oracle (vv. 27-41) with the double reference to "impossibility" shape the double thema of this entire chapter. On the one hand, the phrase "too hard" looks back to an anticipation of the destruction of the city and of the king (vv. 3-4) which is reiterated in vv. 23-24, 28-29. The loss of Jerusalem is indeed a major fact in Israel's faith and in Israel's experience. The city long regarded itself as privileged and guaranteed by God, but now has been devastated by God. The experience is visible and incontrovertible.

On the other hand, however, the prayer and oracle both dare to look ahead in hope to God's second resolve of restoration. This resolve is voiced in v. 15 and is reiterated in vv. 25, 37-41, 42-44. The text dodges or denies nothing of Judah's trouble. It insists, however, that the trouble is not the end of the tale. Thus in every element of this long reflective statement,

---

82. George Steiner, *Real Presences: Is There Anything in What We Say?* (Chicago: University of Chicago Press and London: Faber & Faber, 1989), 231-32.

83. On the use of "good" *(tob)* in exilic theology, see Walter Brueggemann, "The Kerygma of the Deuteronomistic Historian: Gospel for Exiles," *Interpretation* 22 (1968): 387-402.

84. The regions named are the same as those named in 33:13.

beginning at v. 6, the crucial issue is that God has promised and will enact complete restoration. That promise is rooted in God's own resolve and in nothing less. The action of the prophet in vv. 6-15 vouches for God's promise in the most concrete way possible. The text is a massive reflection which moves Israel into the displacement, and out of it, both by the resolve of God for whom nothing is too hard. Israel's destiny is to lose what it treasures, and then to have it handed back by God in mercy, massively broken and then powerfully blessed.

Restoration for Judah and Jerusalem (33:1-26)

This chapter consists in seven promissory oracles, each of which announces God's resolve to invert the fortunes of Judah and to create a new season of well-being for Jerusalem. While these several oracles differ in detail, two factors are constant. First, the voiced resolve of the text is indeed God's very own resolve, rooted in God's long-term intention and uttered in God's own speech. Second, that resolve of God concerns precisely the public, historical, sociopolitical future of the community. Thus these promissory statements join together the resolve of heaven and the future of the earth.

33:1-10 The word comes "a second time" while the prophet is still under arrest. The "first time" is reported in 32:2. The formula joins together (through editorial activity) the narrative, prayer, and oracle of ch. 32 and the present chapter. These promissory passages, according to the introduction, are situated in a hostile confinement. A poet held as a political prisoner writes poems of hope, resolutely contradicting not only the present condition of his people, but resolutely overriding his own personal circumstance.[85] Such a rhetorical act stridently asserts the freedom and effectiveness of God's intent, against all apparent limitations imposed by "realism." These promises have little patience with or respect for conventional "realism."

The oracle begins by God's self-assertion and self-identity (33:2). The speaker of promise is not just any God, but the God who had the

---

85. The utterance of promises rooted in faith from prison is not unlike some of the epistles of Paul in the NT. Moreover, in our own time some of the most important and dangerous poetry has come from those imprisoned and politically at risk. See Nicanor Parra, *Emergency Poems* (New York: New Directions, 1972).

power to make the earth, to form the earth, to found the earth. This is a God who has moved decisively against chaos (cf. 5:22). The name of this God is Yahweh, a name associated in doxologies with the power to bring order out of chaos and life out of death. This large claim for Yahweh's identity is reminiscent of 32:17, 27.

This powerful God in whose will the world lives, now promises to be available precisely to the exiles who thought they were God-abandoned.[86] The creator of heaven and earth is the God who assured attentiveness to and care for the exiles. The God of all power is the God who attends to the powerless. The God who seemed to be absent is present, findable, and approachable. (See the exilic theme in Deut. 4:29-31; Jer. 29:12-14; Isa. 55:6-9; and subsequently Isa. 65:24.) The "call" that is invited and authorized is Israel's call of need, petition, and distress.[87] God will answer such a call; when God answers, it will not be an innocuous assurance, but it will be a disclosure of what is not yet known in Israel, that is, a disclosure of the future which is certain in God's resolve, even if not yet visible in Israel. If exilic Israel acts in faith, God will make available God's intent for the future.

Then follows the very disclosure that has been promised. Jeremiah 33:4-5 provides the context for talk about the future by a brief review of the recent past. The recent past is filled with houses torn down to provide emergency military equipment and supplies, with defense maneuvers, with invading Babylonians, and with an abundance of corpses, military casualties.[88] That utter disorder has occurred because of God's hidden "face."

86. Thus the Exile is an experience of Jerusalem's God-forsakenness in response to Jerusalem's having abandoned God. This dialectic perhaps provides a model for an interpretation of the cross in the NT. Jürgen Moltmann, *The Crucified God* (New York: Harper & Row, 1974), 243, concludes: "The Fatherlessness of the Son is matched by the Sonlessness of the Father. . . ." *Mutatis mutandis,* such a formulation is not unlike the situation of God and Jerusalem in the Exile.

87. Karl Barth, *Church Dogmatics,* III/3 (Edinburgh: Clark, 1960), 262-288, has most powerfully urged that petition is the center of biblical prayer. Petition which God will hear is the proper mode of speech in exile. Barth asserts, "Prayer, or praying, is simply asking" (268). See Perry LeFevre, *Understandings of Prayer* (Philadelphia: Westminster, 1981), 28-45, for a discussion of Barth on prayer.

88. In this usage, "house" bespeaks influence, affluence, power, and stability. Such houses are sure to be the target of an invading army; they are also the target of prophetic criticism, because they embody social inequality, indifference, and exploitation. Cf. Jer. 22:13-17; Amos. 3:15; and the counterreality of the Rechabites in Jer. 35:7-9.

That is, God has withdrawn from the city the sustaining power of God's promise, making the city available for and vulnerable to massive destruction. The city without God's face, that is, without God's own self, is left to the outworking of its own wickedness. And that wickedness, without the protective hedge of God, has inundated Israel. If vv. 4-5 can be related to the rhetoric about creation in v. 2, then we have a picture of the creator God who has withdrawn ordering governance and abandons life to the surging power of chaos which takes the form of Babylonian invasion. Babylon is simply the power of chaos which Yahweh has finally unleashed against God's own people. Israel's enacted evil has caused God to relinquish this beloved city to the surging power of cosmic evil.

All of this analysis and threat in vv. 4-5, however, is background and context for the oracle. The chaos of evil has indeed worked its will. The "great and hidden things" of v. 3 are only now approached in v. 6. The interlude of vv. 4-5 tells of things not hidden (which everyone can see), and of things not great. The "great and hidden things" concern God's unexpected but sure resolve to quench the evil and to move against and beyond the destruction.

The "great and hidden things" now disclosed concern God's resolve to act with powerful, beneficent verbs (vv. 6-9). God now resolves to bring healing in the face of the destructive powers which have wrought chaos, and to give to the city utter well-being, a well-being *(sh-l-m)* marked by God's own fidelity (*emet;* RSV "security"). The language of the promise envisions a complete inversion of the destruction of the recent past. Thus the promise uses the programmatic formula, "I will restore the fortunes," that is, renew the good conditions of old (v. 7). The formula is given more concrete substance by three verbs: "I will build [rebuild], I will cleanse, I will forgive" (vv. 7b-8). The first verb refers to the physical reconstruction and rehabilitation of the city; the other two refer to making the city religiously, ritually acceptable to God, so that God can again be available and present in the city. God will do for Israel and Judah what they cannot do for themselves: make them qualified for God's good gifts and God's powerful presence. Verse 8 is saturated with the language of guilt and sin, using all three standard words for sin: "sin" *(ht'),* "guilt" *('on),* and "rebellion" *(p-sh-').*[89] These words,

---

89. See the same three terms in Exod. 34:7, in one of Israel's primary articulations of the seriousness with which God takes Israel's infidelity. In the old confession, such sin is punished; here it is forgiven. Thus this text plays against the old warning.

however, are overpowered by the strong verbs which permit God's newness. The outcome of God's resolve and God's action is the rehabilitation of Jerusalem. The city had become a place of grief and wretchedness, and now comes joy! It had become a place of shame and humiliation, and now comes glory and splendor! The action of God makes an utterly new Jerusalem. The new city is a gift of life to its inhabitants.

The city is at the same time a powerful and unambiguous witness to the nations. The other nations are always watching Jerusalem, and God knows they are watching. They have watched while God abandoned the city, and they have no doubt drawn ignominious conclusions about Yahweh.[90] Now, however, the nations will notice the newness. They will see the "good" *(tob)* and the "prosperity" *(shalom)*, and they will be required to draw new conclusions about God and about Israel. Through the rescue of Jerusalem, all the nations will see and know that there is a God in Israel (cf. 1 Sam. 17:46). The greatest attestation to be made concerning the rule of Yahweh comes whenever God's power for life vetoes the grip of death.[91] That veto is about to be enacted by Yahweh in Jerusalem and the nations cannot fail to notice. They will be unable to avoid the conclusion that the God of Jerusalem must be reckoned with. Thus healed Jerusalem becomes a theological datum which requires the nations to reposition themselves vis-à-vis Yahweh. (This argument in the end leads to the oracles of chs. 46–51, which assert that Yahweh is the key factor in the life of the nations.)

33:10-11 This second promissory oracle states a massive inversion in Jerusalem toward well-being, wrought by God. The promise culminates in the use of the programmatic formula, "restore the fortunes." Leading to that concluding verdict is a concrete example of the inversion wrought by God. The Hebrew text begins with the promise, "There will again be heard," and then the entire negative phrase which constitutes the bulk of 33:10 in English is a dependent clause only identifying the place. The negativity only characterizes the place where the happy affirmation of v. 11

90. The drawing of such conclusions is the basis of the petition of Moses in Num. 14:13-19 and of God's fresh resolve in Ezek. 36:22-32. On the latter, see Brueggemann, *Hopeful Imagination*, 69-87.
91. This is the same claim made in the Christian affirmation of the resurrection of Jesus which breaks the power of death; cf. Acts 2:24; 1 Cor. 15:54-57.

will be heard. The negative designation of v. 10 is stated in a parallelism concerning the cities of Judah marked as a "waste" and the streets of Jerusalem marked as a "desolation." The first of these, the cities of Judah, are characterized by a double *en* (without): without humankind and without animals. The second set concerning the streets of Jerusalem has a threefold use of *en* ("without"): without humankind, without inhabitants, without beasts. The cities and the streets together are five times "without" *(en)*, suggesting that they have been forcibly emptied of all viable life, human and nonhuman. It is in this empty, abandoned, bereft, hopeless place, a place reduced to mute despair, that sounds will again be heard. The good news of the sounds cannot be fully appreciated unless the contrasting situation of mute despair is fully mapped out.

Three times Jeremiah has characterized the destruction of Jerusalem and Judah by anticipating the elimination of the sounds of a wedding (7:34; 16:9; 25:10). The cessation of wedding joy signifies a crushing judgment in which conventional social relations are impossible and the entire infrastructure of the community has failed. The community will cease to practice the most elemental acts necessary for its maintenance through time. In this massive assertion of judgment, there is no will for celebration, not enough security or trust or buoyancy or confidence to undertake a wedding which always constitutes some investment in the future. This particular silence, the absence of celebrative social noise, is as acute as "without, without, without, without, without."

It is in this place of desolate silence that a new sound will be heard. What has not been heard will again be heard, as God's good resolve for viable human community overrides the empty silence. Israel will resume the social practice of mirth, enacting a broad commitment into the future.[92] The desolateness will be overcome enough to foster a season of mirth and celebration, as the reconstituted community overrides the pall of exile.

The voices that sing of weddings also sing a more theological song, for the resumption of social life is intimately linked to the resumption of

92. The recent social transformation in Eastern Europe offers important parallels to the anticipations of these promises. After the "opening" of the Soviet Union, a cabaret was opened after fifty years. A commentator observed that it had been "fifty years of mirthlessness in Moscow." In like manner, Jerusalem has long had "mirthlessness."

life with God (33:11b). Thus the voices that sing wedding songs also sing a song of thanks to God. This thanksgiving song entails a concrete gesture of gratitude, an offering which bespeaks a blessing received. The song of thanks, accompanied by offerings as a gesture of gratitude, sings of the character of Yahweh. Thanks is given because Yahweh is good (does good), because Yahweh's loyal love is endlessly abiding.

Two claims operate in this doxology. First, it is voiced in the Exile, just when Yahweh seemed neither good nor faithful. What Israel believes about God is here not derived from circumstance, but is sung against circumstance. Second, the juxtaposition of wedding song and doxology evidences how Israel's faith is enmeshed in the fabric of life. The two songs are different but they are not unrelated. The joy of futuring human relations derives from and is authorized by the large intention of God about the future. It is God's sure fidelity that permits the practice of human fidelity in a context of abundant fickleness. Both songs together show Israel moving past emptied cities and emptied streets. The outbreak of blessing, joy, and gratitude overrides the silence of desolation.

33:12-13   This third promissory oracle brings together two themes recently voiced in the tradition of Jeremiah and organizes them in relation to a fresh metaphor. On the one hand, the negative characterization of the city and towns echoes that of v. 10. This is the same empty place, void of life. On the other hand, the map of restoration reiterates the same six geographical reference points of 32:44: Benjamin, Jerusalem, Judah, hill country, Shephelah, and the Negeb. These six elements, in the horizon of Judah, mean "everywhere." All the land will be restored and healed.

The fresh metaphor which reshapes the material is that of flock, shepherd, and pasture land. The tranquil pastoral scene of grazing with adequate food, water, and protection will again be established. To be counted by the shepherd means that the shepherd knows the name of each sheep, counts them, and pays attention to any missing one.[93] After a season of chaos, such an image bespeaks a settled, well-ordered, caring, and attentive community with healing governance. While the image of peasant tranquility may be an economic-domestic statement, there is no doubt that the image refers to reordered political life in which there is adequate

93. It is this metaphor with reference to the ingathering of exiles that lies behind the parable of Luke 15:3-7 and the declaration of John 10:1-18.

governance to protect against both rapaciousness and anarchy (cf. 23:1-4; Ezek. 34:1-24). The metaphor serves yet again to witness to the radical, healing transformation intended by God.

33:14-15   This fourth promissory oracle looks back to Jer. 23:5-6. Indeed, this oracle is a simple repetition of that statement (on which see vol. 1, *To Pluck Up, To Tear Down*, 199-200), except for the phrase, "I will fulfill the promise I made to the house of Israel and the house of Judah." This oracle thus refers back to a previous oracle. The reference may be back to the taproot oracle in 2 Sam. 7:8, or it may be an editorial acknowledgement that the promise already appears in 23:5-6 and is seconded here.

In either case, the promise to the Davidic house is peculiar and unexpected in the tradition of Jeremiah, for the larger casting of the Jeremiah tradition regards the dynasty as a main problem for Israel (cf. 22:13-18, 24-30), and does not characteristically envision a David-shaped future. Nonetheless, God's good inclination toward the dynasty and family of David belongs to Israel's central stock of promises. It is therefore included here among the many ways in which Israel voices its hope. Indeed, this chapter seems to want to collect all Israel's possible ways of speaking of God's good future. It is promised that one will arise in that dynasty who will do what kings are supposed to do, namely, practice justice and righteousness (Ps. 72:1-4; cf. Jer. 22:15-17). Thus the Jeremiah tradition draws even the dynasty into its passion for the primary torah guarantees of Israel. Indeed, "justice and righteousness" have belonged to the central mandate of Davidic kings from the outset (cf. Isa. 9:7; 1 Kgs. 10:9). Jeremiah makes that general Davidic promise serve his own passionate sense of covenantal requirements for any viable future with Yahweh.

When the king practices justice and righteousness, the city and the land will be healed and saved. Thus the royal intention of Jerusalem is reshaped for the large covenantal design of the Jeremiah tradition which connects covenantal obedience and covenantal blessing. The prophetic construct of "justice → well-being" is not new. What is new is the assurance that royal Israel will act in ways that make new life possible. The outcome is that this sordid, disappointing city of indifference and exploitation receives a means whereby a new social reality is authorized.[94]

94. See Ezek. 48:35, where the city is renamed and thereby recharacterized. See Klein, 187-89.

33:17-18   This fifth promissory oracle makes only a single statement about a well-ordered future upon which God is resolved. The oracle is of interest to us for two reasons. First, the dynastic future of David and of the priestly order are intimately linked together and both are guaranteed. This intense connection may reflect the way in which priests are functionaries of the kings. More likely it reflects the exilic and postexilic situation of Judah in which civil and priestly authority worked closely together.[95] In that linkage, it is noticeable that whereas the assumed king is given no task to perform, the task assigned to the guaranteed priest is quite explicit and extensive. The function of the priest would seem to be the more important factor in the shaping of the future. This suggests that in the horizon of this oracle, the "state" is on the way to becoming a "church."

Second, the guarantee that "David" "shall never lack a man" is strikingly peculiar in the tradition of Jeremiah. The statement seems to guarantee the dynasty into the future. On the one hand, Jeremiah had explicitly voiced the termination of the monarchy when there would be none to occupy the throne (Jer. 22:30). On the other hand, the general thema of Jeremiah refuses to regard the monarch either as guaranteed or as important. The monarchy is completely dependent on and subordinated to the torah. Thus on both concrete textual and programmatic grounds, this royal promise surprises us in this context. One can only conclude that the crisis of discontinuity in Judah is past and behind Judah. Without denying Judah's great discontinuity worked in 587, the monarchy continued to impact the imagination of Israel. When Israel imagined the future, it could not finally imagine a future without both guaranteed king and guaranteed priest. The promised king is a human agent who is designated to do the human task which will reshape a human future. In contrast to 33:14-15, the king here is not required to do anything. The assurance for the future is simply a gift from God. Clearly the tradition has moved a long distance from the strictures of 22:13-18, 24-30.

33:19-22   This sixth promissory oracle seeks to assure continuity in the community by two large appeals. The assurance of continuity concerns the covenant made with the Davidic house and the covenant with the Levites. The two, king and Levite, are here grouped together as in 33:17-

95. See Roland de Vaux, *Ancient Israel, Its Life and Institutions* (New York: McGraw-Hill, 1961), 376-79; and Holladay, *Jeremiah 2,* 229-230.

18. That linkage likely reflects the realities of power and leadership at the time when the text voices its claim, presumably in or after the Exile. The covenant with David (cf. 2 Sam. 7:11-16; Ps. 89:24-37; Isa. 55:3) has seemed in the Exile to be in jeopardy. Indeed, Jeremiah had placed the Davidic claim in jeopardy by his subversive voicing of reality.

This text, concerned with fidelity and continuity, against much of the Jeremiah tradition, asserts the abiding certitude of these two covenants which legitimate leadership and therefore certify the structure of the community. It is as though a voice of wonderment and disbelief asked, "How sure are these covenants?" — which of course is an inquiry about the reliability of God's promise.

The answer to that question of reliability is twofold. First, the covenants with king and priest are as sure as the covenants of night and day, that is, ultimately reliable. In other words, the rhythms of night and day are not "natural" phenomena, but happen in regular ways because God has promised that each of them will have an assured and regular time of presence. This rhetoric regards the reliability and predictability of night and day to be the most extreme statement possible concerning God's faithful, powerful capacity to do what God promises. God will keep God's word, not only for night and day, but for king and priest about which God has also made promises. Historical structures rooted in God's promises are as sure as cosmic sequences authored by God who creates and presides. God's love to Israel is as sure as God's ordering of creation.

The second guarantee is an appeal to the Abraham-Sarah promise about fertility and productivity into the future (Jer. 33:22). This family is assured of multiplicity as the stars of the heavens (Gen. 15:5) or as the sand of the seashore (Gen. 22:17; 32:12). The text only alludes to the ancestral tradition and explicitly moves directly from "stars/sand" to the royal, priestly families. The threat for all dynasties, royal and priestly, is to be without heirs. Because these dynasties are assured countless heirs, their futures are utterly, utterly secure. These massive and grand assurances of continuity are in amazing and profound tension with the main claims of the Jeremiah tradition and with the threat of the exilic experience. These promises do not resist or deny the reality of discontinuity, but are voices of hope after the breaking point, and therefore speak against the painful judgments of the historical process. The promises of Yahweh are not always and everywhere the appropriate thing to say; they function, however, in particular times and places, times of death and places of despair. The promises rooted in reliable cosmic realities seek to override the despair. Israel's way into the future rests only upon God's good word which abides in the face of disruptive circumstance.

33:23-26 This final promissory oracle in the sequence of this chapter again appeals to the ordering covenant with creation as a criterion for God's fidelity to Israel, as in Jer. 33:20-22 and 31:35-37. This assurance in this text, however, is framed very differently from the earlier statements. The oracle of 33:25-26 is a response to the problem expressed in v. 24. This oracle, unlike the others in the series of this chapter, responds to a specific and stated issue. The problem is that "these people" treat Yahweh's covenant people with contempt. We do not know the identity of "these people." They may be any of the surrounding nations who have observed the recent history of this community, or they may be more specifically the Babylonians who had dismantled the Judean community. The speaker is not interested in identifying the practitioners of contempt. The Israelites have a long history, either of paying attention to what the nation thinks or of alleging what the nations think as a ploy to evoke a response from God (cf. Num. 14:13-16; Jer. 30:17; Ezek. 36:22). The "two families" refers to the north and south of divided Israel, so that the Israelites are being judged as failures in exile (cf. Ezek. 37:15-23).

The important point is not what the nations think (for perhaps they thought very little at all about Israel), but what Israel thinks of itself and what it thinks the nations think of it. That is, the contempt allegedly held by the nations is in fact intrinsic in exile, which is a context evoking Israel's shame, humiliation, and self-despising (cf., e.g., Isa. 54:4). It is the reality of exile that leads to the judgment that God's chosen has become God's rejected (Jer. 33:24). In sum, the Exile evokes the conclusion that Israel's special status as God's beloved has been forfeited. It matters not at all if that conclusion is drawn by the nations or drawn by Israel and projected upon the nations.

It is in response to that theological crisis evoked by the Exile, a crisis concerning Israel's theological identity as Yahweh's people, that the oracle of vv. 25-26 is given.[96] The oracle consists of a protasis ("if") in v. 25 and an

---

96. Thus in a laconic way, these verses are in fact a response to the question of theodicy, making an affirmation not unlike that of Ps. 73. On the issues of theodicy in Ps. 73, see Ronald J. Williams, "Theodicy in the Ancient Near East," in Crenshaw, *Theodicy in the Old Testament,* 50-51; and Martin Buber, "The Heart Determines: Psalm 73," in Crenshaw, *Theodicy in the Old Testament,* 109-118.

apodosis ("then," *gam*) in v. 26. If the ordering of creation (day and night, heavens and earth) was not established, then Yahweh would reject Israel. The oracle appeals back to the negative term "reject" in v. 24. The unstated countertheme is that, since God's ordering of creation manifestly persists, the operative word for Israel persists as "chosen" and not "rejected." Thus creation is offered as argument and analogue for the status of Israel with Yahweh. This argument and analogue decisively reject the verdict of v. 24. Thus the verdict of v. 24 is wrong, whether drawn by the nations or by Israel and projected upon the nations. Exile does not entail rejection. Exile is not the end of Israel's chosen status. Israel's chosenness persists in and through exile!

The specifics of the enduring chosenness in the Exile, on the one hand, appeals to the primal promises to the ancestors in Genesis and, on the other hand, to the Davidic dynasty (v. 26). Thus the promises to David are not rooted in memories and commitments which are undermined in the Exile. The promises and old commitments of God are in force and are powerfully operative in and through the difficult present. Thus the oracle appeals to memory and tradition in order to assert a theological reality that overrides present historical circumstance. The theological reality is that the promise endures. The political fact derived from that promise is the legitimacy of the Davidic enterprise, a legitimacy not undermined by the loss of the throne. Thus the oracle asserts a theological claim that relativizes the present historical moment of negative experience.

That verdict which finally refutes the misreading of v. 24 is reinforced by the concluding formula of v. 26. Not only is the phrase "restore their fortunes" used one more time, but it is reinforced by the final phrase, "I will have mercy upon them." It is precisely in exile, when all seems lost, that mercy comes to the fore as God's primal way with Israel.[97] God's resilient mercy makes the seeming discontinuity of exile less than decisive. The oracle reads reality against observable circumstance.

These seven oracles together comprise for exilic Israel a remarkable affirmation: God's commitment to Israel in the present and God's resolve for Israel's good future are fully asserted and reaffirmed. The editorial process of the book of Jeremiah has gathered together into a powerful collection oracles of God's relentless fidelity as a conclusion to the "Book of Comfort." Those oracles sustained and sustain Israel even in its times of abandonment.

97. See Brueggemann, "At the Mercy of Babylon."

A Case Study in Fidelity

Jeremiah 34:1–35:19

This narrative begins with an address to King Zedekiah (34:1-7), offers two narratives concerning the community — one negative (34:8-22) and one positive (35:1-11) — and two conclusions from the contrasting "case studies" (35:12-19).

34:1-7 These verses deliver yet again a harsh announcement against the city and the king in the face of the threat of Babylon, a threat which the prophet characteristically takes as a threat from Yahweh. The passage has parallels in 21:1-7; 37:3-10; and 38:14-28, where the same points are articulated. In each of these, Zedekiah receives or acknowledges a hard word from the prophet.

This passage is framed by statements about command (34:1-2a) and obedience (vv. 6-7). In the command, the word of the prophet is in a context of massive Babylonian pressure. Note the repeated use of the word "all" (v. 1). The word given to the prophet is congruent with the awareness that *all* the armies and *all* the peoples are against *all* the cities. In vv. 6-7 we are told that Jeremiah spoke as God had commanded him. Again in the conclusion of the section, we are reminded of the context of great military threat. The use of the word "all" — "all these words" (v. 6), "all the cities" (v. 7) — suggests an interface between a context of ominous danger and a message of severe threat. The known world of Jerusalem is under assault both by word and by the imperial army.

The message from God given through the prophet forms the center of the passage (vv. 2b-5). It is this message that is commanded (vv. 1-2a) and performed (vv. 6-7). The message itself is divided into two parts. First, there is a straightforward announcement of judgment and doom (vv. 2b-3). The judgment includes the city of Jerusalem (which will be destroyed) and the king (who will be apprehended by Babylon). There is no escape from Babylon. The judgment against the king, however, is less severe than is promised on the same king elsewhere. It is elsewhere anticipated that the king will suffer a cruel death (21:6-7). Here it is anticipated only that Zedekiah must give answer before the king of Babylon. Perhaps the cruel death made explicit elsewhere is only implied here in the king's appearance at the imperial court. In any case, the judgment is ambiguous, but for that, no less ominous.

Second, however, a different announcement is made which offers a different future for the king (34:4-5). Here it is announced that the king will die a peaceful death, will be honored in death, and appropriately buried and grieved by his kingdom. (On the humiliation of being un-grieved, see the contrast in 22:18-19.)

Scholars have been quick to notice that the verdict on King Zedekiah in 34:4-5 is very different from that pronounced in v. 3. Characteristically, there are two ways to handle the contradiction. On the one hand, the term "in peace" *(b-sh-l-m)* is emended to read "in Jerusalem" *(b-y-r-sh-l-m)*. Such an emendation does not fully overcome the contradiction, for in v. 3 he is to be taken to Babylon and is not to die in Jerusalem. The proposed emendation does, however, eliminate the key word that suggests a tranquil death.

More plausibly, in my judgment, scholars read the statement in vv. 4-5 by assuming a protasis-apodosis construction and implying an "if-then" argument:

[if] you hear the word of the LORD . . .
[then] you shall die in peace.

This construal of the message is congruent with Jeremiah's argument elsewhere concerning obedience and blessing. Moreover, such a reading permits vv. 4-5 to make sense even after the assertion of vv. 2b-3. That is, vv. 2b-3 give the expected sentence, but vv. 4-5 add a proviso for an alternative outcome to altered behavior. The alternative of hearing the word, however, in fact means submitting to Babylon, the urging made all along by the prophet. If the reading of "if-then" be accepted, then vv. 2b-3 assert disaster if there is resistance to Babylon, and painful living until death if there is not submission to the empire. Such an interpretation fits well with what is said elsewhere in the tradition, and provides a clear choice to the king that is both theologically consistent and politically credible. Clearly the cruel fate suffered by Zedekiah suggests, according to the tradition of Jeremiah, that Zedekiah did not listen (39:5-7; 52:11). The king found it impossible to accept the only choice of life offered by the prophet, the choice of submission to the empire.

34:8-22 The narrative tradition now presents a remarkable "case study" in fidelity and infidelity. The whole of 34:8–35:19 may be placed here by an editorial process in order to provide ground for and support the harsh judgment of 34:1-7. The case study consists of two parts, an example of infidelity (34:8-22) and a "control group" as an example of fidelity (35:1-11). The first example comes from the days of Zedekiah (34:8), and the second from the time of Jehoiakim (35:1). Because the two narratives are removed from each other chronologically, it is clear that the narrative is not making a historical-sequential statement, but intends a much more programmatic and didactic statement. The whole can be understood as a proclamation about the nature of fidelity, the cost of fidelity, and the price of infidelity.

The first element in this negative case of infidelity is a narrative summary which sets the context for the subsequent prophetic word (vv. 8-11). Verse 8 begins as though it is a "word of the LORD." In fact, however, that word is not given until v. 12.[1] Before the word announced in v. 8 is given in v. 12, we are offered a narrative report on the social crisis which evoked the prophetic word (vv. 8b-11). King Zedekiah made a covenant to release slaves. We do not know of this act from any other report.[2] The action of the king is based in the old torah commandment that debt slaves can only be held in bondage for six years, and then must be released with

---

1. The deferral of the word from the LORD as a narrative strategy in 34:8 until v. 12 is paralleled in ch. 32, in which the word announced in v. 1 is withheld until v. 6.

2. The closest parallel to this account is the action of Nehemiah in Neh. 5:1-13. These two narratives suggest that the provision for a year of release was at least in the purview of Israel's practice.

3. On the text of Deut. 15:1-11 and its significance for Israel's faith, see Jeffries Mock Hamilton, "Social Justice and Deuteronomy: The Case of Deuteronomy 15" (diss., Princeton Theological Seminary).

their debt cancelled (cf. Deut. 15:1-11; Exod. 21:1-6).[3] Note well that the legal provision and this action by the king relate to "Hebrew slaves" — "Judeans." That is, this narrative concerns fellow Jews who are in hock because they are poor and cannot pay their debts to other members of the Jewish community.

In a remarkable, humane provision, the torah of Moses limited the ways in which the community could exploit such poor persons. And now Zedekiah enacts the provision of liberation and debt cancellation. We do not know what prompted the action of the king, but it is in any case an economically disruptive act, for it simply writes off unpaid debts around which the economy is organized. It is usual to think this was a frantic gesture (foxhole religion), to show in an emergency good faith toward the torah commandments. It is thinkable that in this episode Zedekiah is as responsive as was his father Josiah to the demands of torah (Jer. 22:15-16; cf. 2 Kgs. 22:11). The narrator does not linger over this act of Zedekiah, but takes it only as a premise for what follows.

Zedekiah's political constituency obeyed his covenant and did indeed liberate their debt slaves and cancel their debts (Jer. 34:10). The verse twice uses the term *shema'*; they heard and heeded (RSV "obeyed") and acted differently, at some obvious risk to their economy. (Notice that the protasis of v. 4 concerning Zedekiah depends on "hearing.")

The entire episode concerning the release, however, issues in a surprising reversal of intent and practice (v. 11): "But afterward!" The economic leadership reneged and reinforced slavery, thus violating the torah, nullifying the covenant, and reducing social relations between the haves and have-nots in the community to sheer economic power. Unbridled wealth and greed prevailed over neighbor solidarity. As the covenant is rejected, instead of covenant blessings, Judah receives one more unwelcome oracle from the prophet.

We are not told why the people of Jerusalem reneged, any more than we are told why the king originally took such a positive initiative. If the intent of the king was initially pragmatic (i.e., the action was only to avert judgment), then it may follow that the reneging on the torah initiative was equally pragmatic. Perhaps the leadership in Jerusalem learned only late how costly the action of slave liberation and debt cancellation was. Either they thought the crisis had past, or they decided that the cancellation of debts was irrelevant to the Babylonian crisis, or they acted for their own vested interest because the cost of debt cancellation was simply too high. The narrative does not tell us anything about motivations, but only reports the actions taken and their outcomes. It is as though two views of social relations are caught in a massive struggle. On the one hand, the act of covenanting is an acknowledgement that all persons are members of the community and each must care for all. On the other hand, commodity interest prevails over covenant, and the strong work their will against the weak and at their expense.[4]

The poignancy of the crisis is reflected first of all in the strong and definitional contrast between two modes of social relations, oriented respectively toward covenant and toward commodity. The phenomenon of debt slavery raises the overarching question of social power: are there limits to the ways of the strong against the weak? Are there zones of human solidarity which override and curb raw economic power? The torah of Moses compelled Zedekiah and his cohorts into modes of covenantal thought for just an instant. Their commitment to sheer economic power, however, caused them to yield "afterwards" to the rule of wealth at the expense of community. This strong contrast is made even more poignant by the abrupt and inexplicable reversal of policy and practice, which only sharpens the complete disregard for torah in the community. This is indeed a dramatic form of resistance in Jerusalem to the torah and to the responsible leadership of the king. This dramatic and inexplicable reversal evokes the harsh prophetic word signalled in v. 8.

34:12-22 The prophet now speaks "the word of the Lord" anticipated in v. 8. The initial formula in God's speech is "I [myself] made a covenant." This statement seems likely only an historical introduction. It is, however, precisely parallel to the statement of v. 8, "King Zedekiah made a covenant." Nothing is made of the parallelism. As a backdrop for what follows the parallel is nonetheless important, for it contrasts God's covenantal faithfulness, upon which God did not renege, with Zedekiah's

---

4. By a rejection of covenantal relations, the poor were reduced to a commodity. This act of reneging provides an opportunity to reflect on the ways in which denial of covenant produces commoditization. Karl Marx has provided the decisive analysis of commodity, on which see David McLellan, *The Thought of Karl Marx: An Introduction* (London: Macmillan, 1971, and New York: Harper & Row, 1972), 105-121. See also Franz J. Hinkellammert, *The Ideological Weapons of Death: A Theological Critique of Capitalism* (Maryknoll, N.Y.: Orbis, 1986); and Gregory Baum, *Theology and Society* (New York: Paulist, 1988), 51.

covenant, upon which he did renege. Moreover, the covenants of Yahweh and of Zedekiah are parallel in that they both concern a "proclamation of liberty." In Yahweh's covenant, "proclaiming liberty" is a torah provision (cf. Deut. 15:1-11); in Zedekiah's covenant, "proclaiming liberty" is an implementation of that torah provision. Indeed, in Yahweh's covenant the torah provision is quoted exactly (Jer. 34:14). The parallelism is continued in the narrative comment. "Your ancestors did not listen," that is, they did not heed the covenant provision of cancelling debts on fellow covenant members (v. 14b). In parallel fashion, Zedekiah's contemporaries also did not listen and so refused the costly commandment.

This last point provides the opening for the prophetic word, which alludes back to vv. 9-11. The statements in vv. 15-16 are precisely parallel in construction, but to opposite effect. Verse 15 asserts, "You, you turned" *(tashubu)*. Israel turned back to torah obedience, obeyed the commandment of release, and solemnly swore to practice the commandment in the temple. That is, the economic act is undertaken as a major, self-conscious theological statement. But then that act is promptly countered in v. 16: "You turned" *(tashubu);* you turned away from torah obedience and from covenant fidelity. The oath sworn in "the house which is called by my name" (v. 15) is now profaning my name; that is, it mocks God and diminishes God's reputation by reenslaving fellow Jews who owe money. The interface between theological intent and economic act is intense and remarkable. The two cannot be separated. Reenslaving debt slaves diminishes God's reputation; that is, it profanes God's name.

The careful and complicated rhetoric of vv. 12-16 constitutes a prophetic indictment which asserts the guilt of Judah and Jerusalem. It makes use of five rhetorical devices: (1) the parallel of Yahweh who made a covenant and Zedekiah who made a covenant; (2) the contrast of Yahweh who kept covenant and Judah who violated covenant; (3) the double use of the word *tashubu,* for Judah turned twice in fickleness and inconsistency; (4) the double use of God's name, before whom an oath is taken and which is profaned in the reneging; and (5) the larger contrast between the historical review (vv. 8-11) and the prophetic comment (vv. 12-16). The result of the completed assertion of vv. 8-16 is to establish that Judah has reneged in its oath to Yahweh and in its obligation to fellow Jews. Nothing is stated about motivation. The act of reneging, committed for whatever reason, makes Judah into a disobedient people that does not heed torah and does not honor its own covenant commitments to its needy fellows.

There follows, as we expect, a massive "therefore" (v. 17) and a sweeping, harsh sentence (vv. 17-22). The indictment is restated in v. 17 as a way into the sentence. The first element in the sentence plays on the word "release" *(dror)* and matches the punishment to the crime.[5] "You did not release [your neighbors from their debts], so I will release — sword, pestilence, and famine!" What God releases is the unfettered devastation and unrestrained terror of covenant curses. The list is a classic, highly stylized recital, but it is also reflective of the forms of damage that come in the wake of an invading army.

The second element of the sentence plays on the word "cut." The word is used in vv. 8, 13 as the technical term for "made" a covenant. The verb perhaps refers to a ritual act of cutting an animal as part of an act of blood-solidarity (cf. Gen. 15:7-11). In Jer. 34:18 the prophetic speech seems to refer back to something like the primitive rite of Gen. 15, only now it is the people of Judah themselves who are cast as the ritual calf who is to be "cut," which of course means brutalized and killed.[6] The argument is not very clear, and the wording is elusive. It does seem clear, nevertheless, that in Jer. 34:19 all parts of the population, and especially its leaders and opinion-makers, are the cut animal in this covenant of death now being enacted by Yahweh. Verse 20 explicates the meaning of the foregoing: they will be handed over to enemies who will kill them, and their corpses will be left exposed in dishonor. Both plays on words, "release" and "cut," are simply rhetorical maneuvers to pronounce an awful judgment of death which matches the great affront committed against Yahweh. Clearly, the prophet makes a great deal of the refusal of Judah to release its poor from bondage. Indeed, Judah's whole future turns to curse because of this act which dishonors God and exploits neighbor.

The final judgment pronounced concerns the king who now will be handed over to Babylon (v. 21), and the city of Jerusalem, and the towns of Judah (v. 22). Babylon is described as being "withdrawn" (v. 21), but the LORD will "bring them back." This statement alludes to the previous invasion of 598, after which there was a respite for Jerusalem from Babylon.

5. On the symmetry of the affront and the punishment, see Patrick D. Miller, Jr., "Sin and Judgment in Jeremiah 34:17-19," *Journal of Biblical Literature* 103 (1984): 611-13.

6. I am following the usual rendering. On the textual difficulty in this verse, see Holladay, *Jeremiah 2,* 242-43.

That respite, however, is now to end with a second decisive invasion in 587.

The main plot of this oracle is clear. We should not, however, miss the poignancy of the argument. The practice of torah and the implementation of the commandment of release would generate safety and well-being for the city. Reneging on the covenant and consequently practicing economic exploitation evoke the invasion of Babylon. This is no silly "supernaturalism," but reflects the prophetic conviction that internal disorder invites external threat which implements God's sovereign rule. The first step toward death is internal economic disorder that pits the "haves" against the "have-nots." Such internal economic disorder reflects a fundamental recalcitrance in Judah. The reference to the Exodus (v. 13) is a reminder that God's initial act of rescue was a gesture of liberation in which the slaves of Egypt were rescued from their economic plight of helplessness. Israel is expected to continue to reenact that miracle of new economic beginnings in its own ordering of social life. When it fails to "hear" *(shema')*, when it no longer remembers its rootage or its historical destiny,[7] it becomes vulnerable to the exploitation of more powerful "haves."[8] A failure to order its economic life differently jeopardizes the city, the king, the villages, the temple, and finally the whole people.

35:1-11 The narrative now takes up a contrasting episode, which is located ten years earlier, in the time of Jehoiakim. It is as though the blatant disobedience of Zedekiah and his cohorts evokes in the memory of the narrator a much earlier prophetic act.

The prophet has a remarkable encounter with the Rechabites in the temple at the command of Yahweh (35:2-4). We are told nothing about the Rechabites or why they are summoned into the drama. Jeremiah is commanded to give them wine (v. 2), and he does so (v. 5). It is as though God has deliberately set up a test case for the Rechabites.

The center of the episode is the response of the Rechabites to the

7. On the decisive power of rootage in memory, see Cynthia Ozick, "Metaphor and Memory," *Metaphor and Memory, Essays* (New York: Knopf, 1989), 265-283.

8. While Zedekiah and his cohorts may have been the influential "haves" in Jerusalem, their resources or staying power against Babylon are flimsy and fleeting. In the book of Jeremiah, it is Babylon who is the real "have," which makes all in Jerusalem vulnerable "have-nots."

offer of wine (vv. 6-10). The Rechabites promptly recite the commands of their ancestor and founder. This response is like the recital of a catechism, or a brief series of commands:[9]

- You shall not drink wine,
- You shall not build a house,
- You shall not sow seed,
- You shall not plant or have a vineyard,
- You shall live in tents.

This pentalogue seems designed to warn against accommodation to the values of the dominant society. Thus the Rechabites are something of a "sect" whose identity entails resistance to the comfortable accommodations of settled, urban society.[10] The Rechabites may indeed be regarded as a religious curiosity. In this narrative, however, they constitute a sect that practices an "alternative life-style," which is regarded in a most positive light.

The narrative exhibits no particular interest in the actual practices of the Rechabite community and makes no particular judgment on those commands. That is, the narrative does not debate whether it is right or good to drink wine or live in houses.[11] What counts for our narrative is that the Rechabites live zealously under command (vv. 6-7); they are a community of intense obedience (v. 8):

We have obeyed . . .
[the charge] to drink no wine,
not to build houses to dwell in.
We have no vineyard or field or seed.

Thus the narrative first reports the commands of Jonadab (vv. 6-7) and then reiterates the commands in terms of their being obeyed (vv. 8-10).

9. Erhard Gerstenberger, *Wesen und Herkunft des "apodiktischen" Rechts*. Wissenschaftliche Monographien zum Alten und Neuen Testament 20 (Neukirchen-Vluyn: Neukirchener, 1965), 110-17 and *passim*.

10. This same theological tendency and strategy is voiced in the contemporary discussion by Stanley Hauerwas and William H. Willimon, *Resident Aliens: Life in the Christian Colony* (Nashville: Abingdon, 1989).

11. See my comments on 33:4 in which "houses" are taken as a symbol and metaphor for disobedient power. The policy of the Rechabites no doubt reflects the same critical attitude toward such social fixtures.

The climactic statement is "We have obeyed and done all that our ancestor Jonadab commanded us" (NRSV). Thus in vv. 8-10, the verb *shema'* is used twice. This is quintessentially a community of listeners!

The comment in v. 11 seems extraneous both to the narrator and to the contrast made between ch. 34 and ch. 35. It appears to be a parenthetical comment about why this countercultural movement is in fact in the city of Jerusalem. The Rechabites are in Jerusalem for protection that only a walled city can provide. Clearly the narrator does not regard their presence in Jerusalem as a contradiction to the practices commanded concerning the avoidance of settled urban culture. If dwelling in Jerusalem were to violate the commands of Jonadab, then the whole contrasting case fails; that clearly is not intended by the narrator.

This summary statement about the Rechabites in terms of command and obedience establishes a contrast with Zedekiah, which is the didactic point of the larger narrative. On the one hand, the ancestors of Israel *did not listen* (34:14) and you *did not listen* (34:17). On the other hand, the Rechabites have *listened and heeded faithfully* (35:8, 10). It is the formal act of listening and not the substance of obedience that is accented in this contrast.[12]

35:12-19   The narrative has juxtaposed two episodes, one from the time of Zedekiah and one from the much earlier time of Jehoiakim. We are now prepared for the instructional conclusion that the narrator draws. This section is in fact a militant meditation on the meaning of listening, the requirements of listening, and the costs of not listening. Everything depends on listening.

The argument begins with a question that is part urging and part accusation (v. 13). Could you not "learn a lesson" (RSV "receive instruction")? The term "lesson" is "discipline" *(musar)*.[13] It is instruction that

---

12. The accent of the text falls upon the formal contrast of listening and not listening (RSV "obey"). It is, however, inevitable that the narrator would have also noticed the substantive difference. Not only did the Rechabites listen, but the commands to which they listened constitute a critique of settled culture, the kind of culture the prophet keeps under assault. Thus attention to form includes within it some attention to the substantive contrast between the Rechabites and the community around the king.

13. On the term, see Hans-Joachim Kraus, "Geschichte als Erziehung," in *Probleme biblischer Theologie.* Festschrift Gerhard von Rad, ed. Hans Walter Wolff (Munich: Kaiser, 1971), 267-274. Kraus concludes with a comment concerning "God as Educator," a theme not unlike the usage in this verse.

the older generation offers to the younger as part of inculcation and socialization into the norms of the community. Thus the question is asked with some impatience and indignation: Can you not accept nurture into the true identity of this community? The RSV makes the two phrases sound sequential and synonymous: receive instruction and listen to my words. The Hebrew, however, makes the second phrase derivative from the first, so that accepting discipline means to be prepared to *shema'*. The community is urged to accept what it means to be Israel: to come under discipline means to learn to listen, to become persons and a community whose very life consists in hearing what God addresses. Thus the listening urged is not to a particular command, but it is a posture and habit and inclination of life that acknowledges that the source of life lies outside of self.[14] Thus the question means, "Could you not renounce your fraudulent autonomy?"

Putting that programmatic question (imperative and accusation), the narrator now exposits the significance of that urging. First the narrator cites once again the positive example of the Rechabites who listen (v. 14a). But then it is the negative case with Israel that receives more extended coverage (vv. 14b-15). This formulation concerning recalcitrant Israel contains a complete statement of a prophetic philosophy of history in three parts:[15]

(1) God spoke — but Israel did *not listen.*
(2) The prophets are a mitigating factor inviting repentance to avoid harsh judgment.
(3) Still, even in the face of the prophets, Israel did *not listen.*

Thus this speech is sandwiched with two uses of *shema'*, before and after the prophets; the prophets change nothing and do not cause Israel to listen. In between the double use of the verb *(shema')* is a summary of prophetic

14. See the contrast sharply voiced in Deut. 8:17.
15. Klaus Koch, *The Prophets,* vol. 2: *The Babylonian and Persian Periods* (Philadelphia: Fortress and London: SCM, 1984), 25-32 and *passim,* clearly articulates the shape of prophetic understandings of history. It is telling that Koch, *The Prophets,* vol. 1: *The Assyrian Period* (Philadelphia: Fortress and London: SCM, 1983), 1-6, understands the prophetic enterprise as "The Longing for a Moral World Order." The three points I have listed summarize the prophetic notion of a moral world order.

speech as understood in the tradition of Jeremiah. The prophet summons Israel to repentance *(shub)*, especially to obey the First Commandment. That summons becomes an offer and a condition of staying in the land. The reference to the land alludes to the fact that this tradition has landlessness and land loss (exile) very much on its mind.[16]

In the three great prose chapters of 7, 26, and 36, the mode of prophetic speech here summarized is precisely enacted by Jeremiah, who invites Israel into land-keeping through life-preserving repentance:

> Amend your ways and your doings, and let me dwell with you in this place. (7:3 — author's translation; cf. vv. 5-7)

> It may be that they will listen, all of them, and will turn from their evil way, that I may change my mind about the disaster that I intend to bring on them because of their evil doings. (26:3 — author's translation; cf. vv. 4-6)

> It may be that when the house of Judah hears of all the disasters that I intend to do to them, all of them may turn from their evil ways, so that I may forgive their iniquity and their sin. (36:3 — author's translation)[17]

The concluding part of this didactic section draws a twofold conclusion from the twofold story of *shema'* (35:17-19). The section is introduced with a "therefore," indicating consequences to be announced. On the one hand, Israel receives all the disasters *(ra'ah)* of the entire curse tradition, for not listening and for not answering (v. 17). On the other hand, the Rechabites receive the consequence of their listening, again with a "therefore" in v. 19: because they listen, they are guaranteed a continuing line of heirs and descendants for all foreseeable generations. The opposite consequences for the two parties are not quite symmetrical. If they were symmetrical, Israel would be denied land (as it is) and the Rechabites would be assigned land. The Rechabites, however, are not destined for

16. See Diepold, *Israels Land;* and Walter Brueggemann, "Israel's Sense of Place in Jeremiah," in *Rhetorical Criticism.* Festschrift James Muilenburg, ed. Jared J. Jackson and Martin Kessler. Pittsburgh Theological Monograph 1 (Pittsburgh: Pickwick, 1974), 149-165.

17. On the theology and provenance of the prose units in Jeremiah, see Ernest W. Nicholson, *Preaching to the Exiles: A Study of the Prose Tradition in the Book of Jeremiah* (Oxford: Blackwell, 1970).

land and do not want it, but want only a guaranteed, protected community. The formula of v. 19, "a man shall not be cut off," is not unlike the formula for the guarantees of the Davidic line and heir (Ps. 132:12; cf. Jer. 33:17). Thus the positive assurance to the Rechabites silently and completely suggests an end to the Davidic dynasty, which will indeed "lack a descendant" to stand before Yahweh.[18] Land loss and the end of the dynasty go together in the ominous consequence of not listening.

Thus the didactic conclusion to the narrative is organized in the following way:

The general thesis as question (summons and accusation) (35:13)
 Contrasting actions (vv. 14-15)
  Rechabites *listen* (v. 14a)
  Israel does *not listen* (vv. 14b-15)
  The contrast of *listening and not listening* (v. 16)
 Contrasting consequences:
 "Therefore" land loss for Israel (v. 17)
 "Therefore" promised continuity for the Rechabites (vv. 18-19)

Everything hinges on the ability and willingness to listen. On that basis, we are able to see how this twofold "case study" (34:8–35:19) relates to the oracle to Zedekiah (34:1-7). The whole problem of Zedekiah and his contemporaries is that they *failed to listen* (34:4) and so were captured and brutalized by Babylon. The general theological notion of listening thus is harnessed to a quite concrete policy issue and a very heavy social crisis.

Our interpretive inclination concerning this extended passage may be delineated in four dimensions:

(1) Israel is a creature of God's word voiced *in the torah.* The general theological foundation for Israel's existence in listening is at the center of the theology of Deuteronomy, which believes that Israel is addressed with everything needful for existence, security, and prosperity.[19] Israel is not a

---

18. This devastating announcement of the end of the dynasty reflects the primary tendency of the tradition of Jeremiah. That primary tendency, however, is powerfully countered in the oracles of 23:5-6; 33:14-16; cf. also 33:17-22.

19. The theology of listening is given its clearest rendering in the tradition of Deuteronomy. However, the final form of Jeremiah is deeply impinged upon by the theology of Deuteronomy (as Nicholson has shown) and reflects the same theological inclination.

self-starter and can never exist autonomously. Its life is always derivative as a gift from God which requires responsive obedience. To listen is to resist autonomy.

(2) In the move from the torah to the prophets, or more specifically in the move from Deuteronomy to Jeremiah, the listening that is required is no longer to the word of the torah. It is *the word of God that has come to the prophet,* specifically the word given to Jeremiah. Thus the whole of *shema'*-theology is mobilized to establish and enhance the speech of this known, named individual person. The transference of *shema'*-theology from scroll to specific prophet is a major and daring shift in canonical theology, for it is now claimed and urged that the command of God is not an established scroll, but a fresh utterance issued concretely.[20]

(3) Insofar as *shema'*-theology is in the mouth of Jeremiah and addressed to Zedekiah, its whole substance turns on one concrete affirmation: *submission to Babylon is Yahweh's will* for Jerusalem and is the only route to survival and well-being. Thus the grand "theology of hearing" in 34:8–35:19 boils down to the concreteness of 34:4-7. The book of Jeremiah makes a specific judgment about a historical crisis. It understands that crisis in terms of the entire tradition of covenant, and it reads the entire tradition of covenant in terms of that crisis. In this crisis, so the argument goes, submission to Babylon is the way covenant is kept, covenant blessings are assured, and Yahweh alone is worshipped. It is the folly of autonomy (= not listening) to refuse Babylonian reality.

(4) In our own time, these chapters speak eloquently against the ideology of autonomy so powerful in modernity, against our notions of holding initiative for our life, and our mistaken notion of being self-starters.[21] Our refusal to have our life given or derived from another is a

20. John Barton, *Oracles of God: Perceptions of Ancient Prophecy in Israel after the Exile* (New York: Oxford University Press, 1986), has characterized the way in which prophets assume authority beyond the established claims of torah. The shift here in the voice to which Israel is to listen, from torah to prophet, nicely embodies Barton's thesis. In another context with the third canon of Hebrew scripture, Donn F. Morgan, *Between Text and Community: The "Writings" in Canonical Interpretation* (Minneapolis: Fortress, 1990), has shown how authority is processed through quite intentional hermeneutical maneuvers. I suggest that in our text the tradition of Jeremiah makes a similar interpretive move.

21. Karl Barth, *Protestant Theology in the Nineteenth Century: Its Background and History* (Valley Forge: Judson, 1973), has seen most clearly that the entire "Enlight-

core pathology in our time as in the days of Zedekiah.[22] Modernity has scuttled not only the tradition rooted in a scroll, but the large notion that authority which permits life can be and must be rooted in another who both gives and commands. Indeed, the summons to listen is for us a summons to break with the most foundational presuppositions of modernity. One can make a quite concrete case that in many places in the world (though not yet in the United States), there is savage loss of land and loss of power where the ruling group has imagined itself to be autonomous and has failed to listen either to the requirements of God's justice or to the hurts of God's people.

In ancient and in modern contexts, this call to repentance urged so insistently by the prophet touches core assumptions of social power. It is ironic, but perfectly credible, that the Rechabites — those poor in spirit and poor, who have so little to lose and so little to gain — are viable candidates for listening. The contrast of Zedekiah and the Rechabites, a contrast both in choices made and in consequences received, suggests that visible power and apparent social importance are impediments to listening . . . and therefore to living long or well.

enment Project" was aimed not primarily at objectivity as an epistemological enterprise, but at human autonomy, i.e., the knowing agent who had reference to none beyond the self.

22. In our own time, Robert N. Bellah et al., *Habits of the Heart: Individualism and Commitment in American Life* (Berkeley: University of California Press, 1985), chronicles the same sort of pathology for those who refuse to receive and derive their lives from another. The healthy contrast to such a sense of autonomy is evident in the work of Emmanuel Levinas, *Totality and Infinity: An Essay on Exteriority* (Pittsburgh: Duquesne University Press, 1969), which characterizes healthy human life in terms of serious engagement with "the others." In the tradition of Jeremiah, that "other" is Yahweh, whom Zedekiah and the people of Jerusalem had disregarded.

The "Baruch Document"

Jeremiah 36:1–45:5

Chapters 36–45 (or 37–45), in the common judgment of scholars, constitute a peculiar and intentional corpus of materials.[1] This corpus may perhaps be intentionally organized; it is expressed almost exclusively in prose, and seems to be preoccupied with the life of the prophet Jeremiah.

The organization of this extended narrative includes the following elements. It begins with ch. 36, which narrates an account of the way in which Baruch wrote and publicly read a scroll of Jeremiah.[2] The corpus concludes in ch. 45 with a special promise to Baruch. Thus chs. 36 and 45 provide the brackets and boundaries which contain the entire narrative. Because the beginning and ending chapters both feature Baruch, this entire corpus is conventionally linked to Baruch.[3] He is taken

---

1. The dominant critical judgments of scholarship continue to be those of Bernard Duhm and Sigmund Mowinckel, on which see Childs, *Old Testament as Scripture,* 342-45. A recent consideration of these materials is offered by William L. Holladay, "A Fresh Look at 'Source B' and 'Source C' in Jeremiah," *Vetus Testamentum* 25 (1975): 394-412. It may well be that ch. 36 should not be grouped with the following materials. On that question, see Carroll, *Jeremiah,* 509-510.

2. We have already encountered the role of Baruch in ch. 32. That reference, however, is not germane to the role of Baruch in this extended narrative, for no critical judgment groups ch. 32 with this material.

3. Richard E. Friedman, *Who Wrote the Bible?* (New York: Summit, 1987), 146-49, has rather dramatically suggested Baruch as the author of the book of Jeremiah. Such a claim is a considerable overstatement, but not unrelated to the main tendency of criticism.

variously as either the author or the main character of the narrative, or both.

With these two chapters as the boundaries, we may identify three larger sections of material which seem intentionally organized:

(1) Jeremiah 37:1–40:6 is concerned with *the threat of Babylon* and with Jeremiah's role in urging surrender of Jerusalem to Babylon. This unit culminates in 40:1-6 with a report that Jeremiah was recognized by the Babylonians and given preferential treatment by the invaders. Of special interest in this section is the role of Ebed-melech (38:7-13), who subsequently receives from the prophet a special promissory oracle (39:15-18).

(2) Jeremiah 40:7–41:18 constitutes a central section in the narrative which functions as a transition and a change of focus and subject in the narrative. This material appears to be straightforward reportage concerning *governance and conspiracy in post–587 B.C.E. Judah*. In this section not only is the prophet Jeremiah absent, but there is no element of explicit theological reflection or interpretation. In its present context, this section — which may indeed be strict reportage — functions to switch the locus, theme, and problematic of the narrative.

(3) Jeremiah 42:1–44:30 provides a third and final section. This section concerns the community of Jews who fled to Egypt and who brought Jeremiah against his will to Egypt. The section is constituted by a series of *harsh condemnations of the Egyptian venture* and culminates with a subtle suggestion that this pitiful flight to Egypt is in fact the inversion and negation of the Exodus.

Thus I suggest that there are two major units of prophetic material (37:1–40:6; 42:1–44:30), linked together by the descriptive narrative of 40:7–41:18. The two major units have as their epitomes two preaching articulations in the mouth of the prophet. These two units are organized in the same way and perform the same theological function in the narrative. They do, nonetheless, reflect changed circumstances and therefore changed substantive arguments. On the one hand, 38:17-18, in a double "if-then" statement, functions to offer positive and negative possibilities to the Jerusalem leadership. The prophet offers both a possibility and a warning to Zedekiah. The positive possibility is surrender to Babylon as a way to have life. The negative alternative is to refuse to surrender, that is, to resist, and so to come to a sorry end.

On the other hand, after the transfer of power to Gedaliah and the failure of his leadership, 42:9-17 offers another "if-then" construction with the same basic structure of positive and negative alternatives.[4] In this case, the positive possibility is to stay in the land, and the negative warning concerns flight to Egypt.

Thus the message of the prophetic voice is different in the two summary passages. The positive option in 38:17-18 concerns *surrender to Babylon,* but does not mention remaining in the city. (Presumably refusal to surrender implies remaining in the city to resist.) In 42:9-17 the positive possibility is to *remain in the city* (but the text only alludes to and assumes surrender to Babylon). Thus the issue and argument is different in the two situations because circumstances have changed. The circumstance has been changed through the intermediate narrative (40:7–41:18), in which Gedaliah is established in power and then assassinated. The assassination of Gedaliah is in fact an act of resistance against Babylonian governance.

Despite the two different postures of 38:7-18 and 42:9-17, in the end both pivotal oracles concern submission to Babylon as the only way to survival. In the latter section, remaining in the city implies submission to Babylon, just as flight to Egypt is in fact resistance to Babylon. The middle section of 40:7–41:18 seems to change matters, but does not in fact effect the essential position voiced by the prophet. The entire corpus is committed to Babylonian reality, which must be heeded as the will of God.

The theological and literary intention of this material has been the subject of much scholarly reflection. A number of useful hypotheses are available, each of which contains a useful insight, but none of which adequately accounts for the material as we have it. We may identify the following scholarly contributions as suggestive and useful.

(1) A commonsense view assumes that this material does indeed report developments in the exilic community.[5] There is no doubt that in broad outline the narrative reflects historical developments. That is, no one seriously doubts the governorship of Gedaliah as a provincial arrange-

4. The "if-then" construction of 42:9-17 is not only more extended but also more complex than the comparable unit in 38:17-18. The purpose, intent, and argument of the two passages are nonetheless closely parallel.

5. Holladay, *Jeremiah 2,* is most inclined among contemporary scholars to this view.

ment after the fall of the monarchy.[6] In my judgment, however, the narrative is not such that we may regard it as primarily historical in character. While the broad outline of events is secure, this does not go very far in suggesting why the material is shaped as it is.

(2) Perhaps the most influential interpretive angle is that of Heinz Kremers, who proposes that this extended narrative is the "passion narrative" of Jeremiah, tracing the way in which, as a righteous sufferer and rejected outsider, the prophet comes to an ignominious end.[7] This view places primary emphasis on the person of Jeremiah, who confronts the kings of Jerusalem and is acknowledged by the king of Babylon and then ends, against his will, among the refugees in Egypt. This view can be critiqued because the person of Jeremiah does not seem to dominate the narrative so completely, and the personal suffering of the prophet is scarcely a main theme.

(3) In contrast to Kremers, Martin Kessler and Ernest Nicholson place the account of the narrative not on the person of Jeremiah, but on the speech of Jeremiah which is taken as the word of God.[8] The narrative then traces the way in which that decisive word from God is utterly and consistently rejected throughout the narrative, first by the leadership around Zedekiah (before 587) and then by the Egyptian contingent led by Johanan (after 587). The narrative then is a story about the destiny of the Word. Again, this suggestion greatly illuminates the narrative but does not account for all of the materials. The two emphases on the person of Jeremiah (Kremers) and the word of Jeremiah (Kessler, Nicholson) might usefully be brought together, for the destinies of person and word are not likely to be separated in the intention of the narrative.

---

6. On the rule of Gedaliah, see J. Maxwell Miller and John H. Hayes, *A History of Ancient Israel and Judah* (Philadelphia: Westminster and London: SCM, 1986), 421-25. They suggest that Gedaliah was not only governor but in fact succeeded to the throne of Zedekiah.

7. Heinz Kremers, "Leidensgemeinschaft mit Gott im Alten Testament: Eine Untersuchung der "biographischen" Berichte im Jeremiabuch," *Evangelische Theologie* 13 (1953): 122-140.

8. Martin Kessler, "Jeremiah Chapters 26–45 Reconsidered," *Journal of Near Eastern Studies* 27 (1968): 81-88; Nicholson, *Preaching to the Exiles*. Nicholson writes: "To be more specific, the narrative has for its primary purpose a description of rejection of the Word of Yahweh, here enshrined in the scroll of the prophet's oracles, in the actions of the king who is the personification of the nation" (42).

(4) Gunther Wanke has provided a shrewd and discerning form-critical analysis of the narrative and has paid special attention to the scenes in which the narrative is cast, and to the way in which various characters are assigned roles in the scenes.[9] While this analysis greatly illuminates the artistry of the narrative, it does not help greatly in discerning the larger intentionality of the whole.

(5) Christopher R. Seitz has paid primary attention to the ideological claims and arguments that operate in the narrative.[10] He has observed that a variety of competing and conflicting ideologies are at work there.

It is likely that none of these analyses adequately illuminates the intentionality of the narrative, but a mixed, eclectic model of intentionality may be more useful. Concerning these several hypothesis, I have only one additional suggestion. As Baruch is presented in ch. 36 as a close associate of Jeremiah and in ch. 45 as especially blessed by Jeremiah, so also he appears in this narrative in one other strategic spot.

In 43:1-3 Jeremiah enters into severe dispute with the leadership of the Egyptian venture. They refuse his word of counsel, which is that they not go to Egypt. They dismiss his word as unauthoritative.[11] Their way of dismissing the word of Jeremiah is enormously suggestive. The adversaries of the word of Jeremiah say:

> The LORD our God did not send you to say, "Do not go to Egypt to settle there"; but Baruch son of Neriah is inciting you against us, to hand us over to the Chaldeans, in order that they may kill us or take us into exile in Babylon. (vv. 2-3 NRSV)

It may be, if the text is historical, that Jeremiah is too venerated and cannot be attacked directly. As a result, the attack is diverted and directed against Baruch. Our purpose, however, is not to determine historicity, but to consider narrative intentionality. Taken as a "signature" for the narrative, however, this statement suggests that Baruch was an important operative, and was perhaps the leader or the symbol of the pro-Babylonian commu-

---

9. Gunther Wanke, *Untersuchungen zur sogenannten Baruchschrift.* Beihefte zur Zeitschrift für die alttestamentliche Wissenschaft 122 (Berlin: de Gruyter, 1971).

10. Seitz, *Theology in Conflict;* and "The Prophet Moses and the Canonical Shape of Jeremiah," *Zeitschrift für die alttestamentliche Wissenschaft* 101 (1989): 3-27.

11. Jeremiah himself is treated in this passage as he himself has done to others in chs. 23 and 27–29.

nity of Jewish exiles, that is, the generator of the ideology placed in the mouth of the prophet.[12]

Thus I suggest that there is a convergence in this material of three factors: (1) the centrality of *Baruch*, (2) the decisiveness of the *prophetic word*, and (3) the *pro-Babylonian ideology* that pervades the material. What is neglected in the several hypotheses of Kremer, Nicholson, Kessler, and Wanke is the Babylonian bent of the material. That is, our interpretation requires us to take into careful account the convergence of *the will of Yahweh* and *the reality of Babylon*. Or said another way, the resolve of Yahweh is discerned in, with, and through the socioeconomic-political reality, and any attempt to understand the word and will of Yahweh in this narrative apart from the "Babylonian-Baruch ideology" misunderstands the mode of theology that is offered here. Thus I concur with Seitz that there is an ideological dimension to this narrative. Yet as Kremer, Nicholson, Kessler, and Wanke have missed the political element in the theological affirmation,[13] it appears to me that Seitz minimizes the theological seriousness and import of the ideological affirmation. It is the convergence and interpretation of the two that become the driving force of the narrative.[14] In the two programmatic passages I have cited, 38:17-18 on surrendering to Babylon and 42:9-17 on remaining in the city, it is the alliance of Yahweh and Babylon that counts to force a truth on the community. And in the two special oracles of blessing cited by Seitz (39:15-18; 45:1-5), it is the supporters of the Babylonian view (Ebed-melech indirectly and Baruch directly) who receive their life as a spoil, while the others receive a death sentence.[15]

---

12. For a shrewd and suggestive analysis of the role of Baruch and what he represents in the Jeremiah tradition, see J. Andrew Dearman, "My Servants the Scribes: Composition and Context in Jeremiah 36," *Journal of Biblical Literature* 109 (1990): 403-421.

13. On the "idealist" disregard of the political factor in the theological affirmation, see the strictures of Gottwald, *The Tribes of Yahweh*, 592-607. On the power of ideology in the formation of the text, see Mottu, "Jeremiah vs. Hananiah."

14. On this methodological convergence, see David Jobling, "Sociological and Literary Approaches to the Bible: How Shall the Twain Meet?" *Journal for the Study of the Old Testament* 38 (1987): 85-93.

15. Seitz, "Canonical Shape," 16-24, suggests that Ebed-melech and Baruch assume roles in the text not unlike Joshua and Caleb in the book of Numbers. On the role of the latter in the shaping of the final form of the text of Numbers, see Olson, *Death of the Old.*

Thus the "Baruch document" makes a massive, determined, sustained judgment that the will of God is indeed visible and operative in the flow of international power in the Near East. Refusal to accept this Babylonian reading of the destiny of Jerusalem is taken as a refusal of the prophetic word, and derivatively, as resistance to the will of God. To regard this narrative as a "Baruch document" is not to focus on the person of Baruch.[16] Rather, it is to affirm the theological *Tendenz* which Baruch represents and to accept the way in which theological reality and the conduct of public policy cohere.[17] We can then see why Baruch is so important for this material. It is my judgment that scholars have focused on the right man, but for the wrong reasons.

In the end, then, we can suggest that the accusation made against Baruch in 43:3 and the accusation that Jeremiah is a pawn of Baruch contain a powerful element of truth. The pro-Babylonian cast of the material is not simply political ideology or pastoral sensitivity toward exiles, but it is finally a daring judgment of faith about God's will and work in the world.[18] The blessed, in the end, are those who accept this version of reality.

The Baruch narrative itself is an interpretive act which proceeds on the assumption that theological and socioeconomic political realities are deeply enmeshed together and must be held together in a Yahwistic view of reality. As the Baruch narrative itself practices such an interpretive stance, our own interpretive act concerning the same text tradition must not do otherwise. Thus I suggest that the name "Baruch" signifies exactly that inalienable congruence of theological and political realities.

16. I suggest that Friedman does not probe deeply enough concerning Baruch and the authorship of the Jeremiah tradition. While focus on the individual person of Baruch may suit our individualistic tendencies and notions of writing, it likely does not fully recognize the ideological disputes in which the person and party of Baruch are fully engaged as they fashion the literature.

17. Gottwald, *The Tribes of Yahweh,* 608-621, has nicely suggested the ways in which theological and political realities may be functions of each other in a dialectical fashion. In some of Gottwald's own recent work the dialectic does not seem to be fully honored, as the political tends to reduce the theological in importance. For much of scholarship, however, the greater temptation is in the opposite direction; for that reason, I accent the force of political ideology in shaping the text and its claims.

18. See Brueggemann, "Second Reading," in which I have argued that pastoral and political affirmations come to be taken as a reliable theological claim.

Jeremiah's Scroll (36:1-32)

This chapter occupies a pivotal place in the tradition of Jeremiah, and more broadly in the shaping of Israel's faith for exile. We may identify three related dimensions in its pivotal place. First, the chapter is closely related to ch. 26. In ch. 26, which in turn derives from ch. 7, Jeremiah is on trial for his life. While the prophet is acquitted, he clearly has become *persona non grata* for the royal-temple leadership in Jerusalem. Chapter 36 now completes that process of making Jeremiah an outsider to the establishment, one who is regarded as an unwelcome and unnecessary threat to dominant policies.

Second, the confrontation between the prophet (through Baruch) and the king makes this meeting virtually a classic paradigm for meeting between prophet and king when "truth speaks to power." Whereas the first point above (Jeremiah as a rejected outsider) focuses on the person of Jeremiah, this second point moves our attention away from historical issues to a paradigmatic drama that transcends both the person of Jeremiah and questions of historicity.[19] That is, regardless of what happened, this is how such a meeting between king and prophet should have happened. The meeting shows that the field of perception in which the prophet moves cannot be accommodated to the ways of the king. It is fair to say that this narrative has contributed greatly to our understanding of "prophetic ministry" as essentially confrontational.

A third point has recently received primary attention from scholars. What happens in this narrative is that the scroll of Jeremiah takes on independent authority (i.e., independent of the person of Jeremiah) and comes to have a life of its own. This emergence of an authorized scroll is emblematic of the emergence of a canonical "book," and this development is pivotal in the formation of an authorized canon. That is, ch. 36 functions as a model of "Bible-making," so that interest turns from the personality

19. On the person of Jeremiah as a paradigm, see Sheldon H. Blank, "The Prophet as Paradigm," in *Essays in Old Testament Theology.* Festschrift J. Philip Hyatt, ed. James L. Crenshaw and John T. Willis (New York: KTAV, 1974), 111-130. The person of Jeremiah is no doubt a construct of the canonical process of Jeremiah, heavily influenced by Deuteronomic theology. See Walter Brueggemann, "The Book of Jeremiah: Portrait of the Prophet," in *Interpreting the Prophets,* ed. James L. Mays and Paul J. Achtemeier (Philadelphia: Fortress, 1987), 113-129; and Wilson, *Prophecy and Society in Ancient Israel,* 231-251.

of the prophet to *the book of Jeremiah.* It is the book (scroll), and not the presence of the prophet, which becomes decisive in resisting the king. From now on, establishment leadership must face a book which relentlessly places established power in jeopardy. The scroll is so much more difficult to resist because it cannot, like a person, be intimidated, banished, or destroyed. It keeps reappearing.

36:1-8   The narrative begins with an account of how the scroll came to be written. The narrative is situated in 605 B.C.E., just as the world of the Fertile Crescent was in enormous upheaval[20] and just as Jehoiakim emerged as a perverse king (v. 1). That is, the "Bible" emerges in the midst of social disorder when there is a profound unsettlement in public life. The "Bible" intends to participate in and be a party to that unsettlement.

The scroll is formed at the impetus of Yahweh (vv. 2-3). The Bible itself strains to make the crucial and difficult claim that a human book is at the instigation of heavenly authority (see also 1:1-3). The scroll is not generated by Jeremiah. It is to contain "the words that I have spoken," not the words of the prophet. The purpose of the scroll, moreover, is to move Judah to hear *(shema')* and to turn *(shub),* and so to avoid evil. That is, the scroll is not designed to give information, nor even to make an argument, but it is to authorize, energize, and evoke a transformed life that will avoid and deter the coming evil. The scroll is intended to alter Judah's public existence. That intention, however, is not guaranteed. We do not know if the scroll will be that powerful, and God does not know either. Even for God the scroll only opens a possibility: "It may be" (36:3).

Jeremiah is obedient to the divine command (v. 4). He dictates the scroll which Baruch writes down. This chapter for a second time introduces Baruch, who is pivotal for the formation of the book of Jeremiah (cf. 32:12-16).[21] The introduction of Baruch indicates that the production of

---

20. On the historical interaction between Jehoiakim and Jeremiah, see Miller and Hayes, 403-6. Marion Ann Taylor,"Jeremiah 45: The Problem of Placement," *Journal for the Study of the Old Testament* 37 (1987): 88-94, suggests that the dates linking prophetic material to Jehoiakim are ways of speaking in formulas about the judgment of God.

21. On the person of Baruch, see James Muilenburg, "Baruch the Scribe," in *Proclamation and Presence.* Festschrift G. H. Davies, ed. John I. Durham and J. Roy Porter (Richmond: John Knox and London: SCM, 1970), 215-238; and Friedman, 146-49.

the scroll is a very human, political enterprise, for Baruch himself is a crucial political figure. He is not a mere stenographer, but one who has a deep stake in the argument made by Jeremiah (cf. 43:1-7). As we shall see, the production of the scroll is a deeply political act that advocates a particular slant on policy questions and passionately engages the issues of the day.[22] From the outset, the Bible is not a neutral document and its formation is not a disinterested act. Jeremiah's mandate to Baruch (36:5-7) parallels Yahweh's mandate to Jeremiah (vv. 2-3). Jeremiah needs a go-between, because he himself is unwelcome in the public places of promulgation.

The intent of Jeremiah echoes the intent of Yahweh: "It may be . . ." (v. 7). The scroll is no certain thing. It is not known what Judah's response will be, but it is the only chance for Judah in the face of Yahweh's impatience and anger. The obedience of Baruch to Jeremiah (v. 8) is parallel to Jeremiah's response to Yahweh (v. 4). The formation of the scroll is narrated as a twofold drama of command and obedience. Through this twofold process, what is initiated in God's own intent has now been delivered concretely to the place of public address. The "word of God" is intended precisely to be heard in public places, to impinge upon public policy, and to provoke public transformation. Such hearing, impingement, and provocation require a quite human act. In this case, Baruch makes the word of God available, and Baruch himself is a passionate advocate for how the heavenly word of Yahweh touches public policy.

36:9-14 Baruch is obedient to Jeremiah. He reads the scroll in public, as per instruction (v. 10). He does so on a high holy day, which assures a large hearing. He reads the scroll in the temple in a named chamber. As we shall see, that the place of reading is in "the chamber of Gemariah the son of Shaphan" cannot be either incidental or unimportant. It is not possible to know if this reading is a scheduled public event or if it is an intrusive act of personal assertion.[23] We do not know if such a

---

22. It seems likely that Baruch, in the scroll, becomes a cipher and agent for the arguments and ideology of pro-Babylonian policy. On the political and social location of Baruch, see Dearman.

23. It is not impossible that the presentation of the scroll was like the offer of theses made by Martin Luther, which set in motion the church crisis that became the Reformation. While Luther's act is popularly thought to be a daring act of defiance, in fact he followed a convention in instigating theological discussion and dispute. Baruch's presentation of the scroll may in its context have been such an act of inviting a dispute.

public reading was a routine and acceptable occurrence in the temple or not.

What matters is the response to the reading (vv. 11-14). In such a predemocratic society, appeal is not made to "the masses." What counts is the leadership. The scroll in the "chamber of Gemariah" is heard by the son of Gemariah, Micaiah. He obviously belongs to an important and powerful political family, and has easy access to the high councils of government.[24] Micaiah immediately reports what he has heard to the cabinet of the royal government. "All the princes" are assembled, and we notice in the list of high officials his father, Gemariah.

The impact of the report of the scroll is powerful. It must have been like the report of the "Pentagon Papers" of Daniel Ellsburg.[25] It is enough to get the attention of the leadership, and to evoke a response of interest and of anxiety. Thus Jeremiah's strategy for Baruch is effective. The scroll (the content of which we know nothing specific) contains words and claims that require the serious and sustained attention of the government. The narrative intends to model a scroll that cannot be avoided, and a power structure that must respond to the scroll. Baruch is summoned to the cabinet meeting. He answers the summons of the cabinet, apparently willingly and unafraid. The scroll by dramatic moves is making its way into the presence of established power, where it must have its say.

36:15-19 The action shifts from a temple chamber to a government chamber. The stakes grow higher! Baruch now provides a second reading of the scroll which has been initiated in God's own utterance (v. 15). This hearing evokes "dread" *(phd)* among the listeners, who are establishment figures (v. 16). The scroll requires and receives a serious hearing. It makes its way into the high councils of government, not because of Jeremiah or Baruch, but because of its intrinsic claim. The response of the princes is twofold.

First, the king must know (v. 16)! This seemingly innocent statement may be more freighted than it appears. This urging may, of course, only voice the expectation of the alarmed princes that the king will have to deal with the claims of the scroll, for it belongs to the king and not to the princes to respond to the crisis. If the statement is read more cunningly,

---

24. See Dearman, 411-421.

25. On the Pentagon Papers, see Neil Sheehan et al., *The Pentagon Papers* (New York: Quadrangle, 1971).

the princes may now sense that they have (at long last) an available tool which the king cannot avoid.[26] One cannot determine how the princes are positioned in this tense confrontation. They may be only mediating to the king as innocent functionaries. The narrative suggests, however, that at least some of the princes are sympathetic to the argument of the scroll and are relieved to have their own view voiced in the presence of the king, voiced in a way that does not place them in direct opposition to the king.[27] That is, we should not assume that all the princes are "yes men" to the king, but some represent very different interests and views which may concur with those of the scroll. It may be that the scroll weighs in on a government dispute that was already under way.

The second response of the princes to the reading by Baruch is to investigate the origin of the scroll (vv. 17-18). If the princes are to value the scroll and risk something for it, they obviously need to know of its origin, authenticity, and credibility. They do not want to go out on a limb for a document that may be a hoax. The specific question poses a much larger one. How can such a countergovernment opinion be voiced in a relatively closed society? Who could have authored such a dangerous document? Baruch's answer is direct and reassuring. The scroll belongs to Jeremiah (v. 18). No claim is made by Baruch that the scroll comes from God. Baruch responds concerning the human process of scroll making, for this is a very human confrontation.

26. Whether the decision to take the scroll to the king is an innocent act or a calculating one depends on two things: (1) whether the issues stated in the scroll were already reflected in a tension at work in the government, and (2) whether the scroll is understood by its handlers as enmeshed from the outset in abrasive policy issues. That is, if the scroll is understood in relation to actual policy matters, then the urging of the royal cabinet officers is more likely to be a calculated act. If, however, the scroll is understood only religiously, then the act may be more innocent. I believe political innocence in such a context is not likely.

27. If the family of Shaphan and the family of Baruch are socially located as Dearman suggests (see above, n. 22), then we may imagine they would favor a policy of great prudence which would urge accommodation to Babylon; they may also be very judicious about running personal risks in confronting the king. Thus the strategy reflected in this narrative makes sense when we consider the role of scribes in a royal government. On such functionaries, see Eris W. Heaton, *Solomon's New Men: The Emergence of Israel as a National State* (London: Thomas and Hudson, 1974, and New York: Pica, 1975).

The princes seem satisfied with his response. Their concluding advice to Baruch is telling indeed. They advise Baruch to disappear with Jeremiah, to be safe from the rage of the king which is sure to come, for this is a dangerously provocative scroll. This response on the part of the princes is enormously important. It indicates, on the one hand, that the princes recognize the scroll to be inherently dangerous and troublesome, and sure to evoke the passionate hostility of the king. They not only know something of the scroll, but they know a great deal about the king. They have witnessed his temper tantrums before. On the other hand, this advice suggests that the princes are not neutral parties in this conflict. They align themselves with the scroll-makers, and by subtle action they align themselves against the king. That is, they do not want the king to succeed against the scroll-makers. The princes become protectors of this subversive voice that the king cannot tolerate. The seasoned bureaucrats also know to proceed on a "need to know" basis. If the princes do not know where Baruch and Jeremiah hide, it is safe for Baruch and Jeremiah, because they will not be betrayed. Moreover, such an arrangement leaves the princes unimplicated in the hiding. The strategy of the princes is to cut off any traceable connection between themselves and their "informants." Thus the scroll-makers are decisively removed from the scene, and the king is left with only the scroll.

36:20-26   Finally, through a studied and formal development, the scroll arrives at "the court of the king." Neither Jeremiah nor Baruch is there, only the scroll. The meeting between king and scroll is dramatic and tense. The scroll is read to the king while the princes stand in attendance. The princes know and have orchestrated the reading, but now they assume a courtly posture of deference to the king.

The king waits and ostentatiously cuts columns of the scroll after they are read and burns them (v. 23). The king gives no hint of listening to the reading, but makes a great show of contempt for the scroll. The king enacts an early form of "document shredding." He continues his act of disdain until all the scroll is gone. The king has eliminated the scroll! The scroll is gone, and there is only the king. The narrator adds a poignant observation. Neither the king nor his entourage rend their garments. The word "rend" (*qr'*) is the same word as "cut" in v. 23. The king would *cut* the scroll in disdain, but he would not *cut* his garments in response or repentance. The king would yield nothing of himself to the claim of the scroll. He shut out the scroll and refused to let it touch his life.

The use of the term *qrʿ* makes a deliberate and telling reference to 2 Kgs. 22:11, wherein another king, Josiah, bears another authoritative scroll and does indeed "rend" his garments in penitence.[28] Thus our narrative articulates a sharp and unambiguous contrast between Josiah, the good king who responds to the scroll, and Jehoiakim, the resistant king who refuses the scroll — its great demand, and its offer of life. The king wants to be and is "scroll-less" because he imagines he is autonomous and need give no answer. Whereas his princely advisors had responded to the scroll in great fear *(phd)* (Jer. 36:16), now the king and his entourage exhibit no "fear" *(phd)* (v. 24). The contrast between the frightened princes and the unresponsive king is complete. The contrast serves to show that the king is utterly cynical, utterly in opposition to the scroll and to the God who speaks in the scroll.

The princes, including Gemariah, with what must have required considerable courage, defend the scroll against the willfulness of the king and urge the scroll to be taken seriously (v. 25). The king, however, would not "listen." The word "listen" looms large in this narrative and reflects the entire tradition of listening obedience as championed in Deuteronomy. "Listening" bespeaks readiness and willingness to submit to the claim of torah, to yield one's life to the demands of Yahweh.[29] In refusing to listen, the king resists not only this particular scroll but the whole world of demands and promises and Yahweh's will for life in covenant. In rejecting the scroll, the king refuses life in covenant with Yahweh. Indeed, the king not only refuses to listen. The king takes aggressive action against the producers of the scroll, dispatching members of his party to "seize" Jeremiah and Baruch (v. 26). The king intends to eliminate those who generate words inimical to his regime.[30]

28. Nicholson, 42-46, has clearly seen how this contrast between Josiah and his son works in the text. Cf. also Jer. 22:13-19.

29. For a programmatic understanding of "listen," see Eugen Rosenstock-Huessy, *Speech and Reality* (Norwich, Vt.: Argo, 1969), 16-31, wherein it is seen that living in human community depends on speaking and listening.

30. The elimination of the scroll by the king places Jeremiah (or the tradition of Jeremiah) in the company of those writers, poets, journalists, and novelists who have been silenced by fearful, authoritarian regimes. Such authorities regularly recognize such writers as threats and believe that silencing them can maintain the present order. On contemporary counterparts see Andre Brink, *Writing in a State of Siege* (New York: Summit, 1984); and *The Writer in Human Rights*, ed. the Toronto Arts Group for Human Rights (Garden City: Doubleday, 1983).

In the face of the king's cynical and self-serving action, the narrative adds a laconic note: "Yahweh hid them" (v. 26). This note is telling, in light of the princely advice of v. 19. With a reflexive verb, the princes had urged Jeremiah and Baruch to "hide themselves." Now, however, Yahweh is the active subject of a causative verb concerning the process of hiding. By this phrase, the narrative signals that more is at work here than flesh and blood. The confrontation has been escalated, so that the protection of Jeremiah and Baruch is not simply a matter of political expedience, but it requires providential care for the carriers of an alternative politics. The princes are not directly implicated in the hiding of Jeremiah and Baruch, but their counsel in v. 19 is part of Yahweh's involvement. With the complicity of the princes, the reality of the scroll has taken on very large and very ominous proportions. The king imagines he has prevailed. He has not, however, stayed through to the completion of the narrative.

36:27-32   The king imagined that the burning of the scroll finished what was for him only a minor episode. The scroll had been burned and no longer existed. There was only the king. The narrative continues, however, after the king has departed the scene. Two actions are taken in this post-king narrative. First, a powerful and devastating lawsuit speech is spoken against the king (vv. 29-31). It is the voice of the very God who stands behind the scroll who now speaks the decisive word against the king. The king is indicted: "You burned the scroll" (v. 29). That act of burning turned out to be much more significant than the king suspected, or than even the princes understood. Then a harsh sentence is pronounced against the king (vv. 30-32). The articulation of punishment is heavily formulary. It anticipates an ignominious end for the king, whose dead body will be dishonorably exposed (cf. 22:18-19), an end to the dynasty when the king will have no heir (cf. 22:30), and enormous evil against the city. The judgment seems disproportionate to the affront of burning the scroll, except that burning it is an awesome attempt to eliminate the concrete, sovereign word and will of God. The elimination of the word (scroll) is an act of gross disobedience which can only bring death and destruction.

The second act authorized in this oracle is the writing of a second scroll (36:28, 32). The divine authorization of a second scroll (v. 28) is linked directly to the royal burning of the first scroll (v. 27). Two things are evident in this immediate follow-up. First, God is indomitable. God is not deterred in the least by the king's refusal. God is a scroll-maker and will continue to make scrolls.[31] Any particular scroll from the God of Israel can be dismissed as was this first one; but it will be promptly and boldly reiterated. The king is unable to eliminate the scroll because God intends a scroll to be present, sounded, and heeded. Second, the narrative ends with the freighted words: "Many similar words were added to them" (v. 32). Thus the king's resistant activity only evoked a larger, more comprehensive, more demanding scroll. The king's action did not terminate the threat of the scroll as he intended, but only magnified the problem for the king.

It is clear in this dramatic narrative that scroll-making (i.e., Bible production) is a daring, dangerous human enterprise. It is equally clear that this scroll-making is paradigmatic of the way in which God counters human pretension and resistance. God will not leave the king scroll-less, even if the king wants no scroll. The emergence and reemergence of the scroll thus makes a statement about the theologically constituent elements of the life of this community. Alongside the courage of Jeremiah and Baruch is the resolve and intent of God. God's relentless resolve arises in the form of a scroll summoning to repentance. God will generate as many scrolls as necessary to override the king's zeal for autonomy. The king cannot finally sustain a world where he need not listen. The king's life consists in listening to the reality of the scroll. In this chapter, the power and authority of the scroll have in fact displaced the voice of the prophet. The scroll calls Judah to turn, which is to live.

Jeremiah Arrested and Imprisoned (37:1-21)

The last days of Judah are ostensibly ruled over by Zedekiah, the third of Josiah's sons (598-587 B.C.E.). His rule, however, is of little importance,

31. Jose Faur, "God as a Writer: Omnipresence and the Art of Dissimulation," *Religion and Intellectual Life* 6/3-4 (1989): 31-43, has made a compelling case that Greek religion is metaphysical but that Hebrew religion is literary: "The God of the Hebrews is eminently literate. God communicates in writing" (33). See the more extended study by Faur, *Golden Doves with Silver Dots: Semiotics and Textuality in Rabbinic Tradition* (Bloomington: Indiana University Press, 1986), and the references to Jacques Derrida in his work.

given the larger events of international politics. The great facts of Judah's political situation are the massive powers of Egypt in the south and Babylon in the north. Those two powers are in deep conflict, and the king in Jerusalem sits helplessly in the middle of the conflict. Zedekiah and his city are caught between them and are in fact helpless to effect matters at all. Into this caldron of power politics comes the voice of Jeremiah, carrier of a word from Yahweh. Jeremiah (and the word he carries) are fully cognizant of the international situation. Because the prophet has drawn a conclusion about the shape of that situation, the prophetic word is an urgent, partisan imperative to the king. The king, pitiful political creature that he is, is at risk in the midst of this raging context of great powers, a context made yet more ominous by the prophetic word. The text of Jeremiah is a study of the interface of royal power and prophetic word, and the demanding requirement of daily life in the midst of that inter-face.[32] This narrative chapter portrays the ways in which the prophetic word intrudes upon royal politics.

37:1-2 Zedekiah is a creature of Babylon (cf. 2 Kgs. 24:17). He rules only at the whim of despised Nebuchadnezzar. The fact that he is an imperial puppet must have evoked resistance from "true patriots." This is the first fact of Zedekiah's rule. For the text, however, that Babylonian fact is only a framing piece of data. The central issue is that the king did not "listen" *(shema')*. No one listened — not the king, not his royal entourage, not the city nor its citizens. "Listening" becomes the key motif for this part of the text.[33] In the use of that single word, the text makes present not only the urgent advocacy of Jeremiah but the entire torah tradition of obedience and fidelity. "Listening" is to acknowledge that Yahweh and the torah tradition provide the dominant clues to life and to power. Zedekiah's refusal to listen is a decision to ignore the tradition, to reject

32. Intrusion of the prophetic word into the public life of Jerusalem is a central motif of chs. 37–45. Note also that the word is not only from God but is at the same time a partisan, political verdict. Indeed, in the prophetic faith of Israel, one cannot have one without the other; i.e., one cannot have a word from God unless it is also a word pertinent to the social realities of the day.

33. It is most likely that the focus of this exchange on "listen" indicates that we are dealing with Deuteronomic theology. The Deuteronomic theology is insistent on this single accent in appropriating moral demands within the public process.

the prophet, to scuttle a theological identity, and to disregard a transcendent purpose in power politics. A refusal to listen is to imagine that the king is autonomous and therefore destined for self-sufficiency. In his refusal to listen, so the text suggests, the king has sealed his own fate and that of his people. His future depends not upon his ingenuity nor his power, but upon his readiness to accept the theological reality of his life and his rule, that is, the reality of Yahweh's rule.

37:3-5   It is odd indeed that the king who refuses to listen to the prophetic word nonetheless asks the prophet to engage in intercessory prayer. While we may conclude that the indictment of Jer. 37:1-2 comes from a different literary source than the prayer request, we may also take the two as a deliberate textual tension. Taken together the two items suggest that the king wants *the aid* of the prophet (and of God) (vv. 3-5), but not *the command* of the prophet (or of God) (v. 2). The king's request is a measure of his acute fear and desperation. Verses 3 and 4 nicely juxtapose the reality of the competing armies and the power of prayer. Belatedly, perhaps halfheartedly, the king is driven to appeal for transcendent help when his own devices have failed. His request, however, contradicts his refusal to listen. Such prayer may be desperate; it has, however, no chance of succeeding. Indeed with Jeremiah, the request for prayer is not even acknowledged. The request of the king is simply disregarded by the prophet. The prayers of those who do not "listen" will be scarcely heard, and even their requests for prayer will be disregarded.[34]

37:6-10   These verses constitute the center of our chapter and are representative of the main affirmations of the Jeremiah tradition. This is an oracle which embodies God's intrusion into the crisis of Jerusalem. The king had asked for a word of prayer *addressed to Yahweh* in intercession. Instead, however, he receives from the prophet *a word from Yahweh,* more of the same

---

34. Though it is not explicit, the text suggests yet another example of the correspondence of affront and punishment which Patrick D. Miller, Jr., *Sin and Judgment in the Prophets,* has explicated. Thus Israel's affront is that it did not "listen," though the text does not say so. Jeremiah's disregard of the request for intercession is in turn an act of not "listening," reflecting the nonresponse both of the prophet and of God. Elsewhere Jeremiah is more directly commanded not to pray because God will "not listen" (7:16; 11:14; 14:11-12; 15:1-2).

word to which he would not listen. The king wants God's help, but gets only God's harsh guidance. What he receives is not what he wants. The only help God will give is guidance which the king will refuse to honor.

The oracle is a word to Jeremiah which is then given to the king. The king has no immediate access to God's word, but depends on the word and authority of the prophet. The oracle is astonishing in its threat. Though it is God's own word, it is an analysis of and an anticipation of the behavior of the great empires. The word addresses the king, who is situated exactly between Egypt and Babylon. The present circumstance suggests to the king that Egypt is the significant factor and Babylon is absent. There was a powerful predilection to tilt political-military assessments in Egypt's favor, and Jerusalem is endlessly haunted by Egyptian promises and potential.

The oracle, however, refutes such an analysis. The king has it all wrong, and his entire intelligence establishment has miscalculated. Egypt is no enduring factor in the future, says the oracle. Pharaoh will withdraw, and the Babylonians will come and destroy. The king who relies on Egypt is betting on the wrong horse. The king is advised by those whom Jeremiah regards as false (cf. 27–28). There was an opinion in Jerusalem that the Babylonians would not return to threaten Jerusalem again. Official Jerusalem engaged in a sustained and systemic underestimate of Babylon. Against such a view, Jeremiah is adamant and insistent. The book of Jeremiah is very sure. Babylon will destroy. There is no escape, and there is no alternative. Indeed, if the main force of the Babylonian army does not destroy Jerusalem, a few Babylonian stragglers will, because it is Yahweh's will that Babylon will destroy the city (37:10). The prophet not only identifies the real enemy of the Davidic house. He also announces the outcome of the conflict. Utter destruction! The prophetic word exposes to the king his terrible jeopardy which he apparently had been able thus far to deny. The threat of Babylon is ostensibly geopolitical. It is, however, in fact a theological threat. Yahweh has willed the destruction of God's own people and city. Thus the Jerusalem establishment had not only misread Babylon. It had also misunderstood Yahweh's potential as an enemy.[35]

---

35. That misunderstanding is not simply a mistake of judgment. Rather, the miscalculation derives from ideology which distorted perceptions and categories of interpretation, so that the error is not ad hoc but systemic and programmatic.

37:11-15 The remaining verses of the chapter, with one exception, concern the personal situation of the prophet. The prophet's personal life is deeply enmeshed with the burden of his public words. Though the prophet has just asserted the forthcoming Babylonian destruction, he seizes a moment of respite from the Babylonian controversy to tend to personal business with the king. He returns home to exercise his legal right to the land (37:12; cf. ch. 32). Jeremiah is a public figure in the city. He is known and his words are known. He is known as the one who has forecast and advocated a Babylonian victory. He is apprehended by a guard as he leaves the city and is accused of deserting to the Babylonians. We are not told, but presumably the city was under tight curfew and none could leave. Predictably, a known imperial sympathizer would be detained. There was sufficient reason from his public message for Jeremiah to be suspect. Jeremiah nonetheless denies the accusation made against him (37:14).[36] He is not a deserter! The guard, predictably, will not "listen" *(shema')*. Jeremiah's public word from God has already been rejected (v. 2). Now his personal defense is also not heeded. His contemporaries will not *listen,* either to his public oracle or to his personal defense. He is arrested, arraigned, beaten, and imprisoned. His public message is costly. The royal establishment despises his message and therefore abuses the messenger. They find his words unbearable. The prophet is subject to police brutality! His word places him in deep conflict with the royal ideology which refuses to face its true situation of jeopardy. The "princes" are the ones who keep the charade of national security functioning. Public policy in Jerusalem has become the practice of a corporate lie.[37] Jeremiah protests, and therefore he must be harshly silenced.

36. The opposition to Jeremiah cannot understand how his words could be anything other than treason. They cannot entertain the thought that his words might indeed be true, i.e., that God wills an imperial triumph over Jerusalem. Ideology, when left uncriticized, renders discernment impossible beyond the close interests of its adherents.

37. Jeremiah's adversaries are indeed on a "March of Folly." Barbara W. Tuchman, *The March of Folly,* characterizes such a strategy of "folly" as a public policy which to any objective observer is self-destructive and which has internal critics who point out the inherent destructiveness of policy. In this case, it is Jeremiah (and no doubt others like Uriah) who point out the folly; the proponents of the policy proceed nonetheless on their self-destructive path. The systemic deception is not unlike that chronicled about Viet Nam by David Halberstam, *The Best and the Brightest* (New

37:16-21 These verses provide an odd conclusion to the chapter. By v. 15 one would have thought that Jeremiah had been effectively disposed of by the government. Certainly the princes thought they had silenced him, and we expect the king to follow the princes in this regard. Zedekiah, however, is haunted. He seems to suspect his own authority. He will not publicly challenge the princes, for they give the appearance of being the true "patriots." They are the ones who "wrap themselves in the flag." Zedekiah also will not, however, settle for their easy affirmation of royal propaganda. Perhaps the king knows better than his princes. In any case, the king questions (i.e., consults) with the prophet "secretly" (v. 17).

The scene of the king in secret with the prophet anticipates the drama in which Nicodemus questions Jesus "by night" (John 3:2). In both cases, the establishment figure comes desperately to the outsider. In both cases, the action of the public official is politically risky and therefore is done surreptitiously. The narrative shows dramatically how the king, as the center of power and authority, grudgingly and desperately reaches beyond official channels of intelligence, suspecting that there is more to be known than his associates tell him. Zedekiah's act toward Jeremiah is an acknowledgement not only of the failure of his official intelligence. It is also a recognition that his own royal power is finally penultimate. He is not master of his own policy. In some way matters are being decided and decreed out beyond his administration. It is as though the governance of affairs has been taken out of his hand. That of course is a main point the prophet has been scoring for a long time. There is another governance which is unfettered by royal policy. Thus the narrative quite indirectly confesses and affirms the rule of Yahweh, a rule which the king mutely acknowledges and which the prophet boldly enacts.

The king's question to the prophet is a desperate, pleading one, for it makes clear that the prophet is the senior partner in this conversation. The king is an empty-handed suppliant, hat (crown) in hand. The king now asks for an assurance from the prophet, though last time he had

---

York: Random House, 1972); and Neil Sheehan, *A Bright Shining Lie: John Paul Vann and America in Viet Nam* (New York: Random House, 1988). Note that, unlike the episode in ch. 36, here the princes are solidly opposed to Jeremiah. Perhaps this suggests that the crisis is more acute and so the resistance is solidified (if we seek a historical explanation), or perhaps the narrative simply needs a differently positioned opposition to the prophet (if we settle for a literary strategy).

received another oracle (vv. 7-10), a word which he did not like and which he could not accept. Now he seeks from the same source a second opinion, a better word.

Jeremiah must have delighted in the scene. He slows the pace of the interaction. He relishes the moment and makes the king wait. His first guarded response to the king is as though he toys with the king. It is respectful but terse, not at all forthcoming: "There is." Then Jeremiah speaks the word for which the king had come. It is, however, the same relentless word sounded so many times before: "You shall be delivered into the hand of the king of Babylon" (v. 17). Zedekiah surely had hoped for a different word. A different verdict, however, is not to be. The power of the king will be submitted to this other royal, imperial, hostile power. No explanation is given and no compromise offered. It is a settled conclusion.

That brief exchange about policy is followed by Jeremiah's personal petition to the king. The request of the prophet in fact constitutes a statement of his innocence. Cast in the form of two questions, the prophet voices two lines of defense. First, he is innocent (v. 18). He has not undermined the war effort. Second, he is right. He has not wronged the king, nor has he misled the king. The other prophets who refused to take Babylon seriously are surely the discredited ones (v. 19). Jeremiah is a truth-teller, and as such he does not deserve this brutalizing treatment.

On the basis of this self-defense, Jeremiah makes a petition (v. 20). He asks not to be returned to the prison, for if he is returned there he will die. These verses comment no more on the destiny of Jerusalem or Babylon. In the midst of such public issues, personal safety is nonetheless crucial for the prophet. The king makes no verbal response to the new oracle, even as he does not respond after vv. 7-10 or after v. 17. He receives the hard word of the prophet silently. He does, however, act to provide maintenance for Jeremiah, and he places him in a lesser, more humane confinement (v. 21). The narrative is laconic. There are hints, however, that Zedekiah has come to regard Jeremiah as a support and an ally. Presumably the king is able to recognize, albeit reluctantly, that the prophet is indeed a truth-teller. In the finished form of the book, there is a lean suggestion that the king has conceded the prophet's main point. This understated gesture on the part of the king serves as an affirmation of the prophet. It suggests that it is now recognized that the prophet is not a liar or a traitor. He is a truth-teller who seeks no special favor, but only fairness for and acknowledgement of his public role.

359

In the midst of an urgent public crisis, there is truth to be told. The overriding will of Yahweh cannot be circumvented, certainly not by abusing the messenger. While we are concerned with Jeremiah in this episode, the larger stakes concern the city of Jerusalem. The city is in an awesome jeopardy. The city is not autonomous. God's powerful word matters, and no posturing by king and princes can void that sovereign word. By the end of the chapter the word from the prophet is not heeded. Its bearer, however, receives a modest concession from the king, almost an act of solidarity. That act is very little, but it is no doubt as much as the king dared risk. It is not easy for a king to yield to "another governance." The counterplan of the prophet (and accepted by the king) affirms that, sooner or later, established royal power must yield to the governing word of Yahweh.

Jeremiah and Zedekiah (38:1-28)

It is a late, ominous time for Jerusalem and for its king, Zedekiah. Once more, this narrative concerns a confrontation between the king and the prophet. They are the two principal actors in the narrative, and they embody two contrasting perspectives. The king is fragile and desperate. His concern in this narrative is the development of a policy of survival for Jerusalem. His counterpart, the prophet, is by now *persona non grata* among the Jerusalem leaders, for he is not supportive of the dominant policies. While his position has important implications for the survival of the state, that is not his major preoccupation. His concern is the will and purpose of Yahweh as it impinges upon the public life of Judah. The conclusions he draws from his discernment of the will and purpose of Yahweh are not conducive to the survival of Jerusalem, as that survival is envisioned by Zedekiah.

We are very close to the end of the long rule of the Davidic line. No wonder there is tension, hostility, distrust, and panic among the leaders. While the text may reflect the historical realities of the late period of independent Judah, this chapter is primarily interested in the fate of the prophet who is the carrier of a word from God which counters both royal policy and public opinion. The text offers an intense, dramatic confrontation over policy options. As canonical literature, the text does not concern a concrete policy decision about 6th-cent. Jerusalem, but it concerns the odd, destabilizing effect of prophetic alternatives upon a consensus policy. The crisis in the narrative concerns the way in which the holy purpose of God works against the present, perceived well-being of Jerusalem.

The book of Jeremiah in its main parts has a decidedly "pro-Babylonian" slant. It argues repeatedly that Babylon will prevail. According to this view, the better part of wisdom is to acknowledge the dominance of Babylon, submit to it, and live with it (38:2-3, 17-18, 20-23). Moreover, this positive attitude toward Babylon is not simply prudence, though it is that. Submission to Babylon is proposed as a theological judgment: God has legitimated Babylon. Resistance to Babylon is not only poor politics, but also disobedience to Yahweh. This linkage of politics and faith leads to a remarkable and predictably unpopular judgment: *obedience to God* equals *surrender to Babylon*. The book of Jeremiah has made this massive political-theological connection. It is as though life comes through death, well-being comes through submission, security comes through enormous risk. Clearly the discerned will of God collides with the "war effort" of the government.

In addition to the king and the prophet who deal with each other in this account directly and with a mutuality of interest, the third role in this narrative is played by the princes, the body of influential opinion in Jerusalem which seems to control policy. They appear decisively at the beginning of the narrative wherein they vigorously oppose the prophet (vv. 1-6) and at the end of the narrative wherein they greatly intimidate the king (vv. 24-28). The princes advocate a policy of go-it-alone independence and resistance which sounds like a militant kind of patriotism. This position brings them into frontal conflict with the prophet, who believes that resistance to Babylon is suicide. The king seems largely sympathetic to the view of the prophet but lacks either the courage or the political clout to withstand the princes. In this narrative the prophet gives considerable attention to his own well-being and safety. He does not do so, however, in a way that compromises anything of his subversive political opinion. His personal safety is subordinated to the word that he must speak concerning the will of Yahweh and the legitimacy of Babylon. It is this determined convergence of the will of Yahweh and the legitimacy of Babylon, the intersection of theological vision and political reality, that brings him into conflict with the "patriotic" authorities.

38:1-6 In this first episode, Jeremiah preaches his characteristic word, that God is now the active enemy of the Jerusalem enterprise (vv. 2-3). That preaching invites into the narrative the powerful princes, who now appear as a third character in the drama (v. 1). They and not the king appear to be the shapers of policy. They embody the bureaucracy which is impervious outside its own ideology. The population of Jerusalem has only two policy options. It can surrender to Babylon, or it can resist. Surrender, so the prophet asserts, will permit life. Resistance will mean death. The promised death of the people of Jerusalem is by conventional plagues which come with an invading army, sword, famine, pestilence. The statement of the prophet imagines a scenario in which Babylon will lay siege to the city, and the sure consequences of such a siege will be famine and pestilence. That is, the deathliness to come is not like a bolt out of heaven, but is a predictable outcome of an extended siege by the army of the empire. Such a pragmatic reading of the anticipated siege is no doubt realistic. The intent of the verdict, however, is theological. It is because of God's resolve that the choices are "red or dead." Jeremiah's alternative to "dead" is to submit to the empire, that is, to accept the compromise of "red."

The response of the princes is as predictable as Jeremiah is unwavering (v. 4). Jeremiah is a traitor who deserves to die. He is undermining the war effort, and that cannot be tolerated. His is an effective act of sabotage of royal policy because it combines an intelligent political assessment of the chances for Jerusalem with a claim of theological insight. The government does not — indeed dares not — agree with him. It only wants him silenced. On any "realistic" reading of the situation, Jeremiah is an enemy of the government, preparing a counteroption against the "well-being" *(shalom)* of the city as defined by the government. The issue is joined between the government and this formidable dissent. Indeed, this entire chapter is about the problem of public dissent which claims to be the voice of God.

Only now, belatedly, the king appears in the narrative (v. 5). We might expect that the king would be completely allied with the princes against the prophet, but the narrative is more complex than that. Zedekiah does not resist the opposition of the princes who want to retaliate against Jeremiah, though he signals no agreement with them. He acts, not in resolve, but in weakness. He abdicates in the same way that Pilate is later to do (John 19:6). He (perhaps reluctantly) turns the troublesome dissident over to the more zealous authorities. With the king's tacit approval, Jeremiah is placed in a miry cistern, presumably to die through neglect (Jer. 38:6). This first episode features the king as the hapless, helpless man in the middle between "zealous patriots" and the dissenting prophet. The outcome of this episode, however, is that the prophet is eliminated from public discussion. The narrative thus far has accomplished the silencing of the prophet and the stifling of a critical prophetic word.

38:7-13 The carrier of God's counterword appears to have been defeated (cf. Gen. 39:19-23). Now, unexpectedly, a fourth character enters into the plot. Without any explanation, an Ethiopian in the royal entourage attends to Jeremiah (Jer. 38:7-8). We do not know why. The narrative introduces this fourth character abruptly and without comment. Is his appearance a fortuitous accident? Has Jeremiah a special friend among "the king's servants"? (The name of the man means simply "servant of the king.") Is Ebed-melech dispatched by other powerful interests in the court who favor Jeremiah's policy alternative, for we know that Jeremiah did indeed have powerful governmental friends who were hostile to royal policies?[38] Is the appearance of Ebed-melech an "act of God" to save the carrier of the word, and thereby to keep the word "in play"? We are told nothing and left to draw our own conclusion. The narrator seems to have no curiosity about the question. The narrative is not embarrassed by the sudden appearance of Ebed-melech. The entry of Ebed-melech into the narrative is crucial, for only he stands between Jeremiah and death. His entry foils the death sentence already decided upon by the princes and now being implemented. His appearance in the narrative puts us on notice that this narrative has working through it a purpose other than straight reportage, a purpose that is not subservient to political pressure or persuasion.

This unexpected servant and the king have a brief but decisive exchange (vv. 9-10). Ebed-melech makes a powerful plea on behalf of the beleaguered prophet which is at the same time criticism of the princes.

---

38. On his support among powerful insiders, see Jer. 26:17, 24; 36:19; cf. Dearman, 403-421. On the episode concerning Ebed-melech, see Seitz, "Canonical Shape," 16-27. Both Dearman and Seitz are concerned with the literary, canonical function of these references; it is difficult to determine what operates historically, but we consider the "historical realities" as they are proposed in the final form of the text. Thus the text gives Jeremiah the support of powerful insiders.

The king (who did not readily side with the princes in v. 5) is moved by the plea of his servant and authorizes the rescue of the prophet (v. 10). We are not told why the king responds so readily, but he clearly is not one of the bloodthirsty zealots of v. 4. In v. 5 the king does not resist the princes. Now he yields to Ebed-melech. Perhaps Zedekiah yields to whatever is the current pressure. Perhaps he is relieved at this intervention by Ebed-melech. Zedekiah plays no active role either in the condemnation of Jeremiah (v. 5) or the rescue (v. 10) of the prophet. In any case, the authorization of the king and the intention of the servant controvert the plan of the princes. We are told in enormous detail of the rescue of the prophet (vv. 11-13). It is clear that the rescue is of crucial importance to the narrator. The rescue of the prophet is no act of direct divine intrusion, but a determined, detailed human act. The rescue of the messenger is important; not even the will of the government can eliminate this threatening countervoice. Thus far we have seen the effort to silence the prophet, and we learn that effort could not succeed.[39] The action of Ebed-melech brings the prophet back into public discussion. The word works its unwelcome way in the face of determined opposition.

38:14-28   The two episodes of vv. 1-6 and vv. 7-13 are accounts, respectively, of imprisonment and release, of sentence and pardon, not unlike crucifixion and resurrection.[40] The carrier of the counterword was for a moment nullified (v. 6), but is inexorably restored (vv. 11-13). The two movements of the narrative are like preliminaries for the main meeting between prophet and king. Finally, now that the princes (vv. 1-6) and Ebed-melech (vv. 7-13) have contributed their parts, the narrative must come to this direct confrontation, for the decisive issue must be faced between king and prophet. It is a meeting fraught with both danger and caution. The stakes are very high. It is not, however, a meeting conducted in hostility. There is a genuine effort by both king and prophet to com-

---

39. In the narrative accounts concerning Jeremiah, there are repeated efforts to silence him. Here, as in chs. 26 and 36, these efforts do not succeed because of human intervention on his behalf. Jeremiah is not without important allies, and the word is not without attentive adherents, even in the deep crisis of the city.

40. Parallels to the career of Joseph in Gen. 39–41 are worth noting. There also the authorities who oppose Joseph are unable to resist his destiny. Those designated by God cannot be finally hemmed in by the authorities.

municate and even to accommodate. The stakes are now too high for acrimony. Nobody has anything to win in this conversation by abrasiveness. In the end the prophet and the king share in the struggle for a truth that will save the city.

This extended unit is an intense conversation. The text consists almost entirely of an exchange of speeches. In this section the princes hover behind the king but are not present; Ebed-melech is now completely absent. Now it is head-to-head between the two principals:

Speeches of the King	Speeches of the Prophet
v. 14 Inquiry	v. 15 Fearful reluctance
v. 16 Assurance given in secret	vv. 17-18 The regular prophetic options of submission or defeat
v. 19 Royal fearfulness	vv. 20-23 The regular prophetic options
vv. 24-26 Plea for duplicity	v. 27 Compliance to the king (indirect discourse)

The meeting is between the king, who needs to know what his governmental intelligence cannot tell him, and the prophet, who can provide what the king needs to know. The narrative is crafted to give the prophet the upper hand and to explicate the epistemological embarrassment of the king. The book of Jeremiah is insistent in its claim that the prophet carries the data the king needs, which the king cannot receive from any other source. The government finally must submit to the prophet. The text thus makes a daring epistemological claim. The crucial information is withheld from authorized channels. The government does not "know best."[41]

Jeremiah is not a coward, but he is realistic. He knows his verdict will displease the king (v. 15; cf. Dan. 4:19). If he displease the king, he will again be in a situation not unlike Jer. 38:4. Perhaps Jeremiah imagines

41. The same epistemological inversion takes place in the narratives of Joseph and Daniel, wherein the occupant of the throne must go outside his royal company to an uncredentialed Israelite to learn reality. In the same way, this king must go to the uncredentialed prophet to learn the truth. All these texts witness to the epistemological subversion that is present in the faith and in the text of Israel.

his situation as Thomas More imagined his situation. He thought that speaking would bring jeopardy and so he preferred silence, because silence ostensibly maintains safety. It is better not to speak if the word only enrages the government. The prophet is wisely restrained (v. 15).

The prophet is not excessively courageous. He takes care to protect himself and receives the king's assurance (vv. 15-16). The king makes a secret promise to the prophet (v. 16). The king cannot be caught in public protecting a "traitor." The king, however, desperately needs this man as an ally, and perhaps even respects him. We may wonder whether, in that chaotic moment, the king's promise of safety is to be trusted. Perhaps the prophet wondered as well.

The king's assurance, in any case, is enough for the prophet (vv. 17-18). The prophet delivers once again his terrible word for the king. Upon hearing his pronouncement, we may wonder in retrospect why the king bargained so hard to get the prophetic word, for it is the same harsh verdict already well known from Jeremiah (cf. vv. 2-3). Perhaps the king thought he would get a better, reassuring word this time. He does not, however, for the prophet is intransigent and the word is relentless. The king receives once more the same message from the prophet. There simply is no maneuverability in Judah's situation. There are two options: surrender and live, resist and die. The word of God promises a way of survival; it is not, however, the desired word, but only a grudging, compromised way of survival. If the present form of this narrative is from and for exiles, as seems plausible, then this reiterated word is an assurance to the ones deported to Babylon.[42] They have chosen the only way to live, which is the way of terrible submission. There is no chance of life except in reference and accommodation to the empire (cf. 29:5-7). There is no chance of life through self-assertion and triumphalism.

Oddly, Zedekiah does not flinch from or argue against this prophetic verdict (38:19). The king seems almost ready to submit to this word from God, a word he could not have welcomed. The situation of the king,

42. This word nicely conforms to the pastoral needs and political interests of the community of exiles in Babylon. Thus it makes most sense to assume that this is a word reflective of the faith of the exilic community, i.e., an exilic redaction of the tradition. A notice of such an interest, however, does not diminish the status of the claim as "canonical." This view of Israel's life and destiny may have arisen out of a vested interest, but it is accepted as normative in the final form of the text.

however, is complicated. Zedekiah does not fear the Babylonian army or government, as we might expect. Rather, he fears his own people. In this response, he fears the pro-Babylonian party. Perhaps they are hostile to him because he resisted too long in his refusal to submit to Babylon. Thus Zedekiah does not reject the word of Jeremiah, but recognizes that it is politically impossible for him to be public about it. In his response to the prophet, the king is enormously candid, now treating the prophet as his confidant and ally. The king is immobilized. He is politically incapable of doing what he knows theologically to be correct.

Jeremiah's response to the fear of the king is not terribly surprising, nor does it reflect any great pastoral sensitivity (v. 20-23). Indeed, the prophet sounds the same options yet one more time. The only safety for the king is in surrender (v. 20). The promise is that the king will be safe from his compatriots whom he fears if he heeds the prophet. The alternative to surrender is most severe. Jeremiah envisions that a refusal to surrender will cause a terrible defeat and punishment. In his vision, all the women of the royal entourage will be treated as women prisoners of war are characteristically treated. The exiled (and abused) women will engage in terrible lamentation. The king will be exiled, the royal family taken, the city burned. The only alternative is surrender. One way or the other, God has determined and decreed the end of the Jerusalem project. Jerusalem is over, either in death or in displacement. There is no third alternative. That is, there is no policy alternative that would be acceptable to the hawkish princes surrounding the king.

Again, upon hearing the devastating verdict of the prophet, the king does not argue or resist (vv. 24-26). The king is only aware that his personal situation is tricky and ominous, so he sets about to do "damage control." This time, unlike that in v. 19, he fears not the ones in Babylon but the princes at home, the ones we have encountered in vv. 1-6. The king pledges the prophet to secrecy. The king fears most his own advisers, not Babylon. It is as though the king is in fact persuaded by the prophet about the hard options. Perhaps his response is in order to buy time. In any case, Zedekiah urges the prophet to dissemble, to avoid the additional danger of internal conflict. Moreover, the prophet complies with the king's request (v. 27). It is as though, in this moment, the prophet is concerned for his own well-being. He is willing to compromise with and accommodate his message. Apparently he had yet another chance to sound his word to the princes; but he declines. The princes are vigilant against him, and he relies

367

on the protection of the king. It is as though these two exhausted, beleaguered figures now must make common cause against impossible odds and enormous hostility.

The last verse of the chapter suggests that the king and the prophet both kept their word to each other (v. 28). They are in collusion against the princes. The prophet is under arrest. The king has received a sure word from the prophet which he does not doubt. The king, however, does not share that word with his advisers or act on it. The princes have both the king and the prophet in hock; they seem to be the ones determining policy. The conversation between king and prophet seems to have no influence on policy. For an instant, the resistant princes have silenced the prophet and intimidated the king. For all the princes know or care, it is as though there had been no word from the LORD. The prophetic word can for a moment be eliminated from the narrative.

This chapter traces the three-way struggle for power. The princes for now prevail against both king and prophet. The prophet is rejected, and the king is intimidated. The chapter alternates between the prophet's hard word and the prophet's personal safety. The overarching drama of the chapter concerns the way in which dominant public policy is on a terrible collision course with God's holy purpose. The collision is under way and near at hand, but we do not know yet of the outcome. For the moment, we are made privy to a peculiar moment of human interaction between king and prophet. Both are at a desperate moment of need. In that moment, they make common cause. Their common work is an act of deception that does not change the larger story line of Jerusalem's ending. It does evidence, however, that even in the throes of such a public crisis, real human persons must act, in the presence of faith, fear, and complexity. Now the die is cast. For the moment, the princes have prevailed against king and prophet. We are still waiting, however, to see about the lean options the prophet has offered the king. The word does offer a way out. It is, however, a lean option, a very narrow gate for survival. In the world of prophetic reality, powerful leaders are offered an option of life, often an option that appears to be too costly politically. The prophetic word is uncompromising and unaccommodating of such political cost. A prophetic reading of reality finally makes no deals. It simply waits for reality to be faced.

The Fall of Jerusalem (39:1-18)

The prophet had long since made clear that Jerusalem had only two choices: surrender and live, or resist and die. Under the leadership of Zedekiah Judah exercised its choice, and made the wrong choice. It resisted Babylon. In 38:1-6 it is clear that this policy had the militant support of "the princes." In so doing, according to the prophet, the monarchy resisted Yahweh and therefore died. This chapter describes the "payoff" of that disastrous choice (39:1-10) and adds two personal episodes derived from the public disaster (vv. 11-14, 15-18).

39:1-10 Most recently in 38:18, Jeremiah had detailed to Zedekiah the deep costs of defiance of Babylon. Now all the threats have come to fruition. While the threats are cast theologically, they also voice political realism. The consequence of resistance to the invader is what an invading, occupying army characteristically does. In this account, there is no mention of the prophet nor of the God to whom Jeremiah bears witness. The devastation of the city is presented simply as the working out of imperial strategy. The narrative is offered simply as reportage and closely parallels the accounts in 2 Kgs. 25:1-12; Jer. 52:4-16.

The taking of the city of Jerusalem was the result of a long siege, perhaps as much as eighteen months (39:1-2). The city could not in the end withstand the resolve of the empire. Finally the commanders of the Babylonian armies occupied the city (v. 3).

Zedekiah fled but was readily captured by the Babylonians (vv. 4-7). Jeremiah had long counselled the king to surrender. In 38:24-26 Zedekiah gives the impression of understanding and accepting the word of the prophet. Now, however, in the midst of crisis, the king is without courage, resolve, or resource. He neither resists nor surrenders, but jumps ship in an ignominious way. He abdicates his royal office and his royal responsibility, leaving his people in the lurch. Read more generously, he intends a "government in hiding." Zedekiah does not, however, get very far in his escape. We may imagine that with such an extended siege the land is saturated, not only with Babylonians but with intimidated informers. The fleeing king is apprehended. As an important prisoner, he is taken to the headquarters of Nebuchadnezzar in the north at Hamath. Nebuchadnezzar is actively present with his armies, no doubt directing the campaign. He is not, however, as far south as Jerusalem, and therefore the prized royal prisoner must be transported north to the field head-quarters of Nebuchadnezzar.

Nebuchadnezzar metes out a horrible punishment to this king, who was for so long troublesome to the empire. Zedekiah is forced to watch while his sons are executed, and then he has his eyes put out. The brutal death of his sons is the last thing he sees, the last thing he will ever see, the thing he will see as long as he lives. And then, in his blindness, he is deported. His defiance ends him in Babylon, in any case. It is as though there never was an option for the king except Babylon. Either he would go willingly (as the prophet urged) or violently (as finally happened). Zedekiah is now the second king of Judah in exile in Babylon.[43] One was taken into exile willingly, the other defiantly. The first was treated humanely (cf. 2 Kgs. 25:22-30), the second brutally. Babylon is the place where Judean kings congregate and die. Apparently how they go, willingly or not, influences their treatment in exile.

Having put a decisive end to the royal threat, the Babylonians now seize and raze parts of the city (Jer. 39:8-10). Eight hundred thirty-two persons were deported (52:29). The deportation was not wholesale. The theological claims we are given assert that "significant Judah" was totally in exile. The important elements of society were deported. It is that view of Judah's history which the Bible wants us to accept, being a document produced by the community of exiles. Thus the judgment is not without a self-serving aspect. In fact, life did go on in devastated Jerusalem. Perhaps it was only "some of the poor" who remained, but there were people there. Life, commerce, and religion did resume. This ongoing life, however, figures only slightly in the emergence of exilic and postexilic Judaism. It was the community of Jews in Babylon who had the decisive voice in defining a Jewish future. That continuing Jerusalem operation, however, will in time occupy us in the book of Jeremiah.

Christopher R. Seitz has made a compelling case that the target of the Babylonian invasion was not the city, nor the temple, nor the general populace, but only the Davidic house embodied by Zedekiah.[44] Thus no mention is made of an assault on the temple by the invaders. The Babylonian authorities establish themselves "in the gate" (39:3), presumably to establish and maintain a semblance of civil order; moreover, that some are

43. See 2 Kgs. 24:12 on Jehoiachin in Babylon.
44. Seitz, *Theology in Conflict*, 264-69.

left in the land and given vineyards and fields (v. 10) indicates that the Babylonians were concerned to sustain the economic structure of the community.[45] Seitz has observed the important contrast between the consolidating policies expressed in vv. 3, 10, and the violence toward the king which sustains the view that the target is the monarchy. It was not the city nor the general populace, but the royal clique that made imperial rule endlessly problematic and unsettled. When that body of opinion was crushed and its functionaries eliminated, Babylon had reason to believe Judah could be adequately governed.

Perhaps most noticeable in the report of destruction is the restrained understatement. The narrative offers no interpretive comment about the debacle. No didactic point is scored. No moral explanation is offered. No theological connection is proposed, not even a reference to the prophet Jeremiah. It is as though the narrative wants us to attend only to the dread and brutality present in the scene. There will be ample time later to reflect on what has happened and why. There will be opportunity to notice that what happened is exactly what the prophet had envisioned. This is indeed "plucking up and tearing down." All such commentary, however, is held in abeyance. It is enough for now to take in that the holy city has become the humiliated, devastated, abandoned city. Without any direct reference, the narrative witnesses that Jeremiah's "word" has been enacted as deed.

39:11-14   The narrative moves promptly to Jeremiah, our continuing topic of interest. The destiny of the prophet is closely tied to that of the city, but Jeremiah's future is not identical with the fate of the city. Jeremiah remained where Zedekiah had left him, in "the court of the guard" (38:28). That is where he is now found by the Babylonians (39:14). No doubt there is some irony in the fate of Zedekiah and the destiny of Jeremiah, the two treatments now reported back-to-back. The defeated Zedekiah is brutalized. Jeremiah is found by the Babylonians in a royal prison, an enemy of the king. An enemy of the king, however, figures to be a friend of Nebuchadnezzar.

Before Jeremiah is found in the prison, however, a decree of Nebuchadnezzar is promulgated (vv. 11-12). It is as though Nebuchadnezzar,

45. See Seitz, *Theology in Conflict,* 270, n. 180, and his citation of J. N. Graham, "'Vinedressers and Plowmen': 2 Kings 25:12 and Jeremiah 52:16," *Biblical Archaeologist* 47 (1984): 55-58.

already before Jeremiah is found in the ruins of the city, knows the name of the prophet and shows that he is recognized as a friend of the empire. It is not unreasonable that the news of a favorable voice in Jerusalem should be known through channels of imperial intelligence. And if not that, the book of Jeremiah wants us to perceive its central character in this way. Jeremiah is singled out by the Babylonians from the general deportation. He is to be well treated. The narrative makes nothing of the irony of Jeremiah's position. He had been accused of being a traitor, of "being soft" on Babylon. Now his preferential treatment by Babylon would seem to vindicate the charge made by fellow citizens of Jerusalem. The narrative passes over the problem in silence. Moreover, the prophet is to have the decisive voice in determining his own future. Jeremiah's person now acts out the positive option Jeremiah had announced for the community. He has urged "submit and live." As one who has *submitted,* he is permitted to *live.* His personal destiny is presented as what might have been available for Zedekiah and for all his cohorts, had they not believed their own war propaganda — their silly, false notion of "well-being" *(shalom).*

Jeremiah is permitted to choose his own future. In a time of chaos and turmoil, his life has become a zone of free choice. His chosen future is marked in two ways. First, he aligns himself with Gedaliah, scion of an influential family, long an important support for the prophet.[46] Gedaliah embodies what was left of "independent Judah." Gedaliah and Jeremiah embody together a middle way for Jews, between the self-destructive shrillness of "the princes" and the easy resignation of the deserters and accommodators. More than that, Jeremiah himself lives out his message. He had proclaimed "submit and live." He had entrusted his future to Babylon, as Nebuchadnezzar here knows. And now he lives, with a decisive say about his future.

The last phrase of v. 14 is telling: "He dwelt among the people." Of course, Jeremiah is not a deserter or one who betrays. He is the one who cared most about his people and who risked the most for them. In the end, there is perhaps an ironic reversal of positions. The king who seemed to care about the survival of his people is now removed from his people

46. Gedaliah is the heir of the family of Shaphan and Ahikam. Cf. Dearman, 410-11. This family is closely allied with Jeremiah and with the views he advocates. Thus Babylon would have been glad to have such a cooperative advocate occupy the new position as governor.

and incapable of helping them. Jeremiah, who seemed a defeatist, is the one who now lives in solidarity with the people and who survives in the city. Without any obvious didactic message, the narrative bears witness to the truth, validity, and effectiveness of Jeremiah's message. Jeremiah is indeed the prophet whose word has come to pass (cf. Deut. 18:22). The apparently strong one is nullified, the apparently weak one in this crisis persists and prevails.

39:15-18   These verses appear abruptly and refer back to Jer. 38:7-13. Jeremiah is still in "the court of the guard" (38:28), even though Gedaliah should "take him home" (39:14). In the midst of the destruction, Jeremiah remembers Ebed-melech, who had abruptly and without explanation rescued him. This last episode is such an utter contrast to vv. 1-10. We had been watching the large, public drama of the empire against the state. Now we have an oracle addressed to one, solitary individual who has no standing and about whom we know practically nothing.

The oracle is in two parts. On the one hand, God is relentless in the resolve against Jerusalem (v. 16). God's action will be for evil and not for good. There is no vacillation or reprieve given by the prophet concerning the city. On the other hand, Ebed-melech is singled out for exceptional treatment. He will be delivered *(n-ts-l)*. "I will save you" *(mlt)*. The oracle uses two powerful verbs for God's rescuing action. God promises to do for Ebed-melech exactly what God would not do for Zedekiah or for Judah. Ebed-melech is singled out, an exception is made. The reason for the exception is that Ebed-melech trusted in Yahweh *(batah)*. Long ago, Jeremiah had warned Jerusalem not to "trust" in the claims of the temple (7:4). Jerusalem, however, had misplaced its trust and so was destroyed. Ebed-melech's trust, however, entailed not simply a good attitude, but a quite concrete act. He intervened for Jeremiah; he saved the prophet. He made the presence of the prophet viable. Thus it is his daring service on behalf of the prophet that is his act of trust. He not only trusted God, but trusted God's concrete way in the world.

Jeremiah 39 as a whole makes a complete contrast between Zedekiah, on the one hand, and Jeremiah and Ebed-melech, on the other hand. In the shaping of the chapter, 39:1-10 contains a general report that is unexceptional and known elsewhere. The tradition of Jeremiah has nothing to contribute to that. That report, however, is previously a foil for vv. 11-14, 15-18, which is peculiar to the tradition of Jeremiah and which narrates a certain history which is wrought through fidelity to the prophetic word. Thus vv. 1-10 is history in disobedience to the word and vv. 11-18 is history in obedience to the word. The destruction of Jerusalem is sweeping and comprehensive (vv. 1-10). A critical exception is nonetheless made. Ebed-melech constitutes an important remnant.[47] The destruction wrought by God through Nebuchadnezzar is not morally indifferent or undifferentiated. Even in such a moment of institutional failure, faithful acts of courage matter and are salvific. The chapter ends in a great affirmation of trust, trust which serves and substantiates the person, tradition, and book of Jeremiah.

The saved ones are the ones who adhere to a Jeremianic discernment of reality. Those who are allied with this faith have their life as "warbooty."[48] All the others become "war booty" for the Babylonians. Trust as evidenced by Ebed-melech is a limit and alternative to Babylonian power and devastation. The contrast is sharp even if left without comment: the resisters in the monarchy come to a sorry end. The alternative for a good end comes to Jeremiah, who is uncompromising in his vision of reality, and to Ebed-melech, who allies himself with the prophet and the prophet's word. The chapter as it stands is a belated invitation that others could separate themselves from a deathly royal vision of history and embrace a counterhistory which leads to life.

Jeremiah's Release (40:1-6)

In ch. 39 the event toward which the book of Jeremiah persistently pointed has happened (39:1-10). The "end" anticipated by the prophet has happened and is narrated in detail. The prophet is thereby vindicated. God will not be mocked. For mocking God, Jerusalem is destroyed.

Life, however, goes on. The deportation did not empty the land.

47. Seitz, "Canonical Shape," 16-27, suggests that Ebed-melech and Baruch constitute a remnant not unlike Caleb and Joshua in the book of Joshua; indeed, they may be intentionally patterned after those figures. As such they provide for the community in the harsh transition to exile, as did Joshua and Caleb through the wilderness.

48. The phrasing was used generally in 38:2 and now is applied specifically. The language is war rhetoric, but the image has now been completely transformed as a way of speaking of a surprising rescue from the general destruction of war.

People still lived there, and because people still lived there, there was need for order and governance. A different governance was required which, unlike the monarchy which was endlessly troublesome to the empire, would be loyal, trustworthy, and committed to Babylon. Babylon now had the "right" and power to have its own kind of government in Judea.

40:1-6 First, however, there is one more telling of the special treatment accorded Jeremiah by the empire, a treatment already told in 39:11-14.[49] His treatment contrasts completely with the fate of Jerusalem. This narrative, as elsewhere, moves back and forth between public events and quite personal matters. Even in the upheaval of 587 B.C.E., the life and destiny of individual persons is not nullified or disregarded.

The narrator reiterates once more in simple, direct fashion the theological significance of the destruction of the city (40:1-3). The narrative even places the theological warrant and explanation in the mouth of a Babylonian military officer, perhaps not unlike the Marcan strategy of placing a final confession of Christ in the mouth of a Roman soldier (Mark 15:39). The Babylonian officer articulates standard prophetic Deuteronomic theology:

> Because you did not obey *(shema')*
> [Therefore] this thing has come upon you. (Jer. 40:3)

The reasons for the devastation are thoroughly covenantal, and in this moment are clear even to the Babylonian. The Babylonian captain of the guard sounds strangely like the prophet.[50]

The narrator, however, is interested in the personal destiny of

49. The two versions of the capture and release of Jeremiah in 39:11-14; 40:1-6 differ somewhat in detail. Both accounts conclude with Jeremiah's entrustment to Gedaliah, i.e., with those who now come to power and who share his ideological orientation. Thus Jeremiah is in the care of the same family who has long been his advocate. Before that conclusion, however, 40:1-6 shows Jeremiah subjected to the more threatening experience and fate of the exiles.

50. The indictment of v. 3 addressed to Jeremiah is odd indeed. Carroll, 699-700, has rightly seen that these verses intermingle a narrative about deportation and an oracle from Jeremiah. In the conflation of the two, however, the oracle of the prophet is placed in a Babylonian mouth and is addressed to the prophet, rather than coming from him.

Jeremiah (vv. 4-6). The contrast of general and personal concern is expressed in v. 4 by "now, behold" *(we'attah)*. The conquerors are attentively deferential to him, as Nebuchadnezzar has commanded (39:12). Jeremiah is released and given the options of going to Babylon or remaining in the land. The important point is that Jeremiah is free and can choose his own future. In this special treatment, there is no doubt high irony. On the one hand, Jeremiah is entirely vindicated. On the other hand, to be well treated by the occupying army can hardly be a popular outcome. It is the treatment given to someone who has become a traitor. Thus Jeremiah, in the very moment of his vindication, is marked as a traitor by the "hawks" among his own people (cf. 26:11; 38:4). Jeremiah 40:5 suggests not only that Jeremiah is given freedom of choice, but also a government allowance.[51]

Jeremiah exercises his choice and identifies himself with the provisional government of Gedaliah, which Babylon had authorized and installed. In making this choice, Jeremiah is consistent with his own past urgings. He does not flee,· and he does not resist Babylon. He occupies a middle position which is politically prudent and, in his reasoning and in the reasoning of the book of Jeremiah, theologically faithful. Persistently, the interpretation given these events by the tradition of Jeremiah is counter to the popular view that all pro-Babylonian postures are in fact treasonable. The Jeremiah tradition never finishes sorting out the vexed challenge that faithfulness to God seems to some to be treason to royal Jerusalem. Jeremiah's choice about the future must have given powerful, much needed legitimacy to the regime of Gedaliah.

Gedaliah's Governorship (40:7–41:18)

This distinct narrative unit is a straightforward account of the brief and tragic history of Gedaliah's governorship. Most scholars take the main outlines of the account as historically reliable, though there clearly is redactional activity. It is most striking that in this narrative about the quick "rise and fall" of

---

51. On food guarantees from the king, see 2 Sam. 9:7; 2 Kgs. 25:27-30. In both parallel cases, the guarantee is more than a little threatening and ominous. On material provision given in the moment of release, see Deut. 15:1-11; and David Daube, *The Exodus Pattern in the Bible* (London: Faber & Faber, 1963), 55-61 and *passim*.

Gedaliah, Jeremiah is completely absent. Nothing is said in the narrative that leads to any direct theological interpretation. The narrative traces the sorry events after the occupation by Babylon. One may conclude that the violence and disorder reported here are the residue of a community that long has imagined itself to be autonomous and free to do what it wants.

40:7-12   These verses narrate the solidification of the provisional government of Gedaliah.[52] It is clear that Gedaliah comes from one of the powerful and respected families of Jerusalem politics. His grandfather Shaphan and his father Ahikam have been highly visible before him, and have taken positions that seem sympathetic to the voice of Jeremiah.[53] The posture of his family seems regularly to be a sane, moderate position that is rooted in covenantal tradition and that is not attracted to the more urgent ideologies of its contemporaries. That is, his family is not tempted with the "extremity" of those who would foolishly resist the power of the empire, that is, the ones who in the end evoked the destructive occupation of Babylon. Gedaliah appears to be sober enough to be trusted by Babylon, stable enough to be trusted by his own people.

The political position of Gedaliah is delicate and mediating. He and his compatriots are forced by circumstance to recognize and come to terms with the power of Babylon. The government of Jerusalem has been defeated and has no bargaining maneuverability. In such a circumstance, it is possible on the one hand to continue to be a firebrand of resistance, but such persons are never permitted power by the conquering command. Zealots in such a situation quickly become irrelevant. On the other hand, it is possible to become a "Quisling," who excessively accommodates foreign power for the sake of personal advantage and who, in the process, betrays the identity of his people and earns their scorn. A mediating possibility is difficult but crucial. It is a position of leadership that cooperates with the occupiers, but which is vigilant for the well-being and independence of his people.

52. See Miller and Hayes, 421-430.
53. Apparently Gedaliah occupied something of a middle position politically that made it possible for him to govern. He is both trusted by the Babylonians and capable internally of governing. His sorry fate, however, suggests that he could not win over or cope with his "right wing," which anticipated independence from the empire.

It is plausible to assume that Gedaliah occupied, or sought to occupy, this middle ground. He belonged to a family which had not been empire-baiters. We may imagine, moreover, that he was not excessively an accommodationist, but was respected and trusted by the main body of opinion among his people. Of course, much depends on perception. No doubt he was perceived by some, no matter what he did, as a despicable compromiser. Perhaps in the end his is a "no-win position," sooner or later sure to evoke either the hostile, angry sentiments of independence or the harsh, heavy hand of the empire.

These verses portray the initial consolidation of Gedaliah's authority. There is no doubt that he is a creature of the empire (40:7). In any case, because of his claim to power his contemporaries, especially the military officers, must deal with him, no matter what their sentiment, ambition, or bias may be. Verse 8 tells of the rallying of a number of significant political forces in Judah to Gedaliah. Of these, the first named, Ishmael and Johanan, will be prominent in the narrative to follow.

Gedaliah receives the leading military figures and enunciates his policy (vv. 9-10). This constituency, as will soon be evident, is crucial to his regime, for this can make him or break him. Gedaliah anticipates and assures that the hegemony of Babylon will not be heavy-handed or unbearable. Of course this is no new conviction on his part. It is a long-held assessment held by those who clustered about Jeremiah. Gedaliah begins his statement with an assurance (v. 9). He promises that submission to Babylon will cause well-being. He issues a nicely balanced statement about "as for me" and "as for you" (v. 10). He nicely differentiates functions and responsibilities, "mine" and "yours." Concerning his own position, Gedaliah asserts not that he will represent Babylon to the Jews, but that he will represent the Jews to Babylon. He will be an advocate for his people. He is not Nebuchadnezzar's man, but he is a man for his people and with his people. The statement evidences strength and resolve to be a faithful and independent agent over against the empire which has authorized him. This enunciation hints at the suspicion with which his office must have been greeted.

The acceptance of this risky role as Judea's advocate, however, also requires something of his restless cohorts: "as for you." They are to work and to be productive in order to make the economy work and generate prosperity. It is as though Gedaliah bargains with the military functionaries who can be either his allies or his adversaries. He nicely distinguishes between political and economic functions. He claims the former for himself and will not compromise; he summons his fellows to economic responsibility. His forceful assertion on the one hand warns his listeners away from any political meddling or interference, and on the other hand it reminds them that they have important work to do. Gedaliah's statement is an assertion of policy that neither asks nor receives assent. Gedaliah's main work is the revival of the economy, and for this he needs a committed, productive work force.[54]

Verses 11-12 report on a generally positive response to the governance of Gedaliah. Apparently many people from Jerusalem had evacuated to avoid the coming Babylonian upheaval and were waiting to see what would happen. For them, the designation of Gedaliah by Nebuchadnezzar evokes a positive response, confidence, and willing allegiance. That so many returned meant that they accepted his authority. Moreover, they went to work (v. 12), as he had hoped (v. 10). Two central issues occupied Gedaliah. On the one hand, he had to secure his own authority and public support. That is, he had to demonstrate that he was serious, could be authoritative, and was not an imperial stooge. On the other hand, his political claim signified nothing if the economy did not recover. Gedaliah's approach to legitimacy is moderate and realistic. His intent is to practice good faith in a context where political independence is not a realistic possibility. Jeremiah had anticipated that the people of God must live on terms other than their own. Gedaliah provides the procedures and structures for this possibility. His moderate government was the best option available, though the arrangement must have been disconcerting, even galling, to those who had treasured memories of better days and who entertained ambitious visions not schooled in present reality.

Gedaliah's modest, moderate regime seems to give concrete political embodiment to Jeremiah's expectations. Jeremiah has eschewed both independence and excessive subordination to Babylon. Gedaliah seems to have struck exactly the right balance. Thus his intentions may be understood as prudential and pragmatic. They also conform to Jeremiah's vision

---

54. The enumeration of wine, summer fruit, and oil indicates attention to "money crops." That is, revival of the economy depends upon production of goods that are useful as export. Attention to such money crops speaks against a self-support peasant economy. This suggests that the economic policies of Gedaliah may have been controversial, thought by some to be too beholden to imperial needs and expectations.

and so reflect an indirect vindication of the prophet. It is telling that, after the Babylonians appoint Gedaliah, he is indeed left on his own without imperial interference. The Jews are given a chance on their own to "make it work."

40:13-16 Gedaliah's government was not only provisional; it was also exceedingly tenuous and, as it turned out, short-lived. It had the backing of the Babylonians (v. 7); it also had the visible support of Jeremiah, who now aligned himself with this government that was a creature of the occupying army (v. 6). The government turned out to be untenable, and the backing of Babylon and Jeremiah must have been distinct liabilities in terms of public support in Jerusalem.

The enduring political questions in Judah now surfaced once again, with enormous passion. The recurring options in Jerusalem were either fierce independence or accommodationist submission.[55] The troubles which now surfaced for Gedaliah may have been in part personal, as his personal advancement through imperial support no doubt blocked the careers and ambitions of others. But the troubles are not primarily personal. They are no doubt deeply felt ideological, partisan disagreements. Gedaliah embodies accommodationist policy, as Jeremiah had earlier championed the same policies. While that policy may have appeared prudent and pragmatic to cool heads, to others it no doubt smelled of betrayal, much as General Philippe Petain was regarded in France. From such a perspective, the theological endorsement of Jeremiah would count for little. Interpretation of this text must pay close attention to the political nuances that are beneath the surface of the narrative. The narrative makes clear that biblical faith, including Jeremiah's advocacy, must be understood and practiced in the midst of real and difficult political realities. There was no supernaturalist or transcendentalist perspective which proved that accommodation was the will of God. The concrete specification of God's will is a judgment call made in a situation of political emergency. It is always in such an emergency that a decision must be made about the will of God. Thus it does not surprise us that such a call does not command universal and immediate assent in the community.

55. A third troublesome and always available option was alliance with Egypt. That option, however, is not visible in this particular narrative.

Gedaliah receives an intelligence report from his loyal colleague, Johanan (vv. 13-14). The report is that an assassination plot has been instigated against Gedaliah. It is not news to Gedaliah that he has powerful adversaries. No doubt he already knows their names. The Ammonites must have resisted a "Babylonian satellite" as close as Jerusalem, for this is what Gedaliah represents in international politics. That is, what might be workable for Jerusalem may constitute a threat for its neighbors. That Babylon can plant its governor in Jerusalem constitutes an implied threat to Ammonite independence. Ishmael no doubt was also a known adversary to Gedaliah. Perhaps he is only an opportunist. Because he is identified as "of the royal family" (41:1), however, he surely is not only an opportunist, but the embodiment of an alternative political opinion and likely the leader of a rival party. We are not surprised that a member of the deposed royal family would vigorously dissent from accommodationist policy. Both adversaries, Baalis and Ishmael, are known and no doubt were under steady surveillance.

What is new in the report of Johanan is that the specific plot and plan are now uncovered. Johanan, like many intelligence agents, is prepared to take a preemptive strike against the instigators of the plot.[56] Gedaliah, however, demurs.

We do not know why Gedaliah resists Johanan's eagerness to act. The use of the word "false" (40:16), a characteristic word in Jeremiah, suggests that Gedaliah does not believe the report. Perhaps there were too many such rumors of threat, and the governor could not spend his energy responding to such ostensible threats. Or perhaps at a moment of acute and delicate transition, Gedaliah stands for unity and consensus and so does not want to acknowledge division or vulnerability. We may believe that Gedaliah's rejection of the report and refusal to act on it were not romantic. His was more likely a calculated political judgment, one that had enormous implications for the future. Of such judgments, made at great risk, is the story of Israel's public faith constituted.[57]

---

56. See the close parallel in 2 Sam. 3:22-27. As in the case with Joab, here also political assassination is not a disinterested act.

57. The courage of Gedaliah and the political decision to disregard the known threat is not unlike the decision of John F. Kennedy to go to Dallas, where he was murdered. He made the decision on political grounds, with full knowledge of the danger.

41:1-3   The discussion of Johanan's report (40:13-16) is preliminary to the main action in the crisis. Gedaliah is warned, but boldly adopts a very different strategy. He conducts himself as though he were above such a threat. Ishmael is a member of the deposed royal family and apparently a leader of some significance, and so cannot be excluded from visible attention. Perhaps Ishmael has dynastic intentions; such ambition required political independence for his people and had no patience with the accommodationist governor. Ishmael is in any case a political force with which Gedaliah must reckon. At Mizpah, Gedaliah's locus of government, there is a high-level meeting. Gedaliah is engaged in consolidating his power, seeking allies, and building a consensus which is necessary to his government. It is not improbable that hard bargaining between rival factions was anticipated, but the public meal indicates that there was a prospect either that Ishmael would join in support of the government or at least acknowledge its legitimacy.

Gedaliah, however, completely misread his situation and underestimated the opposition of Ishmael. Both in rejecting the intelligence report of Johanan and in conducting a public parley with Ishmael, Gedaliah misread the danger to himself from Ishmael. The narrative portrays Ishmael in the most ruthless and despicable terms possible. He violated the hospitality of Gedaliah. He exploited a friendly public gesture from the governor and, in complete dishonor, committed an act of outrage. Jeremiah 41:3 is at pains to celebrate Gedaliah both for his long, honorable pedigree and for his legitimacy from Babylon. He is a noble man who stands in contrast to Ishmael, who is presented as nothing more than thug, albeit a royal thug. Gedaliah had made a beginning in new governance, but he had no chance. There was still active (though unrealistic) public opinion that believed Babylonian power could be thwarted.[58] The same unrealistic judgment which earlier had so troubled Jeremiah now destroyed a responsible accommodationist effort at governance. Thus Gedaliah's brief effort at governance ends in a bloodbath.

41:4-10   Ishmael, however, is not yet finished with his violence. He is an eager, ruthless man and is increasingly a desperate one. Pilgrims from

---

58. In a quite different context and different form, the unrealistic ambition of Ishmael continues the perspective of Hananiah (Jer. 27–28). In both cases, the more hopeful option may be rooted in sound, dynastic faith, but it fails to reckon with the political reality of the empire.

the great northern cities and shrines came to Jerusalem, dressed in mourning clothes.[59] They did not know of the bloodbath committed the day before; they knew only of the destruction of the city. Their visit reflects the continuing power and attraction of Jerusalem, even for northerners who had been cut off from Jerusalem for more than a century. They came with good intentions and in innocence. They knew nothing of Jews killing Jews; they knew only of Babylonian violence against Jerusalem, and they had come to grieve the wound to the city. Their public gesture is an act of bold solidarity with the suffering city. That gesture, however, is ruthlessly mocked, exploited, and dismissed by Ishmael.

The good intentions of the northern pilgrims contrast sharply with Ishmael's violence. He has no reason to fear these visitors, no cause to despise them or injure them. Perhaps they took him by surprise. Perhaps they disrupted his plans or inconvenienced him. Perhaps they were potential informers against him. In any case, their innocent, good intentions contrast with his vile, negative intention. Ishmael deceives them by word as he invites them to meet Gedaliah, whom he has already killed. He deceives them by deed, for he presents himself sharing the grief which they grieve. His deception is only a device to seduce them into the city. Then he kills them. Ishmael's action is almost inexplicable. We are never told what Ishmael is after, but he seemingly will stop at nothing to secure what he wants. Perhaps the narrative offers this report to exemplify the deep disorder present in a society that will not listen.[60]

Ishmael pauses momentarily to receive a bribe from ten of the visitors (41:8). For the sake of their "wheat, barley, oil, and honey," he spares them. He is indeed an unprincipled man. But that pause is only momentary. The narrative is preoccupied with the man's actions, which are deathly. He made dastardly use of a large cistern, one known to the readers of this

59. This episode may be taken as evidence that the operation of the cult in Jerusalem did not terminate in 587. See Enno Janssen, *Juda in der Exilszeit.* Forschungen zur Religion und Literatur des Alten und Neuen Testaments 69 (Göttingen: Vandenhoeck & Ruprecht, 1956), 46-56 and *passim.*

60. If, as Seitz proposes, the real trouble for Babylon is not the city or its people but the Davidic dynasty, then Ishmael may be an extreme case of the enduring, self-destructive power of the royal ideology which has already provoked the empire and brought destruction upon the city. If that is correct, clearly Ishmael is impervious and will risk yet another imperial intrusion into Jerusalem for the sake of his ideology and his ambition.

text. And he filled it! He filled it with corpses. He filled it with the innocent dead. In their death, Ishmael has killed off whatever chance there may have been for some measure of Jewish autonomy from the power of Babylon. For good reason, Ishmael flees. He goes toward his patrons, the Ammonites. There he will be safe. He takes with him a remnant, no doubt as hostages. Ishmael's moment in the narrative is brief and ugly. He completes the devastation wrought by Nebuchadnezzar. It is as though he wants to save Jerusalem from Babylon and will decimate (or destroy) the city in order to save it. His intervention which destroys Jerusalem is the last gasping measure of the old dynastic ideology which Jeremiah had for so long refuted.

41:11-18 Ishmael fled, and Johanan pursued after him. Ishmael's motives are never probed, and we do not learn either what he wanted or what he accomplished. The pursuers catch up with the pursued at the great pool of Gibeon.[61] But they do not apprehend him. Ishmael escapes to the Ammonites. In the perspective of the narrator, Ishmael is thoroughly discredited both by his violence and by his appeal to the Ammonites.

Johanan, with the death of Gedaliah, has now emerged as a leader to counter Ishmael. Johanan is warmly welcomed by the hostages of Ishmael who had been taken against their will. Johanan is perceived as their savior and rescuer (v. 13). He does not eliminate Ishmael, but he does end his moment of terror. The land, however, is in shambles. The political situation is one of chaos. While abruptly stated, it does not surprise us greatly that Johanan proposes to go to Egypt, as far away from Babylon as is possible (v. 17). The Jews expect that Babylon will fiercely retaliate because their appointee, Gedaliah, has been murdered. The Jews then seek safety in the only place they can think of, Egypt.

The narrative proceeds in great detail. What is most to be noticed is that there is no stable political order. Public life is in total disarray. None of the available options is very attractive. Johanan opts for the extreme alternative to Babylon, namely, Egypt. Notice that this chapter is presented as reportage. There is no reference to the prophet or to the God of the prophet. The action of the chapter is an interplay of principle and prudence. It is time for the prophet to intervene yet one more time, reminding

61. The parallel should not be pressed too far, but cf. 2 Sam. 2:13 and another political crisis at the pool of Gibeon.

us that the public life of Judah cannot be reduced to mere political calculation.

Jeremiah had long since made clear the only workable option for his people. The three dominant figures of this narrative, Gedaliah, Ishmael, and Johanan, embody these policy options: Gedaliah is a Babylonian accommodator, Ishmael is a fierce actor for resistance and independence, and Johanan now opts for Egypt. While flight to Egypt appears to be the most plausible remaining option, Jeremiah, as we shall see, is unwavering in his pro-Babylonian insistence.

Judah Refuses to Listen (42:1–43:7)

The extended narrative which begins in ch. 37 revolves around three themes: (1) the public adjustment of Judah to the new situation after 587 B.C.E., (2) the intrusion of the word of God into public issues through the speech of Jeremiah, and (3) the personal fortunes of Jeremiah. Jeremiah as an identifiable voice in the narrative was most active in chs. 37 and 38, boldly speaking a pro-Babylonian option to the king and the princes. In chs. 39–41, however, Jeremiah is only marginally visible in the text. In 39:11-14; 40:4-6 Jeremiah is treated carefully and respectfully by the Babylonians and casts his lot with the government of Gedaliah, thereby giving his measure of legitimacy to the new regime. His only other entry in these chapters is in 39:15-18, a remembrance of Ebed-melech, likely functioning as an earnest of "remnant theology" which now emerges in the narrative. As an active voice concerning public policy, Jeremiah is virtually silent in chs. 39–41.

The reportage of chs. 39–41 serves to vindicate the primary witness of the book of Jeremiah: the "Babylonian card" will be played and change all other options. That has turned out to be true. The decisive impingement of Babylon has happened. In its wake have come in sequence Gedaliah, Ishmael, and now Johanan, but none can reorganize the ruins created by Babylon. By the end of ch. 41 the post-587 venture of Gedaliah has failed, and the *de facto* leadership of the community (first Ishmael and then Johanan) seems to have run out of options. It is exactly when the visible leadership runs out of options that Jeremiah is invited back into the narrative (42:1-2). In the formation of the narrative, the centrality of Jeremiah in ch. 42 (after his silence in 40:7–41:18) seems to connect back to 38:17-18, 20-23, where Jeremiah stated his last argument against King Zedekiah. It is now time for the prophet again to state his Yahwistic option, which again seems too costly and is rejected.

After 587 as before 587, Jeremiah is consulted when the community knows nowhere else to turn. After 587 as before 587, Jeremiah makes a response the community does not want to hear and cannot bear. The response of the prophet is not unchanging and fixed. Before 587 his urging is to *submit to Babylon*. After 587 his urging is to *remain in the land of Judah*. Both responses are unpopular and counteract the easier choice. Moreover, even the latter response, *remain in the land*, is tantamount to submission to Babylon, for the territory is under Babylonian control. Thus, even with a changed response, the large vision of the future in this tradition is unchanged.

The long unit of 42:1–43:7 is framed as a narrative by a *request* for guidance (42:1-3, 5-6) and a *rejection* of that guidance (43:1-7). The community asks for guidance but cannot bear the response it receives. Between the request and the rejection is Jeremiah's long oracle of guidance (42:7-22), which is divided at v. 18 into two distinct speeches. This unit is strikingly different from chs. 39–41, which, even where Jeremiah is mentioned, is cast as a direct report on public events. In our present unit, the text contains very little narrative and no report on public events. It consists primarily of speech which follows a sequence of invitation (42:1-6), response (42:7-22), and rejection (43:1-7). The speech, rather than the narrative, permits Jeremiah direct voice in the life of the fearful, desperate Jews. It does not surprise us that it is in the speech that the text is more directly concerned with theological dimensions of Israel's life. This long response of the prophet is in important ways a summation of Jeremianic theology.

42:1-6 Even before our unit begins, we are told that Johanan and his company "intended to go to Egypt" (41:17). From the perspective of the community of Johanan, Egypt is the premise and conclusion of the entire transaction. The consultation with the prophet seems to be preempted by a decision already made. On the face of it, this seems a simple, concrete decision about geography. It immediately becomes clear, however, that in the purview of Jeremiah such a decision is not simply a political option but is fraught with theological gravity and risk. It is odd that the decision seems to have been made in 41:17, yet in 42:1-3 guidance is sought from the prophet.

The peculiar arrangement of 41:17 before 42:1-3 (i.e., the conclusion before the guidance) is a narrative setup for the harsh polemic of the prophet that is to follow. That is, this community is impervious to prophetic counsel and will work its own stubborn way. Perhaps the request of the community is only a ploy, anticipating Jeremiah's quick blessing. Perhaps the request also reflects the bewilderment and confusion of the leadership in a moment of profound chaos. In any case, the turn of the narrative back to Jeremiah (who has not been consulted since Zedekiah did so in ch. 38) is striking. The turn to Jeremiah is abrupt. It is as though consultation with the prophet seems to all persons as the obvious, uncontested thing to do. That clarity, however, simply reflects the perspective of the book of Jeremiah. Outside the prophetic literature, such an act of consultation might seem less than obvious. When people are fleeing for their lives, prophetic consultation does not always happen — except that it will surely happen in this canonically recommended reality. Because all of Jewish life is lived under God's aegis, consultation with the prophet is not only appropriate but indispensable.

The request of the community is abrupt, wholehearted, and enormously serious. It is made by the entire community, "from the least to the greatest." It asks Jeremiah to pray and seek guidance, fully certain that such guidance will be given and can be followed (cf. Deut. 30:11-14). The request is a statement of profound confidence and trust. The speakers now recognize themselves as "this remnant" (Jer. 42:2). The book of Jeremiah is framed to recognize that after 587 the carriers of Jewish faithfulness are a small, vulnerable community. What that small, vulnerable community does matters enormously, for it carries the future of Jewishness. The statement of self-description is most suggestive: "We are left but a *few of many*" (v. 2). The move from "many" (in times past) to "few" (in the present) is decisive for their situation, and it contrasts programmatically with the celebration of the Exodus which asserts "we were few and became many" (cf. Deut. 10:22).

Thus the phrase "few of many" is a code phrase indicating that this community is a reversal or undoing of the Exodus. That is, the phrasing is not a population report, but a recognition that the whole history of deliverance is now in deep jeopardy and is in a process of reversal.

Jeremiah's response to their request is positive and eager (Jer. 42:4). He will pray, and he has no doubt that an answer will be forthcoming. The exchange assumed that prayer is a mode of guidance, and that the prophet is crucial to that process of guidance. In the time before 587 Jeremiah has been explicitly prohibited from prayer, for God was cut off from and uninterested in the destiny of Jerusalem (7:16; 11:14; 14:11-12; 15:1-2). The devastation of 587 seems to have cancelled that prohibition.[62] In a situation of genuine need and supplication, Jeremiah is free again to exercise his prophetic function of intercession.[63] Jeremiah thus takes their request at face value and agrees to cooperate.

The response of the commanders and the people to the cooperation of Jeremiah is a vow of unconditional obedience (42:5-6), echoing the response Israel previously made to Moses (Exod. 24:3, 7), to Joshua (Josh. 24:21, 24), and to Samuel (1 Sam. 7:4, 6, 8; 12:19). The language of this exchange suggests that this meeting with Jeremiah is not an incidental conversation. Rather, the text casts this meeting as one of the great dramatic moments in the life of Israel that is community-forming.[64] This "remnant" now pledges to be obedient Israel, to live according to the will and purpose of Yahweh, and to heed the word of the prophet. Yahweh is invited to witness its oath and to hold it to the oath.

The language of the oath is formal, formidable, and even exaggerated: "May the LORD be a true and reliable (RSV 'faithful'; *emet wenne'eman*) witness." This meeting is indeed serious business. The pledge is that Israel will hear *(shema')*, no matter what the command of God is, no matter if it is good or evil, pleasing or not pleasing. This radical pledge made to the prophet is a blank check to follow the will of Yahweh, no matter what. It is as though the narrator seizes the opportunity to sketch out what genuine obedience would look like, since the tradition of Jeremiah looks in vain for compelling models in contemporary Jerusalem (cf. Jer. 5:1). In retrospect, it is clear that the purpose of the narrative is to expose a radical

---

62. The change whereby the silenced Jeremiah can again intercede is not unlike the change in Ezekiel, who is reduced to dumbness and with the fall of Jerusalem is once again permitted to speak. On the latter, see Klein, *Ezekiel,* 37-40.

63. For a review of the role of prophet as intercessor, see Samuel E. Balentine, "The Prophet as Intercessor: A Reassessment," *Journal of Biblical Literature* 103 (1984): 161-173. See his references to Burke O. Long and Georg C. Macholz on 169, n. 24.

64. It is impossible to assess this meeting historically. In terms of the textual tradition of Jeremiah and the canonical intent of the text, it is the voice of the prophet and the derivative text that creates the community. That is, the text serves to assert and enhance the authority of the prophet (and the prophetic text) as the way in which faithful Israel is formed.

model of *dis*obedience. The textual tradition thus envisions a remnant community prepared to obey, committed to torah, responsive to the prophet. This meeting is their "Sinai," and they will now go to their wilderness (exile), fully faithful.[65] That is, the exchange within the text ostensibly reports a full and ready obedience. But the text as text uses the example of ostensive obedience in order to demonstrate rank disobedience.

42:7-17 Jeremiah reconvenes the assembly of Israel after ten days. We are told nothing about Jeremiah's reception of God's guidance, for the Bible simply takes such a reception for granted (42:7). There is now convened a formal "assembly," which is not a private or casual consultation. It is a meeting of all Israel from the least to the greatest, now being reconstituted after the debacle of recent events (v. 8).

This speech of Jeremiah is constructed around a series of "if-then" pronouncements, positive and negative, which affirm that public policy choices have profound public consequences, for they are in the end acts of faith and unfaith.[66] The skeletal structure of the speech consists in three "if-then" statements. First, there is a positive "if-then" statement in vv. 10-12, matched by a negative "if-then" statement in vv. 13-15a. That negative statement, however, is then commented upon in greater detail by a second negative "if-then" statement in vv. 15b-17. The threefold rhetorical pattern of protasis and apodosis (vv. 10-12, 13-15a, 15b-17) is employed to make a clear policy recommendation and to issue a stern warning. The rhetoric of this speech, in the long tradition of Moses, Joshua, and Samuel, is a pattern of blessings and curses which is determined completely by covenant obedience *(shema')* or disobedience *(lo' shema')*.

65. Seitz, "Canonical Shape," helpfully demonstrates how the tradition of Jeremiah appeals to the wilderness tradition as a type for the exile Israel now faces. The juxtaposition of Joshua-Caleb and Ebed-melech–Baruch shows how the same issues are again present at a crisis point when the community faces the issue of continuity and discontinuity. The abrasive quality of this conversation in 42:1-6 is evident in the reference to "your God" (v. 5) and "our God" (v. 6).

66. The "if-then" structure of the rhetoric reflects an assumption and affirmation of a "deeds-structure" notion of the relation of actions and outcomes. On that notion, see Klaus Koch, "Is There a Doctrine of Retribution in the Old Testament?" in Crenshaw, *Theodicy in the Old Testament,* 57-87. On the power and problem of such a practice of structure legitimation, see Walter Brueggemann, "A Shape for Old Testament Theology, I: Structure Legitimation," *Catholic Biblical Quarterly* 47 (1985): 28-46.

Jeremiah first states his positive recommendation, which is God's intention for the remnant. The "if" is terse: "Remain in the land" (v. 10). This is the sum of God's command, expressed with the intensity of an infinitive absolute. This is the key statement of the entire unit, and everything else follows from this decision. The "then" that follows is more extended and exceedingly rich. It consists in four rhetorical patterns, each of which carries extraordinary theological force:

(1) The oracle reverts to the four verbs which seem to govern the book of Jeremiah, "build, break down, plant, pluck up" (cf. 1:10; 18:7-10; 24:6; 31:28). If the remnant remains in the land, Yahweh will implement the two good verbs, "build and plant," and not work devastation. One might have thought the work of "breaking down and plucking up" had already been completed in the Babylonian occupation. But no, more such destructiveness is in purview, unless the remnant stays in the land. The choices of the people can change the resolve of God. Moreover, a decision to remain in the land of the devastation will evoke new life from God. This quite explicit theological reasoning is anticipated in the syllogism of 18:7-10, which asserts that Israel's decisions impinge upon God's intentions. Now that general theological pattern is given quite concrete substance.

(2) God can and will change course, that is, "repent."[67] The "evil which I did to you" refers to the destruction of 587. So quickly God pulls back from that harsh act. Faithful obedience does change God's mind. The anger of that occasion of destruction (587) does not fate Israel forever to judgment (cf. 31:27-38). God now pines to do good for Israel, but God's goodness will require obedient residence in the city. Already here are the seeds of restoration. The destroyed city is immediately the object of God's positive and attentive concern. It is, however, a concern that depends upon Israel's decision to stay present to the crisis. If Israel changes, God will change.

(3) The prophet then delivers a salvation oracle with a twice stated "do not fear."[68] This speech echoes the initial promise made to Jeremiah

---

67. On God's capacity for repentance, see Fretheim, *The Suffering of God*. Overtures to Biblical Theology 14 (Philadelphia: Fortress, 1984); and Francis I. Andersen and David Noel Freedman, *Amos*. Anchor Bible 24A (Garden City: Doubleday, 1989), 638-679.

68. On the form in this text, see Conrad, *Fear Not Warrior*, 49-55.

(1:8, 19; cf. also 30:10-11), which is now transferred from the prophet to the whole community. God will be a decisive force to intervene on Israel's behalf. The rhetoric is more intense than those initial assurances in ch. 1, for in addition to the verb "deliver" *(n-ts-l)* which was previously used, it is seconded by the verb "save" *(y-sh-ʿ).* God will be an active, intervening agent. In 1:13-15, however, Jeremiah's danger did not come from "the north," but from his compatriots.[69] Thus our oracle forms a counterpart to 1:13-15. Babylon was sent by God, and now God intervenes to protect the community from Babylon. The salvation oracle quite concretely and practically assures exilic Judah that God will prevent Babylon from being the threat it fears.

(4) Finally, in a most remarkable statement, God promises "compassion" for the displaced community (cf. Isa. 54:7-8). Then, dramatically, it is asserted that because Yahweh gives mercy, therefore "he" (i.e., Babylon) will have mercy and "let you remain in your own land." The statement is crucial because it witnesses to the precise convergence of *Yahweh's covenantal resolve* and *Babylon's foreign policy.* It is the mercy of Yahweh which will make Babylon a merciful overlord, who will make living in the land a viable option.[70] The prophet inserts a theological, covenantal dimension into the fearful realities of international politics.

This entire statement is an argument that the remnant must not leave, but must stay in the land and in the city, present to its troubles and open to its future. The exiles, it is argued, have no other future and no other business. Moreover, Yahweh's own commitment to the rehabilitation of land and city is massive and overriding. The oracle gives every thinkable theological warrant for not running away from the trouble. God wants God's people present both to the trouble and to the possibility.

The prophetic oracle proceeds like a syllogistic argument. Finally the negative "if-then" is voiced, stating the costs and risks of leaving the land (Jer. 42:13-15a). The "if" equates not staying with not listening *(shemaʿ).* That is, departing, especially to Egypt, constitutes disobedience to Yahweh. The seduction of Egypt is the assumption that such "flight" is an escape

---

69. In that text there is, to be sure, an enemy and a threat to come from the north. The salvation oracle, however, is to protect the prophet from his own people, who react against his word of threat and judgment.

70. On the interplay of mercy and Babylon, see Brueggemann, "At the Mercy of Babylon."

from punishment, threat, and curse. Egypt appears to this desperate, frightened community to be a peaceable place, where there is no threat of war and no famine. Egypt regularly offers itself as an escapist alternative, both from the troubles of the land and from the dangers of Babylon.

The "then" that follows from this negative "if" is rhetorically complex. The "then" is stated in v. 15 but is further developed into an additional, albeit derivative, "if-then" formulation. The derivative "if" of v. 15 is simply a reiteration of v. 13. The "then" of vv. 16-17 in fact completes the "if" of v. 13. That is, the protasis is a proposal to escape the curse and the apodosis is an assertion that Egypt is saturated with deathliness. When the remnant flees to Egypt, it will find death waiting, in three stylized forms: sword, famine, pestilence. In Israel's long theological tradition, Egypt is a place from which to escape, not a place to which to flee. To go to Egypt now will be to rush to receive deathly curses. An inclination to go to Egypt as an escape from deathliness is a grievous misreading of social reality. While the "then" clause is stated in stylized and formal theological language, the argument is that Egypt is not a hospitable place; to go there is to go from the frying pan into the fire. To go to Egypt is to act out a death wish, for it is a sure way to guarantee the complete eradication of the Jewish community.

The threefold pattern of "if-then" argument is simple, forceful, and direct:

positive:	*if:*	remain in the land
	then:	mercy, life, and well-being.
negative:	*if:*	we will not remain
	then:	hear,
negative:	*if:*	you enter Egypt
	then:	death!

Jeremiah has previously stated simple, unambiguous options to Zedekiah (38:17-18, 20-23). Now, in a quite different context, a parallel pronouncement is given. The proclamation is thoroughly theonomous: God wills a concrete community policy. The proclamation is cast in conventional covenantal formulations of blessing and curse. This formalistic theology is also a thoughtful "judgment call" about concrete sociopolitical reality. The land, dangerous and devastated as it is, is Israel's destiny. Anything else will lead to death. Israel must learn to live in this land, even though

Babylon looms large and threateningly. The fidelity of Yahweh counters the Babylonian danger, as Yahweh will not counter the deathliness of Egypt.

42:18-22   As is characteristic of stern covenantal (Deuteronomic) theology, the negative warning of the prophet receives much more extensive coverage than the positive invitation. In 42:7-17, vv. 10-12 voice a positive invitation, whereas all of vv. 13-17 is negative warning. In the second speech (vv. 18-22) there is no positive invitation at all, but only severe warning.[71] A parallel is drawn in this second speech between Jerusalem already destroyed and the remnant now under threat of like destruction. (The preaching of ch. 7 had earlier made the same argument, drawing a parallel between already-destroyed Shiloh and about-to-be-destroyed Jerusalem. Only now, Jerusalem is not in the role of the about-to-be-destroyed, but embodies what has already been destroyed. Thus the parallelism is even more poignant here than in ch. 7.) The appeal to Jerusalem destroyed and the warning against further destruction constitute the claim that God will not be mocked and disobeyed. The flight to Egypt, which seemed like an escape, is in fact a sure death sentence. The sequence of the curse is not unlike the formal recital of Deut. 28:37. The remnant community, when it disobeys, will become an object of scorn and derision, utterly humiliated. The outcome of the anger of God finally is this: "You shall see this place no more" (Jer. 42:18). No doubt the remnant community, any remnant community, imagines its displacement is temporary; there will come a time, sooner or later, when there will be a return to the homeland.[72] The prophetic oracle rejects such a hope. This remnant, if it leaves the land, will never come back. The present moment is the only chance for life in the land; if that chance is forfeited, there will be no other chance.

71. The disproportion of the length of the curse in relation to the blessing is not unlike the disproportion in length in the recitals of Lev. 26; Deut. 28, where the curse passage is so much longer than the blessing statement. Our passage has important parallels to the curse recital of Deut. 28.

72. The imagination and therefore expectation of an imminent return to the homeland is, I suspect, inevitable among exiles. This is certainly the case with contemporary communities of exile, including deposed monarchies and communities of refugees.

In v. 19 the verdict of the prophet escalates covenantal rhetoric as much as is imaginable. It is as though the prophet said, "A new commandment I give to you." This is a new command, cast in the characteristic language of commandment: "Thou shalt not go into Egypt."[73] This is as strong and unambiguous as the prophet can be. It is a remarkably concrete statement and leaves nothing to the imagination. The conclusion is consistent with the earlier advocacy of the book of Jeremiah, though the issue is somewhat reconfigured. The earlier command had been "Do not resist Babylon." The command against going to Egypt in fact serves the same social policy and is another version of the same perspective. Not going to Egypt inevitably means submission to Babylon and to its occupying force.

The theological claim of this prophetic assertion is enormously important. It affirms (1) that new commandments are given; (2) they are given through prophetic authority, the voice of newness, even when the command is not rooted in old tradition; and (3) the new command concerns concrete issues of public policy in the midst of public crisis. The prophet reminds the listeners that they have promised allegiance to his teaching. Now they are reneging. The danger is double. It is wrong to go to Egypt. It is wrong to vow to listen to the prophet and then to disobey. On both counts, this remnant community has placed itself in profound jeopardy.

The final verses of this speech voice a clear prophetic lawsuit (vv. 21-22). The indictment is that the community did not *shema'*. The indictment is sweeping and comprehensive. Israel's refusal to listen is massive and systemic. It pertains to everything the prophetic tradition has ever uttered. The sentence is the standard list of covenant curses. The remnant is under death sentence for its policy decision. It has made the wrong historical decision and now lives under an inescapable death sentence. Death by sword, famine, and pestilence is the predictable outcome of enemy occupation. These curses are caused, however, by not listening.

43:1-7 The negative rhetoric of Jeremiah in 42:13-22 has prepared us for the outcome of this confrontation. We are led by Jeremiah's indictment to anticipate a gross act of disobedience, for the rhetoric clearly expects

---

73. The negative, to be sure, is *'al*, bespeaking an immediate provision, and not *lo'*, which would suggest a permanent prohibition. That is, the prohibition is something less than an abiding command. On the two negative particles, however, see Gerstenberger, *Wesen and Herkunft*, 50-54 and *passim*.

such a negative response. And that is what we find in the concluding section of the narrative (43:1-7). The prophetic oracle had been so earnestly sought and devoutly yearned for by the fugitive community (42:1-6). The response made to the prophetic oracle by the community, however, is immediate, total, belligerent rejection (43:1-7). One wonders: Did the remnant think it would receive a different oracle? Did it imagine Jeremiah would not reverse course and become oddly and capriciously anti-Babylonian? If we stay inside the text, which is clear and uncompromising, we have the simple, predictable process whereby the prophet condemns this errant remnant community.

We may, however, step outside the text and ask about the intended sociopolitical function of the text. It becomes plausible that the voice of Jeremiah in this text is in fact the voice of the Babylonian community of exiles, in deep dispute with its counterpart, the Egyptian community of exile.[74] The dispute in the midst of the Exile is not between simply prophet and people (as the text ostensibly has it), but between two communities who vie for legitimacy as the true carrier of the Jewish tradition. That is, the text is a witness and party to a conflict about legitimacy. Clearly the figure of Jeremiah has become a mouthpiece for the community of Babylonian exiles, which seeks to assert its own exclusive legitimacy and the corresponding illegitimacy of every rival community. The canonizing process has clearly settled the matter of legitimacy in favor of the Babylonian community.[75] The interplay of *vested interest* and *theological affirmation* is both evident and unavoidable. The text is not disinterested, but it operates on the conviction that the intent of God and the interest of this community of Babylonian exiles do indeed converge.

The response of Jeremiah (and the community for which he speaks) to the Egyptian community of exiles, therefore, is predictable. The text loses no time in labelling the adversaries of Jeremiah. They are "insolent

74. The sweeping claim of the narrative is that the land was completely emptied. "All the people . . . all the remnant of Judah" went to Egypt. The ideological character of the narrative asserts that there was no third alternative and forces this simple, sharp either/or. Either one succumbed or one fled with this party to Egypt.

75. Clearly the canonizing process is a political process: in this case it represents achievement and triumph for the community of Babylonian Jews. To say that the process is political does not in principle deny that the final shape is theologically faithful. Theological faithfulness and political interest are not by definition mutually exclusive.

men," that is, they presume on their own to know better about what to do (v. 2). They set themselves against the authority of God (or Jeremiah) which is given to us as canonical.

Jeremiah has with due solemnity announced the will of God in the form of a command: "Do not go to Egypt" (42:19). There is no room in the command for hermeneutical playfulness. It will not do to argue about the meaning of such a command. The only way to counter such a command is to reject it. It must be dismissed wholesale. That is what the Egyptian community does. It labels the command "a lie" *(sh-q-r)*. It rejects the notion that Yahweh would give such a command. The use of the term "false" *(sh-q-r)* in this way is remarkable. Characteristically, it is Jeremiah who labels other opinions as "false" (cf. 23:14; 27:10; 28:15; 29:21). Now the word is turned back on Jeremiah, and he is the one who is dismissed as a fraud. We note, of course, that there is no objective ground by which to adjudicate this dispute.[76]

In severe fashion, Jeremiah's earlier controversy with "false prophets" is now turned against him. Of Jeremiah himself and therefore the exilic community for which he speaks, this recalcitrant group led by Johanan can have God say to Jeremiah, as Jeremiah earlier said himself:

> I did not send the prophets,
> yet they ran;
>
> I did not speak to them,
> yet they prophesied. (23:21)

From the perspective of the Egyptian remnant, the verdict against going to Egypt is not God's word, but is the self-serving ideology of a counter-community for which the prophet has no transcendent authority. Of course! How could it be otherwise? Each side in this deep conflict argues that the other side is acting autonomously and claiming its own perspective as God's will. We have no way to adjudicate these claims (as they did not), except to note the canonical outcome of the dispute. In the canonical outcome of this text, the Babylonian opinion is accepted as God's truth.

In a desperate attempt to establish "the lie," 43:3 makes an unexpected accusation. It is as though Jeremiah himself is too powerfully

76. See Crenshaw, *Prophetic Conflict*, 48-61.

situated to attack successfully, and therefore the attack is turned on Baruch. This is a stunning maneuver on the part of Jeremiah's adversaries, though perhaps if we knew more we would understand better. All we know is that Baruch is Jeremiah's faithful colleague who shared in the risks of his vocation. We have had no evidence heretofore that Baruch, beyond his loyalty to Jeremiah, represents a political or ideologically partisan position. Indeed, we would not even know that Baruch is a known political figure. This reference suggests to us that Baruch, and therefore the entire productive process of the book of Jeremiah, is not an innocent enterprise but is an ideological assertion that champions some positions and counters others.[77]

We may make no claim that Jeremiah's (and Baruch's) theological position is less than reputable and faithful. That theological position, however, if it has any significance at all, inevitably takes sides on public questions. That is, the book of Jeremiah is not neutral in the great contested issues of the day. In the circumstance of this text, it was impossible to speak of God's will among the exiles without in the same moment taking sides on the conflict among exilic communities and therefore recognizing that no claim is politically disinterested. Thus while the accusation in v. 3 may be overstated and/or gratuitous, it is surely not unfounded. Baruch and the pro-Babylonian party not only stood against the Egyptian remnant, but were also decisive in the formation of the book of Jeremiah and in its canonizing powers. This is not an argument that they were simply political operatives; it is rather to recognize the inescapable fact that interpretive questions (i.e., questions of God's will and questions of canonization) are always set in the midst of and intimately connected to difficult public issues. That is how the Bible came to be and where it came from. Johanan and the others of the Egyptian remnant understood well the process. Since they are losers and outsiders to the canonical verdict, they do what they can to discredit both the process and the outcome. As a last effort, they employ one of Jeremiah's best words in order to critique ideology. They label the entire position of the Jeremiah-Baruch community as "false" *(sh-q-r)*. In that utterance, the Egyptian remnant dismisses the entire canonical process of Jeremiah and disengages itself from the powerful legitimating advocacy of the Babylonian community of exiles.

77. That ideological reality is evidently pro-Babylonian; moreover, it seems linked to the great scribal families, of which Baruch is a representative member.

The argument of Johanan in vv. 2-3 is situated in the canonical text, however, to refute the charges made against Jeremiah. The speech of the Egyptian remnant is sandwiched in v. 2 by the label "insolent" and in v. 4 by "they did not listen/obey." The Egyptian remnant refused to submit to what was becoming a canonical judgment.

Acting against the word of the prophet, the community led by Johanan went to Egypt (vv. 5-7). They themselves went, with considerable resolve. They also took all those who had been exiled and had returned. They took all those who remained under the regime of Gedaliah. They took the entire population! Astonishingly, they also took Jeremiah! And they took Baruch! The report ends in indignation and sadness (v. 7). We do not know why they took Jeremiah. It is sometimes said that they did so to protect the prophet, but his life was not in any danger in Jerusalem. Perhaps Jeremiah and Baruch are taken as hostages against the dangers from the pro-Babylonian party. Surely Jeremiah and Baruch must have been taken against their will. The Egyptian company forced Jeremiah and Baruch to act and to live exactly against their own deep conviction. There must be powerful irony in this last act. Jeremiah, all through the book, has been "over against" some dominant ideology (cf. 1:18). He has been powerless in the face of dominant ideology. He has been endlessly rejected and in jeopardy. And now, at the end, even as he is vindicated by the outcome of events in Jerusalem, he is once more abused, rejected, dishonored, and powerless. He is, so the text says, utterly defeated, certainly not delivered and protected as had been promised him at the outset (1:8, 19).

The text adds its terrible verdict: "They did not listen!" (43:7). They imagined they were autonomous. Even when they had sworn to listen to the prophet, they did not. In marginality as in power, in jeopardy as in strength, Jeremiah's constituency always and characteristically resisted his word. The text has no doubt that in its failure to heed Jeremiah the remnant failed to heed Yahweh. And "not listening" can only lead to death.

"They arrived at Tahpanhes" (v. 7)! Of course they did. That is where they had been headed. That is where they were resolved to go. That is where they wanted to go, even against the counsel of the prophet. That is where they went to be "out of reach" of the Babylonians. The culmination of this confrontation is indeed ironic. Johanan and his companions imagined they had escaped the threat. Jeremiah had made clear that they had chosen poorly. In pursuit of life, they had chosen death (42:22). According to the prophet, they were closed off forever to the homeland.

They had, on such a reading, no future. They ended up where the story of Israel had begun, back in Egypt, back in a bondage they misread as freedom.

No doubt the text intends to report geographical specificity. It names the place of their arrival. Israel, however, can never read such geography without attending to the historical drama that surrounds the geography and works through it. In such a dramatic reading, the end has come. Johanan has opted out of Yahweh's saving drama. The scenario or rescue that began with Moses in this pitiful moment ends in exhaustion, failure, defeat, and despair. Jeremiah at the end, like Moses at the beginning, had labored mightily to preserve another option for his people.[78] For all his fidelity, however, Jeremiah is defeated by the power of a false reading of reality which he could not finally counter. The end result is not only a defeat for Jeremiah. It is an awesome defeat for the God whose work has begun in an escape from Egypt. Defeat for the prophet and for God all pivots on "not listening." And the end of not listening is death!

Jeremiah in Egypt (43:8-13)

The community led by Johanan ended in Egypt (Tahpanhes) against the strong counsel of the prophet. Jeremiah himself arrived with them, against his will and against his perception of the will of Yahweh. In 43:8-13; 44:1ff. Jeremiah repeatedly rebukes the community of Jews in Tahpanhes for what he perceives as its utter defiance of the purposes of Yahweh. According to Jeremiah, continued presence in Jerusalem under the hegemony of Babylon is Yahweh's intention for the Jews, which this community has blatantly defied. Our present text is organized as a symbolic act (43:8-9) and an oracle occasioned by the symbolic act (vv. 10-13).

43:8-9 This report of a symbolic act is not unlike Jeremiah's earlier actions concerning a broken pot (19:1-13), an iron yoke (27:2), and especially a hidden loincloth (13:1-7). This act is like the latter act, in that it consists in hiding something that has no immediate power or significance

---

78. See Richard E. Friedman, "From Egypt to Egypt: Dtr[1] and Dtr[2]," in *Traditions in Transformation. Festschrift Frank M. Cross,* ed. Baruch Halpern and Jon D. Levenson (Winona Lake: Eisenbrauns, 1981), 189-192.

but which is left as a sign and gesture, the power and significance of which will emerge only later. It is not helpful, as some interpreters do, to regard such acts as "magic," as though they could only be committed or only matter to a primitive, precritical mind. Such a reading of a symbolic act reflects a kind of positivism which is unaware of the strange power exercised by such acts. It is more helpful, in taking the text seriously, to see the act as a poetic, sacramental gesture.[79] Such a gesture makes an assault on presently construed reality, and stakes out a power-laden expectation for the future that works in the imagination of the observing community. It is the kind of gesture that is characteristically committed by communities of marginality and oppression. Such communities possess no conventional form of power and must rely on sacramental gestures as modes of power which the dominant power cannot resist. Such gestures often take on enormous social power and significance, enough to reshape the community.

In this sacramental gesture, the prophet places large stones underneath the mortar pavement of Pharaoh's palace. In doing so, the prophet dramatically "undermines" the palace, the throne, and the authority of Pharaoh. What is "underneath" Pharaoh — more basic, more reliable than Pharaoh's throne — works to destabilize and threaten the perceived absoluteness of Pharaoh and his governance.

43:10-13 The gesture itself could admit of other significance than "undermining." It is the interpretive oracle that gives the act its subversive thrust. The oracle depends upon the stones for its concrete poignancy; the stones depend upon the oracle to gain this special significance. The commentary on the symbolic act is in the mouth of Yahweh: "Behold, I." The "I" of Yahweh becomes the basis and premise for all that follows. In this extended oracle, Yahweh enacts only two verbs: "I will send, I will take." The object of those verbs is Nebuchadnezzar, who is identified in two ominous ways. Nebuchadnezzar is "king of Babylon" and "my servant." Nebuchadnezzar is the carrier of imperial might and authority, and is the embodiment of Yahweh's resolve; *imperial might* and the *resolve of Yahweh*

79. The reported action must be accepted as given in this narrative account. That is, it is not useful or possible to determine the "historicity" of the event. The textual report may be simply a literary presentation, but that does not detract from the cruciality of the event in bringing this part of the Jeremiah tradition to closure.

converge. The utterance of the twofold identity on the one hand threatens the political claims of Egypt. On the other hand, the utterance jeopardizes the religious legitimacy of the empire which appeals to Egyptian gods. Thus the twofold title for Nebuchadnezzar is an act both of political critique and of theological subversion.

It is a daring act to utter the name of Nebuchadnezzar in the throne room of Pharaoh. The mere utterance of this awesome name already deabsolutizes Pharaoh, for there is now another, more powerful name in the presence of which Pharaoh must exist. Nebuchadnezzar's primal act, according to the oracle, is to engage the stones of the symbolic act. The hidden stones, now brought into public play, are the base (and warrant) for Nebuchadnezzar's throne which is now to be established in Egypt. The throne of Nebuchadnezzar does not belong in Egypt and has no right to be there. The prophet, however, has provided a place to put the throne, a place not borrowed from Pharaoh, but newly formed by prophetic authority and prophetic speech. Thus the prophetic act (43:9) makes the political act of Nebuchadnezzar possible (v. 10).

The hidden stones are the base for the throne of Nebuchadnezzar, and they have been put there by the prophet. That is, the prophet has symbolically created the "place" for this odd throne. The stones are hidden as they wait for a revolution in power. They are as hidden as is Nebuchadnezzar's promised and inchoate power. But what is hidden will be revealed, to the great cost of the pharaoh. What is hidden cannot be stopped. Nebuchadnezzar will come here to power.[80] His power will be public, visible, magnificent, expansive, embodied in a spreading "royal canopy." The canopy will be a sign of awesome royal power which must be protected. Nebuchadnezzar will establish a magnificent presence, in the very throne room of Pharaoh!

Then follows a series of harsh verbs, specifying how this new rule will be conducted. Nebuchadnezzar will "ravage" (*nkh*; RSV "smite") the land of Egypt. The verb is the same as that used with the old plagues of Moses (Exod. 3:20; 7:25; 9:15; 12:13; Ps. 136:10). The land of Pharaoh will be visited with a severe threat, as it was in the beginning of Israel's life, when the Egyptian government was confronted by a power it could not resist. Nebuchadnezzar will come and place the empire of Egypt under

---

80. On the historical ground for this alleged episode, see John Bright, *A History of Israel,* 3rd ed. (Philadelphia: Westminster and London: SCM, 1981), 351-52.

curse, the curses most threatening in Israel's rhetoric (cf. Jer. 15:2), the curses that come with an invading army: pestilence, captivity, sword. Egypt has always imagined itself protected, isolated, and immune to danger (cf. Ezek. 29:3). It is so no longer. The power of death will have its intrusive way in the empire, as it did with Moses (cf. Exod. 11:4-6).

Nebuchadnezzar will carry out a complete devastation of the religious symbols of Egypt, the symbols of legitimacy, the signs of ideology, the emblems that maintain the claims of the imperial order. Fire will burn the temples where the symbolic power of the empire is housed. The gods of the empire will be confiscated, shown to be not only vulnerable but finally powerless. Nebuchadnezzar will possess the Egyptian gods; that is, he will possess their power and authority to govern. Moreover, he will "delouse" the land, in the way a shepherd shakes out his coat.[81] A shepherd, living very close to the sheep, may get fleas and vermin, and the coat must be shaken out. So Nebuchadnezzar will shake out the vermin of Egypt, which may mean both the gods of the empire and its enormous wealth. The imagery thus denigrates what Egypt values, dismissing it as "lice," and it places the denigrated wealth and gods of Egypt under threat. Nebuchadnezzar will destroy ("break, burn") all the imperial symbols of power and authority. This recital of verbs of violence and destruction is not unlike the command of Deut. 12:1-3, in which Moses commands Israel to destroy all religious symbols of Canaan that seduce Israel and resist Yahweh. In a parallel way, Nebuchadnezzar will break all the symbolization which supports Egyptian power, in order that his own power may prevail.

Thus the act (Jer. 43:8-9) and the oracle (vv. 10-13) open Egypt to the threat of Nebuchadnezzar. It is worth noting that nowhere in this unit are the Jewish fugitives mentioned. They are not on the horizon of this oracle. The larger threat against Egypt, however, does indeed touch the Jewish community in Egypt. On the one hand, the oracle asserts that Egypt is no safe place to which to flee. It is a place of deep danger, and the Jews with Johanan have gone from the frying pan into the fire (cf. Amos 5:19). On the other hand, the oracle asserts that there is no place in which to hide from Babylon. Thus the Babylonian accent of the Jeremiah tradition persists until the end. It reaches into the most unlikely place; Egypt, in geopolitical terms, is the furthest extreme from Babylonian power. As the Psalmist cannot finally escape from God (Ps. 139:7-12; cf.

81. On this rendering, see Holladay, *Jeremiah 2*, 302-3.

Amos 9:2-4), so the Jews cannot finally escape Nebuchadnezzar, who is "my servant."

In the end, this oracle is one more reiteration of a consistent claim of the Jeremiah tradition. Because Yahweh governs, Jews must live in a Babylonian world. This assertion of *Babylon over Egypt* is an anticipation of the first of the Oracles against the Nations in Jer. 46:1-28. In that long poem, Egyptian power is broken by Yahweh because of Egypt's inordinate arrogance. In the prose commentary of 46:2, 13, 25-26 that Yahwistic threat is embodied in Nebuchadnezzar and the Babylonians. The mistake of the Egyptian community of Jews is that they thought they could have Yahweh without Babylon. This text, like much of Jeremiah, insists that Yahweh is regularly and inescapably accompanied by Babylon. The fugitives have completely miscalculated. They stand under the threat made against the Egyptians, for it is with Egypt that they have placed their misinformed trust.

Jeremiah's Last Known Words (44:1-30)

The narrative account of Jeremiah's life ends in 43:7 with the arrival of the Johanan community in Tahpanhes. The so-called "Baruch document" concludes with three oracles (43:8-13; 44:1-30; 45:1-5). In these oracles there is no more narrative account, only a voice. The three oracles are summary theological statements, as though the shapers of the canonical book want to have one last chance to make their powerful, partisan statements of advocacy.

The most extended, elaborate, and interesting of these concluding statements is 44:1-30. It is divided into three statements by Jeremiah (vv. 1-14, 20-23, 24-30), with one "answer" given to the prophet by his Egyptian adversaries (vv. 15-19). This material is aimed, in the first instance, at the Egyptian community whom it purports to address.[82] It has a wider interest, however, because it makes a more general theological

---

82. To state the matter this way means that the historical dimension of the reported oracle is bracketed out. Our concern is with the canonical placement of the oracle and the canonical function of the oracle as a form of theological advocacy and instruction. Its canonical placement and function focus attention on its enduring assertion and not its meaning for the first alleged listeners.

point. Because the material makes a general theological point, it may indeed be that the ostensive answer to the prophet (vv. 15-19) is in fact not an answer but a deliberate foil designed to serve the larger argument. In general, the point of this extended discussion is that Israel must be committed *only to Yahweh.*[83] Any compromise of this singular loyalty is unacceptable and is sure to bring trouble and death.

44:1-14 This section makes an argument that assumes a world of cause-and-effect payoffs governed by Yahweh. It is filled with conventional covenantal language which affirms that "evils" committed against Yahweh will produce "evils" wrought by Yahweh.[84] The statement appeals to recent judgments enacted by Yahweh against Jerusalem and Judah as a didactic example and warning for the Egyptian community of Jews.

The basic argument of the oracle is succinctly stated in vv. 2-3, in a conventional lawsuit pattern. The sentence implemented by Yahweh is "evil" (NRSV "disaster") worked against Jerusalem and the cities of Judah, that is, the destruction wrought through the Babylonian invasion (v. 2). (Note well, the Babylonians are not mentioned.) The indictment against Judah which caused the destruction is the "evil" (RSV "wickedness") committed by Judah, which is essentially the violation of the First Commandment (v. 3). That is, loyalty to Yahweh has not been singular and unambiguous. Such divided loyalty has caused the failure of Jerusalem.

This tight syllogism, reflective of a morally rigorous notion of historical reality under Yahweh's governance (vv. 2-3), is momentarily modified in vv. 4-5 by the standard mitigating factor of prophetic theology.[85] Though vv. 2-3 present a closed and compelling case, in fact Yahweh has

83. The "only Yahweh" theological position is powerfully articulated in the tradition of Deuteronomy and in the part of the book of Jeremiah governed by that theology. It likely is rooted in the role and memory of Moses in the community, and has not only theological but also socioeconomic politcal implications. Robert M. Polzin, *Moses and the Deuteronomist* (New York: Seabury, 1980), has explored some of the interpretive issues involved in the "only Yahweh" theology.

84. The term "evil" *(ra')* is variously rendered in the NRSV as "disaster" and "wickedness." Such varied translations are unfortunate, because they destroy the rhetorical effect of matching the offense with the punishment. On the close and intentional connection between offense and punishment, see Patrick D. Miller, Jr., *Sin and Judgment in the Prophets.* In this passage, the correlation is evident in vv. 2-3.

85. Cf. 2 Kgs. 17:13-14; Zech. 1:3-6.

been gracious over a long period by sending prophets who warn Israel and seek to provoke repentance.[86] (This is the intent of Jeremiah, according to Jer. 7:4-7; 26:3; 36:3.) That is, the prophets are not a threat against Israel, not a negative force, but are God's gracious gift through which repentance and rescue might occur (44:4). The prophets, however, in fact make no effective difference in the future of Israel, because Israel characteristically will not listen (v. 5). Indeed, "not listening" is a foundational attitude of Israel. The outcome of v. 6 is the same as in v. 2, a massive judgment wrought by God, who will brook no rival and who will act against those who engage a rival.

Thus vv. 2-6 are built around very conventional themes, and are arranged in chiastic fashion:

    a   God does "evil" (v. 2)
      b   Israel disobeys (v. 3)
        c   God sends prophets to rescue (v. 4)
      b′ Israel refuses and does "evil" (v. 5)
    a′ God works destruction (v. 6).

The prophets constitute God's "second effort" to save, but to no avail. This argument in vv. 2-6 is a reflection on the past. It is not an assault on Jerusalem, but reflects on a judgment that has already been implemented and that is well known among the Jews in Egypt here addressed.

Now the text ends its review of Jerusalem's destiny and focuses on the present implied audience in Egypt: "And now" (*we'attah,* v. 7). The Egyptian community is invited to order its present life differently because of this review of the past. While the shift of v. 7 leads us to expect an imperative, in fact the tone of vv. 7-9 is accusatory. The Hebrew poses an accusatory question in vv. 7 and 9, while the two elements rendered as questions by the RSV in v. 8 properly reflect the tone of the whole. Thus four questions are asked: Why? Why? Will you? Have you? All of the questions imply that the addressed community is indeed doing "evil," much like the earlier community in Jerusalem. Moreover, this "evil" will

---

86. The Deuteronomic assumption reflected here is that there was an intentional, identifiable series of prophets all with the same charge. This assumption is rooted in Deut. 18:9-22 and comes to its culmination in the Deuteronomic casting of Jeremiah. Cf. Wilson, 156-252.

lead to being "cut off," that is, excommunicated and declared illegitimate. We likely hear in this threat the strident voice either of the community of exiled Jews in Babylon, which regards all other Jews as less than adequate, or the community of Jews who remained in Jerusalem, which regarded Egyptian Jews as outside the pale. The cause of illegitimacy is attentiveness in the Egyptian community of Jews to other gods which were indeed attractive and which led to a compromise of "pure Yahwism," sponsored by the accusing party. In effect, this community of Jews in Egypt had learned nothing and has refused to change, thus rejecting the torah (v. 10).[87] Thus what purports to be a probe and invitation by the prophet is, in the end, a severe condemnation, with the verdict rendered in v. 10.

The verdict in v. 10 is now given a full and exceedingly harsh response in vv. 11-14. God says, "I will set my face" (v. 11). God is utterly resolved to bring "evil" on this community. The reference is to "all Judah," but that seems in this context to refer only to all those who did not yield to Babylon but opted for Egypt. For that community, according to this text, there are no longer any options, no choices, no alternatives, no escape. The term twice rendered "perish" (*tmm;* RSV "be consumed") means "completed." That is, the community will be "totalled," with nothing left, nothing salvageable. The totality of destruction will be accomplished by sword, famine, and pestilence. The reiteration three times of "sword" and "famine" may indicate redactional activity. More likely it suggests the passion of the verdict. The outcome will be a community which is an utter humiliation. In v. 13 the text asserts a historical analogy, not unlike vv. 2-9: as with Jerusalem in the past (vv. 2-6), so with Egypt in the present (vv. 7-9). What Yahweh has done in the recent past that everyone can already see, now Yahweh will again do here. None will escape . . . except a few fugitives. If the community is a rescued remnant as it thought itself to be, now there will be only a remnant of a remnant, survivors who are not of any value (cf. a like figure in Amos 3:12).

44:15-19   The prophetic oracle receives a defiant answer from the community. This may be a genuine answer, and if it is, it is a very bold response

87. The concrete data that the Egyptian community of Jews broke the torah is presumably offered in evidence of the Elephantine community; cf. Miller and Hayes, 434-36. The theological verdict of the text may follow such evidence. It is nonetheless at the same time a highly polemical, partisan verdict made by a rival community.

to the prophet. But because the answer is so recalcitrant, it may rather be a response placed in the mouth of the Egyptian community by the prophetic tradition.[88] That is, such resistance in action by the opponents of the Jeremiah tradition is credible. Such determined resistance in actual speech, however, is more difficult to imagine, because one would expect at least a surface effort at compromise. This resistant response either reflects a very hard-nosed community, prepared to challenge the prophet, or it is a device by the framers of the text to make the community of Egyptian Jews appear as ignoble as possible. In this answer (either a serious one or a contrived one to thicken the dispute) there is no signal of accommodation to the prophetic word. From the perspective of the Jeremiah community, this response is resistant, arrogant, and death-choosing. The community is portrayed as completely and militantly resistant to the prophetic program of "Yahweh alone."

This community of response blatantly and defiantly answers, "We will not listen" (Jer. 44:16). That statement constitutes a rejection of Jeremianic theology. The book of Jeremiah (especially its prose elements) has endlessly accused the community of "not listening," and now here is an explicit, frontal refusal, without embarrassment or shame or any mitigating factor. The alternative to "listening" (i.e., keeping the torah) is to keep faith with alternative gods, in this case with "the queen of heaven."

With this defiant assertion, the answering community now makes a programmatic theological defense of its religious commitment. The reason for holding to this alternative faith is simple: It works (v. 17)! The queen of heaven delivers the goods. The worship of this god has led to "peace and prosperity." Negatively, the neglect of the worship of this god has led to the loss of well-being (v. 18). The point seems irrefutable. It is the argument that every religion seeks to make, that a god is judged by the gifts that are given. On its own terms, the argument is unanswerable.

44:20-23   Jeremiah will nonetheless answer. His answer does not engage the argument just offered, for one cannot challenge an argument made on those premises. Instead, perhaps wisely, perhaps of necessity, Jeremiah

88. On the practice of placing a quote in the mouth of an opponent, see Hans Walter Wolff, "Das Zitat im Prophetenspruch," *Gesammelte Studien zum Alten Testament.* Theologische Bücherei 22 (Munich: Kaiser, 1964), 36-129. Such a device often creates an adversarial position against which the prophet can then speak.

ignores the assertion of his opponents and simply restates his own Yahwistic, covenantal, prophetic argument. The oracle accepts the analysis just made by his opponents, but turns the argument on its head and draws an antithetical conclusion.

The offering made to other gods does indeed matter decisively for the community, as the opponents have asserted. These offerings are not, however, causes of well-being. They are rather causes of covenantal curse. The very religion that the community of Egyptian Jews thinks has caused it to prosper is in reality the religion that has brought trouble. The worship of this other god is in fact the trigger for the evil that will be worked against them by Yahweh. Thus there is indeed blessing and curse; the disagreement is over which god can bless and which god will surely curse.

44:24-30 The text adds one more paragraph, yet another oracle to clinch the argument. The prophet now sarcastically acknowledges that the resolve of this recalcitrant Egyptian community is fixed; the prophet will no longer dispute with them (44:25). The statement of the prophet includes a twofold infinitive absolute that greatly strengthens the verse: "you shall *surely keep* your vow and you shall *surely do* your sacrifices." The tone of this concession by Jeremiah is not unlike the prophet's concession to Hananiah, when Jeremiah finally recognizes that an argument is futile (28:6). Thus the prophet abandons the community to its own deathly choice, and will protest no longer.

Given that unshakable conclusion drawn by the Egyptian community of Jews and now grudgingly accepted by the prophet, we are not surprised that this severe God will speak yet again (44:26-28). Now Yahweh makes a statement that disassociates God's own self from this community. God no longer evidences a concern for this community, but now God is preoccupied only with Yahweh's own sovereignty and authority.[89] Yahweh will completely withdraw from this community and will be for it an absent, unavailable God. Or perhaps we may even say a "dead God." The community will no longer say, "As Yahweh lives," for they will have no reference points for such a bottom-line statement. This community is alone and without God in the world.

God is, in this oracle, not yet finished with this community. God will do what God has been doing since the beginning of the book of

89. See the same self-concern on God's part in Exod. 14:4, 17; Ezek. 36:22-32.

Jeremiah. God is "watching," that is, staying at an attentive distance, overseeing the working out of God's resolve (cf. 1:11-12). For the community of exiles presumably in Babylon, God is "watching" for good (cf. 24:6-7; 29:11; 31:28). But for this community in Egypt, the same "watching" will yield only evil. The statement of 44:27 employs for negative use two statements made positively in other, earlier contexts. Thus "for evil and not for good" (v. 27) inverts "for welfare and not for evil" (29:11). Moreover, the negative "watching" here counters the watching of 31:28, in which the watching is for planting and building. Thus God is not absent nor dead for this community, but worse: God is alive and attentive to work a terrible destiny for this community. That terrible destiny will be termination.

Jeremiah 44:28 constitutes a climactic statement in two ways. The phrase "few in number" is a direct reference to Israel's miraculous origin in Egypt, when it was clearly Yahweh alone who took "the few" and made a people (cf. Deut. 10:22; 26:5).[90] Yahweh was the only reason Israel happened at all. Now that whole saving process is being inverted.[91] The community is reverting to "few in number," which inevitably happens when the strong support of Yahweh is absent, for Yahweh is the only source of life and well-being for this community. This community has cut itself off from that one reliable source, and now Yahweh will let this community have its choice . . . complete nullification.

The last phrase of Jer. 44:28, "mine or theirs," is an acknowledgement that the difficult theological issue has been joined in vv. 15-19, that more than one argument has been made, and that no conclusive point has been scored. "Their" argument is in vv. 17-18; "my" argument is in vv. 21-23. The community must wait to see how the pragmatic outcome of the case will finally adjudicate the argument.

Finally this dismissive statement by Yahweh accepts the criteria by which the theological question will be decided. Yahweh offers a "sign" for the future, a piece of future concrete data which will decide the large theological issue (vv. 29-30). The "sign" is a deed wrought by Yahweh.

---

90. Deut. 28:62 has a curse quite parallel in its intent.

91. The "return to Egypt" thus is not simply a geographical development, but constitutes the nullification of the Exodus. In this terminal moment, Israel is as it was before God's primal event of rescue. This foolish community has, by its conduct, cancelled Israel's entire history of rescue.

Pharaoh Hophra (Apries) will be done to death. To be sure, Pharaoh does have enemies, but Jeremiah argues (as he earlier argued concerning Babylon as an enemy) that it is Yahweh who will dispatch these enemies.[92] Thus the test of "mine" or "theirs" (i.e., the vindication of Yahweh or the queen of heaven) will be manifest in the destiny of the pharaoh who hosts this refugee community of Jews. The reference to Zedekiah as a model for Hophra is a reiteration of the "then-now" "there-here" argument of vv. 2-9. That is, the argument about the fate of Jerusalem (vv. 2-6) is used as an argument about Egypt (vv. 7-9).

The die is cast; but the community must wait, as the biblical community must always wait, to see how the die lands.[93] The recurring problem of biblical faith, upon which the prophets always insist, is that the community of faith must act in the middle of things. This community of faith does not have the luxury of waiting until the end to see how things turn out. Thus a decision for Yahweh or for the queen of heaven cannot wait until the destiny of Hophra is clear. A decision of faith must be made now. And of course, the prophets know that a refusal to decide, a decision to wait for more data, is itself a decision, usually a wrong one as well as a cowardly one.

We may pause over the serious theological adjudication which is invited by this chapter. For the question between "mine" or "theirs" is in fact the large question of prophetic faith and is in contemporary theology the crucial issue between "foundationalism" and confessional theology.[94]

92. The same argument is made in Jer. 50–51; there it is Babylon who is attacked by enemies dispatched by Yahweh. In every case, the destruction can be understood in political, military terms, but the tradition of Jeremiah insists upon a Yahwistic construal of such political, military events.

93. The actual turn of events concerning Hophra did not in fact turn out as this text anticipates; cf. Bright, 347-352. If, however, the text be taken canonically and not historically, then the crucial point is that the future of Jews cannot rely upon Egypt which this pro-Babylonian text perceives as disobedience to Yahweh. In the end, the judgment here pronounced against Egypt is matched by the final judgment against Babylon in chs. 50–51.

94. For a judicious review of that contemporary debate, see William C. Placher, *Unapologetic Theology: A Christian Voice in a Pluralistic Conversation* (Louisville: Westminster/John Knox, 1989). The vexed question of "foundationalism" is not unlike the debate here conducted between Jeremiah and his opponents.

That is, it is a question of what "reasons" and warrants can be given for faith in the God of the Bible. I suggest three useful lines of reflection.

(1) In the first instance, it is clear that intellectually Jeremiah's case is no more convincing or compelling than is that of his opponents. The argument is a stalemate, moving from different assumptions, waiting for data. Each side operates from premises that the other side cannot afford to grant. James Moulder has made a powerful case that arguments about God acting in history are impossible arguments that cannot be made convincingly, and that are not needed by anyone.[95] Every such argument is in fact not an argument from data, but is an argument imposed on the data, which insists that the data must be read in a certain way. Robert P. Carroll takes considerable delight in the recognition that the same "experience" can be used by two conflicting ideologies, because each ideology presses the experienced data into its service.[96] At the level of logical analysis, there really is no serious issue that can be joined, and the two sides talk past each other. The outcome is that each party remains convinced, not by experience or by data, but by its own premise, assumptions, and interests.

(2) Such a reading of the matter, however, does not take us very far in interpreting the text. Our interpretation of Jeremiah cannot leave the matter there if the text is to be taken on its own terms. For into this rather sophisticated intellectual argument there intrudes the matter of canon. At a second level, it is the text of Jeremiah that has emerged as a "classic," [97] that is, as an important and prevailing text to which we continue to turn for authorization and reflection. The matter of "canon" does not require a theory of inspiration or revelation, nor is it an escape hatch to defend an absolutist ideology. Rather, the canonical shaping of the argument insists that the canon both (a) recognized the serious nature of the argument and (b) proposed an answer which intended to refute the counteranswer. Our interpretation must at least reflect on why the canon came to this conclusion and what it means that the canon so decides. That is,

95. James Moulder, "Skepticism and Agnosticism about Theology and Historiography," in *Being and Truth.* Festschrift John Macquarrie, ed. Alistair Kee and Eugene T. Long (London: SCM, 1986), 437-452.

96. Carroll, 737-38.

97. On the notion of classic, see David Tracy, *The Analogical Imagination: Christian Theology and the Culture of Pluralism* (New York: Crossroad, 1981), 99-229.

to conclude simply that one answer is as good as another is to ignore the fact that the argument is lodged in this way in this text. If we are to hear this text at all, it requires — at least for a moment — standing inside that community of interpretation to give its rendering a serious and preferential hearing. Whatever the outcome may be, the canonical nature of the text makes the matter more complex than simply calling the argument a draw.

(3) If we seek to go underneath the intellectual "balance" of the question about "which God" and beyond the formal fact of canon, we are led to theologically substantive issues. That is, the matter of "Yahweh versus the queen of heaven," or more broadly, "Yahweh versus other gods," is not simply a multiple-choice question among gods with different names, one of which is as credible as another.

The question of "which god" is a question which has a long- term history and a theological density, a history and a density which the book of Jeremiah seeks to exposit.[98] That is, each God is embedded in a certain history, and when one chooses a god, one chooses with it a history.[99]

The claims of Yahweh (as voiced in vv. 21-23) are rooted claims, and not just the ideological self-serving, ad hoc arguments of one party to an exilic dispute about power. The rootage of the claim goes back behind Jeremiah and the prophetic traditions to the earliest recitals of Israel, to Moses, and to some fundamental decisions about covenant at Sinai. These are not merely the biases of contemporary religious authorities (though that factor is not absent), but they are claims about the moral, communal dimension of social power and social order, and the force of religious legitimation that supports certain moral, communal claims.

98. I use the term "density" here with deliberate reference to the notion of "thick description" so crucial to Clifford Geertz. Geertz has written of the social process and reality in many places. I find especially helpful "Blurred Genius: The Refiguration of Social Thought," *American Scholar* 49 (1980): 165-179. In this article Geertz variously proposes that life is "a game," "a stage," "a text." For his more programmatic statement, see Clifford Geertz, *The Interpretation of Cultures* (New York: Basic Books, 1973), 3-30.

99. Manifestly the "queen of heaven" lacks a history, i.e., produced no continuing community of interpretation. In Tracy's terms, the queen of heaven generated no "classic." In adjudicating the rival claims of the two parties at this late date, it is evident that Yahweh and Yahwism has a kind of historical density not matched by the queen of heaven. It is the difference in density that tells in the canon-making claim of Yahwism.

To put the matter another way, the argument between the two claims concerns an intense interface between theological symbolization (creedal recital) and socioeconomic, political practice that brings together the holiness of God and the value of the neighbor. Such a claim in which the tradition of Jeremiah stands may or may not be true, but it is not a matter of indifference. The counterclaim of the queen of heaven (which has yielded no canonical, classical literature and no interpretive community) makes no witness about the holiness of God which refuses harnessing holy power for immediate social ends, and makes no claim about the value of the neighbor who is an end and not a means. In the end, a cavalier notion that one argument is as good as another is not wrong, but it is terribly innocent. It is innocent because it imagines that theological choices are not choices about social power. It is innocent because it imagines that an even-handed refusal to choose is in fact also a choice, not only about theological symbolization but also about social power. Such a perspective finally does not understand the linkage, explicit at least since Karl Marx, that every theological claim carries with it a socioeconomic claim.[100] And these claims are not a matter of indifference to the ongoing work of interpretation.

This chapter is remarkably honest in recognizing the difficulty of an advocated theological claim and in refusing to voice an easy answer. The last verses of the chapter do invite reflection. How is it that Zedekiah fell? Is the end simply raw power, so that Nebuchadnezzar finally has his turn? Or is there a moral texture even to such imperial power? The text intends to leave the Egyptian community of Jews haunted by that question. It may also leave us haunted in the same way for the same reason by the same question.

Baruch's Despair (45:1-5)

This brief chapter brings to a close the section of the book of Jeremiah commonly called the "Baruch document." Chapter 46 is the beginning

---

100. Marx's programmatic statements as quoted in McLellan, *The Thought of Karl Marx,* 22, are the criticism of heaven as thus transformed into the criticism of earth, the criticism of religion into the criticism of law, and the criticism of theology into the criticism of politics. See the comment on the passage by McLellan, 21-27.

of the Oracles against the Nations, which obviously constitute a very distinct body of material. Chapter 45 is not only dated to 605 B.C.E. ("the fourth year of Jehoiakim," v. 1), but explicitly refers to Baruch's writing of the Jeremiah scroll, an event described in ch. 36 (45:1). Moreover, the dating formula is exactly the same as in 36:1. Thus chs. 36 and 45 are explicitly related to each other, both of which feature Baruch. It is probable that these two chapters are placed as they are to provide brackets at the beginning and at the end of the narrative material commonly referred to as "the Baruch document." Thus ch. 45 gives closure to an account begun in ch. 36.[101]

This chapter is of peculiar interest because it expresses the concern of an individual, and shows the prophet responding to that individual. For our interpretation, the most important issue is to inquire about the identity of Baruch, to wonder why he merits special attention for the prophet and why he is given such structural importance in the redactional shaping of the book of Jeremiah. The easiest and perhaps most convincing thought about Baruch is that he was a person close to Jeremiah and loyal to the prophet at great risk. That is sufficient reason for this good word to him. Baruch greatly aided the prophetic vocation of Jeremiah, and now the prophet responds appropriately.

If, however, we pay careful attention to 43:2-3, we may suggest another way of understanding the Baruch of ch. 45. In 43:2-3 Baruch is blamed by the adversaries of Jeremiah for inciting Jeremiah to betray Jerusalem to the Babylonians. This has the effect of softening the direct criticism of Jeremiah. I suggest that the name "Baruch" may also have come in this material to be a cipher for all that body of opinion and all those persons who championed a pro-Babylonian view of the crisis in Jerusalem. Thus Baruch may be a tag-word for all those "right-minded" people who with Jeremiah equated the purpose of Yahweh with the oppression of Babylon. This is not to deny that Baruch is a person, but to suggest that he is a representative person. Mention of Baruch is a convenient way of referring to all those who stood with Jeremiah in his radical "Babylonian reading" of his time and place in God's history. This concluding oracle then is a commendation and vindication of those who have shared the faith and discernment of Jeremiah.

After the identification of the time and place of the oracle (45:1-2),

101. On the placement and function of this narrative unit, see Taylor.

the oracle itself combines two quite different rhetorical maneuvers. On the one hand, there is the intimate transaction of lament and response concerning Baruch. The lament of Baruch is ostensibly quoted and reiterated by Jeremiah, perhaps prayed to God by Jeremiah on behalf of Baruch. It is a cry of exhausted, unrequited faith which has run great risks, but without any good response from God. That Baruch finds "no rest" means that he has gotten the consequence appropriate to the wicked, but he himself is a righteous, obedient man. Thus the complaint of Baruch voices a question of theodicy, not unlike the question of Job, already anticipated in Jer. 12:1-4.

The response of God to Baruch through Jeremiah consists of two distinct phases. First, Baruch is rebuked for expecting and demanding too much.[102] The RSV expresses the warning in 45:5 as an interrogative. But it is not a question; it is, rather, a reprimand. Baruch seeks "great things" for himself, and he should not, because they are not to be given, and he has no ground on which to make such an insistence. That is, Baruch's risky faith is an end in itself and should not be utilized as a means toward a self-serving end.[103]

Second, soon after the rebuke by the prophet comes a promise (v. 5). Baruch will receive his life as "spoil." The phrase "prize of war" is a military phrase referring to captive booty that victorious soldiers can take home from their enemies. Baruch will not be given material war booty. There is indeed a victory, and there will be "booty." What Baruch will receive is more lean than normal war booty, but also more precious: his life! God promises Baruch that the outcome of risky faith is survival into the future. As is often the case in Jeremiah, the response of God does not adequately meet the terms of the complaint. Baruch is not the promised rest for which he prayed, but survival.

That promise of personal survival, however, is more poignant if we consider the countertheme of the divine oracle. In addition to the personal,

102. The uncompromising response to the complaint of Baruch, which is a reprimand, is not unlike the response made by Yahweh to the complaints of Jeremiah, which are also characteristically reprimands rather than reassurance; cf. 12:5-6; 15:19-21.

103. We do not know what "great things" are for Baruch; perhaps it is some ambition for leadership in the community of Babylonian Jews. The argument of Dearman, 411-421, suggests that such an ambition could be credible and cogent, given Baruch's apparent family ties. The same term *gedolot* is used in the same way in Ps. 131:1.

intimate word to Baruch, the occasion of the personal address is used for one more public oracle in vv. 4-5. Again, this prophetic response from God is in two parts. The oracle utilizes four of the strong verbs of 1:10.[104] The two negative verbs "break down and pluck up" will prevail over "plant and build." One last time, Jeremiah recites the sentence of death which God has decreed. In this odd usage of the four verbs, the action of "plant and build" is regarded as all in the past, for the present and immediate future belongs to the verbs of destruction. Moreover, the hard sentence now pronounced is not aimed simply at Jerusalem and Judah, but the scope is "all the land," perhaps "all the earth." That is, the known world of power arrangements in its totality is under assault from God; nothing will be spared.

This massive negative message is reinforced by the second public element in the oracle: "I am bringing evil upon 'all flesh.'" The "evil" (disaster) God will bring is commensurate with the evil found in the human community. The term "all flesh" is used elsewhere in exilic texts to refer to the whole of creation (cf. Gen. 6:12; 9:15; Isa. 40:5).

The public element of this oracle has a forward thrust as the Hebrew text of the book of Jeremiah is now arranged. The reference to "all the earth" and "all flesh" suggests a transnational scope to the oracle which anticipates the Oracles against the Nations in Jer. 46–51. Thus the themes of "prophet to the nations" and "pluck up and tear down" from 1:10 are here taken up to give closure to the book of Jeremiah.

In light of that massive judgment which dominates much of the tradition of Jeremiah, we are in a better position to appreciate the promise made to Baruch. There will be wholesale destruction, but there is an exception. The exception (remnant) is for those who have supported and accepted Jeremiah. The formula "your life as a prize of war" is used in 38:2 to refer generally to all those who submit to Babylon, who are a party to a Babylonian reading of Yahwistic reality. More specific use is made of the formula only in our text and one other time, to refer to Ebed-melech (39:18). Ebed-melech is also a functionary in Jerusalem who intervened to save the life of Jeremiah (cf. 38:7-13). Thus the two recipients of the formula, Ebed-melech and Baruch, have in common only that they have been allied with Jeremiah. It is clear that both of them did so at enormous personal risk.

104. See the analysis of these verbs in their several contexts by Taylor, 90-91.

Thus this brief oracle asserts *massive judgment* and an *exceptional rescue*. Christopher R. Seitz has suggested that the two recipients of the rescue formula, Ebed-melech and Baruch, function in the book of Jeremiah as did Caleb and Joshua in the book of Joshua.[105] That is, they are the two who had faith in the promises of God, who ran risks for their faith, and who therefore became the only survivors into the next generation of Israel, when all the others had been abandoned by God to death. This formula signals a self-conscious remnant theology and identifies the two addressees (Baruch and Ebed-melech) as the means by which God will open a faithful way into the future. The oracle concerns not only remnant theology but also a practical way forward in the community of faith, identifying those who are the carriers of real faith for the future. That these two have their lives ensures a survival of a faithful community in the midst of massive destruction.

There can be little doubt that Baruch at least (and perhaps Ebed-melech) is situated in the Babylonian community of Jews who are the wave of God's future (cf. Jer. 24).[106] This good word to Baruch thus offers a direct counterpoint to the oracles of 43:8-13; 44:1-30, which dismiss the Egyptian Jews to death. The destruction there is wholesale, as indicated by the unrestrained rhetoric of those oracles. Conversely, the good hope of Baruch, perhaps the quintessential Babylonian Jew, is voiced in very lean verbiage because it is a very lean hope. It is nonetheless hope, the most hope given in the midst of a world now destined for upheaval and chaos. The Oracles against the Nations which follow choreograph that coming upheaval and chaos. This little oracle asserts, in the face of the upheaval, that there is still a live hope and a concrete chance for faithful Jews.[107] That hope, as always for Israel, is based only in the promissory word of God.

---

105. Seitz, "Canonical Shape," 16-27; cf. Olson.

106. See Jer. 51:59-64, where the brother of Baruch is mandated to go to Babylon, so that it is not unreasonable that Baruch also went there.

107. Perhaps this oracle performs the same function as the concluding narrative report of 52:31-34 (2 Kgs. 25:27-30). On that passage, see Gerhard von Rad, "The Deuteronomic Theology of History in *I* and *II Kings*," *The Problem of the Hexateuch and Other Essays* (1966; repr. London: SCM and Philadelphia: Fortress, 1984), 219-220.

The Oracles against the Nations

Jeremiah 46:1–51:64

It is conventional in the prophetic literature of the OT to have collections of oracles which are Yahweh's word to (and against) the nations, as in Amos 1–2, Isa. 13–23, and Ezek. 25–32.[1] The history and development of this genre of prophetic speech is not well known to us.[2] It may be that the oracles emerged in the midst of liturgic celebrations of the sovereignty of Yahweh, and served to voice the claim that God's sovereign rule extended not simply over Israel but over all peoples. Thus in Ps. 96:10 the imperative is issued: "Say among the nations, 'The LORD is king!'" (NRSV).[3] The oracles may then be the concrete way in which it is announced to the nations that "The LORD is king."

That genre, which no doubt has liturgical antecedents, is utilized

---

1. A splendid introduction to the genre and various texts is Norman K. Gottwald, *All the Kingdoms of the Earth* (New York: Harper and Row, 1964). In this volume Gottwald is still focused on historical-critical questions and does not greatly reflect the penetrating social criticism of his later work.

2. The origin of the genre is perhaps liturgical. See one bold proposal in that regard by Aage Bentzen, "The Ritual Background of Amos 1:2–2:3," *Oudtestamentische Studiën* 8 (1950): 85-99.

3. See the discussion of the psalm and this formula in Walter Brueggemann, *Israel's Praise: Doxology against Idolatry and Ideology* (Philadelphia: Fortress, 1988), 29-53. There is no doubt that the formula used in the Jerusalem temple carried with it triumphalist tendencies for the Davidic house; cf. John Mauchline, "Implicit Signs of a Persistent Belief in the Davidic Empire," *Vetus Testamentum* 20 (1970): 287-303.

in the book of Jeremiah to implement the assertion of Jer. 1:10 that Jeremiah is summoned to be "a prophet to the nations." Indeed, the book of Jeremiah makes very little coherent sense unless the claims of the text are set initially in the context of the history and politics of the Near East. The life of Israel and Judah in the 7th and 6th cents. is dominated by Babylonian policy and power. It is the work of the book of Jeremiah to relate that imperial policy and power credibly to the claims of Yahwism.[4] The book of Jeremiah makes use of the genre Oracles against the Nations to assert the rule of Yahweh over the nations as well as over the people Israel.

In the present ordering of the Hebrew text of the book of Jeremiah, the Oracles against the Nations (chs. 46–51) are situated following the end of the Baruch narrative in ch. 45.[5] Indeed, ch. 45 functions in its present locus as a transition between the Baruch narrative and the Oracles against the Nations. As the last word of the Baruch narrative, ch. 45 asserts that Baruch, great defender of Jeremiah's message (and perhaps generator of pro-Babylonian ideology), will have his life as a prize of war (45:5). In contrast to that comforting word to Baruch, however, the same oracle asserts that God is about to bring disaster *(ra'ah)* against "all flesh" (v. 5). The phrase "all flesh" is paralleled in v. 4 with the phrase "the whole land."[6] That is, God is about to disrupt all present power arrangements. The statement provides an appropriate lead-in to the Oracles against the Nations.

These oracles in chs. 46–51 voice a single recurrent theme: God is sovereign. The nations must honor Yahweh's sovereignty. Honoring Yahweh's

4. I take this in a quite general sense concerning the broad flow of geopolitical power. I am most reluctant to become as specific or precise as is Holladay, *Jeremiah 2.*

5. The LXX, which places these texts in the midst of ch. 25, does not concern us here. It is evident that the collection of Oracles against the Nations was something of a free-floating collection. Differing placements in the final form of the text no doubt serve different canonical intentions.

6. The phrase can be rendered "all the land."

7. The oracles often concern abuse of Israel, but not always. Thus the other nation may be an agent of Yahweh against Israel, or the judgment of a nation may concern cruelties not perpetrated against Israel. This is noticeably the case in some of the oracles of Amos 1–2. Israel may be a subject of such oracles but is not necessarily present. The horizon of the genre can be more comprehensive.

sovereignty often entails positive regard for Yahweh's people.[7] Nations which do not honor God (and God's people) stand under judgment and will be destabilized. This argument is articulated in a variety of stylized forms. Because Yahweh is sovereign, no nation, no matter how powerful, is finally and ultimately an absolute value.

This theological argument is exceedingly difficult in our context of modernity, where the rule of Yahweh in public matters is intellectually problematic. I suggest, however, that Paul Kennedy's study, *The Rise and Fall of the Great Powers,* may be understood as a contemporary, secularized form of the same affirmation.[8] Kennedy proposes that every nation-state, because of its population, territory, and natural resources, is entitled to a certain share of the world's wealth. When a nation-state overreaches that share in an act of self-aggrandizement, that nation places itself in jeopardy and stands at risk in the process of world politics. To be sure, Kennedy bases his argument completely on economic, political, and military considerations; as might be expected, he introduces no explicit theological categories into his argument. In the end, nonetheless, Kennedy's argument is that no nation-state dares to conduct itself as though it were an ultimate end in itself. A viable and survivable nation-state must understand its own life and security in the context of a larger dynamic to which it must submit and of which it is a part.

Mutatis mutandis, I suggest that the argument of Kennedy is the same as the argument in the prophetic Oracles against the Nations. That "larger dynamic" which relativizes and endlessly jeopardizes every absolutist political claim is articulated in the prophets as the will of Yahweh. The prophet Jeremiah and the other prophets were not obscurantist supernaturalists. Perceiving the world theologically, they were able to discern that when a nation violates the larger dynamic of the political process which has a coherent moral purpose, trouble comes. Thus it is indeed possible to understand the role of Babylon in terms of Yahweh's governance, or alternatively (with Kennedy), in terms of a larger relativizing dynamic. My point is not to claim Kennedy for the theological process, but to suggest that the prophetic categories of criticism of the nations are not remote from our own sense of the historical process. Yahweh is the character in the drama of world history who overrides national pretensions and chastens every self-serving idolatry. It is this

8. Kennedy, *Rise and Fall.*

character to whom the nations must finally make reference, and with whom they must come to terms.

Having affirmed the theme of Yahweh's sovereignty, the Oracles against the Nations in Jeremiah require a more nuanced consideration. As we have seen in the Baruch narrative, the pivotal reality of Babylon decisively shapes the view of international reality held in the book of Jeremiah. Thus it will not do simply to treat chs. 46–51 as an undifferentiated mass of materials on a common theme. We may make three differentiations in the materials that are appropriate in the context of the book of Jeremiah.

(1) The oracles concern Egypt, the Philistines, Moab, Ammon, Edom, Damascus, Kedar, Elam, and Babylon. Although all these oracles belong to the same genre, a distinction is to be made in the context of the book of Jeremiah between the oracle against Babylon (chs. 50–51) and all the other oracles (chs. 46–49). Two formal grounds for such a distinction can be noted. First, the oracle concerning Babylon is much longer than any of the others. Second, that oracle stands in the final position, clearly designed to conclude the collection.

The primary distinction, however, is not finally formal but substantive. In the context of Jeremiah, it is Babylon who is "the destroyer" of all the other peoples. That is, Babylon is likely the agent of Yahweh in working trouble for the nations in chs. 46–49. Such a view is congruent with the historical performance of Babylon under Nebuchadnezzar, who did indeed trouble the other nations. Moreover, such a role for Babylon fits the conviction of the Jeremiah tradition that Nebuchadnezzar is the servant of Yahweh working the will of Yahweh (cf. 25:9; 27:6; 43:10). Thus Nebuchadnezzar is the tool of Yahweh in governing and chastening the other peoples. The text implicitly voices the triumph of Babylon over the nations, and a great affirmation for Babylon. That is, I suggest, the first point concerning the oracles of chs. 46–49. Yahweh triumphs over the nations through the work of Babylon.

In the second part of this corpus, however, the tradition does a complete about-face. The second point is that in chs. 50–51 Babylon in turn is decisively crushed and its power is nullified. Penultimately, the purposes of Yahweh converge with the interests of Babylon. Ultimately, God's purposes converge with no earthly arrangement, and certainly not with Babylon. Thus the book of Jeremiah is penultimately pro-Babylonian, until the very end. At the end, however, in an act of profound hope and assurance for exiled Jews (exiled by Babylon), Babylon is nullified — which permits a homecoming for exiled Jews.[9]

The prose commentary in the Babylonian oracle (cf. 50:8-10, 18-20, 44-46) anticipates the rise of the next world power (Persia) who will overwhelm Babylon. This oracular tradition, however, does not simply provide political commentary on the coming and going of nations. It is a theological assertion that finally no world power, not even mighty Babylon toward whom Jeremiah (and Baruch) are so well disposed, can claim special privilege with Yahweh. The text asserts that Babylon has finally run afoul of Yahweh in its pretension. Alternatively, Kennedy might say that Babylon has overreached in its pretension and is sure to fall. The very Babylon so useful to Yahweh (and to Jeremiah) finally is destroyed by Yahweh (Persia). Such a sovereign destruction is the ground of hope for Jews in the 6th century. The oracles are arranged in a two-stage way, first celebrative of Babylon (chs. 46–49), then utterly dismissive (on theological grounds) of Babylon (chs. 50–51).

(2) The oracles against the other nations (chs. 46–49) seem to be all of a piece. We may only notice that Egypt stands in the first position (ch. 46). Assuming such an arrangement is not happenstance, we may suggest two reasons for this priority. First, Egypt is named first as the major power which is able to counter and cope with Babylon. Given the pro-Babylonian propensity of the book of Jeremiah, Egypt as the main counter to Babylon would be perceived as the greatest threat, and so needs to be dealt with first and most decisively. Of all the powers who resist the Yahweh-Babylon axis, Egypt is foremost.

Second, the Baruch narrative ended in chs. 43–44 with harsh words against Egypt and against the Jews who fled to Egypt. In 43:10-13; 44:30 the text is specific and concrete in its dismissal of Egypt. To be sure, there stands between the concrete judgment of chs. 43–44 against Egypt and the oracle of ch. 46 the Baruch oracle in ch. 45. Nonetheless, the placement of the oracle against Egypt in ch. 46 helps make a direct connection between the Baruch narrative which ends with Egypt and the Oracles against the Nations which begin with Egypt. Yahweh has pledged to work

9. In a later generation, Isa. 40–55 celebrates the fall of Babylon as a permit wrought by God so that the exiled Jews can go home. In Jer. 50–51 the tradition of Jeremiah moves toward this affirmation, but does not yet make such a complete affirmation.

a judgment against "all the earth" (45:4) and against "all flesh" (45:5). Such a massive judgment begins against Egypt.

Thus the primacy of Egypt in the Oracles against the Nations lets the rule of Yahweh be initiated most aggressively against Yahweh's (and Babylon's) greatest enemy. The capacity of Egypt to evoke such hostile commentary is no doubt rooted in 7th-6th cent. politics, where Egypt is a primary threat to a pro-Babylonian reading of political reality. That historical-political reality concerning Egypt is perhaps reinforced for the prophetic text by seeing the ignoble flight of the Jews to Egypt (chs. 42–44) as the full circle which began in Exod. 1–15.[10] All the pharaohs from the time of Moses until the 6th cent. fall under a common negative symbolization in ancient Israel. All of them are dismissed as the quintessential enemy of Israel and of Yahweh. For all these reasons, historical-political and symbolic, Egypt receives special focus in this corpus. Egypt is a primary cipher for all that resists the purposes of Yahweh.

(3) The Oracles against the Nations end with an odd narrative in Jer. 51:59-64. Such a narrative is not at all usual in such a collection, and it clearly departs from the genre. Our purpose is not to comment on the historicity of the narrative about Seraiah. Rather, we consider the function of the narrative in the arrangement of the text in the book of Jeremiah. This remarkable narrative permits the text concerning Babylon to stand as an enduring testimony against Babylon. It is as though chs. 46–49 are only prelude to chs. 50–51. In the end, it is the defeat of Babylon and none other that matters to the exiled Jews and to the book of Jeremiah. If Yahweh is to evidence sovereignty anywhere, it will most compellingly be sovereignty over Babylon.

The role of Seraiah, brother of Baruch, is especially important for the shape of the book of Jeremiah. (Again, our concern is a structural, not a historical one.) The text is arranged so that the two brothers, Baruch and Seraiah, are preoccupied with two scrolls which well embody the two-stage philosophy of history in the book of Jeremiah (cf. ch. 36 on Baruch's scroll and then, to a lesser extent, Baruch with the property document of ch. 32). On the one hand, as we have seen, Baruch is the great pro-Babylon voice who believes Jerusalem must submit in order to trust Yahweh. As a pro-Babylonian, Baruch can see that it is indeed God's will that Jerusalem be "plucked up and torn down" by Babylon. On the

10. See Friedman, "From Egypt to Egypt," 189-192.

other hand, the future of the Jews, the future of "building and planting," depends upon being free and having the power of Babylon broken. This latter requirement is the burden of the scroll and witness of the second brother, Seraiah. Thus the two brothers in turn are custodians of two scrolls that celebrate Babylon and then nullify Babylon.

In the two-stage view of Babylon, the two brothers evidence how it is that God, through the historical process, first "plucks up and tears down" (through Babylon) and then "builds and plants" (beyond Babylon). Both turns of history vis-à-vis the empire are evidence of Yahweh's rule over Israel and over the nations. In the end, the Oracles against the Nations are a theological statement, not to be explained away by historical correlations. In the end, the historical process, the rise and fall of the great powers, is an unmistakable witness to the relentless rule of Yahweh.

Oracle against Egypt (46:1-28)

In the Oracles against the Nations Yahweh's governance over the international world around Jerusalem is asserted. In the assertion of this claim, Egypt is addressed first. In the pro-Babylonian tendency of the Jeremiah tradition, Egypt is the main diplomatic alternative to Babylon, and is considered a deathly alternative.[11] Thus on political grounds Egypt most needs to be brought under the aegis of Yahweh. Moreover, Egypt has come to be a primal metaphor for worldly power that is organized against the purposes of God. For both political and metaphorical-theological reasons, Egypt is named first in this list of nations, for when Egypt is brought under the rule and purpose of Yahweh, in effect Yahweh's governance will be fully established. This extended discussion concerning Egypt is organized into three rhetorical units (46:3-12, 13-24, and 25-26). After this relentless and sustained address concerning Egypt, the unit culminates with a good and reassuring word to Israel (vv. 27-28). Before the good word for Israel can be spoken, however, the hard word against Egypt must be effected.

Before taking up the actual oracle, the text in its present arrangement is introduced by two editorial comments, first a general foreword to the collection (v. 1) and then a historical note concerning Egypt (v. 2).

11. On the theological issues in the Exile as pertains to the Jeremiah tradition, see Seitz, *Theology in Conflict*.

46:1 This verse functions as introduction to the entire unit of chs. 46–51, connecting the rule (word) of Yahweh and the future of the nations. Jeremiah, the speaker of these oracles, is the one who connects *the rule of Yahweh* and *the future of the nations*. That connection is not self-evident; it is established by the daring and critical oracles that follow. The final phrase of 46:1, "concerning the nations," provides an important clue to the final form of the Jeremiah text, for this phrase deliberately refers back to the mandate of 1:10. From the outset, according to the "call narrative," the prophecy (and book) of Jeremiah have been concerned with God's governance of the nations through the words of Jeremiah. Thus 1:10 and 46:1 form an inclusio, framing the book of Jeremiah and providing a literary context for the concern for Israel and Jerusalem within the inclusion. These framing verses suggest, in tension with the materials in between, that the book of Jeremiah in the end is concerned with the rule of Yahweh and the coming of Yahweh's kingdom over the kingdoms of the world (cf. Rev. 11:15). A serious hearing of this textual tradition requires us to think again about that large governance which in the end transcends even the well-being of Israel.[12]

46:2 The text moves specifically to implement the mandate of 1:10 and the concrete substance of 46:1. The initial words, "concerning Egypt" (NRSV), are daring and abrupt. Indeed, the utterance of this phrase makes an outrageous theological claim, for it is not easy or obvious that Yahweh and Egypt belong together in the same world of power or in the same utterance. By the utterance of this phrase, the text preempts our field of perception. The claim, that a speaker for Yahweh should address the great Egyptian empire, should leave us dazzled. The warrant given for the utterance is no more compelling warrant than we have seen heretofore in the book of Jeremiah: it is a speech from Yahweh. It is the "word of Yahweh," a word beyond known reason and conventional logic that dares draw the empire into Israel's theological discourse.

This verse seeks to give historical placement for the oracle that follows, though the specific historical placement is subordinated to the canonical-

---

12. It is envisioned that all the nations will be either willingly or reluctantly brought under the rule of Yahweh. This is evident in the Enthronement Psalms, in the Yahwist theology, as well as in the prophets. On the rule of Yahweh as a political construct, see Wright, "The Nations in Hebrew Prophecy."

theological claim asserted. The claim concerns the rule of Yahweh over the empire in every time and in all times. The historical specificity asserted is the battle of Carchemish in 605 B.C.E., when Babylon emerged as a world power, thus jeopardizing Egyptian hegemony.[13] This prose editorial comment appeals to the outcome of that battle as a reference point for Yahweh's governance amid world powers. That is, the outcome of the battle is claimed as a show of Yahweh's will and power. Notice that the connection between *theological claim* and *historical experience* depends on the large, bold assertion of the prophet.[14] The Egypt now addressed is a "Carchemish-conditioned" empire, when everything about the old hegemony had become unglued, and its vaunted power was now exposed as fraudulent. Everything is placed in danger for Egypt, and everything is now open for the peoples long intimidated by Egypt. The danger and the openness are here acknowledged to be Yahweh's fresh action in the world. The prophetic world governed by Yahweh becomes more daring and imaginative, and in such a casting, more ominous for the empire.

46:3-12   The poem invites us into the middle of a dangerous and uneven battle. The poem is not completely clear, because the antecedents of the pronouns are ill-defined. The poem is not a report of a battle, but it is an act of imagination whereby the poet construes a harsh conflict and a rout of the great empire. The purpose of the poetry is to redescribe international reality. International powers seem so stable, so entrenched, so enduring. The poetry intends to subvert all such presumed political givens and to propose an alternative scenario for the shape of worldly power.

In vv. 3-4 we do not know who is addressed with the series of imperatives. It is a summons to battle, a summons and dispatch of well-armed, well-prepared, responsive troops. They are to move immediately into action; they are to do so because the speaker has already noticed that the enemy is in frantic retreat (vv. 5-6). Early in the Jeremiah tradition the poetry speaks of a great invading army and the humiliating rout of

13. On the battle, see Miller and Hayes, *A History of Ancient Israel and Judah*, 403.

14. It is evident that the claim of the oracle is not self-evident. It is rather an imaginative construal that reads reality in this way rather than in some other way. On the power of imagination to "take as," see David J. Bryant, *Faith and the Play of Imagination* (Macon: Mercer University Press, 1989), 115-128 and *passim*.

Judah and Jerusalem (5:15-17; 6:1-8, 22-26). Now the poetic strategy is to take up the same sort of language and apply it to the seemingly invincible Egyptians. The rhetoric of invasion and attack is the same as in the earlier poems, but now the rhetoric has been redirected from Judah toward Egypt. The attacked are said to be in complete panic; their situation is so desperate that they cannot even escape. They are indeed in a hopeless situation.

The poet has shrewdly withheld identification of any of the actors in this scenario. We do not know who is attacking (46:3-4) or who is retreating (vv. 5-6). Now in vv. 7-9 we are to have the earlier dramatic portrayal specified. In v. 7 we are asked about the cast of characters. The question provides a hint of the answer: "Who is this rising like the Nile, the great surging river?" (author's translation). The "Nile question" (v. 7) prepares us for the "Egypt answer" (v. 8). Now finally we are told: Egypt! That is who is surging desperately in retreat. Egypt — arrogant, powerful, threatening — had thought to "cover the earth" with its aggressive drive for domination (v. 8). Verse 9, however, counters that imperial intention with disaster and abrupt imperatives. Horses, chariots, warriors with shield and bow, all are now summoned and addressed. They are addressed like the invader in v. 4, only now it is the one attacked who is addressed. The question is asked (v. 7), the answer is given (v. 8), and now in a mocking way the Egyptians (men of Ethiopia, Put, and Lud) are addressed and advised to go out in retreat (v. 9). Thus vv. 7-9 portray an international conflict between the old established power of Egypt, now on the run, and the new power of the north that arises ominously against them. We are able to see that the new power in the north is addressed in vv. 3-6, and the old fading power in vv. 7-9. The shape of the rhetoric helps present a drastic contrast between awesome power and frantic retreat, between Babylon on the attack and Egypt in desperate withdrawal.

Thus far the poem could be only ordinary war poetry, dramatizing the waxing and waning of battle, the rise and fall of nations, the sudden disarray of a long vaunted power.[15] It is not until we reach v. 10, however,

---

15. The sudden disarray of a long vaunted power seems on the face of it to be implausible. Yet in our very own experience, the abrupt demise of the power of the Soviet Union makes clear such a realistic possibility. The text itself does not depend on concrete examples, but proceeds in confidence of the power of its own speech to redescribe reality. We can nonetheless observe a convergence between the intention of the poetry and our own recent, observable public experience.

that the prophetic claims of the oracle are made explicit. We could have forgotten, in the poem and in the powerful imagery of battle, that this poem is prophetic, Jeremianic, Yahwistic. Now abruptly in v. 10, everything is named and becomes focused. The day of battle is a day with a special reference and sponsor and purpose. The day belongs to the LORD, "Yahweh of hosts." The naming of God is in an exaggerated military formula (twice named LORD, God of the troops) to accent God's powerful, decisive presence in the conflict. This assertion redescribes what is happening. What we witness at first glimpse is simply a conflict between Egypt and "the north." The naming of the name of Yahweh now provides a clue for what is in fact happening. This is no ordinary context, no routine battle. This is not simply a battle between world powers, war as an instrument of state politics. This is a theological happening, attesting to the decisive power and purpose of Yahweh.

And the purpose? It is that God may avenge God's own foe! That is, the real enemy of Egypt is not the Babylonians; it is the God of Israel. We are not told wherein Egypt has offended Yahweh. We only know that the full establishment of Yahweh's governance requires the terrible demise of Egypt.[16]

Perhaps the poetry against Egypt takes Judean listeners clear back to the Exodus, and we are hearing one more reiteration of the old, foundational hostility between Pharaoh and Yahweh, a hostility primally voiced in the Exodus liturgy (Exod. 1–15). More likely we are in the midst of a theological verdict pertaining to the 7th-6th cents., when the flow of the future is to Babylon (cf. Ezek. 28).[17] Egypt is judged by the Jeremiah tradition to be a deathly impediment to the coming ordering of world power. Either way, as an allusion to the Exodus or as a more contemporary critique of Egyptian power, we have a theological verdict and not simply a political analysis. That verdict is that God will take up the whole of the Egyptian army as a bloody "sacrifice" (Jer. 46:10).

The rhetoric shocks us. This is not the sort of poetry that suits our propensity to reconciliation. This is indeed brutalizing rhetoric. I suggest three ways to understand what happens in such a text. First, the poetry is

16. On the ways in which Yahweh established rule, see Mendenhall, *The Tenth Generation*, 69-104.
17. Cf. Donald E. Gowan, *When Man Becomes God.* Pittsburgh Theological Monograph 6 (Pittsburgh: Pickwick, 1975), 69-92.

no doubt making use of rhetorical conventions.[18] This is the stock formulation of war poetry that inevitably includes a theological (self-serving, ideological) dimension. The convention mocks the enemy for the sake of our well-being. Second, such brutalizing poetry does not claim to be evenhanded and nonpartisan, but no doubt reflects a quite partisan judgment made in the midst of heavy conflict where one cannot abdicate or practice neutrality. In this poetry, there is no ambiguity about where the future lies and where the right is being enacted. Third, however, this use of literary convention and the partisan judgment of the poem are in the service of a larger theological claim. Yahweh stands at the center of this harsh dispute. Yahweh stalks the map of the Near East as only Yahweh is authorized to do. The nations will sooner or later have to come to terms with Yahweh's powerful will. International politics does not consist simply in power and cunning and strategy and ruthlessness. There is a purpose that overrides all such human posturing. Whoever stands over against that transcendent purpose, as Egypt here does, is sure to fail.

After the massive theological assertion of v. 10, vv. 11-12 provide a dramatic contrast. Now there is almost a tone of pity and momentary sympathy. The poet again uses the old formula concerning healing in Gilead. As there had been no healing in Gilead for beloved Israel (cf. 8:22), so Gilead offers no remedy for Egypt! As Israel had been beyond healing, so Egypt is utterly beyond healing. Egypt now receives what God's own people had received earlier. There remains for the empire only shame and cry, a cry that fills the earth (cf. Exod. 11:6). In the end there is "stumbling and falling" (Jer. 46:12), the same words sounded in v. 6. The poet crafts the way in which Yahweh prevails; and when Yahweh prevails, Egypt is gone!

46:13-24 The same themes of conflict and defeat are sounded again, though now the imagery is more poignant. The prose introduction of v. 13 provides a simple political summary: it is Babylon (Nebuchadnezzar) against Egypt. That is so simple, and anyone could have seen such a visible development. Poets, however, can never stand so far outside events and take them so simply as would other observers. The poet wants us to go

18. On the genre of war oracles in relation to Jeremiah, see Duane L. Christensen, *Transformations of the War Oracle in Old Testament Prophecy.* Harvard Dissertations in Religion 3 (Missoula: Scholars Press, 1975), 183-280.

inside the text, inside the experience of pain and defeat and humiliation. Our work is not just to draw a geopolitical conclusion (easy enough), but to linger over the hurt that belongs to imperial arrogance, and to notice the futility of such restless domination.

In the initial statement (vv. 14-17) the invading enemy is not even mentioned. The poet focuses completely on Egypt. The key cities of the empire are named — Memphis, Tahpanhes — centers of power, now to be centers of pain and shame.[19] The poet speaks in ironic imperative. These great imperial cities are to "stand ready and be prepared," but prepared only for wholesale defeat. The massiveness and depth of defeat are evidenced in the retreat of the god Apis (v. 14). As the god leaves the field in shame, so the armies of the empire become hopeless. And why has the god fled? Because Yahweh has defeated him. Yahweh has done so directly, according to this rhetoric — no enemy army, no mediating agent. This is the rhetoric of a daring poet who is willing to read historical reality theologically. As in the old exodus, the holy God overrides the gods of the Egyptian empire. And when the gods of the empire are defeated, the empire is indeed lost.

One more time the word pair "stumble-fall" is repeated (v. 16; cf. vv. 6, 12); Egypt's last strategy is a retreat back to the safety of the invulnerable homeland. The ambitious imperial claims of Egypt, which extended far up into the Fertile Crescent, far beyond its conventional sphere of influence, have been defeated. The poet cannot resist one more cutting jab at the failed empire. Verse 17 is almost like a political cartoon in which the pharaoh is mocked as the boisterous leader who fails in the moment of crisis. Of course such a ruler will fail, because he seeks to act against the purpose of Yahweh. Israel's poets have known since Moses that pharaohs will always lose when Yahweh prevails.

The next section of the poem begins with an oath or decree in the mouth of God (vv. 18-24). This is Yahweh's only substantive appearance in this section of the poem. Yahweh does only one thing, but it is done in the name of Yahweh's massive military authority. The one who swears is the

---

19. The mention of Tahpanhes is here made without special emphasis. Nonetheless, the attentive reader cannot fail to remember that it was to Tahpanhes that the Jews led by Johanan fled and to which they carried Jeremiah (43:7-8; 44:1). Thus in connecting the Oracle against the Nations corpus (chs. 46–51) to the Baruch document (chs. 36–45), that Egyptian city is now mentioned as a place under threat. Almost incidentally, the threat sounded in chs. 43–44 is here given added emphasis.

"LORD of the troops." Yahweh authorizes one "who will come" (v. 18). That is all. Yahweh does nothing more; the coming one is not named anywhere else in this poem. All else that happens is human action, all conflict enacted by human agents. But what a coming one! He is like Mt. Tabor towering all alone over the hills, like Carmel, jutting out prominently and all alone into the sea, massive in presence, sure to be noticed, unavoidable, dominating the entire landscape. The struggle for power and domination in the Fertile Crescent is an uneven one. The poet, however, does not explicate. The poet avoids concrete political reference, because he wants Yahweh (specified only once) to be the key factor in this geopolitical revolution. The "coming one" evokes a pathos-filled imperative for Egypt: "prepare for exile" (v. 19)![20] The judgment on Memphis echoes the earlier judgment on Jerusalem. God has decreed a terrible dismantling of royal power; the same "coming one" who ended Jerusalem will also end Memphis.

The juxtaposition of vv. 18-19 is telling. In v. 18 the "coming one" is sketched out with powerful, exaggerated rhetoric. The counterpart of Egypt (v. 19) bespeaks failure and defeat, a pitiful counterpart to Yahweh, unable to perform any effective role in the drama of power.

Verses 20-24 are framed with the ominous phrase "from the north" (vv.· 20, 24; cf. 1:13-15). The one who comes is not named. We know his identity. It is not his identity that counts, however; it is his detailed characterization that interests the poet. This ominous one from the north is like a "gadfly" who comes to sting, before whom Egypt, the "beautiful heifer," is helpless.[21] The image then changes abruptly. The "gadfly" (46:20) becomes "enemies marching in force" with axes, attacking the land and destroying primitive forests (vv. 22-23). The figures of an insect (v. 20) and an invading army (vv. 22-23) are brought together by the poet in the image of the locust (v. 23). The locust is both a pesky insect and an invading, irresistible army, too numerous to count, irresistible, destructive, intimidating, making one utterly helpless.

Against that awesome power from the north, Egypt is a "beautiful heifer," attractive, dumb, helpless, vulnerable, and exposed (v. 20). The image of Egypt shifts slightly; the "beautiful heifer" is now the "fatted calf" (v. 21). The first image was of the empire, the second is of the soldiers.

---

20. The phrasing and imagery of "baggage for exile" is the same as in Ezek. 12:7-16; only here it is the great empire who is to pack for deportation.

21. Holladay, *Jeremiah 2,* 331-32, reads "horsefly" instead of "gadfly."

They are the ones entrusted with resistance to "the coming one," but they are in fact only a valuable, attractive sacrifice, to be done handily to death. At the edge of the images of heifer and fatted calf, military language again intrudes language of retreat, calamity, and destruction (v. 21).

The image of Egypt now changes. The heifer has become a serpent, quietly, stealthily sneaking away, sneaking to safety, but a creature whose very name is one of shame and humiliation (v. 22). The serpent may seek to hide in the underbrush, but the coming one will destroy it. Even in the form of a devious, hiding snake, Egypt cannot escape.

This poet voices a remarkable richness of images: beautiful *heifer*, exposed to the pain-inflicting *gadfly*, the *fatted calf* vulnerable and designed only for sacrifice (cf. v. 10), the *serpent* vulnerable to the woodsmen, utterly exposed; finally comes the *locust* devouring all that is still standing (cf. v. 14; 5:17 on devouring). The richness of the imagery serves to dramatize and detail the uneven contest, the hopelessness of Egypt and its sure defeat before the irresistible invader. The images of Egypt are all of passivity and vulnerability. There is nothing Egypt can do or will do. The images of the "one who comes" bespeak aggressive and effective activity. The conflict is so uneven, and the outcome is so unavoidable. Jeremiah 46:24 does not advance the rhetoric, but only reiterates the now familiar themes and drives to the inevitable conclusion: "Egypt will be handed over!"

46:25-26   These prose verses now draw the explicit historical verdict that has been sketched in the foregoing poetry. It is as though the prose intends to name and identify (and inevitably flatten) the metaphors of the preceding. This explanatory comment is dominated by two powerful first person verbs, the first a participle and the second a perfect verb. These two verbs place Yahweh at the center of the action, attributing to Yahweh both enormous resolve and enormous power. The first verb asserts Yahweh's mustering of power against Egypt: "I am bringing punishment" *(pqd)*. The verb is followed by six uses of the preposition "against" *('yal)*: against Pharaoh, against Egypt, against its gods, against its kings, against Pharaoh, against all who trust Pharaoh. The grammar could not more relentlessly voice Yahweh's "againstness."[22]

---

22. See the same negative preposition in a series in Isa. 2:12-16; Jer. 1:15; and in 48:18 with a weaker preposition. In each case God is said to be "against" everything that is established.

This sweeping negative assertion is then explicated in v. 26 with the second strong verb, "I will deliver" *(ntn)*. Now we learn that the "againstness" of God is to be by the hand (power) of Nebuchadnezzar, who is now explicitly named as "the coming one" (v. 18; cf. v. 13). In this section the strong verb is followed by a threefold use of "the hand of"; "into the hand of those who seek their life, into the hand of Nebuchadnezzar, into the hand of his officers." This threefold usage matches the sixfold preposition of v. 25. The two series of uses thus juxtapose the unequal adversaries. In v. 25 the sixfold inventory names all those who are now at risk. The threefold usage in v. 26 counters by naming those who will prevail. Thus vv. 25 and 26 respectively explicate the "beautiful heifer," who is six times vulnerable, and the "gadfly," who is three times powerful. The outcome of this confrontation could hardly be more dramatically articulated.

At the end of v. 25 we are offered one more surprise: "afterward!" (cf. 25:12; 27:7, 20). The text dares to comment upon ancient Near Eastern politics, to anticipate the destiny of Egypt after the hegemony of Nebuchadnezzar which has been the subject of the poetry. One can, of course, imagine that this concluding assertion only reflects historical experience after Nebuchadnezzar, for the Babylonian threat against Egypt could not be sustained very long. On such historical grounds, the line seems to retreat from the sweeping rhetoric of the preceding. The line, however, need not be taken simply as a reflection of subsequent historical events. It can be taken canonically as awareness that even Nebuchadnezzar and even Babylon are penultimate. The Babylonian army and empire are not the real determinants of the historical process, and even such a massive political construct as Babylon finally cannot endure.

If the Babylonian achievement is penultimate, then what is ultimate? Who is then ultimate? It is Yahweh who governs the two strong verbs of 46:25-26. It is Yahweh who speaks this oracle, who concludes "says the LORD." It is Yahweh and not Babylon who will fix the long-term destiny of Egypt. That long-term destiny willed by Yahweh is that Egypt will live as in "the days of old." The Babylonian invasion is an episode for Egypt, not an irreversible development. After this episode which lacks staying power, God intends even Egypt to live in its own land, as it used to be. Egypt had indeed been too ambitious (cf. v. 8). When that imperial ambition is defeated, however, Egypt can return to its proper role in its proper sphere.[23] God does not want to destabilize this great power endlessly.

The great powers, however, must learn (again and again, it appears) that they are not autonomous agents free to act according to their unbridled power. The historical process, governed by Yahweh, will in savage and cunning ways curb such arrogance, leaving the aggressor unhealed (v. 11) and displaced (v. 19). The large future of the historical process cannot be nullified, even by imperial pretension. The purpose of Yahweh, who stands sovereign within the historical process, cannot be mocked. There is indeed an "afterward," even for Egypt. The route from self-serving aggressiveness to well-being in one's own proper sphere, however, is a route of terror, brutality, and suffering. Egypt stands, in the final form of the text, as a cipher for all the great powers, who learn again and again, so reluctantly and so painfully.

The poem, cast in the voice of Yahweh, exhibits a sober, balanced view of the public process of history. It refutes and rejects a view which says that the historical process is endlessly submissive to raw power. It asserts, as the only viable alternative to raw power, an ordered governance from Yahweh which limits, curbs, and chastens. One option for the public process (embodied here by Pharaoh) allows no Yahweh to speak or act. The other option, carried in the mouth of the prophet, portrays Yahweh indefatigably at the center of the international process. To be a prophet "to the nations" (cf. 1:10) means to portray the process of public power as a process under a larger purpose and not as an end in itself.

The final phrase of 46:26 is telling: "says the LORD." Yahweh is the ultimate and decisive speaker of the historical process. Yahweh does not want to force the great powers out of history, but Yahweh does relentlessly insist that the great powers must accept their proper and therefore limited role. That Egypt will again be inhabited means that it belongs inalienably in the public process. Egypt's life and power are, however, penultimate, as is Nebuchadnezzar's great conquest. What prevails in the end is only "says the LORD."

23. A return to a proper sphere of power, influence, and ambition is what Kennedy, *The Rise and Fall of the Great Powers,* urges and believes possible. That is, an overextended great power need not disintegrate. It can be changed for a realistic chance at life. The anticipation of this text and the analysis of Kennedy are agreed in an alternative to destruction.

46:27-28 Throughout this long poem Israel, Judah, and Jerusalem have not been mentioned (except for the historical notation of v. 2). Indeed, Israel, Judah, and Jerusalem are nowhere on the horizon of this poem. The issue of the poem concerns the imperial power of Egypt coming to terms with the governance of Yahweh, without reference to any privileged role for the biblical community. Verses 25-26 have provided something of an interpretive conclusion for the poem.

Then, however, vv. 27-28 appear at the end of the poem as an extrapolation from the preceding action. These verses constitute an odd, unexpected development in the poem. Two things are clear. First, the assertion of the rule of Yahweh over Egypt has crucial derivative implications for Israel. It is not that Yahweh has taken action against Egypt for the sake of Israel; God's actions are only because of Egypt's arrogant overextendedness, which mocks Yahweh. Nonetheless, when Egypt comes under the governance of Yahweh, as it now will do through the agency of Babylon, Israel finds itself in a new position. Thus the odd continuation of the Egyptian poem in vv. 27-28 dramatically asserts that benefit to Israel is derivative from Yahweh's sovereign dealing with the nations. This odd derivative effect is nowhere more clearly articulated than in Ezek. 36.[24] God's actions are undertaken not because God loves Israel, but because Yahweh will be honored (Ezek. 36:22, 32). Yahweh's desire to be honored by the nations benefits Israel. So in our passage, God's actions are not because God loves Israel, but these acts nonetheless benefit Israel.

Second, the benefit to Israel in the preceding poetry is stated in a traditional formulation we have already considered in Jer. 30:10-11. As the "war oracle" against Egypt in 46:3-4, 9 uses old formulations which were used against Judah in chs. 4–6, so now the good news for Israel also uses an old formula already used in ch. 30. What interests us is not the text itself (already discussed in its locus in 30:10-11), but the placement, use, and intent of the text in this location.

These verses constitute a salvation oracle, with the double assertion, "Fear not" (46:27-28).[25] Each assuring imperative is followed (as is characteristic of the form) with a reason why Israel should not fear. The reasons are (1) "I will save you," and (2) "I am with you." This is the God who

24. See Brueggemann, *Hopeful Imagination,* 68-87; and Gowan, *Eschatology in the Old Testament.*

25. See Conrad, *Fear Not Warrior,* 108-115.

will end exile, bringing Jacob safely home and giving security. This is the God who will deal severely with the exile-causing nations. Thus the oracle concerns the end of Judah's exile. In terms of its specific statement, this is an odd announcement here, because it seems concerned with Babylon who caused exile, rather than with Egypt, the subject of vv. 1-26. That, however, only evidences that these two verses are an old poem reused and redirected.

Now the salvation oracle, the homecoming, and the gift of well-being and security are connected to the judgment against Egypt. The oracle of Yahweh against Egypt has made the world a safe place for Israel.

As v. 28 sorts out Yahweh's intention for the nations and Israel's benefit, the poem uses two rhetorical structures which are very different. On the one hand, there is a contrast between the host nations of exile and the people of Jacob. For the former, there is "a full end." For Jacob there is no "full end," that is, Jacob can and will endure beyond exile.[26] On the other hand, the last two lines of the unit concern only Jacob, the other nations now being absent. The destiny of Jacob at the hands of Yahweh is twofold and delicate. There will be appropriate chastening, as when a father chastens a son. The historical process has abundantly delivered the chastening. Jacob will not be off scot-free (cf. Isa. 40:2). The counterpoint to this verse is unstated. We expect a statement that says, "but I will not destroy." This is not stated but is perhaps implicit in the adjective, "in just measure" *(mishpat);* that is, the chastening is appropriate punishment, but not capricious or ultimate nullification. This carefully wrought verse delicately asserts that Judah's position vis-à-vis Yahweh is very different from the position of the nations that host the Exile. That difference is perhaps rooted in the old covenant tradition, though nothing is said of covenant.

26. On the contrast of "make an end" and "not make an end," see also Amos 9:8; Jer. 4:27; 5:10, 18. The prophetic tradition struggles relentlessly with the question of God's making an end of God's people. Cf. Frank Crüsemann, "Kritik an Amos im Deuteronomistischen Geschichtswerk," in *Probleme biblischer Theologie.* Festschrift Gerhard von Rad, ed. Hans Walter Wolff (Munich: Kaiser, 1971), 57-63; Rudolf Smend, " 'Das Ende ist gekommen': Ein Amoswort in der Priesterschrift," in *Die Botschaft und die Boten.* Festschrift Hans Walter Wolff, ed. Jörg Jeremias and Lothar Perlitt (Neukirchen-Vluyn: Neukirchener, 1981), 67-72; and Klaus Koch, "Das Profetenschweigen des deuteronomistischen Geschichtswerks," in Jeremias-Perlitt, 115-128. To be sure, these reflections concern *qets,* not the word for "end" in our text. The questions nonetheless are much the same with the use of the two terms.

Or perhaps Judah's special future is rooted in the difference Yahweh makes between perpetrator nations and victim nations, as though God cares differently for the victim nations. No such distinction, however, is explicit in the poem. What is clear is that after the massive rhetorical assault on Egypt (Jer. 46:3-26), there is here a modest counterpoint. God values the little one, God notices the abased one, and God gives to this oppressed one a future. Egypt is given a future: "Egypt shall be inhabited as in the days of old" (v. 26). Jacob is given a future: "Jacob shall have quiet and ease" (v. 27). Both the great power and the beloved community are given futures, and the two futures are not incompatible.[27]

It is as though the poem witnesses to and sanctions a moment in geopolitics which is chaotic and disruptive, when power is turned loose against all established normalcies. The poem, in the end, envisions a settled normalcy when all the powers are back in their proper places and proper perspectives. When that happens, Jacob can resume its life. For both the empire and the beloved community, everything depends on Yahweh's sovereign rule. Without that sovereign rule, all these states are left in disarray and under threat. When Yahweh's sovereign rule reemerges, as it does through this poem, well-being comes. Both the long military mock-sing (vv. 3-26) and the brief salvation oracle (vv. 27-28) are rhetorical acts in the service of God's reestablished order. That order in the end will serve both Egypt and Israel well. It is worth noting that Babylon, the agent of reestablished order, receives no word of a future here. That comes later in the tradition of Jeremiah (chs. 50–51). The "prophet to the nations" has reenvisioned the ancient Near East as a map of well-being where there is just chastening but not an end. Rather, Yahweh's reestablished rule is a new beginning. There must be endings, but here they serve only to begin again.

Oracle against the Philistines (47:1-7)

The Philistines are an old, traditional enemy of Israel, especially prominent in the time of Saul and David. Later, by the time of Jeremiah, they do

27. In a quite different tradition (Isa. 19:24-25), the great powers and the beloved community finally come to share in the favor and blessing of the God who presides over the affairs of both.

not figure as a political force, but are pawns of the great powers. The region of the Philistines, however, continued to be a strategically crucial position in the path between Egypt and the threatening power "of the north." In practice, the Philistine region had become a satellite of Egypt, exercising no independent political position. As satellite, it was of course exposed to and vulnerable before the same threat as was Egypt. Consequently it is useful to regard this brief poem of ch. 47 as a satellite to the larger poem of ch. 46.

This is a poem that does not develop very much; that is, it contains no plot. Its single idea is to assert in the most vivid way possible that the Philistines are under threat "out of the north" (47:2). The poem uses highly stylized formulas to convey that single motif.

47:1 This verse again identifies the poem as God's word to Jeremiah; in other words, we are again hearing "the prophet to the nations." The timing of the oracle "before Pharaoh smote Gaza" is a curious one. That phrasing suggests a threat from Philistia's south, but the poem itself concerns the threat "from the north." We lack sufficient data to determine what is intended by the phrasing of v. 1.

47:2-7 The poem begins with the metaphor of "waters, overflowing torrent" (v. 2). The image of "waters" bespeaks the surging threat of chaos that is relentless, irresistible, and endlessly destructive. Already in Isa. 8:7-8 Assyria had been pictured as a great chaotic threat against Judah, and now the same image is used to allude to a subsequent power from the north which will again bring chaos, destruction, and death. The waters of chaos will fill the land and inundate the cities. Nothing will be exempt from the threat to come. The danger will evoke terror and fear, dread and grief — an enormous cry of need, helplessness, and hopelessness.

The image is changed in Jer. 47:3, or perhaps better, the metaphor of surging waters is now connected to a concrete reference. The "chaotic waters" are in fact the onslaught of a savage army. Again using the standard formulas of military poetry, v. 3 evokes a sense of ominous power and massive danger — of huge stallions, rushing chariots, and rumbling wheels. The poet seeks to bring the listeners into the specific action of the one-sided battle. That picture of brutal and determined force from the north is sharply contrasted with the Philistine fathers, the ones formerly of military prowess, now unable even to protect their own children, now utterly weak, and failed, and helpless. The rhetoric draws a powerful and complete contrast between power and weakness, between success and shame, between action and passivity.

The metaphor of rushing waters and the image of charging soldiers finally converge at the first poetic climax. It is "the day" (v. 4; cf. 46:10)![28] It is Yahweh's day, the day of armed assertiveness, of vengeance, of raw unrestrained power. It is Yahweh and none other who dares this awesome deed of destruction. The name of Yahweh is now evoked for the first time in the poem. It is Yahweh who comes against the Philistines. (The reference to Tyre and Sidon here is enigmatic; apparently these coastal cities are here grouped with the Philistine cities, also subject to the terrible threat of the day.)

The juxtaposition of 47:2-3 and v. 4 reiterates what we have seen in 46:3-10. The ostensive enemy is "from the north," that is, Babylon. The theological accent of these poems, however, makes clear that the real destroyer is not Babylon, but Yahweh. It is Yahweh who is at work to establish or reestablish Yahweh's own hegemony. The poem is a theological act that insists upon a drastic rereading of political reality.

The Philistine response to the massive threat of Yahweh is pictured in a derisive way (v. 5). Reference is made to two Philistine cities, Gaza and Ashkelon, which have been centers of power, but are now centers of grief. The third line of the verse appears to be mocking. The men of the Philistines had been powerful and formidable, before whom the ancient Israelites stood in awe. Now, because of this massive reversal wrought through an invasion, there is only a remnant, only the feeble descendants and leftovers of the great ones. Perhaps this is a comment on how few they are. More likely the phrase suggests that the great ones have come upon pitiful days. Indeed, David's grieving song, which he did not want overheard by the Philistines, said of Saul and Jonathan, "How are the mighty fallen!" (2 Sam. 1:25, 27). Keeping that poem in mind, there is perhaps high irony here.[29] The Philistines were the mighty ones, and now

---

28. The notion of "the day" is rooted in military references that indicate the coming of massive devastation dispatched by God. See von Rad, *Old Testament Theology*, 2 (1965):119-125.

29. The same inscrutable reversal of the Philistines is narrated for an earlier period in the "Ark narrative" of 1 Sam. 4:1–7:1. The Philistines have their season of success and power, but they are pitiful and helpless when Yahweh's power is mobilized against them.

the mighty ones among the Philistines have fallen. They are reduced not only to ordinary folk, but to pitiful soldiers who cringe before the invasion, who have not the energy ever to be effective fathers! Their characteristic acts are "baldness" and "gashing," either desperate attempts to bring and motivate their impotent gods or, more likely, acts of terrible grieving over the loss of their known world.[30] Either as desperate religion or as pitiful grief, the former "giants" are now helpless. The rhetoric helps render them helpless, making their impotence and hopelessness palpable. Indeed, no "helper" remains (cf. Jer. 47:4). The poet carefully offers a sketch of an old power that has failed; warriors now grieve, soldiers falter, fathers fail even their own little children. The poem itself is a powerful rhetorical act of diminishment. The great ones are indeed fallen, and their own pious acts of impotence measure their futility and despair.

The poem concludes with a harsh vocative (vv. 6-7): "Ah, sword of the LORD!" The one addressed is unnamed, indeed not named anywhere in the poem. In v. 2 we know of one "out of the north," but that is all. From the context and from ch. 46, we surmise that the one addressed is Babylon, or even Nebuchadnezzar who is to be "Yahweh's sword." The poet, however, is either restrained or judicious, leaving everything open and unspecified. The one addressed is some human agent, some historical threat, authorized by Yahweh to move "against Ashkelon and against the seashore" (47:7).

The vocative address performs a trick. The ostensive question of v. 6 is "When will you stop your destructiveness? When will you have done enough? When will you finally desist, either in exhaustion or in satiation?" The question is put as though the questioner (the poet, Yahweh) is exhausted with the feverish activity of "the sword of Yahweh" and wants the devastation to stop. The question implies an exasperated "Enough!" Or perhaps the question is wishful thinking in the mouth of the Philistines? Or if the questioner is in fact Yahweh, then the question sounds as though Yahweh's destructive sword is autonomous, out of control, and no longer subordinate to Yahweh. Then the question suggests that the sword is indeed "out of hand."

Whatever the intent of the question, it receives a harsh answer. How

---

30. In 1 Sam. 6:1-9 the Philistines are portrayed as helpless and frantic to avoid the threat of God. On frantic ritual activities in the face of God's power, see 1 Kgs. 18:28-29.

can the sword be quiet? How can the sword rest or how can it be sheathed? It cannot be rested; it dare not be, because it has been mandated (commanded) by Yahweh and must do its terrible work for Yahweh against the Philistines. The sword is not out of control. It is appointed and authorized by Yahweh, and it must do its obedient work. That is, the destruction now happening in the Philistine cities is not just northern aggression. It is an act commanded by Yahweh.

The poem revolves around one idea, namely, destruction from the hand of Yahweh. No reason for the destruction is given. There is nothing here of Philistine arrogance or brutality or disobedience.[31] The poem simply anticipates terrible military devastation; four times the poem connects the devastation to the purpose of Yahweh: "day" of Yahweh (v. 4), "Yahweh destroys" (v. 4), "sword of Yahweh" (v. 6), and "Yahweh gives charge" (v. 7). Everything that is happening is credited to Yahweh. The historical process is not on its own.

The poet ostensibly wants the Philistines to notice and understand what is happening. The poet intends that the Philistines should be theologically alert. Behind that ostensive purpose, however, the poem is an acknowledgement of Yahweh's unqualified governance, wrought here as terrible violence.

Interpreting this text requires both candor and criticism. The candor is to confess that the poem affronts us. It is so severe and so raw, and indeed shameless, unbothered about the theological authorization of brutality. We might wish it otherwise, but this is what we have. The criticism we must do is to ask what is intended in this speech. What response does the poem intend to evoke? Perhaps the poet wishes only to assert the unqualified and unprincipled rule of Yahweh, unprincipled because in this text we are given no warrant or sanction for what Yahweh is doing.

More likely, in the assertion of Yahweh's unqualified role, the poet intends to establish a ground of hope outside all established normalcies. Yahweh is not domesticated by any of our conventionalities, but acts in sheer freedom, owing no one anything. Listeners to this poem are invited to face this undomesticated God who may violate our sensitivities, this

31. This is in contrast to the Oracles against the Nations in Amos 1–2, where there are reasons for the destruction, reasons related to barbarism and massive cruelty. Such reasons may be inferred here, but they are not stated.

God who may be the only hope for the Philistines as for Israel. Of course the point is not to do "theology." The poet wants to understand and embrace life in the world. It is evident that a force of chaos is set loose, flowing like volcanic lava. The foe from the north may be only sheer chaos. The poet dares to assert, without denying the severity of the threat, that even this flow of chaos has a name, an unmocked name. The brutality evident in this poem is nothing less than brutal. It is in the end, however, a "connected brutality," connected to the name of Yahweh and therefore to large purposes. It is an odd way *in extremis* to assert moral coherence in public reality. Whatever moral coherence there is depends on the undomesticated one, who works God's own way, savagely and relentlessly. Moreover, all the calculated response of the Philistines (baldness, gashing) does not curb this raw holiness, which permits no explanation but only evocative, shrill speech of testimony.

Oracle against Moab (48:1-47)

Upon finishing with the Philistines in ch. 47, the text moves abruptly east across the hill country and the Jordan River to address Moab. When the address begins, it goes on and on, yielding a long and complicated poem, longer even than that addressed to mighty Egypt.

This long poem is exceedingly difficult, and scholars are uncertain on a number of preliminary points: (1) It is exceedingly difficult to locate *political-historical events* that correspond to the poetry, though William L. Holladay makes a characteristically valiant effort.[32] (2) It is impossible to identify geographically many of the *place names,* and the poem invites considerable speculation among scholars. (3) The poem is disordered so that a *literary analysis* is complicated, even assuming that sense can be made of it. There is no doubt that this poetry utilized traditional materials that must have belonged to an established pattern of rhetoric concerning the nations and especially concerning Moab. (4) It is difficult to determine why *this poem concerning Moab is so extensive,* compared to any of the others in the corpus. Clearly the poem became a "catchall" for traditional materials, variously judged "authentic" and "secondary." Very likely Moab

32. Holladay, *Jeremiah 2,* 353-364.

as a close competitor and immediate rival evokes a hostility and resentment greater than found elsewhere.

Because we can reach no reliable conclusions concerning political-historical, geographical, or literary matters related to the poem, we are largely limited to the claim of the text itself (not a bad limit), which requires no great speculation about matters outside the text. We may better ask, what rhetorical effect does the text intend to evoke in its listeners, listeners who ostensively are Moabites but who are likely to have been Judeans?

48:1-9   This poetic unit makes an abrupt beginning, linking two unlikely items (48:1a). First, the subject is Moab! The utterance of the name no doubt evokes in Judah a host of negative sensitivities. Second, Israel's "LORD of the troops" is about to speak. In quick fashion, the *destiny of Moab* is drawn into the sphere of *Yahweh's sovereign speech*. That national destiny will be powerfully impinged upon by this sovereign speech.

The first word this ominous God speaks is "Woe," that is, trouble, death, judgment (v. 1b). The long chapter to follow is a complicated exposition of this simple utterance. The "woe destiny" of Moab is presented, in the beginning, by two rhetorical devices (vv. 1b-5). On the one hand, the cities, the great centers of economic power and military pride, are named: Nebo, Kiriathaim, Heshbon, Madmen, Horonaim, Zoar, Luhith. The poem sounds like an intelligence report for a coming invader. The poem knows the terrain of Moab well. On the other hand, the poetry couples with the naming of centers of power and pride phrases concerning suffering, destruction, and death: "Laid waste, put to shame, taken, put to shame, broken down, cut off, brought to silence, pursued by a sword, desolation, great destruction, destroyed, cry, weeping, cry of destruction." The connection between the *centers of power and pride* and the *phrasings of loss* pound at the listener. What had seemed permanent and secure is rhetorically undermined and placed in jeopardy. Indeed, these two incongruous rhetorical elements fight each other; in their fight, the poem accomplishes a massive inversion, for the centers are, through the poem, emptied of pride and power.

Having anticipated the devastation, the poem now addresses those who live in the midst of the devastation (vv. 6-9). Verses 6 and 9 provide an inclusio; v. 6 is an imperative urging flight out of the city to escape the

443

devastation;[33] v. 9 oddly differentiates between "Moab" (presumably its people) and the destroyed cities. The people are urged to separate themselves from the cities (and perhaps from the royal-urban ideology which drives those cities toward destructiveness). In both verses the listeners are urged to escape, for the coming attack will focus on those centers of power and pride.

Within that inclusio, vv. 7-8 voice a prophetic lawsuit. The indictment in the first line focuses on "false trust" *(bth)*, which is in fact idolatry. The sentence now announced is that Chemosh, the Moabite god, will go into exile *(glh)*, along with priests and princes. Thus the assault is upon the power structure, its leaders, and its religious ideology which has fostered and legitimated a false perception of reality. In v. 8 the poet utters the ominous "the destroyer" *(sh-d-d)*. The term *sh-d-d* is the same as the term "laid waste," which began the deathly recital of v. 1b. "The destroyer" is not named, but the threat is real and concrete. Though the focus of the poem has been on cities and strongholds, now the horizon of the "destroyer" includes cities, valleys, and plains, that is, everything everywhere. The assault is twofold, as is characteristic in Judah, for it includes both the prospect of exile and the danger of devastation. Thus the destiny of Moab is the same as the fate of Judah previously announced in the book of Jeremiah. Both Judah and Moab receive the same from the hand of Yahweh, and both receive the same from the action of Nebuchadnezzar. Both receive for the same reason: "Because you trusted . . . !"

48:10-13 These verses provide a reflective pause, an interlude, in the poetry. They consist in a brief poetic statement (v. 11) enveloped in what appear to be two prose elements (vv. 10, 12, 13). The poetic element presents the situation of Moab under the metaphor of wine-making (v. 11). Moab has had a long, pleasant career as a winemaker and producer. The winemaker has been at ease, prosperous, and indolent, content not to remove the sediment in the wine (lees). On "ease," see Amos 6:1 for the same term of complacency applied to Zion. On complacency concerning the process of wine-making, see Zeph. 1:12. In Zephaniah the indiffer-

---

33. See Robert Bach, *Die Aufforderung zur Flucht und zum Kampf im alttestamentliche Prophetenspruch.* Wissenschaftliche Monographien zum Alten und Neuen Testament 9 (Neukirchen-Vluyn: Neukirchener, 1962); and Patrick D. Miller, Jr., "The Divine Council and the Prophetic Call to War," *Vetus Testamentum* 18 (1968): 100-107.

ence and complacency is because it is believed that "The LORD will not do good, nor will he do ill." That is, the indifference and indolence are because the God of Israel is not taken seriously as a norm, a demand, or a threat. The life of the complacent and indolent winemaker has been unbothered and untroubled, perfectly at ease. Now the poem shifts the image. Now Moab is not the winemaker, but the wine that has been left undisturbed, not moved around, not poured out, that is, not taken into exile *(glh)!* (Again that ominous word!) The result of the lack of disturbance is that the taste and smell of the winemaker has gone unchallenged and unchanged. Moab has gone to sleep in its well-being.

That idyllic picture of untroubled Moab is juxtaposed to the two incongruous prose verses. Everyone is to do the destructive work of Yahweh with vigor (Jer. 48:10)! The time is coming for the ominous days of dismantling (vv. 12-13). The text returns in v. 12 to the imagery of the middle portion of v. 11. There will be poured out Moab, poured out like wine, and the containers will be empty, broken, smashed. The theological conclusion is that the Moabite god Chemosh will have failed (cf. v. 7). This odd sequence of statements holds together poetic metaphor (wine-making), political analysis (exile for Moab), and theological verdict (failure of Chemosh). The destiny of Moab (like the destiny of Israel) partakes of and requires all three elements for its full articulation. The last word in v. 13 is "confidence" *(bth),* the same root as the powerful indictment of v. 7. Thus Moab trusted in its own strength (v. 7) and in the power of its god who sustained that strength (v. 13), even as Israel placed its trust in the wrong object. Both politically and theologically, the season of Moab's ease is over, brutally terminated.

48:14-20   In this poetic section the language and images echo vv. 6-9. Again it is the "LORD of hosts" who speaks (v. 15). This time the title is escalated. Yahweh is "the King," thus providing a direct challenge to the rule of Chemosh, who is in process of being dethroned and displaced. Twice in connection with the mention of Israel's God there is also mention of "the destroyer of Moab" *(sh-d-d,* vv. 15, 18). By the verdict of Yahweh, the God of Israel, a terrible destructive force has been unloosed in the political arena against Moab.

Again the rhetoric engages in sharp reversals to voice the dismantling of Moabite power and pride. The mocking address is to the "heroes," the "mighty men," "the choicest of his young men," "the mighty scepter," "the glorious staff." The poet with great extravagance names and acknowledges all the well-being, prestige, and grandeur of Moab. Such a naming, however, is part of a larger strategy of humiliation. The great ones are named only to be attacked.

The poem urges Moab to change its speech, in order to bring its speech into contact with the new reality caused by Yahweh. They did say, "We are heroes" (v. 14). They are now urged to say, "How the mighty scepter is broken" (v. 17). The first speech is obsolete and now illusionary; the poet urges Moab's speech to embrace the new reality of devastation. The poet seeks to break the power of ideology which keeps speaking about a reality that no longer exists. There follows once again a rich vocabulary of devastation: "calamity, affliction, bemoan, destroyed, flee, put to shame, broken, wail, and cry." This collage of words contrasts totally with the preceding cluster of "heroes, mighty men, choicest, and so forth." What had been is no more. What will be is deathliness, wrought by "the King" (v. 15). Between what has been and what will now be stands the decree of Yahweh and the unnamed "destroyer." The unit ends with "laid waste" (*sh-d-d,* v. 20), thus referring back to the opening of v. 1b. The whole poem thus far is situated between "laid waste" (v. 1b) and "laid waste" (v. 20); between these two dread-filled verbs lies Moab's future.

48:21-28   These verses in prose (except the conclusion, v. 28, in poetry) introduce no new themes, but state the issue of Yahweh against Moab with rich and varied metaphor. It is helpful to see that these lines express the two motifs of a prophetic lawsuit, indictment and sentence.

The indictment against Moab is twofold. First, Moab made himself great against Yahweh; that is, Moab asserted autonomy from Yahweh (v. 26). The indictment, on the face of it, is more than a little curious, because Moab would not have imagined itself in any way in relation to Yahweh. The text, however, never reflects upon or explains why Moab should be responsive or submissive to Yahweh. The text simply assumes this to be the case, and further assumes that Moab should know about this definitional relation. That Yahwistic claim, which is foundational to all these "Oracles against the Nations," is a daring act of rhetoric which insists upon connections where others do not notice or acknowledge them. Moab's failure is a failure to come to terms with the rule of Yahweh, a rule which is the driving power of this poetry.

Second, the specific way in which Moab "magnified itself" is that it made a laughingstock of Israel. The language is not unlike that of the Psalms of Lament, which complain of people treating Israel with contempt (Ps. 59:8; Lam. 1:7; Jer. 20:7). Moab has treated Israel with contempt. This is the way in which Moab has violated Yahweh. Thus sin against the "brother" here is indeed sin against God. Moab does not love the brother whom it has seen, and surely does not love God whom it has not seen (cf. 1 John 4:20).

From such a foundational indictment comes a severe sentence. The punishment for defying Yahweh and mocking Israel is stated in three sets of metaphors. First, "judgment" *(mishpat)* of a political-military kind is described which is massive and comprehensive (Jer. 48:21-25). The attack envisioned includes the "tableland" and "all the cities." That utter devastation has broken the power ("horn," "arm") of Moab (v. 25), so that Moab is reduced to a helpless subject state.

The second set of metaphors is more venturesome. Moab will be made drunk and will wallow in his vomit (v. 26). The image suggests humiliation, weakness, helplessness, and instability, the depth of pitiful degradation. The third element in the characterization of Moab's new situation is to be "held in derision" *(sh-h-q,* v. 26), that is, treated with contempt (a punishment which corresponds verbally to the indictment of v. 27). That is, Moab will now be treated the way Moab has cynically treated Israel.[34] It is no wonder that this section concludes in v. 28 with poetry echoing v. 9. The only counsel the poem offers is to leave, escape, and go hide in remote places in the hinterland, for the destruction is severe and wholesale. There is no hope except to flee.

48:29-33   The poetry now resumes after the prose unit, utilizing lines from Isa. 16:6ff. This unit is a lawsuit which turns on the "therefore" in Jer. 48:31. Verses 29-30 are the indictment, which is completely lacking in specificity but which piles up the vocabulary concerning defiance, arrogance, and autonomy. This language is an extrapolation from the pivotal indictment of v. 26. Moab is guilty of "pride, pride, loftiness, pride, arrogance, a haughty heart." All but the last of these six words either is derived from the same root or sounds alike. The rhetorical effect is cumulative. Moab has thought it was outside the arena of Yahweh's sovereignty

---

34. Again, notice the precise correspondence between offense and punishment, as noticed programmatically by Patrick D. Miller, Jr., *Sin and Judgment in the Prophets.*

and could do what it wanted, for the indictment of haughtiness and insolence has substance only in a world where Yahweh is the decisive point of reference. The conclusion of the indictment in v. 30 is terse and abrupt: "not so in his hand, not so they do" (author's translation). What Moab does has no substance, because there is a quality of unreality about its life, an unreality rooted in a lack of reality about its relation to Yahweh. Moab treats Yahweh as unreal; the outcome, however, is not that Yahweh is made unreal by Moab, but that the life of Moab becomes a self-destructive unreality. Yahweh stands "real" in the poem, to the harsh cost of Moab.

The sentence against Moab bespeaks the coming devastation and suffering (vv. 31-33). Verse 32 hints at the well-being and effectiveness of the Moabite economy, which in the past was extensive and productive. Against all that prosperity, however, "the destroyer" has come. Again the poet uses the term as we have seen repeatedly, *sh-d-d*. We do not know if "the destroyer" is Yahweh or some human agent designated by Yahweh. The poet gives us no hint and lets the rhetoric make its own intimidating case.

As a result of "the destroyer" who will devastate Moab, there is occasion for mourning, weeping, crying. The poet conducts a national funeral. This motif of sadness over the ruin was already anticipated in the first word of the poetry, "Woe" (v. 1b). The word bespeaks the sadness and grief of death, and now the poet explicates that large initiatory word. Thus the coming practice of grief, sadness, and mourning (vv. 31-32) is nicely juxtaposed with the gladness and shouts of joy which have been heard but which now are silenced (v. 33).[35] The harvest time is a time of exuberant celebration, a time of rich profit, an assurance of blessing, and no doubt of exaggerated drinking. All of that extravagant celebration, however, will now cease. The wine-making will stop, and with it all glad occasions of profit, blessing, and imbibing. The poet anticipates an abrupt end to all joy and celebration so characteristic of the community. The regular patterns of social life which generate celebration, well-being, and identity are all halted; in their place come grief and mourning. By the cluster of the words for *mourning* and for *joy*, the poet has enacted a dramatic reversal of the fortunes of the community.

35. On the contrasting sounds of grief and joy, see the suggestive metaphor of Jer. 7:34; 16:9; 25:10; 33:11. On similar imagery for drastic reversal, see Luke 6:20-21; John 16:22.

The poem has made use of the figure of wine-making in different ways. In vv. 11-12 the images are mixed, whereby Moab is a producer of wine but then is also the wine poured out (in exile). In v. 26 Moab is the victim of wine. Now in these verses the reference is the joy evoked in wine-making time. By the use of this metaphor, along with other images, the poet has effected a complete and dramatic reversal. In both the positive reference to joy (now terminated) and in the negative reference to grief (now anticipated), the vocabulary is reiterative and cumulative. Indeed, in this unit we may identify three clusters of terms which express intensity, passion, and certitude about the future:

Moab's offense:	Moab's loss:	Moab's destiny:
pride		summer fruits / wail
proud		vintage / cry out
loftiness		gladness / mourn
pride		joy / weep
arrogance		wine
haughtiness	shouts of joy	
insolence		shouts of joy

These clusters of words revolve around a very simple argument urged by the poet. *Arrogance* causes enormous *loss,* which evokes profound *grief.* At the center of the process of arrogance-loss-grief stands Yahweh in uncompromising sovereignty.

48:34-39 These verses are dominated by the first person asseverations of Yahweh: "I will bring an end to Moab" or, alternatively, "I will cause a sabbath to Moab" (v. 35). Yahweh's resolve is to cause Moab to disappear. That verdict of God dominates this section and, indeed, the entire chapter. From that verdict, the other elements of this unit follow: (1) There is grief over Moab, because of its wretchedness and death (v. 34). (2) Moab is indicted as a worshipper of false gods (v. 35). (3) There must be deep grief (moaning) of a ritual kind (i.e., set to music) because of the massive, visible reversals of fortunes (v. 36).

From the verdict comes an outpouring of overwhelming grief (vv. 37-38). Four acts of public grief are named: shaving heads, cutting off beards, gashing hands, and dressing in sackcloth (cf. 47:5-6). The extremity of the lament indicates the depth of the loss. The reason for the loss is that God's own self has broken the vessel "no one wants" (NRSV). The poem uses a metaphor used earlier for Israel, for Jerusalem, and even for a deposed king.[36] Jeremiah 48:39 seems to be almost a quote of the lament itself. In grief, this is what the mourner might say: "How it is broken!"[37] The poet comes close to the edge of language, beyond which nothing dare be uttered. The rhetoric provides no coherent statement, but almost an ejaculation of disconnected words: "broken, wail, shame, derision." Moab is completely dismantled; nothing coherent can even be voiced about it.

48:40-47 The concluding poetic unit on Moab again sounds the notes of devastation and ruin. In vv. 40-43 we have a description of the threat. The one who is to come (we are not told whom) comes as a massive, hovering dangerous eagle, who will swoop up Moab. The metaphor of eagle quickly yields to more concrete, graphic description. The attack will be against the centers of power (cities and fortresses), and the hearts of the Moabite soldiers will melt in fear. The poet uses a startling metaphor to contrast the would-be valor and courage of the soldiers with the anguish and hurt of labor pains. This metaphor is not unlike that of the failed fathers of 47:3. The outcome of such a terrible threat that reduces to helpless trembling is "terror, pit, and snare" (48:43), that is, places of utter defeat and hopelessness. The poem does not linger long to tell us why this will happen. The reason, already stated in v. 26, is that Moab has magnified itself against Yahweh, that is, acted in defiance against the rule of Yahweh. Such an act of self-magnification can only bring ruin and devastation.

The theme of "terror, pit, and snare" is an especially powerful alliteration in Hebrew: *phd, pht, ph.* While the triad is offered in v. 43 only as a conventional formula,[38] in v. 44 the poem arranges in a more meaningful sequence. Now one moves from one danger to the next. The cumulative effect of the three terms is a sense of inescapability and therefore hopelessness. There will be no way to circumvent the harsh destiny of judgment now set in motion. The general theme of inescapability of

36. See 22:28; 30:12-17. On the latter, see Brueggemann, "The 'Uncared for' Now Cared for."

37. On the same imagery, though with different terminology, see 19:11. Here the broken pot is Moab; there it is Israel and Jerusalem. In this oracle Moab receives the same devastating treatment earlier enacted against Israel.

38. On one member of this triad, see Hillers, *Treaty-Curses,* 69-70.

judgment echoes Amos 5:18-20, but the specific wording of these verses is more paralleled by Isa. 24:17-18, in which the same phrasing is utilized in an apocalyptic context.

The long rhetorical assault on Moab culminates in Jer. 48:45-47. These lines refer again to Heshbon, center of power (v. 45). Heshbon, however, is now surrounded by desperate fugitives trying to escape the devastation. The great city is burning; the monarchy is up in flames. The threat reaches to the center of power, of autonomy, of arrogance. It touches the crown and core of what had been limitless pride. The "sons of tumult" have, by the end of the poem, reached their sorry destruction.

The "political job" done on Moab in v. 45 is matched in v. 46 with a theological reference. The verse begins with "woe," reiterating the ominous beginning point of v. 1b.[39] Moab is now "undone"; in other words, Moab will perish as a vulnerable, helpless community, sons and daughters (i.e., everyone into exile). It is stunning that this is now "the people of Chemosh," Moab as known by its god. In v. 7 it is Chemosh who goes into exile. In v. 13 Moab is ashamed of Chemosh. The defeat of Moab is in actuality the defeat of this god who is no god at all. The fall of Moab is in fact the defeat of Chemosh at the hands of Yahweh, thus replicating once again the theological conflict of Yahweh over the Egyptian gods (Exod. 5–15), of Yahweh over Dagon (1 Sam. 4–6).[40]

The poem ends, oddly enough, with an act of hope (Jer. 48:47). The phrase, "I will restore their fortunes," is a common Jeremianic term for restoration after exile (cf. 29:14; 30:3, 18; 31:23; 32:44; 33:11, 26).[41] Now the phrase is applied even to Israel's enemy. In Hebrew the phrase is *shabti shebot,* a phrase not unlike the double use of "captivity" *(shebi)* in v. 46. Thus the same sound is used to voice exact opposites, exile (v. 46) and return (v. 47). The concluding verse, however, cannot be understood simply as a play on words. The point of the reverse is a theological one. There are, even for Moab, "latter days." There is more promised for Moab than ultimate destruction. The assertion of v. 47 can of course be understood simply as an editorial maneuver to tone down the awful threat of

39. Here the term is *'oy*, whereas in v. 1 it is *hoy*, but the connection seems clear enough.

40. On the Ark narrative as a struggle between Yahweh and Dagon, see Miller and Roberts, *The Hand of the Lord*, 40-51.

41. See Bracke, "Coherence and Theology," 148-155.

the foregoing. Read theologically, however, the verse suggests that Yahweh's primary business with Moab is not destruction. The destruction so passionately voiced is a "strategic necessity" in order to establish Yahweh's sovereignty, out of which will come Yahweh's powerful newness.[42] The final verse of the poem hints at a reestablished international order in which Moab has a positive role to play and in which Moab will have better days of well-being as a gift from Yahweh.

This complex and difficult poem voices in an acute way the question raised by all of the Oracles against the Nations. The question is acute here because the oracle goes repeatedly over the central points. We are left to ponder the intent of such an oracle that seems to work a rhetorical "overkill." Two suggestions about the intent of the poem come readily to mind. First, the poem voices deep Israelite venom felt toward its near and troublesome neighbor. The poem is an act of vengeful ventilation and catharsis. No doubt this element is present whenever the poem is recited. Such a view, however, does not reckon with the clear claim that this is God's speech, though it is not difficult to imagine such passionate ideology placed in God's mouth.

Second, it can be suggested that this oracle (and others like it) are not addressed to the ostensive addressee, but are designed for Judah's hearing and overhearing. No doubt there was "overhearing" and some intended overhearing, but the poem is too specific and didactic for that to be an adequate explanation of the poem.

If we are to be "realistic" and take the poem on its own terms, this is an oracle from God's mouth. Then the question is, Why does God speak this way? The answer is that God, this particular God, speaks this way because the establishment of Yahweh's hegemony over the nations is crucial to their well-being. One does not need to deny the operation of Israel's political ideology in this claim, but such ideology does not exhaust the theological claim expressed. The God who speaks in this poem is not simply a petty partisan and patron of Jerusalem. There is more to the speech of God than the political claim of Jerusalem. This is the God of

42. On "vengeance" for the sake of sovereignty, see Wright, "The Nations in Hebrew Prophecy"; and Mendenhall. The burden of Wright and Mendenhall is that Yahweh's destructive action is not capricious but is an instrument of policy, legitimated by a rightful claim to sovereignty. The conclusion of this poem supports such a scholarly verdict.

the whole Israelite tradition, the LORD of heaven and earth, the initiator of the Exodus who withstood the Egyptian empire for the sake of the slaves. This is the God who destabilizes and deabsolutizes every pretentious and petty political claim for the sake of a larger ordering that makes human life possible.[43]

To be sure, this large claim of Yahweh's sovereignty ill fits with the harshness of the threat against Moab. The threat mouthed by Yahweh anticipates the awesome policy of "destroying villages in order to save them." Governments in the real world of power, however, act in such a way. This poem is exactly the voice of the government of Yahweh that intends to reestablish its authority and prerogative. Moab's failure, according to the poem, is that this kingdom resisted Yahweh's authority by trusting in "strongholds and treasures" (v. 7), by magnifying itself at Yahweh's expense (vv. 26, 42), by treating Israel in derision (v. 27), and by pride and arrogance (vv. 29-30). Such policy will not work! Nations in the end cannot act in such a way with impunity. There is a terrible accounting.

That theological claim which interprets the international order according to the intention of Yahweh finally leads us to an observation about these oracles in their present place in the book of Jeremiah. The corpus of chs. 46–51 makes a decisive canonical statement in the tradition of Jeremiah. The book of Jeremiah wants to assert that there is indeed the free, unfettered, dangerous power of Yahweh released into the public process. That free, unfettered, dangerous power will not be domesticated or disregarded. Israel may try to domesticate the power of Yahweh, and Moab may seek to disregard Yahweh. Judah and Moab both try to treat Yahweh as irrelevant. And both bring upon themselves massive danger. In the end (i.e., the end of the canonical corpus), however, this free and dangerous One does speak and act decisively. In that speech the whole of the world, even the particular claims of the kingdoms, is sharply reshaped and even preempted. Moab, like all the nations, must come to terms with Yahweh's sovereign resolve. A mocking disregard of this holy intention will

---

43. Notice that in the oracle against Moab in Amos 2:1 the indictment concerns Moab's brutal treatment of Edom. The indictment thus suggests an international governance in which Israel, at least in this oracle, is not even a player. Yahweh's moral agenda is not coterminal with Israel but has a direct connection to the nations and their policies.

bring deep trouble, visible even in the public process. From the beginning, Jeremiah had struggled with the public reality of "exile" (1:3) and was a "prophet to the nations" (1:10). Now the theme of *exile* plays heavily among the nations. There may be a restoration of destiny (48:47), but first there is an exile (48:7, 11, 46). Because there is a powerful, passionate Yahweh, there will be an inescapable exile.

Oracles against Other Nations (49:1-39)

This chapter includes oracles concerning five peoples. None of these peoples receives the extended attention of Moab in ch. 48. All of them, however, are discussed with reference to the same themes as were present concerning Moab.

49:1-6 The oracle against *the Ammonites* falls into two distinct units, plus a conclusion in v. 6. Verses 1-2 are dominated by the fourfold occurrence of the root *yarash*, variously rendered as "heir" (v. 1), "dispossess" (v. 1), and "dispossessor" (v. 2 twice). In v. 1 the first three lines are introduced by an interrogative triad characteristic of Jeremiah, *ha-, 'im, maddua'*.[44] The first two questions, "has . . . has . . . ," require a negative response: no, it is not true that Israel has no sons or no heirs. The third line then functions as an indictment against Ammon, based on the implied answers to the first two questions. If Israel had been without sons and heirs, then Ammon and its god Milcom might rightly take over the land. But because Israel does indeed have heirs and sons, Milcom (and Ammon) have wrongly, improperly, and illegitimately taken over the land of Israel (Gad). The indictment thus is that Ammon has wrongly seized Israelite territory and disregarded Israel's legitimate claim as heir of the land. Ammon has taken what is not rightly his. Thus land-taking military aggression is voiced in a metaphor concerning sons, heirs, and family rights.

The sentence against indicted Ammon is introduced, "Therefore, behold . . ." (v. 2). God declares war on Ammon, causes a savage cry of attack, and dispatches armies which will devastate and destroy Ammon.

44. On the form, see Walter Brueggemann, "Jeremiah's Use of Rhetorical Questions," *Journal of Biblical Literature* 92 (1973): 358-374.

In the end, Israel will dispossess those who dispossess; the term *yarash* can be rendered "possess" or "dispossess," so that Israel will now possess that from which it has been dispossessed.

Thus the indictment concerns illicit seizure of the land, no doubt as royal policy. The sentence concerns the reseizure of the land by Israel, which implies a great loss to Ammon. The oracle lives amid the recurring tension over land among peoples, tensions which may be very old, but which continue to be passionately felt by succeeding generations. Families and tribes never forget when an unfair land seizure has been perpetrated, whether by war or by dishonest adjudication. Ammon will not in the end be able to hold the land inappropriately taken. Moreover, because of its aggressive greed, Ammon will not only lose that land but will have its homeland abused as well, burned and reduced to an abandoned heap. These two verses offer a reflection on a primary dynamic of world history. That dynamic consists in (1) illicit land seizures and (2) sudden, inexplicable reversals whereby land is given back to those to whom it rightly belongs. The poet discerns the story of Judah within this recurring dynamic.

In vv. 3-5, the second element of this oracle, the mode of rhetoric is very different. Verse 3 is a summons to public ceremonies of grief: "wail, cry, gird, lament, run." Ammon is summoned to respond to its grief-evoking situation. The reason for the grief is that both its god (Milcom) and its human leaders (priests and princes) will go into exile, that is, will experience severe defeat and humiliation. Verse 4 is a taunting dismissal of Ammon, which has been excessively complacent, which trusts in its own resources, and which feels utterly secure (cf. 48:11). The security reflected in 49:4 is in fact a terrible illusion. The key term is again "trust" *(bth)*. Ammon has placed its confidence in its own powers, powers which are inadequate when real trouble comes.

Verse 5 counters that illusion with a heavy dose of theological reality. The central reality is introduced by "Behold, I." This is the historical power and purpose with which Ammon has not sufficiently reckoned. It is this "I" of Yahweh who cracks the complacency of Ammon and breaks open the illusion. Yahweh will cause exile and displacement, that is, a dispossessing of this settled people. There are no alternatives to Yahweh, who will prevail. Thus vv. 3-5 bespeak the terrible loss and hurt that derives from the lawsuit of vv. 1-2. Because of its infringement upon Israelite land, Ammon is in deep jeopardy.

The conclusion in v. 6 reflects a complete change of tone. It looks beyond the present moment of vexation. The verse anticipates the reversal of Ammonite destiny. The One who will do a good deed of rescue for Ammon is the same One who will cause the exile. Thus Yahweh will do for Ammon as Yahweh will do for Judah, causing both exile and home-coming (cf. 31:10, 27-28 for these actions toward Israel). The oracle concerns both Ammon's immediate fate (devastation) and Ammon's long-term destiny (well-being). Both are in the hands of Yahweh.

49:7-22 This more extended oracle concerning *Edom* seems to be built out of a variety of traditional pieces.[45] Jeremiah 49:7-16 constitutes an extended poem interrupted by the prose argument of vv. 12-13.

Verses 7-10 make up something of a rhetorical unit. Edom is tradi-tionally a place of wisdom and understanding.[46] The rhetorical question of v. 7 appeals to that tradition. The wise decision now for Edom, if indeed Edom still possesses wisdom, is to flee from the coming trouble (v. 8). Thus the question of v. 7 does not clearly imply a certain answer. If there is still wisdom, Edom will flee. Not to flee would be "foolish." Whether Edom flees from the devastation will evidence whether wisdom is still present in Edom. The threat announced is the "calamity of Esau" (v. 8). No specifics are given. We only know that the unspecified threat is very large and very grave.

In vv. 9-10 the poet engages two images to accent the threat Yahweh poses to Edom. Grape-gatherers do not pick the vines completely clean, but leave a residue (cf. Deut. 24:19-22). Thieves in the night do not take everything available, but only what they need. Both grape-gatherers and thieves leave something behind.[47] Yahweh, however, is unlike conventional grape-gatherers and thieves. Unlike grape-gatherers, Yahweh will leave no residue in Edom. Unlike a thief, Yahweh will take everything from Edom.

---

45. Verses 9, 14-16 are closely related to Obadiah. It is not necessary or possible to determine the direction of influence.

46. See Hans Walter Wolff, *Amos the Prophet* (Philadelphia: Fortress, 1973), 37, n. 91.

47. The argument itself is cast in a sapiential mode. That is, the argument proceeds by questions, anticipating that the answer will come from the expeience of the listener. If there is sufficient reflection, the listener can find the answer which condemns without being told directly.

Thus the images of grape-gatherer and thief are involved in order to make a contrast, to state how radical and massive will be Yahweh's actions — so radical and massive that nothing will survive and life is not possible.

In light of that massive warning and threat, Jer. 49:11 voices an odd footnote. In such a war-devastated society, there will inevitably be orphans and widows, without resources or protection. They are the predictable products of war. These, however, unlike the subjects of vv. 7-10, will be safe with Yahweh (cf. Hos. 14:3b). They are invited to trust *(bth)* Yahweh, and Yahweh will give them life. The inclination of Yahweh in Jer. 49:11 is quite in contrast to the ferocious Yahweh of vv. 9-10. The contrast is a strange one, indicating that only the abandoned and defenseless will find succor in Yahweh; all others will be devastated. Thus even this exceptional note functions in the total context of the poem to underscore the destruction everywhere else anticipated.

The prose interlude of vv. 12-13 seems again to underscore the imminent danger to Edom. The "cup" is a cup of suffering and devastation (cf. 25:15-29). Innocent peoples have had to drink from that cup; that is, innocent peoples have been caught in the flow of international upheaval caused by Yahweh. How much more will Edom drink such a cup, Edom who deserves the upheaval! There will be no escape for Edom. The punishment is as sure as God's own oath; it is aimed first against Bozrah, a proud capital city now to be utterly dismantled, subject of a massive curse, object of Yahweh's devastating action (cf. Deut. 28:37).

In light of the "no exception" statement of Jer. 49:9-10 and the curse formula of v. 13, vv. 14-16 now simply restate the threat. The poet "reports" on a "rumor" that has gone among the nations (v. 14). God is mobilizing all the nations together against Edom. This daring verse thus suggests a convergence of divine resolve and savage international strategy. The rumor among the nations is rooted in God's own resolve (v. 16). Because of pride and arrogance, there will be no escape, no hiding place, no refuge. God and God's agents will search out every hiding, fleeing Edomite.

In the reprise against Edom, three powerful metaphors are employed (vv. 17-22). First, Edom will be *like Sodom and Gomorrah,* utterly devastated, without any qualification or rescue (vv. 17-18). Second, God will be *like a lion* who will attack the flock of sheep that is Edom and will devastate and terrorize (vv. 19-20). No shepherd (king) in Edom can withstand the terrible threat. The sheep are completely exposed when the lion comes. Third, the one who will attack (i.e., a human agent) will be *like a great eagle,* who with huge wings will intimidate and terrorize, causing warriors to quake like women in labor (v. 22).

Sodom and Gomorrah, lion, and eagle are all images summoned in order to voice the impending threat against Edom. Behind the threat in these various images is the intention of Yahweh. In vv. 19-20 the poem comes to theological focus in the awesome person of Yahweh. The claims made for Yahweh in this assertion are threefold. First, there are first person verbs: "I will cause to run, I will appoint." Second, there are three interrogatives of defiance: "Who is like me, who will summon me, what shepherd can stand before me?" The questions are in fact assertions of authority and defiance. The claim implicit is "none like me, none can summon me, no shepherd can withstand me." Third, it is asserted that Yahweh has a "plan" against Edom, that is, a resolve from the very throne of heaven. All three of these devices — the verbs, the questions, the "plan" — establish the lion-God who dispatches the eagle-scavenger as the key actor in Edom's life. Against such a force Edom has no option, no chance, no future. This is an extraordinarily powerful statement of destruction. Its passion is matched by a complete lack of concrete reference or reason. We only hear of the "calamity of Edom," but know nothing about its motivation. That "calamity" looms large in the purpose of Yahweh.

49:23-27   Damascus here represents all of Syria (cf. Isa. 7:8). Syria is now named among those under assault from Yahweh. Three cities are named which refer to all of the kingdom: Damascus, Hamath, and Arpad. All of these have heard "rumors" of threat, all are anxious, all are uneasy (v. 23). Damascus receives more particular attention than the other two cities named (vv. 24-26). The great city and fortress of Damascus is feeble, unstable, and upset as a woman in labor (cf. v. 22). The mocking lament of v. 24 leads to the great reversal of vv. 25-26, contrasting "before" and "after." The joyful city is forsaken.[48] The best young men are now dead. Soldiers are destroyed. Strength is gone; the glory is departed. The mood is not even one of threat, but only of grief, for a great city has been destroyed. Verse 27 concludes the poem with a standard formulary against Damascus and its king (cf. Amos 1:4). This brief poem lacks every his-

---

48. The same language of reversal concerning Jerusalem is expressed in Isa. 62:4-5, though there the reversal is a positive one.

torical reference, every cause for such an action on God's part. The poem functions to destabilize every historical-political claim. The poem asserts that even great concentrations of human power (as in monarchies) are enormously pliable and tentative in the face of Yahweh's "tidings" and Yahweh's "plan." None can withstand the resolve of God.

49:28-33 The horizon of the poet now makes a sweep toward the Arabian tribes of the East. "Kedar" is generally taken to refer to Bedouin peoples of the East, indeed, as far East as is thinkable in the geography of the ancient world.[49] "Hazor" is less certain. Apparently it cannot here refer to the great Palestinian city of the book of Joshua. Holladay proposes that the term refers not to a specific city but to the sedentary Arabs who are not nomadic, and Robert P. Carroll, following Jer. 49:31, leaves it as "unwalled villages."[50] The reference is in any case indefinite.

This oracle is again an announcement of invasion and devastation. It includes the two standard elements: (1) an imperative which mobilizes the enemies of the addressed people (vv. 28-29), and (2) an urging that the inhabitants under attack should escape to safety (v. 30).

The most interesting element in this poem is the explicit reference to Nebuchadnezzar, who is said to have a "plan" and a "purpose." This reference is worth noting, because in none of the other oracles in this collection has Nebuchadnezzar been explicitly named. (He has been named, to be sure, in some of the editorial introductions). Even here, however, the mention of Nebuchadnezzar may not be secure, for the LXX lacks the name. If the historical reference to Nebuchadnezzar is retained, then we have a more concrete setting for the oracle. If not, then we have, as in other places, a large theological assertion about Yahweh's resolve. And indeed, after v. 30, the poem concludes with a claim for Yahweh, not for any human agent.

Thus Nebuchadnezzar is in any case not pivotal for the primary assertion of the oracle, which is theological. It is Yahweh who speaks the imperative, "Rise up" (v. 31), as in v. 28. It is Yahweh who attacks this people who dwell secure (*bth,* v. 31). It is Yahweh who claims the verbs "I will scatter, I will bring" (v. 32). Because of Yahweh's resolve, the loss of camels and herds is reported, and the utter devastation of the city is

49. See Jer. 2:10, where "Kedar" is juxtaposed to Cyprus as the furthest thinkable reference to the eastern edge of reality, as Cyprus represented the western edge.
50. Holladay, *Jeremiah 2,* 382-83; Carroll, *Jeremiah,* 809-811.

accomplished. At best, Nebuchadnezzar is a "bit player" in Yahweh's large intention. There is no doubt that Nebuchadnezzar hovers over and around these oracles against the nations. The poet, however, is never confused on the name of the primary actor. Nebuchadnezzar may indeed have a plan and purpose. It is, however, Yahweh who presides in plucking up and tearing down, as Yahweh has done even in Judah.

49:34-39 In the last of these brief oracles, the poet reaches the far northeastern horizon of the available world. No reason and no historical occasion is given for this harsh pronouncement of judgment against *Elam*. Unlike the preceding oracles in this collection, this oracle is rhetorically simple. Most of the rhetorical features found in the other poems are absent here. The poem is dominated by a single rhetorical pattern, namely first person verbs with Yahweh as the subject. After the initial "behold" (v. 35), the sequence of verbs is impressive:

> I will break,
> I will bring,
> I will scatter,
> I will terrify,
> I will bring (evil),
> I will send . . .
> > until I have consumed,
> I will set . . .

The recital is unambiguous, without reservation, unqualifiedly negative and destructive, and without any historical agent. Yahweh resolves to nullify the power and the governance of Elam, and to replace it with Yahweh's own direct rule.[51] The language is thoroughly military. The fate of Elam is sealed in Yahweh's assertive intention.

---

51. The political threat involved in "direct rule" is enormous. It happens when a hegemonic power loses patience with its underlings. Such a loss of patience suggests that "direct rule" will be much more severe and serve to squelch any autonomy or move toward independence. A recent case in point has been the refusal of the Soviet Union to allow independent rule in the Balkan states but to insist upon direct rule. Ezekiel 34:11-16 is a case in which Yahweh as the hegemonic power undertakes direct rule at the expense of the Jerusalem "shepherds." In that case, however, the direct rule of Yahweh will be benign.

The oracle, however, adds one other active verb for Yahweh, which follows after the threat (v. 39). For Elam, as for Egypt (46:26), Moab (48:47), and Ammon (49:6), there are more days, other days, better days intended by Yahweh. After the massive devastation, Yahweh will restore the fortune of Elam. God's ultimate resolve is the well-being even of Elam. That well-being can only happen, however, when Yahweh's throne is firm in the land and all other claimants to the throne have been eliminated.[52]

Oracle against Babylon (50:1–51:58)

This extended and complex oracle concerning Babylon belongs to the same genre as other "oracles against the nations" in chs. 46–51. Indeed, it is regularly grouped in interpretive discussions with all the others in this corpus. The argument of this oracle is not unlike the others: Yahweh summons new enemies against Babylon and decrees the downfall of the arrogant empire, much as Yahweh has summoned enemies against the previously named nations in chs. 46–49.

Though this oracle is like the others in the corpus in terms of genre and rhetoric, it is a mistake to group it with the other Oracles against the Nations in the book of Jeremiah. Indeed, chs. 50–51 represent a counter-theme in the book of Jeremiah, counter to chs. 46–49. In the end, in the final form of the text, Babylon dominates the book of Jeremiah, as the empire of Babylon dominated the politics of the period of Jeremiah.[53] Babylon is the superpower par excellence, and it utterly preoccupied Jeremiah and his contemporaries, as well as subsequent generations of Judean exiles who established the final form of the text of Jeremiah. Babylon is everywhere in the text of Jeremiah, explicitly in much of the prose, by allusion and implication in much of the poetry. Moreover, the argument of the book of Jeremiah is that Babylon is implementing the judgment of God against Jerusalem.[54] For that reason, Jerusalem's obedience to God entails submission to the power and policy of Babylon.

52. On this rule, see Patrick D. Miller, Jr., "The Sovereignty of God."
53. See Miller and Hayes, 416-436.
54. Seitz, *Theology in Conflict,* has shown that the interpretive disputes concerning the meaning of the Exile pivot on divergent understandings of the role of Babylon and the place of the exiles within that Babylonian hegemony.

In the Oracles against the Nations, the situation is not different for the other nations from the situation of Judah and Jerusalem. As Babylon dominates the horizon and destiny of Judah and Jerusalem, so in chs. 46–49 Babylon will dominate the future of the other nations. The central threat of the book of Jeremiah is that *the resolve of God* and *the policies of Babylon* converge completely and are to be equated. Thus a Yahweh-governed world is a Babylon-dominated world. The religiopolitical outcome of such an argument is that for Jerusalem there can only be a Babylon-shaped future, even as the nations must face a Babylon-dominated future. Babylon is indeed Yahweh's mode of sovereignty. Neither Jerusalem nor the other nations can entertain any alternative to Babylon. Thus the political preeminence of Babylon, in itself overwhelming, is given theological legitimacy by the tradition of Jeremiah, seemingly to perpetuity.

Chapters 50–51, however, provide an unexpected and decisive turn in the final form of the text of the book of Jeremiah. The poetry which has so consistently summoned the "foe from the north" (i.e., Babylon) now turns against the "foe from the north," and thereby transforms the role and position of Babylon. That great empire now is not the means of attack, but the object of Yahweh's attack.[55] Yahweh, who has made such good and sustained use of Babylon, now acts against that same Babylon. All the pro-Babylonian sympathy of the Jeremiah tradition is in this utterance nullified and negated. A sharp divergence is voiced which breaks apart the sovereign purpose of Yahweh from the imperial policies of Babylon. The two do not converge, but are at strong odds with each other. By the end of the book of Jeremiah, trust in and obedience to Yahweh do not equal submissiveness to Babylon, for Babylon now stands under judgment and will soon disappear from the map of world power. Babylon is therefore not the shaper of the future, not the perpetual power with which to reckon, but only one more pretender to power who cannot endure the ultimate power of Yahweh.

55. Brevard S. Childs, "The Enemy from the North and the Chaos Tradition," in *A Prophet to the Nations,* ed. Leo G. Perdue and Brian W. Kovacs (Winona Lake: Eisenbrauns, 1984), 151-161, has observed that the nature of "the enemy" is expressed in rhetoric in chs. 50–51 different from the rhetoric of chs. 46–49. In chs. 50–51 the rhetoric becomes apocalyptic and the enemy "has taken on a trans-historical, apocalyptic coloring" (159). Such a difference may be required because of the stature and massive threat of Babylon. In any case, Childs's analysis supports the important distinction between the two bodies of text.

Thus by the end of the book of Jeremiah we are left not with *Yahweh and Babylon,* but with *only Yahweh.*[56] At the most, Babylon has been for Yahweh only a convenience; at the worst, Babylonian power has been a brutalizing interlude which cannot be sustained or extended. This oracle in chs. 50–51 thus makes two claims. First, only the sovereign power of Yahweh matters. That sovereign power is allied with nothing else and is dependent on no other power (cf. Isa. 25–28).[57] That sovereign power will on its own terms and in its own way prevail, and must be accepted. Second, adherence to Yahweh's sovereign power is not only unavoidable. It is good news for Judah and Jerusalem, for it makes a post-Babylonian, postexilic future thinkable, available, and do-able. In this shaping of the final form of the text, Jer. 50–51 not only play against chs. 46–49. They also exercise a theological role in the book of Jeremiah disproportionate to their extent, for they counter much of what has gone before in the book. They make the claim that the dynamic of public history is indeed a theological dynamic, and not a matter of power politics. There is a purposefulness to the public process that is not coterminous with raw power. Thus the appearance of Babylonian power is not to be taken at face value.

The passing of such a superpower is good news for the little, subjugated peoples who had resigned themselves to long-term domination. The passing of a superpower, such as happens in this text, raises large questions not only about political possibilities, but about moral coherence in the world. These two chapters assert that a profound moral coherence continues in, with, and beyond Babylon. That profound moral coherence is visible not only in the emergence of the power of Babylon, but in the disappearance of Babylon as well.

---

56. Thus in a very odd way even the Oracles against the Nations serve the "Yahweh alone" theology voiced in the tradition of Deuteronomy which is so decisive in shaping the final form of the book of Jeremiah. While the Oracles against the Nations contain none of the rhetorical marks of Deuteronomic shaping, the theological import of the oracles is congenial to that theology.

57. In his comments on Isa. 40:13-14, R. Norman Whybray, *The Heavenly Counsellor in Isaiah XL 13-14* (Cambridge: Cambridge University Press, 1971), has shown how in the Exile Israel reasserted "Yahweh alone" theology. In Isa. 40 the poet intends to refute any claim of credibility for the gods of Babylon, thus making a point parallel to that of Jer. 50–51.

50:1   These chapters receive a formal and ponderous introduction. The structure of this introduction is not unlike 1:1-3; in both cases we deal with *the word of Yahweh* and with *the role of Jeremiah,* who is explicitly named in both introductions. The two sources of text are intimately linked to each other, but the two are not to be equated. The explicit naming of Jeremiah here suggests a reflective, canonical intention. The framers of this text know they are "making Scripture." They seek to balance the *"Exile"* (1:3) with an address concerning the proximate *cause of exile* (i.e., Babylon) and the *end of exile* when that proximate cause is overpowered by the ultimate cause of exile, that is, when Yahweh overpowers the ostensive superpower, Babylon.

50:2-10   With a mixture of poetry and prose, these verses announce the main themes for the two long chapters to follow. Instruction is given to the implied messengers: "declare, proclaim, set up, proclaim, do not conceal, say" (v. 2; cf. Isa. 40:9; 52:7 for a like implied messenger). The poem proposes a major announcement which is the outcome of a battle that is now completed, an announcement which is stunning in its import, unexpected but to be eagerly received by "the nations," that is, by the subjugated peoples.[58] The battle has been fought elsewhere (we are not told where or how), but the news will now change the circumstance and destiny of those addressed in the announcement.[59] The whole of the ancient Near East was contained in the Babylonian hegemony, and the Babylonian gods seemed beyond challenge. Now, in an instant, only as long as it takes to issue the news bulletin, that brutal hegemony is ended, and with it the seemingly all-powerful Babylonian gods are terminated. This is a moment the bondaged peoples savored!

The announcement is terse and to the point. First, Babylon is cap-

---

58. As Babylon is larger than life, so the report of the defeat of Babylon is voiced in speech that is larger than life, or as Childs ("The Enemy from the North," 161) has observed, Israel has "'mythologized' an historical tradition." The report requires Israel to push to the limits of language to speak adequately about this most welcome, quite unexpected turn of the historical process.

59. On the battle there being effective here, and the battle then being effective now, see Brueggemann, *Israel's Praise,* 29-38; and Garrett Green, *Imagining God: Theology and the Religious Imagination* (San Francisco: Harper & Row, 1989). The capacity to transfer the effect of the battle from there to here, from then to now, is operative in the imagery of apocalyptic which Childs finds in this text.

tured! The verb is passive. No agent is named. What counts is that the invincible one has been overthrown. Second, the fall of the empire has a theological dimension. The failure of Babylon is the failure of its gods, Bel and Merodach.[60] The verbs are each repeated, "put to shame, dismayed." Politically and theologically, the announcement completely revamps the landscape of public life. There will be ample time later for details. This is only the lead bulletin, but it says all that needs to be said.

Verse 3 provides a modest explanatory note. Babylon has fallen because a nation has come "out of the north." The phrase is filled with irony. In terms of *Realpolitik,* the reference is to Cyrus and the Persians. What counts for the text, however, is not the concrete political reference, but the fact that Babylon which has for so long been the ominous foe "from the north" should now be displaced by a new "foe from the north" which in turn threatens Babylon. History has turned decisively, and the turn is bad news for Babylon. The new "foe from the north" makes the old "foe from the north" helpless, wretched, and devastated.

Now the oracle reflects on the implication of the news bulletin concerning Babylon for Israel and Judah (vv. 4-5). The defeat of Babylon entails the end of displacement and exile for the Jews, and the capacity to come back home! The book of Jeremiah has had as its central theme the Exile (cf. 1:3). In a moment, in the twinkling of an eye, exile is over. The deported ones are now returning in weakness, grief, and penitence to Jerusalem, to the site of the temple, to God. The return home signifies a return to covenant with God, a relation disrupted by exile. The covenant is now said to be "everlasting." It is precisely at the end of the Exile that the renewed, restored relation with God is celebrated as everlasting and beyond disruption.[61] That is, at the very moment of discontinuity deep continuity is asserted.[62] The rhetoric of return clearly intends that the Exile is not one of many disruptions, but is the only one of its kind. Such a rupture will not happen again (cf. Isa. 54:7-10; Gen. 9:8-17). Judah and Israel are now assured a solid, enduring destiny with Yahweh.

The poem reflects on the circumstance of exile (Jer. 50:6-7) and on

60. See Carroll, 819.
61. See Gen. 9:8-17; Lev. 26:40-45; Jer. 31:35-37; 33:19-26; Ezek. 34:25-31; 37:24-28.
62. On continuity in the midst of the discontinuity of exile, see Brueggemann, "A Shattered Transcendence?"

the reversal and return (vv. 8-10). Verses 6-7 reflect on the reasons for exile. "My people" are understood as a flock of sheep; the sheep, however, have been at the mercy of their shepherds (= kings; cf. 22:22; 23:1-4; Ezek. 34:1-10). The Exile has been caused by the terrible failure of Israel's kings. Indeed, even the conquering enemy, Babylon, knows the cause of exile. The Babylonians here are presented as theologically astute enough to understand both Israel's *sin* and the certitude that Yahweh is Israel's *hope*. The Babylonians understood better than Israel's kings both the cost of sin and the root of hope.

The oracle, however, does not linger over the Exile and its causes. It wants rather to assert the end of exile and the capacity for homecoming (Jer. 50:8-10). It is time to leave Babylon! Those addressed are urged to act as "he-goats." "He-goats" are the strong leaders of the flock who take bold initiatives and act with courage, in order to lead the flock in a determined way. The departure from exile will require strong courage and resolve, and will therefore necessitate determined leadership. Thus v. 6 is an authorization of leaders who must dare to act against the residue of Babylonian power which continues to be intimidating. The imperative of the poem urges an end to fearfulness. The ground for such daring action is that Yahweh is creating an enemy against Babylon who will now plunder Babylon. For that reason, emerging leadership among the exiles need not be intimidated. Thus the daring Israelite action now authorized and required takes place in a context of enormous international upheaval.[63] The Jewish leadership can reckon with unnamed allies authorized by Yahweh who make their escape possible.

50:11-16 This poetic unit in turn addresses two different subjects. First, Babylon, the defeated and humiliated power, is addressed (vv. 11-13). It is Babylon who has been a reckless plunderer (v. 11), acting as greedy as a hungry cow which can gorge itself to death, as aggressive and brazen as a lusting stallion. Both the heifer in pasture and the lusting stallion act for their appetite and know no restraint or boundary to their desire. Babylon has imagined it could do whatever it wanted by way of abuse and self-serving exploitation; now, however, comes the reckoning of shame and disgrace and

---

63. Childs, "The Enemy from the North," has seen that the upheaval is not only international but transhistorical. The poem strains to find imagery and language adequate for the deep turn that is here anticipated.

dismantling (v. 12). Babylon's autonomy has failed to reckon with Yahweh, with Yahweh's anger which now retaliates against Babylon. Babylon has for too long violated Yahweh and Yahweh's "heritage." The richness and power of the images assert that Yahweh's overriding purpose and sovereignty will curb and limit Babylon's self-indulgent freedom. The empire must now answer for its self-indulgence. Such self-serving license can run loose in history only for so long, and then Yahweh acts against the violator.

In vv. 14-16 there is a second address, this time to the new unnamed enemy of Babylon. This address is largely a series of imperatives, urging and authorizing brutal military action against Babylon. Yahweh is portrayed as a king who declares unconditional war against the empire. No doubt such poetry reflects the accumulated hostility of the Jews toward their oppressor. The poetry, however, is more than a venting of resentment; it is a theological assertion that Yahweh will not finally tolerate such a strident abuse of public power. Thus the series of authorizing imperatives is marked by utterances about Yahweh. Babylon has sinned *against Yahweh* (v. 14). The coming action is *the vengeance of Yahweh* (v. 15). The poem refuses the notion that, to paraphrase automaker Henry Ford, history is "just one damn empire after another." History is the working out of Yahweh's righteous will. Because Babylon has stridently violated that righteous will, a turn in the public process is now authorized and will not be resisted.

50:17-20 These prose verses provide an explicit review of Israel's history under the metaphor of sheep and shepherd. Israel is a vulnerable flock, exposed to ravenous lions. (One can detect various philosophies of power at work in this material. Whereas v. 6 has asserted that Israel's own shepherds have caused the trouble, here the problem is marauding lions from the outside. These lines do not acknowledge, as earlier prophets including Jeremiah had asserted, that these imperial lions were indeed dispatched by none other than Yahweh. Here the lions are presented as greedy self-starters.) The history of Israel has consisted in the long-term threat of Assyria and more recently the dangerous, destructive presence of Babylon.[64] Israel's life has been lived under the threat of and shaped by

---

64. The history of Israel and Judah as portrayed by Miller and Hayes, and by J. Alberto Soggin, *A History of Ancient Israel* (Philadelphia: Westminster and London: SCM, 1985), makes clear that Israel and Judah are states characteristically dominated by larger powers who decisively impinge upon and shape Israel's life and policy.

the reality of these two empires for a very long time. The relation of Israel to these empires (much like the relation of Lithuania to the Soviet Union or the relation of Nicaragua to the United States) is as sheep to lion. In that unequal relation, the sheep is exposed and helpless, and the lion would seem to be authorized to govern to perpetuity.

But now, all of that sheep-to-lion relation is to change (v. 18)! In turn Babylon, like Assyria, will be "visited" by God. When the great powers are "visited" by God, good things happen for Israel. Israel returns to its land, which has been occupied and exploited. The flock receives back its pasture from the real shepherd. The very flock which had strayed (v. 6) is now free, safe, innocent, and unmarked by sin. Israel going into exile and Israel coming out of exile are two different peoples. The difference is that Yahweh will pardon. The pardon from Yahweh permits Israel's life and history to begin again, afresh, with new potential. In these few verses the oracle reflects on recent imperial history. In doing so, however, it insists that the real determinants for Israel's life are not the policies of the empires, but the purposes of Yahweh. It is Yahweh, the good shepherd, who gives Israel its life and restores its good pastures. Unlike much of the book of Jeremiah, here Babylon is not a tool of Yahweh, but only a rapacious lion. Yahweh presides over all such threats and then pardons.

50:21-34 This section, made up of quite different and distinct literary units, is largely preoccupied with Yahweh's direct dealing with Babylon. The oracle reflects the standard genre of taunt songs and victory songs. Only in vv. 28, 33-34 is there comment on Israel, which is a by-product of the main theme. The oracle concerns Yahweh's relation to and governance of the empire, almost without reference to Israel.

In vv. 21-27 three themes interplay. First, the unnamed attacker is authorized to proceed against Babylon in a most determined way. That agent of Yahweh is to "slay, and utterly destroy" (v. 21), to seize grain and "destroy . . . utterly" (v. 26), to kill all its bulls and destroy all its wealth (v. 27). Babylon is to be showed no mercy. "Bull" here may be taken to mean all the potency of the empire — sexual, military, and economic.

Second, the countertheme of the attack is to taunt and gloat over the massacre of Babylon. This is especially evident in vv. 23-24. The rhetoric is the voice of lament and grief, but the expression of grief is ironic. It is as though Yahweh, the perpetrator of destruction, can say with mock innocence, "I can hardly believe what has happened to Babylon!"

In v. 24 Yahweh addresses the empire directly, so that there is no misunderstanding. The core argument is reiterated: "Babylon is taken."

The authorization of the attack and the taunting of Babylon are held together by a third rhetorical feature asserting that this action is indeed the action of Yahweh. Thus the attacker does "all that I have commanded you" (v. 21). It is Yahweh who has "opened his armory" (i.e., his stock of weapons; v. 25), who has had work to do. Indeed, the fall of Babylon is for a theological reason: "You strove against Yahweh" (v. 24). The term "strive" elsewhere refers to political, personal, or military conflict of a physical kind. Here it is an odd usage, for no such conflict is identifiable between Yahweh and Babylon. This oracle suggests, however, that Yahweh and Babylon have been in dispute over who should control Israel and the land of Israel. In that hard dispute, Babylon has lost and must now be punished. Clearly the theological interpretation of Babylon at the end of the Exile is very different from the role earlier assigned to Babylon in the days of Zedekiah. The intent of the whole is to assert the sovereign rule of Yahweh, now implemented through an unnamed attacker whose role is to destroy the usurping empire of Babylon.

Verse 28 adds an isolated note that is derivative from the poem. The double use of the word "vengeance" suggests that Yahweh's vengeance consists in the reestablishment of Yahweh's rule and Yahweh's honor, both against Babylon and for Jerusalem (the temple). Thus "vengeance" is the abrasive factor in sovereign rule and order. Political authority depends on the capacity to enforce! It is in Zion that this vengeance/rule of Yahweh is now to be proclaimed. Yahweh is back in charge. Note that in the exilic proclamation of Isa. 40:9 it is Zion who receives the news of Yahweh's reasserted governance.

Again, in a prose reflection, the familiar triangle is mobilized. There is in this interaction *Babylon,* who is to be destroyed; there is the *unnamed attacker,* who is summoned and authorized by Yahweh; and there is *Yahweh,* who initiates the action of the one against the other. At a human level, the anticipated action is simply one superpower against another superpower. Read theologically, however, as the oracle insists, the key actor in the world of the superpowers is none other than Yahweh. Read theologically, two factors are decisive. On the one hand, Babylon has "proudly defied" *(zd)* Yahweh. Indeed, Babylon's very existence as an aggressive, arrogant imperial power is an act of defiance (cf. Dan. 4). On the other hand, there is in the historical process requiting *(sh-l-m).* That is, even great powers may expect to receive back in kind for their actions and policies. The great powers finally are not free and autonomous. Thus the triangle serves in a dramatic way to articulate that even the superpowers live in a world of theological, moral accountability. The world around Jerusalem is theologically ordered; none can escape or circumvent that resilient ordering.

In the following poetic section (Jer. 50:31-32) the oracle takes up the theme of the "proud one" (*zd*, as in v. 29). Babylon is the arrogant one par excellence. Such presumptious, rebellious posturing inevitably makes Babylon the sworn enemy of Yahweh, who will not tolerate such posturing.[65] Yahweh is definitionally against such arrogant power. In such an enmity, Babylon cannot prevail. Those who resist Yahweh, so the poem insists, will always lose and always pay. Verse 32 then offers a consequent lament which is largely in stylized, formulaic language. The second line is not unlike an earlier lament over Israel (Amos 5:2), a statement of total hopelessness and helplessness. The only difference is that instead of the subject being "virgin Israel," now it is proud Babylon (cf. Isa. 47:1-3 on the disrobing of "virgin" Babylon). The intent of this poem is to accomplish and enact the rhetorical dismantling of the empire, so that the speech itself makes available and visible the terrible ending of the empire.

Again, the demise of Babylon yields the liberation of Israel. This brief unit begins with a powerful abruptness, with an inverted word order in the Hebrew (Jer. 50:33): "Oppressed is the people of Israel." Verse 33 characterizes the oppression. Verse 34 counters the oppression with a strong first word: "liberator" (*ga'al;* RSV "Redeemer"), the one who ends oppression. Thus the resolve of God is to override the practice of the empire.

This little unit (vv. 33-34) is crafted around four rhetorical features. First, the central one of "oppress/liberate" is decisive. Second, the terms "held fast" and "strong" are the same Hebrew word *(hzq).* Thus as the oppressor is strong to confine, so the Redeemer is strong to release. Third, the phrase "surely plead their cause" is made of three uses of Hebrew *rib (rib yarib et-ribam).* The Redeemer goes to court in order to secure the right of the one illicitly held captive. Fourth, the contrast of "rest/unrest"

65. See Gowan, *When Man Becomes God,* 22, for the term *zd* and more generally on the arrogance of states which mock Yahweh. It is instructive that most of Gowan's exposition concerns precisely Babylon.

is expressed in a Hebrew wordplay: "rest" = *rg*, "unrest" = *rgz*. The term rendered "earth" may mean "land" (i.e., the land of Israel), so that when the land is set free of Babylon it also can become a peaceable land. The lines nicely develop the total contrast between two systems of power which have enormous implications for the future of Israel.

50:35-40 In a stunning and remarkably disciplined piece of poetry, we are offered an "ode to a sword." This poem is striking first because it has no verbs in its main clauses; the phrase concerning the sword is reiterated in all its stark power. Second, the sword is not identified politically or linked to any historical process. It stands barren as a contextless threat. That is all there is, just a sword. It is a sword, perhaps from Yahweh's armory (cf. v. 25), which will do its singularly devastating work. It is attached to no human agent. This sword as a bald threat is aimed at every significant element of imperial society — princes, wise men, diviners, warriors, horses, chariots, mercenaries, treasures. Every part of public life is to be denied power and stability. And in each case, there is to be a radical and total reversal, so that diviners (wise men) become fools,[66] warriors are shattered, troops become women, treasures are plundered, waters are dried up. Everything is reduced to weakness, lifelessness, and dysfunction. One can imagine a slow, eerie camera shot silently scanning the lingering ruin, Babylon, "stumbled and fallen" and "none to raise him up" (v. 32). All of this will happen because of images and idols (v. 38), all because of self-deceiving ideology that seduced the empire into a false discernment of its place in life.

The upshot of this sword-visited state follows with a "therefore" (vv. 39-40). The land is now emptied of all agents and symbols of power, life, and effectiveness. Instead there are only the most despicable scavengers who can live where there are no life supports: wild animals, hyenas, ostriches, and nobody else, now or ever.[67] Like Sodom and Gomorrah, Babylon is now emptied of human life and human possibility — no

---

66. The ultimate foolishness is to imagine that one is autonomous and self-sufficient. Von Rad, *Wisdom in Israel*, 65, terms such foolishness "practical atheism"; cf. Isa. 10:12-14.

67. Here I am following the NRSV. For a very different rendering, see John Bright, *Jeremiah*. Anchor Bible 21 (Garden City: Doubleday, 1965), 355; and Holladay, *Jeremiah 2*, 420-21.

people, no persons, nobody, no future! The language strains to convey the utter nullity of the old order, an order which so recently seemed so settled and so secure (cf. Isa. 47:7-10).

50:41-46   This section consists of two quotations of materials we have already considered elsewhere. First, Jer. 50:41-43 reiterates 6:22-24. The quote is verbatim with only minor changes. Obviously the names are changed, so that "daughter of Zion" becomes "daughter of Babylon." What is most important in the reuse of the material is that the poet accomplishes an exact inversion of the role of Babylon. In 6:22-24 it is to be assumed that the enemy people from the north is indeed Babylon who terrifies and who will show no mercy. In the present passage it is Babylon who is terrified and to whom no mercy will be shown. In 6:24 it is Babylon who devastates Jerusalem and "we" who have pain as in labor. Now it is the "king of Babylon" (no less) who hears and who is reduced to pain and anguish. The poem deftly makes the strong one into the weak one and portrays for us the total reversal of power in public history. The first one dramatically becomes the last one! We are permitted to watch while the great king of Babylon, a syllable at a time, is reduced to frailty, intimidation, weakness, and dysfunction.

The prose section of vv. 44-46 is likewise a quote, this time paralleled in 49:19-21. Again the inversion is total, for in ch. 49 the invader is presumed to be Babylon, whereas here it is Babylon who is the helpless, vulnerable flock. What counts now is the "plan" and "purposes" of Yahweh made against Babylon. No shepherd, no king — not even a Babylonian king — can withstand the purpose of Yahweh. Yahweh will appoint whomever God chooses. In 2 Isaiah the one chosen and appointed is Cyrus (Isa. 44:28; 45:1). Here the candidate is not named. In any case, Babylon has no voice in the coming leadership. The phrase "appoint whomever I choose" is taken up in Dan. 4 as a threat against Nebuchadnezzar (Dan. 4:17, 25, 32). The claim is powerfully made that Yahweh and not Babylon will order power in the world. The nations will hear and will know that the old ordering of public reality, which was dominated by Nebuchadnezzar, has come to an abrupt, decisive ending. The poet must work intensely so that this chapter can counter the main claims of the book of Jeremiah. When this chapter is finished, it is clear that *the purpose of Yahweh* and *the role of Babylon* are no longer compatible. It is that startling incompatibility which is the theme of the poem and which becomes the basis for new hope on the horizon of Jeremiah. Jerusalem is invited to look beyond the Babylonian episode to the future intended by Yahweh.

51:1-23 This long unit consists of several distinct pieces that could be variously divided. The main themes, however, are abundantly clear.

The sovereign voice of God begins with a statement of resolve (Jer. 51:1-5). The initial "behold" alerts us to a new, decisive announcement which entails a new action. The word is followed by two first person verbs: "I will arouse, I will send." The remainder of vv. 1-4 concerns the result of these two promised actions. The one aroused, that is, stirred to action (so RSV) and authorized, is a destroyer who will utterly destroy Babylon. In v. 1 it is a single destroyer who is aroused; in vv. 2-3 the destroyer comes with other agents, no doubt elements of an invading army. The ones sent will come to "winnow," that is, to judge and devastate the land. No one will be spared, not even the chosen youths (v. 3). Babylon will become an area for massive suffering and death because of the resolve of God. This rhetorical unit ends with a motivational clause in two parts (v. 5). Positively, this action is taken because Israel and Judah are still the object of God's concern. The term rendered "forsaken" is an adjective form of "widow." That is, this people is not without the strong protective husband who will intervene on its behalf.[68] Negatively, the action against Babylon is because of the guilt of Babylon (contrast 50:7). Thus the poem contains a triangle:[69] Yahweh is for Israel; Yahweh is against Babylon. We are given no specifics, but we may imagine that Babylon's guilt that is "against the Holy One of Israel" was enacted as abuse against Israel (later on; see 51:49). Thus Yahweh's forceful ultimatum is because of the violation of Israel, Yahweh's "wife." Babylon becomes the outsider in this triangle, at great cost.

68. On "widow" as a designation for the socially vulnerable, see Paula S. Hiebert, "'Whence Shall Help Come to Me?': The Biblical Widow," in *Gender and Difference in Ancient Israel,* ed. Peggy L. Day (Minneapolis: Fortress, 1989), 125-141.
69. On "triangling," see Murray Bowen, *Family Therapy in Clinical Practice* (New York: Aranson, 1978); and Edwin H. Friedman, *Generation to Generation: Family Process in Church and Synagogue* (New York: Guilford, 1985). Claus Westermann, *Praise and Lament in the Psalms* (Atlanta: John Knox and Edinburgh: T. & T. Clark, 1981), 169 and *passim,* has shown that the Psalms of Lament in Israel are triangles of God, speaker, and enemy. In the laments the speaker asks God to triangle with the speaker against the enemy. The outcome of such triangling is evident in our oracle.

The same voice of sovereign resolve now makes direct address (vv. 6-10). The addressee is not clear. Verse 6 suggests, in characteristic fashion, that the inhabitants of Babylon are urged to flee the coming attack. However, in v. 9 the address suggests the exiles (Israelites and others) who have been forcibly gathered in Babylon are now urged to leave, because the coming trouble is not aimed at them. In either case, the urging to flee serves to underscore the coming judgment. This unit is framed in juridical language. In v. 6 the coming judgment is identified as Yahweh's "vengeance" (i.e., restitution of rule) and as "requital" (i.e., as an equitable response to the acts of Babylon). In v. 9 it is "judgment" against Babylon that is being enacted, and in v. 10 the vengeance, requital, and judgment against Babylon are said to be "Zion's vindication" *(tsedeqah)*. Thus the action against Babylon is at the same time action for Israel, again the same triangle operative as in vv. 1-5.

At the center of this unit (vv. 7-9a), Babylon is characterized in a way that sharply contrasts its previous state and its present crisis. Previously, Babylon was "Yahweh's golden cup," that is, the means whereby God punished other peoples (v. 7).

It was through Babylon that all the other nations were required to drink the punishment that made them reel in drunkenness, helplessness, and humiliation. The entire unit turns dramatically at the beginning of v. 8: "Suddenly!" In an abrupt way, almost beyond explanation, Babylon has now been broken and devastated and worthy of grief. When healing was offered, Babylon in its recalcitrance refused. This unit offers something of a ring composition and pivots on the transition in v. 8. In an instant, the prosperous empire has become pitiful and ineffective. The changed circumstance of Babylon has come about because Yahweh is now reestablishing order and paying attention to the well-being of Israel. The reference to the righteousness *(tsedeqah)* of Israel in v. 10 is parallel to the mention of Israel and Judah in v. 5. While Yahweh deals directly with Babylon, the spin-off of that relation for Israel is never far from the horizon of the poem.

Now Yahweh addresses both parties to the coming conflict (vv. 11-14). On the one hand, the attacker is summoned (vv. 11a, 12a). On the other hand, Babylon is addressed in order to be forewarned that it faces "your end" (v. 13). Yahweh manages the battle so that the fate of both the attacker and the attacked are centered in Yahweh's rhetoric. In v. 11 we are given a prose interpretive commentary to identify the parties to the coming conflict. It is Yahweh who stirs up the Medes against Babylon (cf. v. 1 on the same verb). In the end, it was the Persians and not the Medes who nullified Babylon, but the confusion or uncertainty about these historical references is not crucial to the rhetorical intent of the text. In both the prose of v. 11 and the poetry of v. 12, attention is focused on Yahweh's "purpose." That is matched in v. 14 by reference to Yahweh's "oath" to destroy Babylon. Thus the named people (Medes) are proposed as the concrete way whereby Yahweh's intention is implemented!

We have seen attention given to Israel in vv. 5, 10, and less directly in v. 11. In the next poetic unit (vv. 15-19) the climactic statement of this unit again concerns Israel. This entire unit is a quote from 10:12-16, which celebrates Yahweh's power, contrasts that power with the powerlessness of the idols who lack "breath," and asserts the special status of Israel (51:19). The same triangle is again asserted, with the claim that God is indeed actively partisan to this people, while punishment comes to the other peoples. The power, wisdom, and understanding of Yahweh, which have cosmic proportion, are in fact correlated to the well-being of Israel. The connection between v. 15 and v. 19 suggests that the great, cosmic power of Yahweh through which the world exists is now mobilized for and developed toward the well-being of Israel. Sandwiched between the claim for Yahweh (vv. 15-16) and the assurance of Israel (v. 19) is the acknowledgement that the image-worshippers have neither power from God nor capacity to recognize the special place of Israel (vv. 17-18). Notice that in this poetic unit there is no reference to Babylon nor any concrete reference to punishment. It is striking how much the context of chs. 50–51 causes us to read the text (from ch. 10) with reference to Babylon, while the poem itself is silent in its reference.

51:20-24   The poem of 51:20-23 is one of astonishing intensity and discipline, paralleling 50:35-38. The opening line is difficult only because the pronoun "you" lacks a clear antecedent. The poem is addressed to one who will destroy the empire. In context that would seem to be the new attacker/destroyer named in 51:11, but that is never specified. Whoever is addressed is a "war club" (NRSV) in the hand of Yahweh to work havoc on Yahweh's enemies.[70] The term rendered "hammer" is from the same root as "break" *(n-p-ts)* in vv. 20-23. Whoever is addressed is instrumental

---

70. See Isa. 10:15, where the image of "axe" is used for the same purpose.

to the active resolve of Yahweh. The verb "I will shatter" (RSV "break") dominates the poem, being reiterated in each line. The direct object of the verb in vv. 20-23 indicates (as in 50:35-38) that every and all aspects of the life of the enemy will be terminated. This includes military power (51:21), every facet of the civilian population (v. 22), and the operators of the rural economy, as well as the urban managers of power (v. 23). This is one of the most extreme cases of God's massive assault against God's sworn enemy. The term "shatter, break" recurs in Ps. 137:9, where it is conventionally rendered "dash," while it might better be rendered "smash," as the NRSV does in Jer. 51:20-23. In both the Psalm and in this poem, the violent verb is used with reference to Babylon.

Verse 24 adds a prose commentary, perhaps to justify the brutality of the preceding lines. In this verse Yahweh will repay *(sh-l-m)*, that is, settle accounts. The evil to be repaid has been perpetrated against Zion, that is, Babylon has violated Judah and Jerusalem. The response of Yahweh is to violate Babylon. Here the theological connection is made explicit that is implicit throughout this long oracle. The theological connection made is daring indeed. It asserts that the fall of Babylon is related as cause and effect to the damage done to Jerusalem.[71] This daring claim is like a claim that the Soviet Union will be leveled because of the violation of Prague, or the United States because of its violation of Managua. Babylon cannot outflank the resolve of Yahweh concerning the ordering of the nations. Any effort to escape Yahweh's rule leads to massive brutality against the perpetrator.

51:25-33 The opening line of this section announces the main point, and it does so even without a verb: "Behold, I (am) against you." Out of that clearly articulated premise, everything else follows. Babylon is a destroying mountain who destroys. (The term "destroy" *[mashhit]* is the same as the one mobilized naming the agent against Babylon in v. 1.) Yahweh announces only one action against this destroyer, with one strong verb: "I will stretch out my hand" (v. 25). Yahweh will mobilize and enact Yahweh's full power. As Yahweh has saved with an outstretched hand (Deut. 4:34; 26:8; cf. Jer. 21:5), so Yahweh will now destroy in the same way. Because God acts so frontally and so decisively, the power of Babylon is completely

71. On the direct connection of cause and effect, see Koch, "Doctrine of Retribution," 57-87. On the verb *sh-l-m*, see Koch, 60.

broken. Nothing from its proud ruins can be salvaged. Nothing will be of any worth at all — no stone for the corner, no stone for a foundation, nothing useful. The imagery is extreme, for it takes enormous devastation to so crush stones that they cannot be reused. It is difficult to imagine a more comprehensive or total act of savagery beyond any salvage. The crushing of the stones may appeal back to the verb "shatter" *(n-p-ts)* in 51:20-23.

Through a series of seven imperatives, Yahweh now authorizes those who will move against Babylon. Among the imperatives, the verb "prepare" *(q-d-sh,* i.e., to "sanctify") is used twice, suggesting that this is indeed God's holy war — holy in its purpose, holy in its stratagem. While the military vocabulary and the naming of historical enemies is evident, v. 29 makes clear that it is Yahweh's *purposes* that are the main issue. It is clear in Isa. 55:6-9; Jer. 29:11 that at the end of the Exile Yahweh has "purposes" for Judah, that is, purposes of homecoming. The purposes of Yahweh against Babylon here form a countertheme, for Babylon's demise makes Jerusalem's homecoming possible.

We now have described for us in vivid detail the outworking of Yahweh's purposes for Babylon (51:29b-32). The poem makes an inventory of the aspects of the life of Babylon which now have failed. Verse 29b is a large thematic summary statement. To be "a desolation, without inhabitant," includes the complete failure of the army, which has been as weak and cowardly as women.[72] Moreover, the walled cities are in flames. Verses 31-32 dramatically suggest a relay arrangement of royal messengers. They have news to bear, and it is as urgent as it is ominous. The news of defeat cascades in and must be reported, in all its power and detail. The messenger carries this report to the king: "The city is taken." The phrase is the same as the theme line of 50:2. This devastating piece of news which terminates Babylon as a world power is the theological counterpart of the announcement, "Your God reigns" (Isa. 52:7). "His city is taken" and "Your God reigns" are two renderings of the same news. For the exiles it is good news; for the king of Babylon it is unbearably bad news. Because the city is

72. The reference to women refers to weakness and cowardliness. There is no doubt that such a reference bespeaks a macho, sexist horizon. Such a usage does not need to be defended, but can be understood amid the savage rhetoric of war. The usage ironically reflects arrogant masculinity and wants to make the contrast as sharply as possible.

taken, the poet can detail the scene of fire and pain and confusion, perhaps not unlike the most desperate scenes from *Gone With the Wind*.

This unit concludes with an ominous and awesome statement: "Yet a little while." The phrase moves to the edge of apocalyptic rhetoric, anticipating a "time of harvest," that is, a full and total judgment against the city.[73] There will be trampling on the city like the trampling of a threshing floor, only the trampling will be of the pride, power, and prestige of the imperial city.

51:34-58   This long poem consists of many smaller units that make use of various literary conventions.

In Jer. 51:34-40 the poem is a lawsuit structured in two parts. The first part, the indictment, is placed in the mouth of an inhabitant of Zion and constitutes a lament concerning Babylon's maltreatment of Jerusalem (vv. 34-35). In this indictment cast as lament, Nebuchadnezzar is explicitly named as the perpetrator. He is the subject of harsh verbs, "devour, crush, swallow." The accusation made against Nebuchadnezzar is that he has emptied Jerusalem (i.e., deported its people) and swallowed the city whole. Nebuchadnezzar has behaved like a sea-monster, like the very embodiment of chaos and evil. Verse 35 brings the cosmic metaphors down to concrete cases. Nebuchadnezzar has wrought enormous violence in Jerusalem. The last line of the verse is a formula assigning bloodguilt to the Babylonian king.[74] That is, Nebuchadnezzar must answer for the blood he has shed. What he regards as state policy is redefined by this poet as murder. The whole of the indictment-lament is an enormous condemnation of Babylon for its wholesale abuse of Jerusalem.

The second part of this unit is a juridical sentence in the mouth of Yahweh, introduced by "therefore" (vv. 36-40). The statement of Yahweh, in response to Zion's lament, begins with juridical language concerning a

---

73. Such a phrasing belongs congenially with the apocalyptic tilt given to the text by Childs, "The Enemy from the North."

74. On the power and acknowledgement of bloodguilt, see H. Graf Reventlow, "Sein Blut komme über sein Haupt," *Vetus Testamentum* 10 (1960): 311-327; and Klaus Koch, "Der Spruch 'Sein Blut bleibe auf seinem Haupt' und die israelitische Auffassung vom vegossenen Blut," *Vetus Testamentum* 12 (1962): 396-416. On a major narrative effort to avoid "bloodguilt," see Walter Brueggemann, *Power, Providence, and Personality: Biblical Insight into Life and Ministry* (Louisville: Westminster/John Knox, 1990), 49-85.

lawsuit. Yahweh will go to court on behalf of Jerusalem. The language moves immediately toward "vengeance" and the implementation of terrible judgment against Babylon. Yahweh promises to dry up the sources of water and of life, until the great city shrivels and dies and becomes only a habitat for jackals, without human life and without political power. Thus in one terse verse, the poet brings a dramatic and decisive end to the empire.

Then Yahweh details the additional punishment (vv. 38-40). This little section begins with lions and ends with lambs and he-goats. The poet imagines the Babylonians to be desperate for food and for drink, starved, ravenous, and parched with the passion of a hungry lion, ready to gulp down everything and everyone within reach. Yahweh, however, will give the lion bad, destructive food that it will immediately seize and consume. From that bad food the lion will become drunk and die in a perpetual sleep. Then Yahweh will slaughter and offer the Babylonians like helpless sacrificial animals, done to death at the hand of Yahweh. The drama of these verses is like the injection of a tranquilizer into a ferocious animal that is quickly reduced to helplessness. When the wild animal turns to drunkenness and sleep, Yahweh can do the act of termination as easily as a lamb is slaughtered.

Upon the execution of Yahweh's judgment against Babylon, the poet gloats over and taunts the defeated, destroyed city (vv. 41-44). The lead phrase echoes the governing theme of 50:2. Jeremiah 51:41 narrates a total reversal: Babylon as an object of praise has become Babylon as a horror. The "sea" is the primordial threat of chaos which has now inundated Babylon (v. 42). Though the language is cosmic and mythical, the actual mode of such inundation is likely a historical enemy, even though no reference to such an enemy is made. The delicacy of interpretation is to see that such cosmic claims are not at all removed from concrete experience into an irrelevant supernaturalism. The sweeping power of chaos (embodied in an invading enemy) destroys all the infrastructure and life-support systems of the empire, and reduces a once productive region to a lifeless wilderness (cf. 2:6).[75]

Jeremiah 51:44 returns to the sweeping themes of vv. 41-42. With the fall of the city, the patron god of the empire is also brought under

75. The imagery of chaos requires an awareness, as Childs sees, that this is more than one nation invading another. This poetry concerns the reappearance of primordial powers of chaos which Babylon had thought tamed.

severe judgment. It has been this empire-god who has swallowed Jerusalem (v. 34). Now Yahweh takes out of the mouth of the Babylonian god the city that has been swallowed but not digested. It is as though Jerusalem is unchewed meat in the mouth of this god and Yahweh retrieves it from such a destructive chewing. That is, the monster-god-empire is forced to relinquish the city of Jerusalem and is not free to devour it. Yahweh has snatched the life of Zion out of the mouth of the empire in the same way that a shepherd snatches a lamb out of the mouth of a lion (cf. 1 Sam. 17:37). On the one hand, the imagery suggests that Jerusalem was saved very late, at the last minute. On the other hand, the image exhibits Yahweh as strong and determined, and in the end stronger than the monster-god of Babylon. Yahweh has prevailed! The last lines of Jer. 51:44 return to the sober verdict of v. 41. Babylon no longer commands the respect or obedience of the nations, receives neither their booty (tax) nor allegiance nor amazement. Babylon has been emptied of its capacity to dominate its world. It has fallen (cf. 50:32).[76]

This section of the poem is arranged in something like a chiastic fashion.

    a the verdict (51:41),
      b mythic allusions (v. 42),
        c the city as wilderness (v. 43),
      b′ mythic allusions (v. 44a),
    a′ the verdict (v. 44b).

Now the abused exiles are addressed as "my people" (vv. 45-46). The exiles are now admonished to depart the empire. Yahweh is about to execute fierce anger against the empire.[77] That "fierce anger" is not now aimed at the Israelite exiles, but they must leave Babylon to avoid the general destruction that is to come. The admonition to flee the general destruction is not unlike the rescue of Lot in the face of the destruction of Sodom (Gen. 19:15-23). The exiles are beset by endless "rumors" (*nishma'ah,* used three times; RSV "report") concerning the empire, its violence, its instability, and its patterns of intrigue. The exiles are tempted

76. Bel is now emptied (51:44), as Jerusalem had been emptied (v. 34).
77. The phrase in v. 45 is the same as in 4:26. Childs, "The Enemy from the North," 157-161, notes the connection between chs. 50–51 and 4:23-26.

to get caught up in such turmoil; paying need to such gossip, however, can only compromise and weaken the resolve of the exilic community. Thus these imperatives urge the exiles to become involved in no imperial games, to remember their own identity, and to act only in response to the initiative of Yahweh. The mandate from Yahweh is to "go out," a word already used for the Exodus (cf. Isa. 49:9; 52:11-12).

The concluding poetry in the oracle is a reassertion that Babylon will be defeated, destroyed, and terminated (Jer. 51:47-58). Twice the poet uses the awesome anticipatory formula, "Behold, the days are coming" (vv. 47, 52). Three times the poet invokes a coming "destroyer" (vv. 48, 53, 56, twice in the plural). The defeat of the gods of Babylon, who are empty, powerless images, bespeaks the fall of a haughty imperial power everywhere feared and deeply resented. The defeat of the gods who legitimate such power will be welcomed everywhere, in the heavens as on earth (v. 48).[78] The elimination of the theological, ideological intimidation of Babylon will permit the whole world to breathe a sigh of glad relief.[79] The specific reason for the defeat of Babylon is that the empire has produced the "slain of Israel" (v. 49). The fall of the empire is connected to the peculiar treasure which Israel is to Yahweh. While the second line of v. 41 does acknowledge that the imperial destruction has not been confined to Israel and has the larger destruction in purview, it is the "slain of Israel" which is the specific ground for the end of the empire.

In vv. 50–51 the surviving Jews are addressed, the ones who were not already destroyed by the empire. They are admonished to go out and not to linger in the empire. A basis for their departure is that they must remember. If they forget, they will try to come to terms with the empire. When these Jews remember, they remember Yahweh, even though they are distanced from the holy place. They are to remember the holy city, and they are to remember the shame and humiliation of the abused temple

78. The rejoicing in heaven and on earth is not unlike the rejoicing in Ps. 96 when the news comes that "Yahweh is king." While Ps. 96 is liturgic and cosmic whereas this oracle is more political and historical, the point of celebration is the same. Babylon is crushed and Israel is free precisely because the rule of Yahweh has been decisively reestablished.

79. The sigh of glad relief on a cosmic scale is like the sigh of glad relief when any totalitarian oppressor finally falls. The cosmic dimension of this fall expressed in apocalyptic language permits all of creation to rejoice, even the nonhuman creation, as is evident in Ps. 96:10-13.

(cf. Pss. 74, 79). That is, they are to remember that they are Jews, to remember the peculiar hurt and desperation of recent time and then to act as Jews.[80]

The departure urged upon the Jews may indeed be geographical. It may also be a departure, the hard part of which is emotional. The victimized exiles may have come excessively to terms with Babylon, both by being excessively fascinated and by being excessively dependent and therefore grateful. An embrace of Jewish memory is the ground for disengagement from geographical, economic, political, and emotional connections to the empire.

Jeremiah 51:52-53 reiterate themes already heard. The poem knows about the "coming time." God will work justice against the empire. Babylon will suffer and the destroyers will come. There is nothing Babylon, even in its best strength, can do to resist the coming destruction, because God has authored the destroyers.

The large hope of vv. 52-53 is "at hand" in vv. 54-57. The poet is the one who hears before others hear. What this poet hears, well ahead of anyone else, is a voice, a cry of Babylon (cf. Exod. 11:6). It is a cry of fear and terror and wretchedness. It is the shriek of people under assault, fleeing from the fire and from trampling horses. It is a cry among the secure and serene who suddenly find themselves in deep jeopardy, utterly helpless, bewildered, and with no resources.

The cry is an appropriate response. The cause of the voice is that Yahweh is destroying Babylon. The word NRSV renders "laying waste" (*shoded,* "destroy") is one we have seen earlier in this long oracle. Now it is Yahweh alone who destroys, the sure and determined enemy of Babylon. It is Yahweh who is denying voice to the empire. Wave upon wave of enemy assault lap at Babylon and drown out the cry. The cry of need and hurt is drowned out by the waves of chaos unleashed by Yahweh. The whole of the political-military establishment is terminated.

The ruin evoked here is not wrought through any identifiable

80. On the cruciality of memory for the survival and buoyancy of Jews, see Yosef Hayim Yerushalmi, *Zakhor: Jewish History and Jewish Memory* (Seattle: University of Washington Press, 1982); and Ozick, *Metaphor and Memory,* 265-283. On Ps. 137 as a powerful act of memory among exiles, see Stephen Mitchell, "Lamentations," in *Congregation: Contemporary Writers Read the Jewish Bible,* ed. David Rosenberg (New York: Harcourt Brace Jovanovich, 1987), 387-390.

geopolitical means. It is wrought solely and singularly by Yahweh, the God of recompense, the God of requital *(sh-l-m),* the God who repays, who gives people what they have coming. It is Yahweh who defeats and places in a deathly stupor the entire power structure — princes, wise men, governors, commanders, warriors, all the great and significant ones now rendered innocuous, helpless, and pitiful.

The oracle ends with a magisterial formula: "says the King" (Jer. 51:57). This is the real king.[81] The others, including Nebuchadnezzar, have been transitory pretenders. This One is the one with the name of power, "LORD of hosts," "ruler of the troops," before whom empires cannot stand and before whom oppression and violence will not be tolerated. History in the empire is bent irresistibly toward the undiminished rule of Yahweh.

This long oracle ends in an understated reprise (v. 58). This same LORD of the troops speaks one more time, offering a simple, descriptive verdict. The walls are levelled, and the gates are burned. The efforts of such as Babylon (peoples and nations) are utterly futile in the face of Yahweh. It is worth noting that this last reference to "peoples and nations" is plural. It is as though the poem at the last moment looks beyond Babylon, which has been the insistent agenda of the oracle, to a larger, more comprehensive horizon. The concrete word has become a more philosophical, comprehensive reflection. Perhaps this concluding formula provides a conclusion to the larger corpus of chs. 46–51.[82] Perhaps the verse expresses a canonical awareness, so that the text makes the Babylonian statements reusable in other contexts. In any case, the concluding term rendered "nothing" (NRSV) is Hebrew *riq,* "emptied." The efforts of the nations as autonomous agents are empty efforts. The world cannot be enacted without God. Power cannot be claimed without Yahweh. That affirmation is good news for displaced Jews. For Babylon, it is a late lesson learned repeatedly at enormous cost.

---

81. Reference to "the King" concerns Yahweh. Thus the text asserts the authority of the real king and the dismissal of the pseudo-king, Nebuchadnezzar. The juxtaposition of the two is not unlike Isa. 6:1, wherein Yahweh the real king displaces Uzziah, who was not the real king. On Yahweh as king, see Marc Zvi Brettler, *God is King: Understanding an Israelite Metaphor.* JSOT Supp. 76 (Sheffield: Sheffield Academic Press, 1989).

82. See the same affirmation in Hab. 2:13.

A Weighty Letter (51:59-64)

This prose passage has in purview the oracle against Babylon just completed (50:1–51:58). The prose paragraph seeks to guarantee the future significance and effectiveness of that just completed oracle for the community of exiled Jews. At the same time, however, this paragraph is a redactional piece that is concerned with the canonical shaping of the book of Jeremiah. The text is quite aware of the need to give closure to the corpus of Jeremiah and knows that this is Jeremiah's last utterance (51:64b). The prophet will be permitted to say nothing more.

The unit begins with the identification of Seraiah, who is pressed into the service of the prophet and who is commissioned to preside over Jeremiah's crucial document. Seraiah is a son of Neriah and therefore, presumably, a brother to Baruch. It is therefore inevitable that the transaction of this narrative concerning the scroll should be related to the oracle of ch. 45 and to the involvement of Baruch in two of Jeremiah's crucial documents (32:12-16; 36:4-32).[83] This connection of Seraiah and Baruch supports my suggestion that Baruch is representative of the Babylonian community of Jews. In any case, Seraiah is charged with Jeremiah's (now written) words, to make them available and effective in Babylon as they have been uttered and written (perhaps by Baruch) in Jerusalem. The text self-consciously knows that the text must be promulgated to have a future.

The paragraph then deals with the preparation, administration, and deposit of the scroll. (1) *The preparation* of the scroll attributes to Jeremiah the actual writing of the scroll (51:60), unlike ch. 36 where Jeremiah orally dictates the scroll. What matters most is that Jeremiah has now opted for a written medium, surely reflective of the fact that we are well on our way toward a canonical literature.[84] The editors of this material (if not Seraiah) know that they are involved in producing something like "Scripture." The

---

83. This family, which includes both Baruch and Seraiah, was presumably a family of scribes. See Dearman, "My Servants the Scribes." It seems plausible that this family was both instrumental in championing the role and significance of Jews exiled to Babylon (cf. 42:2-3) and active and instrumental in the canonical production of the book of Jeremiah.

84. On the significance of the move from oral to written communication, see Werner H. Kelber, *The Oral and the Written Gospel* (Philadelphia: Fortress, 1983); and Walter J. Ong, *Orality and Literacy* (New York: Methuen, 1982).

substance of the scroll concerns "evil" (disasters) against Babylon, which surely indicates that the scroll refers to chs. 50–51, the prophet's climactic word against the empire.

(2) *The administration* of the scroll is quite specific and equally odd (51:61-62). First, Seraiah is to read (proclaim) the scroll, that is, to make it a matter of public record (as in chs. 32, 36). Clearly Seraiah is to do something as dangerous as the action of his brother Baruch in ch. 36. Whereas Baruch acts in defiance of the king in Jerusalem in ch. 36, Seraiah acts in defiance of the empire. Second, Seraiah is to "say" to Yahweh, that is, to pray. The prayer is to remind God of what God has said in God's resolve to destroy the Babylonian Empire. The act on the part of Seraiah suggests a most interesting motif concerning God and a telling theological understanding of the scroll.

The point about the character of God is that the prophet is concerned to remind God what God has resolved to do. It is as though God might neglect or even forget, unless God is reminded.[85] But then, when did God issue this threat against the empire? Presumably in chs. 50–51. We are given a picture of the scroll being waved in God's face in order to remind God of what God has decreed in the preceding oracle.

The scroll is brought into play because the scroll itself is where God issued the threat. That is, the scroll is indeed God's word.[86] Thus the scroll comes to exercise a pivotal role not only for Jeremiah and for the community of the canon, but in God's own life. The tone of this reminder to God seems not unlike Moses's prayer in Num. 14:17-19, in which God is reminded of God's own verbalized commitment in Exod. 34:6-7. The theological function of the scroll is to provide a guide and norm for Yahweh's exercise of sovereignty. It is as though the scroll functions to say to God, "This is what it means to be God, and this is how to be God."

(3) *The deposit* of the scroll follows its administration (Jer. 51:63-64a). The deposit of the scroll is presented as though it were a formal, public, and sacramental act. The scroll is to be thrown into the Euphrates, the river which is the lifeline of Babylon. It is, however, to be thrown into the river with appropriately ominous words. The deposit of the scroll into

---

85. On God's memory, the chance of forgetting, and reminders to God, see Ralph W. Klein, *Israel in Exile: A Theological Interpretation*. Overtures to Biblical Theology 6 (Philadelphia: Fortress, 1979), 135-36; cf. Isa. 63:7-9.

86. On God's own work in and through scrolls, see Faur, "God as a Writer."

the river evokes an announcement that Babylon will sink (like a scroll with a stone tied to it), sink to death, never to rise . . . because of evil.

The speech accompanying the deposit of the scroll evokes two connections. On the one hand, the sinking is not unlike the sinking of Pharaoh, the imperial embodiment of evil now assigned into the powers of the chaotic waters.[87] On the other hand, the scroll in the Euphrates which bespeaks the termination of Babylon is parallel to the waistcloth in the Euphrates bespeaking the termination of Judah (13:1-11). Thus the river is a place where the prophet deposits more than one ominous, deathly message. The scroll, the speech, and the deposit together tell decisively against the empire.

The act of the deposit need not be dismissed as "magic." It can as well be understood as a freighted political act which serves both to undermine the absolutist claims of Babylon and to invite Jewish hope away from its mesmerizing fear of the empire. Insofar as the act is a short-term political act, observers are put on notice that this is a moment when changed allegiance is possible. Insofar as the act is a long-term political act, it creates an abiding clue about the way history will work. Against all present available data, this is an awesome reminder that God, who seems so irrelevant, has taken a profound decision that eventually and inevitably will prevail.

We have, however, no access to the event itself. What we have is a paragraph describing an alleged event. We, with the long succession of interpreters, struggle with the narrative report which is strategically placed in the book of Jeremiah to enhance the oracle of chs. 50–51 and to indicate that, of all the things Jeremiah said or could have said, this is his last testimony to his people. It is a testimony that invites Israel to perceive itself in a peculiar way in a historical process where the sovereign, hidden power of God is decisively at work. It is a testimony that moves beyond most of the book of Jeremiah, which has seen Babylon as God's great partner in judgment. Now, against all of that, Yahweh terminates Babylon. This testimony reminds the community that the shape and clue to life is not given by the will or whim of an empire. Babylon is penultimately significant. In the end, however, Babylon faces a demise with no Easter, a sinking with no rising. After the empire has sunk like a rock into the river,

87. The image is not unlike that of Exod. 15:4-10, though the verb is not the same.

Israel still has the scroll, the promise of the scroll, and the God who speaks in and through the scroll.

No wonder the words of Jeremiah ended (51:64)! Nothing more need be said. This act is like a great belated, exalted cry: "It is finished" (John 19:30)! The empire is finished, and the God of Jeremiah has finished the painful rescue of Israel. This is not "magic." It is a political act of a special, lyrical kind. We must not reduce the power of communal symbol into our straitjackets of rational positivism. Such an act as the deposit of the scroll in the river is a gesture which lingers with power in the community of remembering and hoping. The act invites courage, and it resists resignation. It gathers the community in energy and focuses on its identity, not as the people of Nebuchadnezzar but as the people of Yahweh.

In the end this narrative is, however, not only awesome politics. It is faithful testimony to the God of exile and homecoming, of death and new life. The sinking of Babylon will indeed happen. As the empire sinks from view into chaos, new futures are opened for Israel. They are opened by the God who is both a God "nearby" and a God "far off" (Jer. 23:23). For much of the book of Jeremiah God was far away, in the company of the empire. Now this same God has come near to this subjugated, intimidated people. The river keeps bubbling as the scroll sinks. It bubbles the death of the empire. It also bubbles the rule of Yahweh and the future of Israel. No more need be said; for that reason the prophet stops. His words are ended!

An Ending and a Chance

Jeremiah 52:1-34

This chapter, which serves as a conclusion to the book of Jeremiah, is derived from other historical sources and does not mention the prophet Jeremiah at all. With the exception of Jer. 52:28-30, the material is parallel to 2 Kgs. 24:18–25:30, and most scholars believe is derived from it. In the construction of the book of Jeremiah, however, material pertinent to the final events of Jerusalem has already been included in Jer. 39:1-10. Moreover, the material on Gedaliah in 2 Kgs. 25:22-26 is not used in Jer. 52, but appears earlier in 40:7–41:18. Thus questions of literary priority are exceedingly difficult. We can only recognize that the material has had a complex editorial process. With that recognition, we can consider the material as it is presented to us. For even if the process has been complex, it does not follow that the present shaping is unintentional.

52:1-3a This material, which is paralleled in 2 Kgs. 24:18-20, reflects the standard royal formulas from the book of Kings. The harsh verdict rendered upon Zedekiah is noteworthy in two regards. First, Zedekiah receives major credit for the royal policies which led to the destruction and is likened in his destructive effort to Jehoiakim. Both Jehoiakim and Zedekiah are mentioned in Jer. 1:1-3 in relation to the Exile. In general, Jehoiachin may be reckoned as the more troublesome of the two (cf. 2 Kgs. 23:36–24:7), but here the two kings are linked together. Zedekiah receives primary blame in a way that seems to override even the verdict on Manasseh (2 Kgs. 21:1-16). Second, the concluding line of Jer. 52:3a renders an

488

unqualified theological verdict with the verb "cast out." The Exile is Yahweh's work, evoked by anger, not just with the king but with the city and with the nation. At last Yahweh does what the book of Jeremiah has long anticipated. In doing so, a major bonding between God and this people is harshly nullified. It is remarkable that this is the last and only time in this extensive chapter that the intervention of Yahweh is mentioned. The remainder of the account proceeds on the basis of human, historical action.

52:3b-11 While vv. 1-3a rendered a theological verdict concerning the anger of Yahweh, vv. 3b-11 render a political verdict concerning the provocation of the Babylonians. The juxtaposition of the two, vv. 1-3a and vv. 3b-11, political and theological verdicts, is dazzling in its twofold statement of cause and in the ill-defined connection between the two.[1] Clearly there is a link between the theological and political verdicts. Clearly the text intends a connection between the two. We are, however, given no clue or indication about that connection. Likely we are to conclude that the provocation of the empire is derived from the anger of Yahweh, but we have no hint of that. Verses 3b-11 are completely disciplined as a political description which carefully avoids any theological allusion. There are two renderings of the crisis, and either interpretation is valid and permissible. In the context of the book of Jeremiah, the two cannot be separated and likely they are understood to be synonymous. Thus Yahweh's "expulsion" of Judah is not a "supernatural" act, but happens in a perfectly understandable way which everyone can observe. Given either interpretation, or given both interpretations together, the political project of an independent Jerusalem initiated by Yahweh in fidelity to David is now effectively and decisively finished. We are at a terrible and irreversible ending in Israel's life.

The account of the Babylonian ending of Jerusalem is closely paralleled in 2 Kgs. 25:1-7 (see also Jer. 39:1-7). It is the story of a powerful, determined empire using its force and authority against a recalcitrant patronage state. In the wake of the invasion and occupation comes famine

---

1. The relation between the two is left unspecified, which permits an enormous range of interpretive options. For these two renderings of the treatment of Jeremiah, the narrative account employs a parataxis, so that the grammatical connection between the two is left deliberately unspecified.

(52:6), one of the usual threats (curses); of the other two traditional curses, the "sword" is implicit in the events of destruction, but pestilence is not mentioned explicitly. In any case, Judah and Jerusalem receive all the threats that characteristically come with such an invasion. In the ensuing crisis Zedekiah did not distinguish himself by his courage or nobility. He ran for his life, but not fast enough (vv. 7-11). He was apprehended and treated to an ignoble, cruel ending. Verse 11 reports (as the parallel accounts do not) that he was in prison until his death. The narrative does not explain to us, as would be plausible, that this terrible ending to the life of the king derives from the theological force of v. 3a.

52:12-16 While vv. 3b-11 have been preoccupied with the fate of the king, these verses describe the fate of the city at the hands of a ruthless occupying army. Whereas vv. 3b-11 had been located by the chronology of Zedekiah ("his ninth year"), now the reckoning is by the chronology of Nebuchadnezzar ("his nineteenth year"). Likely the change in chronological reckoning reflects a shift in the horizon of power, for Nebuchadnezzar has now become the point of political reference. It is his power and his longevity on the throne which now determine the shape of events.

Three items are reported from the occupation. First, there was a great destruction of the temple, the walls, and many houses (vv. 13-14). The narrative offers a poignant statement with a fourfold use of "house," suggesting massive destruction by fire, destruction of all that gave stability and security. Second, there was an extensive deportation from the city (v. 15). This verse does not support the conventional wisdom that deportation involved only leading citizens, as this company of deportees seems much more to be a cross section of the population. Third, there were left in the land some whose responsibility it was to continue the work of the agricultural economy (v. 16). This is congruent with the directive of Gedaliah, who worked at revitalization of the economy (40:10-12), though that report does not make the remnant in the land sound as marginal and pitiful as is suggested here. In any case, enough persons are left in the land to make clear that the deportation was part of an imperial strategy for a continued economy in the land, not designed to "empty" the land.

Thus the policy of Babylon reflects political realism, for the empire had a stake in the continuation and revitalization of the economy. Such political stratagems are likely to be less extreme than theological verdicts, one of which might be that the land was "emptied." In such a verdict,

theological rhetoric overruns the political realism of the empire. In any case, the fabric of communal life was not destroyed, but every element of the population which might give encouragement to resistance or autonomy was obviously dispatched.

52:17-27 Now the narrative becomes more specific about the action of the occupying force against the city. Two elements are noted. First, there was seizure and confiscation of the temple vessels (52:17-23). This act of violation involved two dimensions. On the one hand, the temple vessels constitute a great storehouse of wealth. We may imagine that the occupying army greedily took what was of value. Invasion is profitable! On the other hand, however, that the wealth is in the temple artifacts adds a theological dimension to the act.[2] The seizure of the temple vessels signifies a removal of all the small signs of theological legitimacy of the temple. The loss of the temple vessels means the loss of prestige for the God who presides over the temple. Writ large, the confiscation asserts that the Babylonian gods have prevailed over the God of Israel. This seizure of the temple artifacts is a highly symbolic as well as highly profitable act that must have been salt on the open wounds of Jerusalem. Peter R. Ackroyd has traced through the literature the fact that the loss and restoration of the temple vessels is a literary device for asserting continuity of the community through the Exile.[3] Here, however, because there is only loss and no restoration, their seizure bespeaks discontinuity. The wealth of the city and the prestige of Yahweh are both forfeited in a single act. This is indeed the Good Friday of the temple!

The second element of the abusive occupation is the seizure and execution of leading citizens (vv. 24-27). The ones seized are enumerated quite specifically. This must have been an act that was highly visible in the city and one that was passionately remembered. The company of those arrested includes the two ranking priests, three lesser priests ("keepers of the threshold"), a military officer, seven members of the king's cabinet, a military secretary, and sixty other citizens. We are not told why the violence is against these seventy-four men. Perhaps this is an accidental roundup of those who happened to be available; perhaps these particular persons were sought out as known resisters to imperial policy. We are not told.

---

2. This may indeed be an example of "commodity fetishism," for transcendent value is attached to these objects.

3. Ackroyd, "The Temple Vessels."

We only know that it is a company of influential people. They are given the same ruthless execution as the king, at Riblah. The empire is thorough and ruthless in destroying not only the wealth and structures of legitimacy in Jerusalem, but in destroying any political will for independence among the Jews. The symbols of legitimacy and the possible candidates for leadership are together brought under total and harsh imperial rule.

52:28-30 This concluding statement now adds a summary of the three waves of deportation undertaken by the empire. The reckoning (as in v. 12) is now according to the time line of Nebuchadnezzar, perpetrator of the deportations:

"in the seventh year"	= 598 B.C.E.	3023 persons
"in the eighteenth year"	= 587 B.C.E.	832 persons
"in the twenty-third year"	= 582 B.C.E.	745 persons
Total		4600 persons

This material does not appear in the parallel accounts. Three things strike one about the material.

First, the double use of the term "exile" *(glh)* rings in our ears. This has been the target of the book of Jeremiah since 1:3. The goal of the entire Jeremiah tradition is to tell the tale toward exile, and now the tale is completed.

Second, the numbers are relatively small. (Of course, they are not insignificant numbers for those taken away, or for those whose families were taken away. The situation of exile was no doubt a threatening one and must have been experienced as something like the end of a world.[4]) Small numbers notwithstanding, the structure of the OT is organized around this event which is given a significance all out of proportion to its data. Most specially, the deportation of 587 is the smallest. It is nonetheless that event which has taken on paradigmatic theological significance which has become definitional for Jewishness.[5] Thus in this chapter we are

4. Daniel L. Smith, *The Religion of the Landless: The Social Context of the Babylonia Exile* (Bloomington, Ind.: Meyer-Stone, 1989), has argued persuasively that the Exile was indeed an experience of acute hardship.

5. On the paradigmatic significance of the Exile for all Jews, see Neusner, *Understanding Seeking Faith,* 137-141.

witnessing the primal event for Jewish identity, an event matching in significance the crucifixion of Jesus for the identity of Christians.

Third, the care and comprehensiveness of the dates and numbers of exiles gives a sense of completeness and finality to the summary statement. Nothing is said of all those who remained in the land. They are not counted in the recorded numbers, and they do not count in the horizon of this narrative. The deported ones are the ones who are counted in this reckoning, and they are the ones who count in this version of Jewish reality. The text is reflective of and perhaps generative of the decisiveness of exile for the shaping of long-term Jewish imagination. Nothing is said here of God's absence or God's fidelity. The Exile is a political event worked by Nebuchadnezzar. Nonetheless for Jewish sensitivity, it is the verb "cast out" *(sh-l-k)* in 52:3a that looms over all these statistics: only Yahweh can be the subject of that awesome, decisive verb.

52:31-34 This final paragraph is chronologically removed from the preceding narrative. The last datum in v. 30 concerns 582. Now in v. 31 we are suddenly at 561. The king exiled in 598, Jehoiachin, is alive and still recognized as king after thirty-seven years, but still in exile, still not free, still not able to return home, still not on his throne. He is king, but something less than fully king. His Babylonian overlord is Evil-merodach (Awel-Marduk). Thus we have moved to a new generation after Nebuchadnezzar, whose son now will reign only two years (562-560). It is this new king who "lifted up the head" of Jehoiachin (v. 31).[6] The Babylonian overlord "spoke kindly," that is, acted as a friend toward him. Jehoiachin is treated with recognition and with dignity, as a royal person cared for and sustained by his benefactor . . . "until the day of his death" (v. 34). He died, then, without ever going home (cf. Jer. 22:24-30, where Jehoiachin is called Coniah).

The text is uncommonly laconic about this boy-king now grown older in exile. It is as though the narrative managed to balance finely and delicately the awareness that he is a captive with the acknowledgement that he is a recognized, royal captive. The narrative does not claim so much as to sound hopeful, but the narrative also does not claim too little to end in despair.[7]

6. On the phrase "lift up the head," see the rich wordplay in Gen. 40:16-23.
7. On the promissory dimension of this text, see von Rad, *Old Testament Theology,* 1:343, n. 22; and the comments of Frank Moore Cross, *Canaanite Myth and Hebrew Epic* (Cambridge, Mass.: Harvard University Press, 1973), 275-78.

Beyond the fact of theological sensitivity and cunning, this narrative articulation is perhaps precisely faithful to the realities, with the outcome unknown.

The last paragraph in the narrative states a modest outcome to what has preceded in this chapter. The main line of the plot of ch. 52 is one of destruction, despair, and deportation. In the midst of that sorry plot line, this little paragraph permits an opening which may let God keep God's powerful promise.[8]

The most important and most difficult question of ch. 52 is its intentionality in its present locus. Why did the shapers of the book of Jeremiah include this historical data which is securely recorded elsewhere? Very likely the chapter intends to make a theological statement, so that we will misread if we focus too much on the historical data.

The book of Jeremiah does not end easily or quickly, which suggests that many hands were at work deciding how to end the book. One ending might have come in 43:8-13; 44:1-30, an ending dismissing the Jews in Egypt and implicitly celebrating the Jews in Babylon. A second ending might have come in ch. 45, which anticipates a "disaster" for "all flesh." Such an anticipation opens the way for the Oracles against the Nations (chs. 46–51). We have seen that these oracles are organized in a two-stage arrangement, (1) the victory of Babylon over all the nations, including Egypt (chs. 46–49), and (2) the harsh demise of Babylon (chs. 50–51). The arrangement of these texts favors Babylonian Jews at the expense of the Egyptian Jews and to the neglect of those who remained in Jerusalem. The narrative also asserts, however, that Babylon as a world power is a provisional and passing matter, because Yahweh gives rule to whomever Yahweh will (cf. 49:19; 50:44). Thus God can give dominion to Babylon (chs. 46–49) ("my servant," 43:10) and God can take it from Babylon (chs. 50–51). In 52:1-30 power is given to Babylon. In 52:31-34 Babylon still has power; but there is another visible king, Jehoiachin, who continues to be present and known. Might Yahweh choose to give power back to him? We do not know. Such a turn is politically unlikely; it is nonetheless theologically possible.

8. This paragraph thus seems to play upon the great promise of 2 Sam. 7:1-16. Although the statement of Jer. 22:24-30 anticipates the end of the dynasty, it is evident from 33:14-16, 19-22, 23-26 that the promise made to David is still active and visible in Judaism. The closing paragraph of the book of Jeremiah makes an allusion to that promise but does not make any precise claim.

Thus the book of Jeremiah thinks and speaks intensely and in various voices about a Babylon-dominated world. That empire might be acknowledged as uncommonly powerful, but not ultimately powerful. Thus the tradition asserts that on occasion the rule of Yahweh and the policy of Babylon converge and are identical. (That is the meaning of the juxtaposition of 52:1-3a and vv. 3b-11.) But the two do not converge everywhere, not always, not finally. Finally it is Yahweh and only Yahweh who governs. Jer. 1:3 introduces us to the tale of exile. Now the story culminates in exile, but the story is not yet ended as we reach the end of the text.

The last paragraph is a theological acknowledgement of Yahweh's sovereignty (vv. 31-34). With that acknowledgement comes a vindication of Jeremiah as well. Jeremiah has known first and most clearly that the city of Jerusalem would fall. Well, it has fallen (vv. 1-30)! It has fallen in every way possible. The prophet cannot finally say "with one to raise it up" (cf. 50:32; Amos 5:2). Perhaps, but perhaps not. Jeremiah is exactly right. Jeremiah knows fully about the sovereignty of Yahweh, but he does not imagine he knows how that sovereignty will out. In Jer. 52:31-34 neither Evil-Merodach nor Jehoiachin knows how Yahweh's rule will out. History is cunning and inscrutable. It is nonetheless the arena where power is given and taken back, assigned and reassigned. In the end, both the great empire and the exiled king must deal with the God of the powerful verb in v. 3a. The verb "cast out," however, is not the only powerful verb in the vocabulary of this God. There are others, which we know from 1:10. The God of the powerful verbs is visible and active nowhere else in this chapter except in v. 3a. Nonetheless, this is the God who dispatches empires and reassigns human power (cf. 49:19; 50:44). At the end we do not know about the destiny of Jehoiachin. Our inability to know, however, is not a problem of failed reportage, so that we wish the narrator had told us more. Rather, our inability to know is a function of Yahweh's sovereignty that requires listening and waiting. More than that we cannot do. This people, because of the odd way of its life with Yahweh, must listen and wait.

495

Selected Bibliography

Books

Bracke, John M. "The Coherence and Theology of Jeremiah 30–31" (Ph.D. dissertation, Union Theological Seminary, Richmond, 1983).

Bright, John. *Jeremiah,* 2nd ed. Anchor Bible 21 (Garden City, N.Y.: Doubleday, 1978).

Carroll, Robert P. *From Chaos to Covenant: Prophecy in the Book of Jeremiah* (London: SCM and New York: Crossroad, 1983).

———. *Jeremiah.* Old Testament Library (Philadelphia: Westminster and London: SCM, 1986).

Holladay, William L. *The Architecture of Jeremiah 1–20* (Lewisburg, Pa.: Bucknell University Press, 1976).

———. *Jeremiah: Spokesman Out of Time* (Philadelphia: United Church, 1974).

———. *Jeremiah 1.* Hermeneia (Philadelphia: Fortress and London: SCM, 1986).

———. *Jeremiah 2.* Hermeneia (Minneapolis: Fortress, 1989).

Ittman, Norbert. *Die Konfessionen Jeremias: Ihre Bedeutung für die Verkündigung des Propheten.* Wissenschaftliche Monographien zum Alten und Neuen Testament 54 (Neukirchen-Vluyn: Neukirchener, 1981).

Janzen, J. Gerald. *Studies in the Text of Jeremiah.* Harvard Semitic Monograph 6 (Cambridge, Mass.: Harvard University Press, 1973).

496

McKane, William. *Jeremiah*, 1. International Critical Commentary (Edinburgh: T. & T. Clark, 1986).

Nicholson, Ernest W. *Preaching to the Exiles: A Study of the Prose Tradition in the Book of Jeremiah* (Oxford: Blackwell, 1970).

Overholt, Thomas W. *The Threat of Falsehood: A Study in the Theology of the Book of Jeremiah*. Studies in Biblical Theology, 2nd series 16 (Naperville: Allenson and London: SCM, 1970).

Perdue, Leo G., and Kovacs, Brian W., ed. *A Prophet to the Nations: Essays in Jeremiah Studies* (Winona Lake, Ind.: Eisenbrauns, 1984).

Polk, Timothy. *The Prophetic Persona: Jeremiah and the Language of the Self.* JSOT Supplement 32 (Sheffield: University of Sheffield Press, 1984).

Reventlow, Henning Graf. *Liturgie und prophetisches Ich bei Jeremia* (Gütersloh: Gerd Mohn, 1963).

Seitz, Christopher R. *Theology in Conflict: Reactions to the Exile in the Book of Jeremiah*. Beihefte zur Zeitschrift für die alttestamentliche Wissenschaft 176 (Berlin: de Gruyter, 1989).

Skinner, John. *Prophecy and Religion: Studies in the Life of Jeremiah* (1922; repr. Cambridge and New York: Cambridge University Press, 1955).

Welch, Adam C. *Jeremiah, His Time and His Work* (1928; repr. Oxford: Blackwell, 1951).

Articles

Ackroyd, Peter R. "The Book of Jeremiah — Some Recent Studies," *Journal for the Study of the Old Testament* 28 (1984): 47-59.

Anderson, Bernhard W. "'The Lord Has Created Something New': A Stylistic Study of Jer 31:15-22," *Catholic Biblical Quarterly* 40 (1978): 463-478. [Repr. in *A Prophet to the Nations: Essays in Jeremiah Studies,* ed. Leo G. Perdue and Brian W. Kovacs (Winona Lake: Eisenbrauns, 1984), 367-380.]

Brueggemann, Walter. "The Book of Jeremiah: Portrait of the Prophet," *Interpretation* 37 (1983): 130-145. [Repr. in *Interpreting the Prophets,* ed. James L. Mays and Paul J. Achtemeier (Philadelphia: Fortress, 1987), 113-129.]

———. "Israel's Sense of Place in Jeremiah," in *Rhetorical Criticism.* Festschrift James Muilenburg, ed. Jared J. Jackson and Martin

Kessler. Pittsburgh Theological Monograph 1 (Pittsburgh: Pickwick, 1974), 148-165.

————. "Land, Fertility, and Justice," in *Theology of the Land,* ed. Bernard F. Evans and Gregory D. Cusack (Collegeville, Minn.: Liturgical Press, 1987), 41-68.

————. "A Second Reading of Jeremiah after the Dismantling," *Ex Auditu* 1 (1985): 156-168.

————. "A Shattered Transcendence? Exile and Restoration," in *Biblical Theology: Problems and Prospects.* Festschrift J. Christian Beker, ed. Steven Kraftchick et al. (forthcoming).

————. "The 'Uncared for' Now Cared for (Jer 30:12-17): A Methodological Consideration," *Journal of Biblical Literature* 104 (1985): 419-428.

Childs, Brevard S. "The Enemy from the North and the Chaos Tradition," *Journal of Biblical Literature* 78 (1959): 187-198. [Repr. in *A Prophet to the Nations,* ed. Perdue and Kovacs, 151-161.]

Dearman, J. Andrew. "My Servants the Scribes: Composition and Context in Jeremiah 36," *Journal of Biblical Literature* 109 (1990): 403-421.

Gerstenberger, Erhard S. "Jeremiah's Complaints: Observations on Jer. 15:10-21," *Journal of Biblical Literature* 82 (1963): 393-408.

Holladay, William L. "The Covenant and the Patriarchs Overturned: Jeremiah's Intention in 'Terror on Every Side' (Jer. 20:1-6)," *Journal of Biblical Literature* 91 (1972): 305-320.

————. "God Writes a Rude Letter (Jeremiah 29:1-23)," *Biblical Archaeologist* 46 (1983): 145-46.

————. "The Years of Jeremiah's Preaching," *Interpretation* 37 (1983): 146-159.

Kessler, Martin. "Jeremiah Chapters 26–45 Reconsidered," *Journal of Near Eastern Studies* 27 (1968): 81-88.

Lemke, Werner E. "The Near and the Distant God: A Study of Jer. 23:23-24 in its Biblical Theological Context," *Journal of Biblical Literature* 100 (1981): 541-555.

Ludwig, Theodore M. "The Shape of Hope: Jeremiah's Book of Consolation," *Concordia Theological Monthly* 39 (1968): 526-541.

McKane, William. "משא in Jeremiah 23,33-40," in *Prophecy: Essays Presented to Georg Fohrer on His Sixty-Fifth Birthday,* ed. John A. Emerton. Beihefte zur Zeitschrift für die alttestamentliche Wissenschaft 150 (1980): 35-54.

Miller, Patrick D., Jr. "Sin and Judgment in Jeremiah 34:17-19," *Journal of Biblical Literature* 103 (1984): 611-13.

Mottu, Henri. "Jeremiah vs. Hananiah: Ideology and Truth in Old Testament Prophecy," in *The Bible and Liberation,* ed. Norman K. Gottwald (Maryknoll: Orbis, 1983), 235-251.

Overholt, Thomas W. "King Nebuchadnezzar in the Jeremiah Tradition," *Catholic Biblical Quarterly* 30 (1968): 39-48.

Rowley, Harold H. "The Prophet Jeremiah and the Book of Deuteronomy," in *Studies in Old Testament Prophecy* (Edinburgh: Clark and New York: Scribners, 1950), 157-174.

Seitz, Christopher R. "The Prophet Moses and the Canonical Shape of Jeremiah," *Zeitschrift für die alttestamentliche Wissenschaft* 101 (1989): 3-27.

Taylor, Marion Ann. "Jeremiah 45: The Problem of Placement," *Journal for the Study of the Old Testament* 37 (1987): 79-98.

von Rad, Gerhard. "The Confessions of Jeremiah," in *A Prophet to the Nations,* ed. Perdue and Kovacs, 269-284.

Other Works

Ackroyd, Peter R. *Exile and Restoration: A Study of Hebrew Thought of the Sixth Century B.C.* Old Testament Library (Philadelphia: Westminster and London: SCM, 1968).

Alter, Robert. *The Art of Biblical Poetry* (New York: Basic Books, 1985).

Blank, Sheldon H. *"Of a Truth the Lord Hath Sent Me"* (Cincinnati: Hebrew Union College Press, 1955).

Bright, John. *Covenant and Promise: The Prophetic Understanding of the Future in Pre-Exilic Israel* (Philadelphia: Westminster, 1976).

Brueggemann, Walter. "At the Mercy of Babylon: A Subversive Rereading of the Empire," *Journal of Biblical Literature* 110 (1991): 1ff.

———. *Hopeful Imagination: Prophetic Voices in Exile* (Philadelphia: Fortress, 1986).

———. *Israel's Praise: Doxology against Idolatry and Ideology* (Philadelphia: Fortress, 1988).

———. "The Kerygma of the Deuteronomistic Historian: Gospel for Exiles," *Interpretation* 22 (1968): 387-402.

————. "A Shape for Old Testament Theology, II: Embrace of Pain," *Catholic Biblical Quarterly* 47 (1985): 395-415.

Childs, Brevard S. *Introduction to the Old Testament as Scripture* (Philadelphia: Fortress and London: SCM, 1979).

Cogan, Morton. *Imperialism and Religion: Assyria, Judah and Israel in the Eighth and Seventh Centuries B.C.E.* SBL Monograph 19 (Missoula, Mont.: Scholars Press, 1974).

Crenshaw, James L. *Prophetic Conflict: Its Effect upon Israelite Religion.* Beihefte zur Zeitschrift für die alttestamentliche Wissenschaft 124 (Berlin: de Gruyter, 1971).

Diepold, Peter. *Israels Land.* Beiträge zur Wissenschaft vom Alten und Neuen Testament 95 (Stuttgart: Kohlhammer, 1972).

Fretheim, Terence E. *The Suffering of God* (Philadelphia: Fortress, 1984).

Friedman, Richard E. *Who Wrote the Bible?* (New York: Summit, 1987).

Gottwald, Norman K. *All the Kingdoms of the Earth* (New York and London: Harper & Row, 1964).

————. *The Tribes of Yahweh: A Sociology of the Religion of Liberated Israel, 1250-1050 B.C.E.* (Maryknoll: Orbis, 1979).

Gowan, Donald E. *Eschatology in the Old Testament* (Philadelphia: Fortress, 1986).

————. *When Man Becomes God: Humanism and Hubris in the Old Testament.* Pittsburgh Theological Monograph 6 (Pittsburgh: Pickwick, 1975).

Greenberg, Moshe. *Biblical Prose Prayer* (Berkeley: University of California Press, 1983).

Hardy, Daniel W., and Ford, David F. *Praising and Knowing God* (Philadelphia: Westminster, 1985).

Heschel, Abraham J. *The Prophets* (New York and London: Harper & Row, 1962).

Kitamori, Kazo. *Theology of the Pain of God* (Richmond: John Knox and London: SCM, 1965).

Klein, Ralph W. *Israel in Exile: A Theological Interpretation.* Overtures to Biblical Theology 6 (Philadelphia: Fortress, 1979).

Koch, Klaus. *The Prophets.* Vol. 1: *The Assyrian Period* (Philadelphia: Fortress and London: SCM, 1983). Vol. 2: *The Babylonian and Persian Periods* (1984).

McKay, John W. *Religion in Judah under the Assyrians, 732-609 B.C.*

Studies in Biblical Theology, 2nd series 26 (Naperville: Allenson and London: SCM, 1973).

Mendenhall, George E. *The Tenth Generation: The Origins of the Biblical Tradition* (Baltimore: Johns Hopkins University Press, 1973).

————. "The 'Vengeance' of Yahweh," in *The Tenth Generation* (Baltimore: Johns Hopkins University Press, 1973), 69-104.

Miller, J. Maxwell, and Hayes, John H. *A History of Ancient Israel and Judah* (Philadelphia: Westminster and London: SCM, 1986).

Miller, Patrick D., Jr. "The Human Sabbath: A Study in Deuteronomic Theology," *Princeton Seminary Bulletin* New Series 6 (1985): 81-97.

————. *Sin and Judgment in the Prophets.* SBL Monograph 27 (Chico, Calif.: Scholars Press, 1982).

————. "The Sovereignty of God," in *The Hermeneutical Quest.* Festschrift James L. Mays, ed. Donald G. Miller. Princeton Theological Monograph 4 (Allison Park, Pa.: Pickwick, 1986).

Miskotte, Kornelis H. *When the Gods Are Silent* (New York: Harper & Row, 1967).

Neusner, Jacob. *Understanding Seeking Faith.* Vol. 1: *Debates on Method, Reports of Results.* Brown Judaic Studies 116 (Atlanta: Scholars Press, 1986).

Niditch, Susan. *The Symbolic Vision in Biblical Tradition.* Harvard Semitic Monograph 30 (Chico, Calif.: Scholars Press, 1983).

Oded, Bustenay. "Judah and the Exile," in *Israelite and Judean History,* ed. Hayes, John H., and Miller, J. Maxwell. Old Testament Library (Philadelphia: Westminster and London: SCM, 1977).

Ollenberger, Ben C. *Zion, the City of the Great King.* Journal for the Study of the Old Testament Supplement 41 (Sheffield: JSOT Press, 1987).

Olson, Dennis T. *The Death of the Old and the Birth of the New.* Brown Judaic Studies 71 (Chico: Scholars Press, 1985).

Smend, Rudolf. *Die Bundesformel.* Theologische Studien 68 (Zurich: EVS, 1963).

Smith, Daniel L. *The Religion of the Landless: The Social Context of the Babylonian Exile* (Bloomington, Ind.: Meyer-Stone, 1989).

Trible, Phyllis. *God and the Rhetoric of Sexuality.* Overtures to Biblical Theology 2 (Philadelphia: Fortress, 1978).

von Rad, Gerhard. *Old Testament Theology.* 2 vols. (New York: Harper & Row and Edinburgh: Oliver & Boyd, 1962-1965).

————. *Wisdom in Israel* (Nashville: Abingdon and London: SCM, 1972).

501

Wanke, Gunther. *Untersuchungen zur sogenannten Baruchschrift.* Beihefte zur Zeitschrift für die alttestamentliche Wissenschaft 122 (Berlin: de Gruyter, 1971).

Wilson, Robert R. *Prophecy and Society in Ancient Israel* (Philadelphia: Fortress, 1980).

Wright, G. Ernest. "The Nations in Hebrew Prophecy," *Encounter* 26 (1965): 225-237.